SYRIA, THE STRENGTH O

The Syrian crisis has confounded political leaders and experts who forecast a rapid fall of the regime. This monumental error of interpretation has had tragic consequences for the unfolding of the crisis and its slide into a frightful civil war with regional and international ramifications. This book looks at Syrian reality in a new light. By analysing twenty-five constitutions and constitutional texts and proposing an innovative classification of the different political regimes that have shaped Syria over the last 100 years, the author retraces the country's intense history and the persistence of a Syrian model defined by the Founding Fathers. If, on emerging from this war, Syria maintains its unity and gives itself a democratic regime reflecting its society, then the concept of Syria may find a new lease of life and Syria will once again be perceived as an idea full of promise.

KARIM ATASSI is an expert in Syrian contemporary politics and constitutions. He holds a Ph.D. in Public Law on Syrian constitutions, is a former foreign student at France's École Nationale d'Administration, graduated in Political Science, and holds a degree in Information and Communication. He is an international civil servant.

SYRIA, THE STRENGTH OF AN IDEA

The Constitutional Architectures of Its Political Regimes

KARIM ATASSI

Preface by
JEAN MARCOU

Translated from the French by
CHRISTOPHER SUTCLIFFE

CAMBRIDGE
UNIVERSITY PRESS

University Printing House, Cambridge CB2 8BS, United Kingdom

One Liberty Plaza, 20th Floor, New York, NY 10006, USA

477 Williamstown Road, Port Melbourne, VIC 3207, Australia

314–321, 3rd Floor, Plot 3, Splendor Forum, Jasola District Centre, New Delhi – 110025, India

79 Anson Road, #06-04/06, Singapore 079906

Cambridge University Press is part of the University of Cambridge.

It furthers the University's mission by disseminating knowledge in the pursuit of education, learning, and research at the highest international levels of excellence.

www.cambridge.org
Information on this title: www.cambridge.org/9781107183605
DOI: 10.1017/9781316872017

© Karim Atassi 2018

This publication is in copyright. Subject to statutory exception and to the provisions of relevant collective licensing agreements, no reproduction of any part may take place without the written permission of Cambridge University Press.

First published 2018

Printed in the United Kingdom by Clays, St Ives plc

A catalogue record for this publication is available from the British Library.

ISBN 978-1-107-18360-5 Hardback
ISBN 978-1-316-63501-8 Paperback

Cambridge University Press has no responsibility for the persistence or accuracy of URLs for external or third-party internet websites referred to in this publication and does not guarantee that any content on such websites is, or will remain, accurate or appropriate.

The views expressed here are the author's and do not necessarily represent those of any organization.

CONTENTS

Preface *page* xv
List of Abbreviations xvii

Introduction 1

1 The Syrian Question 10
   1.1 Ibrahim Pasha's Syria 12
   1.2 The Lessons of Ibrahim Pasha's Syrian Campaign 17
   1.3 A Wasted Opportunity to Create an Independent Syria 21
   1.4 The Gradual Assertion of a National Identity 23
      1.4.1 The Arab *Nahda* 23
      1.4.2 The 1913 Arab Congress in Paris 26
   1.5 The 1915 Damascus Protocol 28
      1.5.1 Arab Nationalists in Damascus 30
      1.5.2 From Decentralization to Independence 30

Part I Parliamentary Constitutions and Liberal Regimes 35

2 The Syrian Monarchy 37
   2.1 The Establishment of an Arab Authority in Damascus 38
      2.1.1 Faysal, an Arab Sovereign 39
      2.1.2 An Arab Government 41
      2.1.3 Internal Political Life and the Construction of the State 44
      2.1.4 The Christian and Jewish Authorities' Allegiance to Faysal 45
   2.2 Foreign Policy under the Monarchy 46
      2.2.1 The Differing Interpretations of the 1915–1916 Hussein–McMahon Correspondence 46
      2.2.2 The Sykes–Picot Agreement 49
      2.2.3 The Revision of the Sykes–Picot Agreement 52

         2.2.4 The Faysal–Weizmann Agreement   55
         2.2.5 The Faysal–Clemenceau Agreement   57
    2.3 The General Syrian Congress   59
         2.3.1 The Origin of the Congress   59
         2.3.2 The Election of the Members of the Congress   60
         2.3.3 The Functions of the Congress   61
    2.4 The Damascus Programme   62
    2.5 Independence and Proclamation of Faysal
         as King of Syria in 1920   65
    2.6 The 1920 Constitution   69
         2.6.1 The Drafting of the 1920 Constitution   69
         2.6.2 Analysis of the 1920 Constitution   71
    2.7 The End of the Arab Kingdom of Syria   80

3 The First Republic   84
    3.1 The French Mandate   86
    3.2 Artificial Nations   88
         3.2.1 Early Military and Political Resistance to the
               Mandate   89
         3.2.2 The Partial Piecing Together of Syria   90
         3.2.3 The Great Revolt and the Assertion
               of National Will   92
    3.3 The Fight for the 1928 Constitution   96
         3.3.1 The 1926 Partial Elections   96
         3.3.2 The Ahmad Nami Government's Ten Points   98
         3.3.3 The 1928 Elections   99
    3.4 The 1928 Constitution as an Instrument for National
         Liberation   101
         3.4.1 The National Question   102
         3.4.2 Legislative Power   104
         3.4.3 The Executive   105
         3.4.4 France's Objections   108
    3.5 The Fight for the Franco-Syrian Treaty
         to Supersede the Mandate   109
         3.5.1 The 1931–1932 Elections   109
         3.5.2 The Assembly of Deputies and the Election
               of the President of the Republic in 1932   111
         3.5.3 The Beginning of Negotiations on the 1932
               Franco-Syrian Treaty   112
         3.5.4 The 1933 Version of the Franco-Syrian Treaty   114
         3.5.5 The 1936 General Strike   116

- 3.6 The 1936 Franco-Syrian Treaty   118
- 3.7 The Era of National Institutions 1936–1939   121
  - 3.7.1 The 1936 Elections   122
  - 3.7.2 Growing Dangers   122
  - 3.7.3 The Sanjak of Alexandretta Crisis   124
  - 3.7.4 Institutional Crises and the End of the National Era in 1939   128
- 3.8 The Institutions during the Second World War (1940–1945)   132
  - 3.8.1 The Fratricidal War between Vichyists and Gaullists   133
  - 3.8.2 The 1943 Elections and the Restoration of the Constitution and Institutions   136
- 3.9 The Difficult End to the Mandate   137
- 3.10 France's Legacy   142
- 3.11 From Independence to the Fall of the First Republic   143
  - 3.11.1 The Splitting of the National Bloc   144
  - 3.11.2 The 1947 Legislative Elections   146
  - 3.11.3 The 1948 Revision of the Constitution   148
  - 3.11.4 The Effects of the Palestine War   150

4 The Second Republic   153

- 4.1 The Advent of the Second Republic   155
  - 4.1.1 The First Coup d'Etat   156
  - 4.1.2 The Constitutional Referendum   159
  - 4.1.3 The 1949 Draft Constitution   160
  - 4.1.4 Domestic and Regional Policy of Husni Al-Zaim's Regime   163
  - 4.1.5 The Second Coup d'Etat   165
- 4.2 The Regional Question during the First Phase of the Second Republic (1949–1951)   167
  - 4.2.1 The Election of the Constituent Assembly   168
  - 4.2.2 The 1949 Provisional Constitution   170
  - 4.2.3 The Third Military Coup   171
  - 4.2.4 The Uneasy Cohabitation of Military and Civilian Authorities   172
  - 4.2.5 Government Appointments and Resignations   174
- 4.3 The 1950 Constitution   179
  - 4.3.1 The Social Question: Towards a Welfare State?   179
  - 4.3.2 The National Question   184
  - 4.3.3 Sovereignty   185

CONTENTS

- 4.3.4 Legislative Power 186
- 4.3.5 Executive Power 188
- 4.3.6 The Judiciary 191

4.4 Return to the Regional Question during the Second Phase of the Second Republic (1954–1958) 192
- 4.4.1 The 1954 Legislative Elections 193
- 4.4.2 The Second Legislature of the Second Republic 195
- 4.4.3 The Second Presidency under the Second Republic 198
- 4.4.4 The March Towards Union with Egypt 200

4.5 The Social Question during the Third Phase of the Second Republic (1961–1963) 203
- 4.5.1 The Coup of 28 September 1961 203
- 4.5.2 The Legitimization of Power 204
- 4.5.3 The Social Compact 206
- 4.5.4 The 1961 Provisional Constitution 208
- 4.5.5 The Election of the Assembly and President 210
- 4.5.6 The National Security Council 211
- 4.5.7 The Coup of 28 March 1962 212

4.6 The 1962 Constitution – An Emergency Constitution 215
- 4.6.1 The Adoption of the 1962 Constitution 217
- 4.6.2 The Meeting of the Assembly Outside the Chamber 218

4.7 The Fall of the Second Republic 220

Part II Presidential Constitutions and Authoritarian Regimes 223

5 The Third Republic 225

5.1 Establishing the Regime 226
- 5.1.1 The Military Republic 227
- 5.1.2 The Regime's Ideological Foundations 229

5.2 The 1953 Presidential-style Constitution 231
- 5.2.1 Democratic Guarantees 233
- 5.2.2 The Organization of National Wealth 236
- 5.2.3 Legislative Authority 237
- 5.2.4 The Executive 241

5.3 The End of the Regime 244
- 5.3.1 The Constitutional and Presidential Referendum 245
- 5.3.2 The Electoral Law 246
- 5.3.3 The Legislative Elections 247
- 5.3.4 The Regime Crisis 248

6 The Fourth Republic   252
  6.1 The Revolution of 8 March 1963 and the Coming to Power of the Ba'th   255
    6.1.1 The Founding of the Regime   256
    6.1.2 Legitimization of the New Order by Arab Nationalism and Socialism   259
    6.1.3 The Ba'thist Governments   263
    6.1.4 Political Life within the Ba'th between 1963 and 1966   265
    6.1.5 The 1964 Provisional Constitution and Collegiate Rule   270
    6.1.6 The End of the Regime of 8 March 1963   277
  6.2 The Neo-Ba'th Seizure of Power and the Radicalization of the Revolution (1966–1970)   281
    6.2.1 The Constitutional Arrangement of February 1966   281
    6.2.2 Political Life under the Neo-Ba'th   283
    6.2.3 The 1969 Provisional Constitution and the Institutionalization of the Ba'th   290
    6.2.4 The End of the Neo-Ba'th Regime   296
  6.3 The 'Corrective Movement' and the Institutionalization of the Revolution (1970–2000)   299
    6.3.1 The 1971 Provisional Constitution and the Legitimization of the Regime   299
    6.3.2 The Reorganization of Political Life   304
    6.3.3 The 1973 Constitution   308
    6.3.4 Political Stability and the Final Challenges to Hafez Assad's Power   318
    6.3.5 The Assad System   325

7 The Pan-Arab Constitutions   338
  7.1 The 1958 Constitution of the United Arab Republic (Syria and Egypt)   339
  7.2 The 1963 Charter of the United Arab Republic (Syria, Egypt, and Iraq)   344
  7.3 The 1971 Constitution of the Federation of Arab Republics (Syria, Egypt, and Libya)   348

8 Towards the Fifth Republic   354
  8.1 The Settling in of the New President and the Announcement of Reforms   356
  8.2 The Plans for Political Reform during the Damascus Spring   358

        8.2.1 The Statement of 99   359
        8.2.1 The Statement of 1000   360
        8.2.3 The Social and National Charter   361
        8.2.4 The Damascus Declaration   362
        8.2.5 The National Salvation Front Project   363
    8.3 From Partial Reforms to Revision of Ba'th Economic Doctrine   365
    8.4 Interpretations of the Ba'th Trilogy   367
        8.4.1 The First Interpretation (1947–1963)   369
        8.4.2 The Second Interpretation (1963–1970)   372
        8.4.3 The Third Interpretation (1970–2005)   375
        8.4.4 The Fourth Interpretation (2005)   376
    8.5 The Missed Opportunity to Reform the Political System in 2006–2007   378
    8.6 The Crisis of March 2011   381
    8.7 The 2012 Constitution or Continuity in the Midst of Change   386
        8.7.1 Title I: 'Basic Principles'   387
        8.7.2 Title II: 'Rights, Freedom, and the Rule of Law'   394
        8.7.3 Title III: 'State Authorities'   398
        8.7.4 Title IV: 'The Supreme Constitutional Court'   405
        8.7.5 Title V: 'Amending the Constitution'   407
    8.8 The 2011 Laws on Elections, Political Parties, and the 2012 Legislative Elections   408
    8.9 The New Electoral Law and the 2014 Presidential Election   412
    8.10 The 2016 Legislative Elections   418
    8.11 The Draft Constitutions Proposed by the Opposition   419
        8.11.1 The Syrian Reform Party's 2006 Draft Constitution   419
        8.11.2 Anwar Buni's 2011 Draft Constitution   424
        8.11.3 The Labwani–Muqdad Draft Constitution of 2011   426
    8.12 What National Compact for Syria?   429
9 Towards the Sixth Republic   434
    9.1 The Search for a Unifying Political Project   437
        9.1.1 The Cairo 1 and 2 Opposition Meetings   437
        9.1.2 The Moscow 1 and 2 Consultative Meetings   441
        9.1.3 The Vienna 1 and 2 Conferences   443

      9.1.4   The UNSCR 2254   445
9.2 The Search for a Constitutional Formula   446
      9.2.1   The Carter Center's Proposed Revision of the 2012 Constitution   447
      9.2.2   The Carter Center's Suggested Provisional Constitution   450
      9.2.3   Russia's Constitutional Proposal   451
      9.2.4   The 2015 Iranian Initiative   454
9.3 The Search for Post-war Partners   455
      9.3.1   The Joint Military Council   455
      9.3.2   The Moderate Armed Groups   456
      9.3.3   The Kurdish Component   458

Conclusion: Return to the Syrian Question   462

Annex: Summary Table of Constitutional Architectures   470
Arabic Bibliography   472
French and English Bibliography   478
Index   483

PREFACE

The publication of Karim Atassi's work on Syrian constitutions, which was the subject of a PhD thesis in public law (December 2012) that I had the pleasure of supervising at Grenoble University (France), is a very welcome event. When this research was first undertaken, Syria, long isolated and little known, appeared in many ways to be totally left out of the transformations of the contemporary world. When Karim Atassi completed his work in 2012, Syria was unfortunately headline news, with the uprising against the backdrop of the Arab Spring having changed into a frightful civil war that is emptying the country of its population and threatening its very existence.

Given this context, readers opening this book might think that taking an interest today in the Syrian constitutional question is somewhat anachronistic, not to say derisory. Yet, both for those simply seeking to understand the current Syrian crisis a little better and for specialists and experts trying to come up with a solution to it, Karim Atassi's book will be a valuable reference work. For this work, far from being a positivistic exegesis of Syrian constitutional texts, deals, through its analysis of them, with the construction of the Syrian state and results in a decoding of the latest events. What the author tells us of is ultimately the failure of constitutionalism in the country despite some considerable endeavours, especially when Hashim Atassi was active. Through both observation of the increasingly intense involvement of the army in the Syrian political system and analysis of the transformations of the Ba'th party, Karim Atassi shows how an authoritarian regime builds itself up and veers away from a constitutionalist project. Drawing on Ibn Khaldun's theory of the state and the brilliant analysis of it by the late Michel Seurat, he underscores the social dimension of the failure of the various Syrian regimes, liberal and authoritarian alike.

English translation of the Preface to the 2014 French edition.

This book has the merit of addressing a subject that is truly novel. No work to date, whether in French, English, or Arabic, has covered all of Syria's constitutions. In this respect, Karim Atassi's developments soon take readers beyond any *idées reçues* that assume somewhat hastily that a country like Syria can do without a constitutional architecture and the complex procedures that it necessarily generates. The author has examined seven permanent and five provisional constitutions, three constitutional arrangements, and four draft constitutions. The bold undertaking shows that even a state in which constitutional power has largely failed can produce a substantial constitutional literature of interest for research.

The author is impressive in his ability to provide readers with keys to interpreting such complexity, because it was not easy to become immersed in so many texts and unravel their storyline. Very methodically, by writing a preliminary chapter on the Syrian question and tying the country's constitutional inconsistency to the difficulties inherent in its existence, Karim Atassi comes up with an astute means to set the scene for the successive Syrian constitutional documents. He then manages to come up with a complete and finally very understandable synthesis of Syrian constitutional history through a meaningful categorization (liberal and authoritarian constitutions) that avoids a purely chronological account and makes it easier to identify and analyse the various texts. Far from drawing on second-hand sources, the study is based on meticulous and comprehensive spadework involving the original texts. This is what makes it so valuable. Through the excerpts of this constitutional literature that the author systematically puts into context, readers discover the key moments in the construction of the Syrian state, its leading actors, its major challenges, its accomplishments, and its missed opportunities. This journey to the heart of the country's constitutional writings provides an opportunity to revisit Syrian political history in a particularly thorough and above all novel way.

Professor Jean Marcou
Sciences Po Grenoble

ABBREVIATIONS

AFS	Arab Federal State
ALM	Arab Liberation Movement
BMA	Ba'th Bureau of Military Affairs
BMC	Ba'th Military Committee
CUP	Committee of Union and Progress
FAR	Federation of Arab Republics
NCRC	National Council of the Revolutionary Command, highest authority governing Syria from the coup of 8 March 1963 to the coup of February 1966
NPF	National Progressive Front
NRC	National Revolutionary Council set up in September 1965 and extended in February 1966. Legislative body and authority controlling the executive, created by the 1964 provisional constitution
NSC	National Security Council
NSF	National Salvation Front
PLA	Palestine Liberation Army
PRC	Ba'th Provisional Regional Command
PYD	Democratic Union Party
SARCAF	Supreme Arab Revolutionary Command of the Armed Forces
SCP	Syrian Communist Party
SDF	Syrian Democratic Forces
SSNP or SPP	Syrian Social Nationalist Party supporter of a Greater Syria also called the SPP or Syrian People's Party
UAR	United Arab Republic of Syria and Egypt (1958–61) and Syria, Egypt, and Iraq in 1963
UNSCR	United Nations Security Council Resolution

Introduction

Syria has been headline news since March 2011, yet, because it has not been readily accessible for half a century and is therefore poorly understood, it is still a mysterious and enthralling country. Although much has been written about Syria, its centres of power and decision-making processes remain opaque to foreign observers. Is Syria run by the military or civilians? Is it a republican or a hereditary regime? Are its politics right- or left-wing? Is it really a minority regime? Is it supported by the majority? There are no easy answers to any of these questions.

Syria's remote and recent history has been described in the most eloquent of terms. Ancient Syria is often described as the crucible of civilizations, the cradle of religions, the crossroads of three continents. Ancient Syria's contribution to the advancement of humankind is immense and includes the invention of both the alphabet and algebra. Syria has had a glorious history since ancient times. It saw the first city states and the first empires. Syria has been Hittite, Egyptian, Aramean, Assyrian, Persian, Babylonian, Greek, Roman, Byzantine, Arab, Seljuk, and Ottoman. Omeyyad Syria stretched all the way to Andalusia. Saladin's Syria fought the Crusaders and liberated Jerusalem and Palestine. Baibars' Ayyubid Syria became Mamluk, then Ottoman, and then the modern Syria that Egyptian President Nasser, in his customary flights of oratory, called its capital, Damascus, 'the pounding heart of Arabism'.

The term Syria has always been geographically indeterminate from the time of Ancient Syria until the time of Levantine Syria encompassing present-day Lebanon, Palestine/Israel, Jordan, Syria, and certain Turkish territories. Ever since the Arab provinces were wrested from the Ottoman Empire in 1918, many have expounded their views about what Syria should or should not be as a political entity. These are sore points that leave no one indifferent in the Near East, where most of the borders are contested. This is not the place for value judgments about diverging opinions as to the geographical extent of Syria. What is important about modern Syria is not its spatial extent. What sets it apart from the region's other political entities is not its geographical size but the very idea of Syria: a generous and embracing idea in a region often characterized by sectarianism and exclusion; an idea that rallies and integrates without assimilating, in a region that is split and tending to disintegrate.

Syrians themselves know little about their own constitutions.[1] Precious little has been written about them. Even the rare specialists and academics seem to have given up on constitutional law. Sadly, even the constitutional law textbook recently used to teach at Damascus University devotes just 30 of its 721 pages to Syria's constitutions. The previous textbook had just 56 out of 603 pages on Syrian constitutions.[2] Regrettably, then, a part of the country's rich history is deliberately blacked out, condemned to oblivion, and concealed.

This book has been written in part to try to fill this gap. It is a combined study of Syria's constitutions and the political regimes they underpinned. It encompasses the history and analysis of the political regimes, their constitutions, electoral laws, and laws on political parties. The task is a complex one. Not so much because of any intrinsic difficulty in the subject matter but because of the profusion of constitutional texts. I examine twenty-five constitutional texts drafted in less than a century. They include seven permanent constitutions (1920, 1928, 1950, 1953, 1962, 1973, 2012), five provisional constitutions (1949, 1961, 1964, 1969, 1971), three pan-Arab constitutions (1958, 1963, 1971), three constitutional arrangements (1949, 1951, 1966), and seven draft constitutions (1949, 2006, 2011, 2012, 2016 (2), 2017). This multitude of constitutional texts reflects the country's intense political history.

Few of these texts had been translated so most of the research has been done using Arabic sources. For want of textbooks on Syrian constitutional law or comparative studies of Syrian constitutions, my research into the historical circumstances peculiar to each of the constitutions was based on manuscripts in Arabic by the actors of the time. Some periods were better covered than others. I also took advantage of my stays in Damascus to interview prime witnesses and actors in Syrian political life over the last fifty years.

---

[1] This book is an updated, revised and shortened English version of *Syrie, la force d'une idée. Architectures constitutionnelles des régimes politiques* (L'Harmattan, Paris, 2014). The French book was an updated, shortened and revised version of the author's 2012 PhD thesis *Etude comparée des constitutions syriennes depuis 1918* directed by Professor Jean Marcou at Grenoble University.

[2] Kalthoum, *Studies of Constitutional Law and Political Regimes* (Arabic); Al-Ghali, *Principles of Constitutional Law and Political Regimes* (Arabic).

Understanding constitutional texts requires knowledge of their causes, origins, and purposes. Each of the texts relates to a particular political regime that ruled the country. Those regimes were as different as can be (monarchic and republican, liberal and authoritarian, right- and left-wing, military and civilian, unionist and sovereignist). Yet despite this diversity, all Syrian regimes for close to a hundred years shared the same values in the shape of a national project outlined by the Founding Fathers of modern Syria in a crucial but often overlooked document, the Damascus Programme, given by the Syrian congress to the King–Crane commission, which was despatched by US President Woodrow Wilson in 1919 on behalf of the Peace Conference to enquire into the wishes of the Eastern populations previously part of the Ottoman empire.

The Syrian congress claimed to represent the aspirations of the 'Syrian' population in the former Ottoman provinces that included not just present-day Syria but also Lebanon, Jordan, Palestine/Israel, and certain Turkish territories. All the successive political regimes, all the constitutions, and virtually all the draft constitutions were fully in keeping with this spirit and in one way or another took up the main points of the national project. These points can be summarized as the coexistence of all the component parts of Syrian society in the form of a Syrian secularism, the refusal of the partitioning of Syrian geographical space, the refusal of any foreign hegemony, and the dismissal of Zionist ambitions for Palestine. All Syrian national and regional policies were developed within this general framework with variations on the theme depending on the period and circumstances. Two further consensus-based items were subsequently added to these four initial points of the Syrian national project, namely social justice and then individual and collective liberties.

The original points developed in the Damascus Programme shaped the values and principles to which generations of Syrians to come were attached. These themes are the unchanging component underpinning all the political contingencies and all the regimes and their legitimizing constitutional texts. The permanence of these themes reflects the fact that, wittingly or not, Syrians have the impression that the national project remains unfinished to this day, preventing the foundation of a full-fledged modern state and focusing Syrians' attention on the container instead of its contents. It has weakened all rulers and promoted forms of power that are antagonistic by nature to the concepts of state and citizenship and not dissimilar to what Ibn Khaldun described in the fourteenth century.

Syria's constitutions and political regimes should first be examined in the context of the Syrian Question and the Founding Fathers' national project because the first constitutions were drafted to address them and not to regulate the executive and legislative branches of power. The earliest reference to any intention to create a constitutional form of power dates from 5 October 1918, just two days after Emir Faysal's triumphal entry into Damascus following the departure of Ottoman troops. On that day, Faysal declared in the name of his father, Sharif Hussein, that he was establishing an independent constitutional government for all Syrian territories, which would respect the rights of minorities. Faysal added that the government would abide by the principles of justice and equality and would treat all Arabs the same regardless of their religion or sectarian origin and would not discriminate in law between Muslims, Christians, and Jews. It was a remarkable declaration in many respects, for from the outset Faysal declared his intention to create a non-despotic, non-religious, civil constitutional state that would promote multi-sectarian coexistence.

This declaration was taken up and developed in the Damascus Programme prepared by the Syrian congress in July 1919 and given to the King–Crane commission, which was officially mandated by the Peace Conference but in fact comprised exclusively US delegates despatched by President Wilson. It was for the Peace Conference again that, after declaring Syria's independence and proclaiming Faysal King of Syria, the Syrian congress drafted the 1920 monarchical constitution. The point of the exercise was not to regulate power between the executive (king, government) and the legislature but to force the hand of the Peace Conference and present it with a *fait accompli* – the independence of Syria, the proclamation of a king, and the adoption of a modern secular constitution.

The manoeuvre was miscalculated and failed tragically. The Syrian nationalists were irredentist and unrealistic; colonial France was intransigent and blind. The outcome was pitiful. Syrian nationalism and French colonial tutelage in the form of a mandate were to be at loggerheads for a quarter of a century. Against this background the second – republican and not monarchic – Syrian constitution was drafted in 1928. Republican France could not spawn a monarchy. Again the purpose of the constitution was not to balance executive and legislative powers. For Syrians its purpose was to express their refusal to the carving up of their country and their rejection of the French mandate. Under the mandate charter granted by the League of Nations in 1922, France had to bestow on Syria an organic law (constitution) in agreement with the population within three years, that is by 1925. The policy by which France sliced up Syrian geography (into the State of Damascus, State of Aleppo, Greater Lebanon, the Alawite State, and Druze Territory) and then reshaped it (Syrian

Federation in 1922, State of Syria in 1925) and the Great Revolt of 1925 had strained relations between French representatives and the Syrian population. This constant strain had prevented any constitution being written and adopted within the time frame set by the international organization. It was not until 1930 that the 1928 constitution, revised and corrected by the high commissioner, was submitted to the League of Nations.

The 1928 constitution was an instrument in the fight against the French mandate. The institutions it created (parliament, government, presidency) led the struggle for independence and the reunification of the Syrian territories. In this, the 1928 constitution kept all its promises. It was after independence that its shortcomings began to show. The flaws lay not so much in the actual text of the constitution and its mechanisms, but rather in the lack of vision of the political class, which was incapable of identifying the challenges and setting the priorities for national action. The political class gave the disastrous impression that it was just looking after itself and its privileges and disregarding the most pressing social needs of a young and largely rural population.

Against this backdrop, the army decided to overthrow the regime and seize power in March 1949. This frightful year for Syria saw three *coups d'état* by the armed forces. The military had entered the political arena, where it has remained, save for the period between 1954 and 1956 when it was confined to barracks and left power to the civilian authorities.

When civilian rule was restored with the second coup d'état in August 1949, the political class called almost unanimously for a new constitution. A constituent assembly was elected and bestowed a provisional constitution on Syria that took up the provisions of the previous constitution on constituted powers. Then a second republican constitution was adopted in 1950 and remained in force until 1962, with two interruptions. The first of these was between 1951 and 1954 further to the coup d'état by Colonel Shishakli setting up a military republic and then a presidential regime. The second interruption was from 1958 to 1961 during the union between Syria and Egypt that gave rise to the United Arab Republic. The end of the union brought a return to the main provisions of the 1950 constitution in the form of a provisional constitution, before a new constitution was adopted in particularly testing circumstances in September 1962.

The 1950 constitution remains the only Syrian constitution that actually sought primarily to regulate and limit the exercise of power beginning with executive power. The intention was laudable but the context hardly conducive. The country had just experienced three *coups d'état* in less than a year and the army, like the constituent assembly, overtly claimed to represent the will of the people. Under the circumstances, it was probably unwise to weaken the executive, which ought instead to have been strengthened so that it could fully assume its role and resist the demands of the military. This was not the way the constituent assembly chose to go in 1950. This was an error of judgment, yet, even so, this constitution still has its supporters who call for it to be re-enacted.

The 1950 constitution should be credited with attempting to put social issues and especially the agrarian question at the heart of the Syrian political system. But the governments of the time made no effort to implement the generous social provisions in the constitutional programme, thereby giving the impression that no social advance, no meaningful reform could be made without a violent shift in the established political and social order, in other words, without regime change. The insensitivity of the traditional political class to the social question led in 1962 to the fall of the last liberal assembly that had been democratically elected in 1961. Instead of amending the 'socialist' laws (agrarian reform, nationalizations) enacted during the union with Egypt, it purely and simply rescinded them. The 1962 constitution was adopted in these highly dramatic circumstances. It took up virtually all of the provisions of the previous constitution. Its article 59, however, granted the president the power to govern by decree, whereas the 1950 version of that same article had formally prohibited this. It was a derisory constitutional disguise for a political reality that completely escaped the civilian authorities despite the full powers granted to the executive. Independent, Ba'thist, and Nasserist officers met with no resistance to their coup d'état on 8 March 1963.

The coming to power of the Ba'th turned the page in the history of a liberal, pluralistic, and parliamentary Syria and ushered in an era of authoritarian, presidential, monolithic regimes of the popular democracy type found in eastern Europe in Cold War times. The notorious exceptions to the previous liberal period were the brief interlude of General Husni Al-Zaim in 1949 and the regime established by Colonel Shishakli between 1951 and 1954, the forerunner of all Arab military regimes and especially those of Nasser in Egypt and Qassem in Iraq. Regime change in Syria was naturally mirrored in the constitutional texts, all of which became authoritarian. The first period of Ba'th rule was that of a supposedly collegiate leadership among comrades. This did not preclude a relentless struggle for power among the various clans, each with its ramifications within the party and the army.

It was not a foregone conclusion that the Ba'th would engage in constitutional window dressing. The Ba'th was a left-wing reformist type of political movement and the proponent of liberal, parliamentary, representative democracy. Its party constitution, its ideology, and its parliamentary history attested to this. It was mostly the Syrian Communist Party renegades who joined the Ba'th when it came to power who gave it a Marxist-leaning ideological line legitimizing an authoritarian regime. This ideological turn-around came at the Sixth National Congress in October 1963 and was reflected in a 'A Few Theoretical Foundations', the publication that heralded the constitutional window dressing to come.

The first two constitutional texts under the Ba'th – the 1964 provisional constitution and the constitutional arrangement of February 1966 after the neo-Ba'th came to power – both reflected the collegiate aspect of their rule. The 1969 provisional constitution was to maintain that collegiality. Although never really applied, that constitution was still the parent of all the ensuing Ba'thist constitutions. The next two, the 1971 provisional constitution and the 1973 constitution were tailor-made for Hafez Assad. The first restored the office of president of the republic instead of the 1969 provisional constitution's head of state. This was a harbinger of the personalization of the regime reflected in the next constitution, which bestowed the widest-ranging powers any Syrian president had ever enjoyed. This constitution brought stability not so much because of the strength of the institutions it put in place or the mechanisms governing relations among them but because of the strength of the regime. That stability was based on the army, the intelligence services, the party, and a bold but cautious regional policy. Moreover, Hafez Assad's regime developed and maintained a broad social base through an informal social compact.

Some of the crucial factors behind that earlier stability vanished under Bashar Assad. On coming to power, the young president announced his intention to make reforms, but the leadership had no ideological foundation for doing so. All the partial reforms initiated (regarding the economy, public sector, and administration) were ultimately attempts to modernize what had become an obsolete system. A return to the ideas of the Founding Fathers of the Ba'th before 1963 could have provided an ideological basis and a general framework for change. That ideological basis could have combined economic and political reforms. An opening up of the economy to the private sector should have been accompanied by an opening up of politics to the opposition. The opportunity for such change came – and went – with the Ba'th Tenth Congress of 2005 at which the party adopted the principle of a 'social market economy' but with no political outreach and it clung to its comfortable role as the party that ran the state and society under the terms of the 1973 constitution. That constitution had enshrined the Ba'th trilogy (Union–Freedom–Socialism) and had integrated it into the constitutional text. What had initially been simply a partisan slogan acquired constitutional standing. The Ba'th trilogy was variously interpreted before and during Ba'th rule. Each of these interpretations reflected the orientations of the time. The latest interpretation was that of the Ba'th Tenth Congress, which modified the concept of 'socialism' without changing the idea of 'freedom', which remained confined to an outmoded meaning of the popular democracy type.

This failing was to have tragic consequences when crisis broke out in March 2011. The regime was distraught and ideologically disarmed when confronted with legitimate demands for political reform. Intellectually, the authorities were not ready for dialogue, concessions, or compromise. It would have meant discarding the dogma in which it had been steeped since 1963. Accordingly, laws inspired in principle by liberal thinking – on peaceful protest, political parties, the press, and a new electoral law – were rushed through with virtually no discussion. But those laws proved highly restrictive, and the changes made since the outset of the crisis amounted to continuity.

In February 2012 a new constitution introduced a multi-party regime and the election of the president by universal suffrage. It also introduced a control over the constitutionality of law by enabling citizens to file objections, the starting point of constitutionalism. However, it failed to meet the expectations of those hoping for an emancipated parliament and a shift in the balance of power between executive and legislature. Despite some irrefutable advances, it is likely that this will be no more than a transitional constitution which, when the time comes, will be superseded by another constitutional text to end the crisis.

Describing Syrian constitutions and political regimes chronologically is only a first step towards understanding them. They still have to be classified, analysed, and their internal architecture examined. The classification used here is inspired by the traditional ordering of political regimes in France: the monarchy followed by a chronological ordering of republican regimes. Such a classification proved feasible as Syria experienced a monarchical constitution followed by several republican constitutions. I have therefore called the 1920 constitution and the Faysal period from his entering Damascus in 1918 the Syrian Monarchy (Chapter 2); the 1928 constitution and the regime it established the First Republic (Chapter 3); and the 1950 constitution and its regime the Second Republic (Chapter 4). I have included the 1962 constitution in the Second Republic because it is virtually a copy of the 1950 constitution. I have called the 1953 constitution and its presidential-style regime the Third Republic (Chapter 5);

the Ba'th constitutions (1964, 1969, 1971, and 1973) and their regimes the Fourth Republic (Chapter 6). I have inserted a separate chapter on the pan-Arab constitutions to which Syria adhered (Chapter 7). I have termed the 2012 constitution and the present-day regime in Syria the Fifth Republic (Chapter 8). I have ended by analysing the dynamics for the establishment of the Sixth Republic (Chapter 9).

The structure of the book reflects the history of Syrian political regimes, namely liberal parliamentary regimes and authoritarian presidential regimes. There is obviously no necessity for a presidential-style regime to be authoritarian, but that is how things have been in Syria. I therefore address the parliamentary constitutions and liberal regimes in Part I. This includes the Syrian Monarchy and the First and Second Republics. I cover the presidential-style constitutions and authoritarian regimes in Part II. This includes the Third and Fourth Republics, a brief chapter on the pan-Arab constitutions, then the Fifth Republic and the march towards the Sixth Republic. To introduce the subject, I have thought it necessary to begin with a first chapter on the Syrian Question since the early nineteenth century by including it in the context of the Eastern Question more generally.

The events that have shaken Syria since March 2011 are evoked in Chapters 8 and 9 and in the conclusion. I deplore the loss of human lives in both camps, just as I deplore the militarization of the crisis by the protagonists. It is true that the Syrian political system was sclerotic, obsolete, authoritarian, and required far-reaching reforms. But did that justify a civil war that may well, albeit inadvertently, bring an end to the national project of the Founding Fathers? What Syria needed was not a war but a gradual, well-thought-out process of political development that could preserve its national unity and the idea of Syria. Unless, of course, the hidden agenda in the war is to put an end to the national project of the Founding Fathers and perhaps to the very existence of a Syria that has often proved rebellious. A Near East without Syria would be a terrible step backwards for everyone without exception. Despite its imperfections, the Syrian model has proved to be a stabilizing force, protective of minorities, and an antidote to the region's disintegration. A regional order without Syria would give free rein to primal instincts and sectarian exclusions. In this sense, Syria remains more than ever an ideal to be attained and a forward-looking idea.

1

The Syrian Question

Whether the proponents of a natural Syria like it or not, contemporary Syria is the outcome of a deliberate although not always rational work of construction. All the protagonists who participated in forming it over the last two centuries – politicians, officers, men of ideas or men of faith, popular movements, foreign powers, and others – sought to build something to reflect their inner convictions or their overt or covert interests. Some preferred a fragmented and multiple Syria; others saw it as a single entity around which to rally. For the latter, who were in the majority in the local population about a century ago, Syria had to be an ideal political construction bringing together the whole population in all its diversity. But for others, a unitary Syria was something to be avoided at all costs; or at least being part of it was. Colonial-style compromise among European powers, sometimes corrected by Syrian nationalists' victorious struggles in the field, ultimately decided the scope, nature, and shape of contemporary Syria. Between dream and reality, construction and abstraction, Syria was to become a fact while continuing to be an ideal to be achieved – for Syria remains, more than ever, an unfinished creation.

The history of contemporary Syria begins with the history of the Syrian Question, which was an integral part of what Europeans called the Eastern Question throughout the nineteenth and into the early twentieth centuries. It is generally accepted that the Eastern Question began with the peace of Küçük-Kaynarca in 1774 between the Ottoman empire and Russia and ended with the 1923 Treaty of Lausanne that consecrated the dismemberment of the empire.

Chronologically, the Eastern Question falls into two main periods. The first extends from the 1774 peace to the Greek crisis of 1827; the second from 1827 to the end of the Ottoman empire in 1923. In the first period, the Eastern Question was a matter of finding and maintaining some sort of balance among the five major European powers (Austria, France, Great Britain, Prussia, and Russia) who were all eager to parcel up the Ottoman empire's possessions. With the 1827 Greek orthodox uprising and their fight for national independence supported by European states and public opinion, and by Russia in particular, the Eastern Question changed nature. It was no longer a matter of wars between the Ottoman empire and a European power, nor of diplomatic protection of certain Christian subjects of the Sublime Porte by a European power. For the first time ever, Europe interfered directly in Ottoman internal affairs and promoted separatism of a part of the population. European intervention in the Greek affair had weighty consequences for the empire's future. The Eastern Question now took on a new dimension. The traditional issue of an external balance among European powers was now compounded by in-fighting among rival Ottoman factions, which themselves gradually came to be closely tied in to the interplay among European powers.[1]

The internationalization of the empire's internal crises was again strikingly evident in the Syrian campaign (1831–41) of Mohamad Ali, viceroy of Egypt. This military campaign, theoretically conducted by a vassal against his sultan, saw direct intervention by European powers in an Ottoman crisis, this time not to support an emancipation movement in the eastern Mediterranean as with the Greek orthodox uprising, but on the contrary, to quell one.

The 1860 crisis was an opportunity to create a great Syrian entity. Great Britain made a proposal along these lines but France would have preferred a Syrian Arab kingdom under Emir Abdel Kader. In the end, taking advantage of the divergent views of the French and British and of Abdel Kader's refusal to ascend the Syrian throne, the sultan recovered control of the Syrian provinces while granting local autonomy to Mount Lebanon.

After the two nineteenth-century Syrian crises of 1831–41 and 1860, it was not until the early twentieth century that the Syrian Question arose again on the international stage. This time it was settled within a decade (1913–22).

The formation of modern political Syria began in 1918 with the separation of the Ottoman empire's Arab provinces after more than four centuries of shared history. The break with the Sublime Porte was experienced as a liberation by the Arabs who, during the final years of the empire, had suffered tremendously under the Young Turk government's policies of domination and discrimination and the ferocious repression ordered by its local representative, Jamal Pasha. Political oppression and endeavours to bring Turkish rule to the Arab provinces had intensified with the

---

[1] Laurens, *Le royaume impossible*, p. 80.

loss of the European provinces (the Balkans) and the transformation of an empire that was initially multi-ethnic and multi-religious into a Muslim empire with a Turk–Arab majority governed by Turks.

1.1 Ibrahim Pasha's Syria

The characteristic features of a modern and unitary Syria (in terms of territory, population, and administration) began to emerge with the Syrian campaign led by Ibrahim Pasha against the Sublime Porte in the name of his father, Mohamad Ali, viceroy of Egypt. At the same time, the European powers were taking on a paramount role in the eastern Mediterranean and their interventions began to have an impact on both the unfolding and the outcome of the Syrian crisis. The geographical location of Syria at the crossroads of three continents – Europe, Asia, and Africa – bordering the eastern Mediterranean and crossed by two major rivers, the Euphrates and the Tigris, had made it the cradle of ancient civilizations and a strategically important route for intercontinental trade. This channel of communication was coveted by all powers wishing to project their influence or having economic and political interests in the Old World. If there was one rule in geopolitics that had changed little from antiquity to modern times it was that, to assume fully their role and defend their interests, the dominant powers at any given time had to control this route interconnecting the three continents. At the time of Mohamad Ali's 1831 campaign, Ottoman Syria formed a buffer zone between several leading regional players: Ottoman Anatolia, the heart of the empire that still encompassed large swaths of the Balkans and eastern Europe; Egypt, which was formally under the Porte's control but which, under Mohamad Ali's energetic command, aspired to political autonomy; the Arabian peninsula torn between the Ottoman caliphate and the new Wahhabite sect practising a strict Islam and who for a time dominated the Najd and the Hejaz and even launched razzias into Syria; and finally Persia, concerned about the development of this new sect on the other shore of the Gulf. Each of these regional actors had its own interests to defend and Syria appeared to be high stakes for at least two of them, Cairo and Istanbul.

The Syrian campaign saw two wars. The first lasted from 1831 to 1833 and the second from 1839 to 1841. Some historians argue the origins of the Syrian campaign are to be sought in the Greek crisis from 1821 to 1827. At the time, the Ottoman sultan Mahmud II, being unable to put down the Greek uprising, sought military aid from Mohamad Ali, who sent his fleet and army. But because of the unanimous support from the

European powers, the war turned to the advantage of the Greeks despite the reinforcements from Egypt. The Egyptian fleet was sunk at Navarino and Mohamad Ali's army was routed. In consideration of his support and the heavy losses he incurred, Mohamad Ali expected to receive Syria or at least the Pashalik[2] of Acre from the sultan. Instead, he received the Pashalik of Crete by way of recognition and compensation, which somewhat embittered the viceroy of Egypt.

Ottoman Syria was divided administratively into five pashaliks: Damascus, Acre, Saida, Tripoli, and Aleppo. The population of Syria had always been religiously and ethnically diverse. In some places, the population enjoyed a degree of autonomy from Istanbul, as was the case on Mount Lebanon, which was only nominally associated with the Sublime Porte and where Druze and Maronites cohabited under the authority of Emir Beshir Shehab. Christians living on the mountain and in the cities and countryside enjoyed traditional privileges associated with their status. Elsewhere the Arab population was mostly Sunnite, with some Muslim minorities not recognized by the Ottoman rulers, such as the Shiites, Alawites, and Ismalians. Sunnite Arabs were treated as equals in theory with Sunnite Turks.

The European powers were familiar with the context of the Syrian campaign of 1831 to 1841. The regime of Capitulations inaugurated by Suleiman the Magnificent had granted François I of France protection over the Maronites in 1536. This undertaking was renewed in 1553 and 1740. Great Britain had secured protection of the Druze in 1583 and Russia that of Orthodox Christians in 1774.

Ever since ancient times, Syria had been strategically important for Egypt. For Mohamad Ali, it enabled him to protect his domain by creating a buffer zone between him and the sultan. It also enabled him to control the growing trade between the Euphrates and the Mediterranean. Syria was of strategic importance for Istanbul, too. As the crossroads of the empire, it linked the empire's European territories and the Nile Valley and it commanded the route to Arabia and Islam's two holiest sites of Mecca and Medina. The Ottomans held Damascus to be the fourth holy city of Islam, after Jerusalem.

Seizing the pretext of a quarrel with the Pasha of Acre, who allegedly gave refuge to almost 6,000 Egyptian fellahs who had fled the Nile delta to avoid paying taxes, Mohamad Ali sent his son Ibrahim Pasha

---

[2] An administrative division governed by a pasha appointed by the sultan.

to invade Syria in October 1831 at the head of an expeditionary force of 30,000 men. Ibrahim was a battle-hardened warrior and formidable military leader, adulated by his men and feared by his enemies. He had already participated in the Sudan campaign in 1821–22, but it was primarily in the expedition against the Wahhabites in 1816–19 that he had distinguished himself. He had driven them from the holy cities of Mecca and Medina, pursued them to their capital Diriyah in the heart of the Najd, where Riyadh now stands, and razed it to the ground on his father's orders. He had also fought in the campaign against the Greek insurgents from 1824 to 1827.

The expedition conquered Gaza early in 1832 and then made for Haifa, Jerusalem, and Nabulus. After a siege of several months, Acre, which had valiantly held out against Bonaparte in 1799, finally fell to Ibrahim in May 1832. Ibrahim then headed for Damascus, which was rising against Ottoman rule. He entered Damascus in June and pursued the Ottomans as they fled north. A month later, Ibrahim defeated an Ottoman army of 50,000–60,000 men near Homs in central Syria and marched on towards Anatolia. After liberating Hama and Aleppo, he crossed the Taurus mountains and took Adana before making for Konya in central Anatolia in December 1832, where he defeated nearly 55,000 Ottoman troops. After a few weeks' break, he resumed his march towards Istanbul and on 2 February 1833 he took Kütahya, just 240 km from Istanbul. Being cautious, Ibrahim halted at Kütahya and awaited his father's instructions. Panic-stricken, sultan Mahmud II called on Great Britain to send its fleet to the Dardanelles and Alexandria. But the British cabinet was against this. In desperation, the sultan asked the czar for help in protecting Istanbul. For the first time in its history, the Russian fleet entered the Bosporus in February 1833. Once the danger of Ibrahim Pasha had receded, before withdrawing from Istanbul the Russians signed an eight-year non-aggression treaty with the Ottoman empire on 8 July 1833. This Treaty of Hunkar Iskelesi prompted acute concern in the other European capitals.

The European powers, worried about the czar's maritime expansion towards the strategic straits connecting the Black Sea and the Mediterranean, realized that to get the Russian fleet to stand down and leave the Bosporus, Sultan Mahmud II would first have to come to an understanding with Mohamad Ali. They therefore acted as go-betweens for the overlord and his vassal. Mohamad Ali would have liked to declare his independence as the Greeks had done a few years earlier, but the European powers dissuaded him for fear of the collapse of the Ottoman empire and the Russians laying hands on the Bosporus straits in the aftermath. A realist, Mohamad Ali finally accepted a compromise signed at Kütahya on 4 May 1833 (an agreement known as the Peace of Kütahya) bestowing on him Egypt and the five pashaliks of Syria for life and granting the Adana region to Ibrahim Pasha. No sooner was the agreement concluded than Mohamad Ali abolished the five pashaliks and entrusted the administration of his new territory to his son, Ibrahim Pasha. For the first time ever, Syria formed a single province with Damascus as its capital. This Syria, under Egyptian administration, stretched from the Taurus in the north to Sinai in the south, and from the Mediterranean in the west to the Euphrates in the east. Although nominally still dependent on the Porte, power no longer lay with the Turks but with the Arabs, whether Syrian or Egyptian. Syria was part of a vast Arab-speaking territory controlled by Cairo and stretching from the eastern Mediterranean to the Euphrates and also encompassing the Nile Valley and the Red Sea.

The Egyptian administration soon proved far more effective than the Ottoman administration that had preceded it because of strong central rule that was tried and tested in Egypt. Syria under Ibrahim Pasha was divided into four constituencies (Damascus, Aleppo, Tripoli, and Saida) with Adana enjoying special status. Representative councils of the population were created on which Christians and Jews sat alongside Muslims. Syria experienced its first modern industrial development, increased trade, the beginnings of public education in Arabic, the opening of schools (for boys and girls) and university departments (600 students in Damascus, 600 in Aleppo, and 400 in Antioch), and Christian missionaries were also authorized to open schools. Measures were implemented to drain marshland, develop agriculture, organize regular tax collection without distinction between Muslims and Christians, reform customs duties, begin the settlement of the bedouin who had for generations plundered the countryside and robbed travellers on the highways, introduce mandatory conscription (except for Christians), develop the postal service, and open up Damascus and Jerusalem, which were not among the Ports of the Levant, to Europeans.[3]

But a combination of internal and external factors made this first experience of Syrian unity a failure. The drawbacks of a centralized and modernized administration were not slow to show through. The notables of the big cities did not appreciate losing their traditional role to mere

---

[3] On the achievements of Ibrahim Pasha's government in Syria see Soulaiman Abou Izz Al-Din, *Ibrahim Pasha in Syria* (Arabic), pp. 149–64.

government officials. Muslim resistance to mandatory conscription was heightened by the unpopularity of the new personal taxes, which were thought humiliating because of their similarity to the poll tax imposed on non-Muslims. The interference from Great Britain to bring about the failure of the Egyptian administration in Syria and its almost open support for the Druze revolt, the endemic irredentism of certain groups of the population to any form of central power, the intrigues of the Porte that incessantly fomented domestic disorder and aspired to recover control of Syria were all challenges facing Ibrahim and that weakened his rule before and after the second Syrian war triggered by the sultan (1839–40). The Porte began the war in May 1839 to recover possession of Syria, but once again Ibrahim won out masterfully at the battle of Nizip in 1839, which some commentators have called the 'Austerlitz of the East'.[4]

After the victory at Nizip the entire Ottoman fleet went over to Mohamad Ali. It seemed nothing could stop Ibrahim in his march on Istanbul or Mohamad Ali in his quest for the independence of Egypt and Syria. But as in 1833 the fear of the collapse of the Ottoman empire and of Russia seizing the straits prompted the other European powers to intervene. This intervention, which was first diplomatic and then military, forced Mohamad Ali to withdraw his troops from Syria, so ending the experience of a unified Syria.

In addition to their incitement to internal disorder, the European powers' intervention intensified from diplomatic persuasion (ultimatums) followed by military intimidation (gunship diplomacy) to direct intervention (landings). The Syrian crisis turned international in the summer of 1840. Representatives from Austria, Great Britain, Prussia, Russia, and the Porte met in London, without France, whose July Monarchy was deemed too favourable to Mohamad Ali. They adopted the Treaty of London on 15 July 1840 in agreement with the sultan. Under the treaty, the five powers offered Mohamad Ali Egypt on a hereditary basis and the Pashalik of Acre for life[5] in exchange for his withdrawal from the rest of Syria, Arabia, and the region of Adana in Cilicia. The powers gave Mohamad Ali ten days to accept. After that, the offer was to be withdrawn and replaced by the concession of Egypt on a hereditary basis alone. The second offer was valid for just ten more days, after which it was to lapse and the powers

---

[4] Sinoué, *Le dernier pharaon*, p. 460.
[5] The London Treaty determined the boundaries of the Pashalik of Acre, termed 'southern Syria', which corresponded to the borders of the territory that was to become Palestine under the British Mandate in 1922. For details see Laurens, *Le royaume impossible*, p. 102.

would take concerted measures to enforce the arrangement (Treaty of London, art. 4).[6]

The first offer was made to the viceroy by a representative of the Porte and the consuls general of the four powers on 14 August 1840. The viceroy declined it and the clock began to tick. After ten days, Mohamad Ali lost the possibility of maintaining the Pashalik of Acre for life. When the second deadline began to run, the viceroy left matters to the sultan's will, which was construed as a second refusal.

Consequently British warships bombarded Beirut on 3 October 1840. On 5 October, 1,500 British naval troops and some 8,000 Turkish troops landed at Juniyah and Nahr el Kaleb north of Beirut. On 10 October the allied troops occupied Beirut. Emir Beshir Shehab, the Maronite lord of Mount Lebanon and ally of Mohamad Ali from the outset, surrendered on 11 October and was exiled to Malta. On 6 December 1840, the allies made their final offer to Mohamad Ali, to evacuate Syria and return the Ottoman fleet in return for keeping Egypt. France urged him to accept. He did so on 10 December 1840. Finally, on 13 February 1841, the sultan granted hereditary rule to the viceroy of Egypt and Mohamad Ali's army withdrew from Syria.

1.2 The Lessons of Ibrahim Pasha's Syrian Campaign

The Syrian campaign involved some valuable lessons for the future. It was the first experience of a unitary Syria, which admittedly was not independent because it was subject to the Cairo government and in theory still Ottoman; but it was the first time that the various 'Syrian' provinces, as they were generally known, were united within an administrative entity stretching from the Taurus mountains in the north to the Sinai and Arabia in the south and from the Mediterranean coast in the west to the Euphrates in the east. This province that had Damascus as its capital was unusual in including a near-autonomous region, Mount Lebanon, and experienced fairly harmonious multi-sectarian coexistence. In the aftermath of the Great War, after the Arab provinces separated from the Ottoman empire, the Arab-Syrian independence movement attempted to construct a kingdom of Syria with Faysal as its constitutional monarch within virtually the same boundaries as Mohamad Ali and Ibrahim's Syrian province.

---

[6] See Sinoué, *Le dernier pharaon*, pp. 490–1 for the principal articles of the Treaty of London.

Unitary Syria was constructed and later deconstructed based on a combination of international, regional, and local factors. Foreign interference came either through direct intervention or a subtler form of involvement by setting sectarian communities one against the other.

Despite its brief existence, unitary Syria served as a framework for the emancipation of Christians. It also served as a framework for asserting equal treatment and equal rights and duties among the inhabitants even before the beginning of the Ottoman reform era and the announcement of the *Tanzimat* (Reorganization) by the 1839 Edict of Gulhane proclaimed by Sultan Abdul-Majid.[7] This modern Syria has proved a suitable framework for multi-religious coexistence of its various component parts.

It was also during this period that the 1840 Treaty of London defined contractually a region called 'southern Syria' and that by coincidence had the same boundaries as what was to become Palestine under British mandate in the next century.

One of the reasons for the failure of this first Syria was that it was not perceived by the local population or by Europeans as embodying a struggle for Arab national emancipation and independence from the Turks, nor indeed was it presented by Mohamad Ali and Ibrahim in that way. Yet it had all the characteristics of such a struggle. But the idea of a nation – the dual heritage of the Enlightenment and the French Revolution – was not yet the yardstick of identity in Syria. Religion and membership of Sunnite Islam were still the primary sources of identity. The national factor was later to become the paramount feature of identity in the final years of the empire. Yet the Syrian campaign probably had all the hallmarks of a fight for national independence, comparable to the fight the Greeks had waged a few years earlier. For while the religion was the same on the two opposing sides in the Syrian campaign, the war against the Sublime Porte for independence for Egypt and Syria largely coincided with a geographical and linguistic divide that can be summarized as Arabs versus Turks. Mohamad Ali only became aware of this towards the end of the Syrian campaign around 1838, but his son Ibrahim was attuned to it long before then.

Several facts and testimonies illustrate this claim. Three serve as examples. First, after the 1832 battle of Homs in the first war of Syria, Ibrahim allegedly proclaimed, 'I shall go as far as I can make myself understood

---

[7] See the text of the Edict of Gulhane in Laurens, *L'Orient arabe*, pp. 58–61.

when speaking Arabic'.⁸ It is not yet Arabism nor the demand for a nation-state but it is a boldly asserted awareness of Arab identity. Then, in 1833, he received France's special envoy, Boislecomte, who reported his conversation with Ibrahim in detail:

> He [Ibrahim] openly announces his intention to revive an Arab nationality, to truly give the Arabs a homeland, to admit them to all positions, whether in the domestic administration or in the army; to make them into a self-supporting people, enjoying a share of public revenue and sharing in the exercise of power, as in the charges required to maintain the state.⁹

Lastly, in 1838, Mohamad Ali sent a letter to the Austrian consul general in Cairo via his foreign affairs minister, stating that, 'the viceroy notifies the representatives of foreign powers that he is compelled to proclaim independence because the Sublime Porte seeks only to undermine his power and authority. Only definitive separation between the two states, Turks and Arabs, can avert for their capitals the baneful consequences of a civil war and foreign invasion.'¹⁰

Great Britain's dogged intent to terminate this Syrian province under Egyptian administration at any price is noteworthy. The European powers, except perhaps France, had every reason to want the viceroy of Egypt to withdraw from Syria. Those reasons were related to the necessity of maintaining a balance among the powers by perpetuating the status quo in the eastern Mediterranean and the Bosporus. Great Britain and France wanted to prop up the Ottoman empire for fear that if it fell apart Russia might grab the straits connecting the Mediterranean to the Black Sea. These strategic considerations were compounded for London by substantial economic interests. The Syrian crisis coincided with the early development of British imperialist doctrine under foreign secretary Lord Palmerston. This policy did not involve acquiring colonies, which was to come later, but defending British interests wherever they were threatened.¹¹ Accordingly, the extension of Mohamad Ali's control over territories from Syria to the straits of Bab El-Mandeb between the Red Sea and the Indian Ocean was perceived as a direct threat to British commercial interests, not because Mohamad Ali opposed the passage of British goods, but because of the taxes levied on them. In 1838 Great Britain

---

⁸ Cited in Sinoué, *Le dernier pharaon*, p. 384.
⁹ Laurens, *L'Orient arabe*, p. 94.
¹⁰ Sinoué, *Le dernier pharaon*, p. 441.
¹¹ See Mansfield, *A History of the Middle East*, pp. 56–7.

convinced the sultan in the Treaty of Balta Liman to dismantle the system of state monopolies and authorize European powers to trade throughout the empire at a 3 per cent tax rate. Mohamad Ali refused to apply the agreement in the territories under his control so as to protect the nascent local industry.

For Palmerston, in addition to objective reasons of state because of the interplay among the great powers and incipient British imperialism, there was a more personal and subjective ground for wishing to see a unitary Syria connected to Cairo disappear. Palmerston belonged to a millennialist evangelistic Christian movement that believed that the return of the Jews to Zion, that is, the Holy Land, would hasten the coming of the Messiah. This Christian Zionism, which was a forerunner of Jewish Zionism, was quite widespread in some British circles at that time. Palmerston's personal convictions would not have needed mentioning had they not impacted British foreign policy during the Syrian crisis from 1831 to 1841. The concern with restoring the Promised Land to the Jews gave British foreign policy under Palmerston a near-mystic quality that made Great Britain God's instrument.[12] Furthermore, once Mohamad Ali's armies had withdrawn to Egypt, Palmerston asked the sultan to place the Protestants and Jews in the Holy Land under Great Britain's protection. The sultan refused. This conjunction between British political interests and the personal religious convictions of some British leaders about the return of Jews to Palestine arose again in the twentieth century with Lloyd George's policy in Palestine.[13] This policy was to lead to the 1917 Balfour Declaration and Lloyd George and Clemenceau's 1918–19 revision of the 1916 Sykes–Picot agreement entailing the carving up of Syria and promoting the creation of a Jewish national homeland in Palestine.[14]

---

[12] According to the leading authority on Palmerston's diplomacy, his policy 'became connected with a mystical idea, never altogether lost in the nineteenth century, that Britain was to be the chosen instrument of God to bring back the Jews to the Holy Land'. Sir Charles Webster quoted in Fromkin, *A Peace to End All Peace*, p. 268. Anthony Ashley-Cooper 7th Earl of Shaftesbury, who was closely related to Lord Palmerston, wrote in July 1853 to Prime Minister Aberdeen that Greater Syria was '"a country without a nation" in need of "a nation without a country ... Is there such a thing? To be sure there is, the ancient and rightful lords of the soil, the Jews!' See Mary Grey, 'Preparing the Ground for Balfour – the Contribution of Shaftesbury', in balfourproject.org. It is believed this has later inspired the Zionist description of Palestine as being 'a land without [a] people for a people without a land'.

[13] On Palmerston and Lloyd George's Christian Zionism see Fromkin, *A Peace to End All Peace*, pp. 268–9.

[14] The Sykes–Picot agreement is discussed in Chapter 2, 'The Syrian Monarchy'.

1.3 A Wasted Opportunity to Create an Independent Syria

The idea of creating a politically independent Syrian entity recurred fleetingly after the 1860 religious crisis that shook Syria and Lebanon. First France then Great Britain suggested creating an Arab kingdom of Syria or Greater Syria.

The 1860 crisis began in the areas of mixed Maronite and Druze settlement of Mount Lebanon. Although initially a Maronite peasant revolt against Christian and Muslim landowners, the disorder quickly became religious and Druze massacred Christians. This blaze of religious violence quickly spread to Damascus where certain fanatical Muslims also slaughtered Christians. There were several reasons for this sudden outburst of violence in regions used to centuries of multi-religious coexistence. First was the Muslims' mistaken perception of the purpose of the sultan's reforms from the 1839 Edict of Gulhane to the 1856 Hatt-i Humayun.[15] The ensuing emancipation of Christians, favouritism towards them from European powers in commerce and education, the abusive extension of the system of Capitulations by European consuls, the change in the millennial order of things based on the distinction between Muslims and non-Muslims, the centralization of the state with mandatory conscription for Muslims alone, Christians being exempted from certain tax payments, and the new fiscal arrangements, were all factors that exacerbated inter-community tensions in Lebanon and Syria.

The exemplary conduct of Emir Abdel Kader during this crisis and his protection of the Christian population and the French consul in Damascus earned him the praise of Napoleon III, the French press, and European public opinion generally. Napoleon III despatched the French fleet to the Syrian coast. He was in favour of creating an Arab kingdom in Syria with Emir Abdel Kader at its head. But Abdel Kader wanted none of it. So the plan never materialized and the Sublime Porte seized the opportunity of this crisis of 1860 to take the Syrian provinces back in hand. The French expedition, presented as an armed humanitarian intervention, was followed by the establishment of an international commission tasked with establishing a new regime for the Syrian provinces.

---

[15] See Laurens, *L'Orient arabe*, pp. 65–6 on the Hatt-i Humayun. As stated earlier, the emancipation of the Christians in Syria started under Ibrahim Pasha before the Sultan issued the Edict of Gulhane in 1839.

In reaction to the 1860 religious massacres and fearing that France might grasp the chance of imposing a protectorate on Syria, Great Britain's representative on the international commission on Syria proposed creating a unified Greater Syria administered by a governor general appointed by the sultan but approved by the European powers.[16] This Ottoman Syria, which was much like the Egyptian Syria of Mohamad Ali and Ibrahim Pasha which, ironically, London had actively helped to dismantle in 1840–41 would, like Egypt, become gradually autonomous and eventually independent. Paradoxically, the British proposal was made when the government was headed by Palmerston, who, as foreign secretary two decades earlier, had gone to great lengths to destroy Mohamed Ali and Ibrahim Pasha's Syria. France, hoping to create an Arab kingdom in Syria under Abdel Kader, was hostile to the plan. Exploiting the opposition between France and Great Britain, the Sublime Porte used the 1860 crisis to recover and intensify its control over the Syrian provinces while granting autonomy to Mount Lebanon in 1861 where a *mutassarifia* was set up governed by a Christian official appointed by the Porte with the agreement of the European powers.

After the failure of the plan to create an Arab kingdom in Damascus and until the outbreak of the Great War in 1914, France was not to have a specific Syrian policy but merely an Ottoman policy encompassing Syria. Paris continued to support the *Tanzimat* reorganization process undertaken by the Porte and stood as guarantor of the empire's territorial integrity. France had everything to gain and under the aegis of the Ottoman empire her interests thrived. In the final fifty years of the empire, France multiplied its cultural, educational, medical, and charitable infrastructures,[17] developed a network of religious missions, and furthered its economic interests. French educational establishments and schools provided a basis for cultural and political influence that relied largely on a mainly Christian clientele, educated in French schools scattered throughout the empire in cities such as Istanbul, Beirut, Aleppo, Damascus, and Mosul.

All of these relations woven by France within the Ottoman empire formed an 'auxiliary France' or 'France of the Levant' which could not be territorialized because it had no geographical basis. A partition of the empire would have forced France to territorialize its influence, which it

---

[16] Laurens, *Le royaume impossible*, p. 126.
[17] French charitable establishments, hospitals, dispensaries, and schools were often referred to at the time as 'les œuvres françaises'. See Riffier, 'Les œuvres françaises et l'invention de la littérature de la Syrie', pp. 223–40.

refused to do before 1914. Alongside this, Paris was not slow to remind the other powers that might have had views on Syria that France had more interests there than any other European power and that in the event of a carve up it intended to stand by them. A 1909 memorandum of the Quai d'Orsay summarizes French policy up until the outbreak of the First World War:

> Since we hold more than ever to the integrity of the Ottoman empire, we must guard ourselves against seeming to contemplate laying hands on Syria. But our standoffishness must not comfort the other powers in concluding that they might themselves lay their hands on this country without having us to deal with. It is good that it should not be forgotten that we have abandoned to no one the traditional interests we have in Syria.[18]

The 1912 Balkan crisis had entailed a degree of agitation in Syria and Mount Lebanon. Fearing that Great Britain might take advantage of the unrest to internationalize the Syrian question, France secured a formal declaration from foreign secretary Sir Edward Grey that his country had no intention to act, nor any design or aspiration of any kind in Syria.[19] Britain, being tied to France by the *Entente cordiale*, respected its ally and pulled out of the eastern Mediterranean on the eve of the First World War.

1.4 The Gradual Assertion of a National Identity

The 1860 crisis gave the sultan an opportunity to strengthen his hold on the Syrian provinces. While they were not to experience any crisis similar to that of 1860 again, they were to form the crucible in which the feeling of a Syrian national identity was slowly forged.

1.4.1 The Arab Nahda

Arabs living in the Ottoman empire gradually began to show an awareness of nationhood in several ways before the outbreak of the Great War. Some historians date the national awareness of Arabs to the onset of the *nahda*, that is, the Arab renaissance movement that began in the nineteenth century with the arrival of the ideas of the Enlightenment and the French Revolution during Bonaparte's 1798 Egyptian campaign. This

---

[18] M.A.E., Turquie, 112, 82, memorandum by Jean Gout, sub-directorate Asia–Oceania, 26 May 1909, cited in Cloarec, *La France et la question de Syrie*, p. 21.
[19] Cloarec, *La France et la question de Syrie*, p. 33.

renaissance was accentuated by the political determination of the master of Egypt, Mohamad Ali, to modernize his country and escape as far as possible from cumbersome Ottoman tutelage. The Syrian campaign launched by his son Ibrahim Pasha in 1831 was the opportunity to project the power of the political ideals of the Arab *nahda* in a Near East where the population had still not become fully aware of nationhood.

But the Arab *nahda* also had a substantial religious dimension and other historians date the onset of the Arab renaissance to the work of Jamal Din Al-Afghani, the nineteenth-century advocate of reformism and the renewal of Islam. Al-Afghani held the Ottoman imperial order that had governed the nation for more than three centuries responsible for Islam's backwardness compared with Europe.[20] The torch he lit was taken up by his faithful disciple of Syrian origin, Ahmad Abdo, who found fertile ground in Egypt for propagating his ideas based on a liberal reading of Islam. Before him, Rifaa Tahtwai, sheikh of Al-Azhar, on returning from a stay in Paris between 1826 and 1831, had published *The Gold of Paris* in which he developed the theme of a possible synthesis between European innovations and ideas and the spirit of Koranic revelation.[21]

The Arab renewal was also manifested by a sizeable strand of literary and artistic thinking involving Syrian and Lebanese creators of all sectarian origins and especially Orthodox Christians, some of whom did not hesitate to go into exile so as to be able to express themselves freely. Cairo, Beirut, Damascus, and Baghdad created Arabic cultural clubs and religious study groups in the late nineteenth and early twentieth centuries. These associations were tolerated by the Ottoman authorities as long as they did not undermine loyalty to the empire and they confined themselves to promoting Arabic or calling for a renewal of Islam under the sultan. Some of these clubs were created in Istanbul and for a brief time enjoyed the freedom offered to the empire's subjects when the 1876 constitution was restored in 1908.

The first movement created by the Arabs in the wake of the 1908 coup d'état and the coming to power of the Committee of Union and Progress (CUP) or Young Turks was the Association for Arab–Ottoman Brotherhood. It set itself up as a defender of the 1876 constitution, while asserting its loyalty to the sultan. It advocated equality and brotherhood

---

[20] Other Syrian thinkers advocated similar ideas, such as Abdel-Rhaman Al-Kawakbi, author of the celebrated *Om al-koura (Mother of Cities)* (i.e. Mecca), published in 1902.
[21] Sorman, *Les enfants de Rifaa*.

among Arabs and Turks and sought to propagate teaching in Arabic. It was authorized to open branches throughout the Arab provinces and to publish its own newspaper. But the honeymoon between Arabs and Young Turks did not last. The centralizing power of the CUP and the determination to Turkify the Arab provinces soon alienated the support they had enjoyed among the enlightened Arab elite in 1908–09. The Association for Arab–Ottoman Brotherhood was dissolved. Arab associations now split into two groups: those advocating a renewal of Islam remained within the Ottoman fold while those calling for the national emancipation of Syrians changed into secret political societies or emigrated to more sympathetic countries.

Christians of the Orient played a leading part in associations asserting Arab and Syrian identity. The two terms were perceived as largely interchangeable at the time. Two countries, France and Egypt, became places of refuge for the exiled associations. Five of these associations deserve a mention because they played an important role in the gradual emergence of the national identity factor:[22]

(1) The Ottoman Administrative Decentralization Party was created in Cairo in 1912. Ever since the imposition of a British protectorate in Egypt in 1882, the primary political activity of nationals of the land of the Nile had been to free their homeland from British domination. Because all of the Egyptian nationalists' energy was mobilized to achieve this objective, they left to the Syrian and Lebanese nationals responsibility for the Arab national struggle for liberation from Turkish domination. Cairo became a place of refuge for Syrian and Lebanese exiles fleeing the repression of the Ottoman authorities.[23] This is how Syrian exiles in Cairo created the Ottoman Administrative Decentralization Party, which, as its name suggests, called for the decentralization of the empire's Arab provinces. The party set up branches in the utmost secrecy in the main cities of Syria, Lebanon, and Iraq. In Lebanon, the party worked with the Reform Committee, a secret nationalist association established in 1912.

(2) Al-Kahtania was formed in Istanbul in 1909 in reaction to the CUP's centralizing policy. The association sought to transform the Ottoman empire into an empire with two crowns, one Turk and the other Arab. The planned scheme was similar to the Austro-Hungarian empire

---

[22] See Wadi', *Syria, Creation of a State and Birth of a Nation* (Arabic), pp. 221–6.
[23] It was a Lebanese exile of the time who began the famous Cairo newspaper *Al-Ahram*.

model. Turks and Arabs would each establish their own kingdom with their own constitutions, parliaments, institutions, and languages under the authority of the sultan, who would wear the crowns of both kingdoms. This association was made up mostly of Arab officers of the Ottoman army.
(3) Al-Arabia Al-Fatat (Arab Youth) was formed in Paris in 1911 by seven Muslim students from Damascus, Jenin, Beirut, Nabulus, and Ba'albek. Its purpose was to secure full independence for the Arab provinces. The association's head office was transferred to Beirut in 1913 before being finally settled in Damascus. The association was to play a leading part in the political developments in Syria between 1915 and 1920.
(4) The Reform Committee was formed in Beirut in 1912 and comprised members from all sectarian origins. It advocated the decentralization of the Arab provinces and the use of Arabic, including in the Istanbul parliament. It also demanded that Arab conscripts should do their military service in their home province in peacetime. The committee set up branches in Damascus, Aleppo, Nabulus, Acre, Baghdad, and Basra.
(5) Al-'Ahd (The Covenant) was formed in Istanbul early in 1914 by former members of Al-Kahtania. It recruited mainly from the officer corps of Iraqi origin. It set up secret branches in Baghdad and Mosul. Al-'Ahd recommended the same objectives as Al-Arabia Al-Fatat but the members of the two associations, one military and the other civilian, were unaware of each other's existence until 1915. They made contact in Damascus in 1915 and decided to join forces to free the Arab provinces from Ottoman domination.

1.4.2 The 1913 Arab Congress in Paris

On the eve of the First World War, the themes of the Arab renaissance movement, the *nahda*, had already propagated in one form or another – political, religious, or literary – in all the Arab provinces of the Ottoman empire. The national project began with an initial phase calling for mere administrative autonomy within the Ottoman empire before taking the shape of a political programme of action that soon took on all the characteristics required for the formation of a true national project.

In reaction to the determination of the Istanbul government dominated by the CUP to stifle calls for reform from the Arabs, Al-Arabia Al-Fatat took the initiative of inviting members of the Party for

Ottoman Administrative Decentralization and members of the Reform Committee as well as independent figures including representatives of the Syrian–Lebanese community in exile in America to participate in a Syrian congress in Paris in the first half of 1913.[24] A preparatory committee (comprising four Muslims and four Christians) was appointed to prepare for the congress. The committee was tasked with contacting participants and explaining the objectives. The need to hold the congress outside the empire's territory was self-evident. The Ottoman authorities under the CUP would not have countenanced it. Paris was chosen as it was host to Al-Arabia Al-Fatat and a sizeable Syrian community.

The congress was held in Paris from 18 to 23 June 1913. The main points on the agenda were (i) national life and the refusal of Turkish hegemony; (ii) the rights of Arabs within the Ottoman empire; and (iii) the need to reform the empire on the basis of decentralization. The twenty-four participants were all Christian and Muslim Syrians, save two Iraqis, whose presence meant the congress became officially at the last minute the 'Arab' rather than 'Syrian Congress' as originally planned. The name change because of the presence of two Iraqi delegates is indicative of how nationalists at the time perceived Arab and Syrian identity. Syrians, Lebanese, and Palestinians were all considered Syrians, who were different from Iraqis, although all were Arabs.

In accordance with the agenda for the congress, all the interventions focused on the need to decentralize the Ottoman empire. At no time was the separation or secession of the Arab provinces evoked. The points most addressed in the interventions were the need to set up an Ottoman government that was neither Turk nor Arab, equal rights and duties of all Ottoman subjects, and the absence of discrimination among subjects of the empire because of their ethnic or religious origins.

The main conclusions of the congress were the need to reform the empire in depth, the recognition of Arabs' political rights to participate effectively in the central administration of the empire, the recognition of Arabic as an official working language in the Istanbul parliament, the recognition of Arabic as the official language in the empire's Arab provinces, the assignment as a matter of principle of Arab conscripts doing their military service in the Ottoman army to the Arab provinces of the empire, save in exceptional circumstances, and support for Armenian claims for

---

[24] Sultan, *History of Syria* (Arabic), pp. 168 ff.

decentralization of their province.²⁵ The conclusions of the congress may seem timid and its demands limited. But they were consistent with the organizers' initial objectives. The congress was an important step in developing awareness of a Syrian national identity. It was also the consecration of years of effort by the network of Syrian associations, cultural clubs, and political societies.

The greatest achievement of the Arab Congress of Paris was probably the convergence of interests and objectives expressed for the first time by Syrian Christian nationalists, who were traditionally proponents of the secular Syrian nationalist strand, with Syrian Muslims, who could a priori be seen as more favourable to a more Arab-Muslim nationalist strand. In this, the Paris congress was an important step towards political emancipation and the assertion of the national identity of Syrians of all creeds, Christian and Muslim, without distinction or discrimination based on religion. This fundamental feature was to be inseparable from the very idea of Syria from then on.

1.5 The 1915 Damascus Protocol

The Istanbul government despatched an emissary to Paris to discuss the recommendations adopted by the congress with the representatives there. He accepted them all and they were ratified by the sultan's government. But in practice, implementation of the recommendations was very hesitant and confined to a few measures such as the appointment of certain Arabs to honorific positions in Istanbul.²⁶

The second stage in the development of a Syrian political project was the call for national independence. This radical change of outlook was embodied in the drawing up of the 1915 Damascus Protocol.

The First World War began in the East in November 1914. After a short period of reflection in the aftermath of the outbreak of war on the European front, the Ottoman empire opted to side with Germany and the Austro-Hungarian empire. One of the very first decisions by the Ottoman authorities, even before they officially entered the war, was to abolish the Capitulations. By siding with Germany, the Young Turks hoped the war would end the economic tutelage of France and Great Britain, remove the military threat from Russia, and restore the Sublime Porte's influence in Egypt. There were many theatres of military

---

[25] Sultan, *History of Syria* (Arabic), pp. 175 ff.
[26] See Kayali, *Arabs and Young Turks*, pp. 177–8.

operations in the East. In 1914 the British landed in Basra to ensure the control of the oil fields and began a long and painful trek to Baghdad. In 1915 the French and British attempted to occupy the Dardanelles so as to then attack Istanbul. But this attack ended in failure at Gallipoli. In February 1915, Jamal Pasha, the Turkish governor of Syria, tried in vain to take the Suez canal through raids from Sinai. The capture of the canal was intended to foreshadow the Ottoman empire's reclaiming of Egypt.

The Arabs soon appeared as one of the important stakes in this war for both sides because of their supposed ability to muster support from Muslims worldwide. France and Great Britain, through their colonial empires, were Muslim powers, albeit secondary ones compared with the Ottoman empire, the sultan's caliphate, and his control over Islam's holy places. But even so they had considerable areas of influence in the Muslim world. The Ottoman authorities wanted Sharif Hussein of Mecca, descendant of the prophet and guardian of the holy places of Islam, to declare *jihad* on the Allies. For their part, the Allies tried to persuade him to rise against Turkish domination and declare *jihad* on the Ottoman empire. On the spot, relations between Sharif Hussein and the Ottoman representative in Medina became strained. The Young Turks did not have complete faith in the sharif's loyalty to the empire. The sharif disapproved of the Young Turks' stated intention to Turkify the Arab provinces. He resisted the Sublime Porte's demands to declare *jihad* on the pretext that the Hejaz needed Egypt for its supplies.

In 1914 correspondence began between the British representative in Cairo, Lord Kitchener, and the Sharif of Mecca. The British tried to convince him not to support the Ottoman empire's war effort. In January 1915, the secret society Al-Arabia Al-Fatat sent an emissary from Damascus to gauge the sharif's readiness to head an Arab revolt against the Turks that the Syrian civilian and military nationalists were preparing. In March 1915, Sharif Hussein sent his son, Emir Faysal, on a mission to Istanbul officially to meet the Ottoman leaders and complain of the misdeeds of the governor of Medina.[27] Unofficially, Faysal was instructed to make contact with Damascene nationalists and try to glean information about the Syrian revolt being prepared against the Turks mentioned by the emissary of Al-Arabia Al-Fatat.

---

[27] Sharif Hussein suspected the Sublime Porte wanted to replace him at the end of the war. See Fromkin, *A Peace to End All Peace*, pp. 425 ff.

1.5.1 Arab Nationalists in Damascus

En route to Istanbul, Faysal stopped off at Damascus for nearly four weeks. As agreed, he used his time to meet discreetly the Syrian nationalists and especially the most eminent members of the two main secret societies, Al-Arabia Al-Fatat and Al-'Ahd, who were fighting Turkish domination. They explained that they had the trust of most Arab officers stationed in the Arab provinces. Faysal was won over. He joined both secret societies and swore allegiance to them.[28]

Faysal was to inform the Syrian nationalists of the contacts already made by his father with the British and the two letters exchanged with Lord Kitchener. The nationalists noted this important development with interest, but were reluctant to break ties with the Ottoman empire and turn against the Turks, fearing European ambitions for the Arab provinces. Having lived with Turks within the same state for almost four centuries, if it meant choosing between Europeans and Turks, the Syrian nationalists would prefer to remain within the framework of the Ottoman empire. The state of mind of the Syrian nationalists at this particular time reflected contradictory feelings towards the Ottoman empire, mixing moral considerations, such as loyalty towards the Sublime Porte and religious solidarity, with political considerations, such as the fear of European aims and yet ample complaints about Ottoman policy and administration in its Arab provinces.

On his return from Istanbul in May 1915, Faysal again stopped off in Damascus for a few days. But he was to find a whole new situation. During Faysal's time in Istanbul, the two secret societies Al-Arabia Al-Fatat and Al-'Ahd had jointly come to a major decision for the region's future: to sever the ties between Arabs and Turks and to accept British support in the war should Britain accept the independence and unity of the Ottoman Arab provinces. The two secret societies of Damascus drew up a common document that they handed to Faysal to give to his father upon returning to Mecca. The document, known as the Damascus Protocol, was to be of great importance subsequently in the correspondence between Sharif Hussein and the British and for rallying the Arabs to the Allied cause.

1.5.2 From Decentralization to Independence

The Damascus Protocol is a brief text containing the terms on which the Arabs might contemplate joining the Allies against the Ottoman

---

[28] Sultan, *History of Syria* (Arabic), pp. 425 ff.

empire. These conditions reflected the change in the nationalist movement and Syrian Arabs' awareness of their identity. The deal was to be independence and unity of the Arab provinces in exchange for a long-term alliance with Britain. The document is novel in that it outlines the geographical borders of the future Arab state. This demarcation was to be fully endorsed by Sharif Hussein and taken up in his correspondence with McMahon, the high commissioner in Cairo, in the following weeks and months. The Protocol called on Great Britain to recognize the independence of a great Arab Asian state in the Middle East and the Gulf with the very understandable exception of Aden, a British colony of capital strategic importance on the route to India. Under the terms of the Protocol, the Arab state was to extend to the Taurus mountains in the north, the Arabian Gulf in the east, the Indian Ocean in the south, and the Red Sea and Mediterranean in the west. Just as with Aden, it was not asked that the Arab state should extend to African Arab territories (Egypt, Sudan, Libya, North Africa) then under Allied (British, Italian, and French) domination.

The Damascus Protocol also called for the abolition of all privileges granted to foreigners. It proposed the signing of a defence agreement between Great Britain and the future Arab state and the preference for Great Britain over any foreign power in economic projects.[29]

The Damascus Protocol is surprising and unprecedented for three reasons. First, this was when the Arab secret societies first called for separation from the Turks. The Damascus Protocol no longer called for simple administrative decentralization of the Arab provinces and recognition of Arab linguistic and cultural rights within the Ottoman empire as the Paris Congress had done, but, on the contrary, advocated a complete break with the Sublime Porte and the alliance of the Arabs with Great Britain in the Great War in exchange for recognition of their national rights to independence and unity.

Second, the peculiarity of the Damascus Protocol – which seemed surprisingly bold to both the Sublime Porte and the allied powers, who only discovered much later that the Arab revolt had been suggested by Syrian nationalists and that Sharif Hussein's claims had been formulated by those same nationalists – was that it sealed an alliance between the nationalists of Damascus and Sharif Hussein of Mecca. As a true association between

---

[29] See the full Arabic text of the Damascus Protocol in Wadi', *Syria, Creation of a State* (Arabic), p. 231.

political modernity and historical-religious tradition, this geopolitical alliance brought the Hejaz region close to the Bilad Al-Sham (or geographical Syria) and for a time bound the Arab nationalists of the major urban centres of the Near East, beginning with Damascus, to the bedouin tribes of the Arabian peninsula under the authority of the Sharif of Mecca.

Third, the other peculiarity of the Protocol is the request from the Damascus nationalists to Sharif Hussein to take command of the Arab revolt in recognition of his incontrovertible legitimacy as descendant of the prophet Muhammad and protector of the holy places of Islam. The Damascus nationalists saw Sharif Hussein as a saviour, or at least as the emblem behind which the whole region might rally. It is interesting that almost a century earlier, during the first Syrian crisis of 1830, Mohamad Ali, viceroy of Egypt, had already briefly contemplated resorting to the Sharif of Mecca to support and legitimize his rebellion against the Porte. Mohamad Ali's line of argument was to deny the legitimacy of the sultan-caliph in Istanbul who, unlike Sharif Yahia of Mecca, did not descend from the lineage of the prophet.[30]

Syrian nationalists were quite confident in 1915 of their ability to move into action at the right time and to trigger an Arab revolt because most of the Ottoman units stationed in Syria were composed of men and officers of Arab origin who were broadly favourable to their cause. Faysal expressed his enthusiasm for the organization of Al-'Ahd, most of whose members were Arab officers of the imperial army. However, as a precaution or out of necessity, Arab troops were transferred by the Ottoman governor Jamal Pasha to remote fronts, and especially to Gallipoli, where one of the major battles of the Great War was fought. That deprived the nationalists of the possibility of triggering themselves the insurrection against the Turks from Syria. This powerlessness to act was to be intensified by the ruthless repression they suffered from Jamal Pasha in the form of persecution, arrest, imprisonment, and execution of nationalists in Damascus and Beirut. In the future, any Arab revolt could only be started from the Hejaz by the Sharif of Mecca. This occurred in June 1916 on the basis of what was to say the least an ambiguous agreement between the Sharif of Mecca and the British.

The full inclusion in the correspondence of Sharif Hussein with McMahon of the geographical boundaries of the future Arab state was to

---

[30] Laurens, *Le royaume impossible*, p. 88.

be the main reference for Syrian territorial claims at the end of the war.[31] The creation of this future Arab state was to rally fighters from Arabia, the Near East (Syria), and even Mesopotamia (Iraq) in revolt against the Turks. This later prompted Faysal to say that while it was the men of the Hejaz who triggered the Great Arab Revolt, it was the Syrians who were its soul and inspiration.

The British and French knew nothing of the part played by the Syrian nationalists in developing the objectives of the revolt and their prior understanding with the Sharif of Mecca. This major failing meant that London and Paris were unable to properly understand the Arabo-Syrian national phenomenon. The French underestimated it and saw in it an epiphenomenon created by the British services to have the Arabs rise against the Turks so as to eliminate French influence in the region. The British underestimated the influence of Syrian nationalists and put all their hopes in the Hashemites whom they considered the true heralds of the Arab revolt, whereas the heart of Arab nationalism lay in Damascus, as they were later to discover.

Faysal returned to Damascus in January 1916 at his father's request to meet the nationalists discreetly. The situation he discovered had changed radically since his previous visit. The Ottoman governor Jamal Pasha had in the meantime transferred the Arab regiments stationed in Damascus and Aleppo to the remote fronts of the First World War and replaced them with Turkish-speaking units who were judged to be more loyal. On his return, Faysal informed his father that the revolt could no longer be triggered from Syria and had to come from the Hejaz.

The Great Arab Revolt was begun in June 1916 from the Hejaz by Sharif Hussein, who conferred command on his son Faysal. After a difficult start, the revolt was triumphant with the decisive aid of allied forces under General Allenby.[32] Upon entering Damascus, Allenby divided the Arab provinces liberated from the Ottoman empire into three separate occupied zones (east, west, and south), covering the four major cities of the interior (Damascus, Homs, Hama, and Aleppo) and east of the Jordan river (Irbid, Amman, Al-Kark, and Aqaba) for the eastern zone; the Mediterranean coast and Cilicia for the western zone;[33] and Palestine for the southern zone. It was these three occupied zones that Emir Faysal,

---

[31] The ambiguities of the correspondence between Hussein and McMahon are examined in Chapter 2.
[32] For a detailed account of the Great Arab Revolt see Kauffer, *La Saga des Hachémites*.
[33] Cilicia was later detached from the western zone to form the northern occupied zone.

commander-in-chief of the Arab forces and future king of Syria, sought in vain to unify as the Arab Kingdom of Syria.

Less than a century separates the Syria of Ibrahim Pasha (1831–42) from that of Emir Faysal (1918–20). The first had conquered Syria by force of arms at his father's command while the second freed it for his father with the decisive help of the British. This could only restrict his control over the liberated zones. The territories conquered by the former and claimed by the latter were largely the same. This Syrian geographical area covers what are now Syria, Lebanon, Jordan, Palestine/Israel, and part of Turkey.

Ibrahim's main strength lay in his army whereas Faysal's strength lay in Arabo-Syrian nationalism. Between Ibrahim and Faysal the perception the population had of its national identity had changed. Although the emancipation of Syrian Christians began under Ibrahim, his promotion of equal rights between Christians and Muslims in the context of religious coexistence within a modern administrative framework encouraged a gradual collective awareness of a common Syrian national identity. This national sentiment was made manifest by the participation of members of both communities in Arab political and literary clubs in the late nineteenth and early twentieth centuries and in the Arab Congress of Paris in 1913. Faysal's short reign confirmed this intention of Muslims and Christians to live together and for the first time introduced into the history of the Near East, through the 1920 constitution, the principle of a civil, non-religious state and laid the foundations for Syrian secularism.

The Syrian Christian and Muslim elites began by calling for administrative decentralization before demanding national independence. This change reflected the transition from Arab-ness to Arab-ism. This Arabism encompassed a larger area than geographical Syria. It was manifested by the Damascus Protocol and the alliance between Syrian nationalists and the Arabs of the Hejaz. The challenges faced by Syrians in the aftermath of the Great War changed it into sovereignist nationalism that was little inclined to compromise.

These features of Syrian identity that gradually emerged between the nineteenth and early twentieth centuries – a Near Eastern geographical space, a diverse population, and an idea – were reflected in a Syrian national project that the Founding Fathers were to develop during the brief but intense period of the Syrian monarchy.

PART I

Parliamentary Constitutions and Liberal Regimes

2

The Syrian Monarchy

I shall refer to Faysal's reign in Damascus from October 1918 to July 1920 and the regime established by the Syrian congress as the Syrian monarchy. The political history of the monarchy can be divided into two periods – that of the emirate and that of the kingdom of Syria proclaimed by the Syrian congress. The first began early in October 1918 after the withdrawal of Ottoman troops from Damascus and Emir Faysal's triumphal entry into the former capital of the Ummayads. The second began on 8 March 1920 with Faysal being proclaimed king by the Syrian congress, ending in tragedy on 24 July 1920 with the battle of Maysalun and the entry of French troops into Damascus the following day.

The brief history of the monarchy was rich in events that were crucial for the future of the Near East, the effects of which continue to be felt a century later. The challenges facing the founders of the monarchy were colossal: controlling the geographical area in which to build their state, developing a federating national project that respected diversity and in which all of the components of the society making up the future state could find their place, and establishing modern representative institutions. The material, financial, and military means available to the men of the monarchy to achieve such a programme and withstand the stated intentions of the French and British were fairly limited. But they had unshakeable faith in the righteousness of their cause and were naive enough to believe the wartime promises made by the Allies, and primarily the British.

The period of the monarchy marked the coming together of a geographical space with uncertain boundaries and an idea to be developed within it – the idea of Syria. It also sealed the coming together of a man, a prince of the desert, Faysal, descendant of the prophet, and a Muslim, Christian, and Jewish Arab population with a past stretching back thousands of years, which was both urban and rural, and which recognized itself in Faysal and proclaimed him king of Syria. The founding fathers of the Syrian monarchy and the French and British colonial powers were engaged in a frantic race against time. The former wanted to establish institutions representing a modern, independent, federating state, with a king, government, parliament, and constitution, as soon as possible so as to pull the rug from under any foreign domination. France and Britain sought to neutralize any hankerings for independence by destroying the incipient institutions and dividing the population the better to rule, and they sought to carve up the geographical area of Syria and reshape it at their own convenience, thereby distorting it.

The political history of the monarchy coincided only partly with the post-Ottoman military history of Syria. The Allied troops, who were mostly British and imperial, remained in the eastern occupied zone (Damascus, Homs, Hama, and Aleppo) until September 1919 before withdrawing to Palestine and east of the Jordan and handing over power within the space formed by the four main cities of inland Syria to the authority of Faysal. But it was not until six months later, in March 1920, that the Syrian congress announced Syria's independence and proclaimed Faysal king. From September 1919 to July 1920, France and the nascent Syria confronted one another without finding ground for agreement, although at one point they did reach a compromise. Had that agreement been applied it might have avoided much misfortune for both sides and would probably have altered the relations between France – and the west more broadly – and Arab nationalism. The young Syrian monarchy was in a somewhat intransigent nationalist mood, although not wholly opposed to a compromise with the mandate holder. The France of the Third Republic was still in an active colonial phase, which did not prevent some from trying, although in vain, to reach a compromise with Syria.

2.1 The Establishment of an Arab Authority in Damascus

Three institutions dominated the twenty-two months of the Syrian monarchy. First, there was King Faysal, a complex but sincere character, whom most of the population saw as a hero and liberator. But being inexperienced and little exposed to international politics, it was during this key period in the history of Syria and the region that he learnt about the niceties of international politics the hard way. Second, there was the Arab government in Damascus. Save for the brief reign of Ibrahim Pasha from 1831 to 1841, this was the first Arab government for more than four centuries in the city that was the fourth-holiest place of Islam. This government had an ambiguous status during the first period of the monarchy. Was it the government of an enemy region under military occupation by the Allies or a national government of a free territory? Third, from June 1919 there was the Syrian congress, which played a leading role during this period and left as its heritage an impressive collection of political texts of paramount importance that enlighten us as to the vision the Founding Fathers had for modern Syria.

2.1.1 Faysal, an Arab Sovereign

Faysal, the son of Hussein, was reportedly born in the Hejaz in 1883 or 1885. According to the Hashemite genealogy, Faysal was the thirty-eighth direct descendant of the Prophet Muhammad via the lineage of his daughter Fatima Al-Zahra and her husband Ali Bin Abu Taleb.[1] He spent his early years in the village of Rehab in the Hejaz, where he was initiated into the hard life of the desert bedouin, horse-riding skills, and the art of combat. In 1893 his father was summoned to Istanbul by the sultan, Abdul Hamid II, after he had contested the Sublime Porte's appointment of another member of the Hashemite family as Sharif of Mecca. Hussein went to Istanbul with his children and was placed under house arrest. They remained in Istanbul until the Young Turk coup in 1908. Hussein was finally authorized to return to the Hejaz and appointed Sharif of Mecca by Sultan Abdul Hamid in 1908.

During the fifteen years spent in Istanbul, Faysal completed his education. He learnt mathematics, geography, and history. His father taught him the Quran. He learnt to speak fluent Turkish, and a smattering of French. He spent time with officers of the Ottoman army and intellectuals, politicians, and men of letters, who regularly visited his father to discuss current events.

Faysal began his political career after returning to Mecca. In 1909 he became the member for Jeddah of the Istanbul Council of Representatives. His brother Abdullah, the future king of Transjordan, was elected member for the holy city of Mecca. Faysal made regular trips to Istanbul to attend sessions of the Council of Representatives.

The turning point in Faysal's political life that affected the rest of his career and the future of the entire region was his encounter in Damascus in 1915 with the nationalist societies Al-Arabia Al-Fatat and Al-'Ahd, which had been formed along the Turkish secret societies model in Istanbul.[2] Faysal had several meetings with them in Damascus in March 1915 on his way to Istanbul and in May 1915 on his way back to the Hejaz.

---

[1] For a biography of Faysal, see Alaywi, *Faysal Bin Al-Hussein* (Arabic), p. 24.
[2] See Chapter 1, 'The Syrian Question'.

He informed the nationalist groups of his father's first contacts with Lord Kitchener, the former British representative in Cairo. Between these two sets of meetings the nationalists' position changed markedly and became more radically opposed to the Ottoman empire. When Faysal first met the nationalists in March 1915, they confined themselves to claiming more rights for Arabs within the Ottoman empire. This moderate position was in line with the conclusions of the 1913 Congress of Paris. The nationalists' stance changed radically in the second series of talks in May 1915 when they informed Faysal of the joint decision by Al-Arabia Al-Fatat and Al-'Ahd to break all ties with the Ottoman empire and rise against the Turks in the event of the British supporting the principle of independence and the unity of an Arab state in Asia.

At that time, the nationalists were still fairly confident of their ability to conduct the revolt against the Turks without outside help. The members of Al-'Ahd, most of whom were in the armed forces, explained to Faysal that the majority of the Ottoman regiments stationed in Syria were composed of men and officers of Arab origin who would readily rally to the Arab cause. What the nationalists needed was for his father, Sharif Hussein of Mecca, as the highest moral and political authority in the Arab and Muslim world, to head the insurrection and the movement to liberate the Arab provinces of the Ottoman empire. The nationalists handed to Faysal for his father the Damascus Protocol, which determined the goal of the Arab revolt and delimited the boundaries of the future Arab state. This protocol was soon taken up almost word for word by Sharif Hussein in his subsequent correspondence with McMahon.

The revolt was triggered in the Hejaz in June 1916 with Faysal, at his father's request, as its military commander. Faysal was not a professional soldier but he had already had the opportunity, since his return from Istanbul in 1909, to distinguish himself in several punitive expeditions against local insurrections in the Hejaz (the Assir region) challenging the authority of the Sublime Porte.[3] The Arab revolt was supported materially by Great Britain, which supplied arms and advisers including the famous T. E. Lawrence, who became known as Lawrence of Arabia.[4] The first year of the revolt took the character of a local insurrection aimed at liberating the Hejaz from Ottoman military presence, although a number of Arab supporters and volunteers, mostly from Syria and Iraq but also from Egypt, joined Faysal's local forces, subsequently named the Arab army.

---

[3] Alaywi, *Faysal Bin Al-Hussein* (Arabic), pp. 43 ff.
[4] See his account of the Arab revolt in Lawrence, *Seven Pillars of Wisdom*.

It was in 1917 that the Arab revolt took on a truly regional and national character with the capture of the city of Aqaba. This conquest opened the gateway to the entire Near East and Syria for the Arab and Allied forces. British troops from Egypt landed in Palestine and joined the Arab army in Syria.

Faysal was welcomed as a liberator by a jubilant crowd on his arrival in Damascus on 3 October 1918. Allenby informed him that the western occupied zone would be under French control, the southern occupied zone under British control, and the eastern occupied zone under the control of Faysal's Arab forces with French assistance. Faysal objected to this territorial division into three occupation zones inspired by the Sykes–Picot agreement, of which he claimed to know nothing because he had not been officially informed of it. He refused for Syria to be landlocked, with the Palestine coast in the hands of the British and the Lebanese and the north-western coast as far as the Turkish border in French hands. Allenby could not settle the matter on its merits and answered that in any event the division of the region into three separate occupation zones was only a military operational arrangement and that the final political arrangements would be discussed with the competent authorities at the end of the war.[5]

2.1.2 An Arab Government

On 5 October 1918, two days after arriving triumphantly in Damascus, Faysal proclaimed the creation of an 'independent constitutional government ... in the name of Sultan Hussein extending over all Syrian territories'.[6] He appointed General Rida Rikabi to head the government, which depended de facto on Faysal. The main points of the communiqué were (i) the formation of an independent and constitutional Arab government in all Syrian lands; (ii) the appointment of Rida Pasha Rikabi as head of government; and (iii) the solemn affirmation that the government was built on the principles of justice and equality, that it would treat all Arabs the same regardless of their religion or creed and would not differentiate in law among Muslims, Christians, and Jews.[7]

---

[5] For details of the meeting between Faysal and Allenby in Damascus on 3 October 1918, see Fromkin, *A Peace to End All Peace*, pp. 330–9.
[6] Alaywi, *Faysal Bin Al-Hussein* (Arabic), p. 67.
[7] See the text of the communiqué in Al-Husri, *The Day of Maysalun* (Arabic), pp. 196–7.

Emir Faysal's first proclamation as leader of Syria was to have important implications for the future. First, Faysal addressed his message to all Syrians and so attempted to delimit his field of political action on the basis of his interpretation of his father's correspondence with the British. This field of action extended to all the Arab provinces freed from the grip of the Ottoman empire and covering in his own mind regions (Palestine, Lebanon, the Syrian coast) that stretched well beyond the eastern occupied zone of enemy territory that Allenby, as commander-in-chief of the Allied forces in Syria and Palestine, had conferred on him two days before. In appointing Rida Rikabi as head of government, Faysal merely confirmed indirectly a decision taken by Allenby to appoint Rikabi as military governor of the eastern occupation zone under the direct orders of Faysal as commander-in-chief of Arab forces.

Rikabi therefore had two official positions, one military in the context of the occupation of enemy territory and the other political, with the task of putting in place the institutions of an independent state.[8] The choice of ministers of the first Arab government was to be crucially important. The geographical origins of the members of the Rikabi cabinet confirmed Faysal's determination to cover all three occupied military zones, and even Iraq and the Hejaz. The ministers appointed by Faysal were of diverse origins. The cabinet included Syrians, Lebanese, Jordano-Palestinians, Iraqis, and Hejazis. The ministers were Christians and Muslims alike.[9] Thus Faysal indirectly confirmed the goal of the great Arab revolt set out in the Damascus Protocol and the Arab interpretation of the correspondence between his father and McMahon, namely to create an Arab state in Asia stretching from the Taurus mountains to the Indian Ocean.

In addition to Faysal's insistence on covering all the regions claimed by his father, the solemn proclamation of 5 October 1918 contained the seeds of one of the prime characteristics of the future Arab state: it was to be a constitutional state based on equal rights for all Syrians of all religions (Muslims, Christians, and Jews). This was of some reassurance to the minorities.

---

[8] Rikabi's government was composed of administrative directors and not formal ministers. In August 1919, Faysal created the council of directors as the precursor of a future national government. It was not until the creation of the kingdom of Syria in March 1920 that a political cabinet of ministers appeared.

[9] For the full list of Rikabi's cabinet members and their origins, see Al-Hakim, *Syria under Faysal's Reign* (Arabic), pp. 35 ff. The Druze complained the cabinet included none of their coreligionists.

This first communiqué published by Faysal after liberating Syria from four centuries of Turkish domination and Ottoman caliphate was very well received by the population. Although the liberating hero belonged to the lineage of the Prophet Muhammad, he proclaimed he intended to form a modern constitutional type of nation state and not a religious state based on Islamic law. The proclamation of equal rights for all citizens without any religious or sectarian distinction was well received by the Christian and Jewish communities. Equal rights reflected the collective will of the Arabs for all communities to live together and to create objective conditions to facilitate the inclusion of citizens in a modern national crucible that respected all identities.[10]

Rikabi's government soon set to work under the benevolent watch of the British authorities.[11] But Rikabi's double appointment by both Faysal and Allenby was to create confusion as to the nature of the authority being set up in the liberated Arab provinces. For the Allies, the division into three occupied zones, although largely inspired by the Sykes–Picot agreement, was purely military and operational and in no manner predetermined the political future of the region nor future national sovereignties. For Faysal and his supporters, the formation of this first Arab rule in Damascus was the outline of the future state for which the Arabs had revolted against the Ottoman empire. In the nationalists' view, the Arab government established in Damascus by Faysal was not just the government of the eastern occupation zone but should eventually extend to all three occupied zones. This confusion grew in the following months as the view that Faysal and the nationalists had of Syria's future diverged from that of Great Britain and of France especially, who stood by the wartime agreements signed between them. The confusion about the nature of Rikabi's cabinet ended when British troops left the north of the eastern occupation zone and redeployed east of the river Jordan in Palestine in September 1919.

The first Arab government maintained as far as possible the administrative structures inherited from the Ottoman empire and simply changed the personnel. Thus instead of the tutelary ministers of Istanbul overseeing the administration of the vilayets, the government created 'general directorates' of the interior, justice, education, finances, general security,

---

[10] See Edmond Rabbath, *The Historical Formation of Political and Constitutional Lebanon* (Arabic), pp. 492–3.

[11] See Al-Hakim, *Syria under Faysal's Reign* (Arabic), p. 70 on British financial aid to Faysal's Arab government in Damascus.

and war. The government also created a State Shura Council, the equivalent of supreme administrative and judicial courts, like those in Istanbul.

2.1.3 Internal Political Life and the Construction of the State

Post-Ottoman Damascus was a thriving city under the monarchy. It was the centre of political and cultural activity of the entire Near East. Dignitaries, politicians, soldiers, and intellectuals flowed in not just from the western and southern occupation zones towards Damascus but also from neighbouring Iraq. Multiple political parties were formed and newspapers flourished. The political class became impassioned for Syria's independence and unity. There was open discussion in the press and the congress of subjects including women's suffrage in a way unthinkable just a few months earlier. Faysal had no difficulty building a very broad pro-independence consensus among the various components of Syrian society. He endeavoured to reassure all the minorities, particularly Christians but Jews too.

The main characteristics of this nascent state were to be found in the various documents produced at the time by the national and religious constituted authorities and in Faysal's public stance. Just days after the liberation of the northern part of Syrian territory and the signing of the armistice of Mudros on 30 October 1918 between the Turkish troops and Allied forces, Faysal went to Aleppo, the leading city of the north. There he made a major speech taking up some of the themes already set out in Damascus and developing others that shed light on the precise views he then held about the priorities for organizing Syria and the other Arab territories.[12] Referring to the great Arab revolt and the end of Ottoman domination, Faysal called the liberation of the Arabs a renaissance. 'We were asleep for six hundred years, but we were not dead. We were awaiting the opportunity to be born again.' Faysal insisted that the form of rule he meant to establish was based on Arabism and not religion. 'I repeat what I have said at all times – the Arabs were Arabs before Jesus, Moses, and Mohamed. Religions order us on Earth to follow the path of truth and brotherhood. Whoever tries to sow discord among Muslims, Christians, and Jews is not an Arab.'[13]

---

[12] See the text of Faysal's Aleppo speech of 11 November 1918 in Al-Husri, *The Day of Maysalun* (Arabic), pp. 197–203.
[13] *Ibid.*

Faysal set out the priorities for building an Arab state. This would mean the formation of a government, army, police force, gendarmerie,[14] and the provision of education throughout the country. Faysal gave reassurances about his future way of governing. He announced that it was only normal for martial law to apply in wartime to ensure order until a government could be formed. So as not to leave a legal vacuum, he proclaimed that the previous laws adopted during the Ottoman period would be maintained until new laws could be drawn up by the Council of the Nation (the future parliament). Faysal acknowledged that in terms of priorities, he should probably have begun by convening the institution tasked with drafting the laws, but those Arabs who were experts in this area lived abroad, and he appealed to them to return to play their part in full.

Faysal was already contemplating a highly decentralized organization for the Arab provinces freed from Ottoman domination:

> Arabs are formed from various nations and populations in their regions. The Aleppan is unlike the Hijazi and the Damascene different from the Yemeni. This is why my father has decided that the country shall be divided into territories in which special laws shall apply depending on the frame of mind and circumstances of their inhabitants. The lands of the interior shall have laws appropriate to them and the coastline shall also have laws reflecting the wishes of its population.

These pragmatic provisions were designed primarily to reassure the Christians of Mount Lebanon that the new ruler's intentions towards them were sincere.

2.1.4 The Christian and Jewish Authorities' Allegiance to Faysal

Shortly after the publication of the communiqué of 5 October 1918, Faysal received the religious authorities representing the Christians and Jews of Damascus. They wished to go over some of the themes developed in the proclamation of the day before. The religious representatives asked Faysal seven questions before granting him their support. The questions concerned obedience to God, respect of religions, consultation before introducing laws and regimes relating to religious affairs, equal rights, reinforced security, education provision, appointment to public office, and employment based on merit. Once Faysal had replied positively to all

---

[14] 'The gendarmerie and police are the pillars of the country,' Faysal said. 'Policing is a noble occupation.' *Ibid.*

seven questions, the Christian and Jewish religious authorities proffered their unanimous support.

On 8 March 1920, the day the independence of the kingdom of Syria was proclaimed, the Christian and Jewish religious authorities of Damascus again met Faysal, now king of Syria, and swore allegiance and loyalty to him. The text of the oath of allegiance referred to the choice of the Syrian nation to appoint Faysal king of Syria within its natural borders and recalled the terms of the encounter of those same religious authorities with Faysal on 7 October 1918, just days after his entry into Damascus, and the answers he gave to the seven questions. This oath of allegiance was set down in writing and signed by the religious representatives in the name of their congregations (Syriac, Catholic, Orthodox, Protestant, Armenian-Catholic, Maronite, Armenian).[15] It was published at Faysal's order in the Official Journal on 11 March 1920.

2.2 Foreign Policy under the Monarchy

Foreign policy under the monarchy can be summarized in the post-war arrangements. The French and British considered the Near East to be compensation for their war efforts and their victory over Germany and its Ottoman ally. The peace conference, initially characterized by the promising presence of the United States and the generous ideas of President Woodrow Wilson, changed with the San Remo conference in April 1920 into a simple recording chamber for a new Franco-British agreement revising the Sykes–Picot agreement of 1916 and granted France and Great Britain mandates – a new form of colonial tutelage – over the territories of the kingdom of Syria. It was during the peace conference that Faysal first called for the creation of a Syria covering the Near East independent from the Hejaz and Iraq. But before coming to this, it would be helpful to recall the correspondence between the British and the Sharif of Mecca and the negotiations between the French and British during the First World War.

2.2.1 The Differing Interpretations of the 1915–1916 Hussein–McMahon Correspondence

When war broke out in 1914, France's ultimate intention for the Ottoman empire was not immediately obvious but emerged gradually. French diplomacy hesitated over the future of the Ottoman empire and was

---

[15] See the text in Al-Hakim, *Syria under Faysal's Reign* (Arabic), p. 143.

initially inclined to preserve rather than dismantle it. There was no shortage of reasons for maintaining the empire because it had permitted France to project its economic, cultural, and linguistic influence, and to form a clientele in the Balkans and the Orient over a period of four centuries. Besides, the Sublime Porte's loss of the Balkans in 1912 had resulted in France's eviction from this part of south-eastern Europe to the benefit of other powers, especially Britain and Greece. The prevailing feeling in France was that the bitter experience of the Balkans should not be repeated in other provinces that were separating from the empire. Similarly, it took the British authorities time to establish a precise position on the post-war future of the Near East. In April 1915, the prime minister, Asquith, created a ministerial commission led by a diplomat, Sir Maurice de Bunsen, which reported in June 1915. The Bunsen commission recommended abandoning the traditional British position of maintaining the territorial integrity of the Ottoman empire and recommended that the region of Smyrna go to Greece, Adalia (Antalya) to Italy, the southern Taurus and northern Syria to France, Palestine and Mesopotamia to Britain, and the remainder to Russia.[16]

Before the Bunsen commission met, Great Britain had already begun corresponding in autumn 1914 with Hussein, the Sharif of Mecca, through McMahon, the high commissioner in Cairo. After the return of his son Faysal from Damascus,[17] Hussein proposed during the summer of 1915 to lead an Arab rebellion and side with the Allies in exchange for the promise of Arab independence in a unitary state whose bounds would correspond to the borders defined by the Damascus Protocol given to Faysal by the Damascus secret societies when he travelled through Syria in May 1915. London immediately grasped the significance of the Sharif of Mecca's defection and the impact it might have on the Arab population within the Ottoman empire and the Arab troops fighting on the various fronts within the imperial army. Since the territory claimed by Hussein included Syria, London could make no specific promise without consulting France, which before the war had already expressed an interest in the region that it confirmed many times over. But so as not to miss the opportunity of the Sharif of Mecca rallying to them, London authorized McMahon to make him certain promises and invited Paris to send an emissary to London to negotiate post-war arrangements for the East.

[16] Cloarec, *La France et la question de Syrie*, p. 33.
[17] Fromkin, *A Peace to End All Peace*, pp. 146 ff.

London's instructions to McMahon were hazy, prompting him to answer Sharif Hussein in vague terms that caused controversy and were variously construed and translated by the different sides after the war. The main controversy was over the limits of the future independent Arab state. To Hussein, who called for a state in accordance with the Damascus Protocol, McMahon replied in October 1915 that the two districts of Mersine and Alexandretta and those portions of Syria west of the districts of Damascus, Homs, Hama, and Aleppo could not be said to be purely Arab, and had to be excluded from the bounds demanded. Palestine was not promised to Hussein either. As for Mesopotamia (Baghdad and Basra), McMahon simply asserted it must come under special administrative arrangements.

For McMahon and his team in Cairo, the Damascus-Homs-Hama-Aleppo line marked the boundary between Arab and Levantine lands.[18] The population west of the line was supposedly Levantine, Arabic-speaking, and Francophile, but not truly Arab. This naive and mistaken view of things was challenged by Hussein in his answer to McMahon in November 1915. Hussein accepted the British position on the two districts of Anatolia, but refuted the idea that the population west of the Damascus-Homs-Hama-Aleppo line was not Arab. Hussein said there was no difference between Muslim and Christian Arabs and that the population of the coast was Arab. McMahon answered in a letter of December 1915 noting his position on the Christian Arabs and affirmed that the question of the vilayets (provinces) of Aleppo and Beirut (that governed all the Syrian coast from Alexandretta to the sanjak of Jerusalem) would have to be discussed subsequently with France because of the interests that country had in these regions.

Hussein and McMahon's correspondence ended without any precise agreement on the bounds of the future Arab state and in particular the western zone – the Mediterranean coastline of Syria – and Palestine. This approximation of the agreement, whether deliberate or not, engendered a series of misunderstandings between the Arabs and British over the post-war arrangements. At no time did McMahon indicate in his correspondence with the Sharif of Mecca, which went on largely in parallel with the negotiations in London between the French and British leading to the Sykes–Picot agreement, that the post-war Near East would be divided into zones of direct British and French influence and control.

[18] Laurens, *L'Orient arabe*, p. 141.

Confident that a firm alliance had been established with Great Britain, the Sharif of Mecca triggered the Arab revolt on 10 June 1916 and called for *jihad*, holy war, against the Turks.[19] The promises made to Sharif Hussein were repeated on several occasions until the end of the conflict, firstly by Great Britain, such as those in the Declaration to the Seven, made to seven Syrian nationalists including Dr Shahbandar in Cairo on 22 June 1918, and even by France in a joint Franco-British communiqué of 8 November 1918.[20]

2.2.2 The Sykes–Picot Agreement

The negotiations that were to lead to the Sykes–Picot agreement began in London in November 1915 in parallel with the correspondence between Hussein and McMahon. The French delegation was led by Georges Picot and the British delegation initially by Sir Arthur Nicholson, who was replaced in December 1915 by Mark Sykes, a protégé of Lord Kitchener, who had become minister for war.

Picot's aims in the talks can be summarized as follows: (i) to keep the Ottoman empire intact as far as possible but weak and so amenable to French economic expansion; (ii) if partition of the empire became inevitable, to claim for France all of Syria including Palestine;[21] (iii) to extend the French zone from the Mediterranean coast in the west to Mosul in the east; and (iv) to ensure the French zone consisted of a direct occupied zone that had to include the Mediterranean coast, Lebanon, and a zone of French influence under Arab administration in inland Syria.

---

[19] Actually, Hussein may have had his doubts but at that point he no longer had any choice. The Porte had decided to replace him or even physically eliminate him. See Fromkin, *A Peace to End All Peace*, p. 174.

[20] See the text of the Declaration to the Seven and the joint Franco-British Communiqué in Al-Hakim, *Syria under Faysal's Reign* (Arabic), pp. 33–4 and 37–8.

[21] These are the instructions given to Picot concerning the boundaries of Syria from the records of the Quai d'Orsay: 'This reservation made (neutralization of Jerusalem and Bethlehem), the simplest solution seems to be to settle on Syria its current administrative bounds. Its territory would thus include the vilayets or mutasarrifiyya of Jerusalem, Beirut, Lebanon, Damascus, Aleppo, and to the north-west, all of the part of the vilayet of Adana south of the Taurus. Particularly fertile regions or Adana, the node of routes of Asia Minor, would thus be secured for us and give our new possession its full value. The new Arabian sovereignty (peninsula) would thus have for bounds Syria so drawn.' And again: 'The name Syria has from all time been understood in France in a broad sense. And the 1840 treaty merely reproduced the general opinion, giving the name of southern Syria to Palestine. It would therefore not be understood that we should abandon any part of the Syrian coast. And please insist that our possession ends only at the Egyptian border.' In Hajjar, *La Syrie (Bilad Al-Cham), démembrement d'un pays*, pp. 12–13.

Sykes' objectives can be summarized as: (i) to maintain the unity of the four inland cities promised to Sharif Hussein (Damascus, Homs, Hama, and Aleppo); (ii) to claim direct administration over the provinces of Baghdad and Basra; (iii) to claim the port of Alexandretta; (iv) to set up a French buffer zone north of Syria to protect the British zone in the south of Syria from future Russian ambitions; and (v) to secure Palestine for Britain, although Kitchener considered Palestine of no interest and wanted none of it.

A compromise was struck. First, the port of Alexandretta remained in the French zone in exchange for which Britain received the ports of Haifa and Acre in Palestine. Second, the holy places of Palestine (Jerusalem, Bethlehem, and the neighbouring areas) were to be given international status. Third, France had direct administration over the zone extending from the north of Palestine to Cilicia including the Mediterranean coast and Mount Lebanon and a part of Anatolia. It also received a zone of influence (Zone A) stretching to the Persian border and covering an independent Arab state including the four cities of inland Syria (Damascus, Homs, Hama, and Aleppo) and Mosul. Fourth, Great Britain received a direct administrative zone encompassing Baghdad and Basra and a zone of influence covering an Arab state connecting Palestine to Mesopotamia and extending from Aqaba to Kirkuk (Zone B).

The main weakness of this arrangement was that the Arabs of Syria and Sharif Hussein had not been consulted as to whether the population of the four Syrian cities of the interior (Damascus, Homs, Hama, and Aleppo) and the coastal cities (Tyre, Sidon, Beirut, Tripoli, Tartous, and Latakia) wanted to be part of the zone of direct administration or under French influence. Except for the Maronites of Mount Lebanon, most of the Syrian population was hostile to France and preferred British tutelage. By a cruel irony of history, the Syrians, who had urged Sharif Hussein to lead the Arab revolt and ally with Britain and had suggested the borders of the future independent Arab state, were to find themselves a few years later under French tutelage.

The other great weakness in this arrangement was the haziness of the borders. Where exactly did the bounds of the direct administration zones (Zone A for France and Zone B for Britain) stop and where did those of the future independent Arab states under British or French influence begin? Although this did not raise any particular difficulty in the case of the British zone, it did cause violent opposition from the Syrian population of the interior in the case of the French zone. As a result of the French interpretation of this agreement, Syria was to lose the four districts of the Beqaa valley east of Mount Lebanon (Zahlah, Ba'albek, Rashaya, and Hassbaya) in 1919. Moreover, under this agreement, Syria was deprived of access to the sea.

The agreement reached between Picot and Sykes was ratified by the French and British governments in February 1916 and kept secret. To finalize it required the Russian government's consent. This was secured in April 1916 and it became the Sykes–Picot–Sazanov agreement that gave Armenia and eastern Anatolia to Russia. A year later, the agreement was extended to Italy at the Saint Jean de Maurienne conference. Under the finalized agreement, Italy was to have a zone of direct control and a zone of influence over southern Anatolia bordering the Aegean Sea. In June 1916, the Sharif of Mecca triggered the great Arab revolt, knowing nothing of the agreement between the French and British about the future of the region that he sought to liberate from Turk domination.

The British view of the importance of the Middle East in the conduct of the war and the arrangements among the Allies for the post-war period was overturned when Lloyd George came to power late in 1916. With Lloyd George at the head of the British government, the architecture among the Allies was changed from top to bottom. Unlike his general staff, Lloyd George did not see the theatre of operations in the Middle East as marginal or secondary to military operations in Europe but as a central or even crucial front in the war against Germany and its Ottoman ally. In addition, Lloyd George did not believe it would be possible to secure gains in Europe in the event of an Allied victory. The European continent was devastated by war and any annexation or new territorial acquisition by the victorious powers would have to be made elsewhere. The Middle East was the ideal compensation for the expanding British empire. That was where the British crown could look to make the greatest gains after the war.

Strategically, Palestine was the final missing link to connect overland British possessions from the Cape of Good Hope to India via Sudan, Egypt, and the former German colonies of East Africa that had fallen into British hands (Rwanda, Burundi, and Tanganyika) during the war. After the occupation of Mesopotamia by troops from British India and the alliance with the Persian empire, only Palestine was missing to link British territories from the Atlantic to the middle of the Pacific.[22]

Lastly, Lloyd George was a committed Zionist. As with Palmerston in the nineteenth century, this personal conviction might have remained private had it not influenced his public action as prime minister. Palmerston shared the opinion of a strand of British thought of Puritan, Protestant, and

---

[22] See Fromkin, *A Peace to End All Peace*, pp. 281 ff.

Evangelical tradition which, since the eighteenth and nineteenth centuries, had advocated the return of the Jews to the Holy Land. Lloyd George came to Zionism by a different road.[23] Before entering politics, Lloyd George had been the attorney of the Zionist movement in Great Britain and negotiated in the name of the movement with Lord Balfour in 1913 the securing of land for Jews in Uganda. An agreement was made to this effect and Lord Balfour made a solemn declaration. This Balfour Declaration on Uganda had little effect, however, so in 1917 a second Balfour Declaration promised the creation of a Jewish national homeland in Palestine.[24]

2.2.3 The Revision of the Sykes–Picot Agreement

The revision of the clauses of the Sykes–Picot agreement began when Clemenceau and Lloyd George met in London in December 1918 a month after the signing of the armistice at Rotondes. It was then that Lloyd George – observing the change in Russian circumstances after the Czar's fall and the scant interest the Bolsheviks showed in the Near East and the Sykes–Picot agreement in which the former regime had been involved – claimed Mosul, which was initially to have been part of the zone of French influence, and Palestine including Jerusalem, which was to have been placed under international administration. Clemenceau accepted outright. This verbal agreement was confirmed by Clemenceau in a memorandum to Lloyd George on 15 February 1919[25] and then in discussion within the Council of Four (Woodrow Wilson, Lloyd George, Clemenceau, and Orlando, Prime Minister of Italy) at Versailles in March and June 1919 as part of the peace conference.[26]

Before the conference's work began and after a short stay in Paris, Faysal went to London in January 1919 where he had talks with the foreign secretary, Lord Balfour. Faysal voiced his fears about French ambitions in Syria and asked for British help. He added that he would fight the French even if the forces were manifestly disproportionate and that if they had to be under foreign domination he would prefer it to be that of the Turkish government, no matter how bad.

---

[23] As Asquith put it, sourly but accurately, 'Lloyd George ... does not care a damn for the Jews or their past or their future, but he thinks it would be an outrage to let the Christian Holy Places – Bethlehem, Mount of Olives, Jerusalem &c – pass into the possession of "Agnostic Atheistic France"!' Barr, *A Line in the Sand*, p. 35.
[24] On Lloyd George's Zionism see Fromkin, *A Peace to End All Peace*, pp. 263 ff.
[25] See Kasmiyé, *Memoirs of Aouni Abdel-Hadi* (Arabic), p. 56.
[26] Mantoux, *Les Délibérations du Conseil des Quatre*, pp. 137–59.

Faysal knew nothing of the Franco-British revision of the initial terms of the Sykes–Picot agreement. Lord Balfour failed to mention that the French and British had already come to an a priori agreement on the new lines along which the region was to be sliced up.[27]

After London, Faysal returned to Paris. His stay in the French capital was the opportunity to meet Clemenceau, who assured him that France had no colonial aspirations regarding Syria and that in exchange for Syria accepting a French mandate, France would be ready to recognize Syrian independence. The encounter between Faysal and Clemenceau ended with a loose gentlemen's agreement that Faysal would use his influence to bring this about.[28] Faysal's few weeks in Paris were also an introduction for him into French political and intellectual life. He met politicians, Quai d'Orsay diplomats, and intellectuals including Anatole France, with whom he had many meetings.

In his intervention at the peace conference and in his two written communications, Faysal no longer called for a unitary Arab state in southwestern Asia stretching from the Taurus mountains in the north to the Arabian Gulf in the east, the Indian Ocean in the south, and the Red Sea and Mediterranean in the west, as had been claimed by his father in his correspondence with McMahon and in the Damascus Protocol.[29] Instead Faysal called for the creation of several separate Arab political entities but related by contractual bonds (economic and trade-related, among others), namely an independent Syria with foreign advisers, but without outside tutelage, and Arab governments for Iraq and the northern part of the Arabian peninsula, which might in addition have recourse to a foreign power for help with developing domestic administration.[30]

Faysal did not address the fate of the Hejaz or the Nejd in the Arabian peninsula, nor that of Yemen. The British supported Faysal's demands, but France vehemently opposed Syria's independence, invoking the Sykes–Picot agreement. To break the deadlock, President Woodrow Wilson proposed a compromise that involved sending a commission of enquiry to Syria to ascertain the wishes of the population. What was to be the King–Crane commission was composed solely of two US representatives, as the French and British declined to take part. Faysal was to pin great hopes on

---

[27] Kasmiyé, *Memoirs of Aouni Abdel-Hadi* (Arabic), p. 87.
[28] From the account Faysal gave to Clayton in May 1919 and cited in Kasmiyé, *Memoirs of Aouni Abdel-Hadi* (Arabic), p. 102.
[29] See the full text of Faysal's communications to the peace conference in Laurens, *L'Orient arabe*, pp. 156–8.
[30] Kasmiyé, *Memoirs of Aouni Abdel-Hadi* (Arabic), p. 96.

the commission and President Wilson's ability to see his precious principles about the right of the people to self-determination prevail. The future was to prove him wrong on both points.

Further to the King–Crane commission's tour of the region in June and July 1919, Franco-British relations deteriorated seriously. France was very disappointed at the turn events in Syria and at the vast majority of the population's rejection of the French mandate in favour of a US, or failing that a British, mandate. France openly accused Faysal of pulling strings for the British. It was the foreign secretary, Lord Balfour, who took the initiative of making the gesture Paris was waiting for to improve relations. On 11 August 1919, Balfour submitted a memorandum to Lloyd George explaining the reasons for the dispute with France. The cause, he argued, lay in the contradictions inherent in five commitments made by Britain – the Sykes–Picot agreement, the correspondence between Hussein and McMahon, the Franco-British common declaration of 9 November 1918, the Covenant of the League of Nations, and the instructions given to the King–Crane commission. Balfour concluded by asserting that Britain's interests in the region were limited to an agreement with France and the implementation of the commitment to the Zionist movement to create a Jewish national home in Palestine. As for the Arabs, meaning here Faysal and the Syrians, they would have to come to an understanding with France.

On the basis of this memorandum, Lloyd George met General Allenby in Deauville on 9 September 1919. For two days, the two men discussed British policy in the region and decided to withdraw British troops from the northern part of the Near East, that is, from the eastern and western occupation zones, from 1 November 1919. Great Britain held on to just Palestine and Mesopotamia. British forces stationed west of the dividing line drawn by the Sykes–Picot agreement, that is, Mount Lebanon and the remainder of the Syrian coast except for Palestine, were replaced by French troops. British forces located east of the Sykes–Picot dividing line withdrew and were superseded by the Sharifian Arab army, that is, inland Syria with the four major cities of Damascus, Homs, Hama, and Aleppo but without the zones east of the Jordan (Irbid, Amman, Al-Kark, and Aqaba), which remained under British control, although this region had always been an integral part of the vilayet of Damascus.[31]

Syrian territory was similarly eroded when the decision to withdraw British troops from the west was implemented. As stated earlier, Paris

---

[31] British troops also withdrew from Cilicia and southern Armenia.

and London changed at will the western border of Syria and included the Beqaa plain (the four cazas of Ba'albek, Zahlah, Rashayia, and Hasbayia) in the territory of Lebanon, which had also always been part of the vilayet of Damascus.[32] This withdrawal of British forces and their replacement by French troops on the basis of the Sykes–Picot agreement revisited by Lloyd George and Clemenceau, an act of gross hypocrisy and bad faith, was presented to the Syrians as a military redeployment and a readjustment of the occupation zones that in no way predetermined the peace conference's final decision.

Although its territory had just suffered the amputation of its southern parts (east of the Jordan and Palestine), all of its coastline, Mount Lebanon, the Beqaa valley, not to mention Cilicia and Mosul, at this time the embryo of an Arab political entity carrying the values of the great Arab revolt still existed in the Syrian interior. The Syrian territory controlled by Faysal was homogeneous and the vast majority of the Arab-speaking Muslim and Christian population supported his cause.

Lloyd George invited Faysal back to London in September 1919. He informed him of Britain's decision to withdraw its troops from the northern part of the Near East in accordance with the Sykes–Picot agreement and to hand over the western occupation zone to France and the eastern occupation zone to the Arab troops. Lloyd George advised Faysal to come to some arrangement with France about the future of the independent Arab state-to-be because it was in the French zone of influence under the Sykes–Picot agreement. Faysal's protests made no difference. The nationalists considered that, having laid hold of Palestine and given the northeastern Mediterranean coast to France, Great Britain delivered up Faysal and inland Syria to France bound hand and foot.

2.2.4 The Faysal–Weizmann Agreement

Faysal's lack of experience in international affairs and diplomatic negotiations showed starkly in the signing in January 1919 of a conditional agreement with Chaim Weizmann of the World Zionist Organization.

---

[32] On 27 November 1919 Faysal and Clemenceau agreed on the non-occupation of the Beqaa valley by French troops and the withdrawal of Arab troops stationed there. Only the administration and the Sharif's gendarmerie were to remain. The agreement also provided for the creation of a mixed Franco-Arab committee for security-related questions. But just days later French troops reoccupied Ba'albek using an assault on a French liaison officer as pretext.

Although it was a putative agreement, contemporary Arab politicians a century later have still not forgiven Faysal.[33]

The circumstances surrounding the signature of the agreement attest that London used all of its considerable influence with Faysal to urge him to reach an understanding with Weizmann. During Faysal's short stay in London in 1918 and early 1919, the Foreign Office asked Colonel T. E. Lawrence to arrange for Faysal and Weizmann to meet. The two had already met through the British on 4 June 1918 at the Al-'Awal camp in the Al-Ghoueira region between Aqaba and Ma'an, in what was to become Transjordan. Weizmann recorded that Faysal was aware at the time of the Zionist plan for Palestine but not the details of the national state to come. According to Weizmann, Faysal told him that Jewish colonization in Palestine would have to be done under Arab sovereignty because Palestine was an Arab country, while acknowledging he had no mandate to discuss political matters as these were in the care of his father, the Sharif of Mecca.[34] Aouni Abdel-Hadi asserted in his memoirs that Weizmann told Faysal at this interview that the Jews had no intention of creating a state in Palestine.[35]

The meeting between Faysal and Weizmann set up by Lawrence in London took place on 3 or 4 January 1919 or on the following days, the exact date is uncertain. The two signed an agreement that detached Palestine from the Arab state (art. I), the frontiers of which would have to be negotiated between the two parties after the peace conference (art. II). The agreement provided for the implementation of the Balfour Declaration (art. III) including intensive Jewish immigration (art. IV) that was not to call into question the rights of 'Arab peasants'. It further provided that no law or regulation would interfere with the freedom of worship of all (art. V), that Muslim places of worship would remain under Muslim administration (art. VI), and it set out the bases for Jewish–Arab cooperation on economic development (art. VII).

Aouni Abdel-Hadi asserts in his memoirs that the wording of the agreement was drafted by Colonel T. E. Lawrence in his own hand, in English, a language Faysal knew nothing of, and that no Arabic translation of it was

---

[33] See Khaddam, *The Contemporary Arab Regime* (Arabic), pp. 181 ff.
[34] Reported in the memoirs of Aouni Abdel-Hadi, a close assistant of Faysal who was at his side during both his trips to Europe in 1918–19 and 1919–20. He sat as a representative of the Hejaz at the peace conference. He was the first minister of foreign affairs of King Faysal in Damascus in 1920 and later became Jordan's minister of foreign affairs. See Kasmiyé, *Memoirs of Aouni Abdel-Hadi* (Arabic) pp. 55 ff.
[35] Ibid.

provided to him. Before signing the agreement, Faysal added in his own hand in Arabic the sentence:

> If the Arabs obtain the independence they have claimed under the memorandum of 4 January 1919 and that was handed to the foreign secretary of Great Britain, then, I accept the content of the articles [of this agreement], but should there be any change or alteration [to that memorandum] then I would not be bound by any commitment, this agreement would be null and void and I would be liable for nothing.[36]

The memorandum Faysal referred to was handed to the Foreign Office on 4 January and took up the Arab interpretation of the correspondence between Hussein and McMahon and the Arab demands of the Damascus Protocol, namely, the creation of an Arab state in Asia Minor that would extend from Alexandretta and Diyarbakir in the north to the Indian Ocean in the south. As the memorandum was handed to the British authorities on 4 January, the Faysal–Weizmann agreement could not have been signed on 3 January, unless Faysal's handwritten proviso was added later.

The Faysal–Weizmann agreement never came into effect therefore. In his speech to an assembly of notables in Damascus on 5 May 1919 on his return from Europe, Faysal guarded against telling the audience of the agreement signed with Weizmann. From the second half of 1919, Faysal changed perspective completely and claimed Palestine as an integral part of Syria and dismissed Zionist designs on the territory out of hand.[37] Thus Faysal approved the Damascus Programme handed by the Syrian congress to the King–Crane commission of enquiry in July 1919 that formally dismissed Zionist aims for Palestine.

2.2.5 The Faysal–Clemenceau Agreement

In October 1919, Faysal went to Paris for a second time, where he had uneasy discussions with the French authorities further to the decision to redeploy British forces. The negotiations were difficult but Faysal still managed to save what was crucial, that is, the unity and independence of inland Syria, at the price of major territorial and political concessions. On 6 January 1920, Faysal and Clemenceau signed an agreement, the content of which was not made public and by which France recognized the right

---

[36] All English translations throughout the book of Arabic text citations including constitutions and political documents are informal and not official.
[37] See Faysal's correspondence with Allenby in Laurens, L'Orient arabe, pp. 168 ff.

of the Arab populations settled on Syrian territory to govern themselves as an independent nation. In exchange Syria would ask France for advice and technical aid. The borders of the future state were left to the peace conference, but Syria henceforth recognized the independence and integrity of Lebanon under French mandate.[38]

For a long time it was impossible to say whether this agreement was merely initialled or actually signed. On returning from his interview with Clemenceau on the evening of 6 January, Faysal told his close collaborators he had not signed anything.[39] Rustom Haidar, who attended the signature of the agreement in person, kept largely silent and said very little in his memoirs several decades later.[40] It was only once the diplomatic records in Nantes were opened that it was possible to establish for certain that the agreement had indeed been signed and not just initialled by Clemenceau and Faysal.[41] Clemenceau told Faysal verbally that the secret agreement was valid for three months during which time Faysal had to convince his supporters in Damascus that it was in Syria's interest to reach an understanding with France. Thereafter, both parties would be released from any commitment. It was therefore a temporary agreement. Faysal left Clemenceau in the hope that he would return to Paris within three months to sign a public agreement with France.

The agreement was fiercely opposed by France's colonial lobby and especially by Robert de Caix, general secretary of the French High Commission in Beirut, who was passing through Paris in January 1920 and rallied opponents to the agreement to have it changed. It was also dismissed by the nationalists of the secret society Al-Arabia Al-Fatat in Damascus in February 1920.[42] When Clemenceau stepped down in March 1920, his successor Millerand, who was receptive to the colonial lobby's arguments, did not feel bound by his predecessor's commitments. Paris changed policies radically and instead of maintaining a unitary Syrian Arab entity, it opted for the *petite politique*, the creation of small political entities on sectarian bases. The Faysal–Clemenceau agreement lapsed into oblivion on the French side although it was approved by the second

---

[38] See the full text of the Faysal–Clemenceau agreement in Laurens, *L'Orient arabe*, pp. 162–3.
[39] See the daily account of Faysal's negotiations in Paris in Haidar, *Rustom Haidar's Memoirs* (Arabic).
[40] In his memoirs, Rustom Haidar cites Dr Kadri congratulating himself on having convinced Faysal not to sign the agreement with Clemenceau. *Ibid.*, p. 541.
[41] See Khoury, *La France et l'Orient arabe*, pp. 271 ff.
[42] On this episode, see Moussa, *The Arab Movement* (Arabic), p. 537.

government of the Syrian monarchy in May 1920.[43] It was too late, however, because the San Remo conference of April 1920 had already granted France a mandate over Syria and Lebanon.

2.3 The General Syrian Congress

The liberation of the Arab provinces from Ottoman domination had marked the beginning of a long and difficult political fight to secure the unity and independence of the liberated provinces. The General Syrian Congress was in the vanguard of this struggle.

2.3.1 *The Origin of the Congress*

It was during his first trip to Europe from November 1918 to April 1919 that Faysal became aware of the importance and indeed the necessity of having a representative body for the Syrian people.[44] Upon returning to Damascus and preparing for the imminent visit of the King–Crane commission of enquiry proposed at the peace conference by President Wilson, Faysal called for the formation of an institution to represent the Syrian people. It was officially the General Syrian Congress, but was commonly referred to as the Syrian congress. Faysal wanted to secure from the congress an unequivocal mandate from the Syrian population in the three (eastern, western, and southern) occupied zones to be able to speak in its name with the European powers who were still meeting at the peace conference and no longer to be simply the representative of his father, Sharif Hussein of Mecca, King of the Hejaz, as had been the case in February–March 1919.

Faysal's other objective for the congress was to endow the future Syria with a constitution and so prove to the powers at the peace conference that Syria could govern itself without a mandate power, and accordingly the provisions of article 22 of the Convention of the League of Nations should not apply to Syria.

On his return from Europe, Faysal made an important address regarding the Syrian congress on 5 May 1919.[45] At the time, Faysal sincerely believed that the harmful effects the Sykes–Picot agreement had done to the region

---

[43] See Al-Hakim, *Syria under Faysal's Reign* (Arabic), p. 162.
[44] On the various versions about how this idea formed in Faysal's mind, see Sheherstan, *The General Syrian Congress* (Arabic), pp. 33 ff.
[45] For Faysal's full speech, see Al-Hakim, *Syria under Faysal's Reign* (Arabic), pp. 85 ff.

would be attenuated or even erased by the despatch of the peace conference's fact-finding commission to enquire into the population's preference as to a mandated power.

The speech was made at the seat of government to a gathering of notables and representatives from the different Syrian provinces including figures from the western and southern occupation zones. Faysal spoke of his talks with the Allies in Europe and gave his assessment of the present situation and future challenges. He explained his new approach to the Arab question and that, for practical purposes, the Arab lands would have to be divided into three separate political units – the Hejaz, Iraq, and Syria – linked by contractual agreements. Faysal defended the European powers, explaining that the decisions they made about Arabs stemmed from their ignorance of the real situation in the Arab lands and not from any ill will. He informed his audience of the need to go beyond the customary form of political life and establish a new form of governance based on national consultation and representation. He called for the creation of a Syrian congress in anticipation of the arrival of the US commission of enquiry. Lastly, in reference to the position of Christians and especially the Christians of Lebanon, he insisted that minority rights had to be observed by the majority.

2.3.2 The Election of the Members of the Congress

As Ottoman legislation continued to apply in Syria, members were elected to congress by the method used for electing members of the council of representatives, in force in the empire since the 1908 Young Turk revolution and the restoration of the 1876 constitution. Any change would have required a great deal of time and the fact-finding commission was to arrive imminently in the region. The voting method provided for two tiers of elections. The electors first had to vote for their delegates (one delegate for 500 electors) and the delegates in turn had to elect the members who would sit on the council of representatives in Istanbul. In the last Ottoman elections of 1913, Arab membership had been set at 27 per cent of the assembly members.

The head of government, Rida Rikabi, acting on instructions from the Emir Faysal, convened the same delegates as in 1913 to elect the members of the Syrian congress. But because the Damascus government only had de facto control over the eastern occupation zone and because France – which controlled the western occupation zone (Lebanon and the Mediterranean coast) – and Great Britain – which controlled the southern occupation zone (Palestine) – were both opposed to the elections, they were held in the eastern zone under Arab government control only. The occupying authorities, and especially the French, were opposed on principle to the holding of elections and preferred to abide by the Sykes–Picot agreement. But their refusal was also based on the fear that the results might not be favourable to them.

The elections in the eastern zone were held swiftly. The delegates of the former vilayets of Damascus and Aleppo elected in the Ottoman elections of 1913 were convened to elect the members of the Syrian congress. Many of the members elected to the congress were former members of the Ottoman council of representatives.

Although elections could not be held in the southern and western zones occupied by British and French forces, private initiatives were taken in the major cities. Elsewhere, representatives of associations or local literary and political clubs duly mandated by the notables and former local delegates from the last Ottoman elections were chosen and sent to the congress.[46] Most but not all were able to travel to Damascus; the French authorities in the western zone prohibited some from travelling. The congress was therefore composed of elected or co-opted notables mandated by the local population. The first session of the Syrian congress was held in Damascus on 3 June 1919. Hashim Atassi, member for the city of Homs, was elected to preside the congress.[47] The congress held two official sessions, one in 1919 and one in 1920. In the absence of any rules and regulations, the congressional sessions were not organized around any pre-established procedure. Meetings were convened by Faysal, by the president of the congress, or by members, depending on circumstances.[48]

2.3.3 The Functions of the Congress

The first task of the congress was to prepare the document to be handed to the King–Crane commission on its visit to Damascus in July 1919.

---

[46] For details of the elections in the eastern zone and co-opting or elections in the western and southern zones, see Sheherstan, *The General Syrian Congress* (Arabic), pp. 35 ff.

[47] Some commentators claim that Mohamed Fawzi Al-Azzem was the first elected president of the Syrian congress a few weeks before his death and that Hashim Atassi subsequently became its second president. This claim is contradicted by other records of politicians of the time asserting that Hashim Atassi was the first elected president of the Syrian congress. For details, see Sheherstan, *The General Syrian Congress* (Arabic), pp. 51 ff.

[48] On the congressional sessions and on the number held, two or three, see Sheherstan, *The General Syrian Congress* (Arabic), pp. 59 ff.

A delegation of twenty-one congressional members was formed, presided by Hashim Atassi, to speak with the commission and hand it the document containing the views of the congress about the mandate power preferred by the population and the future of the Syrian provinces detached from the Ottoman empire. The document was to be known as the Damascus Programme. But the congress went much further than simply expounding the people's wishes to the American commission. The following year it declared independence and proclaimed Faysal King of Syria. It assumed the functions of a constituent assembly and gave the kingdom of Syria its first modern constitution. The congress also assumed the functions of a traditional legislative assembly by controlling the governments appointed by the king and holding votes of confidence. Finally, the congress stated its opinions on foreign policy and commented on the position of the European powers with regard to the Syrian question.

2.4 The Damascus Programme

After the call for administrative decentralization of the Arab provinces of the Ottoman empire, and then the call for their independence and unity within an Arab state, there came the moment to define the Syrian national project proper. This was the reflection of the encounter between a man – Faysal – and a people – the Syrian people – sharing a common vision of the future and especially of the formation of a modern state. As soon as it was created, the Syrian congress designated a commission of twenty-one members to write a memorandum to be handed to the American delegation. This text, which was to be named the 'Damascus Programme' in the King–Crane commission's final report, contained the following main points:[49]

1. The total independence of Syria within its natural frontiers with no protectorate or mandate. Syria being bounded to the north by the Taurus mountains; to the south by Rafah and a line from Djof to Aqaba; to the east by the Euphrates and Khabur rivers passing east of Abu Kamal to the east of Djof; and to the west by the Mediterranean.
2. Syria aspired to become a decentralized, parliamentary, civilian kingdom guaranteeing the rights of minorities, the king of which was the Emir Faysal.

---

[49] For the full text of the Damascus Programme see Al-Hakim, *Historical Records on the Syrian Question* (Arabic), pp. 85–8.

3. The Syrian people were in a similar situation to the Bulgarian, Serbian, Greek, and Romanian peoples with respect to their independence and rejected the application of article 22 of the Covenant of the League of Nations (as a country requiring a mandate) for Syria.
4. Were the peace conference to fail to endorse Syria's objection concerning article 22, pursuant to President Wilson's declaration rejecting occupation and colonization, Syria should consider the mandate as mere technical and economic aid that in no manner precluded its full independence. In that event, Syria's first choice would be for the United States as mandatory power to provide technical and economic aid for a period not exceeding twenty years while respecting Syria's political independence and unity.
5. Were the United States to decline the mandate, Syria's second choice would be to have the United Kingdom as its mandatory power.
6. Dismissal of all French claims as to any right over any part of Syrian territory. Rejection of any assistance in whatever form from France.
7. Refusal to transform the southern part of Syria – Palestine – into a Jewish national state. Refusal of Jewish immigration to Palestine, but equal treatment of 'our Jewish brethren' originally living in the country.
8. Refusal of the separation of the southern part of Syria known as Palestine and the western part on the coast that also included Lebanon. The unity of the country had to be ensured and it had not to suffer any partition.
9. Call for the total independence of Iraq. Refusal of any economic barrier between Iraq and Syria.
10. Denunciation of all secret agreements, pursuant to the principles of President Wilson, and in particular those agreements aiming to carve up Syria (Sykes–Picot) and any specific promise (Balfour Declaration) intended to strengthen the Zionists in the south of the country.

The importance of the Damascus Programme lay in the fact that the document was drafted by a body that had a strong claim to representative legitimacy and, despite the flaws in its formation because of the presence of foreign armed forces in some regions, it still faithfully reflected the aspirations of most of the population living in the three occupation zones in the east, west, and south, at a particular moment in their history, with the notable exception of a large number of Christians of Mount Lebanon. The other particularity of the document is that it set out for the first time the geographical boundaries of Syria. In this, the Syrian congress confirmed Syria's separation from Iraq and the Hejaz, as Faysal had done in his communication to the peace conference in January 1919. Interestingly, the delimitation of Syria by the Damascus Programme corresponded largely to the Syrian province of Mohamad Ali and Ibrahim Pasha from 1833 to 1841. The geographical extent of the region known as Syria has always been ambiguous, but the bounds set out in the Damascus Programme corresponded roughly to what it was understood to be in ancient times.[50]

The four major themes in the Damascus Programme that were taken up in one form or another by all Syrian constitutions and regimes for the next century and marked Syria's domestic and regional policies were: multi-sectarian co-existence with recognition of the rights of minorities, the refusal of any foreign tutelage or hegemony, the refusal of any carve-up of the territory, and the dismissal of Zionist intentions with regard to Palestine. For all these reasons, the Damascus Programme remains one of the most important texts in the history of contemporary Syria. It was the mainspring for the political action of the Founding Fathers during Faysal's time and is rightly referred to as a Syrian national project.[51]

The King–Crane commission's final report gave credit to the Damascus Programme saying it was one of the most important documents given to it during its enquiry in the region. The report endorsed the main demands of the Syrian congress. It recommended that the Syrian state should be a monarchy, that Faysal should ascend the throne, and that the territories that now make up Syria, Lebanon, Jordan, Israel, the Occupied Palestinian Territories, and part of Turkey should be integrated under the Syrian monarchy. The commission also recommended a special autonomous regime for Mount Lebanon within the kingdom of Syria and warned of the dangers of intensive Jewish immigration to Palestine and the creation of a Jewish state. The King–Crane commission submitted its report in the autumn of 1919. But it was too late as the USA had withdrawn from the peace conference. The report was not published until 1922[52] after the French and British mandates had been distributed and the US House

---

[50] For details, see Sartre, *D'Alexandre à Zénobie*.

[51] The principles laid before the King–Crane commission by the Syrian congress are considered to be the 'founding instrument of Syrian Arab nationalism'. See Donati, *L'exception syrienne*, p. 25. She cites three of these principles – the refusal to see 'natural Syria' broken up, opposition to the establishment of a Jewish homeland in Palestine, and the rejection of any foreign tutelage. To these three basic principles should be added the equally important multi-sectarian existence, the cornerstone of Syrian secularism.

[52] *Report of American section of inter-allied commission of mandates in Turkey*, 2 December 1922.

of Representatives and Senate had voted in favour of the establishment of a national Jewish homeland in Palestine on the terms of the Balfour Declaration.

The Damascus Programme was severely criticized by certain Christians of Mount Lebanon. The assignment of the US commission of enquiry to Syria worried the Maronite patriarch Monseigneur Hoyeck and prompted him to go to Paris to call on the French authorities to create a Greater Lebanon independent of Syria. His demand was accepted without much difficulty.

2.5 Independence and Proclamation of Faysal as King of Syria in 1920

The Damascus Programme drafted by the Syrian congress in July 1919 in many respects heralded the Declaration of Independence proclaimed by the congress in March 1920. During Faysal's second trip to Europe in late 1919 to early 1920 and as the situation in Syria was becoming ever more critical after the agreement between Lloyd George and Clemenceau concerning the withdrawal of British forces and their replacement by French troops, the Emir Zeid, Faysal's brother who was in temporary charge during Faysal's absence, asked the head of government to inform the congress of the debates going on in Europe. On 22 November 1919, Rida Rikabi addressed the members of congress along those lines. Two days later, on 24 November 1919, the congress responded by recommending that Syrian independence should be declared within the boundaries as indicated to the King–Crane commission and that a sovereign state should be created in the form of a constitutional kingdom with a government accountable to the nation and its representatives. Faysal declined at this point to take this step to create unilaterally a kingdom of Syria so as not to jeopardize the complex negotiations he was conducting in France.

On his return from Europe, Faysal convened the Syrian congress in late February 1920. The political climate was tense. Britain had jettisoned Faysal since the agreement between Lloyd George and Clemenceau in September 1919. The wartime promises made to the Arabs had evaporated. Faysal, who had signed an agreement with Clemenceau in January 1920, had been unable to impose it in the face of nationalist aspirations in Damascus.[53] Even in France, the agreement was strongly contested by

---

[53] Faysal submitted the agreement signed with Clemenceau to the secret society Al-Arabia Al-Fatat. It was rejected. See Moussa, *The Arab Movement* (Arabic), p. 537.

the supporters of a colonial policy for Syria. At the time of the signing of the agreement, Clemenceau was on the point of standing down from the presidency and leaving the position to Millerand, who did not consider himself bound by the agreement between his predecessor and Faysal.

Faysal and the nationalists therefore decided to declare Syrian independence and unity in the form of a constitutional kingdom with Faysal as king. The purpose of the manoeuvre was to present the Allies and the peace conference that was about to decide the fate of the Arab provinces of the Ottoman empire with a fait accompli. It is interesting to observe that chronologically and historically it was the Syrian congress that created Syria and not the other way round. This primacy of the assembly over the state formed a precedent in the region that was taken up by Mustapha Kemal's Turkey three years later when the Grand National Assembly created the Republic of Turkey.

Faysal was far too diplomatic and conciliatory by nature to risk colliding head on with his main European interlocutors and especially France with which he still hoped to be able to reach an agreement. Faysal therefore consulted Paris and London separately about the proclamation of independence.[54] The French authorities were consulted by Nouri Al-Saïd, a close adviser of Faysal, through their liaison officers in Damascus, Colonels Toulat and Cousse. They in turn informed General Gouraud, the high commissioner in Beirut, who made no explicit objection and merely forwarded the news to Paris. Nouri Al-Saïd had presented the declaration of independence to the French in its most positive light for France. He told his interlocutors that once independence had been declared, Syria would ask France for assistance. Nouri Al-Saïd also insisted on the advantages inherent in the declaration of independence, namely, the effective separation of Syria and the Hejaz and consequently the political distancing between Faysal and his father, Sharif Hussein of Mecca, to which he added the distancing of Faysal from his former British protectors.

The British authorities were consulted at Faysal's request by Reda Rikabi. The British opposed outright the declaration of independence, which they thought premature and liable to spread to neighbouring Iraq. London was of the mind that the fate of the Arab provinces of the Ottoman empire should be decided collectively at the peace conference and not unilaterally by the Arabs.

The Syrians saw the declaration as the political acknowledgement of the actual state of affairs on the ground. The eastern occupation zone, except for the east of Jordan was militarily in Arab hands. Things were

---

[54] Kadri, *My Recollections of the Great Arab Revolt* (Arabic) pp. 177–8, cited in Sultan, *The History of Syria 1918–1920* (Arabic), pp. 273 ff.

quite different in the western and southern occupation zones, which were under French and British control, respectively. The Syrian nationalists nurtured the ambition to see these two zones join the kingdom of Syria later. It was under these circumstances that a very broad consensus arose within the Syrian congress to declare independence without further ado.

The inaugural session of the congress was held in Damascus on 6 March 1920 amid general enthusiasm and in the presence of Faysal, who had his collaborator Aouni Abdul Hadi read a speech in his name. Faysal prompted the congress to declare independence and justified the initiative by recalling the Allies' commitments and in particular the Franco-British declaration of 8 November 1918. He also evoked in his address President Wilson's principles and the right of peoples to self-determination. He stated that independence was a right for the Arabs, who had fought bravely alongside the Allies during the war. He insisted on the need to develop a constitution to regulate the institutions of the future Syrian state and added that Syria's policy would be aimed at reconciliation and peace.

The Declaration of Independence was passed by the congress the next day, 7 March 1920, and solemnly proclaimed at Damascus town hall the day after that, 8 March 1920, in the presence of elected representatives, local notables, and many foreign dignitaries including French representatives but, of course, in the absence of the British.

The text of the Declaration of Independence took up the points raised by Faysal in his speech made two days before. It proclaimed the creation of the kingdom of Syria within its 'natural borders', but without setting their limits. This kingdom expressly included Palestine and Mount Lebanon, the latter being granted broad autonomy. Faysal was proclaimed king of Syria. Lastly, the Declaration of Independence emphasized the need to draft a constitution for the kingdom at the earliest opportunity.

The main points of the Declaration of Independence and the proclamation of Faysal as the first king of Syria were:[55]

- The Syrian congress reaffirmed its representative legitimacy and considered itself to be representative of 'the Syrian nation' in these three geographical regions, namely the inland, coastal, and Palestinian zones.
- The Declaration evoked the bravery, abnegation, and sense of sacrifice shown by Arab fighters of all origins (from Syria, Iraq, and the Hejaz) who had participated alongside the Allies, facilitated victory over the

---

[55] See the French translation of the Declaration of Independence in Laurens, *L'Orient arabe*, pp. 165–6.

Turks, and established national governments even before Allied troops arrived.
- The Declaration recalled the meaning given by the Allies to the division of the Arab lands into three separate occupation zones (east, west, and south) as a provisional, military measure, in no way predetermining the future and destiny of Syria, its independence, or its unity. The Declaration recalled that the peace conference had decided to send the King–Crane commission to enquire about the wishes of the people.
- The congress solemnly and unanimously declared the independence of Syria within its natural borders (without specifying what they were) including Palestine on a civil and representative basis.
- The congress took into consideration the desires of the Lebanese patriots concerning the administration of their province, Lebanon, within the bounds recognized before the war, provided that Lebanon stayed clear of any foreign influence.
- The congress dismissed the Zionist claims to make Palestine a Jewish national homeland or a land of immigration.
- The congress proclaimed Faysal constitutional king of Syria.
- The congress declared the end of military governments in the three occupation zones and their replacement by a royal parliamentary government accountable to the congress for all matters relating to the total independence of the country and until such time as the government successfully convened a parliament and governed the various provinces on the basis of administrative decentralization.
- The congress proclaimed its solidarity with Iraq, called for its independence, and invited it to form a political and economic union with Syria.
- The congress reaffirmed its friendship with the Allies.

The Declaration of Independence was a text of great significance in the history of Syria and deserved to be called also the National Covenant.

After the Declaration of Independence of 8 March 1920, the first monarchic government was formed under Rida Rikabi on 9 March. It presented its programme to the congress on 27 March and secured a vote of confidence. The make-up of the first royal government reflected the congress ambitions to unite the three occupation zones (east, west, and south) into a single entity. The cabinet included ministers from Damascus, Aleppo, Homs, Latakia, Beirut, and Jerusalem.

In the purest parliamentary tradition, the Rikabi government resigned on 2 May 1920 after the congress had lambasted the lack of military preparation to face up to French threats. The Rikabi cabinet was replaced on 8 May 1920 by a government formed by Hashim Atassi, president of the congress. The new government presented its programme to the congress, which approved it unanimously. The Atassi cabinet included ministers from the eastern zone. It did not include any from the southern zone (Palestine), probably so as not to upset the British. The replacement of Hashim Atassi as president of the congress was the representative for Tripoli in the western zone, Rashid Reda, who was a fierce opponent of the French mandate for Lebanon and Syria.

The Atassi cabinet remained in office until the battle of Maysalun and the French army's entry into Damascus on 25 July 1920. Before leaving the Syrian capital for good, Faysal named as his third prime minister Alaa' el-Din Droubi, who was to begin a policy of collaboration with France until assassinated by nationalists barely four weeks after taking office. Of course, the Droubi cabinet did not convene the Syrian congress to secure its investiture because France did not recognize the existence of the congress.

2.6 The 1920 Constitution

In addition to being a 'Founding Father' of the kingdom of Syria, the Syrian congress also assumed the function of a constituent assembly. From July 1919 it appointed a constitutional commission from among its members chaired by Hashim Atassi and tasked it with drafting a constitution, 'qanun assassi' (or basic law).[56] The commission set about its work in 1919 and continued to meet periodically. After the proclamation of independence on 8 March 1920 its work intensified to complete promptly the drafting of the constitution. The draft was finished in June 1920 and approved by the members of the congress in its first reading early in July 1920. By the time the congress suspended its work on 19 July 1920 because of the deterioration of the situation with France, it had only managed to adopt the first seven articles in its second reading.

2.6.1 The Drafting of the 1920 Constitution

Some non-Arabic speaking commentators question whether an original version of the 1920 constitution is still extant.[57] They refer to the French

---

[56] The commission was composed of Hashim Atassi (chair), Saadallah Jabri, Abdel Kader Keilani, Wassfi Atassi, Ibrahim Kassem Abdel Hadi, Saïd Haidar, Othman Sultan, Abdel Azim Trabulsi, Théodore Antaki, and Ezzat Darwaza.

[57] See Picaudou, 'La tradition constitutionnelle arabe', pp. 24 ff.

translation of the text in the 1923 thesis by Philippe David,[58] which it is claimed was subsequently translated back into Arabic.[59] Arabic-speaking commentators[60] base their works on the 1920 constitution on its Arabic version published by the Arab League in Cairo.[61] Those commentators also rely on the records of Hassan Al-Hakim, on an explanatory note of the 1920 constitution drafted by Othman Sultan, the member for Tripoli, who sat on the constitutional commission,[62] and the press reports of the time on the commission's work, especially from March 1920 onwards.[63]

The 1920 constitution was drafted by the Syrian congress between July 1919 and June 1920. It logically completed the impressive major political texts already drawn up by this body such as the Damascus Programme, the Declaration of Independence, and the proclamation of Faysal as constitutional monarch of Syria. The constitution was never applied. The French army entered Damascus after the battle of Maysalun before the congress, which had adopted the constitution at its first reading, had finished adopting all its articles at the second reading. Even so, this doomed text still has symbolic value. The constitution sought to strengthen the legitimacy of the kingdom of Syria and keep it in existence. Although it was unable to fulfil its purpose, it clearly indicated the direction Syrians would have taken if they had been allowed to govern themselves.

The 1920 constitution faithfully reflected the state of mind of the Founding Fathers of Syria and the national covenant they wished to establish among its citizens. It still seems astounding nowadays that the Syrian congress should have named the Emir Faysal King of Syria and drafted the 1920 constitution for him although he was not Syrian by origin. This can be explained not just by the popularity of Faysal, who won over the Syrians, but also by what his family stood for in the collective memory of the Arabs, and particularly the Muslims, and by his commitment alongside the Syrian nationalists from as early as 1915.

---

[58] David, *Un gouvernement arabe à Damas*.
[59] Rabbath, *The Historical Formation of Political and Constitutional Lebanon* (Arabic), p. 513.
[60] See especially Kasmiyé, *The Arab Government in Damascus* (Arabic), pp. 291–309.
[61] Constitutions of Arab countries, pp. 3–22 cited in Khouri, *Plans for Arab Union* (Arabic), pp. 35 ff.
[62] See the Arabic text of the explanatory note to the 1920 constitution in Al-Hakim, *Historical Records* (Arabic), pp. 214–28.
[63] On the almost daily press reports from March 1920 onwards about the advancement of the commission's work, see Sheherstan, *The General Syrian Congress* (Arabic), pp. 179–93.

2.6.2 Analysis of the 1920 Constitution

The 1920 constitution was designed to introduce a constitutional monarchy as in a liberal parliamentary regime. It was inspired by both the French Third Republic and the 1876 Ottoman constitution. The explanatory note on the 1920 constitution by one of its authors provides real insight into the text and a better understanding of the intentions of the constituent assembly.

From the outset, the note states the objective of the constitution is to protect the rights of minorities and to remove any pretext from the arguments of those trying to impose a new form of colonial domination on the Syrian nation under various guises such as tutelage, mandate, or protectorate. The note recalls the procedure agreed for drafting the constitution before further analysing the advantage for Syria in adopting a civil parliamentary regime and confirming what the Syrian congress had already announced in the Damascus Programme given to the King–Crane commission of enquiry in 1919, namely that a parliamentary regime was what best suited the Syrian people.

The note affirms that by establishing a civil parliamentary regime, the constitution sought to put power into the hands of the nation so that it might govern by itself and not allow purely religious interests to interfere in politics and public affairs, while observing the freedom of all religions and confessions without differentiating among communities and leaving to them issues relating to worship and personal matters. These provisions were designed to separate politics and religion while leaving to the different sectarian communities the regulation of the personal status of their members, as was the case during the Ottoman period. This was the Syrian version of secularism and the separation of Islam and the state. This form of secularism was remarkable for its day. Less than two years earlier, Syria had still been part of the Ottoman empire and the drafters of the constitution still subjects of the Sublime Porte, for which no similar provision existed on the separation of politics and religion. Turkish citizens had to wait until Mustapha Kemal Ataturk took full control in 1923 for Turkey in turn to introduce secularism albeit in a more radical form.

The note goes on to analyse the most appropriate form for the Syria state, recalling that the country had been ruled for centuries by a sultan and that it was only to be expected after the country had won its freedom and independence that some would want to establish a republican regime to make a complete break from the former authoritarian despotic regime. However, the social education and level of knowledge in the country did not allow it to go down this dangerous road because of the risk of chaos and destruction of the nation. Accordingly, it was firmly decided that the country would follow the path of parliamentary monarchy so that it would experience a gradual shift from despotic monarchy to monarchy with limited powers. Given that such a regime required as the head of the executive power a king or sultan equidistant between the seat of power and the nation and who represented the kingdom abroad, the Syrian congress offered the crown of Syria to Prince Faysal, son of King Hussein of the Hejaz, saviour of the Arab nation, by reason of his qualities, descending as he did from the noblest of Arab families, who commanded the Arab armies, and fought for and defended the Syrian cause in international organizations.

In this spirit, article 1 of the 1920 constitution states that 'the government of the Arab Kingdom of Syria shall be a civil, parliamentary, monarchic government. Its capital shall be Damascus and the religion of the king shall be Islam'. The note emphasized the importance of this first article because it defined Syria as a parliamentary monarchy in which the nation governed itself and religion did not come into public affairs.[64]

Article 2 stated 'The Kingdom of Syria shall be made up of provinces that form an indivisible political unit'. Article 3 added that 'The Kingdom's official language shall be Arabic'. The constitution did not expressly define the Syrian provinces. The constitution's intention was to create a unitary but decentralized state in which the various provinces would enjoy very broad autonomy, multiply economic trade among themselves, and rally around the person of the king, who would be the guarantor of the defence of the frontiers and would organize the business of the general government in the domains of public administration, the economy, and the army. Under this system, the provinces would enjoy wide internal autonomy with an elected parliament and a governor general appointed by the king. The terminology used to describe the national institutions (general assembly of deputies, general government) as opposed to the provincial instances (assembly of deputies, governor general) and the competences attributed to the authorities at national and provincial level suggested that the 1920 constituent assembly was out to establish a largely decentralized monarchy probably inspired by the programme of the Independence Party, which was the political façade of the secret society Al-Arabia Al-Fatat, which had planned to create a federal type of parliamentary

---

[64] Al-Hakim, *Historical Records* (Arabic), pp. 216–17.

The Declaration of Rights

As the first constitution of an independent Syria, the 1920 basic law had to have a Declaration of Rights. This featured in the third chapter, just after the General Provisions (Chapter 1) and the King (Chapter 2). The Declaration of Rights took up the classic themes generally found in any constitution. Article 10 stipulated that 'all Syrians shall have equal rights and duties in law'. Article 11 stated: 'Personal safety shall be guaranteed, no one shall be arrested without legal grounds.' Article 12 stated that torture was prohibited, while article 13 added: 'It is prohibited to oppose the freedom of belief and religions or to oppose religious celebrations unless they disturb public order or interfere with worship by other religions.' The law set out the way to run religious courts, sectarian councils that determined personal status according to their own rules, and the way to govern *wakf*, that is, Muslims' religious property (art. 14).

According to article 16, status shall determine the way to form associations, hold meetings, and form companies. Interestingly, the 1920 constitution did not expressly mention the formation of political parties although, at the time it was drafted, congress members were divided into two main political groups: the Progress Party – most of whose members were from the former secret society Al-Arabia Al-Fatat or from the Independence Party – and the Democratic Party.[65] It is possible that the constituent assembly considered political parties to be particular forms of association covered by article 16 of the constitution. This is a plausible hypothesis because most political parties were created from the spring of 1919 onwards and, although called political parties, took the form of organizations or associations such as the famous Arab Club.[66]

Regarding rights, homes were to be inviolable other than in circumstances laid down by law (art. 17). Financial assets of individuals were guaranteed and private property were only to be confiscated in the general interest after payment of compensation in accordance with law (art. 18). Publications were unrestricted within the framework of law (art. 19).

---

[65] See Darwaza, *On the Modern Arab Movement* (Arabic), pp. 115–16 and pp. 86–92 on other political parties and associations.

[66] On the main movements and political parties of the time, see Russell, *The First Modern Arab State*, pp. 75–9.

Education in the state and private schools of the kingdom was to be based on national principles throughout the Syrian provinces (art. 20). Primary education was to be compulsory and free-of-charge in state schools (art. 21). No one was to be compelled to pay tax, duties, or any other form of aid other than on the basis of law (art. 23). Judgments were to be based on law (art. 25).

Interestingly, the rights in this Declaration were in principle, because of their nature and their position in constitutional law, guaranteed rights. At least that is what can be inferred from analysing the wording of constitution. This inference was not to be borne out by actual deeds, however, as the constitution was never implemented.

Executive Power

The executive provided for by the constitution had two heads, the king and the general government.

As regards the king, article 4 stated:

> The dynasty of the King of Syria shall be restricted to the male children of King Faysal I and passed on by the right of birth order. Should there be no direct descendant of King Faysal I, the eldest of his relatives shall become king of Syria. In the absence of any such eldest relative of King Faysal I, the Congress shall elect by a two-thirds majority a king of Syria descending from the dynasty of King Hussein I, King of the Hejaz. Successors to the king shall be chosen from among his descendants in the same way as for King Faysal I.

Article 5 added:

> The King shall ascend the throne at the age of eighteen years. If the throne falls to an heir below the required age, the Congress shall elect by an absolute majority a viceroy who shall govern the kingdom in the King's name. The viceroy shall be a member of the armed forces.

Article 7 stated that the king was accountable to no one and article 8 provided:

> He is commander-in-chief. He declares war, signs peace treaties and other treaties, and submits them to the Congress for approval. Treaties are only applicable after approval by the Congress. The King may declare a general amnesty after approval of the Congress. The King names the prime minister, approves the composition of the cabinet, and accepts its resignation. He appoints and receives ambassadors. He approves statutes and regulations. He decrees special amnesties and reduces the sentences of convicts. He inaugurates and closes the Congress. He extends the meetings of the Congress as need might be and dissolves the Assembly of Deputies. He

strikes money, grants decorations, appoints military rankings and has royal offices in his grant.

As for the general government, the 1920 constitution sought to establish a parliamentary monarchy in which the government was accountable to the lower house alone. Article 27 stipulated that 'the general government of the Syrian provinces is constituted by the cabinet, which is accountable for its acts to the Assembly of Deputies'. The king could therefore not dismiss the government.

The prime minister was to choose the ministers and submit their names to the king (art. 28). Each minister was required to submit his plans once composed to the Assembly of Deputies (art. 29). Each minister was individually accountable for his ministry to the Assembly of Deputies (art. 30). No statute or regulation could be published unless signed by the prime minister, the relevant minister, and endorsed by the king (art. 31). The King's orders were to be jointly signed by the prime minister and the minister tasked with their enforcement (art. 32). No member of the royal family could be part of the government (art. 33).

Article 34 stipulated: 'The army, navy, foreign affairs, postal and telegraph services, customs, public telephones between the provinces, railways, ports, mines, mint, stamps, treasury bonds, creation of a central bank, manufacture of armaments, weaponry, and explosives, and the highways are all matters for the general government'.

The general government would create, manage, and finance university departments of the sciences and fine arts. The general government was to have the right to oversee the uniform character of basic teaching and education in all the Syrian provinces (art. 35).

Without expressly stating as much, article 39 actually introduced the practice of government by decree:

> In the event of danger for the kingdom or infringement of public order when the Congress is not sitting and if it is impossible to convene it to adopt the necessary statutes, the cabinet shall adopt the necessary measures, have them approved by the King, and enforce them as statutes that shall be submitted to the Congress at its next meeting.

Article 40 added:

> In the event of revolt in any of the provinces of the Kingdom or in the event of a declaration of war by the general government, or general mobilization, the general government shall temporarily decree martial law as defined by legislation adopted by the Congress. In the event of revolt, martial law shall be confined to the area concerned by the disorder.

Ministers were entitled to attend the deliberations of the Senate and General Assembly of Deputies whenever they wished and could speak (art. 41). Ministers were required to answer in person or through a representative any request by the Senate or Assembly of Deputies concerning the activities of their ministry (art. 42). Only the Assembly can dismiss the government.

Article 43 stipulated:

> Should a minister who is invited by the Assembly of Deputies to furnish explanations on a particular subject fail to secure a majority vote after that explanation, he shall resign. In the event of the prime minister resigning, the whole cabinet shall be deemed to have resigned. A minister or the cabinet may apply to postpone an answer on which their responsibility is at issue.

The constitution provided a specific procedure for investigating ministers by a Supreme Court (art. 44) and for the consequences of such investigations (art. 45).

Legislative Power

The 1920 constitution was unique in that it sought to establish a parliamentary monarchy with two chambers, the General Assembly of Deputies and the Senate. All the Syrian constitutions that followed had just a single chamber.

The Congress was to be constituted by the Senate and the General Assembly of Deputies (art. 47) and the king was to pronounce the inaugural speech of the parliamentary sessions (art. 49). The Senate and the General Assembly of Deputies were required to verify that their members had been validly elected (art. 51).

Article 54 stated: 'Deliberations may only take place in either chamber if a majority of members is present. Decisions shall be taken by the majority of the members present except when a two-thirds majority is required.' Decisions were to be taken by secret ballot after approval by the majority of members (art. 55).

Article 60 provided:

> Civil, criminal, commercial, maritime statutes, statutes relating to public health, written matter, artistic creation, publications, state and private education, associations, assemblies, companies, emigration, insurance, nationality, weights and measures, money, the right to work, and statutes pertaining to the domain of the general government are adopted by the Congress and enforceable in all the provinces.

Article 61 provided:

> In the event of a divergence of views between the General Assembly of Deputies and the Senate on a bill, a committee consisting of equal number of members from both houses shall be established to resolve the conflict, if it fails to agree the opinion of the Assembly shall prevail after two readings in both chambers provided that the vote of the lower chamber is by a two-thirds majority. Referral of bills between the chambers shall be limited to a single reading for a budget bill.

Article 63 added:

> Statutes adopted by both chambers are enforceable and forwarded to the King for approval. The King may refer them back to the General Assembly of Deputies explaining why he invites the lower chamber to reconsider them. Statutes characterized as urgent shall be approved or sent back within one week. After re-reading by both chambers, statutes shall be sent back to the King for approval within the time provided.

As for the Senate, article 65 provided for the provincial Assemblies of Deputies to elect its members in a proportion equal to one quarter of the representatives in the General Assembly of Deputies. The king was to appoint the other members of the Senate in a proportion of half of the members elected by the provincial Assemblies of Deputies.

The number of senators belonging to minorities was to correspond to one quarter of the members of the General Assembly of Deputies. The election of senators representing minorities and quotas per province were to be determined by a statute voted by the Congress and this proportion was to be observed for members appointed by the king (art. 67). 'A senator's mandate shall last nine years. One-third of the members of the Senate shall be renewed every three years' (art. 68).

Deputies were to be elected by secret ballot in a two-tier election (art. 73). Legislative elections were to be held every four years (art. 74). In accordance with article 77, elections were free and the government had no right to interfere in them.

Article 78 gave rise to impassioned debates within the commission tasked with drafting the constitution, in the press, and in what we would nowadays call civil society. The question was whether or not to give the vote to women. Supporters and opponents of women's suffrage confronted each other and petitioned the commission from Damascus, Beirut, and other Syrian cities. The local press blazed with the debate that at one point almost turned in favour of women. In the end, the commission did not grant the right to vote to women and moved on to examine the other articles of the constitution. Had female suffrage been granted, Syria would have been a pioneer in this field in stark contrast to the position of women at the time in other Arab countries, Turkey, and even France.[67]

Article 80 stipulated that members of the armed forces on active duty were not permitted to participate in elections. State employees were not entitled to stand or be elected in the constituency in which they held a position unless they resigned their position two months before the election (art. 82). Serving as a member could not be combined with being a state employee except for ministers (art. 83). Each member was deemed to be the representative of all Syrians (art. 85).

Article 87 stated: 'Each mudiriyya [subdivision of a province] is an electoral constituency. Mudiriyyas of fewer than 40,000 inhabitants and more than 20,000 inhabitants shall elect one deputy. Mudiriyyas of fewer than 20,000 inhabitants shall be merged with the nearest mudiriyya.' This system was borrowed from the Ottoman electoral law that had been used for the elections of 1877, 1908, and 1914.

Each province constituted a district for minorities. According to article 88, the quota for each deputy was 30,000 inhabitants. Every 200 first-tier electors were to elect a second-tier elector (art. 89). Each mudiriyya was subdivided into several electoral sectors, each with 200 first-tier electors (art. 90). The electoral law laid down the particulars of the electoral procedure and minority votes (art. 91).

Article 93 stated:

> In the event of divergence between the General Assembly of Deputies and the government and if the government fails to secure the confidence of the General Assembly of Deputies, the government shall resign. If the new government persists in the same opinion as its predecessor, the dispute shall be passed on to the Senate. If the Senate supports the Assembly, the government shall concede. If the Senate does not support the Assembly, the King shall dissolve the Assembly and call new elections to be held within three months. If the new Assembly supports the opinion of the previous one, its decision shall become binding.

In accordance with article 95:

> Any deputy may ask for the creation of a parliamentary commission to investigate any serious incident that may arise in a ministry, a department, or province. If the request is agreed by the majority of deputies, a commission of enquiry shall be set up. It shall submit its conclusions and its works to the Assembly.

---

[67] See Darwaza, *On the Modern Arab Movement* (Arabic), p. 116. On the various requests to the constitutional commission relating to women's suffrage, see Shehrestan, *The General Syrian Congress* (Arabic), pp. 165 ff.

The Provinces

The provinces were to be governed on the basis of broad decentralization limited by matters which, under the Constitution, fell within the ambit of the general government (art. 122). 'Each province has a parliament that controls its finances, lays down its local laws and regulations according to its needs, and controls its government. The local parliament cannot legislate in domains that are reserved to the Congress under the provisions of the Constitution' (art. 123). It should be noted that no other article of the constitution defined a provincial government. This 'oversight' was probably because the drafting of the constitution was completed in a state of emergency at a time when relations with France were extremely tense just days before General Gouraud's ultimatum and the battle of Maysalun.

Article 124 stipulated that each province must have an area of at least 25,000 km^2 and 500,000 inhabitants. Local deputies were to be elected by one-round, direct, uninominal ballot (art. 125) for a period of two years (art. 126). Each local deputy represented 20,000 people (art. 127). The number of deputies representing minorities in each province was determined by 'the number of people belonging to minority groups in the ratio of one elected representative for 15,000 people' (art. 128). The electoral law for the election of provincial parliaments was determined by each province (art 129).

Statutes adopted by provincial parliaments were to be forwarded to the king via the governor general for their promulgation within one month (art. 131). Article 132 added: 'In the event a law is not promulgated but referred back by the King on the grounds that it violates the Constitution or the general laws, the provincial parliament shall revise it in a second reading. Should the provincial parliament confirm the law and the King again refuse to promulgate it, the matter shall be brought before the Senate which shall make the final decision.'

Article 134 stipulated that 'the provinces shall be directed by a governor general appointed by the King' and the governor general was to appoint the local heads of services who reported to his administration (art. 135) and was to be responsible for applying the budgetary laws (art. 136). Each year the governor general was required to present to the assembly of deputies of the province the programme of activities his government had implemented and the one he intended to conduct the following year (art. 137).

Article 138 provided: 'In the event of disagreement between the governor general and the provincial assembly, it shall be for the Senate to make a final decision, including by revoking the governor general if necessary'.

Under article 140, 'The governor general and the deputies of the provincial assembly may propose laws', while under article 143, 'The provinces may form courts and tribunals at all levels'.

This constitution was drafted by the Syrian congress between 3 June 1919 and 19 July 1920. Its 148 articles were adopted at its first reading by the congress on 3 July 1920. But after General Gouraud's ultimatum to King Faysal on 19 July 1920, the congress was only able to discuss the first seven articles of the constitution at the second reading. It rejected article 3, which had been adopted at first reading, on the grounds that it was a repetition of what was stipulated later in the chapter on the provinces.[68] The 1920 constitution therefore consisted of a text of 147 articles that were never applied.

2.7 The End of the Arab Kingdom of Syria

Nationalists wished for the total independence and unity of Syria within its natural borders, that is, in the three (eastern, western, and southern) occupation zones. After Faysal was abandoned by the British and the Sykes–Picot agreement was redefined by Lloyd George and Clemenceau in 1919, Faysal could obtain no more than the contents of the agreement of 6 January with Clemenceau, namely partial independence, limited geographically to inland Syria and limited politically by special relations with France. This text was rejected by the nationalists, because it amounted to less than the wartime promises made to the Arabs and less than their legitimate ambition for independence after four centuries of Ottoman domination. Their fierce opposition to the French mandate could be explained by the fear that Syria would experience the same fate as the protectorates of Morocco and Tunisia. The nationalists saw in the mandate merely a new form of colonial domination. This is why they rejected the agreement in February 1920. In May 1920, the Atassi government accepted it, but it was by then too late and France had changed its mind.

The reason for France's change of tack was not just the change at the head of the government with the departure of the committed anti-colonialist Clemenceau and his replacement by Millerand. France's shift

---

[68] Article 3 adopted at first reading stated that the provinces should be independent administratively on the basis of the constitution and that the congress should set out by statute the boundaries of each province. The numbering chosen to describe this constitution is that containing 147 articles and featured in Al-Hakim, *Historical Records* (Arabic), pp. 194–213. For numbering with 148 articles, see Shehrestan, *The General Syrian Congress* (Arabic), pp. 245–62.

in outlook was a response to developments in Cilicia and the successful revolt by Mustapha Kemal against French occupying troops. Gouraud feared the formation of an alliance between Syrian and Turkish nationalists against France. The harbingers of such a danger were many: the Syrian authorities' refusal to allow French troops to use the Riyyak–Aleppo railway to carry men and equipment to the north;[69] visits to Damascus by high-ranking Turkish officers and the possible connection between those visits and the decision by the Syrian authorities to decree mandatory conscription and create the national defence committee;[70] and Turkish support with logistics and equipment for the revolt led by Ibrahim Hanano in northern Syria from the autumn of 1919. All of these events worried France at a time when it was facing setbacks in Cilicia and especially in Marash after Kemalists had seized control of the city of Mersin.

Political developments in France, the recalcitrance of nationalists in Damascus, and military developments in Cilicia put paid to the final hopes of the French and Syrians coming to any understanding. The San Remo conference attributed to France a mandate over Syria and Lebanon in April 1920. The die was cast. France would apply its mandate by force if need be should the Syrians decide to resist. The story of the final weeks of the kingdom of Syria is a series of ultimatums issued by General Gouraud from his Beirut headquarters and the usually positive responses from the Syrian government, which was torn between the will to try to save what could still be salvaged and the determination of the majority of the congress, the nationalist political circles, and the majority of public opinion not to yield.[71]

This rise of extremism, despite the Syrian government's acceptance of the terms of the ultimatum of 14 July 1920, was to lead to the battle of Maysalun on 24 July 1920, the defeat of the nascent Syrian army, which was largely underequipped and ill-trained, and General Gouraud's entry as conqueror the next day into the Umayyad capital, which even the crusaders had been unable to take.[72] The battle of Maysalun that ended

---

[69] Members of the Syrian government diverged in their opinions on this, but the defence and foreign affairs ministers persuaded the cabinet to side with them. See Al-Hakim, *Syria under Faysal's Reign* (Arabic), pp. 170 ff.

[70] See Khoury, *La France et l'Orient arabe*, pp. 322–3.

[71] For a Syrian version of General Gouraud's ultimatums and the Syrian authorities' responses, see Al-Hakim, *Syria under Faysal's Reign* (Arabic), pp. 178 ff. For a French version of events, see Khoury, *La France et l'Orient arabe*, pp. 376 ff.

[72] One of General Gouraud's first acts in Damascus was to go to Saladin's tomb next to the Umayyad mosque in the old city and declare, 'We have returned, Saladin. My presence here symbolizes the victory of the cross over the crescent.' Cited in Mardam Beik, *Jamil*

the Arab kingdom of Syria is still steeped in meaning and symbol. It was the first confrontation between Arabo-Syrian nationalism and a western power in the twentieth century. It was followed by repeated resistance and uprisings (in 1920–22, 1925–26, 1936 and 1945) against the French mandate. The Faysal–Clemenceau agreement was a French attempt to develop an Arab policy based on understanding between France and Arab nationalism by replacing France's Ottoman policy. The regrettable abandoning of this attempt in favour of another orientation, based on an understanding with the minorities and the exacerbation of local and sectarian specificities could only lead to a head-on clash between colonial France and Arab nationalism represented by the kingdom of Syria.[73]

The tragedy of Maysalun arose largely from the colonial lobby in France underestimating the Arab national factor within the Syrian population. This battle – which could have been avoided – bore the seeds of misunderstandings and incomprehension that continued to develop in the following decades in the Near East and North Africa between Arab nationalism and the western powers, and especially France. For the Syrians, Maysalun was truly traumatic. For the second time within a century, the attempt to create a united Syria proved impossible. After the destruction, mainly because of the British, of the first non-independent but autonomous unitary Syria under Ibrahim Pasha and Mohamed Ali's Egypt, the second attempt to create a unitary and independent Syria was thwarted this time by France in agreement with Britain.

As the first Arab constitutional monarchy to declare itself independent after the Great War, the Arab kingdom of Syria proved ephemeral. But although short-lived, Faysal's monarchy bequeathed an impressive legacy to future generations. It delimited Syrian geographical space by separating it from Mesopotamia and the Arabian peninsula. It claimed as its national territory a geographical space made up of the three Allied military occupation zones (east, west, and south) that it considered as forming natural Syria. The borders of that area largely coincided with those of the Syria of 1831 to 1841, the autonomous province administered by Ibrahim Pasha for his father, Mohamed Ali. It gave the territory a separate personality from the other Arab lands, which was reflected in the Damascus Programme, a true national project that defined the concept of the Syria that the Founding Fathers had sought to create. This was to be a

---

Mardam Beik's notes (Arabic), p. 47. This tactless and inopportune declaration was to have the most deplorable effect on the Syrian population.

[73] Khoury, *Une tutelle coloniale*, pp. 93–4.

state that was not based on Islam, but rather a state in which all religious communities would coexist harmoniously within a framework of modern citizenship. A state that would reject all foreign hegemony, all territorial division of its lands into tiny political entities on a sectarian basis, and would reject Zionist designs on Palestine. These ideas continued to grow in Syrian minds and were passed down the generations. A century later, these characteristics still underpin the Syrian national project today as the heir to the monarchy of the previous century.

The kingdom of Syria also left as its legacy the 1920 constitution, which was the only Arab constitution at the time it was adopted, and a true national covenant between Syrians of all origins and their king.[74] That eminently modern constitution was designed to establish a largely decentralized monarchy that would abide by the particularities of its various provinces and the beliefs of all of its citizens, and rally them without discrimination around the king's person. The tragic end of the Arab kingdom of Syria meant the constitution never came into force. It vanished together with the monarchy, forever leaving the bitter feeling of a great injustice, a missed opportunity, and an incomplete achievement.

---

[74] The first Arab countries to have constitutions were Tunisia (1861–64) and Egypt (1882–83). But the regimes they set up did not endure. For an analysis of these two constitutions, see Brown, *Constitutions in a Nonconstitutional World*, pp. 16–20 and 26–9.

3

The First Republic

I shall call the political regime established by the constituent assembly elected in 1928 under the French mandate the First Republic. This regime ended three years after the last French troops had left with General Husni Al-Zaim's coup d'état in March 1949.

The mandate was established on the ashes of the kingdom of Syria and against the wishes of the vast majority of the population. The battle of Maysalun was the first military confrontation of the twentieth century between a colonial-style French policy and Arab nationalism in its Syrian version. Maysalun remained the original sin of the mandate that no French policy towards Syria, however liberal – and such policies were rare at the time – could atone for. The Syrian nationalists attempted with Faysal to establish an inclusive, modern, constitutional monarchy that respected the religious diversity of the Arab provinces recently separated from the Ottoman empire. The mandate policy did the exact opposite. It promoted disintegration and advocated separatism; it exacerbated regionalism, communitarianism, and sectarianism.

Just as in the previous period which saw the ephemeral rise and fall of the Syrian monarchy, France continued to largely underestimate the importance of the national factor. The mandate's ideologically blinkered vision of Near Eastern realities led to the creation of artificial political entities of which Lebanon alone survived the departure of French troops. The nationalists, supported by almost all the population, fought tooth and nail for reunification and independence. They turned to insurrection, armed struggle, a general strike, elections, dialogue, cooperation, and negotiation with the mandatory power. They mobilized in their favour the republican institutions created in agreement with France. They fought to impose their constitution, which they used to serve two great national causes that during this period jointly symbolized the national question: independence and the reunification of Syrian territories. Despite the proliferation of artificial mini-nations, the Syrian question was neither dead nor buried.

But the history of the French mandate in Syria cannot be confined to just a Franco-Syrian stand-off. Other regional actors interfered more or less openly, foremost among which were Great Britain – the mandatory power occupying the Syrian territories of the south (Transjordan) and south-west (Palestine), and controlling Mesopotamia (Iraq) – and Ataturk's victorious Turkey. They intervened not to bring the French and Syrians closer together but rather to stoke their differences and take advantage of them. Their objectives were diverse – to weaken France in the East and delay the emergence of a free and reunited Syria for as long as possible.

The kingdom of Syria had been destroyed, dismantled, and torn apart, but the idea of 'Syria' was still alive and stood for an ideal to be achieved. The heart of Syria continued to beat beneath the 'little Syrias'. Resistance fighters and nationalists were determined to revive a Syria whose greatness would not be due to its geographical extent, which now hung on British and French colonial policies, but on the values Syria embodied. These values were those of the Founding Fathers of the kingdom of Syria expressed in the Damascus Programme (1919) and the Declaration of Independence (1920), at the forefront of which featured harmonious, secular coexistence among citizens from different religious communities within a modern, civil, parliamentary nation state respectful of all religious, sectarian, ethnic, and political diversities.

After twenty-six years of struggle, the Syrian republic finally won its independence in 1946 within its current borders. The fight for independence was led by the nationalists who, despite all the challenges, managed to reunite most of the Syrian territories hived off by France at the beginning of the mandate in 1920 (Damascus, Aleppo, the Jabal Druze, and the Alawi territory). However, the new Syria no longer included the sanjak of Alexandretta, ceded to Turkey by France in controversial circumstances, and Lebanon, which opted for its independence. Nor did it include the former Syrian territories under British mandate. Transjordan became the kingdom of Jordan and the mandate of Palestine, having been demographically altered beyond recognition, with the active benevolence of the British, was militarily conquered by Zionist armed bands that founded the State of Israel there.

The 1928 constitution governed the institutions of independent Syria for the three years from 1946 to 1949. It was to be abolished after the first coup d'état by the army in 1949 and replaced by a new constitution the following year.

3.1 The French Mandate

The Sykes–Picot agreement on the share-out of the Arab provinces of the Ottoman empire into protectorates and French and British zones of influence was drafted in accordance with the provisions of international law in force before the outbreak of the Great War. However, the concepts of international law inherited from the nineteenth century changed rapidly during the war under the impetus of President Wilson. In his famous Fourteen Points, the US President suggested a novel formula for the non-Turk nations under Ottoman domination. Instead of the classical pre-war forms of domination based on annexation or protectorates, Wilson came up with a new formula that involved accompanying these young nations on their road to independence.[1] This principled stance by the USA somewhat complicated the task of France and Great Britain, which had already shared out the remains of the Ottoman empire, but without calling into question the principle of their 1916 agreement.

The system of mandates, enshrined by article 22(4) of the Covenant of the League of Nations was a compromise between President Wilson's idealism and France and Britain's determination to parcel up the Near East into zones of influence and occupation as provided for in the Sykes–Picot agreement.

The paternity of the ambiguous concept of the mandate fell to the future prime minister of South Africa, General Jan Smuts.[2] Theoretically, the League of Nations was to take via a mandate the legacy of the German colonial empire in Africa and the Arab territories detached from the Ottoman empire. The mandatory power was to act as a tutor with its ward and report regularly to the League of Nations on the progress achieved. This idea was accepted by President Wilson. Clemenceau and Lloyd George raised no objections.

Article 22 of the Covenant of the League of Nations defined the 'Mandate' as follows:

---

[1] Point 12 of President Wilson's Fourteen Points related to non-Turk territories under Ottoman domination: 'The Turkish portion of the present Ottoman empire should be assured a secure sovereignty, but the other nationalities which are now under Turkish rule should be assured an undoubted security of life and an absolutely unmolested opportunity of autonomous development'.

[2] Christian Zionist South African general and future father of the policy of apartheid in his country. Lloyd George considered him to lead the 1917 Palestine campaign to free the territory from Ottoman domination. Smuts accepted but his government refused. See Fromkin, *A Peace to End All Peace*, pp. 280–3.

> To those colonies and territories which as a consequence of the late war have ceased to be under the sovereignty of the States which formerly governed them and which are inhabited by peoples not yet able to stand by themselves under the strenuous conditions of the modern world, there should be applied the principle that the well-being and development of such peoples form a sacred trust of civilisation and that securities for the performance of this trust should be embodied in this Covenant.
>
> The best method of giving practical effect to this principle is that the tutelage of such peoples should be entrusted to advanced nations who by reason of their resources, their experience or their geographical position can best undertake this responsibility, and who are willing to accept it, and that this tutelage should be exercised by them as Mandatories on behalf of the League.
>
> The character of the Mandate must differ according to the stage of the development of the people, the geographical situation of the territory, its economic conditions and other similar circumstances.
>
> Certain communities formerly belonging to the Turkish Empire have reached a stage of development where their existence as independent nations can be provisionally recognized subject to the rendering of administrative advice and assistance by a Mandatory until such time as they are able to stand alone. The wishes of these communities must be a principal consideration in the selection of the Mandatory.

As Henry Laurens put it, 'By its very nature, the Mandate sought to be a liberal enterprise of colonization.'[3] France saw in this a convenient way to impose its presence, and to perpetuate and assert its pre-war influence in Syria and Lebanon under the Sykes–Picot agreement as revised by the Clemenceau–Lloyd George agreement, even if it meant denaturing the very conception of the mandate by considering it to be a new form of domination to be likened to the more familiar protectorate. Besides, most of the personnel in the French army and administration sent out to Syria, including the high commissioners, except perhaps for Henri de Jouvenel and de Martel, behaved in Syria and Lebanon as if they were in Morocco or Tunisia. Ultimately the mandates issued by the League of Nations in the Near East did not serve as a framework for the betterment of the people. They were rather a new form of colonial-type domination by the mandatory powers, which used them to reinvent the region so as to serve their own interests and to reshape it in accordance with their subjective outlook.

---

[3] Laurens, 'Le Mandat français sur la Syrie et le Liban' in Méouchy (ed.) *France, Syrie et Liban 1918–1946*, p. 414.

3.2 Artificial Nations

Pursuant to the decision of the San Remo conference of April 1920 confirming the Lloyd George–Clemenceau agreement of September 1919, which in its turn revised the clauses of the 1916 Sykes–Picot agreement, the Arab kingdom of Syria that Faysal was endeavouring to build was set asunder into French and British mandates. Then two months after the battle of Maysalun and the occupation of Damascus by French troops, the French part of Syria was dismembered by the high commissioner into five separate political entities:

- The creation of the State of Aleppo in northern Syria in September 1920. The former Ottoman mutasarrifiyya of Zor became Deir Ezzor and was attached to it. Alexandretta became a sanjak and was attached to the State of Aleppo while holding on to its administrative autonomy.
- The creation of the Alawi Territory with Latakia as its capital. This territory was formed from two mutasarrifiyya, that of Latakia (cazas Latakia, Jablé, Banias, and Mussiaf also called Omrania) and that of Tartous (cazas of Tartous, Safita, and Al-Hosn). The Alawi Territory was to become an independent state in 1925.
- The State of Damascus was formed by the remainder of the former eastern occupation zone, including the three large urban centres that form the Syrian hinterland, Damascus, Homs, and Hama.
- The Jabal Druze east of the Hawran plateau enjoyed autonomous administration from 1922 with Emir Selim Pasha Al-Atrash at its head and later became an independent state. The caza of Ajlun was separated from the Hawran and attached to the neighbouring caza of Karak, so passing from Syria to Transjordan.
- The creation on 1 September 1920 of Greater Lebanon comprising the former mutasarrifiyya of Lebanon (Mount Lebanon), the four cazas of the Beqaa valley detached from Damascus (Ba'albek, Zahla, Rachaya, and Hasbaya), the north of the sanjak of Saida (the south becoming part of the mandate of Palestine), the sanjak of Beirut, the caza of Tripoli, the part of the caza of Akkar south of Nahr El-Kebir, and a part of the caza of Hosn Al-Akkrad.

The dismembering of Syria illustrated France's new *petite politique* in the Orient, which superseded its grand Ottoman policy. The latter sought to maintain the unity of the Ottoman empire whereas the former, on the contrary, recommended the carving up of the Arab territories derived from the break-up of the empire. France pushed to the limit the local autonomy of certain religious minorities, which were suddenly raised to the status of national minorities at the expense of the basic unity of the Syrian population.[4] Most of the population failed to understand this division of the territory, viewing it as arbitrary. It was 'divide and rule' applied to the letter. The division of the geographical area could not, as its proponents wanted, objectively be characterized as nation building or the birth of viable national entities. The artificial character of these micro-states was obvious and most of these constructions, largely inspired by Robert de Caix,[5] were soon to reveal their limitations. The resistance movements that were soon to flare up in some regions promptly showed that the carve-up of Syria was neither viable nor realistic. Only Greater Lebanon managed, with mixed success, to survive as an independent political entity. For the remainder, the history of this time could be characterized as a search for the lost Syria.

3.2.1   Early Military and Political Resistance to the Mandate

The defeat of Maysalun and the division of Syrian territory into several political units caused several localized armed insurrections. When French forces entered Damascus on 25 July 1920, the high commissioner found an unexpected wholehearted collaborator in Alaa'el-Din Droubi, the last head of the government appointed by King Faysal before he left Damascus, but the Syrian prime minister was assassinated four weeks later during a visit to the Druze region in the south of the country. In the west, on the Mediterranean coast and in the Alawi mountains, resistance led by Sheikh Ali Saleh had begun well before the battle of Maysalun. It commenced on the arrival of French troops in 1918 and lasted until October 1921. In the north, around Aleppo, resistance to French troops was organized from 1919 by the political leader Ibrahim Hanano who made contact with Mustapha Kamal and obtained logistical support (arms, munitions, and officers) from Turkey for a while. The revolt ended in 1921 with the Ankara agreement between Turkey and France and the withdrawal

---

[4] Oddly, the official title of the French representative of the time was 'High Commissioner in Syria and Cilicia' even though one of the high commissioner's first decisions was to wipe Syria from the map as a political entity. A year later, the French government signed the Ankara agreement (October 1921) abandoning Cilicia to Turkey. Subsequently, the French representative's title became 'High Commissioner in Syria and Lebanon'.

[5] See Khoury, *Une tutelle coloniale*.

of French troops from Cilicia. Turkish aid ceased and the French army intensified its campaign with some 15,000 troops to put down the armed insurrection. In the east, in the area of Deir Ezzor and the Syrian desert, the uprising was directed by nomadic tribes and only ended in 1921. In the south, in the Jabal Druze, an insurrection was launched in July 1922 by Sultan Atrash that ended in April 1923. In the south-west, the introduction of the mandate prompted an uprising in some of the territories detached from the vilayet of Damascus and attached to Mount Lebanon. Emir Mohamed Abu Fa'aour launched an armed revolt against France in the cazas of Rashiya and Hassbaya which had become Lebanese.

The population accepted neither the mandate nor the division of its territory. This weakened France's position both internally in its administration of the territories under its authority and internationally with the League of Nations, which had given France three years to draw up a basic law (constitution) in agreement with the populations of the new political entities.

The rejection of the new geographical and political order by the majority of the population meant there was ready support for violent action by the most committed nationalists and resistance forces with the complicity of the authorities of the neighbouring lands.[6] The two Hashemite monarchies set up by Great Britain in Transjordan and Iraq were decidedly hostile to France and their leaders did not conceal their sympathy for Syrian militants resisting the French mandate.

3.2.2 *The Partial Piecing Together of Syria*

Confronted with this build-up of internal and external challenges and calls for reunification from the Syrian people and notables, France resigned itself to trying another territorial and political recipe. In June 1922, General Gouraud created a Syrian Federation grouping the States of Aleppo and Damascus and the Alawi territory (Order No 1459 bis of 28 June 1922). A federal council was appointed by the high commissioner comprising fifteen members (five for each), which elected Subhi Barakat, a leading notable from Antioch, as president. Justice, land matters, wakf (religious endowment), public works of common interest, and administration of state property were all federal matters. The federal council was

---

[6] The prime minister of Transjordan, Rida Rikabi, Damascene by origin and former prime minister of King Faysal, who in the meantime had been placed on the throne of Iraq by the British, offered asylum and refuge to the Syrian insurgents fighting the French mandate.

responsible for all proposals concerning the passing of unitary legislation on points with a common interest for the states. Bills previously studied by the three governments had to be presented to the federal government if they were acceptable to two out of three states.[7]

Syria was re-emerging as a political entity. The process of reintegrating small political entities into a larger whole was under way to the satisfaction of the majority of the population, who considered the federation a first step towards Syrian unity and not as an end in itself. General Weygand, who succeeded General Gouraud as high commissioner, decided in 1923 to bestow representative councils on the states of Damascus and Aleppo, which were to be elected by the population and with a consultative capacity. He set up a new procedure that provided for the election in each caza of a representative in the first tier for 6,000 voters, taking account of a proportional system of representation for the various religions and minorities. Each candidate for the first tier had to be at least twenty-five years old and thirty years old for the second tier. The proportion of second-tier elected representatives was set at 1:100, which worked out at twenty-eight representatives for Aleppo and thirty for Damascus.[8]

The elections for the representative council of the State of Damascus were widely boycotted. Some council members relayed the call of the majority of their fellow citizens in demanding the reunification of Syrian lands, the election of a constituent assembly, and the formation of a government accountable to a parliamentary assembly.[9] These personal standpoints foreshadowed what was later to become the Great Revolt of 1925–26, a programme of national demands. The councils of Damascus and Aleppo passed resolutions in favour of reunification, but not the Alawi council, which twice voted for autonomy.[10] The two years of separation of Alawi territory had begun to give rise to regionalist sentiment, but subsequently, the vast majority of the population clearly showed that it was fundamentally attached to its Syrian identity.

The stance taken by the representative councils of Damascus and Aleppo and the attitude of the population that boycotted the elections

---

[7] For details on the institutional mechanisms, see Anonymous, *La Syrie et le Liban*, pp. 35 ff.
[8] On the two-tier electoral procedure decreed by the high commissioner for the election of the representative councils of the States of Damascus and Aleppo, see Order 2144 of 30 August 1923 and for the activity of the councils see Qarqout, *The Development of the National Movement* (Arabic), pp. 56–7.
[9] See the declarations by Fares Khoury, Rashed Barazi, and Faydi Atassi in Qarqout, *The Development of the National Movement*.
[10] Anonymous, *La Syrie et le Liban*, p. 35.

finally persuaded the mandate authorities that even the federation was not the most appropriate scheme for governing Syria. In January 1925, the high commissioner created the State of Syria by merging the States of Damascus and Aleppo. He also created an independent Alawi State (Decree No 2980 of the high commissioner of 5 December 1924 promulgated on 1 January 1925). The sanjak of Alexandretta was attached to Syria but under an autonomous arrangement. The two elected councils in 1923 were also merged. They assumed the functions of a parliament and were based in Damascus. Subhi Barakat was appointed by the mandatory power as head of state and formed a cabinet comprising five ministers.

These successive rearrangements of Syrian territory revealed the difficulties besetting the policy of dividing up the land that had been followed since 1920. The little Syria made up of Damascus and Aleppo was not slow in engendering new armed resistance movements calling for the reattachment of the other Syrian territories. These insurrections were led by local political leaders, who gradually made national claims that can be summarized by the terms reunification and independence.

3.2.3 The Great Revolt and the Assertion of National Will

After the localized uprisings of 1920–23 when the mandate was being introduced, France was confronted with a second, more centralized wave of opposition in what was called the Great Syrian Revolt of 1925–26.[11]

The uprising began in southern Syria, in the Jabal Druze in July 1925 for reasons relating to the administration by the local representative of the mandatory power. It changed into a national Syrian revolt that spread rapidly to the centre and north of the country. The news of the early military successes by the insurgents under Sultan Atrash (surrounding French troops at Suwayda, the capital of the Druze mountain and routing a force of 3,000 men sent from Damascus to rescue them) spread like wildfire and drew a large number of politicians, intellectuals, and nationalists throughout the country to join the revolt.

The insurgents set up embryonic political institutions and made their movement's political objectives known. Sultan Atrash was proclaimed commander-in-chief of the revolt and Abdel-Rahman Shahbandar was appointed political head of the movement. In the early days of the revolt, Sultan Atrash published three communiqués calling on the Syrian people

---

[11] On the Syrian insurrections see Hallak, *The Great Syrian Revolts* (Arabic).

to rise against the mandatory power, for the unity of Syrian lands; recognition of its independence; the establishment of government by the people tasked with convening a constituent assembly to draw up a basic law (constitution) based on the principle of national sovereignty; the withdrawal of occupying forces and the formation of a national army; and the assertion of the principles of the French Revolution and of the Rights of Man to liberty, fraternity, and equality.[12] The third communiqué took up a quote from Faysal – 'independence is to be taken not given' – and set out concrete measures for local administration in the parts of the territory freed from French presence.[13]

The people's government that was announced was never formed. But what was important about the three communiqués was that they set out the main aims of the insurrectional movement and the main political demands of the revolt, namely, the formation of a national government, the election by direct universal suffrage of a constituent assembly, and the drafting of a basic law (constitution).[14] So after the personal claims by the members of the Council of Representatives in 1923, the Syrians for the first time developed a programme of national claims in the context of an armed insurrection with massive popular support.

The nationalist forces were outnumbered and the revolt was quelled in December 1926, but not without having set ablaze most of Syrian territory and even part of Lebanon. France had to send in large numbers of troops to take the situation back in hand. Damascus was on the verge of falling to the insurgents, and French artillery had to shell the city twice. The loss of human life and the destruction caused by the bombardment of Damascus stirred keen emotions both in Syria and in Paris where the government recalled the high commissioner, General Sarrail.

During the twenty months of the revolt, the mandatory power and the insurgents exchanged messages via go-betweens to try to reach a compromise. Gradually, the insurgents adopted a more conciliatory tone with Shahbandar even sending a letter to the foreign ministry in Paris that ended, 'It is my duty to affirm before concluding this letter that France cannot maintain its influence in this part of the Near East by force of arms, but it can do so by adopting a peaceful policy and acknowledging Syria's legitimate rights. I can assure you that most of the Syrian people

---

[12] Al-Hakim, *Syria and the French Mandate* (Arabic), pp. 116–17; Bokova, *La Confrontation franco-syrienne*, pp. 173–6.
[13] Qarqout, *The Development of the National Movement* (Arabic), pp. 70–1.
[14] Al-Ba'ini, *The Druze*, p. 205.

are ready for an understanding with France on the basis of the national sovereignty of Syria while preserving French interests.'[15]

To pacify the situation in Syria, France for the first time appointed a civilian as high commissioner. Senator Henri de Jouvenel was tasked with finding a political outcome for the mandate crisis in Syria. The replacement of a solider with a politician was perceived in Syria as the beginning of a change of style and a new approach to the mandate.

De Jouvenel was favourable to a political arrangement, the first of its kind, between France and the nationalists. But it was no easy matter. The initial positions of the protagonists were so far apart that it took time and considerable goodwill and imagination on both sides to come up with a compromise. France sought primarily to restore order. The insurgents, for their part, wanted a guarantee of independence and reunification of Syrian lands. To break the deadlock, the new high commissioner began a political process with an outstretched hand and indirect dialogue with the insurgents while intensifying the repression of the revolt through the arrival of military reinforcements. The rare political formations in Syria[16] and the figures close to the insurgents suggested schemes for extricating the country from crisis. The Cairo-based Syrian–Palestinian congress,[17] made up of figures hostile to the French mandate, and which saw itself politically as the heir to the 1919–20 Syrian congress, proposed a mediation with the insurgents based on a six-point plan including the reunification of the Syrian states under the French mandate, a referendum on the question of Lebanon being attached to Syria or not, the formation of a provisional national government tasked with organizing the election of a constituent assembly, the adoption by the constituent assembly elected by direct universal suffrage of a basic law (constitution) based on internal and external national sovereignty, the abolition of the mandate and the delimitation by means of agreement of future relations between France and Syria, the withdrawal of French troops from Syrian territory, the recording of the Franco-Syrian agreement with the League of Nations, and Syria's membership of the League.[18]

[15] Shahbandar, *The Syrian National Revolt* (Arabic), p. 128.
[16] When the Great Revolt broke out in 1925, Syria had two main political parties: the People's Party formed in 1925 by Shahbandar and the Istiqlal Party, which was an emanation of the former secret society Al-Arabiya Al-Fatat, created under the Ottoman empire and which became a political party during the monarchic period. The two groups subsequently merged in 1927 to give rise to the National Bloc that was to play a crucial part in the history of Syria until the first military coup in March 1949.
[17] On the Syrian–Palestinian Congress, see Babeel, *Twentieth-Century Syrian Journalism and Politics* (Arabic), pp. 46 ff.
[18] Qarqout, *The Development of the National Movement* (Arabic), pp. 76–7.

De Jouvenel dismissed this over-ambitious scheme, which he deemed unacceptable and some days after arriving in Beirut in December 1925, he appealed to the Syrians: 'Your destiny is in your own hands. That destiny consists in imitating what is happening in Lebanon and electing a constituent assembly, electing a government, and adopting a basic law.'[19] Most of these points already featured in the three communiqués from Sultan Atrash at the time the revolt begun in June 1925. They were also taken up in a slightly modified form by a delegation of Damascene notables who went to Beirut to meet the new high commissioner at his request. The delegation put a four-point plan to de Jouvenel: the formation of a provisional national government, the election of a constituent assembly, the reunification of Syria within its natural borders, and a moratorium on sanctions related to the revolt.[20] On the eve of this meeting, Subhi Barakat, president of the State of Syria appointed by the previous high commissioner, tendered his resignation. Although he was considered a moderate and a great friend of France, he still took up in his letter of resignation certain demands made by the insurgents that he characterized as 'justified demands', such as the formation of a constituent assembly, the adoption of a constitution based on national sovereignty, the formation of a constitutional government, a general amnesty, and Syria's membership of the League of Nations.[21] His letter of resignation also raised the issues of the Syrian nationalists' demand for the reunification of the Syrian governments (Syrian, Alawi, and Druze) and the fate of the territories detached from Syria by France and attached to Lebanon.

In his response to the notables who had come to meet him in Beirut, the high commissioner accepted the principle of a constitution and a partial amnesty. He announced elections would be held in areas not affected by the revolt and offered the insurgents having committed no serious public order offences two weeks to lay down their arms and participate in the elections. As for the leaders of the revolt, he did not guarantee them an amnesty but stated that their lives would be spared if they surrendered.

The insurgents rejected the offer and continued the revolt for nearly a year. However, de Jouvenel's method based not just on the use of force as with his predecessors but on dialogue and the search for a compromise created a precedent for future relations between France and the nationalists. For the first time, nationalists and the mandatory power talked and

---

[19] *Ibid.*, p. 78.
[20] *Ibid.*, p. 80.
[21] *Ibid.*, p. 81.

negotiated indirectly. This constructive dialogue, characterized by nationalists as 'honourable cooperation' gradually gave way to direct dialogue and became the preferred method of both camps, most of the time, to attempt to manage the situation in Syria.

De Jouvenel's method had led to the adoption of a road map for the future satisfying France's two priorities, namely, the conclusion of an agreement with Syria similar to the 1923 Anglo-Iraqi agreement and an organic law for Syrian territories under the League of Nations' mandate. For this, the mandatory power had to promote the establishment of legitimate institutions on the basis of a constitution adopted freely by the population like that of Lebanon in 1926. The nationalists saw the future constitution and the institutions that would derive from it as an important step forward and as new instruments in their quest for independence.

3.3 The Fight for the 1928 Constitution

The Great Revolt (1925–26) had shown that nothing could be achieved by armed struggle alone, the nationalist forces being greatly outnumbered. It had also made France realize that the policy followed since the battle of Maysalun in 1920 had led to a dead-end and that the Syrians would not accept the mandate or the partition of their country. Negotiation was the only way out of the deadlock. As high commissioner de Jouvenel initiated a political process, for their part the nationalists gradually abandoned their position of 'no negotiation with the mandate'. Two crucial elections in 1928 and 1931 symbolized the political process of 'honourable cooperation'. The main challenge of the 1928 election was to adopt a constitution and the challenge of the 1931–32 election was to conclude a Franco-Syrian agreement to supersede the mandate. Alongside these objectives, the nationalists continued to call for the reunification of Syrian lands. But before the 1928 and 1931–32 elections, the high commissioner organized partial elections early in 1926, without any prior agreement with the nationalists, which were a hopeless failure.

3.3.1 The 1926 Partial Elections

De Jouvenel's political open-mindedness and personal style had made it possible to work towards an honourable outcome to the Great Revolt, which lost impetus as French military pressure built up. Through the Damascene delegations that had come to meet the high commissioner in Beirut, the nationalists had suggested appointing a government to prepare elections for a constituent assembly, adopting a constitution, and concluding a treaty to supersede the mandate. De Jouvenel was not fundamentally opposed to this, but in order of priority he preferred first to hold elections for a representative council, probably so as to better measure nationalist influence in the country, before appointing a new government.

De Jouvenel therefore called elections in Syria for 8 February 1926 except in the region of Damascus where a state of siege had been proclaimed. Elections for the Damascus region and its surroundings were in principle to be held a month after the lifting of the state of siege. Although the siege was subsequently lifted, the elections were never held.

The partial elections went ahead in the remainder of Syria early in 1926 by the two-tier voting system in force since the 1923 order. They were largely boycotted by the populations of the major cities (Aleppo, Homs, and Hama) at the request of nationalist leaders.[22] These elections confirmed the popularity of the nationalists and prompted the high commissioner to come to an understanding with their leaders. He began by proposing the position of head of government to Hashim Atassi and then Ibrahim Hanano. Both declined the position and any direct negotiation with France before there was a promise of independence.[23] Having failed to find a credible Syrian to serve as prime minister, the high commissioner offered the job to the Damad Ahmad Nami.

Ahmad Nami stood apart among the political leaders of the time. He had been born in 1878 into a family of Circassian origin, had undertaken military studies in Istanbul, and served for a time in the imperial army before joining the Ottoman administration in Beirut and Smyrna. He married one of Sultan Abdul Hamid's daughters, Princess Aisha, thus becoming a prince, an Ottoman highness, and bearing the title 'Damad', meaning son-in-law in Turkish, although he had divorced by the time he was appointed head of Syria.[24] Ahmad Nami's appointment met with opposition because he was not Syrian. Despite his pro-French affinities, the Damad did manage to win some trust from the nationalists who accepted for a time to work with him.

---

[22] For details on the election, see Qarqout, *The Development of the National Movement* (Arabic), pp. 82 ff.

[23] Moubayed, *The Politics of Damascus*, p. 65.

[24] In 1926, during the Damad Ahmad Nami's rule in Syria, the last Ottoman Sultan Vahideddin Mehmed VI passed away in San Remo, Italy, and was buried in Damascus.

3.3.2 The Ahmad Nami Government's Ten Points

The process of drafting the 1928 constitution was triggered after the high commissioner's appointment of Ahmad Nami in May 1926. As soon as his cabinet was formed, comprising six ministers, three of whom were nationalists, and with the Damad combining the positions of prime minister and head of state, Ahmad Nami, in agreement with the high commissioner, made known the ten points of his government's agenda. The main points were the election of a constituent assembly; the replacement of the mandate by a treaty between Syria and France for a term of thirty years that would safeguard the rights and duties of both parties in an identical way to the agreement between Great Britain and Iraq and that would be submitted for approval to the Syrian parliament; the completion of Syrian unity; the creation of a national army so that France could gradually withdraw its troops; France's aid in having Syria admitted to the League of Nations, as was the case of Iraq with Great Britain; and a general amnesty for all political crimes, that is all those related to the Great Revolt.[25]

The three governments Ahmad Nami formed between May 1926 and February 1928 were unable to fulfil this ambitious programme. High commissioner Henri de Jouvenel's replacement by Henri Ponsot in September 1926 went along with a change of direction on the Syrian question, not to say a U-turn. The less conciliatory Ponsot decreed only a partial amnesty, contrary to the general amnesty provided for under the Ahmad Nami–de Jouvenel agreement. Moreover, the French authorities arrested the government's three nationalist ministers in September 1926 and exiled them to Lebanon. That was hardly an incentive to the insurgents to lay down their arms or to facilitate the new high commissioner's understanding with the nationalists. The constituent assembly planned for in the government agenda could not be formed under the Damad's successive governments. Only the principle underpinning it was settled. In late 1927, the high commissioner began a series of discussions in Beirut with the main Syrian nationalist leaders Atassi and Hanano about the future constitution, which failed to lead to any agreement. Faced with the deadlock between the nationalists and France, Ahmad Nami resigned. The high commissioner provisionally appointed a new head of state, Sheikh Tajeddine Al-Hasni, who was closer to the positions of the mandatory

---

[25] For details of the Ahmad Nami government's agenda, see Al-Hakim, *Syria and the French Mandate* (Arabic), vol. IV, pp. 148 ff.

power. Ponsot hoped through this appointment to positively influence the forthcoming elections for the constituent assembly.

France was eager to restore order after the successive Syrian crises. Under the provisions of the mandate charter conferred on it by the League of Nations, France had three years to give Syria an organic law, in other words a constitution, in agreement with the population.[26] But the division of Syria into several political entities during the initial phase of the mandate had precluded any dialogue between the mandatory power and the political elites and had led to the Great Revolt of 1925–26. As a sign of the failure of its Syrian policy on two occasions (September 1926 and March 1927) France had to ask the League of Nations for extra time to bestow an organic law on Syria. Hence the mandatory authorities were impatient that Syria should have a constitution at the earliest opportunity. The nationalists were just as impatient because for them the constitution was a pre-condition for negotiating the treaty that could replace the mandate. Moreover, they were determined to make it an instrument in the fight not just for independence but for reunification with the other Syrian lands.

3.3.3 The 1928 Elections

The 1928 elections for the constituent assembly were organized by the pro-French government of Sheikh Tajeddine Al-Hasni without any prior understanding between the high commissioner and the nationalists about the major points of the future constitution or, more importantly, between the nationalists and the head of government. Unlike the previous period and in particular Ahmad Nami's first cabinet, the composition of Sheikh Tajeddine Al-Hasni's government was not based on any understanding with the nationalists, who had no ministerial positions. The mandatory power's hopes for a chamber favourable to its views on the future constitution and the future Franco-Syrian treaty rested entirely with the Al-Hasni government positively influencing electors and securing the election of moderate representatives to the constituent assembly.

---

[26] Article 1 of the French Mandate for Syria and the Lebanon (1922): 'The Mandatory shall frame, within a period of three years from the coming into force of this Mandate, an organic law for Syria and the Lebanon. This organic law shall be framed in agreement with the native authorities and shall consider the rights, interests, and wishes of all the population inhabiting the said territory. The Mandatory shall further enact measures to facilitate the progressive development of Syria and the Lebanon as independent states. Pending the coming into effect of the organic law, the Government of Syria and the Lebanon shall be conducted in accordance with the spirit of this Mandate...' See the full text of the mandate in Haut Commissariat, *La Syrie et le Liban*.

The high commissioner decreed an amnesty before the elections, which he termed a general amnesty but excluded charges relating to the Great Revolt and the main Syro-Lebanese nationalist leaders such as Abdel Rahman Shahbandar, Shukri Qwatli, Ihsan Jabri (Syria), Sultan Atrash (Jabal Druze), Shakib Arslan, Fawzi Qawukji, and Shaib Whab (Lebanon), as well as Mohamed Shureiki and Amin Rouhaiaha (Alawi region). The Syrian leaders of the armed resistance could therefore not take part in the elections.

Accordingly, the partial amnesty did not have the expected effects on the Syrian population during the elections held in the following weeks. In preparation for the elections, the nationalists formed a new political grouping that included the former National Party, certain members of the People's Party (others remained loyal to their leader in exile in Cairo, Abdel Rahman Shahbandar), and independent figures, mostly local notables. The new grouping took the name of the 'National Bloc' and was to play a prime role in Syria's political struggle for independence. The members of the National Bloc elected Hashim Atassi as president of the movement. He was the former president of the Syrian congress of 1919 to 1920 and the former prime minister of King Faysal in 1920.

The elections were held in April 1928. The voting arrangements were those provided for by the order of the high commissioner of 20 March 1928 merging orders 2144 and 2145 of 1923 for the elections in Damascus and Aleppo and order 2844 of 1924 for the elections in Deir Ezzor. The new voting arrangements still provided for two-tier elections as under the Ottoman procedure.[27] The quota for the election of members was 1:6,000 inhabitants. The first-tier constituencies were the *nahie* in the countryside and the districts in cities. The second-tier constituencies were the *caza* for the countryside and the cities of Damascus and Aleppo. The right to vote was restricted to men of more than twenty-one years of age for the first-tier election and twenty-five years for the second-tier. Candidates had to be at least thirty years old and literate. Elections were by relative majority. Soldiers, gendarmes, and assimilated professions could not vote in principle. Under no circumstances could they stand for office. The electoral procedure introduced the principle of special representation for sectarian minorities and bedouins.

The results were not clear cut, being favourable to the nationalists in the cities and the moderates in the countryside. But subsequently, the

---

[27] See Order 1889 of 20 March 1928 in *Recueil des actes administratifs du Haut-Commissaire de la République française en Syrie et au Liban*, 1928, vol. IX, pp. 58 ff.

moderates aligned in the assembly on the positions of the nationalists, united around a clearly defined national programme. The constituent assembly met in Damascus on 9 May 1928 and its members elected Hashim Atassi to preside over it. The members of the constituent assembly set quickly to work and on 11 August 1928 passed on its first reading the text of the first constitution of the Syrian Republic.

3.4 The 1928 Constitution as an Instrument for National Liberation

Drafting the constitution was a far easier job than getting France to accept it. The constituent assembly completed its work within a few weeks, but it took the high commissioner nearly two years to amend and promulgate the text. The nationalists and mandate authorities did not share the same conception of the constitution. For the former, the constitution was first an opportunity to raise the national question again and a tool for reuniting Syrian lands under French (Lebanon, the Druze and Alawi territories) and British (Palestine, Transjordan) mandates before being an instrument for internal regulation of power above and beyond the high commissioner's competences. For the latter, the constitution was first to be a way for the Syrians to legitimize the mandate and the territorial carve-up since the battle of Maysalun and incidentally an instrument for regulating power between the executive, legislative, and judicial powers of the little Syrian Republic.

The 1928 constitution was to be applied on-and-off between 1930 and 1949. Over this period it was suspended several times by France, related to the vicissitudes and relations between the mandatory power and the elected representatives and nationalists. The importance of the constitution lay not in the way it regulated authority, although this was a significant aspect of it, but rather in the way it formed a radical break with the different political orders that the former eastern occupied zone, Syria's predecessor, had experienced after its separation from the Ottoman empire before being split into various mini-entities by the French mandate. In establishing a republic by mutual agreement between France and the elected representatives of the Syrian people, the 1928 constitution turned the page on the short-lived monarchic experiment of 1920. But via its centralized and unifying character, the constitution also confirmed the bankruptcy of the repeated attempts by the mandatory power to carve up Syria into small autonomous or federated entities. The road that was to lead the young Syrian republic towards independence and reunification of the other Syrian lands that were still autonomous (the Druze and Alawi territories) was to be a long and winding one. However, with the institutions of the 1928 constitution, the nationalists now had a sharp instrument for their political combat.

3.4.1 The National Question

Eight years after the tragic disappearance of the kingdom of Syria and the parcelling of its territory between the French and British mandates, the 1928 constitution posed the national question to its full extent. Article 2 stipulated that Syria comprised 'all the Syrian territories detached from the Ottoman empire, without regard to the divisions that arose after the end of the world war'. In this article, the elected representatives to the constituent assembly called for the reunification of Syria with the Druze and Alawi territories, Lebanon, Transjordan, and Palestine. This provision surprised the French authorities, which had consistently thought Syrian nationalism was a transient epiphenomenon manipulated by the British. But the national question was plainly still very much alive in Syrians' minds and included not just the Syrian lands under the French mandate but also those under the British mandate.

Article 4 described the Syrian flag: 'It is made up of three stripes coloured green, white, and black with three red stars on the white stripe.' The colours were those of the flag of the Great Arab Revolt of 1916 dear to the nationalists, but arranged differently. The three stars represented the former states of Damascus and Aleppo and the sanjak of Deir Ezzor where the election for the constituent assembly was held in 1928. This flag, commonly known as that of independence, was adopted by the opposition during the 2011 crisis.

The 1928 constitution contained a classical declaration of rights entitled 'individual rights'.[28] The constitution contained articles relating to personal security, individual and civil liberties, and freedom of worship. These rights were guaranteed. It is noteworthy that the declaration made no distinction among citizens on the basis of their religious background in terms of rights and duties, while maintaining the personal status of individuals depending on their sectarian origin. Thus, the 1928 constitution confirmed the 'Syrian style secularization' already expressed in the 1920 constitution, namely the secularization of citizens' rights and duties and the sectarianization of the personal status of individuals. In addition, the

---

[28] See the text of the 1928 constitution in French in Ajlani, *La Constitution de la Syrie*, pp. 269–89.

1928 constituent assembly, like that of 1920, made no express reference to political parties, merely authorizing instead the formation of associations.

'The conditions for acquiring and losing Syrian nationality shall be determined by statute', stated article 5. 'Syrians are equal before the law. They all enjoy the same civil and political rights. They are bound by the same duties and subject to the same encumbrances. There shall be no unequal treatment among them because of religion, sectarian origin, race, or language' (art. 6).

Individual freedom was guaranteed by article 7: 'No one shall be arrested or detained other than as provided by law' and article 8: 'Anyone who is arrested or detained has to be advised within 24 hours of the reasons for their arrest or detention and of the authority that has ordered it. They shall be afforded all facilities for their defence within the same lapse of time.'

Under article 10, 'No one shall be tried by courts other than those indicated by law'. Corporal punishment was prohibited. 'It is forbidden to remove Syrians from their national territory and to require or prohibit any particular place of residence except in cases provided for by law' (art. 11). The home was inviolable, stated article 12; 'no one may enter unless on the terms and in the forms provided for by law'.

Article 13 stated: 'The right of property is guaranteed by law. No one shall be expropriated except in the general interest, in cases provided for by law, and in exchange for fair, prior compensation.' The general confiscation of property was prohibited (art. 14). 'Freedom of conscience is absolute; the state shall respect all confessions and established religions in the country; it shall guarantee and protect the free exercise of all forms of worship compatible with public order and decency; it shall also guarantee all populations, whatever rites they practise, respect for their religious interests and personal status' (art. 15).

Under article 16, freedom of opinion was guaranteed: 'Everyone has the right to express themselves freely in speech, writing, addresses, and drawings within the framework laid down by law'. Freedom of the press and printing was guaranteed on conditions provided for by law (art. 17); 'Postal, telegraphic, and telephone correspondence is inviolable and shall not be delayed or censured other than as provided for by law' (art. 18).

Article 19 stipulated that education was unrestricted, 'provided it is not contrary to public order and decency and does not affect the dignity of the country or religions'. Primary education was mandatory for all Syrians of both sexes and free in official schools (art. 21); 'The rights of the various religious communities are guaranteed, and those communities may found schools for teaching children in their own language provided they comply with the principles laid down by law' (art. 28).

Under article 24, Arabic was to be the official language in all government services, 'except where other languages are added in this capacity by law or an international agreement'. Freedom of association and assembly was guaranteed on the terms provided for by law (art. 25).

3.4.2 Legislative Power

Parliament was to have a single chamber. This was a major difference between the 1928 constitution and the 1920 monarchic constitution, which provided for a senate alongside the assembly. Single chamber parliaments were to become the rule and were adopted by all subsequent Syrian constitutions.

The Assembly of Deputies

The procedure for election to the chamber is laid down by law, stated article 41. This principle was taken up by numerous subsequent Syrian constitutions, leaving it to the legislature to define the voting system. This was also true of the 1920 constitution, although the constituent assembly of the time had taken the care to define the conditions for two-tier voting (as detailed by arts 87–90). The 1928 constitution specified only that voting shall be by secret ballot according to electoral law (art. 37). Just like the 1920 constitution, the 1928 constitution provided that the electoral law shall also lay down the representation of sectarian minorities (art. 37).

Article 39 provided for legislatures of four years' duration. Each deputy represents the entire nation, stated article 42. Whereas article 44 of the 1928 constitution stipulated that the Assembly of Deputies sit twice a year, the 1920 constitution had provided for just one parliamentary session per year. Article 45 added: The President of the Republic may convene the Assembly for extraordinary sittings. An absolute majority of deputies may ask the President of the Republic to convene an extraordinary sitting.

The Assembly's Responsibilities

The assembly had as its first task to pass statutes. 'Legislation may be introduced by the President of the Republic or by the Assembly of Deputies,' stated article 32. The government, therefore, could not initiate legislation. Bills were to be discussed within commissions of the Assembly (art. 54); 'No bill that is dismissed by the Assembly may be resubmitted for a new vote within the same parliamentary sitting' (art. 55). Under article 56, 'Each bill shall be discussed by the Assembly article by article and then submitted as a whole to a nominal vote'.

In accordance with article 49, the Assembly 'may only take decisions if an absolute majority of members is present'. Decisions were to be taken by a relative majority unless otherwise provided by law (art. 50). Votes were open (raised hands, standing or sitting) except for elections and questions relating to appointments, which were by secret ballot (art. 51).

Each deputy was entitled to question ministers (art. 52). Article 53 added: 'The Assembly of Deputies can hold the government to account. Any censure motion shall be presented in writing and signed by at least ten deputies. Ministers may postpone the debate for eight days. A resolution of no-confidence can only be adopted if it receives the majority of the votes of the Assembly. No censure motion is admissible during the examination of the budget.'

3.4.3 *The Executive*

The executive was made up of the president and government.

The President of the Republic

Article 68 of the 1928 constitution provided: The President of the Republic shall be elected by secret ballot by the majority of members of the Assembly of Deputies. In the third round of voting, the President is elected by the relative majority. In being elected by the representatives of the nation and not by direct popular suffrage, the president owed his political legitimacy to the confidence accorded to him by parliament. By definition, this was less than the political legitimacy of the assembly, which was elected directly by the people.

Article 3 stipulated that the religion of the President had to be Islam. This article can be likened to article 2 of the 1920 monarchic constitution specifying that the king's religion was Islam. Any candidate for the presidency had to meet the necessary requirements for being a deputy. The minimum age for election was thirty-five years, and supreme office was for a duration of five years that could not be renewed without a five-year interruption between the two terms (art. 68). The duration of the presidency exceeded that of the legislature by one year. This article was amended in 1948 to allow President Shukri Qwatli to be re-elected for a second term.

The Attributes of the President of the Republic

The president chooses the prime minister and appoints the ministers upon the prime minister's proposal. He accepts their resignation and appoints representatives abroad. He receives foreign representatives and appoints civil servants and the judiciary (art. 75).

Under article 77, the President has the right to dissolve the Assembly in agreement with the Council of Ministers and under its responsibility. The decree of dissolution shall state its reasons and invite the electoral body to hold new legislative elections within two months. It was not a discretionary power, therefore, because the council of ministers could oppose it. 'The President cannot dissolve the Assembly twice for the same reason,' added article 78. The right of dissolution was therefore restricted.

Article 79 stated: 'The President of the Republic shall publish Acts of Parliament within one month of their being passed by the Assembly and transmitted to the Government. If an Act of Parliament is not published within this time frame, it shall be held to be enforceable as of right. Acts of Parliament that the Assembly characterizes as urgent shall be published within one week.'

In accordance with article 80, the 'President may ask the Assembly for a second reading of a law within the time allowed for its publication. If the Assembly confirms its previous vote by a two-thirds majority, the law shall be held to be enforceable and shall be published.' The president therefore had a provisional veto only. To defeat the presidential veto, the assembly had to confirm its vote by a two-thirds majority. Theoretically, it was difficult to achieve such a majority. In most cases, the law in question would probably require just a relative majority unless legislative provisions stated otherwise. This article therefore gave the president considerable leeway to dismiss any law he disagreed with and that could not secure a two-thirds vote in the Parliament. In practice, that would have been tantamount in many instances to the president having pre-eminence over the assembly, but this provision was never applied.

Article 81 enabled the executive to delay any excessive steps by the parliament: 'The President, in agreement with the Council of Ministers, may adjourn the Assembly for a period not exceeding one month. He may not do it twice during the same session.'

Article 74 stated that the President concluded and promulgated treaties. It added: 'Treaties that involve state security or finances, trade treaties, and all treaties whose duration or effects exceed one year shall be passed by the Assembly before they come into force'.

The Non-responsibility of the President of the Republic

Article 82 provided:

> The President bears no responsibility. The Assembly cannot depose him. The President cannot be prosecuted for acts committed in the exercise of his functions except for violation of the constitution or high treason. He may be prosecuted for ordinary crimes within the frame of the law. Charges may only be brought against him by a two-thirds majority of the Assembly. He may be tried by the Supreme Court only.

While the president bore no responsibility, all acts had to be countersigned by a minister, who assumed full responsibility for them. Article 76 of the constitution specified that any decision taken by the President must be countersigned by the minister responsible, except for the appointment of the Prime Minister.

The Government

Article 75 provided: 'The President of the Republic chooses the Prime Minister and appoints the ministers upon the Prime Minister's proposal. He accepts their resignation.' The constitution did not require a vote for investiture of the assembly. Parliament was therefore not involved in the formation of the government. However, article 90 stipulated that the Prime Minister or a minister must present the Government's plan to the Assembly.

Article 89 set the number of ministers at seven. Article 88 provided that the Government directs all of the state administrative machinery. It meets under the chairmanship of the Prime Minister to take decisions on important questions and article 90 added: 'The cabinet is collectively responsible to the Assembly of Deputies for general policy. Each minister is individually responsible for matters concerning his ministry'.

The presence of two-thirds of the deputies was required for a vote of confidence, greater than that required for the election of the president (an absolute majority). According to the mechanism established by article 93, the Government or a minister may call for a vote of confidence in the presence of a majority of deputies. A minister who fails to secure a vote of confidence shall resign.

Article 94 stated that charges for high treason or abuse of authority against members of the government may only be brought against them by a two-thirds majority of the Assembly. Article 95 added they shall be tried by the Supreme Court.

3.4.4 France's Objections

The high commissioner judged that six articles of the constitution contradicted France's international obligations to the League of Nations concerning Syria and purely and simply ignored the mandate. France rejected articles 2, 73, 74, 75, 110, and 112. Several of these concerned the attributes of the president and the army. Under article 73 the president was vested with the power to grant pardons. The right of general amnesty could only be granted by law. Article 74 provided that the president should conclude and sign treaties, but that treaties concerning state security and finances, trade treaties, and all treaties that could not be abrogated at the end of the year had to be passed by the assembly to be enforceable. Article 75 specified that the president should choose the prime minister and appoint the ministers he proposed. The president accepted their resignation and appointed representatives abroad. He received foreign representatives and appointed civil servants and the judiciary. Article 110 specified that the future army would be the subject of a special law and article 112 granted the president the power to proclaim a state of siege in unsettled areas when proposed by the council of ministers.

The constituent assembly was twice suspended for three months. The high commissioner met with Hashim Atassi and asked him to withdraw the six litigious articles on the pretext that they granted too much power to the president to the detriment of the high commissioner. Hashim Atassi declined, but promised, in exchange for acceptance of the constitution in the form adopted by the constituent assembly, a treaty guaranteeing France a privileged position in Syria.[29] He added that France would continue, as the mandatory power, to be responsible for Syria's foreign relations, but that home affairs were to be dealt with exclusively by a local government.

The constituent assembly was authorized to resume its work on 5 February 1929 without any agreement having been reached with the nationalists. The high commissioner, via his representatives, again asked for the six articles at odds with the mandate to be modified. The deputies again declined.[30] The assembly was adjourned indefinitely by the high commissioner before being dissolved. The constitution was finally proclaimed unilaterally by the high commissioner in 1930 after modifying article 2 and adding an article 116. As soon as it was promulgated, the high commissioner announced legislative elections were to be held

---

[29] Moubayed, *The Politics of Damascus*, p. 83.
[30] Al-Hakim, *Syria and the French Mandate* (Arabic), vol. IV, pp. 216–17.

to elect an assembly, a president, and a government with which France meant to negotiate the treaty that would supersede the mandate.

In the version revised by the high commissioner, article 2 stipulated that 'Syria forms an indivisible political unit' instead of stating that Syria included 'all the Syrian territories detached from the Ottoman empire, without regard to the divisions that arose after the end of the world war'. Article 116 added by the mandatory power stipulated that no provision of the constitution could go counter to the obligations undertaken by France concerning Syria, particularly with respect to the League of Nations. Article 116 was rejected by the nationalists and was finally abolished by the Syrian parliament in 1943 under circumstances to be described later.

The suspension of the constituent assembly's work and the French authorities' refusal to confirm the choices made by freely chosen representatives led to disorder nationwide. During this period, which lasted nearly two years, the struggle for the constitution went hand in hand with the struggle for Syria's independence and unity.

3.5 The Fight for the Franco-Syrian Treaty to Supersede the Mandate

Seven years after members of the representative council of the State of Damascus within the Syrian Federation had timidly asked for the election of a constituent assembly and five years after that call had been taken up by the Great Syrian Revolt, the struggle for the constitution provisionally ended with the adoption of a constitution drafted by the elected representatives of the Syrian people and amended by France. Immediately a fresh struggle began, which was equally decisive for the country's future, that of the Franco-Syrian treaty that was eventually to supersede the mandate. The first stage unfolded in the 1931–32 elections to pick members of the future parliament who would have to vote on the provisions of the future treaty.

3.5.1 The 1931–1932 Elections

The election of deputies was conducted in accordance with the 1928 procedure. The dates for the election were 20 December 1931 for the first tier and 5 January 1932 for the second tier. Several political movements were in the running, including the National Bloc under Hashim Atassi, and Rida Rekabi's monarchist party. Supporters of the mandate were gathered around Sheikh Tajeddine Al-Hasni and Haqqi Al-Azzem's pro-French Reform Party.

One of the immediate questions of the election was whether Syria would remain a republic or become a monarchy again. The 1928 constitution had admittedly opted for a republic as the form of government. But the instinctive irredentism of the Syrians and the difficulty in engaging in constructive dialogue with the nationalist leaders prompted the high commissioner Henri Ponsot to contemplate changing Syria into a kingdom. This idea was subsequently to cross the mind of another high commissioner at another difficult moment between France and the Syrian political class.[31] Ponsot's initial idea was for France to appoint a king who would get on with the country's leaders. Potential candidates included King Faysal, ex-king of Syria and now king of Iraq; his brother Prince Ali, ex-king of the Hedjaz; the former Khedive of Egypt Abbas Hilmi II;[32] and the Damad Ahmad Nami.[33]

For the monarchists, the 1931–32 election was an opportunity not to be missed. Rida Rikabi, twice former head of Faysal's government (in 1918 and 1920) and former head of government of the kingdom of Transjordan (in 1922) led the monarchist electoral bid after his return to Syria in 1924. Faysal, although he had become king of Iraq, had fond memories of the brief years in Syria. He sent his loyal adviser Rustom Haydar to Damascus, then his brother Ali, to weigh up the chances of ascending the Syrian throne again. But unlike the fervour of the Syrian nationalists in 1915 who from the outset rallied to the Hashemite banner, the emerging Syrian political elite was no longer in favour of Faysal's return. Since he had left in 1920, Syria had seen political leaders emerge who had won the trust of the population by opposing France politically and militarily. This new political elite did not intend to abdicate its power and the authority it had earned through struggle to a king who had abandoned the country during one of the worst moments in its history when the mandate was set up and the country divided. Besides, Syrians no longer saw the Hashemites as saviours of the Arab nation because they were compromised with the British. The notables preferred to choose a national leader from among their peers rather than put matters back into Hashemite hands. Even so, the possibility of Faysal's return galvanized some, in particular among the

---

[31] Puaux, *Deux années au Levant*, pp. 41–2.
[32] Moubayed, *The Politics of Damascus*, p. 86.
[33] When the high commissioner accepted Ahmad Nami's resignation in 1928, he asked him to remain neutral between moderate and nationalist Syrians so as to be in a position to be crowned king of Syria in the future. See Al-Hakim, *Syria and the French Mandate* (Arabic), vol. IV, p. 202.

religious and among those nostalgic for the days of the first Arab government in Damascus after four centuries of Ottoman domination.

The election did not turn in the monarchists' favour. Even their leader, Rida Rikabi, although a hero of the Great Arab Revolt, was not elected. The first inklings of the dialogue that the nationalists termed 'honourable cooperation' with the mandate and France's hope to come at last to a compromise with them left the royalist party no hope of playing a leading part and restoring the monarchy.

The monarchists' defeat was not the only feature of the election. Voting was marred by glaring irregularities (intimidation of pro-nationalist electors and ballot boxes stuffed by those collaborating with France) that stirred up unrest in all the major cities (including Damascus, Homs, Aleppo, and Hama). The National Bloc called immediately for the election to be boycotted. Its call was followed en masse throughout the country, demonstrating the National Bloc's hold over the population. The elections were suspended until April 1932, when the National Bloc and the high commissioner agreed on the voting system so that the election would be transparent, free from constraint and fraud. At the insistence of the National Bloc and its president Hashim Atassi, the agreement also included the release of the nationalist leaders arrested by the mandate forces, such as Saadallah Jabri in Aleppo and the return of exiles such as Shukri Qwatli.[34] However, the agreement did not include Shahbandar and Sultan Atrash, the heroes of the Great Syrian Revolt. The high commissioner had continued to oppose their return since 1926. Once the agreement was reached, elections resumed in Damascus, Douma, and Hama.[35]

3.5.2 The Assembly of Deputies and the Election of the President of the Republic in 1932

The election result gave the National Bloc seventeen out of seventy seats. So, as in the previous election in 1928, the nationalists did not have a majority in the chamber. However, as in 1928, their influence proved considerable and exceeded their arithmetical weight alone. The nationalists were the driving force behind the assembly. At its first sitting, the assembly

---

[34] See Atassi, *Hashim Atassi* (Arabic), p. 130.

[35] The vote of the city of Aleppo in December 1931 was marred by blatant irregularities but the nationalists decided not to bring the matter before the assembly and ask for verification under article 47 of the constitution so as not to overshadow the assembly's primary mission, which was to conclude the Franco-Syrian treaty that was to replace the mandate.

elected its speaker, Subhi Barakat, a notable from Antioch, former president of the Federation of Syria (Damascus, Aleppo, and Alawi territory) between 1922 and 1925, of the Syrian State between 1926 and 1928, and someone close to France. The chamber then undertook to elect the first president of the Syrian Republic. The four front runners were Subhi Barakat, the newly elected speaker; Haqqi Al-Azzem, former head of the State of Damascus from 1920 to 1922, who was known for his pro-French position; Ali Abed, a scion of a wealthy Damascene family closely tied to Sultan Abdel Hamid II, and former ambassador of the Sublime Porte to the United States in 1908; and Hashim Atassi, former president of the Syrian congress (1919–20), prime minister of King Faysal, and president of the constituent assembly in 1928. The nationalists were too few to secure the election of their candidate Hashim Atassi. He withdrew after the first round of voting and the nationalists supported Ali Abed, a moderate politician, to block Haqqi Al-Azzem and Subhi Barakat, both notoriously pro-French. The nationalist tactic paid off and Ali Abed was elected the first president of the Syrian Republic on 11 June 1932.

Ali Abed's election was felt as a fresh failure by the high commissioner Henri Ponsot to add to his inability to influence the adoption of a constitution favourable to the mandatory power's views in 1928.

3.5.3 *The Beginning of Negotiations on the 1932 Franco-Syrian Treaty*

The first actions of the young republic took on particular symbolic and political importance. For the first time ever, twelve years after the mandate was established, Syria was at last to be governed via national institutions freely elected in accordance with provisions laid down by the constitution. The population had endured much and waited impatiently for the time it would finally have a parliament, government, and president. It now remained to be seen how these three institutions would coordinate their actions and what their relations with the high commissioner would be.

The nationalists were determined to mobilize all the new institutions in the service of their struggle for independence and reunification of Syrian territories. Although in a minority in the new assembly, the nationalist deputies were united behind the National Bloc, which, after having politically supported the insurrectional fight in 1925–26 and led the fight for the constitution between 1928 and 1930, then the fight for free and fair elections in 1931–32, was preparing for a new and equally crucial fight for the future of Syria. This fight was in principle to take place within the framework of the institutions of the new republic and its objective was to conclude a treaty with France that would ultimately replace the mandate, grant independence, and reunite the country.

Under article 75 of the 1928 constitution, President Abed appointed Haqqi Al-Azzem, his unhappy rival for the presidency, as prime minister. This appointment was due to pressure on the new president from the high commissioner. Two nationalists affiliated to the National Bloc agreed to join the government to counter France's influence, but without having secured the prior approval of their political movement. This sparked vehement protests within the National Bloc. But after weighing the pros and cons of having two nationalist ministers out of the four portfolios in the Al-Azzem government, the National Bloc leader, Hashim Atassi, accorded them his confidence, thereby confirming in an open-handed gesture his cautious policy of dialogue with France.

The nationalists were keen to begin negotiations for the conclusion of the Franco-Syrian treaty. As the French authorities were dragging their feet, Hashim Atassi published a communiqué in the name of the National Bloc asking all its members within the assembly and government to suspend their participation in those institutions until the high commissioner sent him personally a memorandum containing the main provisions of the future treaty. Henri Ponsot, surprised by the manoeuvre and the tone taken by Atassi, sought President Abed's mediation. But Atassi stood his ground. So as not to break off all ties with the president and the high commissioner, the two National Bloc ministers remained in the cabinet but the National Bloc deputies refused to sit in the assembly until Hashim Atassi, in response to mediation by the head of state, asked them to do so. To the satisfaction of the National Bloc, President Abed convened the assembly some days later for a session on the question of the treaty with France. On 5 November 1932, the assembly authorized the head of state to begin negotiations with France for the conclusion of a treaty setting out relations between the two countries and Syria's admission to the League of Nations. Time was pressing, including for France, because a month before, on 3 October 1932, Iraq had joined the League of Nations.

In November 1932, Henri Ponsot went to Geneva and argued in the League of Nations for Syria's membership, but without the Alawite and Druze territories, which he claimed could not be attached to Syria for the time being because of their economic backwardness and need for development. This position caused uproar in Syria. Demonstrations were organized nationwide. Jamil Mardam, one of the nationalist ministers, tried in vain to persuade the high commissioner to change his position on the reunification of Syrian, Alawite, and Druze lands.[36] But Ponsot refused. The two nationalist ministers had no choice and were ordered by the National Bloc to resign, bringing down the Al-Azzem government in April 1933 and putting a temporary end to the policy of conciliation and 'honourable cooperation' between the nationalists and France. The young Syrian republic had just experienced its first government crisis.

Some days later, on 3 May 1933, Haqqi Al-Azzem was tasked with forming a second cabinet, but this time without nationalist ministers. The assembly gave a vote of confidence to the new cabinet, but without the nationalist members who decided to boycott the parliament again. France was embarrassed by the turn events had taken in Syria because it had to submit a report to the League of Nations' mandates commission in June 1933. Paris recalled Henri Ponsot and appointed in his place Count Damien de Martel, former ambassador to China, as the new high commissioner for Syria and Lebanon.[37]

3.5.4 The 1933 Version of the Franco-Syrian Treaty

After taking office, the new high commissioner accorded himself some time for thought and consultation with the main political actors. After several weeks, he revealed to President Abed and the Al-Azzem government the provisions of the treaty that France intended to sign with Syria. This text did not plan for reunification with the Druze and Alawi territories.[38] De Martel asked the president and prime minister to adopt the text of the treaty in cabinet and to submit it to the assembly. The cabinet stage proved more difficult than planned. Two of the five government ministers expressed their disagreement with the treaty provisions and one of them resigned in protest. That did not prevent Prime Minister Al-Azzem from signing the treaty with the high commissioner on 16 November 1933.

On 19 November 1933, President Abed submitted the treaty to the assembly for approval. On 21 November, the chamber held its one and only sitting to discuss it. The session was unruly and soon turned to the advantage of the nationalists who, although in a minority, managed to

---

[36] Moubayed, *The Politics of Damascus*, pp. 103 ff.
[37] Ponsot was subsequently appointed French ambassador to Turkey. He was therefore involved in matters concerning Syria, in particular at the start of the crisis over the sanjak of Alexandretta and its attachment to Turkey.
[38] See the main provisions of the treaty in Al-Hakim, *Syria and the French Mandate* (Arabic), vol. IV, pp. 238–9.

rally a majority of deputies to dismiss the text. Confronted with this turn of events, the high commissioner's delegate asked the speaker to suspend the session for four days. The speaker, although notorious for his pro-French sympathies, refused and continued with the agenda of the assembly, which rejected the text by an absolute majority (46 votes out of 70). A French armed unit entered the assembly and interrupted the session. The speaker invited the members to join him at his residence nearby where a majority (48 out of 70, or close to 70 per cent of the chamber) followed him.[39] They resumed work and signed a petition rejecting the proposed treaty and the closure of the assembly. The deputies opposed to the treaty made it known to the high commissioner that they were numerous enough to call for an extraordinary sitting at the end of the parliamentary session, to which the high commissioner replied that he would dissolve the assembly.[40]

So, De Martel failed to force through a slightly modified version of the treaty, the main points of which had been suggested by his predecessor some months earlier. To the high commissioner's great surprise, the nationalists, in a minority in the chamber, managed with the help of the speaker, Subhi Barakat, to carry most members with them in opposing the treaty. The trial of strength was on. Just as in 1928, the parliamentary institution became an instrument in nationalist hands. On the eve of the planned resumption of the assembly's work, the high commissioner ordered it to be adjourned for the entire period of the parliamentary session under a somewhat peculiar interpretation of article 44 (dates of parliamentary sessions and priority for the vote on the budget during the autumn session) and article 100 (procedure for passing statutes containing new expenditure) of the constitution.[41]

The assembly's dismissal of the treaty, the suspension of the parliamentary session, and the demonstrations that ensued led the high commissioner to ask for the assembly's work to be suspended for a further six months. Just as in 1928, France was censuring a legitimately elected representative assembly. The subject of disagreement in 1928 was the constitution; in 1933 it was the Franco-Syrian treaty.

A congress of the National Bloc met in Homs early in February 1934 and adopted a national pact that took up the nationalists' main demands:[42]

---

[39] See Atassi, *Hashim Atassi* (Arabic), p. 142.
[40] *Ibid.*
[41] See Quarqout, *The Development of the National Movement* (Arabic), p. 142.
[42] See Atassi, *Hashim Atassi* (Arabic), pp. 143 ff.

the unity of Syria with the Jabal Druze, the Alawite territory, the city of Tripoli (Lebanon), and the four cazas detached from Syria and attached to Lebanon in 1920, national and administrative reunification, political and economic independence, and a general amnesty.

Faced with political deadlock and the shutdown of institutions, the high commissioner asked for the resignation of the Al-Azzem government and the appointment of Sheikh Tajeddine Al-Hasni as prime minister. The Tajeddine Al-Hasni government was formed in May 1934 in close consultation with the high commissioner, president, and prime minister. It included figures close to France and independent members respected by the nationalists but no member of the National Bloc. As in 1928, Tajeddine Al-Hasni's 1934 appointment resulted from an absence of dialogue between the nationalists and France.

3.5.5 The 1936 General Strike

No initiative could be proposed to break the deadlock in Syria. Parliament had been paralysed since 1932 and the mandatory power did not contemplate reaching any understanding with the nationalists. The two branches of the executive, the president and the government, supported France, while parliament was suspended for having supported the nationalists in rejecting the treaty. Towards the end of 1935, the population was becoming increasingly frustrated and impatient and protests began to take the shape of boycotts (of the tram company and electricity company, for example), strikes, and repeated street demonstrations. The events that followed the death, from natural causes, of the great nationalist leader from Aleppo, Ibrahim Hanano, in November 1935 were the spark that ignited the powder and transformed the latent protest movement into a general strike.

On 21 December 1935 at the commemoration on the fortieth day after Hanano's death, the National Bloc organized a ceremony in Aleppo at which Fares Khoury, in the name of the National Bloc, gave an address and made public a 'National Covenant'. His speech galvanized the crowd. The National Bloc published the text of the National Covenant, which became the nationalists' political manifesto. The main points were: (1) the liberation of the Syrian territories separated from the Ottoman empire from any foreign power so as to achieve independence and complete sovereignty and the reunification of the separated territories into a single state; (2) the refusal of Balfour's promise and resistance to the establishment of a Zionist national home; (3) the need to work with other Arab states to try to establish a federation.[43]

The National Bloc organized another commemorative ceremony in honour of Ibrahim Hanano on 18 January 1936 in Damascus at which Hashim Atassi and Jamil Mardam made speeches that enflamed the audience.[44] Demonstrators against France filled the streets of Damascus and Aleppo. In reaction, the French authorities closed the National Bloc's offices and imprisoned some of its leaders. This prompted the National Bloc to mobilize students and organize daily demonstrations. Other sectors of civil society and especially shopkeepers decided to strike in support of the movement. The movement snowballed and the entire country was paralyzed.

On 27 January 1936, the National Bloc called on the population to continue the general strike until constitutional life was restored. The National Bloc organized a network of support and mutual aid to enable the population to pursue the strike. The trial of strength continued with no initiative taken to remedy matters. Contrary to all expectations, it was Paris that eased the crisis. Faced with the Syrian population's support for the National Bloc, the Quai d'Orsay asked the high commissioner to work for a compromise with the nationalists. De Martel asked for Prime Minister Tajeddine Al-Hasni to resign and for him to be replaced by Atta Ayubi, an independent member respected by the nationalist leaders. He formed a politically neutral government, but included two nationalists. Although the National Bloc approved the removal of Tajeddin Al-Hasni, Hashim Atassi called for the general strike to continue throughout Syria. The population answered his call.

To ease tensions, the new head of government began mediation between the high commissioner and the National Bloc and secured the promise of a partial amnesty. Hashim Atassi refused the agreement because it excluded some three thousand people arrested by France since the beginning of the great strike and he called for the movement to continue. Finally, twenty-seven months after the break-off of direct contact between the National Bloc and France, the high commissioner had to resolve to negotiate directly with the National Bloc. He asked to meet Hashim Atassi on 29 February 1936. Atassi renewed the Bloc's demands for the signing of a

---

[43] See the text in Arabic in Khabbaz and Haddad, *Farés Khoury*, cited in Quarqout, *The Development of the National Movement* (Arabic), p. 245.
[44] For the speech by Hashim Atassi, see Atassi, *Hashim Atassi* (Arabic), pp. 155 ff. For the speech by Jamil Mardam, see Moubayed, *The Politics of Damascus*, pp. 109 ff.

similar agreement to the 1930 Anglo-Iraqi treaty and the reunification of the Syrian states. Atassi also asked for a delegation from the National Bloc to go to Paris to negotiate the provisions of this agreement directly with the French authorities. The next day, 1 March 1936, de Martel and Atassi met again and the high commissioner accepted the National Bloc's demands. The two sides also agreed to resume parliamentary activity and for free elections to be held. This agreement was signed in a common declaration by Atassi and de Martel.[45]

It was a triumphant Hashim Atassi who announced on 2 March 1936 the release of all prisoners, the return of those in exile, and the forthcoming departure for Paris of a delegation to negotiate with France the future treaty, independence, and the reunification of the Syrian states. The general strike of the entire country had lasted sixty days and costs the lives of many who fell under the bullets of the forces of law and order during the almost daily protests. Material losses were enormous because of the almost total paralysis of the country. Ultimately, the nationalists came out as the winners of this trial of strength. Their representative and legitimate character needed no further demonstration.[46] They had called on the people to strike, negotiated with the high commissioner, obtained satisfaction and then ended the strike. After winning the battle over the treaty in the assembly in 1933, they won a new political battle, but this time outside the institutional framework. The general strike officially ended on 8 March 1936 once all the political prisoners had been released.

3.6 The 1936 Franco-Syrian Treaty

The Franco-Syrian treaty negotiations in Paris were long and drawn out, lasting more than six months. The Syrian delegation was led by Hashim Atassi, president of the National Bloc, and included the Bloc's three main leaders and its two government ministers. The negotiations might have failed if in the meantime the legislative elections of May 1936 had not brought the Front populaire to power in France. The first version of the treaty proposed by the Quai d'Orsay before the legislative elections was dismissed by the Syrian delegation because it failed to comply with the agreement signed in Damascus on 2 March 1936 by de Martel and Hashim Atassi, concerning the unity and independence of Syria.

---

[45] See the text of the agreement in Atassi, *Hashim Atassi* (Arabic), p. 173.
[46] A popular slogan of the time read 'Obedience to God and the National Bloc'.

After a brief interruption because of the legislative elections, talks resumed with the Front populaire government. The French delegation was headed by Pierre Viénot, under-secretary of state for foreign affairs. The negotiating atmosphere was better than that with the preceding team. It took eleven weeks to reach an agreement, with the talks becoming bogged down at times, especially over Lebanon.

The Franco-Syrian Treaty of Friendship and Alliance comprised nine articles plus a military convention and five protocols. The main provisions of the treaty can be summarized thus: Art. 1: peace, perpetual friendship, and an alliance between France and Syria. Art. 2: consultation of French and Syrian governments over all matters of foreign policy that might affect their common interests. Art. 3: the Syrian government succeeds to the rights and obligations contracted by the French government in Syria's name. Art. 4: in the event of a risk of a dispute with a third state, the two governments would consult one another with a view to settling the dispute by peaceful means. If despite these measures, one of the contracting parties were to be engaged in conflict, the other party would lend it support as its ally. Art. 5: for the duration of the treaty, France would lend Syria its military support as provided for by the military convention. Art. 6: the treaty was concluded for a renewable period of 25 years. Art. 7: the treaty was to come into force the day Syria became a member of the League of Nations. Art. 8: when the treaty came into force, the responsibilities and obligations of the mandatory power would be transferred automatically to the Syrian government. Art. 9: the contracting parties would have recourse to a conciliation and arbitration procedure of the League of Nations in the event of dispute over the application or interpretation of any of the treaty clauses.

The military convention included eight articles that could be summarized thus: France would send a military mission to instruct Syrian armed forces; French troops would be stationed in the Alawi region and the Jabal Druze for five years; France would be entitled to maintain two air bases in Syria (in Damascus and Aleppo) for the duration of the alliance; France would supply weapons, equipment, and munitions to Syria.

The reattachment of the Alawi region and the Jabal Druze to Syria raised no difficulties. However, the question of Lebanon was one of the thorniest in the negotiations. The opening of Franco-Syrian talks had raised concern among the supporters of Greater Lebanon. The fear was that the future of Lebanon (federation with Syria and return of the four cazas) would be discussed in Paris. Indeed, the Syrian delegation wished to address the case of the Syrian territories attached to Lebanon by General

Gouraud in 1920, that is, the Beqaa valley (the cazas of Zahlah, Ba'albek, Rashayia, and Habsayia) and coastal Syria (especially the city of Tripoli).

This Franco-Syrian dialogue worried the Maronites. The Maronite Patriarch sent the cardinal of Beirut, Monseigneur Moubarak, to Paris to meet the French authorities and try to obtain guarantees. He easily obtained them and Viénot wired the president of Lebanon to assure him that France's position remained unchanged as concerned Lebanon's borders with Syria. For his part, the high commissioner, de Martel, sent a letter to Hashim Atassi on 27 June 1936 informing him that the French authorities did not intend to address the question of the borders of Syria with Lebanon during the negotiations with the Syrian delegation. Hashim Atassi wrote back on 6 August 1936 asserting that the creation of Lebanon by General Gouraud in 1920 was illegal in international law and undemocratic. Atassi added that the fair and democratic solution would be to hold a popular referendum in which the Lebanese would freely express themselves including on the possibility of reunification with Syria. The next day Viénot rebutted these arguments and gave it to be understood that if the Syrian party persisted in addressing the fate of Lebanon, the talks on the independence of Syria might be discontinued. To avoid deadlock, both sides accepted a compromise. The treaty remained silent on the question of Lebanon. Syria therefore did not recognize Lebanon or the Lebanese borders and France declared that the future relations between the two countries were to be decided by Syria and Lebanon after their independence.

This was a disappointment for the Syrian party, which would at least have established the principle of a Syro-Lebanese federation. However, from the Syrian point of view, the mere fact that the fate of Lebanon was not addressed in the final agreement with the French authorities meant that Syria did not officially acknowledge the existence of a Lebanon independent of Syria.

The 1936 treaty appears in many respects as a novel, unusual, and innovative instrument for the time, heralding what after the Second World War was to become decolonization. For the first time ever, France promised the eventual independence of a territory under its control.[47] Several features attested to this singularity. First, the fact that it was signed by the Front populaire government. The previous government, although it had promised through its high commissioner in March 1936 the independence

---

[47] Fares Khoury, one of the National Bloc leaders, called the Franco-Syrian treaty 'a twentieth-century miracle'.

and unity of Syria, proved very reluctant to sign an agreement to this effect with the Syrian nationalists. But the most important aspect for the Syrians was that this treaty eschewed the policy of dividing Syria pursued by France since 1920 on the pretext of promoting 'local autonomy'. Admittedly, after an initial break-up and dismembering of Syria, France had created the Syrian Federation in 1922 and then a small centralized Syrian state in 1925. But for the first time France agreed to reintegrate the Alawi and Druze territories into Syria and grant it independence. This was not the rebirth of Faysal's monarchic Greater Syria, but even so the 1936 treaty saw the birth of a new and important actor in the region.

This agreement left aside the Greater Lebanon created by France and the other Syrian territories under the British mandate (Transjordan and Palestine). Even so, independence and unity of only of a medium-sized Syria was of concern to the proponents of a Middle East divided into sectarian entities and was likely in the long term to upset certain regional balances and thwart the aspirations of certain actors. Lastly, the 1936 treaty signed by France, as a great colonial power, and the representatives of a territory under its administration was the first form of decolonization of its time. It was hardly surprising therefore that the treaty caused a ragbag of actors and pressure groups whose interests were in jeopardy to rise against it.

The leading opponents of the treaty were the supporters of the colonial lobby in France (such as the right, the military, the church, and the French living in Lebanon and Syria) who feared the Syrian precedent would spread to contaminate French colonies and territories in North Africa (Morocco, Algeria, and Tunisia). The right-wing opposition openly took on the Front populaire and accused it of being weak in its negotiations with the Syrians and selling off France's interests cheaply.[48] This campaign proved successful and the Front populaire government backed away from presenting the 1936 treaty to parliament for ratification notwithstanding the signing of two additional protocols with Syria in 1937.

3.7 The Era of National Institutions, 1936-1939

Eighteen years after the first Arab government was established by Faysal in Damascus when the Arab provinces separated from the Ottoman empire and sixteen years after the fall of the kingdom of Syria and the introduction of the mandate further to the battle of Maysalun, a Syrian Arab

[48] See Homet, *L'Histoire secrète du traité franco-syrien*.

nationalist government come legitimately to power in Damascus through the ballot box. This national government was not just the outcome of the treaty recently entered into with France but also the consecration of sixteen years of sacrifice, political struggle, and insurrection by the Syrian people for their independence and their unity. The Franco-Syrian treaty could not have been concluded in the way it was without the great general strike of 1936. The 1928 constitution could not have come about without the sacrifices of the Great Revolt of 1925–26. It was this accumulation of struggle, resistance, and combat in various shapes that meant the Syrians could finally hope to take their destiny into their own hands.

3.7.1   The 1936 Elections

The return from Paris of the delegation that negotiated the Franco-Syrian treaty was accompanied by scenes of popular joy in Aleppo and Damascus. Celebrations in the capital lasted four days. Pursuant to the Atassi–de Martel agreement that put an end to the general strike, the 1928 constitution was restored and legislative elections organized. Under the 1928 voting system two rounds of elections were held, on 14 and 30 November 1936, giving a crushing majority to the National Bloc candidates. The deputies elected Fares Khoury as speaker at the first session.

The president, Mohamed Ali Abed, realizing that a new era was opening for Syria, presented his resignation to parliament on 21 December 1936, six months before his term of office expired. The chamber elected Hashim Atassi president in the first round of voting (he gained 74 out of 82 votes). Upon taking office, Atassi appointed Jamil Mardam prime minister. In the space of a few days Mardam formed his cabinet of four ministers, including for the first time a ministry of defence and a ministry of foreign affairs. All the positions were given to members of the National Bloc (two from Damascus and two from Aleppo). For the first time ever, the National Bloc was to face the test of government. The government's first action was to sign the Franco-Syrian treaty and send it to parliament for ratification.

3.7.2   Growing Dangers

The 'state of grace' for the national government was short-lived. Events left the National Bloc no breathing space. They were a cruel reminder that the government was only nominally in charge of the country. Yet when the National Bloc delegation had returned from Paris all the signs had been that the period to come would unfold as per the terms of the

Franco-Syrian agreement. In this context, the high commissioner published an order on 2 December 1936 integrating the Druze lands back into the Syrian Republic after ratification of the Franco-Syrian treaty.[49] On 5 December 1936 he published a similar order concerning the Alawite territory.[50] The two texts foresaw eventually a special administrative and financial regime for the Druze and Alawi regions while placing them under the authority of the Syrian constitution. The reintegration of these two territories into the homeland crowned a struggle of more than sixteen years for the Jabal Druze and more than ten years for the Alawite territory.

If Syria was on the verge of achieving unity, independence was still not within reach. The National Bloc government did not have sovereign power. It continued to be dependent on the say-so of the mandatory power. The Syrian government had virtually no means of imposing its authority nationwide. The existence and political authority of the government remained conditional upon the Franco-Syrian agreement being ratified by the French parliament. This proved highly problematic. A series of crises weakened the newly established national government in Damascus.

The national government had to deal with three sectarian or regional crises that broke out almost simultaneously in various parts of the country. In eastern Syria, in the Jazira region between Turkey and Iraq, protest movements were organized by members of the Assyrian community and by Kurds against the appointment of a governor by the Damascus government. The minority groups in the Jazira region, both Christians and Kurds, who had grown accustomed to living under a near-autonomous regime since the introduction of the French mandate, were apprehensive about coming under the authority of a representative of central government, which was perceived as remote and in the main Arabo-Muslim.[51] In the west, in Alawi territory, disorder was fomented by the supporters of a local leader who claimed to be a prophet and took as their target the new governor appointed by Damascus. In the south, in the Jabal Druze, the unrest was organized by members of the Atrash family. In all three instances, in addition to the purely regional claims and the fact that some segments of the population had an interest in extending the regime of autonomy from the capital, it seemed that some French officials

---

[49] Arrêté no. 265 of 2 December 1936. See the Arabic text in Al-Hakim, *Historical Records* (Arabic), pp. 351 ff.
[50] Arrêté no. 274 of 5 December 1936. See the Arabic text in *ibid.*, pp. 355 ff.
[51] For details on religious and ethnic unrest in Jazira, see Moubayed, *The Politics of Damascus*, pp. 133–5.

representing the mandate and opposed to the Franco-Syrian treaty and the existence of a unitary and centralized Syrian national government actively supported, not to say stirred up and encouraged, the disorder.[52] These crises showed that the nationalist leaders had not put enough effort into forging ties with the populations who had enjoyed autonomous status since the beginning of the mandate. But the most serious challenge the national government had to face and that severely affected its credibility and legitimacy was over the sanjak of Alexandretta.

3.7.3 The Sanjak of Alexandretta Crisis

The sanjak of Alexandretta, including the city of Antioch, the seat of the Church of the East for close to two thousand years, was attached to the vilayet of Aleppo until the end of the Ottoman period. After the Arab provinces separated from the Ottoman empire in 1918 and were divided by the Allied forces into three separate occupied zones (east, west, and south), the sanjak of Alexandretta was attached to the western zone that included the Mediterranean coastline and was occupied in 1919 by the French army. The French authorities created separate governments in Beirut, Latakia, and Alexandretta. After France occupied the kingdom of Syria formed by Faysal in the former eastern occupied zone in 1920, the sanjak was again attached to Aleppo, as in the Ottoman period, before being administered directly by the high commissioner, and then again attached to Syria in 1926.

The population of the sanjak of Alexandretta comprised Arabs (Sunnites, Alawites, Christians), Turks, and Armenian refugees since the 1915–16 tragedy and mass deportation by the Ottomans during what the Armenians considered a genocide. The 1920 San Remo conference had included the sanjak among the Syrian lands attributed to France under article 22 of the League of Nations Covenant. The population in the sanjak of Turkish origin did not oppose the establishment of the French mandate in Syria in 1920, and the Franco-Turkish agreement of Ankara signed in 1921, by which France withdrew from southern Turkey and gave up Cilicia, did not challenge the fact that this territory was Syrian. The agreement confined itself simply to indicating that the sanjak's population had to choose its government freely (administrative autonomy) and that the Turkish community was entitled to see its culture thrive. This agreement was amended in 1926 to straighten the Syro-Turkish border at Turkey's

---

[52] See Al-Armanazi, *Syria from the Occupation to Independence* (Arabic), pp. 116–17.

request.[53] Under the mandate charter, France gave the sanjak an organic law in 1930 defining the characteristics of this territory within the Syrian state. In each general election in Syria (in 1928, 1931–32, and 1936), the sanjak was represented by deputies elected by its population. It was only after the 1936 Franco-Syrian treaty was signed that the Ankara government and the Turkish population of the sanjak asked simultaneously for separation from Syria.

On several occasions, the Turkish president, Mustapha Kamal, publicly called for the sanjak to become an autonomous part of Syria and independent of the Damascus government. This claim was addressed primarily to France, as the mandatory power for Syria. After the 1936 Franco-Syrian treaty, the Turkish government began a series of diplomatic consultations with the French government over the sanjak. In answer to Turkish demands and so as not to envenom bilateral relations between the two countries, Pierre Viénot, under-secretary of state for foreign affairs, declared to the League of Nations in December 1936 that the French government was to suspend presenting the Franco-Syrian treaty for ratification to parliament until the council of the League of Nations had ruled on the Franco-Turkish dispute over the sanjak.

For the newly established Syrian government this was a complete surprise. No one in Damascus expected such a turn-around from France over the recent treaty nor over the sanjak, which France had maintained united with Syria since the beginning of the mandate. The Damascus government was also surprised by Turkey making a stance on this issue at that time.[54] The Syrian leaders soon realized that the Franco-Turkish bilateral talks might open the way to separation of the sanjak and have a lasting effect on Franco-Syrian relations. From the onset of the crisis, the French government handled the matter without any prior consultation with the Damascus authorities, merely informing the Syrian president on 19 December 1936 of Ankara's wish to discuss its borders with Syria again and that the matter was to be taken before the League of Nations, where France intended to defend Syrian interests.

---

[53] The 1926 agreement was initialled by the French high commissioner in Syria and Lebanon, Henri de Jouvenel, and by the Turkish foreign minister, Rushdie Aras (see Khadoury, *The Question of Alexandretta* (Arabic), pp. 18 ff.)

[54] When the Syrian delegation travelled through Turkey on its way from Paris to Damascus after negotiating the Franco-Syrian treaty, the Turkish government tried to begin talks over the sanjak. The Syrian delegation refused to initiate such discussions, considering it was not authorized to do so.

In response to France's new approach over the sanjak, the nationalists called for the territory to be integrated into Syria forthwith. President Atassi launched a call for reunification that was taken up by the Arab population of the sanjak, which in turn asked for immediate reunification with Syria. But neither France nor Turkey were prepared for this to happen.

Franco-Turkish discussions related to both legal and political aspects. Léon Blum declared bluntly that legally the sanjak was an integral part of Syrian territory.[55] It was therefore on the political aspect that discussions over the future of the sanjak turned, regardless of France's obligations under article 22 of the League of Nations mandate, its obligations under the 1920 San Remo agreement and the 1922 mandate charter on Syria and Lebanon enjoining it to maintain the integrity of the territory under its authority, and regardless of the legal framework set out by the 1921 and 1926 Franco-Turkish agreements.

Late 1936 and early 1937 saw intense diplomatic activity and Franco-Turkish talks in Paris, Ankara, and Geneva, the seat of the League of Nations. In raising the question of its border with Syria and the future of the sanjak, Turkey was merely asserting in its own way that the Syrian question had reopened following the Franco-Syrian treaty. It was in this spirit that on 11 January 1937 the Turkish foreign affairs minister, Rashid Aras, submitted to his French counterpart a proposal to create a confederation between Syria, Lebanon, and the sanjak.[56] France dismissed the offer and, in a letter of 18 January 1937 to the Turkish ambassador in Paris, Léon Blum proposed to continue direct talks outside the framework of the 1921 and 1926 agreements, with a view to mutually agreeing a special regime for the sanjak that would be submitted for the League of Nations' approval and by virtue of which the council would appoint a French high commissioner to administer the sanjak.[57]

After the French and Turkish governments had reached agreement, with the benevolent aid of the British representative to the League of Nations, Anthony Eden, about the contents of the sanjak's special regime, the League approved it on 27 January 1937, thereby giving international legal personality to the territory. The sanjak was on the way to becoming an independent political entity with respect to its domestic affairs, but whose external affairs remained theoretically administered by the

---

[55] Al-Armanazi, *Syria from the Occupation to Independence* (Arabic), p. 109.
[56] Khadoury, *The Question of Alexandretta* (Arabic), pp. 49 ff.
[57] *Ibid.*, pp. 54 ff.

Damascus government and enjoying customs and monetary union with Syria. On 29 May 1937, the League of Nations bestowed on the sanjak an organic status and a basic law (constitution) that was to come into force as from 29 November 1939. The official language became Turkish. The official use of other languages was to be decided by the League of Nations council.

The two decisions of the League of Nations council of 27 January 1937 and 29 May 1937 created a particularly complicated situation constitutionally and internationally.[58] The sanjak of Alexandretta had three deputies sitting in the Syrian parliament in Damascus. Alongside this, the new organic statute for the sanjak provided initially for sovereignty of the territory to be shared between France and Syria. For so long as the French mandate over Syria lasted, the organic statute theoretically placed the sanjak under a dual Franco-Syrian mandate. Some functions were to be performed by France, others theoretically by Syria. At the end of the French mandate in Syria, the sanjak was to become a protectorate under the joint administration of Syria, Turkey, France, and the League of Nations. France and Syria were in charge of the sanjak's security and had to protect it against aggression. Syria was responsible for the territory's foreign policy. It had to negotiate international conventions in the sanjak's name, ensure its diplomatic representation, and exercise consular functions for it abroad. In addition, Syria was to share its currency and its customs with the sanjak. As for the League of Nations, through its intermediary it had to ensure that the sanjak's legislation and administrative instruments complied with the territory's organic statute and the fundamental law. The League of Nations representative was also empowered to hear Syrian–Turkish disputes involving the common interests of both parties.

This complex regime was never applied. In an exchange of letters dated 4 July 1938, France involved Turkey in preparing the elections to be held in accordance with a decision of the League of Nations council of 29 May 1937. On 25 July 1938, France authorized the Turkish army to enter the sanjak.[59] The elections were held in September 1938 amid controversy after the mass arrival from Turkey of electors who were distantly from

---

[58] *Ibid.*, p. 71.

[59] The situation of the sanjak during this period has been compared to that of Bosnia-Herzegovina during the period 1878–1909, when the sovereignty of the territory was Turkish although it was administered de facto by Austria-Hungary, just as the sanjak of Alexendretta and then Hatay was theoretically part of the French mandate over Syria although the territory was already de facto controlled by Turkey.

the sanjak and after an equally controversial population census.[60] The elections returned a parliament with a Turkish majority that declared the birth of the Republic of Hatay on 7 September 1938. Much of the Arab population headed into exile and found refuge in Syria. The Republic of Hatay officially merged with Turkey on 29 June 1939 under an agreement signed with Turkey a month earlier.

3.7.4 Institutional Crises and the End of the National Era in 1939

The sanjak crisis unfolded in a strained international context characterized by the radicalization of Hitler's Germany and a growing feeling of insecurity among the other European nations including the greater powers such as France and Great Britain. From the early 1930s, Germany sought to rearm. This effort was intensified once the Nazi Party came to power in 1933. In 1935 Germany restored compulsory military service, built an air force, launched its first submarine since the end of the Great War and increased the size of its army. On 7 March 1936, six weeks after general elections in France brought the Front populaire to power, the German army reoccupied the Rhineland. The European states' perception of the increasing German threat directly affected the situation in Syria and prompted the French authorities to backtrack on the generous feelings that had led to the Franco-Syrian treaty. This was no longer a time for concessions. The French right campaigned actively against relinquishing any positions in the eastern Mediterranean and to prevent ratification of the 1936 treaty.

The tension and the growing dangers in Europe between 1936 and 1939 (manifested in the Spanish Civil War, the Nazi annexation of Austria, and the German stronghold of Munich, for example) had repercussions on the development of the sanjak crisis. As Germany became ever more menacing, France, encouraged by Great Britain, showed itself more conciliatory with Turkish ambitions for the sanjak and to the detriment of Syria's rights. Turkish friendship and goodwill towards Paris were essential for France to maintain its positions in the eastern Mediterranean on the eve of the Second World War. This clear interest of France explains its gradual turnaround on the sanjak question from autumn 1936 until the territory was finally attached to Turkey and French troops withdrawn for

---

[60] On the elections and the controversy over recording electors, see Khadoury, *The Question of Alexandretta* (Arabic), pp. 83 ff.

good in July 1939. It was no chance matter that the sanjak's detachment from Syria and attachment to Turkey went virtually hand in hand with the Munich agreements of September 1938. To cite the title of a book on the question, the sanjak crisis was an eastern Munich.[61] The concession of the territory to Turkey under the cover of the League of Nations paid dividends because in exchange Turkey remained neutral during the Second World War.

The crisis of the sanjak of Alexandretta had a devastating effect on the National Bloc in Damascus and continued to poison Syro-Turkish relations for nearly six decades. It weakened Jamil Mardam's government, divided the National Bloc into several factions, and boosted the popularity of the national leader, Shahbandar, who after the signing of the 1936 treaty was authorized to return from his ten-year exile in Cairo and who had become an outspoken opponent of the National Bloc's power and in particular of Prime Minister Jamil Mardam.

The reasons that impelled the French authorities to be conciliatory with Turkey over the sanjak of Alexandretta and those that prompted them not to ratify the 1936 Franco-Syrian treaty were the same. Yet, the National Bloc government in Damascus and Prime Minister Jamal Mardam in particular spared no effort in trying to convince France to ratify the treaty. Twice Mardam had gone to Paris and signed additional protocols to the 1936 treaty to reassure the French authorities as to certain aspects of the 1936 agreement. In 1937 he negotiated with the Quai d'Orsay, on 11 December signing an exchange of letters planning a special regime for religious minorities after the bloody incidents of Jazira. The exchange of letters also confirmed the Syrian government's commitment to enforce the law on the provinces recognizing local specificities and to accept technical assistance from France in organizing certain public administrations. France confirmed that it considered the transition period for application of the 1936 treaty as having started at the beginning of 1937.

The 1937 exchange of letters was excoriated by the political class in Damascus, including within the ranks of the National Bloc. The prime minister was accused of having been too conciliatory in his negotiations with Paris. But despite Jamil Mardam's concessions, France did not ratify the 1936 treaty. This prompted the prime minister to return to Paris a second time in 1938 and resume discussions. This new phase of talks led to the signing of a protocol and a joint declaration of 14 November 1938. The joint declaration confirmed both parties' intent

---

[61] Bitterlin, *Alexandretta: le Munich de l'Orient*.

to apply the provisions of the 1936 treaty and for it to be ratified by the French parliament before 20 January 1939. The additional protocol referred to the necessity to apply the clauses in the 1937 exchange of letters and added further provisions about the central bank, hydrocarbon resources, the permanent regime of the French civil service, observance of freedom of belief in particular for Christians and the non-application of Sharia law to them, the place of French culture and language, the development of bilateral trade, application of the 1936 treaty as from 30 September 1939, and the despatch of a Syrian political representative to Paris after the exchange of the instruments of ratification.[62]

All these annexes to the 1936 treaty were negotiated in good faith by Prime Minister Jamil Mardam in the hope that France would finally ratify the treaty. He signed the agreements without the prior consent of the members of his government, the president, the National Bloc, or parliament. He took an enormous political gamble in the hope of persuading France to ratify the 1936 agreement. But it was a wasted effort. One month after signing the additional protocol and the joint declaration, France announced on 13 December 1938 that it would not submit the Franco-Syrian treaty for ratification by its parliament. This caused disappointment but no real surprise in Damascus as it was part of a general policy of hostility from France towards Syria over more than two years. That hostility was very apparent in the Alexandretta affair. In reaction, the Syrian parliament solemnly rejected on 31 December 1938 all the annexes to the 1936 treaty signed by the prime minister.[63]

It was under these difficult circumstances that Paris appointed a new high commissioner in January 1939, Gabriel Puaux. Upon his arrival, he openly admitted he would prefer a monarchic to a republican regime for Syria. Puaux even contacted King Abdul Aziz of Saudi Arabia and offered the throne of Syria to one his sons, Faysal or Saoud.[64] However, Abdul Aziz had no ambition to reign over Syria and declined the offer.

One of the most intricate questions Puaux had to handle shortly after taking up office concerned the previous high commissioner's orders, signed in December 1938, creating a status for religious communities that authorized a change of religion and mixed marriages. These provisions were contrary to Sharia law forbidding a Muslim to change religion

---

[62] Al-Armanazi, *Syria from the Occupation to Independence* (Arabic), pp. 124–5.
[63] See the text of the declaration in Arabic in Al-Hakim *Historical Records* (Arabic), pp. 374–5.
[64] Moubayed, *The Politics of Damascus*, p. 137.

and a Muslim woman to marry a non-Muslim.[65] Prime Minister Jamil Mardam ordered the courts to ignore the high commissioner's decrees and resigned in protest in February 1939. Faced with the outcry, Puaux signed a new decree in March 1939 exempting Muslims from his predecessor's controversial orders.

After Mardam's departure, President Atassi appointed Lutfi Haffar, a member of the National Bloc, as prime minister, but Haffar resigned after two weeks in March 1939. President Atassi then asked an independent politician, Nassouhi Boukhari, who had the support of the National Bloc, to form a new government in April 1939. The high commissioner continued to pile pressure on the Syrian authorities. In May 1939, he asked to see President Atassi and his prime minister to inform them that France was prepared to ratify the 1936 treaty provided it was amended so that independent Syria would not include the Alawite territory and the Jabal Druze. The Syrian authorities refused this step backwards.

Some days later, on 15 May 1939, the prime minister tendered his government's resignation to the head of state. Atassi realized that France had no intention of ratifying the 1936 treaty or facilitating matters for any Syrian national government after the entry of Turkish troops into the sanjak of Alexandretta on 23 June 1939, after the appointment by the high commissioner of a governor in Latakia, which was supposed to be part of Syrian territory, and, after the unrest stirred by the mandate authorities in the Jabal Druze, he presented his resignation to parliament on 7 July 1939. To palliate the power vacuum until the election of a new president by the assembly and pursuant to article 75 of the constitution, the speaker noted that the resignation of the Boukhari government of 15 May had still not been accepted by the president on the day of his own resignation. Consequently, under article 75, the Boukhari cabinet was supposedly still in charge. And since the president had resigned in the meantime, the functions of head of state in the event of there being no president were to be exercised collegiately by the council of ministers, as provided for by article 84.[66] This reading of the constitution, while accurate, was not in keeping with the intentions of France, which was all too happy to take back direct control of Syria after the resignation of all the constituted authorities. The Boukhari cabinet returned on 8 July 1939, but the next day the high commissioner suspended the constitution, dissolved the assembly, and increased the autonomy of the Alawite and Druze regions.

[65] Puaux, *Deux années au Levant*, pp. 32–6.
[66] Babeel, *Twentieth-Century Syrian Journalism and Politics* (Arabic), pp. 113–14.

For the third time in nine years (1930, 1933, 1939) France dissolved or suspended an elected assembly and for the second time in six years (1933, 1939) it suspended the constitution. As for Syria, it found itself a landlocked country, without access to the Mediterranean and formed solely by the former states of Damascus and Aleppo, minus the sanjak of Alexandretta. At no time since the parcelling up of its territory after the battle of Maysalun in 1920 had it been so small. Even the Syrian Federation (1922–25) had been geographically larger with access to the sea via the sanjak of Alexandretta and the Alawite territory. But once again, despite the shrinking of its territory, the idea of Syria was no less alive among the population and the political elites who continued to fight for the unity and independence of the country.

The National Bloc's first experience of government ended in failure. France found itself, some weeks before the outbreak of the Second World War, without any interlocutor in Syria. The high commissioner appointed a government of administrators formed by the directors of the various ministries under the tutelage of the director of the ministry of the interior, Bahij Khatib.

3.8 The Institutions during the Second World War (1940–1945)

In July 1940, Syria was mourning the assassination of the Aleppine leader Abdel Rahman Shahbandar. Several leaders of the National Bloc suspected for a time of being linked to the assassination fled to Iraq. This tragic incident added to the grave political crisis the country was going through after the curtailing of talks with France, the resignation of President Hashim Atassi, and the dissolution of parliament in July 1939. Alongside the political deadlock in Damascus, Syria and Lebanon were experiencing a serious economic crisis in 1940–41 with rampant inflation, a shortage of basic foodstuffs (wheat, sugar, and rice), and a shortage of petroleum, which could no longer be brought through Marseille because of the maritime blockade imposed by Britain. Part of the population was on the verge of famine. In February 1941, protests were organized by the nationalists calling for the restoration of the constitution, the formation of a representative government, and the abolition of the government of administrators. The new high commissioner appointed by Vichy in December 1940, General Dentz, failed to untangle the political crisis he inherited in Syria. He advised the nationalist leaders that France could not negotiate a final arrangement with Syria before the end of the war.

A general strike was called on 1 March 1941. All the political leaders General Dentz contacted to form a government declined (Atta Ayubi, Hashim Atassi). Only Ahmed Nami, the former head of state from 1926 to 1928, agreed to cooperate with France, but was unable to form a government because the nationalist leaders refused to work with him since he was too favourable towards France. Finally, on 2 April 1941, Khaled Al-Azzem agreed to form a transitional government, which obtained the nationalists' tacit consent. Dentz announced the forthcoming convening of a consultative assembly including representatives of the Druze and Alawite territories. The general strike ended and talks began between Dentz and the British to partially lift the blockade on Syria and Lebanon, raising hopes for economic improvement in the Near East.

3.8.1 The Fratricidal War between Vichyists and Gaullists

On 18 April 1941, France, upon the recommendation of Germany, withdrew from the League of Nations. This withdrawal, effective as of 19 April 1943, was immediately construed by the nationalists as withdrawing from France any legal basis for its mandate in Syria. Vichy's prime objective was to maintain France's position in the eastern Mediterranean. General Dentz's orders were to resist any attack from wherever it came. Vichy's position in Syria was fragile as it was flanked to the south and east by three territories (Palestine, Transjordan, and Iraq) under British control.

The situation on the ground seemed to be stabilizing when a pro-German revolt broke out in Baghdad. The supporters of Germany led by Rashid Ali took control of the country and evicted the pro-British Hashemite regent. Rashid Ali's revolt caused a stir throughout the Near East. It threatened to upset the geostrategic balance of power to the detriment of Great Britain by cutting off the road to India from the Mediterranean.

Germany sought to channel aid to the new rulers in Baghdad and asked France early in May 1941 to authorize its aircraft to fly over Syrian territory and to be refuelled there. The Vichy authorities accepted the request, thereby beginning what was to become the policy of 'collaboration' with Germany. In exchange, Vichy called for and obtained the liberation of certain prisoners of war (veterans of 1914–18 and fathers of large families, making 30,000 men in all), the loosening of the demarcation line, a reduction in charges for occupation, reinforcement of the armistice army's officers and armaments, and the gradual return to French administration of the Nord and Pas-de-Calais départements that were attached to German administration in Brussels. However, despite repeated requests, France did not secure from Germany the guarantee that its colonial empire would be maintained in the context of future peace negotiations.[67]

This first Franco-German collaboration, which had Syria as its theatre of operations, upset the fragile equilibrium that had reigned since 1940 between the French authorities in Syria and Lebanon, who reported to Vichy, and their neighbours in the territories under British mandate or influence. The British baulked at the facilities afforded to Germany in Syria by Vichy to support the insurrection in Iraq. As a reprisal, on 8 June 1941, the British and de Gaulle's Free French Forces entered Syria and Lebanon. Vichyists, Gaullists, and the British fought a fratricidal battle for the control of Syria and Lebanon. This forgotten war claimed 10,000 victims within weeks and 200 aircraft were lost.[68]

On the same day that British and Free French troops entered Syria and Lebanon, General Catroux, in General de Gaulle's name, proclaimed the independence of Syria and Lebanon, adding that Syrians and Lebanese could form either separate states or a single state.[69] But this promise of independence came with a condition attached – a treaty of alliance had to be signed with France. Great Britain immediately approved the declaration of independence. Syrians and Lebanese did not take part in the war. The Syrian and Lebanese governments asked that their respective capitals, Damascus and Beirut, be declared open cities. On 21 June, British and Free French forces occupied Damascus.

The outcome was unsurprisingly in favour of the Allies and from July 1941 onwards Syria was under the nominal control of the Free French, very largely supported by the British. General de Gaulle repeated relentlessly and vehemently until the end of the war, even if it meant creating tension with its British ally, that France remained the supreme authority in Syria and Lebanon.[70] This did not square well with the fact that British forces, being superior in number and military equipment, were masters on the ground in Syria and Lebanon. Throughout the war and even afterwards, de Gaulle suspected the British of using their de facto supremacy to undermine France's authority, encouraging the Syrian and Lebanese nationalist leaders to challenge the mandate, and seeking to supplant Paris in the Levant. For their part, the British, as guarantors of the declaration of independence of Syria and Lebanon, wanted France to act on its

---

[67] Davet, *La double affaire de Syrie*, pp. 71 ff.
[68] de Wailly, *Syrie 1941*.
[69] See the text of the declaration in *ibid.*, p. 221.
[70] Davet, *La double affaire de Syrie*, p. 170.

promises promptly to appease public opinion in the other Arab countries under British domination.

De Gaulle went to Syria in July 1941 to review arrangements for the country. The Syrian political class was highly sceptical about the Free French declaration of independence. Blum in 1936 and Dentz in 1940 had made much the same promises. De Gaulle contemplated three ways of administering Syria. The first was to restore the 1936 institutions (president, government, and parliament), the second was to hold elections immediately, and the third was to confirm the principle of independence already granted, but defer its application until the end of the war and link independence to the signing of a treaty of alliance between France and Syria. De Gaulle dismissed the second solution out of hand although it was the one preferred by General Catroux, who had been appointed delegate general in Lebanon and Syria, the new title for the former office of high commissioner. De Gaulle feared that free elections held with a strong British military presence in Syria would focus matters on independence alone.

De Gaulle preferred to contact the former Syrian authorities and attempted to restore the institutions of 1936, before the constitution had been suspended. He began by meeting the former president, Hashim Atassi, 'the father of the republic'[71] and 'father of the constitution'. They met twice, once in Homs, President Atassi's home city, and then in Shtoura, in the Beqaa valley. Atassi and the other nationalist leaders were not opposed to restoring the 1936 institutions but he refused to sign a new treaty with France as he could not pre-empt post-war Franco-Syrian relations. Atassi considered the 1936 treaty was out-dated. De Gaulle was to meet with the same polite but firm refusal from Jamil Mardam, the prime minister in 1936, who had spared no effort at the time in convincing France to ratify the Franco-Syrian treaty. Again the Syrian political class presented a united front and as in 1928 and 1932 France had to turn to Sheikh Tajeddine Al-Hasni, a notorious Francophile, who was appointed head of state on 17 September 1941 by General Catroux. The principle of independence was confirmed but the constitution was not restored and the elections were postponed. Sheikh Tajeddine Al-Hasni remained in office until his death in 1943. He asked Hassan Al-Hakim to form a government. On 27 September 1941, General Catroux officially handed over to the Syrian government the declaration of the independence of Syria.[72]

---

[71] Davet, *La Double affaire de Syrie*, pp. 213–14.
[72] See the text in Arabic in Al-Hakim, *Historical Records* (Arabic), pp. 376–9.

The cabinet remained in office until April 1942 and was replaced by one led by Hosni Barazi, which in turn was superseded in January 1943, days after the death of the head of state Tajeddine Al-Hasni, by a new government led by Jamil Al-Ulshi.

As a pledge of goodwill, General Catroux reintegrated the Druze and Alawite territories into Syria on 12 December 1942. Over the course of the mandate, France joined and separated these territories from Syria several times as relations with the nationalists ebbed and flowed. This time the Druze territory and Alawite mountains were to remain once and for all part of the motherland.[73]

3.8.2 The 1943 Elections and the Restoration of the Constitution and Institutions

The British criticized the French for lowering the morale of the Allies throughout the Arab world because of their policy in Syria. They pressured the Free French throughout 1942 both through their local representative, General Spears, and their prime minister, Winston Churchill, in London, to organize elections in Syria and Lebanon. De Gaulle was unmoved. He wanted first to settle the problem of the treaty of alliance of the two states with France. General Catroux met again with Atassi, who proved as intractable as he was with de Gaulle. Again he declined to settle future relations of Syria with France according to the provisions of the 1936 treaty, accepting the effects of the agreement only while the war lasted.[74] Finally, the French National Liberation Committee meeting in London in 1942 decided, upon General Catroux's proposal, to hold elections in Syria and Lebanon in summer 1943.

After the demise of Sheikh Tajeddine Al-Hasni, General Catroux restored the 1928 constitution and in March 1943, a few days before he left office as delegate general in Syria and Lebanon, he appointed a new interim government headed by Atta Ayubi, which was tasked with preparing the elections held in Syria in July 1943 and a month later in Lebanon. General Catroux explained in a communiqué that to restore constitutional order in the country he should have restored to office the authorities in place in 1939 when the constitution had been suspended, the chamber dissolved, and the president had resigned. However, the former President

---

[73] Arrêté no 22 FL and Arrêté no 23 FL of 12 January 1942. See the text in Al-Hakim, *Historical Records* (Arabic), pp. 380 and 384.
[74] Davet, *La double affaire de Syrie*, p. 226.

Atassi dismissed this possibility and called for new elections. It was in this spirit that the Atta Ayubi cabinet had been formed to prepare for the forthcoming elections.[75]

The 1943 election was held by the voting system in force since 1928. The nationalists won the elections in Syria and Lebanon. These electoral victories, preceded by the restoration of the Syrian and Lebanese constitutions, were welcomed throughout the Arab world and encouraged recognition of Syria and Lebanon as independent states. The National Bloc won the majority of seats in the Damascus parliament. Two-thirds of the deputies elected had already sat in the 1936 parliament. Fares Khoury was elected speaker. Logically, the president of the National Bloc, Hashim Atassi, should have become president of the republic, but on recommendation of the other Bloc members, he agreed to leave the highest office to Shukri Qwatli.[76] Once elected, Qwatli appointed Saadallah Jabri as prime minister. Both were eminent members of the National Bloc. The Qwatli–Jabri tandem had a logic to it. One was from Syria's largest city, Damascus, the other from the second city, Aleppo. Power was shared therefore on a regional basis. At the same time, in neighbouring Lebanon, two major political figures, Beshara El-Khoury (Maronite) and Riad El-Solh (Sunnite), were setting up another share-out of responsibilities, the office of president for the Maronites and the office of prime minister for the Sunnites. The distribution in Syria between Damascenes and Aleppines was to be short-lived, whereas that in Lebanon, which was based on sectarianism, went down in history as the National Pact.

3.9 The Difficult End to the Mandate

As soon as they were established in Damascus and Beirut and by virtue of their independence declared by France as of 1941 and guaranteed by Britain, the Syrian and Lebanese governments asked almost simultaneously in October 1943 for the French delegation to be changed into a diplomatic mission and for the transfer of all attributes of sovereignty still held by France as the mandatory power. The Lebanese parliament went further still on 8 November 1943 by amending the constitutional articles that contradicted with the country's independence. Some days previously, the Lebanese government had declared that Arabic and not French would

---

[75] See Al-Armanazi, *Syria from the Occupation to Independence* (Arabic), p. 159.
[76] See the details of the interview in Homs between Hashim Atassi, Shukri Al-Qwatli, and Fares Khoury in Al-Hakim, *Syria and the French Mandate* (Arabic), pp. 230–2.

be the country's official language and replaced the flag inherited from General Gouraud with a new national flag. The reaction from the delegate general, Jean Helleu, was brutal. On 11 November, he had the president, prime minister, and the ministers of the interior and the economy arrested and imprisoned in the fortress of Rashaya. The constitution was suspended and the chamber elected three months earlier was dissolved. Emile Eddé, a pro-French Maronite, was appointed by the delegate general as the new head of state. The arrests sparked uproar in Beirut and Lebanon. General Spears threatened to have the Lebanese political leaders released by force and Churchill threatened no longer to recognize the French National Liberation Committee if de Gaulle did not release the Lebanese officials.[77]

On 13 November 1943, de Gaulle ordered General Catroux to restore the Lebanese constitution, release the imprisoned officials, and form a new government with which France could get on. Catroux arrived in Beirut on 16 November and began consultations, which included the president and the head of government, who were still being held in the fortress of Rashaya. On 19 November, the British minister in Beirut Richard Casey and General Spears handed Catroux an ultimatum whereby he was to release the prisoners before 22 November at 10.00 am and restore them to office otherwise martial law would be declared by the British command in Lebanon and the prisoners would be freed. There would then be a conference between the Lebanese authorities and General Catroux under the aegis of Britain in a territory under British administration outside Lebanon to reach a modus vivendi in Lebanon until the end of the war. In no uncertain terms, the British would force the French out of Lebanon. De Gaulle, so as to give the impression of not yielding, reconfirmed his instruction to have the prisoners released but asked Catroux to restore only the president to office. General Catroux executed the orders but also at his own instigation restored the prime minister, Riad El-Solh, to office. He later explained to de Gaulle that he had no alternative if France was not to alienate the populations of the two Levant states for good.

The Syrians monitored developments in Lebanon closely. The victory of the nationalists in the August election, the way the new Lebanese leaders stood up to France, and the November 1943 crisis made a great impression in Syria. The Lebanon created by France was turning on its godfather. This episode changed the view Syrians had of the Lebanese entity. This new attitude towards Lebanon and therefore towards the Syrian

---

[77] See Davet, *La double affaire de Syrie*, p. 236.

national question was reflected in the work of the chamber of deputies in Damascus. One of the first decisions of the new parliamentary assembly after the Lebanese crisis was to abolish the famous and highly controversial article 116 of the constitution imposed by the high commissioner in 1930 and that restricted the powers of the constituted institutions, in particular the president, and limited national sovereignty. The article was deleted without taking the form of a constitutional revision. The chamber considered in a unanimous vote on 27 November 1943 that article 116 had never existed as it had been added to the constitutional text by a foreign authority.[78] However, the chamber raised no objection to article 2 of the constitution although it too had been added by France. This article, amended by the high commissioner, confined Syria's borders to those decided by the mandatory power and not the borders claimed by the kingdom of Syria. By refusing, knowingly or otherwise, to challenge the mandate borders, the Syrian parliament was distancing itself from the heritage of the kingdom of Syria and accepting for the first time de facto not just the creation of a Lebanon that was separate from Syria but also of Palestine and Transjordan. The change in the understanding of the national question fifteen years after the initial drafting of article 2 by the constituent assembly was subtle but crucial. The Syrian nationalists, largely concerned with securing their own independence from France, waived the reunification of Syria with the other entities created by the French and British. Their priority was to be limited to obtaining the independence of Syria with the Druze and Alawite territories.

Parliament's removal of article 116 did not mean, though, that Syria had effectively become an independent state, because of the remaining presence of French and British forces in its territory and France's control of Syrian special troops, and the 'common interests' in Lebanon and Syria. Once the status quo ante had been restored in Beirut, there was no longer anything to oppose the principle of handing over the 'common interests' to the two states. In December 1943, General Catroux signed a protocol with Syria and Lebanon transferring as from 1 January 1944 the public services (police, post office, press, passports, etc.) held by the mandatory power. At that date, France still had troops stationed in Syria and Lebanon (5,000 to 6,000 men) and still controlled the Syrian and Lebanese special troops (18,000 men). It had civilian agents and controlled a network of 395 schools for 60,000 pupils.

---

[78] Al-Ghali, *The Principles of Constitutional Law and Political Regimes* (Arabic).

After the transfer of the common interests, the final phase of the French mandate was played out around the removal of the last French forces in the Levant and the control of the Syrian and Lebanese troops. In October 1944, France dismissed a request from Syria and Lebanon concerning the special troops. General de Gaulle still did not contemplate transferring them to the two states before an alliance treaty was signed ensuring French interests and enabling it to maintain military bases, much as in Britain's treaties with Iraq and Egypt. The French position was presented to the two governments by the new delegate general for France in Syria and Lebanon, General Beynet. Britain did not object in principle to the signing of such a treaty and pressured the Syrian leaders, beginning with the president, to act accordingly. But in vain. President Qwatli withstood Churchill's demands[79] just as former President Atassi had done with de Gaulle in 1941. This refusal by the two leaders to commit to an agreement granting France military installations in Syria simply took up, with some changes, one of the initial characteristics of the Syrian national project of 1919. At that date, Syrians had expressed their refusal of any foreign tutelage. On the eve of their independence, they adopted the same position by refusing any foreign hegemony.

Political life in Syria continued to be subordinated to developments relating to the Second World War. Even so, that did not prevent more personal than political differences arising among government members. The cabinet resigned in October 1944 further to a disagreement between the prime minister and his interior minister, Lutfi Haffar, an eminent member of the National Bloc. The leaders of the three political institutions heading the country (president, speaker, and outgoing prime minister) agreed to confer the next government on Fares Khoury, the speaker, and to replace him with the head of the outgoing government, Saadallah Jabri. That was no problem given that the National Bloc had a comfortable majority in the chamber. The Khoury government resigned six months later in April 1945 again because of a divergence of views among its ministers. The president reappointed the outgoing head of government to office.

Early in May 1945, General Beynet judged the French forces in the Levant insufficient (5,000–6,000 men) and asked for reinforcements. Paris agreed to despatch a further 2,500 men. Britain protested. At the announcement of the imminent arrival of extra troops in Syria and Lebanon unrest broke out in the main cities of both countries. On 10 May 1945, there were riots in Damascus. On 27 May 1945 a French military convoy was attacked and

[79] Babeel, *Twentieth-Century Syrian Journalism and Politics* (Arabic), pp. 220 ff.

destroyed near Homs. During the night of 27–28 May, the population of Damascus rose up and attacked symbols of French presence (such as barracks and legation offices). Fighting went on in Damascus, with the rioters taking over on 29 May 1945 most of the city's public buildings (parliament, Bank of Syria, government offices, town hall, and police headquarters). The Syrian government left the capital. To retake control, General Oliva-Roget, the delegate general in Damascus, ordered the shelling and bombing of public buildings in Damascus including the parliament. On the evening of 30 May, French forces regained control of the capital at the cost of massive destruction and many dead and wounded. The Syrian government put the number of victims at several hundred and asked for Generals Beynet and Oliva-Roget to be tried as war criminals in an international court.[80] For the second time in twenty years, the French army had shelled Damascus. The first time, in 1925, General Sarrail, the high commissioner, had ordered the artillery to shell Damascus lest the city fall under the control of the insurgents during the Great Revolt of 1925–26.

On the evening of 30 May 1945, the French ambassador in London was given an ultimatum by Churchill to stop the bombardment of Damascus. This ultimatum, the second from London to Paris over its Near Eastern policy after that of the Lebanese crisis in November 1943, moved de Gaulle to indignation and anger. Overnight Paris ordered a ceasefire. Even so, on 31 May 1945, Churchill ordered General Paget, commander-in-chief in the east, to intervene. On 1 June 1945, British forces entered Beirut. General Paget gave an ultimatum to General Beynet and threatened to intervene directly unless he ordered a ceasefire and French troops to return to barracks.

Tension in Syria continued to rise between the population and the mandate representatives. The French command handed the Syrian troops over to the Damascus government and evacuated the big cities. The French army henceforth remained confined to barracks and the outskirts of the cities. The end of the mandate was near. On 12 December 1945, the French and British governments signed an agreement in London for the simultaneous withdrawal from the Levant of most of their forces in both countries. In January 1946, General de Gaulle resigned as head of government for reasons unrelated to French policy in the Levant. He was to hold bitter memories of this period and of Franco-British rivalry in Syria and Lebanon, perceptible in many pages of his memoirs.

[80] Davet, *La double affaire de Syrie*, p. 256.

The foreign affairs ministers of Syria and Lebanon petitioned the United Nations Security Council, meeting for the first time in London on 10 January 1946, for French troops to withdraw. The request was examined by the Security Council in February 1946, but no decision was adopted because of a double veto by the USA and the USSR. But there was no doubt about the final outcome, which came about outside the auspices of the new international organization. In March 1946, Britain and France signed a second agreement for the simultaneous withdrawal of troops from Syria and Lebanon. The last of the French troops left Syria on 17 April 1946, a date that was proclaimed a national holiday. The last French forces withdrew from Lebanon on 31 December of that same year.

France pulled out of Syria and Lebanon without having imposed a treaty of alliance with the two countries ensuring it privileged relations and military bases. In this respect, Syria and Lebanon were in a more favourable position upon achieving their independence than Iraq and Egypt, which had been forced into such arrangements with Britain. Winning the independence of Syria and the reunification of four of the five political entities created by Gouraud at the beginning of the mandate in 1920 had taken more than a quarter of a century of combat, struggle, and sacrifice. France's evacuation of Syria marked the beginning of the era of post-war decolonization. The victory, though, left a bitter taste. Having been busy in the struggle against the French mandate, a whole generation of Syrians had been unable to do much to thwart Zionist plans for hegemony in Palestine.

3.10 France's Legacy

France left as its legacy many aspects of modern Syria including the extent of the national territory and the form of its regime. Syria first owes to the French mandate the scope of its territory further to the dismembering and partial recomposition of the area claimed by the kingdom of Syria.

The second characteristic that Syria inherited from France was its republican system of government. The choice of a republic was not self-evident. The first reflex of the Syrian population after the separation of the Arab provinces from the Ottoman empire had been to choose a king. At no time was a republic contemplated. It was not part of the local custom. The destruction of Faysal's kingdom left a political vacuum that was gradually filled by an emerging nationalist elite opposed to the mandate. Faysal's abandoning of the Syrian people to their fate during one of the bleakest moments of their history, his lack of enthusiasm in supporting local resistance including the Syrian Great Revolt of 1925–26, the compensation he received for the loss of the throne of Syria by Britain offering him the throne of Iraq, and the passive attitude of his brother Abdullah towards Jewish immigration to Palestine, finally convinced the Syrians they could hope for nothing from the Hashemites.

The nationalist elite did not give France's representatives on the ground an easy ride. Two high commissioners – Ponsot and Puaux – seriously contemplated putting a king at the head of Syria rather than having to deal with a president elected by a parliament, which was itself democratically elected and so politically legitimate and representative. Gabriel Puaux stated very clearly in his memoirs the advantage for France of dealing with a king rather than the representatives of a republican regime:

> A treaty concluded with a monarch would have far greater chance of enduring: it would not bind a single man or a party but a dynasty. Friendship would arise between France and the Syrian crown, which would be far more stable and more effective, because more humane than some theoretical legal commitment. A king assuming supreme power in oriental fashion would not have to deal with the demands of demagogues. The discretion of French advisers would have facilitated his task on a daily basis. It would have been possible besides to shore up his throne with representative assemblies in harmony with local mores. It might have been expected too that the Druze and Alawites would have accepted to obey a king belonging to one of the great dynasties of Islam rather than a cabinet of Damascan (*sic*) city dwellers. But can the French Republic be a kingmaker?[81]

Such was the dilemma facing republican France that had settled in Syria after destroying Faysal's kingdom.

Royalty might well have facilitated the mandatory power's task to some extent. But coexistence of the various sectarian and ethnic components of Syrian society was successfully facilitated by the republic.

3.11 From Independence to the Fall of the First Republic

The second period of the 1928 constitution began with Syria's actual independence in 1946 and ended with the first coup d'état in 1949. During these first three years of freedom, the young republic's institutions were regulated by the provisions of the 1928 constitution. For the first time, Syrians were masters of their own fate. Just as in 1936 with the first national government at the time of the mandate, all the institutions (presidency,

---

[81] Puaux, *Deux années au Levant*, pp. 40–1.

government, and parliament) faced major challenges. The lack of experience in public affairs on the part of a political class that wore the halo of glory for its past struggles was to be felt very soon after independence. The internal and external challenges with which the young Syria was to be confronted proved difficult for a disunited political class to overcome.

The immediate challenges were both domestic and regional. The National Bloc was to rapidly break apart. This rally of nationalist notables devised in 1927 as a movement of political resistance to the mandate and for national liberation was never structured as a political party with a programme of government and a party-political organization. It failed to withstand the test of the first elections in an independent Syria free from French occupation. Syria's youth, galvanized by the political struggles of their elders, to which they had contributed in the Great Strike of 1936 and the insurrection of May 1945, meant to play a leading role in public affairs. Their intention to take part in running the country was well understood by the new political parties who went to great efforts to persuade the new generation that their ideological programmes were well founded, being generally based on the need from more social justice and a better distribution of wealth. But the most difficult challenges to be overcome and that had the greatest impact on Syria's domestic stability came from outside. The situation in Palestine that was to degenerate into an armed conflict less than two years after independence was to precipitate Syria into a series of military coups. The army and the ideologically based political parties were to be the major actors in the ensuing period, to the detriment of the institutions and traditional political formations and the constitution itself.

3.11.1 *The Splitting of the National Bloc*

The National Bloc, which had been the spearhead of the nationalist struggle for independence for two decades, split into two branches after the 1947 legislative elections – the Damascene branch gathered into a new political formation, the National Party, and an Aleppine branch grouped first around a parliamentary bloc before re-establishing, in August 1948, the former People's Party created in 1925 by Abdel-Rahman Shahbandar. The regional bases of these two formations and their leading members coincided largely with the cities of Damascus and Aleppo. The regional leaning of the Damascene and Aleppine political staff had already shown itself after the 1943 elections, when the members of the National

Bloc agreed to divide the presidency and the office of prime minister between a Damascene, Shukri Qwatli and an Aleppine, Saadallah Jabri. Consequently, they had asked the former president of the National Bloc, Hashim Atassi, from the city of Homs and a veteran of the fight for independence and former president of the republic, not to seek a second presidential mandate.

The National Party

The National Party was formed early in 1947. Its most eminent members were from Damascus, although some were from Aleppo, grouped around President Shukri Qwatli. The new party was led from the outset by the former prime minister Saadallah Jabri and included Nabih Azmé, Jamil Mardam, Abdel-Rahman Kayali, Fares Khoury, Sabri Al-Assali, and Lutfi Haffar. The premature death of Saadallah Jabri before the legislative elections of July 1947 caused a serious crisis within the party and especially in the Aleppine branch, which split between the supporters of Ihsan Jabri, the deceased's brother, and Abdel-Rahman Kayali. This split among the notables of the National Party in Aleppo left the way open to its great rival, the People's Party, which was to become the dominant party in the great metropolis of the north and in Syria generally.

The People's Party

The Aleppine dissidents of the National Bloc were grouped around two major political figures of the city, Nazem Kudsi and Rushdi Kikhyia. They received support from notables of Homs affiliated to Hashim Atassi, who himself remained neutral between the National Party and the People's Party, both derived from the National Bloc he had created and led during the mandate.

The People's Party had an ambitious project for Aleppo and for the whole of Syria. This project, which it was to develop gradually, was named Iraq. From the most ancient times, Aleppo had always stood at the crossroads of trade and transit of goods and merchandise between West and East. The famous silk road between Asia and Europe went through this great city of northern Syria. Because of its geographical position and its trading tradition, Aleppo had suffered enormously from the new borders inherited after the First World War. The sudden separation from Turkey that cut Aleppo off from its hinterland intensified by the creation of Iraq to the east and the attachment of the sanjak of Alexandretta to Turkey in the west meant that Aleppo was cut off from Anatolia, Cilicia and its natural port of Alexandretta, and from Mosul, its outlet towards Baghdad and the rest of Mesopotamia and Asia.

The People's Party was formed in August 1948, one year after the 1947 legislative elections. Three months later, on 23 November 1948, it submitted a memorandum for an Arab federation to President Shukri Qwatli, which was in fact a plan for union between Syria and Iraq to confront Israel, which had just won the war against its Arab neighbours. The national question was to take on a new dimension with the People's Party. Its plan for a union with Iraq was to have a dramatic impact on Syria in the 1950s.

3.11.2 The 1947 Legislative Elections

Syria's government at the time the last French soldier left on 17 April 1946 had been led since the previous September by Saadallah Jabri, one of the historical leaders of the National Bloc and former prime minister in 1943–44. That government remained in power until 30 April 1946. After Jabri's resignation, the president asked him to form a new government that lasted until December 1946. Jamil Mardam, another historical figure of the National Bloc and former prime minister from 1936 to 1939, succeeded him as head of government with the task of organizing the elections planned for 7 July 1947. Seizing this as an opportunity to modernize the electoral law, the assembly defined a new system of voting by electoral law number 325 passed by parliament in May 1947.[82] Henceforth the elections were to be direct, uninominal, with two rounds, for male voters only. The page had been definitively turned on the two-tier system of indirect elections inherited from the Ottoman period, introduced for the elections of the councils of representatives in Istanbul in 1876, 1909, and 1913 and then taken up for the election of the Syrian congress in 1919. France confirmed the principle of two-tier elections while amending the electoral procedure in 1923 and 1928 for the election of the representative councils in 1923 and 1926 and for the assembly in 1928, 1931–32, 1936, and 1943.

This first electoral law introduced a two-round majority list vote. Intentionally or otherwise, this favoured the local notables and candidates of the traditional parties. It was the candidate who obtained the absolute majority of votes in the first round or in a second round organized one week later who was elected. Candidates who won more than 10 per cent of the votes could fight on in the second round. Should turnout not reach

[82] See the Official Journal no. 33 of 24 May 1947, law number 325, pp. 949–53.

60 per cent for the first round in a constituency, voting was extended until the following day.

The basic constituency was the caza, each of which formed an electoral constituency. The main town of each mohafazat and the areas attached to it (village, *nahie*) also formed a caza. The quota for the election of deputies was 1:6,000 inhabitants. The electoral rolls of each electoral constituency were to be revised in December each year. The 1947 law maintained the sectarian representation of minorities and reserved ten seats for bedouins including one for the tribes of the Jabal Druze.

The National Party stood for the 1947 elections without any real manifesto. Its plan was limited to the defence of the interests of the notables of the city of Damascus.[83] Its dominant campaign theme was its fight for independence from France. President Qwatli's opponents, the dissident Aleppine politicians of the National Bloc, who were to create the People's Party some months later, allied with the newly formed Arab Ba'th Party, that was already finding an audience among the young. They joined forces in the 1947 elections in a new formation, the Hizb Al-Ahrar or Liberal Party. The Aleppine politicians had a minimum electoral manifesto that included timid reforms to improve living conditions in rural areas.[84]

The elections gave a relative majority to the opposition to the president (53 seats), to the detriment of the National Party (24 seats). Between these two formations, there was a loosely structured but partisan mass of more than fifty independent deputies, open to external influences and who were to give the majority to the final governments of the First Republic. The bloc of independent members, which reflected how strongly entrenched they were locally and how weak the modern political parties were, was made up of landowners, businessmen, notables, heads of bedouin tribes, and representatives of minorities. Fares Khoury was elected speaker and Jamil Mardam tasked with forming a new government.

It is important to observe that the election results, the relative victory of the opposition, and the defeat of the president's party had virtually no effect on political life and practically no impact on government. After the legislative elections, the head of state restored the outgoing prime minister to office. The prime minister managed without too much effort to win over a number of opposition members and secured a vote of confidence for

---

[83] Seale, *The Struggle for Syria*, pp. 48–9.
[84] For a detailed description of the 1947 elections in the various Syrian provinces and the many contested results, see Babeel, *Twentieth-Century Syrian Journalism and Politics* (Arabic), pp. 311–30 and Torrey, *Syrian Politics*, pp. 90–100.

his government that included three members of the opposition, whereas his own National Party was in a minority in the assembly. Logically, the opposition should have formed the new government, but it was poorly structured and failed to capitalize on the arithmetical advantage it had in the house. The absence of any credible opposition able to transform its majority in terms of seats into a plan for an alternative government and the party-political pirouettes and opportunistic haggling of some members of the opposition tended to discredit the political class in the eyes of the public and cast doubts on the capacity of the political representatives to bring about the social reforms the country needed. This feeling that the political class was detached from the everyday problems of the population intensified and served to legitimize the army's seizing power some months later.

3.11.3   The 1948 Revision of the Constitution

The crisis of representation and the loss of credibility of the political class were to worsen with the 1948 constitutional revision. On 11 November 1947, eighty-seven deputies called for article 68 of the 1928 constitution to be revised so Shukri Qwatli could be re-elected president.[85] This initiative stirred debate among the political class. Should the re-election for a second term be via the assembly or directly by the people by universal suffrage?[86] The assembly selected a committee to revise the constitution and settle the matter. But the committee members failed to reach agreement. This prompted the deputies to seek President Qwatli's opinion. He received the representatives of the parliamentary groups of the chamber on 18 March 1948, but did not make his opinion known on the main matter. He asked the deputies to decide for themselves whether the president should be elected directly by the people or indirectly by the assembly. The committee tasked with constitutional revision went back to work the next day and on 20 March 1948 voted unanimously to revise article 68 of the constitution and re-elect the president for a second term via the assembly. On 17 April 1948, the national holiday commemorating the departure of the last French solider two years earlier, the assembly voted unanimously to modify articles 68, 85, and 89 of the 1928 constitution and remove article 115, as suggested by the assembly's committee for constitutional revision.

---

[85] Al-Kayali, *Study of Syrian Contemporary Political History* (Arabic), p. 311.
[86] See Babeel, *Twentieth-Century Syrian Journalism and Politics* (Arabic), p. 361.

The new version of article 68(1) stipulated that 'the President of the Republic is elected by secret ballot by the absolute majority of the members of the chamber. At the third round of voting, a relative majority suffices. The President's term of office is five years. The President can only be re-elected for a third term after an interval of five years.' This amendment meant the president could be re-elected for a second term.

The new version of article 85 stipulated that 'at least one month and at most four months before the powers of the President of the Republic expire, the chamber shall be convened by its Speaker to elect the new President. Failing such convening, this meeting shall take place as of right on the tenth day before the end of the President's term of office.' This amendment slightly modified the period during which the assembly was to elect a new president, now from one to four months instead of the one to two months as in the previous version of article 85.

The amended version of article 89 stipulated that 'the number of ministers shall not exceed twelve. They may be chosen from outside the parliament'. This amendment raised the number of ministers from seven to twelve.

Article 115 stipulating that 'the first President of the Republic shall be elected by the Chamber of Deputies pursuant to the provisions of the constitution' was abolished.

On the same day that the constitution was revised, the deputies re-elected President Qwatli for a second term as from the end of his first presidential term, which was to be on 17 August 1948. The reason for the support of opposition members, who voted massively for the amendment of article 68 of the constitution and for the re-election of President Qwatli, was questionable. Some explained the vote as a mark of respect for a great political leader who had devoted his life to the national cause since the time Syria had been part of the Ottoman empire. Others argued this support from the opposition was the outcome of a compromise between the head of state and the opposition represented by the National Bloc.[87]

The alteration of the 1928 constitution shifted the balance among the institutions of the First Republic and it may have seemed at first glance to the supporters of the change that it was strengthening the president's hand. But by providing the opportunity to seek a second term, it made

---

[87] Walid Al-Mouallem argues that President Qwatli allegedly promised the opposition four ministers after his re-election. Prime Minister Jamil Mardam, who was not aware of this compromise, gave only one ministerial portfolio to the opposition in his new cabinet. See Al-Mouallem, *Syria 1918–1958* (Arabic), pp. 87 ff.

the president more vulnerable to parliament, at least during his first term of office, because he would be necessarily more attentive to the deputies who had his possible re-election in their gift. What mattered most were not the institutional consequences of the constitutional revision – which could not be ascertained because the regime was overturned less than a year after the beginning of President Qwatli's second term – but its political consequences and the way public opinion perceived this initiative. Those consequences were disastrous. The constitutional revision was presented to parliament four months after the president's party had lost the legislative elections and Shukri Qwatli was re-elected for a second term less than one month before the Palestine war. The timing could not have been worse. Commentators remain divided over the need for this constitutional revision. However, most seem to acknowledge that it was inopportune, harmful for the future of Syria, and that it prevented the political class from concentrating on the modernization and more substantial reforms the country needed.[88]

3.11.4   The Effects of the Palestine War

The defeat of the Syrian army engaged alongside other Arab armies to save Palestine from the ambitions of Zionist armed groups and the creation of the State of Israel was to have incalculable and dramatic consequences for Syria's future, its political regime, its constitution, and its institutions. The political class and not just the government led by the National Party, came out of it weaker. The obvious unpreparedness of the Syrian army, recently formed after the departure of France in 1946, its lack of resources, the rumours of corruption around armaments contracts, and the poor coordination with the other Arab armies were a lasting smear on the credibility of the political class. The direct victims of this policy, the officers and men who participated in the war, harboured undiminishing rancour towards traditional politicians. The *nakba* also fuelled sharp resentment among the population, which engaged in protests and strikes. On 29 November 1948, on the first anniversary of the vote for the partition of Palestine by the General Assembly of the United Nations, there was a stormy session in parliament. Unrest broke out in Damascus and other cities. The police fired on the crowd and the government declared a state of emergency. For the first time since independence, the army left its barracks and stepped in to restore order and impose a curfew from 6.00 p.m. to 6.00 a.m.

[88] See Seale, *The Struggle for Syria*, p. 54.

Ironically, the army, which was highly critical of the government, was called to Damascus by the cabinet to impose a curfew, preserve the institutions, and ensure the survival of the regime that was threatened by the crowd. Political contestation was rapidly to change into a governmental crisis before becoming a regime crisis. The army protected the regime for four months.

Although it did not know it, the government of the First Republic was living out its final days. On 1 December 1948, Prime Minister Jamil Mardam resigned. He was replaced by Khaled Al-Azzem on 16 December 1948. He formed a government of experts chosen from outside parliament. The Al-Azzem government signed a financial agreement with France on 7 February 1949 and with the US corporation Tapline on 16 February 1949 for a pipeline to run through Syria connecting the Saudi oil fields (Aramco) to the Lebanese port of Saida on the Mediterranean. The two agreements prompted violent opposition within parliament which threatened not to approve them and particularly the one with the US corporation because of US support for Israel. But the chamber never had time to accept or refuse the two instruments. On 30 March 1949, Syria experienced its first coup d'état. General Husni Al-Zaim, head of the general staff took power, proclaimed himself commander-in-chief, dissolved the assembly, and abolished the 1928 constitution. The First Republic had been toppled and Syria was moving into the era of *coups d'état.*

The way in which the mandate from 1920 to 1946 had unfolded enabled the emerging political class in Syria to find its feet in the various modes of passive or violent resistance, depending on circumstances, and the art of international negotiations; but certainly, not in that of governing a modern state. In twenty-six years of mandate, Syria only experienced normal constitutional political life with legitimate institutions for intermittent periods. The 1928 constituent assembly exercised its functions for several weeks before being suspended and then dissolved by the mandatory power. The legislative assembly elected in late 1931 and early 1932 operated normally for a few months and was then suspended by the high commissioner in 1933. After the 1936 negotiation and the signing of the Franco-Syrian treaty, the country was to experience for three years a bumpy political life that was marked especially by France abandoning the sanjak of Alexandretta to Turkey. In July 1939, the high commissioner dissolved parliament after the president's resignation. Constitutional political life was restored by France in 1943, that is, three years before actual independence. During the difficult period as the mandate came to an end, all the constituted authorities, the president, government, parliament, and political personnel were mobilized so that a cooperation agreement should not be imposed on Syria. This tension climaxed with the French army bombarding the seat of parliament in Damascus in May 1945. The political class that liberated the country in 1946 did not have the opportunity to acquire the necessary experience to run the state, the public administration, and of course was unable to carry out local political activity as in any normal country in peacetime.

The political class that secured independence had to cope with domestic challenges that it was not always aware of, such as the need to meet the aspirations for social justice from the least privileged parts of the population living in a rural setting and often formed of sectarian minorities. The army was the way out for this underprivileged and politically committed, young, rural population. The political class failed also to mobilize young people in the urban centres and left this function to ideologically based political parties that were to play a prime role in the following period under the Second Republic. The governing class further discredited itself in the eyes of the general public and especially the young and the army by monopolizing the political institutions (parliament, government, presidency) to protect its members' private interests. The discredit of the political class was to reflect on the constitution itself, which was seen not as an instrument for regulating power and political changes of power, but as an instrument in the hands of the ruling class to perpetuate its domination.

The failure to take account of the need to reform the country and the latent crisis of political representation were to prove fatal to a political class of traditional notables that did not know how to manage the effects of the war in Palestine and the defeat of the Syrian army. The Palestinian question, which historically was always an integral part of the Syrian question throughout the nineteenth century and even under the Syrian monarchy of Faysal, was to come to the forefront during the Second Republic. After being pushed into the background under the mandate because Palestine and Syria were both subject to the domination of different European powers, the Palestinian question was to become a priority in the following period and take on a form that very few commentators could have predicted. It was to push Syrians to exceed even the framework of Greater Syria or natural Syria and to seek alliances with Iraq and Egypt.

4

The Second Republic

I shall call the regime established by the constituent assembly elected on 15 November 1949 until the coup d'état of 8 March 1963 that brought the Ba'th party to power the Second Republic. This period was interrupted twice, once from 1951 to 1954 and again from 1958 to 1961. Four constitutions mark the very intense history of the Second Republic. The parent constitution, which had the greatest impact and was the most long-lived, was that of 1950. It was preceded by a provisional constitution adopted by the constituent assembly in December 1949. After discontinuing the union with Egypt in 1961, the new regime adopted a provisional constitution that took up the main provisions of the 1950 constitution. In September 1962, the assembly elected the year before, although dissolved by the army, managed to meet in an extraordinary session outside the parliament building to adopt a new constitution which merely took up the text of the 1950 constitution, amending it slightly to adapt it to the political circumstances of the day.

The 1950 constitution that set up the Second Republic still occupies pride of place in the collective memory of Syrians. It ushered in the golden age of Syrian democracy and a liberal parliamentary type of regime under which political life was seldom as rich and intense either in Syria or elsewhere in the region. Accordingly, many are still nostalgic for the 1950 constitution. It enabled free legislative and presidential elections to be held. It experienced the sole hand-over of power between two freely elected presidents. The great beneficiaries of this space of freedom created by the golden age of democracy in Syria and those who managed to profit most from it were the political parties and in particular the progressive parties whose influence was gradually to dominate.

The other major player of the period was the army. The irruption of the army and the parties as leading actors in political life were the main features of the Second Republic. It was the army that ended the First Republic in March 1949, and it was the army again that put paid to the Second Republic in March 1963. Between those two dates, the army imposed the major political choices on the country via a show of force and several coups. The Second Republic was interrupted twice. The first time was in December 1951 when the army took control for the first time and established a military republic of a presidential character that later inspired other Arab officers in Egypt (1952) and Iraq (1958). This military republic will be discussed subsequently as the Third Republic. It ended with an insurrection by certain senior officers supported by the population in 1954. The second interruption occurred in February 1958 with the union with Egypt, which was largely imposed by the army and then endorsed by politicians and the vast majority of the population. It was again the army, three years later in September 1961, that put an end to this experiment with union that left much bitterness between Damascus and Cairo.

The Second Republic, like the previous one, was consistent with the Founding Fathers' national project. Although Syrians hesitated about the future direction their country should take, they did not question the main characteristics of their national project. These remained unchanged from the time of the Syrian monarchy and then the First Republic, namely sectarian coexistence, refusal to dismember the territory, refusal of all forms of foreign hegemony, and refusal of the Zionist project in Palestine. Syrians soon felt pent up within their borders upon achieving their independence after twenty-six years of the mandate. Their immediate attention did not fall on their nearest neighbours such as Lebanon or Jordan that were part of or claimed as an integral part of the Syria advocated by the Syrian congress in 1919 and King Faysal in 1920. The abrogation by the Damascus government in 1950 of the customs union between Syria and Lebanon, which was deemed too favourable to Beirut's economic interests at the expense of the Damascene merchant class reflected the scant interest Syrians took in Lebanon. For the Syrians saw further afield. They were casting sideways glances at Baghdad and Cairo. Some called for union with Iraq, others with Egypt. Was Syria's calling to be merged into one vast Near Eastern political entity under the aegis of the Hashemites of Iraq or to form the embryo of a future Arab union with Nasser's Egypt? Each project had its supporters within and beyond the borders. Syria became a stake and a prey for the various regional powers (Iraq, Egypt) and their international backers (Britain, France, the USA, and USSR).

The Second Republic also inherited the Palestinian question. The *nakba* and the fate of this southern province claimed by the defunct kingdom of Syria deeply traumatized Syrians in mind and body. The mandate had ended in freedom and independence in Syria, Lebanon, and Transjordan, but in Palestine it was superseded by an occupation coupled with massive immigration, promoted from the outset by the mandatory power, which sought to erase the Arab, Syrian, Muslim, and Christian character of the land. The 1956 war against Israel was to bring to the fore an Arab leader, Nasser, who dazzled the Syrians like no one had done since King Faysal. The Palestinian question became a main component of the national project and influenced the regional and international alliances Syria would make. Could Syrians form an alliance with the friends (the USA, France, Britain) of their enemy, that is, with Israel?

The social question compounded the many debates that divided public opinion. The progressive parties and their electors and civil and military sympathizers made it a paramount question of Syrian political life. The Second Republic attempted to meet the legitimate aspirations of the majority of the population for more social justice for the middle classes and the least favoured, especially in rural areas. But it could only do so in a partial and disorderly manner with no internal consensus about the nature of the reforms to be undertaken and the economic and social policy to follow, in particular on the agrarian question.

One of the great weaknesses of the Second Republic was that its institutions did not have the strength to neutralize the army's forays into politics. The constitutional mechanisms regulating relations between the executive and legislative branches were deficient and unsuited to the political challenges of the time. The political class was divided even over the defence of democratic values and representative democracy. Some politicians openly supported the intervention of the military in politics and legitimized their seizing of power.

The coups and the union with Egypt marked out three separate periods in the Second Republic's history. Each period witnessed the upwelling of at least one of the three questions that unsettled public opinion: the national question, the Palestinian question, and the social question. Unable to overcome the host of challenges, willingly or by force, the Syrians were to sacrifice their freedom and even at times abdicate their independence without immediately realizing what a tremendous loss this was.

4.1 The Advent of the Second Republic

Two successive coups four months apart prepared the ground for the Second Republic. The first coup d'état ended the First Republic. The second ushered in the Second Republic.

4.1.1 The First Coup d'Etat

Syria experienced its first coup on 30 March 1949, which will long remain a red-letter day in its history. It was to be followed by two others before the year was out. This first coup, led by the army chief of staff General Husni Al-Zaim, abolished the 1928 constitution, dissolved the chamber, and ousted the head of state, Shukri Qwatli. The new man in charge stated his intention to give the country a new constitution. But he had no time to do so as his regime lasted just 137 days. On the day of the coup, the army published six communiqués. It was the sixth of these that informed Syrians that the country was led by the commander of the army and the armed forces.[1]

Several factors can account for General Al-Zaim's coup. The war lost in Palestine a few months earlier had rankled with the general staff who blamed the government and president for sending a poorly trained and under-equipped army into combat. The loss of Palestine had largely discredited the entire political class, whom the army, like the rest of the population, saw as putting their own interests before national causes. The revision of article 68 of the constitution so that President Qwatli could be re-elected, just weeks before war broke out, had certainly done nothing to alter that outlook. The new generation had little faith in the institutional mechanisms whether for running the country, standing up to outside challenges such as Israel, or bringing about the social reforms the country needed, primarily agrarian reform. As for the officers who led this first coup, before independence they had witnessed multiple suspensions of the constitution by the high commissioner and France's abolition of normal political life and institutions for extended periods. So why should the national army not do the same? This step was soon taken by ambitious officers who had little regard for democratic principles and values.

As for the proximate causes, analysts generally give three that supposedly decided the perpetrators of the first coup to act on 30 March 1949. First, the government had concluded an agreement with the US petroleum company Aramco for a pipeline to link the Saudi Arabian oil fields to Lebanon via Syrian territory. The agreement had been submitted for approval to parliament where it had come in for fierce criticism from many members because of Washington's support for Israel in the 1948 war. One of the first decisions the new regime took was to confirm this

---

[1] See Babeel, *Journalism and Politics in Syria during the Twentieth Century* (Arabic), p. 425.

agreement. Second, the government had just entered into a financial agreement with France. This too had prompted frenzied opposition from a great many members of the dissolved assembly who accused the government of maintaining too close ties with the former mandatory power. This agreement was also upheld by the new regime. This prompted some commentators to claim the coup was French-backed. Third, the president was closely monitoring a matter of mismanagement or even corruption within the army's procurement office and the chief of the general staff, the coup leader, made no secret of his sympathy for the high-ranking officer involved. Some even said that he was personally involved in this corruption affair.

Upon seizing power, General Husni Al-Zaim announced by decree on 11 April 1949 the dissolution of parliament, the establishment of a constitutional committee entrusted with preparing a draft constitution, and a new electoral law to be followed by general elections. It is strange to observe that most of the political parties supported the coup except, obviously, former President Qwatli's National Party, although some days later eminent members of the party began to work with Husni Al-Zaim.[2] If the majority of the political class was not fundamentally hostile to the coup d'état,[3] it was because it was aware that the Qwatli regime, in power since 1943, had worn thin. The three political formations that supported the new regime were Akram Hawrani's Arab Socialist Party, the Ba'th, and the People's Party, with the notable exception of some of its leaders. For the People's Party, avowed supporters of a union with Iraq, their support for Husni Al-Zaim lasted but a few days, the time it took them to realize that this project was not part of the agenda of the country's new master. The Ba'th withdrew its support for Husni Al-Zaim in May 1949 because of the regime's restrictions on the press and its regional policy choices such as its closer ties with Faruk, King of Egypt, and with Saudi Arabia.

As for the Arab Socialist Party, it supported Husni Al-Zaim until he appointed Mohsen Barazi, a big landowner of the Hama region and local political rival of Hawrani, prime minister in June 1949. Akram

---

[2] Sabri Al-Assali, a member of the National Party, was sent by Husni Al-Zaim on a mission to Baghdad with the Emir Adel Arslan in May 1949 to discuss Syrian–Iraqi relations. See Kourani, *Recollections* (Arabic), p. 202. Sabri Al-Assali and Léon Zemria were appointed members of the second committee tasked with drawing up a new constitution under the rule of Husni Al-Zaim. See Kourani, *Recollections* (Arabic), p. 208.

[3] Kourani, *ibid.*, p. 195, counts as many as 80 out of 131 members of the parliament in favour of Husni Al-Zaim's coup.

Hawrani played an important role in the Second Republic. He was a politician from Hama in the centre of Syria and founded the Arab Socialist Party in 1949. Previously he had led a paramilitary-type youth movement in the wake of the nationalist movements against the French mandate. He established fairly close ties between his movement and the Syrian Social Nationalist Party (SSNP), also known as the Syrian Popular Party formed in Beirut in 1938. In 1944–45 he participated with certain Syrian officers (including the future President Adib Shishkali) and members of the SSNP in sporadic armed resistance movements in the Hama region against French installations. In 1948, Hawrani took part in raids against Zionist settler colonies in Palestine. These armed resistance operations forged close comradeship and friendship between Hawrani and certain officers who were to play leading roles in Syrian politics.

The Arab Ba'th Party was formed in 1947 by two teachers who had studied in France, Michel Aflaq and Salah Bitar.[4] The Ba'th, meaning 'resurrection' in Arabic, was the most remarkable pan-Arab political party. Ba'th ideas spread rapidly among students, the intelligentsia, and the army. They extended well beyond Syria and were broadly taken up some years later by Nasser.

Domestically, Husni Al-Zaim's regime took steps to modernize political and social life in Syria. It gave women the right to vote that was not in the 1928 constitution. It abolished the former Ottoman titles (beys, pashas, etc.), encouraged western dress codes, and initiated the adoption of new civil, commercial, and criminal codes instead of traditional Islamic laws. But Husni Al-Zaim's regime quickly turned into a Latin-American style caricature of a dictatorship. Within weeks, the country's new master broke with virtually all his supporters. Government informers began to proliferate in Syrian society. The army's functions changed during this period. In addition to the traditional job of defending the borders, the army became the country's governing institution. This new role gave rise to a new function within the armed forces, that of the defence of the regime. This function was attributed de facto to those units of the army with Kurd or Circassian majorities that were judged more loyal towards the new president and his future prime minister, who were both of Kurdish origin. These units were entrusted with maintaining order in the main urban centres.

---

[4] His full name was Salah El-Dine Bitar.

4.1.2 The Constitutional Referendum

As stated earlier, on 11 April 1949, Husni Al-Zaim published a decree,[5] as commander-in-chief of the army and armed forces, dissolving parliament and setting up a committee to draw up a new constitution.[6] He asked the general directors of the ministries to run their ministries. On 17 April Husni Al-Zaim formed a government, making himself prime minister and minister of defence. He governed by decree and remained in office until the constitutional referendum of June 1949 that made him president.

The constitutional committee was headed by a renowned jurist, Asaad Kourani. The new constitution had to be endorsed by the council of ministers before being submitted for popular approval by referendum.[7] The committee completed its work on 27 June and handed the draft constitution to the head of state. In the meantime, Husni Al-Zaim had changed his mind and instead of legitimizing his regime by passing a new constitution by referendum, he preferred, on the advice of Mohsen Barazi, his ambassador in Cairo and future prime minister, to organize a constitutional-type referendum with four questions for voters. Mohsen Barazi carefully prepared the details of this consultation, which was designed not just to legitimize the coup d'état of 30 March 1949 and all the decisions taken by the new regime but also to elect a president with a mandate to draft a new constitution that could be adopted either by the people or by the council of ministers. As Husni Al-Zaim was the only candidate for the presidency, the referendum turned into a plebiscite.

The referendum was held on 25 June 1949. Each elector had to answer four questions:[8]

1. Do you wish the president to be elected for the first time by the people by a general secret ballot, chosen from among Syrians in possession of their civil rights who are aged forty years or more at the time of their candidacy and whose election is proclaimed by the council of ministers, and for a duration determined by the constitution?
2. Do you wish the president to receive by a decree adopted in the council of ministers the authority to establish a new constitution within a

---

[5] See the text of the decree in Babeel, *Journalism and Politics in Syria during the Twentieth Century* (Arabic), pp. 426–7.
[6] The committee was composed of Asaad Kourani, Hassan Al-Zein, Georges Jabra, Sami Midani, Abdel-Jawad Sarmini, and Abdel-Wahab Homad.
[7] Kourani, *Recollections* (Arabic), p. 198.
[8] See the Arabic wording in Seale, *The Struggle for Syria*, p. 89. This is my loose translation.

period of not more than four months from the date of his election and that will have to be directly approved by the people or the council of ministers?
3. Do you wish the president to be given authority to promulgate decrees including constitutional decrees taken in the council of ministers until a new constitution is drafted and approved?
4. Do you wish to consider the authority granted to the president as defined in question 3 as having effect for all decrees adopted since 30 March 1949?

With these four questions, political legitimacy certainly reached its limits of elasticity on that day. The outcome of the referendum was unsurprising. Of 816,331 electors allowed to vote, Husni Al-Zaim secured 726,116 votes and the 'yes' came out ahead for all four questions.[9]

Two days after the referendum, the president received the draft constitution from the Kourani committee. Husni Al-Zaim appointed a second constitutional committee under his new prime minister, Mohsen Barazi, to revise the draft prepared by the Kourani committee. The new committee brought in Al-Sinhori from Cairo, a constitutional law specialist to help it with its task. The committee did not have time to complete its work because of the coup d'état that overthrew the regime on 14 August 1949.[10]

4.1.3 The 1949 Draft Constitution

The constitution drafted by the Kourani committee never came into being.[11] Even so it is worth examining its main provisions because they reflect the state of mind of Syrian society and the political elite of the time. Some of the provisions were to be rejected by the next constitution the following year.[12] The Kourani draft constitution ran to 160 articles. It was preceded by a memorandum to the head of state explaining the four principles on which the committee had based its draft. First, the committee considered that a parliamentary regime was better suited to Syria and its history than a presidential regime. The committee, however, thought

---

[9] On the holding of the vote, see Kourani, *Recollections* (Arabic), pp. 204 ff.
[10] The second constitutional committee was chaired by Mohsen Barazi and included Sabri Al-Assali, Léon Mirza, Asaad Kourani, Shaker Hannbali, and Nihad Kassem. See Kourani, *Recollections* (Arabic), pp. 208–9.
[11] It seems the draft constitution was never published. I obtained a copy from the People's Assembly (parliament) in Damascus.
[12] Al-Ghali, *The Principles of Constitutional Law* (Arabic), pp. 539 ff.

that the executive should be reinforced by various measures such as the extension of the presidential term of office, the possibility for the president to stand for an unlimited number of terms, the government was to be accountable to the president, the president would have the power to dissolve the chamber, the government would have the exclusive right to introduce finance bills, and it would be difficult for the government to be held to account before parliament should a no-confidence motion be filed against it. These measures were intended to prevent the legislature from holding sway over the executive.

Second, the committee, inspired by constitutions that arose after the Second World War, included the economic and social dimension in its draft, the aspirations of the population, and the spirit of the coup d'état of 30 March 1949 reflected by the various public stances taken by Husni Al-Zaim. This was captured in the text by the reference to the need for social justice, social protection, family protection, the right to work, the protection of private property and of inheritance in the general interest, encouragement for agricultural smallholdings, medical care, and housing for workers.

Third, the draft included a declaration of citizen's rights ensuring individual freedom, the right to life, dignity, inviolability of the home, freedom of conscience, religion, thought, freedom of assembly and communications, and the immunity of the judiciary.

Fourth, there was no reference to sectarianism including the religion of the head of state and sectarian electoral quotas disappeared because of the feeling of national unity of the Syrian people and the Universal Declaration of Human Rights approved by Syria a few months earlier, which prescribed equal rights and duties for citizens regardless of their religion.

The draft also reflected the uncertainty about the future of the national question and more broadly about national identity. Although most of the population agreed that Syria within the borders inherited at its independence remained an incomplete creation, there were obvious divergences as to how to complete that independence. Was it for Syria to achieve its full independence by merging with other sister political entities in a single Arab project? Or was its future more to merge into a Greater Syrian national project confined to the Near East? These questions were reflected in various articles of the draft constitution without it being possible to answer either way. Thus article 1 stipulated that 'Syria is a parliamentary, democratic Arab republic built on the principles of equality and social justice'. But further on, article 6 stipulated that 'sovereignty is vested in the Syrian nation', and article 7 stated that 'the Syrian nation exercises its sovereignty according to the provisions of the constitution'. It should be recalled that the earlier constitutions of 1920 and 1928 in the initial version adopted by the constituent assembly before being amended by the high commissioner were openly pan-Syrian. By characterizing Syria as an Arab republic, the 1949 draft marked the beginning of a slide in Syrian constitutions and the national project from pan-Syrianism towards pan-Arabism.

Legislative Power

The draft provided for a single-chamber regime. Article 38 stated that the Assembly of Deputies shall exercise legislative power and article 42 added that the Assembly is elected for five years. There was to be a ratio of 1 deputy for 30,000 citizens (art. 39). Article 65 stated that 'The President of the Republic and the deputies shall introduce bills except for finance bills that are the exclusive domain of the President of the Republic'. Article 67 added: 'The Assembly may authorize the government to legislate in some domains by decrees passed in Cabinet' and article 74 stated: 'The Assembly may withdraw its confidence from an individual minister or the government as a whole except during discussion of finance bills'. In addition, according to article 75, a motion of censure shall be presented by at least twenty-five members and may only be discussed after a period of five days. The vote shall be by a two-thirds majority. Article 76 provided that the Assembly may dissolve itself upon a proposal of one-third of its members followed by the approval of two-thirds of the chamber.

Executive Power

Executive power had two heads comprising the President of the Republic and the Government. Article 78 stated that the President of the Republic shall be elected by the Assembly. Article 80 provided that the presidency will be for a period of seven years renewable for an unlimited period. According to article 84, decrees made out by the President shall be countersigned by the ministers responsible for their enforcement except for the decree appointing and dismissing the Prime Minister. In accordance with article 90, the President may ask Parliament for a second reading of a bill. Should the bill obtain a two-thirds majority in a second reading, it shall be promulgated. The president was to appoint ministers upon proposals from the head of government and dismiss them on his proposal too (art. 86), he was to chair the Cabinet meetings and had the right to dissolve the Assembly after agreement of the Cabinet (art. 92).

Once formed, the government had one month to secure a vote of confidence from the Chamber (art. 103); the Ministers shall be collectively accountable to the Assembly on the policy of the cabinet and each Minister individually accountable for his own Ministry (art. 111). The prime minister alone could commit the government on a vote of confidence (art. 112); 'The question of confidence may only be discussed three days after being raised. Confidence shall be withdrawn from the Cabinet as a whole or a specific Minister by a straight majority vote' (art. 112).

Reflecting the historical circumstances under which it was drawn up, the draft constitution provided for the establishment of a parliamentary regime characterized by the hegemony of the executive over the legislature. The draft was 'tailor-made' for Husni Al-Zaim, the country's new ruler. Out of concern for introducing greater stability into political life, the suggested constitution was rigid. It could only be amended by a proposal from the government. Any vote to revise the constitution could only take place one month after the amendment was proposed and had to be approved by a two-thirds majority of the members before being submitted for popular approval by way of a referendum.

Two provisions marked a radical break with the monarchic (1920) and republican (1928) constitutions that Syria had previously known. The first related to the recognition of economic and social rights for citizens as early as the preamble. Article 1 stated that 'Syria is a Republic ... built on principles of equality and social justice'. The second important change was the absence of any reference to the president's religion. The earlier constitutions had both specified that the religion of the king (1920) or president (1928) was to be Islam.

4.1.4 Domestic and Regional Policy of Husni Al-Zaim's Regime

Most of Husni Al-Zaim's promised reforms failed to be enacted. His authoritarian method of government, his personal style, and his choices in domestic but above all regional and international policy saw a united front come together against him in record time. The armistice talks with Israel and Husni Al-Zaim's willingness to meet with Ben Gourion worried the military and in particular the head of the Syrian delegation to the armistice talks, Colonel Fawzi Selo. It was later discovered that Husni Al-Zaim had separately begun talks with the USA about a project to resettle

Palestinian refugees in the Jazira region of eastern Syria.[13] The declared rejection of any kind of Greater Syria or Fertile Crescent advocated by the Hashemites in Amman and Baghdad, the closer relationship of Faruk's Egypt and Ibn Saud's Saudi Arabia, the great rivals of the Hashemites, worried Iraq, Jordan, and Britain.

These regional policy choices bound together opponents of the regime. But Husni Al-Zaim's most serious mistake was to deport Antun Sa'ada, the historical leader of the Syrian Social Nationalist Party (SSNP), to Lebanon. He was tried and executed within twenty-four hours. This deportation had deeply shocked many of the party's supporters in Syria and especially within the army. Antun Sa'ada had officially formed the SSNP in Beirut in 1935. He had been born into a Greek Orthodox Lebanese family and having emigrated to Brazil in the late nineteenth century, Antun Sa'ada returned in 1920 and settled first in Damascus, where he contributed to a newspaper for some time before moving to Beirut, where he founded in 1932 a secret society to create a Greater Syria. The SSNP ideology held that there was a Syrian national identity that had the right to thrive in its natural environment and to create its own nation state. National territory was a prime factor in SSNP doctrine, which defined it extensively as including all of the Near East from the Taurus mountains in the north to the Sinai in the south and from the Mediterranean (called the Syrian Sea) in the west to the Euphrates in the east. In 1947 Sa'ada added Iraq, Kuwait, and Cyprus. The territory claimed by the SSNP was therefore more extensive than Ottoman Syria had ever been even under the reign of Mohamad Ali and his son Ibrahim. It extended well beyond the borders of the kingdom of Syria under Faysal, too.

One notorious peculiarity about the SSNP was its militant secularism, and its stated objective in the 1930s had been to separate the state from all religions. This was quite rare for the region and is worth mentioning because, when it was first formed, the SSNP was to be one of the very rare political parties in Lebanon and Syria to promote secularism and recruit its members without any distinction as to their sectarian origins. In organizational terms the SSNP borrowed its structure and cadres from national-socialist-type parties of the 1930s.

Domestically, the appointment of Mohsen Barazi, a big landowner from the Hama region, as prime minister had alienated from Husni Al-Zaim's regime the support of Akram Hawrani, the leader of the Arab

---

[13] Landis, 'Early U.S. policy', pp. 77–8.

Socialist Party, and his network within the army. Al-Zaim's sending of military reinforcements into the Druze mountain because of his suspicions of plots in the region against the regime and of complicity with the Hashemites in Jordan turned the Druze population against him. As a precaution he dismissed officers who had supported him from the beginning of the coup such as Colonel Adib Shishakli. However, despite its authoritarian character and his sometimes grotesque style, Husni Al-Zaim's regime was not a bloody one.[14] The only case of blood-letting that can be ascribed to him, even indirectly, was the execution of Antun Sa'ada by the Lebanese authorities after his deportation. It was a fatal error that resulted in the fall of Husni Al-Zaim, his execution and that of his prime minister, as well as the assassination two years later of the Lebanese prime minister, Riyad Solh, who had signed the order to execute Antun Sa'ada.

4.1.5 *The Second Coup d'Etat*

During the night of 14 August 1949, armoured vehicles commanded by General Sami Hinnawi entered sleeping Damascus and occupied the capital's nerve centres such as the president's residence, the general staff headquarters, and the radio station. Before dawn, Husni Al-Zaim and his prime minister Mohsen Barazi had been arrested and executed. The coup by General Hinnawi was construed as a British response to the first pro-American and pro-French coup by Husni Al-Zaim. Amman and Baghdad immediately expressed their support for the new regime in Damascus, whereas the royal court in Egypt proclaimed three days' mourning. One of the first decisions taken by the new authorities was to reinstate the officers sacked by the fallen dictator. These included Colonel Adib Shishakli, who was appointed to head the first armoured division.

The perpetrators of the second coup immediately announced their intention to hand power back to the civilian authorities. They set up a supreme war council headed by General Hinnawi and convened a meeting of the country's political leaders, across the board, at their headquarters to discuss how to restore normal political life and hand power back to the civilian authorities. This method was also to be used after the coup of September 1961 that ended the union with Egypt, and again in March 1962 in the wake of the army coup against the constituted authorities. In these three instances, the military convened the politicians to participate

---

[14] For a description of the period under Husni Al-Zaim by his brother-in-law and one of his closest collaborators, see Fansa, *The Days of Husni Al-Zaim* (Arabic).

in what may be characterized as a states-general of the political class and asked them to restore civilian political institutions (parliament, government, and presidency).

Sami Hinnawi and the political leaders invited the former president, Hashim Atassi, a historical figure in the fight for independence, former prime minister under King Faysal, and father of the Syrian constitutions of 1920 and 1928, to form a provisional cabinet to ensure the transition to a legitimately elected government. Hashim Atassi had retired from political life since Syria's independence in 1946. He reluctantly agreed to take on the caretaker role provided he could form a government of national union. His preference was for a return to the position before the coup of 30 March 1949. He favoured restoring former President Qwatli to the office from which he had had to resign after the coup. He also wished for the reinstatement of the parliament dissolved by Husni Al-Zaim before he had accepted the resignation of President Qwatli.[15]

Hashim Atassi's arguments based on the necessity of restoring constitutional continuity as far as possible to the situation before the two coups of March and August 1949 failed to convince the majority of the political leaders and the perpetrators of the second coup. Most participants did not want to see former President Qwatli return. In the end, Hashim Atassi agreed to form a provisional government of national union the majority of whose members belonged to the People's Party but with two ministers from the former president's National Party.[16] The Ba'th Party founder, Michel Aflaq, and the Arab Socialist Party founder, Akram Hawrani, were also part of the cabinet of national unity, whose first task was to organize elections for a constituent assembly. All political parties were authorized again except for the Communist Party and the extreme right Cooperative Socialist Party. The provisional government led by Hashim Atassi was invested with presidential attributes and endowed with executive and legislative powers.[17]

---

[15] On the discussions among the politicians attending this meeting at army headquarters, see Atassi, *Hashim Atassi* (Arabic), p. 315 and Kourani, *Recollections* (Arabic), pp. 229 ff. On further discussions with the provisional cabinet of national union, see Al-Azzem, *Memoirs of Khaled Al-Azzem* (Arabic), vol II, pp. 211 ff.

[16] The National Party declared the two ministers had agreed to join the government in their personal capacity.

[17] See the text of the Atassi government's communiqué in Kasmiyé, *The Arab Vanguard* (Arabic), p. 507.

The debate about whether it was necessary to convene the parliament elected in 1947 and dissolved with the first coup in March 1949 arose again within the provisional government. A majority of ministers was against the idea. The fact that the majority of the members of the former parliament had approved Husni Al-Zaim's coup and participated in the June 1949 referendum legitimizing the coup certainly did not inspire the provisional government to reconvene a largely discredited parliament.

4.2 The Regional Question during the First Phase of the Second Republic (1949–1951)

The regional question, with the Palestinian question as its backdrop, was to arise during this period in the shape of a planned union or federation with Iraq. The need to finish building the nation had continued to weigh on Syrians' minds ever since the separation of the Arab provinces from the Ottoman Empire in 1918 and the carve-up of the kingdom of Syria by the French and British in 1920. Syrians continued to dream of a great scheme and some wanted to complete the independence of the 'Little Syria' of 1946 with closer ties or even a total or partial merger with their powerful Iraqi neighbour. Domestic and regional developments strengthened the conviction of many Syrians about the need to create a vast Syrian–Iraqi entity, especially after Israel's defeat of the Arab armies in 1948. The leaders of the People's Party, who were mostly from Aleppo, which had ancestral commercial ties with Mesopotamia, had made no mystery of their ambition to federate Syria with Iraq within a Fertile Crescent, which would be joined by Jordan and Lebanon. They had handed President Qwatli a memorandum to this effect in late 1948 just months before the coup by Husni Al-Zaim. The idea of the Fertile Crescent had been floated by the Iraqi prime minister of the time, Nouri Al-Said. Hashim Atassi had approved it so as to establish a united front encompassing the Arab states of the Near East able to stand up to the challenges arising from the creation of the State of Israel in 1948.[18] It was argued subsequently that

---

[18] Colonel Mohamad Ma'arouf, then a young officer and member of the supreme war council that preceded the second coup in August 1949, recounts in his memoirs a conversation with the head of the provisional government, President Hashim Atassi, who told him, 'My son, you know that all of the outside world supports Israel militarily and politically. I am sure that Syria will be of no importance unless it unites with Iraq. Iraq is made powerful by its army which is the largest and oldest in the Arab world. Iraq is wealthy with its unlimited resources and is our neighbour. Iraq has always stood beside those who militated against the French mandate. It supported us and was our crutch. Go in that direction; it is the right way. May God be with you.' Cited in Ma'arouf, *Days I Lived* (Arabic), p. 166.

one of the unstated ambitions of the People's Party in seeking a federation with Iraq at all costs was to make the Syrian army toe the line and send it back to barracks.[19] That may have been so, but only after the army had interfered in the political sphere, that is after 1949.

If the planned union with Iraq had its supporters in Syria, it also had its opponents within the political class, government, and army. The two main criticisms of the scheme were that the monarchic regime in Baghdad was incompatible with the republican regime in Damascus and that Iraq was tied to Britain by an alliance treaty, whereas Syria had managed to secure its independence from France without any commitment to the former mandate power. The proponents of this sovereignist approach did not wish to be tied indirectly to Britain, the godparent of Israel, via a union with Iraq.

4.2.1 The Election of the Constituent Assembly

Once democracy was restored the political class saw some intense activity during the second half of 1949. Everything had to be done again as if Syria had just been created. Political circles discussed a new constitution, a new electoral law, and a project for union with Iraq.[20] These debates between supporters and opponents of a union with Iraq and the debates over the country's future constitution and institutions were to be reflected in the work of the government and its foreign policy. The Atassi government set up two ministerial committees, one to prepare the new electoral law for the upcoming elections for an assembly tasked with drafting the new constitution, and one to study Syria's foreign policy. The first committee prepared a draft electoral decree while the second proposed a scheme for a federation with Iraq.

Early in September 1949 the provisional government announced elections for a constituent assembly on 15 November. The Atassi government adopted a new electoral law to supersede the 1947 law via a decree prepared by the ministerial committee.[21] The new law was

---

[19] Al-Azzem, *Memoirs of Khaled Al-Azzem* (Arabic), p. 270.
[20] When the project of union with Iraq seemed to be on the point of materializing after the second coup in 1949, the National Party decided, as a precaution, to revise its articles of association so as to accept that Syria could become a monarchy. Then it changed its articles back a few months later.
[21] Decree 17 of 10 September 1949, see Official Journal no. 46 of 13 September 1949, pp. 2617–21. For details on this electoral law and those that followed under the Second, Third, and Fourth Republics, see Fida'a Haurani's article in Arabic 'Election is our right however …' at www.maaber.org/independance/independance_7.htm.

not without party political afterthoughts. It granted the right to vote to women with a certificate of primary education, a promise that had already been made by Husni Al-Zaim. To satisfy the new progressive political parties it planned to lower the voting age to 18 years. The 1949 law confirmed that it would be two-round majority voting. To be elected, a candidate had to obtain at least 40 per cent of the votes. Otherwise a second round was to be held the following week. Candidates with more than 10 per cent of the votes could stand in the second round. Should participation not reach 60 per cent in the first round in a constituency, voting was extended until the next day. The quota for the election was to be 1 member for 30,000 inhabitants. The basic constituency was the caza. Each caza formed an electoral constituency. The main town of each mohafazat and the areas attached to it (village, *nahie*) also formed a caza. The decree stipulated that all candidates had to have at least their school certificate. The 1949 electoral law partly abolished the system of minority representation by limiting it to religion rather than sectarian origin. It also limited the number of seats reserved for bedouins to six instead of the nine under the previous electoral law. A second electoral decree set the number of members at 108 divided as 86 Muslims, 15 Christians, 1 Jew, and 6 bedouins. Religious quotas were therefore maintained contrary to the draft constitution of the Kourani committee submitted to Husni Al-Zaim, which planned to abolish them.

The second ministerial committee submitted to the members of the government a project for a federation with Iraq. The project planned for the creation of a federation with a president and vice-president. The federation was to have authority for defence, foreign policy, and the economy. There were plans for the creation of a federal council and federal ministers. The project, with its poorly defined contours, was only discussed once in the cabinet. A majority of ministers, prominent among which were ministers of the People's Party, were in favour (eight out of twelve), but one-third of the members of the government were fiercely opposed to it.[22] Confronted with the split on this question, the head of government, Hashim Atassi, thought that such an important decision could not be taken by a provisional cabinet and put off discussions until after the elections.

---

[22] For the debate within the government, see Al-Azzem, *Memoirs of Khaled Al-Azzem* (Arabic), vol II, pp. 291 ff. For discussion within political circles, see Kasmiyé, *The Arab Vanguard* (Arabic), pp. 139 ff.

The People's Party was determined to use the future elections, then the new constitution, and the future institutions to promote the union with Iraq. The elections gave the People's Party a relative majority of forty-three seats and support from a further twenty populist members secured an absolute majority. There were twenty-two independent members. Although officially it boycotted the elections, the National Party could count on thirteen allied members while the Ba'th and Syrian Social Nationalist Party each won one seat.[23] The independents could shift the balance towards the People's Party or the army lobby at will.

4.2.2 The 1949 Provisional Constitution

The first opportunity for the independents to tip the scales arose over the interim government's draft provisional constitution. The majority People's Party leader and interior minister, Rushdi Kikhyia, was elected speaker at the first meeting. The assembly then debated the provisional constitution. The initial version, largely drafted by Rushdi Kikhyia himself and the People's Party, included the following three articles:

Article 1: The Assembly, by an absolute majority of its members or failing that by a relative majority in the second round of voting, shall elect the Head of State who has the rights and powers of the President of the Republic.

Article 2: The Head of State shall appoint the Prime Minister and the members of the Cabinet.

Article 3: The Head of State with the help of the Cabinet shall exercise legislative and executive powers according to the provisions in force since 14 August 1949 until such time as the new Constitution is adopted and comes into force.

The intention ascribed to the People's Party with this draft was to cling to power as long as possible while advancing its project for federation with Iraq. If conditions were right, it could quite quickly finalize the new constitution so as to reflect its views. If circumstances were against it, it could continue to wield power under the cover of a government that would be in its hands and a head of state favourable to its views.[24] The draft provisional constitution was debated by the assembly and amended as below:

---

[23] See the election results in Seale, *The Struggle for Syria*, p. 112.
[24] Al-Azzem, *Memoirs of Khaled Al-Azzem* (Arabic), p. 222.

Article 1: The Assembly, by an absolute majority of its members or failing that by a relative majority in the second round of voting, shall elect the Head of State who has the rights and powers of the President of the Republic defined in the previous Constitution.

Article 2: The Head of State with the help of the Cabinet shall exercise legislative powers, except for international treaties, and executive powers according to the provisions in force since 14 August 1949 until such time as the new Constitution is adopted and comes into force within a period not to exceed three months.[25]

This text limited the period for drafting the new constitution to three months and prevented the new head of state in the meantime from concluding any international agreements, a veiled allusion to possible closer ties with Iraq.[26] It was passed by the constituent assembly at its first meeting on 12 December 1949.

As soon as the provisional constitution was adopted, Hashim Atassi presented his government's resignation. Two days later, he was elected provisional president. Under the provisional constitution, he had the powers granted to the president of the republic by the previous constitution, that of 1928, until the new constitution could be adopted. The constituent assembly was unable to adopt the new constitution within the allotted three months. The commission tasked with preparing the constitution completed its work in April 1950 but the constitution was only adopted in September. Between the provisional constitution of 1949 and the 1950 constitution, Syria was to experience another army coup.

4.2.3 *The Third Military Coup*

After the election of the constituent assembly, the adoption of a provisional constitution, and the election of a president, Syria experienced its third armed coup in less than a year on 19 December 1949. This one came just one week after the first meeting of the constituent assembly and five days after the presidential election. This coup, which was more like a settling of scores among the military, nevertheless had lasting consequences for the first period of the Second Republic. It left intact the three major political institutions, the constituent assembly, the provisional constitution, and the presidency. The only apparent victims of this turnaround

---

[25] Author's translation of the provisional constitution and the text passed by the constituent assembly.

[26] See the text of the provisional constitution and the discussions of it in Al-Azzem, *Memoirs of Khaled Al-Azzem* (Arabic), p. 223.

by the army were the chief of the general staff, General Sami Hannawi, and his loyal pro-Iraqi supporters. But the political consequences for the future of Syria were very significant since the coup was a serious blow for the proponents of union with Iraq.

The officers who carried out the coup were mostly sympathizers of the SSNP and Arab Socialist Party and opposed to any closer ties with Iraq. The spark was the oath that the constituent assembly members and president had to take. A committee of three assembly members proposed the following wording, which was approved by the majority of the constituent assembly on 17 December 1949: 'I swear by almighty God to abide by the laws of the state, to safeguard the country's independence, its sovereignty, its territorial integrity, to safeguard its finances, and to work for union of Arab lands'.[27] This oath made no reference to the republican character of the regime in Syria and was an invitation to union with Arab countries, and by implication Iraq. It worried those opposed to closer ties with Baghdad, who saw in it a sign of the imminent advent of the union with Iraq openly called for by the People's Party, which had a majority in the assembly and was supported by General Sami Hinnawi, chief of the general staff. In fact, this was not at all so.[28] But doubt prompted the officers involved in the putsch to move without delay. In doing so, these officers led by Colonel Adib Shishakli were merely making their own and reinterpreting one of the initial components of the Syrian national project of 1919, namely the rejection of any foreign hegemony over Syria. In this case it was the hegemony of Britain via the Hashimites of Iraq.

4.2.4 The Uneasy Cohabitation of Military and Civilian Authorities

The army faction that had just seized control of the military institution was hostile to closer ties with Iraq. This revolution at the head of the army did not bear the hallmarks of a traditional coup. It was more of a coup with geopolitical dimensions, the regional fallout from which spread far beyond the borders of Syria. Over the next two years, the general staff, dominated by officers opposed to any union with Iraq, and the constituent assembly and then legislative assembly of 1950 after adoption of the new constitution, dominated by the People's Party which was favourable

---

[27] Author's translation. For the Arabic text see Atassi, *Hashim Atassi* (Arabic), p. 331.
[28] On the difficulty of establishing a Syrian–Iraqi federation at the time of the third coup, see Seale, *The Struggle for Syria*, p. 112.

to a federation with Iraq, were engaged in a stand-off over Syria's regional alliances. Between the two institutions, the president was to endeavour to use his good offices to reach compromises between the military and politicians of different sides, so as to safeguard the country's constitutional regime and maintain the normal operation of the institutions.

One of the instigators of this third army coup was Akram Hawrani. Concerned about Syria's political independence if it were to come under the sway of the Hashemites of Iraq and their British ally, Hawrani mobilized the many officers close to him, beginning with Adib Shishakli, himself a former sympathizer of the SSNP.

Five successive governments ran the country during the first spell of the Second Republic, which extended from the Shishakli coup of December 1949 until his second coup in December 1951. The patent antagonism between the general staff and the assembly put all successive governments in an impossible position. Governments had to perform a precarious balancing act between the assembly and the general staff. Between these two institutions with their opposing ambitions, the successive governments attempted to run the country by constantly looking for the lowest common denominator between an elected institution attached to its constitutional prerogatives and a military institution on the verge of rebellion and claiming to embody some degree of popular will. No government could hold on to power without the formal support of the assembly and the informal support of the general staff.

The president was in an unenviable position. From the coup of December 1949 to the adoption of the new constitution in September 1950, his role was confined to political consultations prior to the appointment of prime ministers and to accepting their resignations.[29] The president's main objective was to ensure that no crisis between the government and army should turn into a regime crisis. The system tottered along for two years thanks to this constantly repeated political balancing act.[30]

The 1950 constitution was a unique opportunity for the constituent assembly to bring in a strong executive that could have counterbalanced the army's growing influence. But instead, the 1950 constitution brought in a regime with a strong legislature and weak executive. After the new constitution was adopted in September 1950, neither the president nor

---

[29] For the extent of the president's responsibilities, see Torrey, *Syrian Politics*, p. 156.
[30] For a detailed description of Syrian political life at the time see Babeel, *Journalism and Politics in Syria during the Twentieth Century* (Arabic), pp. 445 ff.

the prime minister could oppose the general staff's constant interference in the choice of government.

A united front of the entire political class might have tipped the scales in favour of civilian power and contained the ambitions of the army. But the political class was divided and the political system in place did not provide it with the means to counter the army and the underhand interference of the leading regional (Iraq, Jordan, Egypt, Saudi Arabia) and international players (Britain, France, USA). Moreover, the new ideologically based political parties (the Ba'th Party, Arab Socialist Party, SSNP, Muslim Brotherhood) and the Communist Party were racing to recruit support among the officers and prompted them to take a stance, by arms if need be, over the main political choices for the country. The traditional parties such as the People's Party, which was still popular in the north (Aleppo) and centre (Homs, Hama), and the National Party, which was firmly established in Damascus, had failed to structure themselves as modern political parties that could attract both urban and rural young people and propose a programme of government and reforms for the country.

To counter the assembly's pro-Hashemite ambitions, the army conducted a parallel diplomacy to bring about closer ties with Egypt and Saudi Arabia, Iraq and Jordan's traditional rivals. While Syrian domestic politics was generally left to the governments in office, although the army did tend to throw its weight behind particular matters, Syria's regional policy was dictated or at least closely controlled, reviewed, and corrected by the general staff, who imposed on all successive governments its choice of defence minister. The army conducted its own foreign policy and strengthened its ties with Egypt and Saudi Arabia to the detriment of closer bonds with Iraq, which had the preference of most of the deputies and often the majority of ministers of the successive governments. The chief of the general staff, Adib Shishakli, went to Egypt, Saudi Arabia, and Lebanon to discuss bilateral relations with Syria without any government mandate to do so. The Syrian army aligned with the Cairo-Riyadh regional axis whereas the civilian authorities mostly preferred the Hashemite Baghdad–Amman axis.

4.2.5 Government Appointments and Resignations

A brief examination of the process of government appointments and resignations over a twenty-four month period reveals that the centre of gravity of political activity in the country was shared between the assembly and the general staff. Governments were formed after consultation between politicians and the military. The assembly's role was often limited to the vote of confidence. No censure motion was filed during the period and no cabinet was removed by a parliament that made timorous use of its constitutional prerogatives. The only initiative that seemed to be left to the head of government was the choice of the date of his resignation.

On 24 December 1949, the head of state tasked Nazem Kudsi (of the People's Party) with forming a new government. After three days of consultations, he informed the president he was unable to do so because of pressures from the general staff. Consequently, the president tendered his resignation to the constituent assembly that had elected him two weeks before. Hashim Atassi's resignation was rejected unanimously by the assembly and he accepted to continue in office in particularly difficult conditions during this troubled period of the country's history. He went before the constituent assembly and was sworn in using the wording approved by the assembly on 17 December 1949.

After Nazem Kudsi's unsuccessful attempt to form a government, the president invited the independent politician, Khaled Al-Azzem, former head of government under the mandate, to form the new cabinet. The general staff did not object but imposed the defence minister in the person of Akram Hawrani, founder of the Arab Socialist Party, and an old friend of Adib Shishakli, the army strongman. The Al-Azzem cabinet was composed of members of the People's Party, the Republican Bloc of the constituent assembly (independents), the Socialist Islamic Front, and independents. The government undertook to uphold the regime's republican character and Syria's independence. In short, the cabinet would not seek to form a federation or union with Iraq.

The Al-Azzem government remained in office from January to May 1950. The one big decision it made was to break off the customs union that had bound Syria and Lebanon since the time of the French mandate over the two countries. This move was approved by most of the political class, the main economic actors, and the army, and it caused no difficulties within the government. Public opinion saw the customs union as favourable to Lebanon at the expense of Syrian economic interests. Disparity within the cabinet and political infighting were to bring down the government. The defence minister (Republican Bloc) and justice minister (People's Party) resigned for different reasons and others threatened to do so. To avoid a government crisis, the president, in agreement with the prime minister, invited a Republican Bloc minister to try to persuade the two resigning ministers to change their minds. But the mediation failed, prompting the head of government to present his cabinet's resignation.

After fruitless attempts with two different candidates including the outgoing prime minister, the president, in agreement with the army, tasked Nazem Kudsi, secretary general of the People's Party, which held the majority in the assembly, with forming the new government. Kudsi put together a more homogenous cabinet than the previous one. All but three ministers belonged to the People's Party. As with the Al-Azzem government, the army imposed the defence minister, this time Colonel Fawzi Selo. The prime minister went to the constituent assembly and outlined his policy, which was debated and a vote of confidence passed. The procedure was remarkable because, in the absence of any constitution, which had still not been completely drafted, nothing more than custom compelled the head of government to act in this way.

The determination to secure a vote of confidence from the constituent assembly at a time when civilian power was contested by the army made the Kudsi government that much more legitimate. But not to the extent that the cabinet could launch major regional initiatives such as closer ties with Iraq. The prime minister considered his government to be provisional until the new constitution was adopted and announced he would expedite current affairs without taking any major political initiative.

The constitution was adopted by the constituent assembly in September 1950. The assembly then elected Hashim Atassi president under the new constitution, after which the assembly became the legislative assembly. This decision divided the political class. The People's Party, which held the majority in the constituent assembly, did not wish for new elections, unlike its rival the National Party and other politicians such as Akram Hawrani, who was close to the army. The president, as an elder statesman, although close to the People's Party, was also in favour of new elections. Finally, the majority of the constituent assembly decided to change into a legislative assembly for four years and Nazem Kudsi was tasked with forming a new government, with all the portfolios going to the People's Party bar three including defence, which the army bestowed on Colonel Fawzi Selo. This second government led by Nazem Kudsi lasted six months.

A combination of foreign and domestic factors soured relations between the government and the army and prompting the prime minister to present his and his government's resignation in March 1951 although he still had a solid majority in the assembly. The government's ambiguous position over Western plans to organize the defence of the Near East in what would become the Baghdad Pact in the face of the supposed Soviet threat worried the army. This Near Eastern defence plan relied on the Hashemites in Iraq and Jordan. The army command was hostile to any closer ties with those two countries. Domestically, control of the gendarmerie poisoned already strained relations between the People's Party and the general staff. The People's Party wanted the gendarmerie to come within the ambit of the interior ministry while the army wanted it to be accountable to the ministry of defence.

The resignation of the Kudsi government marked the first political crisis of the Second Republic after adoption of the 1950 constitution. The president tried in vain to persuade the prime minister to change his mind. He interviewed several figures about forming a new government, including the outgoing prime minister. The army vetoed the latter, forcing the speaker, Rushdi Kihyia (of the People's Party), to resign in protest at the army's interference. After several days of wrangling, an agreement approved by the army was announced. Khaled Al-Azzem was asked to form a new government made up of independent ministers. Logically enough, the People's Party, having a majority in the assembly but prevented by the army from exercising power, was not going to make life easy for the government. This drove the prime minister closer to the army.

The assembly did not grant the necessary resources to the Al-Azzem government. It refused to vote for certain lines of credit and in particular additional spending for defence and public sector wages. This brought on a general strike among government employees. Confronted with the social crisis coupled with distrust between the government and the assembly, the prime minister handed in his resignation in August 1951. Before resigning, Kahled Al-Azzem asked the president to exercise his constitutional right to dissolve the assembly. Under article 85 of the constitution, the dissolution of parliament meant the government also had to resign, which would have created a dangerous political vacuum. Anxious not to lead the country into an even more serious political crisis, the president declined.

Once again the army prevented the People's Party from forming a government by vetoing its candidates. The party leaders advised President Atassi to entrust the task to Hassan Al-Hakim who was an independent, historically close to the Hashemites and especially King Faysal and his brother Abdullah, King of Jordan, and known for his pro-Western sympathies. The army accepted the compromise. Hassan Al-Hakim had already held the position in 1941–42 under President Sheikh Tajeddin Al-Hasni.

Despite the new prime minister's long-standing sympathy for the Hashemites and the fact that the People's Party, proponents of a union with Iraq, were in the majority in the assembly, the government had to restrain its words and deeds to cautious regional neutrality so as not to provoke the general staff. To survive, the Al-Hakim government needed the continued support of the People's Party. It managed to keep it from August to October 1951 when the prime minister and his foreign affairs minister, Faydi Atassi (of the People's Party), diverged over Syria's attitude to Western proposals for Near Eastern countries to form a common defence against the Soviet Union. The People's Party concurred with the army and expressly dismissed Syria's involvement in any such undertaking, whereas the head of government was in favour of it. Through this clear and unambiguous stance, the People's Party for a time refuted all accusations of it being pro-British because it was pro-Hashemite. This tangle of regional and domestic issues and the similar viewpoint shared by the People's Party and the general staff, which was rare enough to rate a mention, compelled the prime minister to resign.

Although the People's Party and the army saw almost eye to eye on regional and international policy, the same was not so for domestic policy. Two days before the cabinet resigned, the interior minister, Rashad Barmada, had resigned in protest at the army's continued insistence on the gendarmerie being directed by the defence ministry. The army took this as a *casus belli*, because without the gendarmerie it could not control the entire territory.

The Al-Hakim government's resignation plunged Syria into a new political crisis. The People's Party insisted the next prime minister should come from within its ranks, that he should exercise his functions in full according to the constitution including matters concerning the defence minister, and that the gendarmerie should be accountable to the interior ministry. These demands were taken as provocation by the general staff who were not inclined to make any concessions. When the new prime minister Ma'aruf Dawalibi (of the People's Party) formed his government on 29 November 1951 with a majority of ministers belonging to the People's Party, he was warned by the army to modify its composition so as to give the defence portfolio to a candidate chosen by the army.

Confronted with Ma'aruf Dawalibi's refusal to accede to the army's demands, the next day, 30 November 1951, the chief of the general staff, Adib Shishakli, set about his second coup in two years. He had the prime minister and People's Party leaders arrested. He demanded the prime minister resign and asked the president to dissolve the assembly. The president sought in vain for a compromise between the People's Party and the army by trying to come up with a new head of government, but given the People's Party's refusal, President Atassi resigned on 2 December 1951 without having dissolved the legislative assembly. It was dissolved that same day by Adib Shishakli by military decree.

Syria was to spend more than two years under military rule. This was to be the Third Republic. The fact that he had not dissolved the assembly before resigning meant Hashim Atassi could reconvene it when the Shishakli era ended in 1954.

4.3   The 1950 Constitution

The assembly Hashim Atassi had refused to dissolve in late 1951 had voted for the new Syrian constitution a little more than a year before. On 15 April 1950, the constituent assembly committee tasked with preparing the new constitution had presented its draft to the assembly. The committee was headed by Nazem Kudsi.[31] Several of the draft articles were debated in the press before being finally amended, such as article 3 stipulating that the head of state's religion was to be Islam and article 5 allowing for a change of the capital, Damascus.[32] Opponents of union with Iraq saw this as an allusion to Baghdad becoming the capital. The constitution was adopted on 5 September 1950 by the constituent assembly.

From the outset, the new constitution, like those of 1920 and 1928, confirmed that 'the religion of the President shall be Islam' (art. 3). The 1949 draft constitution had abolished this provision. Article 3 of the new constitution also stated that Muslim law (*Fiqh* or Islamic jurisprudence) was to be the main source of legislation. This provision did not feature in the previous two constitutions. It was to be taken up by all the constitutions to come. Article 3 added: 'The personal status of religious communities is guaranteed and protected'.

4.3.1   *The Social Question: Towards a Welfare State?*

Just seventeen months separated the repeal in April 1949 of the 1928 constitution that set up the First Syrian Republic and the adoption of the 1950

---

[31] The committee's reporter was Abdel-Wahab Homad, a member of the constitutional committee directed by Kourani in 1949 during the time of Husni Al-Zaim. See Kourani, *Recollections* (Arabic), p. 234.
[32] See Seale, *The Struggle for Syria*, pp. 129 ff. and Kourani, *Recollections* (Arabic), pp. 234 ff.

constitution by the constituent assembly elected in November 1949. But the texts of the two constitutions show that in the meantime Syria had moved from one era to another. Although both set up a liberal democratic regime of a parliamentary type, they were very different. The 1928 constitution was conceived first of all as a weapon against the mandate power, as a first step to replace the mandate by a treaty, in short, as an instrument of national liberation as much if not more than an instrument for regulating the exercise of power. The 1950 constitution reflected the state of mind of a young, vibrant society that had recently won its independence and wanted to mark with the seal of constitutional authority the most urgent social reforms to be carried out by the institutions. The 1950 constitution had the stated ambition, domestically, of bringing about reforms and transforming Syrian society.

But what the 1950 constituent assembly did not realize was that the future of the new constitution and the regime it was to engender would hang not on domestic policy but on Syria's regional role. The military were reluctant to see any closer ties with the Hashemites of Iraq and were not slow to remind the constituted civilian authorities of this, including the constituent assembly. But instead of establishing a regime with a strong executive able to stand up to the army's demands, the civilian authorities produced a weak executive, the weakest in the entire history of contemporary Syria. This fatal error played into the army's hands and it did not hesitate to interfere in politics throughout the Second Republic until the regime finally fell in 1963 after two temporary interruptions in 1951 and 1958.

In many respects, the 1950 constitution foreshadowed the upheavals that Syrian society was to experience in the coming decade through successive coups. Title II of the constitution, 'Fundamental Provisions', collated the usual articles of a Declaration of Rights, as had the 1920 and 1928 constitutions, to which it added articles of an economic and social character. The 1950 constitution purported therefore to be a manifesto and constitution. It aimed to make Syria a welfare state by creating economic and social rights. It provided for modest agrarian reform and limited the major landowners, but with no retroactive effect (art. 22), promoted workers' rights (art. 26), developed education (art. 28), and created a social security scheme (art. 27). In short, the 1950 constitution had as its stated objective from its preamble to set up an economic and social regime that would ensure social justice, protect workers and farmers, ensure equal duties and rights, and implement progressive taxation.

On agrarian reform, article 22 of the 1950 constitution provided: 'in order to ensure rational exploitation of the national heritage and to establish equitable social relations among citizens'(art. 22(1)), legislation would be introduced based on the following principles:

- 'obligation to farm the land. In the event of neglect for a period laid down by law, the right of enjoyment shall be abolished' (art. 22(1)(a));
- 'a law having no retroactive effect shall limit, by region, the maximum extent of landownership by disposal or exploitation' (art. 22(1)(b));
- 'the State shall divide plots of land among landless farmers and against eventual payment of a moderate price to allow them to ensure their livelihood' (art. 22(1)(e));
- 'the State shall encourage the creation of cooperatives and control them' (art. 22(2));
- 'the State shall build model villages and salubrious accommodation for farmers' (art. 22(3));
- 'a law shall be laid down ensuring protection of farmers and the raising of their standard of living' (art. 22(4)).

Article 26 stated:

(1) the right to work for all citizens is a duty dictated by honour. It is the single most important fundamental component of social life. It shall be ensured to all citizens by the State which guarantees it by orienting the national economy and its recovery
(2) The State shall protect work and establish legislation based on the following principles:
    (a) to pay workers' wages proportional to the quantity and quality of work provided
    (b) to define the number of working hours per week and grant workers weekly and annual paid leave
    (c) to set up a special compensation scheme for workers with a dependent family in the event of redundancy, illness, incapacity, and accidents at work
    (d) to lay down special working conditions for women and children;
(3) the State shall provide workers with salubrious accommodation. The law shall determine the resources for doing so
(4) trade unionism is unrestricted within the bounds of the law.

One of the innovations introduced by the 1950 constitution was social security. Article 27 stipulated that all citizens 'are entitled with their families to be protected by the State in exceptional circumstances of illness, incapacity, old-age, involuntary unemployment'. To this end, the state was to regulate welfare insurance through its participation and that of firms and individuals to ensure the necessary funding (art. 27(1)) and the state was to protect citizens' health. To this end it was to build hospitals, sanatoria, and maternity hospitals and ensure citizens have access to health care and protection during maternity and childhood (art. 27(2)).

The constitution paid particular attention to education at all levels, which was recognized as a right for all citizens. Article 28 stated:

> primary education is mandatory and free-of-charge in State-run schools and is unified. Private primary schools shall teach the State curriculum and may teach extra subjects defined by law. Secondary and vocational education is free-of-charge in State schools. The law determines the subjects that private secondary institutions are compelled to teach. Religious instruction for these two tiers shall be taught for each confession in accordance with its beliefs. The State shall make the spread and generalization of primary and vocational education a budgetary priority in rural areas to ensure equality among Syrians. The State shall facilitate access to higher education and its institutions are to enjoy financial and administrative autonomy.

The non-compatibility of policies followed by successive governments under the Second Republic with the generous social objectives proclaimed by the 1950 constitution seriously discredited the regime as a whole and its ability to reform society and establish new social relations. The traditional political class was caught up with regional issues or more simply party-political infighting. It failed to realize there and then that its inability to meet the legitimate social and economic aspirations of the majority of the Syrian population and in particular its rural young people was going to turn them away from the values of liberal-type representative democracy and towards the proponents of radical revolutionary regimes. It probably also failed to realize that social justice was to become one of the main features of the Syrian national project.

To have any hope of implementing these reforms, the Second Republic needed stable governments, an efficient administration, and devoted political staff accepting the rules of democracy. This was not to be. The 1950 constitution did not give the country a strong executive that could have achieved its ambitions.

Title II of the 1950 constitution also included articles that generally figure in a declaration of rights such as equality before the law, personal safety, and individual and collective freedoms. Article 7 stated that 'citizens are equal in law, duties and rights, dignity, and social position' and article 8: 'The State guarantees freedom, security, and equal standing to all citizens'.

Under article 10:

(1) Individual freedom is guaranteed.
(2) No one shall be detained without an arrest warrant or unless caught red handed or without the intention of bringing them before the judicial authorities on charges of some specific crime or offence.
(3) Torture and inhumane treatment are prohibited. The law determines the penalties for anyone guilty of such acts.
(4) It is prohibited for the administrative authorities to make preventive arrests unless in a state of siege, martial law, or war, and pursuant to the law.

The inviolability of the home is guaranteed: 'No one shall enter or search a home without the owner's authorization or without a legal warrant, other than in cases where offenders are caught in the act' (art. 12); 'Postal, telegraphic, and telephone correspondence is inviolable and cannot be confiscated, delayed, or intercepted unless provided for by law' (art. 13).

Article 15 states:

(1) The press and printing and publication are unrestricted within the limits of the law.
(2) Newspapers may not be suspended or closed down other than as provided for by law.
(3) In states of emergency or exceptional circumstances, the law may establish censorship for newspapers, publications, printed matter, and broadcasting, limited to questions relating to public safety and the needs of national defence.

For the first time ever, the 1950 constitution made specific reference to the right to form political parties. The 1920 and 1928 constitutions simply mentioned the possibility of creating associations. Article 16 specified that 'Syrians have the right of assembly and peaceful demonstration without arms within the limits laid down by law' and article 17(1) added: 'Syrians have the right to create associations for purposes not prohibited by law and to join them'. Article 18(1) stated: 'Syrians have the right to create political parties provided they act for legitimate purposes by peaceful processes and adopt democratic principles'.

Article 19 provided that Syrians could not be exiled and article 20(1) stated: 'Refugees cannot be extradited for their political principles and actions in defence of freedom'.

4.3.2 *The National Question*

Like the 1928 constitution, the 1950 constitution had a certain conception of Syrian realities and their interaction with the regional environment. But while the 1928 constitution, like that of 1920, had been drafted from a pan-Syrian national viewpoint, the 1950 constitution had a whole new perception of Syria and was part rather of a pan-Arab national project. Thus article 1 stated that 'Syria is a democratic, parliamentary, sovereign Arab republic ... the Syrian people is part of the Arab nation'.

Originally, the first Syrian constitution, the monarchic constitution of 1920, was drafted by the Syrian congress, which considered itself to be the legitimate representative of the separated Arab provinces of the Ottoman empire, that is, the vilayets of Damascus, Aleppo, Beirut, and the sanjaks of Jerusalem and Deir Ezzor, which later became Syria, Lebanon, Palestine, and Transjordan. The 1920 constitution was therefore by definition a pan-Syrian constitution. The Syrian monarchy saw itself as unitary and decentralized, and it planned a special autonomous status for Mount Lebanon. The ambition was to create a great Syrian state in the Near East, separate from the other Arab political entities of the region such as Iraq and the Hejaz, but linked to them by economic, trade, and political agreements. This great scheme was never to be and the kingdom of Syria, that was to last a mere four months, was limited de facto to the eastern zone of occupation, that is inland Syria.

The second Syrian constitution, that of 1928, tried unsuccessfully to reassert in the constitutional text the great scheme of the Founding Fathers in 1920. The initial article 2 of the 1928 constitution as it was first adopted by the constituent assembly stated that Syria comprised 'all the Syrian territories detached from the Ottoman Empire, regardless of the divisions that occurred after the end of the Great War'. This article was forcefully rejected by the French high commissioner who found it contradicted France's international commitments. But the Syrian constituent assembly did not yield and it was only by using his prerogatives as the mandate power that the high commissioner promulgated the 1928 constitution in 1930 after having amended, among other things, article 2 to read 'Syria forms an indivisible political unit'.

The slow shift of Syrian public opinion from the pan-Syrian to the pan-Arab national project took place between the 1928 and 1950 constitutions. This change was foreshadowed by the 1949 draft constitution that hesitated between the two. Several factors can explain this change.

Pan-Syrianism had long been the Hashemite spearhead in the region. From the fall of Faysal's monarchy in 1920 until the death of King Abdullah of Transjordan in 1951 and the fall of the Iraqi monarchy in 1958, the two Hashemite kingdoms of Jordan and Iraq became the most fervent supporters of the Greater Syria project in the Near East. The projects of Iraq and Jordan took different names and forms but they were similar. The Iraqi project was known as the Fertile Crescent and sought to gather natural Syria and Iraq into a single unit. The Jordanian project was known as Greater Syria and aimed at reuniting the Arab provinces of the Syria claimed by King Faysal under the name of natural Syria, that is, Syria, Lebanon, Jordan, and Palestine. At the time the 1950 Syrian constitution was drafted, the Greater Syria project under the aegis of King Abdullah of Jordan had already run out of steam. Most Syrians for that matter had never believed in it because of the king's supposed complacency with the plans of Zionist armed groups, in particular before and during the 1948 Palestine War. Conversely, many Syrians thought that a union with the Hashemites of Iraq was in the country's best interests. In addition to the Hashemites, the SSNP, which was well established in Lebanon and Syria, advocated the creation of a Greater Syria that would encompass natural Syria, Mesopotamia, Kuwait, and even the island of Cyprus.

Alongside pan-Syrianism, there developed among the intelligentsia, the young, and the army, the outline of an Arab national project for which the Ba'th, the Arab Socialist Party, and later the Nasserists were to be the representatives. Over nearly a decade (1949–58), Syrian political life and its regional relations were dominated by this confrontation between the supporters of a pro-Syrian project favourable to a union with Iraq, and their political opponents, who came together around the pan-Arab project, which was to crystallize in closer ties with Egypt and lead to the union of Syria and Egypt in 1958.

4.3.3 *Sovereignty*

The 1950 constitution was the first to take a stance on the question of sovereignty. The 1920 and 1928 constitutions had not addressed this issue. The 1928 constitution asserted simply in its article 29 that 'the Nation is the source of all power'. The 1950 constitution stated in its article 2 that:

(1) Sovereignty is vested in the people alone. No section of the people nor any individual may take its exercise into their own hands.

(2) The exercise of sovereignty rests on the principle of government of the people, by the people, for the people.
(3) The people shall exercise its right of sovereignty in the forms and limits set out by the constitution.

4.3.4 Legislative Power

Title III of the 1950 constitution addressed legislative power. The 1950 constitution took up the single-chamber approach introduced by the 1928 constitution and provided for an assembly of deputies. The bicameralism contemplated by the 1920 monarchic constitution was therefore abandoned definitively.

The Assembly of Deputies

One of the great differences between the 1950 assembly and that of 1928 was that it was elected by men and women voters. Women's right to vote was granted by the new electoral law. The constituent assembly in 1950 took up the provision. Under article 38 of the constitution, 'the electoral body is made up of male and female Syrians aged 18 years, listed on the civil registry rolls, and who satisfy the conditions laid down by the electoral law'. That law required that women should have their primary school diploma in order to vote. This provision, which was discriminatory towards women and not applicable to men, was subsequently dropped from the 1961 electoral law.

In the same way as the previous constituent bodies had done in 1920 and 1928, the 1950 constitution left it to the legislature to decide on the electoral law. Article 35 stated that 'legislative power shall be held by the Assembly of Deputies, which shall be elected by secret universal ballot in accordance with the provisions of the electoral law'. However, like the earlier constituent bodies, the 1950 constituent assembly laid down certain rules by which the legislature had to abide. Article 40 stipulated that 'the electoral law shall contain provisions on the proper conduct of elections, the right of candidates to inspect voting operations, and the enforcement of sanctions against any falsification of the outcome of the vote'.

Unlike the 1920 and 1928 constituent assemblies, that of 1950 made no reference to the representation of sectarian minorities within the assembly. The 1920 and 1928 constitutions had provided that the electoral law should allow for minority representation. This provision vanished from the 1950 constitution. However, as stated earlier, the electoral law adopted in September 1949 had only partly abolished the system for minority representation by limiting it to religion rather than confession. The representation of sectarian minorities within parliaments had been a constant ever since the 1920 constitution. It is to be recalled that the 1949 draft constitution prepared by the Kourani committee had eliminated sectarian quotas. The mere fact that minority representation was not mentioned in the constitution and was left to the electoral law was later to facilitate the abolition of religious quotas without having to revise the constitution and by merely amending the electoral law.

Article 36 stipulated that the Assembly shall sit for five years and this duration may only be extended by law in the event of war. According to Article 85(2) 'The Assembly cannot be dissolved in the first eighteen months of its legislature'. Article 37 stated: 'Each deputy represents the entire people. His mandate may not be limited under any circumstances and he shall carry it out in good conscience'.

Members of the Assembly

Under article 58, laws shall be promoted by the President of the Republic in agreement with the Government and by each member individually. The right to introduce finance bills and other bills with an effect on public finances lies with the President of the Republic in accordance with the Government or at least twenty members.

Article 56 stipulated that sessions of the assembly could only be held in the presence of an absolute majority of members. Article 57 provided that only the deputies present may vote. Voting shall be by secret ballot. Decisions shall be taken by the majority present except where the constitution and the assembly rules and regulations so provide. In the event of a tie of votes, the bill shall be considered to have been dismissed.

One important provision of the 1950 constitution that marked a change from the 1928 constitution was that it was impossible for parliament to set aside its legislative powers (art. 59). In other words, the assembly could not delegate to the executive the possibility of legislating by decree. This had been common practice under the First Republic.

Article 61 stipulated:

(1) Any law passed by the Assembly shall be promulgated by the President of the Republic within two weeks.
(2) In the event that a law passed by the Assembly by an absolute majority of its members is characterized as urgent and contains a deadline for its promulgation, it shall be promulgated by the President of the

Republic within the allotted time, failing which it shall be published by the Speaker upon expiration of the deadline.

The 1950 constitution instituted a parliamentary regime under which the government was accountable to parliament. Article 67 stated:

(1) The Assembly shall study any motion of censure of the Government or a Minister if the motion is presented by at least fifteen members. The motion of censure shall be discussed by the Assembly two days after being presented.
(2) If the motion of censure is passed by an absolute majority of the Assembly, the Government shall resign.
(3) Any Minister in whom the Assembly votes no confidence shall resign.

Interestingly, in this latter case the constitution did not require any qualified majority.

4.3.5 Executive Power

Title IV of the constitution referred to executive power. The executive was headed by both the president and the council of ministers.

The President of the Republic

As in the 1928 constitution, the new constitution provided that the President of the Republic must be elected by the Assembly of Deputies by secret ballot (art. 71(1)) and by a two-thirds majority (art. 71(2)). The same article adds should he fail to secure the majority in the first round, the President shall be elected in a second round of voting by an absolute majority (art. 71(3)); and should he fail to secure a majority in the second round, he shall be elected in a third round by a relative majority (art. 71(4)). Under article 72 any candidate for the Presidency of the Republic had to be aged 40 years old or more.

The presidential term of office was five years and could only be renewed after an interruption of five years (art. 73). The 1950 constitution therefore returned to the initial provisions of the 1928 constitution and ignored the 1948 constitutional revision that allowed Shukri Qwatli to be elected for a second term.

Article 78 stated: 'The President of the Republic can invite the Council of Ministers to meet under his chairmanship.' Article 90 provided that the President of the Republic appoints the Prime Minister and the Ministers upon proposals from the Prime Minister.

Three provisions weakened the president and the government with respect to the chamber. First, the constitution provided that, should the President of the Republic dissolve the assembly by a decree stating its reasons passed by the Council of Ministers (art. 85(1)), the Government shall resign. The President of the Republic appoints a Government made up of Ministers not having participated in the previous Government tasked with supervising the forthcoming elections (art. 85(3)). This was probably one of the major shortcomings of the 1950 constitution. Dissolution was not considered as a legitimate means for the executive to put pressure on a reluctant or rebellious parliament but as a collective suicide of government. Hence the option of dissolution as the ultimate dissuasive weapon in the hands of the executive was neutralized. In the entire history of the Second Republic, only a single prime minister asked the president to dissolve the assembly. The president refused probably so as not to take the risk of transforming a governmental crisis into a regime crisis with a dissolution of the assembly and resignation of the government. This absence of risk of dissolution meant the necessary collaboration between the legislature and the executive was replaced by a de facto subordination of the executive to the legislature. The 1928 parliamentary regime became an assembly-dominated regime under the 1950 constitution.

Second, the president no longer held regulatory power: 'If the President of the Republic fails to sign the decrees presented to him by the Government within ten days and if he fails to submit them to the Supreme Court for violation of the Constitution or the law, the Prime Minister may then set about their publication and the decrees shall become enforceable' (art. 81(1)). This provision considerably weakened the standing of the president with respect to the government. The two-headed executive of the 1950 constitution was thus tilted in favour of the prime minister and against the president. Under the 1928 constitution, the dual leadership of the executive had worked in favour of the president.

Third, under article 62:

(1) Should the President of the Republic consider that an ordinary, non-urgent bill ought to be reconsidered, he may send it back for a second reading before the Assembly (provisional veto) within the time allotted for its promulgation in the form of a decree stating reasons passed in the Council of Ministers.
(2) If the absolute majority of the Assembly members confirm its opinion, the law shall be promulgated immediately.

This procedure in the event of disagreement between parliament and president about a bill passed by the assembly was different from that of the previous constitution and tipped in parliament's favour. The president could not as before ask for a second reading by the assembly for a bill that it deemed urgent. He could only do so for non-urgent bills. Moreover, the qualified majority required by the assembly to override the president's provisional veto and confirm a bill at a second reading was an absolute majority and no longer the two-thirds majority as under the 1928 constitution. The 1950 constituent assembly clearly wanted parliament to be preeminent and to restrict presidential power.

This procedure was never implemented, just as under the First Republic. But the determination to weaken the head of state at a time when the authority of civilian power was openly challenged by the military remains surprising. It can only be explained, like the other provisions that aimed to weaken the president and government, by inexperience of the political class in constitutional matters, clumsiness, or the deliberate intent of some influential members of the constituent assembly to weaken the executive relative to the legislature and to weaken all civilian institutions for the benefit of the military, who were thought more fit to govern the country and to undertake the most urgent social reforms.

Under article 86:

(1) The President of the Republic is responsible in the event of violation of the Constitution or of high treason.
(2) He is also accountable for any crimes committed under ordinary law.
(3) The President of the Republic can only be tried by the Supreme Court.

The counterbalance of the president bearing no responsibility for his official acts was that all decrees, agreements, and letters concerning affairs of state signed by him had to be countersigned by the prime minister and the relevant minister, except for the appointment of the prime minister and the acceptance of his resignation.

The Government

Under article 90, the President of the Republic chooses the Prime Minister and appoints the Ministers upon the latter's proposal. The government presents its programme to the Assembly which gives it a vote of confidence (art. 91(1)); confidence is granted by the majority of members attending (art. 91(2)). The ex-post intervention of parliament in the formation of the government by a vote of investiture was a new feature. This provision confirmed the 1950 constituent assembly's intention to ascribe a greater role to parliament.

Article 92 stated:

(1) The Council of Ministers directs the policy of the State.
(2) It sits under the Prime Minister's chairmanship to decide on bills, organizational decrees, domestic and foreign policy, questions proposed by the Prime Minister or by a Minister with the Prime Minister's agreement, and other questions determined by law.
(3) Decisions are taken by the majority. Ministers in the minority are deemed to have accepted the decisions unless they resign.

Article 77 provided that the Government negotiated international agreements, and the President of the Republic signed them. It stipulated that the Government must keep the President informed of international talks (art. 77(1)). 'The President signs treaties and promulgates them after agreement of the Chamber' (art. 77(2)).

Article 94(3) stated that the Prime Minister alone may call for a vote of confidence in the Government in the Assembly, while article 98 provided that: The Ministers are collectively accountable to the Assembly for general policy and individually accountable for their own Ministry. Under article 96, 'in the event of the Government resigning or the Assembly voting no confidence in it, the Ministers shall continue in a caretaker role until a new Government is formed'.

Constitutional Revision

Title IX described the unwieldy procedure for revising the constitution. Article 155 stated that the President of the Republic, in the Council of Ministers, and the Chamber may ask for a revision of the Constitution. If the request comes from the Chamber, it shall be signed by at least one in three of the members. The request had first to be adopted by the absolute majority of deputies. But this was only considered a 'wish for revision'. To be definitively approved, the 'wish for revision' had to be adopted by the chamber within six months by a two-thirds majority.

4.3.6 The Judiciary

The judicial authority consisted of the Supreme Court, the Court of Cassation, and the ordinary tribunals. The Supreme Court existed under the 1928 constitution but its responsibilities were extended in 1950. The Supreme Court's mandate included examining the constitutionality of laws, the constitutionality and legality of draft decrees deferred to it by the President of the Republic, judging the President of the Republic and Ministers, validating elections, hearing appeals for annulment of legal instruments, administrative decisions, decrees taken in breach of the constitution, the law, and regulations, from persons having incurred harm or loss from them (art. 122). The other original feature of the Supreme Court was its composition: it is made up of seven members elected for five years by the Assembly of Deputies from a list of fourteen candidates presented by the President of the Republic (art. 116); the members of the Supreme Court elect their President (art. 119). The previous constitution provided for a Supreme Court whose power was confined to sitting in judgment on the president of the republic for violation of the constitution or high treason.

4.4 Return to the Regional Question during the Second Phase of the Second Republic (1954–1958)

Once the constitution was adopted, the constituent assembly changed in September 1950 into a legislative assembly, due to govern for a period of four years. It sat until it was dissolved in December 1951 further to a coup by General Shishakli, as explained earlier. It was to be reconvened in March 1954 after the army coup that overturned General Shishakli's regime.

With the fall of the Shishakli regime began the second period of the Second Republic that saw the golden age of Syrian democracy and ended with a union with Egypt in 1958. On 1 March 1954 President Atassi returned in triumph to Damascus after having withdrawn for more than two years to his home city of Homs where he had been kept under surveillance and for a time under house arrest. It was from his home in Homs that he directed the action of the various political factions opposed to the Shishakli regime. Despite his advancing years, he had successfully mobilized, coalesced, and directed the opposition that put an end to Shishakli's military republic. The army played a decisive role in the regime's overthrow. Once its objective had been attained, it handed back power to the civilian authorities. In this respect, the fall of the Shishakli regime was not unlike the end of Husni Al-Zaim's reign in 1949, although at the time the overthrow of the regime was due solely to the coup by General Hinnawi with no involvement of the political class and the population.

For the second time in five years, the army transferred power to the politicians. But contrary to what had happened in the wake of General Hinnawi's coup of 14 August 1949, this time Hashim Atassi managed to restore constitutional order as before the military coup of December 1951. In the aftermath of the August 1949 coup, Hashim Atassi had recommended restoring the previous political position including the return of the former President Qwatli, the restoration of the 1928 constitution, and the convening of the parliament elected in 1947. The majority of the political class and the army had objected to this. This time no one could prevent Hashim Atassi from restoring the position prior to the Shishakli coup of December 1951.

The 1953 constitution was abolished and the parliament elected in 1953 dissolved.[33] President Atassi's first decision, even before leaving Homs for Damascus, was to officially and retroactively accept the resignation of his former prime minister, Ma'aruf Dawalabi, of 1 December 1951 when he was arrested and thrown into prison. Out of concern for national union, he invited Sabri Al-Assali, leader of the National Party, which had in the meantime joined the ranks of the opposition to Shishakli, to form a new government. The decision to attribute the position of prime minister to the National Party, while it had only a minority in the parliament elected in 1949, had been taken out of concern for national union and in agreement between the People's Party and the National Party, supported at least nominally by the Ba'th.[34]

The 1950 constitution was restored. The assembly elected in 1949 and dissolved by Shishakli in 1951 was reconvened on 16 March 1954 and saw out its term six months later. The day after parliament convened, the Sabri Al-Assali government outlined its policy. Its objective was to lead the country to the legislative elections planned for the autumn. After the deputies had discussed the government's plans, the assembly passed a vote of confidence in the cabinet by an absolute majority (seventy-eight votes in favour).

4.4.1 The 1954 Legislative Elections

The Al-Assali cabinet remained in office until June 1954. Party-political criticism of it in the run-up to the legislative elections showed the need for

---

[33] See Chapter 5 'The Third Republic'.
[34] See Atassi, *Hashim Atassi* (Arabic), p. 374.

a neutral cabinet to run the country. President Atassi tasked Said Ghazi, a former minister, and an independent, with forming a new government. The Ghazi government, made up of technocrats, set itself the main objective of organizing the legislative elections.

After revoking the 1953 electoral law passed during the Shishakli period, the assembly enacted a new one in June 1954 which was similar to that of 1949, but with a few modifications.[35] The number of seats in the assembly was set at 142. Each member represented 30,000 constituents. Quotas for religious minorities were abolished and never again restored. This abolition had featured among the provisions of the draft constitution prepared by the Kourani committee during the rule of Husni Al-Zaim in 1949, but quotas had been reinstated for a time in the electoral law adopted by the provisional government directed by Hashim Atassi in autumn 1949. The caza was the basic electoral constituency. Depending on its size, each caza was to elect two, three, or four deputies. The deputies had to be elected in the first round of voting with 40 per cent of the votes. Should not all the seats find takers in the first round, a second round (a re-run) was to be organized. This law authorized women to stand for the first time. It also introduced the obligation to install voting booths in the polling stations. The polling stations and the electoral rolls for each polling station were to be finalized and made public two weeks before the election. While it abolished minority representation, the law still reserved seats for the bedouins.

The 1954 electoral law was amended in 1957. The new electoral law abolished seats for the bedouins and replaced the two rounds of voting by a majority system with a single-round ballot. The left-wing parties were favourable to this change. They won three out of four seats in the 1957 by-elections under this new arrangement. The left-wing parties had high hopes of winning the 1958 legislative elections by this type of ballot, but Syria decided to merge its future with that of Nasser's Egypt six months before the elections.

Analysts agree that Syria's 1954 legislative elections were the most democratic ever held in an Arab country to that date. The first round of voting was on 24–25 September; the second on 4–5 October. The People's Party won a relative but not absolute majority. In the 1949 elections, it had only commanded an absolute majority with the support of its independent allies. To many people's surprise, the second party in terms of seats was the Ba'th, which during the Shishakli period had merged with

---

[35] Electoral law 188, see Official Journal no. 28 of 28 June 1954, pp. 3199–201.

Akram Hawrani's Arab Socialist Party, followed by the National Party. But the big winners of the elections were, once again, the independents.[36] As in 1947 and in 1949, any government wanting to secure a vote of confidence in parliament and remain in charge had to count on the support of the independents.

The persistence of the large number of independent members in three consecutive elections in the space of seven years (1947, 1949, and 1954) reflected the crisis besetting the political parties and especially the traditional liberal parties such as the People's Party and the National Party, which could no longer attract an expanding electorate that was young, both urban and rural, eager for social reforms, and sensitive to great national causes. The People's Party managed to obtain an absolute majority but only with the alliance of independent members.

From the beginning of the Second Republic, the People's Party's great scheme was the union with Iraq, which it continued to advocate after the 1954 elections. The National Party was made up of former notables of the National Bloc, who were mostly Damascene and grouped around president Shukri Qwatli. The party had been much weakened by the coup led by Husni Al-Zaim in 1949 against President Qwatli. It also lost credibility with public opinion when some of its members agreed to work with the new regime.

The ideological parties (Ba'th, SSNP, Communist Party, and Muslim Brotherhood) were growing stronger with each election, especially the Ba'th. However, the political circumstances of the coming months left them no time to reinforce their electoral base.

4.4.2 The Second Legislature of the Second Republic

The new parliament met in October 1954 and elected Nazem Kudsi (of the People's Party) as the speaker. As the 1954 election did not return a clear majority, the members assembled into two main blocs representing the left and right. Each bloc counted some sixty members. Only a few independents representing bedouins, Islamists, and Shishakli supporters remained outside the two parliamentary formations. The right brought together the members of the People's Party, National Party, and the Constitutional Bloc made up of right-wing independent members led by Mounir Ajlani. The left brought together alongside the Ba'th members

---

[36] For the detailed election results see Al-Azzem, *Memoirs of Khaled Al-Azzem* (Arabic), vol. II, pp. 302 ff.

the former head of government, Khaled Al-Azzem, the Democratic Bloc, which included the left-wing independent members, who were joined in 1957 after a by-election victory by the only communist member of the assembly, Khaled Bagdache, the historical leader of the Syrian Communist Party.

President Hashim Atassi sounded out Khaled Al-Azzem on 14 November 1954 about forming a government. After a few days of consultations, Al-Azzem declined because of the very small majority his government would have had, supported by the left-wing parliamentary bloc alone. President Atassi then tasked Fares Khoury with the mission. He managed to form a government with the support of the right-wing parliamentary bloc. Fares Khoury, former speaker, former minister, and co-founder of the National Bloc, thus became the first Christian to occupy the position of prime minister in an Arab country.

Without the Syrians realizing it at the time, the beginning of 1955 was a pivotal date in their country's history. Public opinion was turning slowly from the pro-Iraqi and pro-Western camp towards the pro-Egyptian camp favourable to the Soviet Union. Two events prompted this shift. In January 1955, Nasser convened a conference of Arab countries in Cairo to discuss Western defence plans for the Near East against supposed Soviet ambitions. By this date, Iraq had already announced its intention to join the Westerners, and Britain in particular, in a common defence pact. Jordan was not opposed to the move. The readiness of the Hashemites of Iraq and Jordan to join the Westerners stirred fear and suspicion in Saudi Arabia and Egypt. The Arabs were divided into two rival camps. The position Syria would take was the only unknown factor that could tip the balance towards one (Iraq, Jordan) or other (Egypt, Saudi Arabia) camp. If Syria sided with Iraq and Jordan, it was the entire Near East that would shift into the Western camp. If it did the opposite, it would be a regional victory for Egypt and, beyond the region, for the Soviet Union. Since 1947, every election in Syria, save that of 1953 during the Shishakli era, had given a majority of parliamentary seats to the People's Party, which favoured a union with Iraq. The 1954 election had also given a relative majority to the People's Party, which had formed the government with its former ally and rival, the National Party, and a group of independent right-wing members. This government was made up of politicians favourable to Iraq and the West, although some of the National Party members had no sympathy with the Baghdad monarchy. The Syrian government was therefore reluctant to take a stance against Iraq and the pro-Western defence project.

At the Cairo conference in January 1955, the Syrian delegation gave the impression of supporting Iraq indirectly by saying it understood the reasons for falling in with the Western defence plans. In Damascus, the People's Party adopted a cautious reserve in this debate. However, in February 1955 the National Party split over the Western defence plans for the Near East. Some National Party members led by Sabri Al-Assali allied with the left-wing coalition (Ba'th, independents) hostile to the Westerners and the future Baghdad Pact. This internal division was to shift the balance in parliament in favour of the left-wing coalition. The Fares Khoury cabinet resigned. President Atassi invited Sabri Al-Assali to form a government. Over the next two years, Syria slid slowly but inexorably towards Nasser's Egypt. Just as Syrian nationalists during the mandate had managed to mobilize all of the institutions under the 1928 constitution to secure independence and reunification of the Syrian lands under French control, Arab nationalists in the late 1950s were to mobilize all of the political institutions under the 1950 constitution to achieve the union with Egypt.

A second event some weeks later shifted public opinion further to the left. The deputy army chief of staff, Colonel Adnan Al-Malki was assassinated. Thought to be close to the Ba'th, Colonel Malki was killed on 22 April 1955 by a member of the SSNP.[37] The assassination provided an opportunity to cleanse the army of many officers who were SSNP sympathizers or had right-wing tendencies and were therefore hostile to the Ba'th, Egypt, and Nasser. The SSNP, as the great rival of the Ba'th among the young and the officer corps, was banned and its members within the army arrested or discharged. This assassination brought the army back into the political sphere from which it had provisionally removed itself since the fall of Adib Shishakli's military republic the year before.

The purge of officers close to the SSNP upset the balance within the army and left the military dominated by Arab nationalist and left-wing (Ba'th, Socialist, pro-Nasser, and pro-Communist) officers. The independent officers gathered for a time around the army chief of staff, General Shawkat Shukeir, a Lebanese Christian. A year later, in July 1956, just weeks before the tripartite attack on Egypt, he resigned. General Shukeir, who had been one of the deputies of Shishakli, was one of the last supports

---

[37] The investigation revealed that the assassination was organized at the instigation of Georges Abdel-Massih, leader of the SSNP, but without consulting the party leadership.

for independent officers within the army, who found themselves increasingly side-lined by leftist officers.

4.4.3 The Second Presidency under the Second Republic

It was in a tense national and regional context that the assembly set about electing the president. President Atassi's term of office was coming to a close and the assembly elected in the second round of voting on 18 August 1955 former president Shukri Qwatli, supported by the right-wing members. The other candidate was Khaled Al-Azzem, who was to be nicknamed the 'red millionaire' and the strongman of the Al-Assali government. Khaled Al-Azzem was to be one of the architects of the closer ties with Egypt and the Soviet Union. He was supported by the Democratic Bloc (Ba'th and left-wing independents) in the chamber. Shukri Qwatli's election was not a foregone conclusion. His National Party was only third in parliament in terms of seats. The People's Party had a relative majority and logically it should have presented its leader, Rushdi Kikhyia, against Khaled Al-Azzem. But the People's Party leader, the natural candidate for the first presidency,[38] did not wish to stand for personal reasons, so leaving the field open to the National Party to present its own candidate in the name of the right-wing members against the left-wing candidate.

Shukri Qwatli, who had returned a few months earlier from his exile in Egypt after the coup against him by Husni Al-Zaim in March 1949, still had many sympathizers in Syria, especially in the capital, because of his past struggles against the Ottomans and the French mandate. But his record as president in the years 1943–49 had been mixed, to say the least. The constitutional revision he had set about so as to seek a second mandate in 1948, the rumours over alleged irregularities in the 1947 legislative elections in Damascus, and accusations of patronage and favouritism had all tarnished his image. His relations with the army had remained strained since the 1948 Palestine war. But the military institution refrained from intervening. General Shawkat Shukeir, still chief of the general staff at the time, neutralized the army's role in the election. In the end, Shukri Qwatli appeared to be the only candidate who could block Khaled Al-Azzem who was supported by the leftist members of parliament.

---

[38] The terminology of the time referred to the office of President of the Republic (president) as the first presidency, the office of President of the Parliament (speaker) as the second presidency, and the office of President of the Council of Ministers (prime minister) as the third presidency. This terminology is still in use in Lebanon.

The presidential election was held in two rounds on 18 August 1955. Under article 71 of the 1950 constitution, for a candidate to be elected in the first round, he had to obtain two-thirds of the votes cast, which neither candidate managed. Shukri Qwatli had eighty-nine votes and Khaled Al-Azzem forty-three. In the second round, Shukri Qwatli secured ninety-one votes and his unhappy opponent forty-one. The new president took office on 5 September. This election is still the only transfer of power between an outgoing president and his successor who were both freely elected by legitimate assemblies.

The day after his investiture, President Qwatli called for the formation of a government of national union and appointed Said Ghazi (an independent) as prime minister. Ghazi had been much appreciated by the entire political class for the even-handed way he had led the government during the 1954 legislative elections. The Ghazi government included representatives from both parliamentary blocs, but no Ba'th minister. In outlining his general policy before the assembly, the prime minister confirmed his government's intention to commit Syria to closer ties with Egypt and Saudi Arabia to the detriment of the Iraqi-Turkish alliance of the Baghdad Pact.

Syria seemed to have recovered from the series of military coups that had punctuated its history since 1949. The 1954 legislative elections and the 1955 presidential election had both gone off without trouble. Syria had a legitimate government, and a democratically elected president and parliament. The political parties and the press enjoyed rare and precious freedom compared with other countries in the region apart from Lebanon. Syrian democracy gave the impression it had triumphed over its enemies. These years were the golden age of democracy in Syria.

But behind this deceptive appearance, Syrian society remained a society that doubted. None of the major concerns had been resolved. Domestically, the various governments had been unable to set about reducing inequalities in Syrian society or implementing the ambitious social programme described in the 1950 constitution beginning with the agrarian reform. The political class was busy recovering power from the military, but with no real determination to make a start on reforms that would affect the lives of ordinary people.

The political class concerned was only unanimous in its fight against the military. On the choice of a regional alliance, the political class was deeply divided. Should Syria side with its Iraqi neighbour or its Egyptian brother? One major reason Syrians looked to Baghdad in the late 1940s was the concern over the Israeli threat after the loss of Palestine. But now the Iraqi monarchy had decided to join a regional alliance against the

Soviet Union led by Britain, Israel's historical protector. Could Syria join its enemy's ally? Was the national question to diverge from the Palestinian question? All of these matters were to be resolved within two years in the swift and irresistible shift towards Nasser's Egypt.

4.4.4 The March Towards Union with Egypt

The regional situation, the discovery of 'plots', and the acute divergences among the general staff led the country steadily towards union with Egypt. Syria underwent some hard tests domestically during the final two years of the second period of the Second Republic (1956–58). Britain, still the dominant Western power in the Near East early in 1956, spared no effort trying to entice Syria, via its Iraqi ally, into its defence scheme against the Soviet Union, the Baghdad Pact, even at the cost of a new coup in Damascus.

Further to a series of resignations by its ministers, the Ghazi government stood down. On 14 June 1956, Sabri Al-Assali (ex-National Party) was tasked with forming a coalition government. As the condition for its participation, the Ba'th demanded that talks begin on a future union with Egypt. Al-Assali formed a left-wing cabinet. Alongside this, upon a proposal from the Syrian Communist Party, a Progressive Front was formed that included the Ba'th, the Communist Party, Khaled Al-Azzem, and left-wing members of parliament. The centre of power shifted from the council of ministers towards the Progressive Front and its supporters within the army.

On 5 August 1956, after meeting Nasser in Cairo, Sabri Al-Assali announced the formation of a three-man ministerial committee to begin talks with Egypt about union. The assembly adopted a statement of support for the government based on article 1(3) of the 1950 constitution, stipulating that the Syrian people was an integral part of the Arab Nation.

At the time of the three-sided attack on Suez by Israel, France, and the UK against Egypt on 23 November 1956, the head of military intelligence, Abdel Hamid Sarraj, announced the discovery of a plot financed by Iraq designed to overthrow the Syrian government and involving the military, members of the assembly, the People's Party, the SSNP, and supporters of former President Shishakli.[39] The

---

[39] It is unclear whether this coup was planned to coincide with the three-sided attack against Egypt. Mohamad Ma'aruf, one of the conspirators, said not. See Ma'aruf, *Days I Lived, 1949–1969*, pp. 247 ff. But Abdallah Sa'ade, future head of the SSNP, claimed the contrary. See Seale, *The Struggle for Syria*, p. 366.

announcement came as a bombshell. Those incriminated included Adnan Atassi, son of the former president, Hashim Atassi, and People's Party member of parliament, as well as the Mounir Ajlani, leader of the independent, right-wing Constitutional Bloc. Some months after the pro-Iraqi plot, intelligence announced the uncovering of a US plot. Conspiracy phobia ran through the population, which believed the country was besieged on all sides and that only the watchfulness of the army, the alliance with Egypt, and the USSR's friendship could save Syria from its enemies.

The assassination in 1955 of Colonel Adnan Malki, who was close to the Ba'th, had provided the opportunity to eliminate the SSNP from the army and prohibit it in the country. This purge of the SSNP contributed to a substantial modification of the balance of power within the officer corps, but had no repercussions on the institutions since the SSNP had little weight in the assembly and no members within the government. However, the situation was very different after the discovery of the pro-Iraqi plot involving leading political figures, members of the People's Party, or its allies within parliament and government. The People's Party had always held a relative majority in parliament, but the announcement of the conspiracy cast opprobrium on it. The left-wing coalition led by the Ba'th made the most of this to implement union with Egypt.

On 31 December 1956, Sabri Al-Assali formed a new government without the People's Party and the Constitutional Bloc (independents), who were accused of involvement in the pro-Iraqi plot. The Ba'th held on to the key ministries of foreign affairs and defence. The prime minister undertook to begin talks for a federation with Egypt. Four by-elections were held in May 1957 to replace the deputies implicated in the Iraqi plot. As a sign of the times and of the leftward shift of public opinion, the results gave three out of four seats to left-wing candidates, whereas the outgoing members had all been right-wingers (from the People's Party and Constitutional Bloc).

The Soviet Union, which so far had kept out of Near Eastern affairs, set about an unprecedented charm offensive directed at Syria on all fronts to try to tip the balance and to make the most of the freedom of action that a democratic regime offered it. The campaign was directed at the army, government, and civil society. Weapons sales to the Syrian army and officer training courses in the USSR and other eastern bloc countries were the Soviet opening move. Politically, relations improved at lightning speed with the opening of embassies, ministerial visits, bilateral agreements with the USSR, the eastern bloc countries, and China, loans on preferential terms, and major projects such as an oil refinery at Homs.

Relations between Syria and Egypt improved at breakneck speed too. In April, June, and August 1957, President Qwatli went to Cairo and reasserted his wish for union with Egypt. In October 1957, Akram Hawrani (of the Ba'th Party – Progressive Front) was elected speaker. In December 1957, the Ba'th proposed a draft agreement for federation with Egypt. The Syrian Communist Party upped the ante by calling for a full merger with Egypt rather than just a federation. This was just so the Communist Party could outdo the Ba'th and position itself as the champion of Arabism. The Communist Party did not expect Nasser would accept. When he said he was in favour, the Syrian Communist Party backpedalled so as not to end up like its Egyptian comrades. It called for a federation preserving the institutions and political life in each of the two states.

In addition to the closer political ties, relations between the two armies developed at an impressive pace. In March 1955, both countries signed a pact and decided to unite their armies. The pact was followed in October 1955 by a mutual defence treaty under which, in October 1957, the Egyptian army landed at Latakia in northern Syria to support the country with its defences against any potential Turkish attack.[40]

Infighting within the Syrian army reached an unprecedented intensity, to the point of threatening the unity of the military institution. The independent officers were grouped around General Nafuri; the Ba'thists and pro-Nasserians around Abdel Hamid Sarraj; and the Communist sympathizers around the chief of the general staff Afif Al-Bizri. On 12 January 1958 a quarrel among senior officers almost degenerated into armed confrontation. Without alerting the defence minister and Damascus government beforehand, the main Syrian military leaders went to Cairo to have Nasser arbitrate and to call for union with Egypt. On 15 January 1958, the chief of staff of the Syrian army declared from Cairo that the Egyptian and Syrian armies had merged.

With their backs to the wall, the council of ministers rushed the foreign affairs minister, Salah Bitar (co-founder of the Ba'th), to Cairo to enquire about the situation but without giving him specific instructions. Syria asked for a federation. Nasser declined. For him, Syria could not maintain its political parties and its liberal democratic parliament but had to adopt Egyptian institutions if it wished to unite with Egypt – therefore forming a union and not a federation. On 25 January 1958, the Syrian president

---

[40] See Seale, *The Struggle for Syria*, p. 398.

and government asked the foreign affairs minister to return to Cairo and argue again for a federal rather than a unitary state. Again Nasser refused.

On 1 February 1958, during a joint meeting of the Syrian and Egyptian governments in Cairo, the union of the two countries was declared. This union was not reflected in a constitution taking account of the two countries' political backgrounds, temperaments, and institutions. The Nasserist Egyptian political system was to be purely and simply extended to Syria. Experience showed that this was not a good choice.

4.5 The Social Question during the Third Phase of the Second Republic (1961–1963)

The third and final phase of the Second Republic began with the coup by a group of officers led by Lieutenant-Colonel Abdel-Karim Nehlawi who, unwittingly, broke the union between Egypt and Syria. Many, beginning with the Arab nationalists, saw this as the political parricide of Nasser, who was still at the height of his glory. The intention of the rebel officers was not to break the union but to correct certain aspects of it, especially the situation of Syrian officers, which they judged discriminatory compared with their Egyptian counterparts.

4.5.1 The Coup of 28 September 1961

During the night of 28 September 1961, several officers, almost all from Damascus, deployed armoured units around the capital. They surrounded and then occupied the army headquarters in which were General Abdel-Hakim Amer, vice-president of the United Arab Republic (UAR), commander-in-chief of the army, and top Egyptian and Syrian officers loyal to the union, including General Jamal Hafez, commander-in-chief of the first army (the Syrian army). The rebel officers began negotiations with General Amer about the conditions for assigning Egyptian officers to Syria and Syrian officers to Egypt as well as the pay and status of Syrian officers in the army of the union. The rebel officers' demands related to the army alone and none concerned the actual principle of the union. By midday, the rebels and General Amer seemed to have reached an agreement. Radio Damascus, under rebel control since the beginning of the insurrection, informed the population in communiqué no. 9 that the perpetrators, who were presented as the Supreme Arab Revolutionary Command of the Armed Forces (SARCAF), and

General Amer had reached an agreement on a series of measures to strengthen the unity of the UAR.

It seemed that things would return to normal. But after communiqué no. 9, General Amer asked the rebel officers to establish a telephone connection for him with Cairo. He spoke with Nasser, who allegedly asked him to make no concessions because the movement was to be crushed. It would seem that Nasser had been misinformed of the situation on the ground by senior Egyptian officers who had been ordered out of Damascus in the early hours and had returned to Cairo. After the conversation, General Amer refused to endorse the agreement previously concluded with the rebel officers. He was taken to the military airport at Mezze and asked to leave Syrian territory. Hours later, Egyptian commandos parachuted into the coastal city of Latakia but were quickly rounded up and sent back to Egypt. The fortunes of the UAR, which had engendered so much hope in Syria and the rest of the Arab world, were turning.

4.5.2 The Legitimization of Power

Initiated by a sectorial demand limited to the army and considered by many at the time as provisional, the coup of 28 September led, despite its perpetrators' stated intention, to the break-up of the UAR. The departure for Cairo of General Abdel-Hakim Amer accompanied by the commander-in-chief of the first army, General Jamal Hafez, left a total hierarchical and political vacuum in Syria. The rebels' immediate objective was to convince the top army officers to fill the vacuum within the military before restoring the country's constitutional and institutional framework. Their attention turned to General Abdel-Karim Zahr El-Din, whom they asked to become the new commander-in-chief of the Syrian army.[41] He accepted and for a few days was the country's de facto leader. As an administrative officer, and politically neutral, General Zahr El-Din played a moderating role during this period from the break-up of the union in September 1961 to the coup of the Ba'th in March 1963. He attempted to have civilians and the military work together to run the country and mediated among the various army factions.

---

[41] General Zahr El-Din was the fourth-highest ranking officer in the Syrian army. The other three were passed over by the rebel officers because the highest ranking, General Basil Sawaya, was a Christian and so could not hold the office of commander-in-chief, the second, General Fouad Kurbi, was considered unsuitable for command because of his weak character, and the third, Philippe Sawaya, was also a Christian. See Zahr El-Din, *My Memoirs* (Arabic), p. 60.

The challenges facing the country's new military and civilian leaders were twofold – to establish sound political institutions able to resist the ambitions of those looking to restore the union with Egypt in its earlier form and to meet the aspirations of a large section of the population and army who had supported the social measures (agrarian reform, nationalizations) implemented under the UAR. These challenges for the new regime were the major items on the agenda of the third period of the Second Republic. The national question and the social question were moving to the front of the political stage again.

Once the new army high command (including commander-in-chief and chief of the general staff) was formed, the rebel leader, Lieutenant Colonel Nehlawi, and the army commander-in-chief, General Zahr El-Din, focused on a still more difficult task, but one of which the Syrian army had gained some experience since 1949, that of legitimizing the new authority and giving the country provisional institutions designed to swiftly restore constitutional order and legitimate political institutions. The aim was to return to democratic life as it had existed before the union with Egypt in February 1958.

The task was arduous because the break-up of the union or *infissal* in Arabic divided the population and the army. Syria was being reborn after having merged body and soul for three years in the UAR. The new army command, under cover of the SARCAF, announced in a communiqué of 29 September 1961 that Ma'amun Kuzbari, former minister, speaker under the Third Republic, and interim president for a few hours at the end of the Shishakli regime in 1954, had agreed to form a transitional government to restore constitutional order. The SARCAF authorized the prime minister to resort to legislative decrees during the transitional period provided they were later submitted to the new legislative assembly when it first met. A similar procedure had followed the army coup of August 1949 that had toppled Husni Al-Zaim. The Kuzbari government was formed on 29 September 1961. It comprised thirteen ministers all on the right of the political spectrum and opposed to the union with Egypt, at least in its previous form of complete union. It was not a good omen that no left-wing minister had agreed to be part of this transitional government and showed that large sectors of the population did not support the break-up of the union.

Syria was reborn as a sovereign political entity in a ponderous fashion, even for the perpetrators of the secession with Egypt. Public opinion and the army doubted the relevance of the action. Some were apprehensive, others wanted the union restored. Syria had committed an act of parricide against Nasser whose charisma dominated the regional and Arab stage. The new leaders realized they had to explain, justify, and try to legitimize their actions if they were to have any chance of winning support of Syrian and Arab public opinion in the trial of strength with Cairo, which did not give up easily on what it still called the 'northern province'. To explain their action, legitimize the secession, and define a project for the future, the army brought together right- and left-wing politicians on 2 October 1961 in a sort of general staff of the political class. They approved the separation (*infissal*) in a joint declaration and saluted the return to Syrian sovereignty. The declaration also included a tribute to representative democracy and individual liberties. It was co-signed by political leaders from across the board: the People's Party, National Party, the Ba'th, and independents. The signatories excoriated Nasser for having denatured the union by imposing a dictatorial regime. This approach by the army was similar to the meeting organized by the military with political leaders in August 1949 after General Hennawi's coup when he handed power back to the politicians to restore the institutions and constitutional order. The military took power and gave it back to the civilians.

Arab union and socialism had been the two main themes of Nasserism. In their explanations, the new leaders had to persuade Syrian, Egyptian, and Arab public opinion that they could do better than Cairo in both domains. The failure of the union with Egypt provided them with the opportunity to draw conclusions so that the same mistakes would not be made again. Several documents drawn up by the Syrian civilian and military authorities attempted to explain the movement of 28 September and a future project for Syria. These included the declaration of support of the Syrian political class for the movement of 28 September 1961,[42] the policy statement by the Kuzbari government,[43] the joint declaration by the Syrian government and the SARCAF on the conditions of a future Arab union,[44] and the joint declaration of the Syrian government and the SARCAF on socialism.[45]

4.5.3 *The Social Compact*

Half a century later, some of those texts look remarkably modern. The declaration on the Arab union is a circumstantial text motivated by the

---

[42] Zahr El-Din, *My Memoirs* (Arabic), p. 92.
[43] *Ibid.*, p. 84.
[44] *Ibid.*, p. 88.
[45] *Ibid.*, p. 133.

great disappointment in the union with Egypt. It provided that any future union among Arab countries should be based on the principle of a decentralized confederation that respected the character of the federated states, which would maintain their own constitutional system and sovereignty.

The joint declaration of the Syrian government and the SARCAF on socialism was more substantive. It contained the new leaders' visions of economic and social questions and recommended a reformist type of socialism. This text purported to be a national compact although its content made it more of a social contract.[46] The declaration took up themes already addressed in the communiqué outlining the Kuzbari government's general policy but in more depth. It defined the characteristics of an Arab socialism adapted to Syria and its relations with democracy and with individual and public liberties. More than fifty years after it was drafted it remains very contemporary in many regards. Its themes and arguments were similar to the early writings of Michel Aflaq from before the union with Egypt. The Ba'th Party founder would probably have adhered to the ideas put forward, namely reformist socialism going along with the principles of liberal democracy, if this text had been drawn up in different circumstances.[47]

The social question had been on the agenda in Syria since the advent of the Second Republic. The need for social reforms had already been expressed in constitutional documents. The draft constitution drawn up by the Kourani committee in 1949 stipulated in its first article that 'Syria is a Parliamentary democratic Arab republic built on the principles of equality and social justice' and contained articles on social rights. The preamble to the 1950 constitution did the same and included detailed

---

[46] Khaled Al-Azzem relates in his memoirs that the political leaders were convened by the army on 29 November 1961 to adopt a national contract. The text had been drafted by right-wing politicians and there was nothing socialist about it. The Ba'th representatives (Salah Bitar, Akram Hawrani) objected. An editorial committee, which included Akram Hawrani, set about revising the initial version. Its work was completed by about 5 a.m. and largely reflected Hawrani's views on agrarian reform and the socialist legislation adopted under UAR. The final text was approved without discussion by the participants whom the army prevented from leaving until the document was completed. However, this national contract was not implemented by the future parliament elected in December 1961 or by the Ma'aruf Dawalibi government. See Al-Azzem, *Memoirs of Khaled Al-Azzem* (Arabic), vol. III, pp. 207–8; Zahr El-Din, *My Memoirs* (Arabic), pp. 143–4; Hawrani, *Memoirs of Akram Hawrani* (Arabic), pp. 2935–7.

[47] Interestingly, Salah Bitar, co-founder of the Ba'th, did not hesitate to sign the declaration of support from Syrian politicians for the officers who had led the secessionist movement of 28 September 1961.

articles setting up a vast social programme. But the state was incapable of financing and applying so ambitious a programme. The social declaration programme of the preamble was dead in the water until the advent of the union with Egypt, which decreed socialist-type measures for peasants, through agrarian reform, and for workers through nationalizations. The redistribution of land and the nationalizations were detrimental to many big land owners and the Syrian middle classes, many of whom headed for Beirut, thereby contributing via the inflow of their capital to the spectacular development of the Lebanese economy during the 1960s. These socialist measures implemented during the union had been welcomed by the rural population, which was widely represented in the army (officers and men) and by the still embryonic proletariat to be found in the country's big cities (Damascus, Aleppo). The army, through its sociological make-up, was very sensitive to the agrarian question and knew instinctively that any sudden backtracking on Nasser's agrarian reform would have repercussions within the military and beyond. The future proved the officers right, but the right-wing politicians were unaware of this.

The reformist socialism advocated by the perpetrators of the ending of the union, who were mostly on the political right, was not very far removed from the concept of the 'social market economy' developed forty-four years later by the Ba'th Party at its tenth regional congress in June 2005, which will be addressed later.[48]

4.5.4 The 1961 Provisional Constitution

Alongside the legitimization of the new authority by a flurry of political statements, the army command and council of ministers agreed on a draft provisional constitution to submit to the electorate for approval. The 1961 provisional constitution comprised eight articles.[49] Article 1 took note of the legacy of the United Arab Republic and changed the country's name from the Syrian Republic to the Syrian Arab Republic. No subsequent regime or constitution changed this name.

Article 8(b) stated that 'the President of the Republic and the Council of Ministers, shall exercise executive power in accordance with the provisions of the 1950 Constitution until publication of the new Constitution'. This procedure is reminiscent of that followed in the aftermath of the August 1949 coup. At that time, the provisional government of national

---

[48] See Chapter 8, 'Towards the Fifth Republic'.
[49] See the text of the provisional constitution in Arabic in Zahr El-Din, *My Memoirs* (Arabic), pp. 148–9.

union led by Hashim Atassi invested itself with executive and legislative powers and drafted a provisional constitution temporarily granting the head of state the powers of the president under the 1928 constitution. The 1949 provisional constitution was submitted for the approval of the constituent assembly once elected. But in this case, the draft provisional constitution of the Kuzbari government was submitted directly to the popular vote for approval by referendum.

The intention of the civilian and military rulers was therefore to resort in part to the provisions of the previous 1950 constitution for a six-month transitional period, as set by article 4 of the provisional constitution, during which the constituent assembly was to draw up the new constitution. While the intention was clearly to adopt in the short term a new constitution, the grounds for not simply restoring the previous constitution remain uncertain. The memoirs left by the main actors of the time ignore the question, despite its political and symbolic importance. This situation was similar to that of August 1949 after the fall of General Husni Al-Zaim, perpetrator of the first military coup four months earlier. At that time, the army had convened the political leaders and consulted them about how to restore the institutions and a legitimate constitutional framework. Just as in August 1949, the political and military elite in 1961 considered the previous constitution was unsuitable for the circumstances of the time and called for a new constitution. In both cases, the new leaders could simply have restored the previous constitution even if it meant changing certain articles.

The constituent assembly had a short and turbulent existence. Article 2 of the provisional constitution stated that 'a Constituent and Legislative Assembly shall be elected by the people for a period of four years'. Article 7 provided that the Assembly shall elect the President of the Republic for a period of five years with the same procedure as the 1950 Constitution. Article 4 stated that 'After adopting a new Constitution within six months period maximum, the Constituent Assembly shall change into a Legislative Assembly'. The change of the 1950 constituent assembly, after having adopted the new constitution, into a legislative assembly by a simple vote of the members had been much criticized by the opposition at the time. On the strength of this experience, the debate was settled in 1961 by the provisional constitution, which provided from the outset for the constituent assembly to become the legislative assembly once the constitution was adopted. Article 6 authorized the assembly to legislate during the period in which the constitution was being drafted as follows:

> bills shall be proposed by the Government or by at least ten members; once passed by the Assembly, the law shall be promulgated by the President of

the Republic and published in the Official Journal. The President of the Republic has the right to send a bill back to the Assembly for a second reading within ten days; if the Assembly confirms the law, it shall be promulgated by the President of the Republic.

No Syrian constituent assembly in recent political history (in 1919, 1928, 1949, nor 1953) had managed to carry out its constitutional task and then end its legislative period. The 1961 constitution fell victim to the same curse. It was the mixing of genres between constituent and legislative assembly that put paid to the 1961 assembly. It discredited itself in the eyes of public opinion and many of the military, and in particular the perpetrators of the coup of 28 September 1961, because of its legislative activity and not because of the drafting of the new constitution, which never really got off the ground.

4.5.5   The Election of the Assembly and President

The constituent assembly was elected by direct suffrage in December 1961. The elections were held on the basis of the 1957 electoral law, slightly amended by the provisional government.[50] Seven seats were reinstated for bedouins, who were supposedly close to the authorities, bringing the total to 172. As after the previous elections, the 1961 assembly included many independent members. The People's Party secured a relative majority enabling the right-wing and their independent allies to command a comfortable majority. The Muslim Brotherhood had several representatives including Issam Attar, the movement's leader. Khaled Al-Azzem, the independent member for Damascus, obtained the most votes nationally followed by Ma'aruf Dawalibi (People's Party), member for Aleppo. At the constituent assembly's first meeting, Ma'amun Kuzbari was elected speaker. This choice was not to the liking of the army, which preferred Said Ghazi, the former prime minister. On 14 December 1961, the assembly elected as president Nazem Kudsi (of the People's Party) almost unanimously. He was the only candidate after the withdrawal of Khaled Al-Azzem, who had been supported by the few leftist members of the assembly and the independents affiliated to them. The head of state appointed Ma'aruf Dawalibi (People's Party) prime minister, further angering the army. Once again the People's Party had been brought to office by the will of the people.

---

[50] The 1957 electoral law was amended by legislative decree 56 of 26 October 1961 and legislative decree 87 of 12 November 1961.

4.5.6 The National Security Council

The great failure of the political class during the *infissal* that followed the break-up of the union with Egypt was their inability to grasp the importance of the social question. This precluded the president, government, and parliament from coming to terms with the military, who, for their part, were very much alert to it despite the army being divided between supporters and opponents of the union, right- and left-wing officers, politically active and neutral officers. There was little trust between the military and the civilian authorities or within the officer corps itself. The army's distrust of politicians deepened as they were perceived as not listening to the country's social demands but merely preoccupied by their own interests. As for the politicians, they distrusted the officers whom they suspected still wanted to impose their views on the legitimate civilian institutions. And yet, despite their mutual suspicions, the *infissal* regime endeavoured to have the military and politicians work together in the context of an original institution created for the purpose, the National Security Council (NSC).

Devised by the army command a few weeks after the break-up of the union with Egypt and created by decree under the interim government led by the prime minister Ezzat Al-Nass, which lasted for thirty-two days from 20 November to 22 December 1961, the NSC was to be a framework for collaboration and reflection between the top military and civilian authorities. The NSC was chaired by the president of the republic and included the head of government, the commander-in-chief of the army, and high-ranking officers, who outnumbered the ministers by design.[51] The NSC was to decide on the major orientations of domestic and foreign policy. The idea was interesting because the great drama of the period before the union had been the lack of symbiosis between the general staff and the civilian authorities, which had been pulling in different directions. The NSC was therefore intended to bring closer together the points of view of the general staff and the government and establish a dialogue in an institutional framework between the two main actors of political life. In the view of the army command, the main political decisions were to be taken within the NSC, leaving it to the government and parliament to carry them out.[52] However, the president, prime minister, and members

---

[51] Zahr El-Din, *My Memoirs* (Arabic), p. 184.
[52] *Ibid.*, p. 152.

of the government had no time for the NSC, which they saw as a body that was imposed on the legitimate civilian authorities by the military to control the political choices of the executive and legislative authorities. They failed to make good use of the institution or to develop it so that it might serve, albeit temporarily, as a framework for the most important discussions and decisions. Besides, the draft constitution drawn up by the constituent assembly made no mention of the NSC among the institutions of the republic.

The NCS was to meet every two weeks in principle.[53] Two of those meetings were characteristic of the atmosphere that prevailed: the meeting to revise the so-called socialist measures and the meeting on the constituent assembly, which will be discussed later.

4.5.7 The Coup of 28 March 1962

Everything had been thought out and put in place to ensure the secession was a success: the provisional constitution, the constituent assembly, transitional government, amendments to the electoral law, new founding texts, and the institutional framework for civilian–military cooperation. But the pursuit of narrow interests by right-wing politicians who were unable to foresee the consequences of their actions and the unpopularity of their decisions, plus the successive destabilization campaigns by Cairo, led to the gradual collapse of the regime beginning with the coup of 28 March 1962.

The failure of the NSC experiment contributed to the fall of the *infissal* regime. One of the biggest setbacks for the institution occurred in the meeting to revise the socialist measures adopted under the union. Early in 1962, the military asked the president and head of government to move bills in the assembly to amend the socialist laws adopted under Nasser. The military wanted to see the joint declaration by the army command and the government recommending moderate socialism embodied in legislation. The president, prime minister, and ministers present were all right-wing and opposed to this. They wished simply to repeal all the socialist measures from the Nasser period. The military insisted and, in the end, the civilian authorities gave in and agreed to amend rather than repeal the socialist measures. The army delegated Colonel Nehlawi to prepare the bills with the help of an expert. Once completed, the bills were submitted to the NSC, which endorsed them. The government then

---

[53] *Ibid.*, p. 184.

submitted them for the assembly's approval. As the majority in the assembly was on the political right, instead of amending the laws it set about repealing them with the tacit consent of the government and perhaps even of President Kudsi.[54] The army felt it had been tricked by the head of state and the government was accused of duplicity. The army's response matched its disappointment. The army command demanded that the president should not promulgate the laws in question and asked him to dismiss the government, remove the parliamentary privilege of certain members of the assembly, reduce the term of the assembly by dissolving it six months after adopting the constitution, and call elections on the basis of the new electoral law.

The army's attitude to the president and government's reneging on their promises was probably disproportionate. It could have settled for asking the president for a second reading of the bills repealing the Nasserist socialist measures under the relevant provisions of the provisional constitution.[55] A second reading might have given the army time to try to bring a majority of members of the constituent assembly and the government round to its views. But application of the constitutional mechanisms was not on the agenda. They were not part of the culture of the military, nor probably of the politicians.

The president rejected the army's demands, claiming he had no intention of interfering in the duties of the assembly or violating the provisional constitution. This response failed to satisfy the military who judged the situation serious enough for constitutional legality to make way for emergency considerations based on the country's best interests.[56] Unrest grew in the army and some days later, on 28 March 1962, Colonel Nehlawi, supported mostly by Damascene officers, carried out his second coup in six months. He had the president, the prime minister, pretty much the majority of the government, and a large number of parliamentarians arrested, and he dissolved the assembly. For the second time in six months he presented the army command and the whole of the country with a *fait accompli*. The president was forced to resign. He did so in writing at army headquarters where he was taken *manu militari* before being transferred and held at Mezze military hospital.

The military communiqués announcing the coup were numbered chronologically in sequence with the communiqués of the movement

---

[54] Zahr El-Din, *My Memoirs* (Arabic), pp. 186 ff.
[55] See article 6(c) of the 1961 provisional constitution.
[56] Zahr El-Din, *My Memoirs* (Arabic), p. 186.

of 28 September 1961 that had brought about the secession and end of the union. They began therefore with communiqué number 26. Like the earlier ones, they were signed by the SARCAF, which confirmed General Zahr El-Din as commander-in-chief of the army. For the second time in six months, the general became the country's de facto leader. Unlike the army coup of 28 September 1961, Colonel Nehlawi's second coup divided the army. Some officers, mostly on the left, approved of it because they wished for amendment of the socialist measures of the Nasserist period, which parliament had purely and simply repealed instead. Pro-Nasserist nationalist officers saw it as an opportunity to restore the union. Yet others clung to a cautious neutrality.

Three days later, on 31 March 1962, army units in Homs rebelled. The insurrection was led by Colonel Badr Alassar, commander-in-chief of the central region who had been joined by units stationed in the region and many officers, mostly Ba'thists and pro-Nasserists, who had been discharged after the break-up of the union in September 1961. The insurrection was not directed against the army command nor against General Zahr El-Din, the country's leader, but against Colonel Nehlawi and the Damascene officers around him, who, it was suspected, wanted to take gradual control of the army and run the country.

Facing the possible spread of the insurrection to other units and the risk of fratricidal combat, General Zahr El-Din convened an army congress in Homs for 1 April 1962. Representatives from all units flowed into Homs. The main decisions were to have Colonel Nehlawi and his supporters in the army removed immediately from Syria; to reorganize the army command; to have the army command examine the terms on which Syria might unite with other Arab countries including Egypt; to have the perpetrators of the insurrection in Homs removed from Syria; to review the dismissal of officers after the movement of 28 September 1961; to form a non-partisan interim government without army participation; and to grant an amnesty for the perpetrators of the Homs insurrection. General Zahr El-Din accepted all the demands made by the congress participants. The officers who were to leave the country did so the next day and, an event rare enough for it to be underscored, the army elected its high command. General Zahr El-Din was confirmed as commander-in-chief.

The congress had saved the unity of the army and probably the country. But as the decisions of the Homs congress were being enforced, a second insurrection broke out on 2 April 1962 in Aleppo. This was led by Colonel Lu'ay Atassi, commander of the eastern region and Colonel Jassem Alouane, a pro-Nasserist officer who had been discharged after the ending of the union in September 1961. Colonel Alouane announced on Aleppo radio the restoration of the union with Egypt and requested logistical and military support for the rebellion from Egypt. The army command despatched a unit of armoured vehicles supported by aircraft to retake control of the northern city. Aleppo was taken back almost without a fight. Jassem Alouane fled and Lu'ay Atassi turned himself in. Like Colonels Nehlawi and Alassar, Colonel Atassi was sent on an overseas mission. The army command decreed an amnesty for all participants in the Homs and Aleppo insurrections.

4.6 The 1962 Constitution – An Emergency Constitution

The restoration of civilian political life in April 1962 after the second coup by Colonel Nehlawi followed by the two armed insurrections came about without the constituent assembly. In accordance with well-established practice since 1949, the army command convened those political leaders not in prison and asked their opinion of how best to restore legitimate political order, while asserting the army had no intention of participating in any government, in accordance with the decisions taken some days earlier by the top officers at their congress in Homs. The politicians advised the army to decline the resignation President Kudsi had handed in on the eve of the coup of 28 March 1962, which would ipso facto allow him to be returned to office. President Kudsi agreed to return provided he received written authorization signed by more than half of the constituent assembly members to exercise executive and legislative powers in conjunction with a transitional government. He also asked for more than half of the assembly members to give their resignations in writing.

The army command laid down its conditions for the release of the president and his return to office. It asked him to sign an agreement that would remain confidential containing the principles of Syrian policy for the coming period. After amending the document, President Kudsi signed together with General Zahr El-Din. The agreement contained the following points: the president would adopt a non-partisan attitude to all political parties including the People's Party;[57] Syria's willingness to establish a union with Arab states, beginning with Egypt, would be reasserted; precedence would be given to social justice, economic development, and revision of the law on agrarian reform and nationalizations; civil rights were to be observed and political and trade union associations allowed;

[57] The president was from the People's Party.

NSC decisions would be considered mandatory until such time as the new constitution could specify the powers and competences of the council; the army commander-in-chief would exercise the powers of defence minister; a draft constitution would be drawn up by a special committee appointed by the president in agreement with the government and the draft submitted for the people's approval by referendum after unrestricted public debate and approval by the NSC; a new electoral law would be adopted and free elections held.[58]

Once this agreement was signed and President Kudsi received the written resignations of more than half the members of the chamber and their authorization for him to exercise executive and legislative powers with a transitional government, he was released from the military hospital of Mezze. Beshir Al-Azzme, a centre-left politician, and former health minister during the union, formed a government by common agreement of the president and the army in April 1962, but without parliamentary approval because the assembly had been dissolved by the army the month before and more than half its members had resigned. He was appointed by presidential decree and remained in office for five months.[59] The most important decision taken by this government was to amend by decree the legislation voted by the assembly repealing the socialist measures of the time of the union with Egypt. The special committee tasked with drafting the new constitution provided for in the Kudsi–Zahr El-Din agreement never saw the light of day.

It can probably be asserted that it was during this period that the principle of social justice became by consensus one of the basic principles of the Syrian national project. The coup organized by right-wing officers in reaction to a right-wing parliament's repeal of social measures adopted under the union raised the principle of social justice to the status of a new component of the Syrian national project alongside secularism and multi-sectarian coexistence, the refusal of foreign hegemony, the refusal of any partition, and the rejection of Zionist ambitions in Palestine. Henceforth all political regimes to come were to comply with it in one way or another.

The Al-Azzme government soon ran out of steam. It had to cope with the hostile propaganda from Nasser's Egypt and the reprobation of most of the Syrian political class who claimed it had no legitimacy and was the lapdog of the military. From June 1962, some members of the dissolved assembly began meeting informally at the home of the former head of government, Khaled Al-Azzem, to discuss current affairs and how to

---

[58] See the text of the declaration in Arabic in Zahr el-Din, *My Memoirs* (Arabic), pp. 242–5.
[59] See the memoirs of Al-Azzme, *The Generation of the Defeat of Memory* (Arabic).

restore the country's constitutional life. To facilitate their return to centre stage of national political life and appease the army, most of them, at the instigation of Khaled Al-Azzem, signed a declaration announcing they had no intention of going back on the Al-Azzme government's legislative decree on socialist measures.[60] When Prime Minister Al-Azzme's resignation became imminent, a group representing the main political strands in the dissolved constituent assembly met with the head of state, Nazem Kudsi. All but Akram Hawrani, one of the Ba'th leaders, wished to restore the dissolved assembly. The head of state was not opposed to this in principle but he knew the army was fundamentally against it.

4.6.1   The Adoption of the 1962 Constitution

The president continued to maintain close ties with some of the members of the dissolved assembly with whom he met frequently. When he wanted to persuade the senior army officers to authorize the assembly to meet one last time to 'self-dissolve',[61] it was agreed that this question would be referred to the NSC. At the meeting, certain right-wing senior officers expressed opinions close to the president's and in contradiction of their commander-in-chief, who did not wish to authorize the assembly to meet once more and off parliamentary premises to 'self-dissolve'.

The president accepted the army's terms and advised the commander-in-chief that informal consultations with the members of the assembly indicated that most parliamentarians wished to see Khaled Al-Azzem form the new cabinet to replace the Al-Azzme government. Zahr el-Din objected to this appointment since Khaled Al-Azzem was not very popular among the unionist army officers because of his opposition since 1958 to the union with Egypt, preferring instead a federation. He had also ceased to be popular with the left-wing officers, after being called the 'red millionaire' in the previous decade, because he actively supported laws repealing the socialist measures of the Nasserist period during the parliamentary debate in March 1962.[62] But the army finally conceded. This in itself showed that democracy continued to operate even if it was only ticking-over with an assembly that was officially dissolved.

---

[60] Al-Azzem, *Memoirs of Khaled Al-Azzem* (Arabic), p. 254.
[61] Constitutionally the assembly could not dissolve itself. Only the president could dissolve it under article 85 of the 1950 constitution, which was taken up by the 1961 provisional constitution.
[62] Al-Azzem, *Memoirs of Khaled Al-Azzem* (Arabic), pp. 241 ff.

The president informed Khaled Al-Azzem, who drew up a list of amendments to the draft constitution already prepared by the assembly and a plan for legitimately transferring power from the outgoing cabinet to the new government. They were then submitted for the approval of the president and main parliamentary leaders:

1. The constituent assembly was to meet at the home of Khaled Al-Azzem to adopt the new constitution in one or two sessions.
2. The amendments to the initial constitutional project were: (a) the Government may exercise legislative power, contrary to Article 59 of the 1950 Constitution; (b) the president of the republic shall choose the prime minister and submit his name to the Assembly for approval. After securing a vote of confidence from the Assembly, the prime minister shall appoint the members of his Government without having to return to Parliament; (c) the Government may dissolve the Assembly and call for legislative elections within one year as from the date of dissolution without the Cabinet that dissolved the Assembly having to resign as stipulated in Article 85 of the 1950 Constitution; (d) legislative decrees in force shall remain enforceable until amended in accordance with the provisions of the constitution.
3. Once the constitution had been adopted, the president was to inform the assembly of its decision to appoint a new prime minister in the person of Khaled Al-Azzem. The parliament was to give him a vote of confidence and authorize the government to legislate for one year, after which the assembly was to be dissolved.[63]
4. In the event the position of prime minister should become vacant, the council of ministers would appoint a new head of government.

4.6.2 The Meeting of the Assembly Outside the Chamber

Once this plan had been agreed by the head of state and parliament's main political leaders, the assembly was convened at Khaled Al-Azzem's home on 11 September 1962. Most of the members participated, with just thirty-nine absentees among the 172 members. As the head of state had expressly asked that the speaker, Ma'amun Kuzbari, should not preside

---

[63] Under article 85 of the 1962 constitution, the assembly could only be dissolved eighteen months after its election. Dissolution required a decree stating the grounds from the council of ministers.

over the session, it was chaired by the deputy speaker, Rafik Bashur. The plan proposed by Khaled Al-Azzem was presented to the parliamentarians who asked for it to be submitted to a special commission. This proposal was accepted by all the deputies.[64] Before closing the first sitting, the assembly voted for the 1950 constitution to be the constitution of Syria with the constitutional amendments suggested by Khaled Al-Azzem.

A short second session was held the next day. Khaled Al-Azzem spoke to reaffirm the legitimacy of this parliamentary session held off parliamentary premises. The session was then closed to allow the special commission to study the constitutional amendments proposed the day before. On 13 September 1962, a third session was held with just fifteen absentees. The special commission presented its recommendations to the assembly. The constitutional revision was approved with the following amendments:

1. The president of the republic shall choose the prime minister and submit his name to the Assembly for approval. A vote of confidence shall take place within the next ten days. The vote of confidence of the Assembly in the person of the prime minister is valid also for the whole of his Cabinet (art. 161). The prime minister could therefore appoint the members of his government without having to go back before parliament.
2. Parliament may delegate, by a vote of the absolute majority of its members, its legislative powers to the council of ministers. For legislative decrees to be adopted by the council of ministers, it shall be presided over by the president of the republic and legislative decrees shall be adopted by a two-thirds majority of the council of ministers (art. 59). This article, warranted by the exceptional circumstances of the adoption of the 1962 constitution, was at the opposite end of the spectrum to article 59 of the 1950 constitution, which stipulated that the chamber could not relinquish its legislative powers. The commission also suggested restoring the Supreme Court of Justice that had been dissolved during the period of union with Egypt (art. 162).
3. The possibility of dissolving the current assembly with, in that event, legislative elections to be held within one year and the non-resignation of the government that performed such dissolution (art. 160). This provision was only to apply for the current assembly. The commission rejected the amendment proposing that the council of ministers should choose a new prime minister in the event of the head of government resigning. The commission suggested that should the prime

---

[64] For the list of commission members, see Al-Azzem, *Memoirs of Khaled Al-Azzem* (Arabic), vol. III, p. 299.

minister or the majority of ministers resign, the assembly would meet as of right for a vote of confidence in the new prime minister (art. 161).

All of the amendments except for that to article 59 were gathered in chapter 10 of the constitution on 'transitional provisions'. They were adopted unanimously. The assembly then ceased to be a constituent assembly and became a legislative assembly as of right (art. 159).

Khaled Al-Azzem took the floor and informed the deputies that the president, in accordance with article 11 of the constitution, had asked him expressly to form a new government. He presented his manifesto and asked for a vote of confidence from the parliament. He obtained it almost unanimously with 156 out of 157 votes from those present. Before closing the session, the former head of government Ma'aruf Dawalibi read a resignation letter from the speaker, Ma'amun Kuzbari. The deputies elected Fawzi Ghazi to succeed him as speaker. Then ten members tabled a bill granting the government legislative power for one year. The bill was passed and the session closed, thus marking the end of this extraordinary session, which was to be the last of this assembly elected in December 1961 and dissolved by the army in March 1962, but nonetheless authorized to meet to adopt a new constitution and vote its confidence in a government that was to be the last of the Second Republic.

The 1962 constitution forms an integral part of Syrian constitutional history. Despite the difficult circumstances of its birth, its filiation, whether legal or natural, with the Second Republic is beyond dispute. Held off the parliamentary premises for reasons of *force majeure*, that extraordinary session of the constituent and legislative assembly remains to this day the final session of any representative assembly of a liberal type of parliamentary regime. The parliamentary assemblies that were to follow were of a different kind, of a popular democracy type inspired by the Soviet Union and Nasser's Egypt.

4.7 The Fall of the Second Republic

The country was ungovernable and the army unmanageable. The sorry circumstances in which the 1962 constitution was adopted and the extreme flexibility of the mechanisms it provided for regulating relations between the executive and legislative powers – which were abnormal for a classical parliamentary-type regime, but dictated by the exceptional circumstances surrounding the adoption of the constitution – reflected the country's general state of decay. The Al-Azzem cabinet failed to achieve its main objective, which was to put the country back on the road to a democratic parliamentary regime. The only important decision to the government's credit was the abolition in January 1963 of the state of emergency, which had been in force since the time of the union with Egypt plus the relative return of confidence of investors because of the prime minister's reputation.

The army continued to be run through with various antagonistic political currents. Colonel Nehlawi, who had been banished from the country since April 1962, slipped discreetly back into Syria early in January 1963 with the complicity of certain officers in the intelligence services and the army. He gathered together his close allies and attempted to organize another coup, the third in fifteen months, with Damascene officers loyal to him. The attempted coup took place on 13 January. Armoured units from the garrisons in the suburbs of Damascus (Kiswe, Qatana, and Qabun) headed for the capital. They were neutralized by the defences of the headquarters which remained loyal to the army command. The coup was a lamentable failure and Colonel Nehlawi had to reconcile himself to returning to exile as a military attaché in Indonesia. All his supporters in the attempted coup were arrested. The army did not come out of the test any stronger. It had managed to counter the coup after having neutralized the two military insurrections in Homs and Aleppo the previous year. Unlike the earlier attempts, this last coup had been the work of right-wing army officers from Damascus alone. That broke the precarious balance of power within the military that had held since the break-off of the union with Egypt. The removal of the right-wing Damascene officers loyal to Nehlawi left the door open to officers from other regions with other political convictions. There were few left-wing officers (Ba'thist or Nasserist) who had not been discharged after the *infissal* and even during the time of the union in the case of the Ba'thists. But they managed to influence and convince neutral, non-politicized officers to support them to overturn the Second Republic for good on 8 March 1963.

Before turning the page on the *infissal*, it should be pointed out that in August 1962, a month before the 1962 constitution was adopted, the Al-Azzme government conducted a population census in Jazira province in controversial circumstances, stripping, according to some estimates, 120,000 Kurds of Syrian nationality. More than four decades later, it was estimated that more than 300,000 of Kurds of Syrian origin continued to suffer from the effects of that discriminatory census. A year after the 2004 Qamishly riots that left nearly sixty-five dead and 165 injured, President Bashar Assad promised a solution to the problem. But it was not until the beginning of the Syrian crisis in April 2011 that President Assad signed a decree facilitating the naturalization of Syrian Kurds and their descendants who had been deprived of Syrian nationality in 1962 and registered as 'foreigners'.

The Second Republic had a very intense political and constitutional life with two constitutions (1950 and 1962) and two provisional constitutions (1949 and 1961). It was punctuated by coups, plots, and military insurrections. The constitutions of the Second Republic finally served more to legitimize the authorities than to regulate them. They laid down a pan-Arab framework for the national question and recognized the importance of the social question, but the successive governments would not or could not make it their priority. The Second Republic came to an end at a time when it was almost totally out of steam, with a political class that was discredited in the eyes of the public, powerless institutions, and a constitution on standby. The various plots, coups, putsches, and insurrections had involved purges and discharges from the army that, in the space of fourteen years, had caused upheaval in the military and the officer corps. The army had become recalcitrant to all authority, beginning with its own.

The social question took on a dimension that it had not seen before either under the First Republic or the monarchy. Like the Palestinian question, it became an integral part of the Syrian question and a paramount feature in any national project. Despite diverging opinions on the direction the national project should take (Iraq or Egypt, reformist or Marxist-style socialism) its characteristics did not change throughout the Second Republic. They remained the same as under the monarchy and the First Republic, namely secularism and multi-sectarian coexistence, the refusal of partition, the refusal of any form of foreign tutelage, and the refusal to acknowledge Israel, to which was added the quest for social justice.

By a strange coincidence of history, the Second Republic that had begun with the People's Party's fruitless attempts to bring about a union between Syria and Iraq was to end at the hands of Ba'thists officers in Syria at a time when Iraq too had been ruled for a month by army officers affiliated to the Ba'th Party.

PART II

Presidential Constitutions and
Authoritarian Regimes

PART III

5

The Third Republic

The Third Republic is the name I shall give to the regime set up by the 1953 constitution between July 1953 and February 1954 that saw Colonel Adib Shishakli rise to high office. This regime was preceded by a military republic established by Shishakli between November 1951 and July 1953.

The Third Republic stands apart in Syria's political and institutional history. It is different in that the 1953 constitution formally establishing the Third Republic sought a presidential type of regime instead of the parliamentary regimes the country had known under the previous (1920, 1928, and 1950) constitutions. This constitution was tailor-made for the regime's strongman, Colonel Shishakli, conferring political legitimacy on him and organizing the political institutions around his person. The other thing that was different about the 1953 constitution was its short lifespan. It was officially adopted by the people by referendum on 10 July 1953 and remained in force until the end of the Shishakli regime some seven months later in February 1954. The Third Republic regime sought to endow itself with an elaborate constitutional architecture by adopting, in addition to the constitution, a new electoral law introducing single-round majority voting and a law on political parties, which was the first of its kind in Syria's history.

The 1953 constitution was preceded by a military republic that was quite close to the regime established by General Husni Al-Zaim after his March 1949 coup d'état, Except that Husni Al-Zaim's military regime lasted just 137 days whereas Shishakli's military republic lasted for almost twenty months and paved the way for the presidential-style constitution of July 1953. Furthermore, Husni Al-Zaim occupied the centre stage himself, whereas Shishakli preferred to run the country from behind the scenes, leaving the role of head of state to General Fawzi Selo for a time. This military republic was a source of inspiration for officers who were to lead future putsches in neighbouring Arab countries such as Nasser in Egypt (1952) and Qassem in Iraq (1958). In this sense, Shishakli's 1951 coup d'état in Syria and the military regime he introduced set a precedent that was imitated in Egypt and Iraq. Even the Ba'thist Syria of Presidents Hafez and Bashar Assad took up certain aspects of Shishakli's presidential regime, even if they did not openly acknowledge any line of descent.

The Third Republic instigated by Colonel Shishakli carried within it the excesses and benefits of military-type regimes. It bore the original sins of such regimes, namely a coup and the establishment of an autocratic regime; but it also had some of their advantages, namely law and order, security, and the possibility of undertaking the reforms necessary for the country that civilian governments had proved unable to accomplish. In this sense, the Shishakli regime's original sins did not prevent many Syrians, for a time, from valuing the reforms undertaken. But the honeymoon period between the regime and the people lasted just months. The regime finally failed when Shishakli's attempted to institutionalize and legitimize his power by adopting a new constitution.

5.1   Establishing the Regime

Colonel Shishakli's hegemony over Syrian political life kicked in gradually after the second military coup in the country in August 1949. This coup was carried out under the command of General Hennawi. In December 1949, Shishakli undertook a third coup, which was more of a bid for power within the army, because it removed his former mentor, General Hennawi, from command of the army, on accusations that he was favourable to a union with Iraq, while leaving the civilian and constitutional authorities in place (president, government, parliament). Having become chief of the general staff, Colonel Shishakli closely monitored the People's Party, which held a majority in the chamber, and prevented it from bringing about a union with Iraq. An open crisis broke out between the military and civilians in November 1951 after a strained two-year period of cohabitation. The proximate cause of this trial of strength was the People's Party's determination to make the gendarmerie accountable to the interior ministry instead of the defence ministry and to appoint a civilian rather than a member of the military favourable to Shishakli as defence minister. Losing the gendarmerie would have meant the army losing both control of the countryside and the potential to influence elections in rural areas. The country's central rural areas were in turmoil because of peasant mobilization and propaganda against the landowners inspired by Akram Hawrani and his Arab Socialist Party.[1] The loss of the defence

[1] Hamdan, *Akram Hawrani, A Man for History* (Arabic), pp. 108–9.

ministry meant the army could no longer rebel against civilian rule and the assembly dominated by the People's Party. The new head of government, Ma'aruf Dawalibi was determined to go down this road and made himself defence minister in addition to his prime ministerial responsibilities. Colonel Shishakli opposed Ma'aruf Dawalabi's ambitions. After three weeks of haggling, he had the head of government and certain other ministers arrested and imprisoned on the day after the composition of the cabinet was announced.

But again, Shishakli did not immediately put himself in the political spotlight. Cautiously, after the resignation of President Hashim Atassi, he formally left power and the presidency to his loyal ally General Fawzi Selo, who in addition to executive power was also invested with legislative authority. It was only in July 1953 that Shishakli set General Selo aside and took on the presidency further to a double referendum organized to approve the new constitution and, for the first time in Syria, to elect the president.

5.1.1 The Military Republic

On 29 November 1951, Colonel Shishakli, then chief of the general staff, had the national radio station read out the army communiqué informing the population that the military had just taken the country in hand. This communiqué was followed by a lengthy communication from the chief of the general staff that was highly critical of the People's Party, which was accused of selling off Syria's independence cheaply by associating it with the Hashemite crown of Iraq, a country whose sovereignty was limited because of its ties with Britain. Although the prime minister designate and part of the political class were imprisoned by the army, President Hashim Atassi tried all the same to save what he could of the democratic regime and mediated between the military and civilians to try to form a new government. But his efforts were unsuccessful. On 2 December 1951, he decided to stand down. He summoned the deputy speaker of the assembly, Said Ishak, and handed his resignation to him. Colonel Shishakli regretted President Atassi's resignation and paid tribute to him.

The Supreme Military Council published its communiqué no. 1 that same day announcing that, further to the president's resignation, the chief of the general staff, General Shishakli, would exercise the functions of head of state and assume all executive power. Later that day, the military council published decree no. 1 on the dissolution of parliament and decree no. 2 announcing that General Selo would take on legislative and executive powers including the competences of president, prime minister, and defence minister. Under the auspices of the military council, the chief of the general staff had just appointed General Selo head of state. Then the military council published decree no. 3 announcing that the permanent secretaries of the ministries would exercise the functions of their ministers until further notice.[2]

Syria was run for the first seven months of the military republic by the equivalent of a cabinet of senior civil servants under General Selo. The country had already experienced something similar between July 1919 and March 1920, before Faysal was proclaimed king by the Syrian congress, and between 1939 and 1941. The first seven months of the Shishakli–Selo era were a period of intense reform and administrative reorganization. The regime also reinforced the army through weaponry provided by France and made it more effective through a policy of recruitment, training, and education to erase the trauma of the 1948 defeat.[3]

The military republic was synonymous with moral order. For the first time in Syria, strict observance of Ramadan was imposed. Measures were taken to control donations from abroad. It was prohibited for youth associations and clubs to engage in political activity. The reforms also affected sports associations and the scouts. Strict rules were adopted to control Syrian private-sector schools and foreign schools. Special dress was required for imams and teachers of Islam. Certain political parties were dissolved in January 1952. The Muslim Brotherhood was prohibited and its offices and schools closed. Faysal al-Assali's extreme right Socialist Cooperation Party was also prohibited in January 1952.[4]

The reforms also affected the press. The written press was reorganized around four daily newspapers. It was forbidden for students, workers, and public sector workers to join political parties. Fiscal reform was based on progressive taxation. This reform sought to reduce indirect taxes on low-income households as far as possible. Authorization was granted to import foreign capital, but it was prohibited for Syrian currency to leave the country. By the same token, land ownership was reformed.[5] In addition to all of these measures, the most heated debates surrounded the agrarian reform decided in January 1952 and the prohibition of political parties in April 1952.[6]

---

[2] See Al-Mouallem, *Syria 1918–1958* (Arabic), p. 154.
[3] Seale, *The Struggle for Syria*, pp. 160–1.
[4] *Ibid.*
[5] Hamdan, *Akram Hawrani* (Arabic), p. 116.
[6] The impact of these two measures will be addressed later.

The intensity and the sheer volume of the reforms by the authorities during these first seven months (275 decrees, or an average of 1.25 per day) soon showed the limits of the council of permanent secretaries. It was therefore replaced by a council of ministers created by decree on 8 June 1952 'to assist the head of state in the exercise of his executive and legislative functions'. The following day, General Selo formed a traditional cabinet with nine portfolios.[7] On 2 August 1952, he created by decree the position of deputy prime minister, made to measure for the regime's strongman, Colonel Shishakli.

5.1.2 *The Regime's Ideological Foundations*

Colonel Shishakli's coup of November 1951 settled for a while the question of what type of Arab nationalism was best for Syria. At the time, the question was whether Syria was to unite with Iraq. Shishakli, who had joined for a time in his youth the Syrian Social Nationalist Party (SSNP), was not opposed in principle to pan-Syrianism but he was not favourable to the Fertile Crescent concept advocated by the Hashemites in Baghdad, which sought to gather first Syria and then Jordan under the Iraqi crown. This Iraqi ambition had superseded in the early 1950s the old initiative of King Abdullah of Jordan to unite Syria and Jordan under his authority to form the Greater Syria that would resemble somewhat the project for the kingdom of Syria that his brother King Faysal had attempted to create in 1920, although of course without Lebanon, which had become independent, and that part of Palestine that had become Israel. Once the risk of union with Iraq had been averted, Shishakli would have to define his conception of Arab nationalism. This was to be a sovereignist conception, respectful of the republican regime and of Syria's independence.

This conception of anti-Hashemite Arab nationalism that was opposed to the British immediately drew Syria closer to Saudi Arabia, Egypt, and France. In regional policy, Shishakli also improved Syria's relations with Lebanon and even with Jordan after consolidating his power at home. In international relations, Shishakli was in principle not against closer ties with NATO, provided they were not detrimental to Syria's sovereignty. His domestic allies, such as Akram Hawrani, were favourable to Syrian neutrality and non-participation in Western plans that were being developed for the defence of the Near East against a possible Soviet threat.

---

[7] See Seale, *The Struggle for Syria*, p. 168 for the composition of the cabinet.

The new regime took up the populist, leftist discourse in favour of workers and farmers of the Arab Socialist Party of Akram Hawrani, a childhood friend of Shishakli's. The most pressing social issue was as ever the agrarian question. The previous regime had tried timidly to settle one aspect as part of the 1950 constitution by restricting the area of future farmland holdings with no retroactive effect. This provision was never acted on and no decision taken to implement it. Decree no. 96 of 30 January 1952 adopted by the Shishakli regime sought to distribute government land to the peasantry. The objective was to distribute 5 million hectares to 50,000 peasant families and so settle 250,000 people on the land thus distributed.[8] The intention was praiseworthy but it was impossible to enforce the decree because the location and area of the land in question had not been established.[9]

Arab nationalism and concern for greater social justice, in particular for the peasantry, were the two main ideological cornerstones on which Shishakli tried to build his regime. But he failed to implement them and the ideological foundations were barely more than slogans. Interestingly, these foundations were not very far removed from the Ba'th doctrine, which, contrary to Shishakli's military regime, was to attempt to implement them quickly once in power, with varying success.

After a few months of military rule that had almost completely erased the former political order, Shishakli felt the need for an intermediary to relay public opinion and an instrument to assert and strengthen his authority within the country. In August 1952, he created the Arab Liberation Movement (ALM). Its doctrine combined militant Arab nationalism with a progressive economic and social policy. The ALM considered that the Arab nation stretched from the Taurus Mountains to the Gulf of Basra and from the Eastern Mediterranean to the Atlantic Ocean. The ALM advocated compulsory conscription, women's liberation, progressive taxation, agrarian reform, bedouin sedentarization, specialized schools for agriculture and trade, and full employment.[10] Not all the measures in the ALM programme were converted into legislation. Even so, many of them already featured in the Ba'th constitution and were taken up by Nasser shortly after.

---

[8] Hamdan, *Akram Hawrani* (Arabic), p. 116.
[9] Seale, *The Struggle for Syria*, pp. 162–3.
[10] Seale, *The Struggle for Syria*, p. 169.

The creation of the ALM marked the end of the alliance between Shishakli and Akram Hawrani, the charismatic leader of the Arab Socialist Party who had encouraged Shisakli's coup in December 1949 against General Hennawi and his November 1951 coup d'état. After his political party was banned, Hawrani turned to the Ba'ath.

The ideological foundations of the Shishakli regime were consistent with the Syrian national project since the separation from the Ottoman empire, namely coexistence among various confessions and communities, the refusal to see the Arab countries broken up, the refusal of foreign hegemony, and resistance to Israel's ambitions. All of these characteristics featured in the 1953 constitution by which Shishakli sought to legitimize and institutionalize his regime.

5.2   The 1953 Presidential-style Constitution

The constitution required by Colonel Shishakli was drawn up by government officials and subjected to a referendum in the name of the Military Council.[11] It was published on 21 June 1953. The press presented it as a modern presidential constitution along US lines. Shishakli sought to establish a presidential-style regime in Syria for the first time ever. Despite the notable differences with the 1950 constitution, the 1953 constitution took up two of the major features of its predecessor, namely the emphasis on social questions and the slow slide away from the pan-Syrianism of the previous constitutions (1920 and 1928) towards pan-Arabism.

The short preamble to the 1953 constitution asserts that the government shall ensure security, justice, freedom of the homeland as well as sovereignty and shall work beyond the borders to achieve the freedom of the Arab nation and ensure its unity and it greatness. This profession of faith in militant Arabism is remarkable in that the regime's two strong men, Shishakli and Selo, were both of Kurdish origin and Shishakli had been a militant in his youth in the SSNP for a Greater Syria.

Title I 'Basic Principles' comprises two chapters. Chapter I, entitled 'The Syrian Republic', contains provisions relating to the republic, sovereignty, the president's religion, and the official language. Chapter II, entitled 'Democratic Guarantees', comprises 'General Rights' and 'The Organization of National Wealth'.

---

[11] Asaad Kourani, a renowned jurist and former minister of justice and president of the constitutional committee that drafted the constitution for Husni Al-Zaim in June 1949, says he did not know who drafted the 1953 constitution. See Kourani, *Recollections and Remembrances* (Arabic).

Article 1 states:

(1) Syria is a sovereign democratic Arab republic.
(2) Syria is an indivisible political entity and it is prohibited to relinquish any part of its territory.
(3) The Syrian people is an integral part of the Arab nation; the state shall work to accomplish Arab unity within the framework of sovereignty and the republican system.

In explicitly asserting the republican character of the state, this last clause sought to close the debate that had stirred Syrian society, the army, and the political class over a possible union of Syria with Iraq under the Hashemite crown.

Article 2 is virtually identical to article 2 of the previous constitution and reads as follows:

(1) Sovereignty lies with the people. No individual or group can lay claim to it;
(2) sovereignty is organized on the principle of government of the people, by the people, for the people;
(3) the people exercises sovereignty in the forms and limits defined in the constitution.

Article 3 continues:

(1) The religion of the President of the Republic is Islam;
(2) Muslim jurisprudence (*fiqh*) shall be the prime source of legislation;
(3) freedom of conscience is guaranteed, the State respects all monotheistic religions and guarantees the freedom of worship provided public order is not disturbed;
(4) the personal status of the various confessions is guaranteed and sponsored by the State.

The second clause of this article takes up the reference already made in the 1950 constitution to Muslim *fiqh* as the main source of legislation. It therefore consolidates this provision that did not feature in the 1920 and 1928 constitutions.

Article 4 provided that Arabic was the official language of the state[12] and article 5 states that Damascus was to be the capital of the republic.

---

[12] A similar provision features in the 2012 constitution, which supplements this provision with a significant article 9 that for the first time recognizes cultural diversity within Syrian society and ipso facto linguistic diversity.

'The territory of the Republic is divided into mohafazats [provinces]. The law sets out their regime, number, divisions, and borders' (art. 6).

Chapter II contains 'Democratic Guarantees' including 'General Rights' and 'The Organization of National Wealth'.

5.2.1 Democratic Guarantees

Several articles deal with 'Democratic Guarantees' including article 7, which stipulates that 'the conditions for acquiring Syrian nationality shall be laid down by law'. This particularly facilitates the acquisition of nationality by Syrian émigrés, their children, and Arabs from other countries. This article reflects the Arab nationalist orientation taken by the 1953 constitution. The similar article in the 1950 constitution stipulated that 'the conditions for acquiring and losing Syrian nationality are determined by law and that émigrés, their descendants, and people from Arab countries enjoy special status' (art. 30(1)). In its 1953 version, the new article on Syrian nationality stipulates that the law must make it easier for Arabs from other countries to obtain Syrian nationality. This provision was to be taken up by all subsequent Syrian constitutions (1962, 1964, 1969, 1971, and 1973) except for that of 2012.

Article 9 set out that the state guaranteed the freedom, tranquillity, and equal chances of all citizens and article 10 guaranteed individual freedom. Article 11 continued: 'Homes are inviolable, no one may enter or search them other than in cases of flagrant offences, after authorization from the owner, or on the basis of a court order, or in the event of emergency and in accordance with the law'. Article 12 stipulated that postal, telegraphic, telephonic, and other communications were inviolable; 'They cannot be delayed, confiscated, or intercepted other than in cases provided for by law'.

Under article 13, the state also guaranteed freedom of opinion:

(1) Each Syrian may freely express his opinion, in speech, writing, pictures, or by any other means of expression;
(2) no one can be held responsible for his opinions unless they exceed the limits authorized by law;
(3) public opinion is sacred, the law protects it from those who would turn it from the truth and from public good, or who encourage dissension among the children of the homeland or who call for a change of regime by force.

This last clause did not feature in the corresponding article of the 1950 constitution.

Under article 14:

(1) The press and publishing are free within the limits laid down by law;
(2) newspapers cannot be suspended or their authorization for publication cancelled unless so provided for by law;
(3) under a state of siege, the law may introduce censorship of newspapers, publications, and broadcasts limited to matters concerning public security and national defence;
(4) the law determines the way newspaper resources are controlled;
(5) the State and the individuals in question are entitled to ask for the publication of a correction or denial in accordance with the law.

Clause 5 introduces for the first time in Syria the right of reply that did not exist in earlier constitutions.

Article 15 provided that Syrians were allowed to assemble and protest peacefully and without arms within the framework of the law and article 16(1) gave Syrians the right to create associations and join them provided that their purpose was not prohibited by law; 'the law sets out the conditions under which administrative authorities are informed of the creation of associations and the way they control their resources' (art. 16(2)). The provisions of these two articles are similar to the provisions of articles 16 and 17 of the previous constitution.

Under article 17:

(1) Syrians have the right to create political parties provided that their purposes are legitimate and their means of action peaceful and democratic;
(2) the law determines the conditions in which the administrative authorities are informed of the formation of political parties and the way they control their resources and the law also guarantees that the members elect the governing bodies at least once per year;
(3) the law considers political parties as schools tasked with the formation of a loyal and educated enlightened elite that is democratically capable of assuming public responsibility and preparing the means for a national instruction of the people that facilitates and supplements its awareness of public affairs and guides it in the pursuit of its interests.

This third clause was absent from article 18 of the 1950 constitution on political parties. It illustrates the populist and moralist vision of the 1953 constitution and the regime it ushered in.

Article 18 stated that Syrians could not be exiled from their homeland and article 19 that refugees could not be extradited because of their political opinions and their action for the defence of freedom. Education at all levels is covered in a lengthy article 21 that is similar to article 28 of the 1950 constitution: primary education is mandatory and free-of-charge in state primary schools; secondary, professional and rural education is free in state schools (art. 21(5)). The 1953 constitution therefore took up the principle of free primary and secondary education in state schools that had been established by article 28 of the 1950 constitution.

Under article 22(1), 'All citizens and their families are entitled to be cared for by the State in exceptional situations of illness, disability, old age, involuntary unemployment, and orphanage'. To achieve this objective, 'a social security system shall be established funded by the State, institutions, and individuals' (art. 22(2)). Clause 1 of this article is similar to the provisions of article 27(1) of the 1950 constitution. Clause 2, however, is an innovation of the 1953 constitution that laid down the basis for modern financing of medical and social care.

According to article 23, 'The State protects citizens' health and for this purpose builds hospitals, hospices, maternity wards, and facilitates citizens' access to care and treatment. The State also protects pregnancy, infancy, and childhood'. The same provisions were found in article 27(2) of the 1950 constitution.

Conscription was mandatory, defined by law (art. 26(1)). Under article 26(2), a National Defence Council was created, its competence and members set out by law (art. 26(2)). These provisions were already in the 1950 constitution, which also contained a description of the army's function. The previous article 30(2) stated that 'the army is the guardian of the homeland and its mission is limited to the defence of the country's borders and security'. This provision no longer features in the 1953 constitution, probably because of the primary role played by the army in the country's internal policy and the establishment of the Shishakli regime. The 1953 constitution therefore remains silent on the army's role. The legislative decree on political parties of 12 September 1953, which will be examined later, stated that it was prohibited for members of the army, police, and any other military order to join a political party.

Interestingly, the 1953 constitution contains a description of treason. Article 27 stipulates that 'treason consists exclusively in bearing arms against the homeland, rallying to the enemy, or affording the enemy help and assistance'. This provision did not feature in any earlier constitution nor was it taken up in any of those to come.

5.2.2 *The Organization of National Wealth*

Several articles deal with 'The Organization of National Wealth'. The Shishakli regime purported to be statist and directive in economic policy and its ambition was to bring about social justice and create a welfare state that was generous towards its citizens. It therefore took up and in some instances expanded on the themes of the articles in the 1950 constitution that was itself inspired by the draft constitution prepared by the Kourani committee at the request of General Husni Al-Zaim in June 1949.[13] Article 29 of the 1953 constitution states that:

(1) property, capital, and labour are the primary components of national wealth. They represent individual freedoms with a social purpose. They must be organized and directed so as to strengthen the homeland and ensure citizens of dignity, mutual support, and a decent standard of living;
(2) the components of national wealth are organized in such a way as to achieve social justice;
(3) economic life is organized in accordance with the interests of the people as a whole;
(4) the law guarantees economic freedom for each citizen within the context of the previously stated objectives.

Article 30(1) made provision for a National Wealth Council to be created 'with the mission of proposing plans and methods for the development of the agricultural, industrial, and commercial potential of the country and to provide work for all citizens'.

Article 33(1) stated that taxes are established for reasons of public utility, while article 33(2) stipulated that taxes were to be paid in cash and exceptionally in kind. Article 33 provided that: 'Taxes are set by law' (art. 33(3)); 'They are established on a progressive and fair basis so as to comply with the principles of equality and social justice while taking account of the number of people in the taxable family' (art. 33(6)). This article is more detailed than article 25 of the 1950 constitution that related to taxation. But the spirit of the two articles remains the same, namely the progressive character of taxation and social justice as the ultimate objective.

Article 34 on ownership of property is similar to article 21 of the 1950 constitution. However, it is interesting that the constituent assembly of

---

[13] See Chapter 4, 'The Second Republic'.

1953 thought it necessary to introduce in clause 3 regarding private ownership the ideas of public interest and social justice and its role in national output. The 1953 constituent assembly also introduced for the first time in Syria the idea of intellectual property, to be protected by clause 5:

(1) Property is publicly or privately owned. The State and legal entities and natural persons can acquire property within the framework of the law;

...

(3) private property is guaranteed so long as it is not prejudicial to the public interest and social justice. The law determines how property can be possessed and enjoyed so as to ensure its social function and its share in national output;
(4) no one can exploit private property in a way that is prejudicial to the public interest;
(5) the law guarantees the rights of individuals to protect their material and moral interests deriving from their material and intellectual output;
(6) expropriation for reasons of public utility is lawful and is based on law which determines the payment of fair compensation.

Title II entitled 'Sovereign Authority' comprises three chapters dealing with 'Legislative Authority', 'Executive Authority', and 'Judicial Authority'. From the outset, it is stated that 'the people exercises its sovereignty through the Assembly, the President of the Republic, and the judicial authorities' (art. 40).

5.2.3 Legislative Authority

The 1953 constitution, inspired by the US constitution, sought to introduce a presidential-style regime characterized by a strict separation between the legislative and executive in which parliament legislates and the president governs. But ultimately the 1953 regime was to establish a more nuanced regime, of a presidential type, with a more flexible separation of powers so as to give the president some legislative competence.

In line with the tradition of the previous two Syrian constitutions of 1928 and 1950, the 1953 constitution introduced a single-chamber legislative body in the form of the assembly of deputies. Article 41 states:

(1) legislative power lies with the Assembly of Deputies which is elected by direct, secret ballot by egalitarian universal suffrage in accordance with the provisions of the electoral law.

(2) Each member represents the people in its entirety; it is not possible to restrict their mandate in any way. Each member shall exercise his mandate according to what his sense of honour and experience dictate.

Article 42 goes on to say:

(1) The legislature shall last for four years as from the date of the decree proclaiming the election results; it cannot be extended except in the event of war by a law proposed by the President and adopted by the absolute majority of the deputies.
(2) The Assembly may decide to dissolve itself by an absolute majority vote of its members.

Giving the chamber power to dissolve itself is an interesting innovation that was used at the end of the Third Republic's brief life after the president resigned and went into exile in February 1954.

Under article 43, 'Voters are Syrian men and women aged eighteen years and over as of 1 January of the year in which the elections are held, listed with the civil registry, and who meet the conditions set out by the electoral law'. As for assembly candidates, 'Anyone with the right to vote, having been educated, aged at least twenty-five years, and meeting the criteria set out by the electoral law may stand in the legislative elections' (art. 44).

Like the 1928 and 1958 constitutions before it, the constitution of 1953 left it to the legislature to decide on the details of the electoral procedure. And like those earlier constitutions, that of 1953 also set out a few guidelines for the legislature to follow. The 1953 constitution provided that the law should define electoral constituency boundaries. However, article 45(1) of the constitution states that the number of members is set so there is at least one member for 50,000 inhabitants. The 1949 electoral law provided for one member for 30,000 inhabitants. Article 45 continues: 'The election consists of a single round of voting and whoever obtains the most votes is considered the winner' (art. 45(2)); 'the electoral law shall contain provisions for voting to be conducted smoothly, equal rights for candidates to supervise elections, and a sanction for the those who change the voters' intentions' (art. 45(3)). On 30 July 1953 the government published by legislative decree an electoral law to replace that of September 1949. A subsequent decree set the number of assembly members at 82 including 69 seats for Muslims, 9 for Christians, and 4 for bedouins.

Article 77 stipulated that the assembly could not hand over its legislative powers to the President. This important provision was to put an end to the situation the country had experienced from December 1951 to July 1953, when General Selo held full legislative and executive powers and he had governed the country through legislative decrees. This article of the constitution unambiguously reinstated the legislative prerogatives of parliament.

Article 50 made provision for the swearing in of new assembly members:

> Before taking office, each member shall publicly swear an oath before the Assembly in these words: I swear in the name of God and on my honour to be faithful to the country's constitution and its laws, to respect and defend them, together with the freedoms of the people, their interests, finances, dignity, and the independence of the nation and its republican regime, and to carry out my mission as member of the Assembly with honour, honesty, and loyalty, and to work to achieve the freedom of the Arab nation and bring about its unity.

Article 58 stipulated that sessions of the assembly could only be held in the presence of the absolute majority of members. Under article 66(1), the president and each member was able to propose legislation. However, article 66(2) added that financial laws 'concerning taxation, reducing it, exempting certain taxpayers from it, or laws intended to assign a part of public funds to a given project, to borrow, guarantee, or spend … may only be proposed by the President or by at least a quarter of the members'. The first clause of this article symbolizes better than any other the true character of the regime introduced by the 1953 constitution. It is a presidential-style regime similar to the dictatorial political regimes in vogue in Latin America rather than a presidential-style regime as in the USA, where the president does not share the right to introduce laws with the congress.

Article 60(3) (4) stated: 'Voting is by secret ballot. Decisions are taken by the majority attending except where so provided by the Constitution and the Assembly's rules. In the event of a hung vote, the bill is deemed to be rejected'. Article 72 stipulated: 'In the event the Assembly dismisses a bill, it can only be presented to the Assembly again from the beginning of the next ordinary session following its rejection'.

One specific feature of the 1953 constitution was to limit parliamentary immunity and introduce 'prosecution for one's beliefs'. Article 61(2) stipulates that 'a two-thirds majority of the Assembly may remove a member from office for their acts or opinions proffered in public that are contrary to the independence of the country or that seek to change the regime by force. Such an application must be presented by at least a quarter of the members of the Assembly'. This clause obviously did not feature in articles 44 and 45 of the 1950 constitution on parliamentary immunity. Its introduction was probably intended to protect the regime from attempts to rekindle the idea of a union with Iraq.

Article 73 provided: 'Any law passed by the Assembly shall be promulgated by the President within fifteen days following its despatch to the President. If the Assembly, by an absolute majority vote of its members, characterizes a law as urgent, it must be promulgated within the time indicated in the act of law'.

Article 74 gives the president a temporary right of veto by asking for a second reading by the assembly:

(1) If the President deems it necessary to reconsider a law, he may send it back to the Assembly during the period allowed for its promulgation stating the reasons for doing so.
(2) If the Assembly reconfirms the law by a two-thirds majority, the law must be enacted immediately. Members vote publicly by yes or no and their votes are published in the Official Journal.

The qualified majority required for the assembly to remove the president's veto at the second reading is two-thirds, which is more difficult to secure than that which is required to pass the law at its first reading, that is, the majority of members present. This provision merely confirms the pre-eminence of the president in the institutional mechanisms of the Third Republic. The 1928 constitution contained a similar provision, but any similarity is merely coincidence because the 1928 constitution introduced democratic parliamentary rule whereas that of 1953 served as a screen for an authoritarian regime.

Article 76 stated: 'If the President fails to promulgate a law within the time allowed under the Constitution, and does not return it to the Assembly or the Supreme Court within this time, it is published by the Speaker and becomes enforceable'.

Article 78 provided that: 'Before the end of each ordinary session, the Assembly elects a permanent commission made up of at least one quarter of the Assembly members, whose mission extends to the beginning of the next permanent session'. This original provision of the 1953 constitution led to the creation of a permanent parliamentary structure between sessions. President Shishakli was to consult some of its members and the speaker and certain ministers before resigning on 25 February 1954.[14]

---

[14] Babeel, *Twentieth-Century Syrian Journalism and Politics* (Arabic).

Under article 69, the president was to send a communication on the country's financial position to the assembly at least once a year. One of the major innovations of the 1953 constitution was the status of the Court of Auditors, described in article 71:

(1) The Court is annexed to the Assembly;
(2) Its budget is included in the overall budget of the Assembly;
(4) The members of the Court are elected by the majority of the members of the Assembly attending the first round and by a relative majority in the second round based on a list prepared by the office of the Assembly and containing twice the numbers of the members to be elected. The Assembly also elects the President of the Court for a period of four-year term of office. The Assembly may revoke a member of the Court by a majority of its members.
(5) The Court of Auditors verifies the State's accounts.

Article 75 of the 1953 constitution put in place a system of control for the constitutional character of laws:

(1) In the event the constitutionality of a law before its publication is challenged by a quarter of the members of the Assembly or by a quarter of the members of its Permanent Commission or in the event it is referred by the President to the Supreme Court as unconstitutional, its publication is suspended until the Supreme Court has ruled on it.
(2) If the Supreme Court rules the law is unconstitutional then it is referred back to the Assembly or the Permanent Commission for the constitutional inconsistency to be corrected.
(3) If the Supreme Court gives no ruling on the law within ten days or within five days for an urgent law, the President shall promulgate the law.
(4) If the Supreme Court rules the law is constitutional, it is considered to have been promulgated from the end of the time allowed for its promulgation.

5.2.4 *The Executive*

Chapter II concerns the executive authority. The executive is the president of the republic alone. The ministers are just collaborators answerable to the president alone.

The President of the Republic

The big new feature with the 1953 constitution was the preponderant role of the president, elected by the people by universal suffrage. In the earlier parliamentary constitutions (1928 and 1950), the president was elected by the chamber and had a secondary role compared with the prime minister. This effacement of the head of state and prominence of a prime minister who was constantly at the mercy of parliament and other pressure groups such as the army led to governmental instability. By strengthening the presidency, the 1953 constitution sought to make up for the shortcomings of the previous regimes and establish a strong executive to counterbalance the legislature.

Article 81(1) stated that 'the President is elected by the people by direct and equal, secret, universal suffrage'. Clause (3) added: 'The candidate obtaining most votes is elected'.

Article 82 set out the criteria for would-be presidents: 'Candidates for the Presidency must fulfil certain conditions: (a) be Syrian by birth, (b) meet the conditions for being a member of the Assembly, and (c) be forty years of age' (art. 82(1)); 'Women are ineligible for the Presidency' (art. 82(2)). This last provision is a regression on the earlier republican constitution of 1950, which in striving to be modern had introduced equality for all citizens and granted votes to women.

Under article 83, the term of office of the president was five years. There was no prohibition on the president seeking a second term, contrary to the provisions of the 1950 constitution. The 1953 constitution therefore aimed to not only restore the provision introduced by the 1948 revision of the 1928 constitution giving the president the opportunity to stand a second time but to broaden it even more.

'Before taking office, the President swears an oath before Parliament in the same words as the members of the Assembly', stated article 78. This article reasserts the republican character of the state and prevents any future attempt at union with Iraq.

Article 79 required the President to exercise executive power in the name of the people within the framework defined by the Constitution. As stated in article 91, 'He is the commander-in-chief of the army and presides over the National Defence Council'.

Other activities feature among the president's competences, as set out in article 92:

(a) the inauguration of Parliamentary sessions by communiqués in which he explains the internal and external situation of the country and the problems facing it, and the plans for solving them;
(b) contact with the Assembly by written communication to the Speaker and that shall be read out at the first session after they are received;

(c) the appointment of public functionaries requiring a decree;
(d) the appointment of ambassadors and plenipotentiary ministers to foreign heads of state;
(e) the declaration of war after consulting the National Defence Council and securing the agreement of the Assembly;
(f) the adoption of necessary measures for defence after consultation of the National Defence Council;
(g) the conclusion of peace after consultation of the National Defence Council and approval of the Assembly;
(h) declaration of the state of emergency after agreement of the Assembly. The President is entitled, in the case of necessity, to declare the state of emergency for a period not exceeding one month provided the Assembly is informed immediately. Only the Assembly may extend the state of emergency;
(i) the President may decree general or partial mobilization;
(j) and grant individual amnesties.

Article 86 required the President to present his resignation in a message to the people and published by the Speaker. This provision was applied when President Shishakli resigned in February 1954.

In certain cases provided for by the constitution, the speaker exercised the functions of a vice president whose office was not provided for by the institutions. In this way, as detailed in article 89(1):

> the Speaker exercises the responsibilities of interim President in the following situations:
> (a) at the request of the President in the event of illness or temporary absence from the country;
> (b) in the event he is to appear before the Supreme Court,
> (c) if it is impossible for the President to perform his duties because of impeachments recognized by a decision stating its grounds taken by a two-thirds majority of the members of the Assembly.

Article 89(2) adds:

> The Speaker also acts as interim President if the impeachments mentioned in clause (c) prove permanent by a decision of the Assembly or if the President is dismissed by the Supreme Court, or in the event of death or resignation. In such cases, the Speaker acting as vice president calls for the election of a new President. An election must be held within two months of the date the office of President becomes vacant for any of the reasons above.

Clause (3) of the same article specified that the speaker must leave the office of speaker to the deputy speaker for the whole time during which he acts as interim president.

According to article 87, the President is not responsible politically. He is responsible in the event of violation of the Constitution, high treason, and for ordinary crimes.

The 1953 constitution contained a special procedure in article 88 for investigating the president that was very similar to the procedure provided under the 1950 constitution.

The Government

Article 94 provided: 'The President has resort to Ministers of State to exercise his executive powers' (art. 94(1)). 'He appoints them, dismisses them, and accepts their resignation by decree and informs the assembly thereof' (art. 94(2)).

Under article 95(3), 'It is not authorized to be a Minister and a member of the Assembly. A Minister cannot stand in legislative elections until having resigned from his position for a period laid down by law'.

Article 97 added:

(1) Each Minister signs the organizational decrees and decrees from the President relating to matters within his area of competence.
(2) Each Minister is accountable to the President for his acts within his Ministry. The Minister is not allowed to dissociate himself from the President by taking decisions within the framework of his Ministry relating to the general policy of the State.
(3) Ministers send reports to the President on the situation within their Ministry.

Finally, article 128 stated: 'The Constitution proclaimed on 25 September 1950 is considered to be annulled as of 29 November 1951 and all measures taken by the authorities since that date are considered sovereign acts'. This provision concerned all the measures taken by the regime from 29 November 1951 to 11 July 1953, a period of nearly twenty months.

5.3 The End of the Regime

Commentators remain divided over this constitution. Some claim it is of little value as it was authoritarian in inspiration and commissioned by the military council, but for others it is a remarkable constitution[15] and could have lasted a hundred years had it been applied in a democratic context.[16]

5.3.1 The Constitutional and Presidential Referendum

Paradoxically it was Shishakli's attempt to legitimize and institutionalize his regime that precipitated his fall. Political opposition to the regime had become organized towards the end of 1952. In December 1952, upon returning from Cairo where he had been for talks with General Neguib, the leader of the free officers who had overthrown the monarchy in July, Shishakli was met at Damascus airport by a young officer, Adnan Maliki, who presented him with four requests in the name of a group of officers and politicians: the restoration of public freedoms, authorization of political parties, dissolution of the ALM, and an end to the collection of private funds for the army's weaponry on the pretext that the sums collected from the public went in fact into the ALM coffers. Shishakli considered this to be an attempted coup.[17] He had the officers and politicians associated with this move arrested.

Having lost all hope in Shishakli, Akram Hawrani began negotiations for the merger of his political formation, the Arab Socialist Party, with the Arab Ba'th Party. Both shared similar agendas, a similar social base, complementary geographical areas of support, and a common ambition to end the army regime. Talks between the leaders led to the two parties merging in November 1952 on the basis of the rules of the Ba'th which added 'socialist' to its name to become the Arab Socialist Ba'th Party. In early 1953, the Ba'th leaders Aflaq, Bitar, and Hawrani fled to Lebanon.

Shishakli's officer arrests alienated part of the army and, of course, the opposition. But having shown his strength, Shishakli was determined to put himself across as more tolerant and even a little liberal out of concern to legitimize his hold on power by adopting a new constitution and through his election as president. Shisakli therefore showed himself to be more conciliatory with the opposition to his regime. The opposition rushed into this narrow opening left by the regime and decided to mobilize all its forces to prevent Shishakli from legitimizing his rule. To do this it rallied around the former president, Hashim Atassi. His home in

---

[15] Professor Edmond Rabbath of Beirut university cited in Kourani, *Recollections and Remembrances* (Arabic), p. 243.
[16] Torrey, *Syrian Politics and the Military*, p. 224.
[17] See Seale, *The Struggle for Syria*, p. 171.

Homs became the headquarters of Shishakli opposition. In June 1953, after Shishakli had stated he intended to submit a new constitution to a referendum and stand for election as president, the leaders of the three main opposition parties, the People's Party, the National Party, and the Ba'th, together with independent figures signed a communiqué endorsed by Hashim Atassi and addressed to Shishakli contesting the legitimacy of the referendum on the constitution and the presidency. The communiqué was published in the Lebanese press. Shishakli ignored it and went ahead with his plans, but he did not interfere with the signatories.

On 10 July 1953 the constitution was approved and Shishakli, the sole candidate, was elected president by referendum with a huge majority (99.7 per cent) with an official turnout of 86 per cent. Five days later, Shishakli formed his first government made up of figures chosen from outside the political inner circle.[18]

5.3.2 The Electoral Law

The government published a new electoral law on 30 July 1953[19] and on 12 September it set the date for parliamentary elections as 9 October. On 14 September, Shishakli lifted the ban on political parties except for subversive parties such as the Communist Party.[20]

The legislative decree of 12 September 1953 was the first legislative text on political parties in the history of modern Syria. It covered associations and political parties and contained certain provisions common to both. The legislative decree authorized Syrians to form and join political parties provided their goals were lawful, their means of action peaceful, and their by-laws democratic. The legitimacy of the purposes of political parties was laid down by legislative decree. Bans were imposed on parties whose aims infringed public order and morality, those that aimed to divide the sons of the nation or that sought sectarian division, those that infringed the state's internal or external security, those that aspired to modify the political, economic, or social form of the country by force or through terrorism, those that sought to deprive citizens of their fundamental rights and their individual freedoms as defined in the constitution,

---

[18] See the list in Seale, *The Struggle for Syria*, p. 174.
[19] See the text of the electoral law in the Official Journal of the Syrian Republic, year 1953, number 43, pp. 3841–50.
[20] Statutory decree of 12 September 1953 published in the Official Journal of the Syrian Republic, year 1953, number 54, pp. 4375–82.

and those that omitted to state their purposes. Also banned were parties with paramilitary structures and secret parties. Financial revenues were strictly controlled. All these provisions were common to associations and political parties. For parties, the legislative decree went even further by prohibiting those whose purposes were contrary to the will of the Arab nation to free itself from foreign domination and unite, or had an ethnic or sectarian orientation. Political parties whose membership was based on religious or ethnic affiliation were not considered democratic. This legislative decree led to the prohibition of parties receiving financial aid from abroad, parties that opposed Arab nationalism, religious parties, the Communist Party, and parties with a military branch.

After setting out the legitimate purposes of political parties, the legislative decree defined what it meant by parties' 'democratic status'. The rules and regulations of a party could not be considered lawful unless they provided for the election of its leaders, and if they expressly or implicitly restricted its membership to a group, sectarian origin, or persons from a given region. The military could not join any political party. Officials could not engage in any political activity while in office. Political activities were prohibited for students in places of teaching.

A statement that a political party was formed had to be filed with the interior ministry. Foreigners had no right to form or to join political parties in Syria. Internal elections to the party were to be by secret ballot at least once a year. The party's general meeting had to be held at least once a year. The rules and regulations of each party had to determine the way its members were selected for legislative elections.

5.3.3 *The Legislative Elections*

Elections were held in accordance with the provisions of the new electoral law. This law set out the arrangement for the general or parliamentary elections and the presidential election by popular referendum. The law accorded great importance to the preparation of electoral rolls. The basic constituency was the *caza*. Each *caza* of more than 25,000 inhabitants formed an electoral constituency. The main town of each *mohafazat* and the areas attached to it (village, *nahie*) also formed a constituency. This electoral law authorized women to stand, and maintained minority and bedouin representations. For the first time, the law provided for a 'first past the post' system that was to become the rule in Syria after a brief return to two-round majority voting in the 1954 elections.

The elections were greeted with almost general indifference by the population and were boycotted by the People's Party, the National Party, and the Ba'th. Only three political formations decided to participate, the ALM, the SSNP, and Faysal al-Assali's Socialist Cooperative Party. The elections gave overwheming victory to the ALM candidates (with sixty seats) and just one seat for the SSNP. The assembly members met for the first time on 24 October 1952 and elected Ma'amun Kouzbari as speaker.

Five days after the government had announced legislative elections for 9 October and three days after the lifting of the ban on political parties, the main opposition to Shishakli held a meeting in Homs on 17 September 1953 chaired by Hashim Atassi. The participants published a convention condemning the Shishakli regime, calling for the restoration of democratic, parliamentary, constitutional life, the restoration of public freedoms, and decided to boycott the future legislative elections.[21] Aflaq, Bitar, and Hawrani, the three historical leaders of the Ba'th, returned to Syria in October under a general amnesty decreed by Shishakli after he was elected president. The political class was determined to continue with its opposition to the regime. Three main centres of opposition defied the regime: the Druze mountain, the fiefdom of the charismatic Druze leader Sultan Atrash, hero of the struggle for independence in Syria and the Great Revolt against the French mandate in 1925–26; Homs, the home city of the former president Hashim Atassi who gathered around him all the opponents to the Shishakli regime; and the city of Aleppo, the great northern metropolis, the economic capital of Syria and fiefdom of the People's Party, which favoured union with Iraq.

5.3.4 The Regime Crisis

In December 1953 disorder broke out in Aleppo. It was violently quelled by the security forces. On 27 and 28 January 1954, the army attacked the Jebel El-Arab, the Druze mountain, on the basis of reports that Sultan Atrash was preparing to trigger an insurrection that would spread throughout the country. The army did not spare Al-Qariye, Sultan Atrash's village. Atrash fled to neighbouring Jordan, where he was granted asylum. His son Mansur and a close relative Hassan Atrash were imprisoned in Damascus, heightening tensions in the Druze region.[22] The country was

---

[21] See the text and the list of signatories in Atassi, *Hashim Atassi, His Life – His Times* (Arabic).
[22] See the memoirs of Atrash, *The Cursed Generation* (Arabic), pp. 169 ff.

slipping into an infernal cycle of protest and repression. Demonstrations multiplied. The army imprisoned several prominent political figures from all sides (People's Party, National Party, and Ba'th) in Damascus. Hashim Atassi was placed under house arrest in Homs. Shishakli declared a state of emergency. Seeing how the situation in the country was deteriorating, Hashim Atassi called for the Arab League to intervene.[23]

The situation stabilized around 31 January and some observers believed the worst was over. The Shishakli regime found support and sympathy in Egypt, Saudi Arabia, and France whereas Iraq and Jordan, and behind them Great Britain, leant rather towards the opposition. But in the final days of February, discontent spread through the army. On 25 February 1954 Commander Mustafa Hamdun read out over Aleppo radio a communiqué signed by Colonel Faysal Atassi, commander of the northern region (Aleppo), calling for Shishakli to resign the presidency.[24] The communiqué contained an ultimatum to Shishakli to leave the country before nine o'clock that night. He also invited the commanders of other regions to rally to these demands. During the day, the commands of the east (Deir Ezzor, Qamishli), west (Latakia), and centre (Homs, Hama) joined the movement.[25] All commentators agree that Shishakli could have resisted because he still had large numbers of loyal troops in the region around Damascus and the south. But, to his credit, he preferred to avoid a bloodbath and fratricidal fighting. Shishakli summoned a few ministers and some members of the permanent parliamentary commission and presented his resignation to the people through the intermediary of the speaker under article 86 of the constitution. He left Syria for Lebanon. The speaker, Ma'amun Kuzarbi, declared himself interim president under article 89(2) of the constitution and left his position in the parliament to his deputy.

Shishakli's hurried departure left a vacuum both at the head of the state and in the army. Some officers close to the outgoing president, disappointed at the turn of events, arrested the chief of the general staff, General Shawkat Shukeir, for a while before releasing him. He released the politicians imprisoned by Shishakli in December and January. The Damascus crowd invaded parliament and left no chance to the assembly,

---

[23] See Seale, *The Struggle for Syria*, p. 184.
[24] Atassi, *Hashim Atassi* (Arabic) pp. 367–8. Some claim the communiqué was drafted by Abdel Fatah Al-Zalt, a close supporter of Akram Hawrani. See Hamdan, *Akram Hawrani* (Arabic), p. 135.
[25] Seale, *The Struggle for Syria*, pp. 190–1.

elected under Shishakli and considered illegitimate by the opposition, to try to organize a transition under the constitutional provisions. The commanders of the military regions sent an ultimatum for the interim president to resign. He complied. His time in office lasted a little over twenty-four hours. Meanwhile the political leaders had met at President Hashim Atassi's home in Homs, which had become the de facto capital of the Syrian revolution. Several proposals were made by the participants to fill the institutional vacuum including convening a constituent assembly to draft a new constitution. Finally, a consensus formed on the need to return to the 1950 constitution, to restore the parliament elected that year for the remainder of its legislature, and to restore President Hashim Atassi to office for the remainder of his term.[26]

On 1 March 1954, a triumphant Hashim Atassi returned to Damascus, escorted from Homs by an impressive convoy of more than 400 vehicles. He resumed the functions he had relinquished on 2 December 1951. Although he was by then eighty-one years old, he stood up to Shishakli and managed to rally the opposition around him until the fall of the regime. He formally accepted the resignation of Ma'aruf Dawalibi, the prime minister he had appointed in November 1951, the composition of whose cabinet had led to the Shishakli coup on 29 November 1951. He asked Sabri Al-Assali (from the National Party) to form a new government and made it his priority to hold legislative elections in August 1954 and the next presidential election the following year. All analysts agree that those parliamentary elections were and remain to this day the freest elections in Syrian history. In 1955 he succeeded in his second task of leaving his position as head of the state to a democratically elected president. To date, it is the only democratic transition between two freely elected presidents that Syria has witnessed.

Hashim Atassi dominated his era like no other politician of his generation. He was at the forefront of Syrian history for thirty-six years from 1919 to 1955, dying in his home city of Homs in 1960.[27] He was the first president of the Syrian Congress, which drafted the Damascus

---

[26] For the discussions among the main three political parties (People's Party, National Party, and Ba'th), see the description by Adnan Atassi cited in Atassi, *Hashim Atassi* (Arabic), pp. 369 ff.

[27] The other three major political figures of the democratic and liberal period in Syria were Shukri Qwatli, who was twice elected president and held national political posts at various times between 1936 and 1958; Kahled Al-Azzem, former prime minister, who held national positions several times between 1941 and 1963; and Jamil Mardam, former prime minister, who held several national positions between 1936 and 1949.

Programme, the main founding texts of modern Syria, plus the Declaration of Independence and the proclamation of Faysal, King of Syria. He became Faysal's prime minister and led the Syrian government that decided to resist the entry of French troops into Syria at Maysalun. He presided over the 1928 constituent assembly, the first freely elected assembly under the French mandate. He presided over the National Bloc and headed the struggle for independence including the Great Strike of 1935–36. He negotiated with the France of Léon Blum and signed the 1936 agreement that was to lead to Syrian independence. He was twice elected president (1936 and 1950). Twice he restored democratic government after army coups (1949 and 1954). As speaker, prime minister or head of state he oversaw the drafting of three liberal Syrian constitutions (1920, 1928, and 1950). As such he remains the father of Syrian constitutions and the father of Syrian democracy.

As for the army, it returned to barracks for a while. But some of the new generation of young officers who played an important part during the Shishakli era rapidly returned to the forefront of politics. The Shishakli experience had shown that the military could not only seize power but could also govern the country for a time. It was all about enduring. The young Ba'th officers who joined the military academy in the early 1950s remembered this when they in turn seized power in 1963, not to relinquish it thereafter.

6

The Fourth Republic

I shall call the regimes established by the Ba'th Party from 1963 onwards the Fourth Republic. Certain differences notwithstanding, these regimes shared the same origins, the same ideology, and the same aspirations. The regimes were institutionalized by three provisional constitutions (1964, 1969, and 1971), one constitutional arrangement (1966), and one permanent constitution (1973).[1]

The year 1963 resembled the year 1949 in Syria's history. In many respects, the two dates marked radical breaks in the country's political history. The year 1949 saw the fall of the First Republic and the lasting incursion of the military into politics; 1963 saw the fall of the Second Republic and the equally long-lasting accession to power of the Ba'th Party.

The country's new masters aimed to change the established order and to stay in power. In order to endure, the Ba'th regimes had to overcome the challenges that had brought down the previous regimes. As the same causes produce the same effects, the new leaders knew instinctively that unless they were careful, they in turn risked having to confront the same coalitions of interests and the same national, regional, and international dynamics that had put paid to the earlier regimes.

Holding on to power seemed impossible a priori. Few specialists would have wagered at the time that the Ba'th rule initiated by the coup d'état of 8 March 1963 would still be in place half a century later. But the new leaders trusted in their destiny because, in addition to armed force, they brought with them an ideology that was fashionable and that was to attract many Syrians. 'All power to the Ba'th' as advocated by Syria's new leaders meant for them not just the full application of Ba'th policy but, above all, power to the Ba'thists alone.

---

[1] This chapter covers the period from the seizure of power by the Ba'th in 1963 until the death of Hafez Assad. The presidency of Bashar Assad will be addressed in Chapter 8, 'Towards the Fifth Republic'.

In March 1963, the Ba'th doctrine as a system of government and programme for radical transformation of society and the economy did not exist. Admittedly, since it was first formed in 1947, the Ba'th had developed abundant political literature, mostly from the pen of its co-founder, Michel Aflaq, and had taken a stance on the main issues stirring Syrian society and the Arab nation. The Ba'th had also proved its worth in the exercise of power by participating in the various governments that had paved the way for the union with Egypt. But in March 1963, the Ba'th was still, by its own party rules and regulations, a reformist socialist type of political party that respected the principles of traditional liberal parliamentary democracy. The Ba'th was not yet proficient in popular democracy.

Although by March 1963 the Ba'th had not developed a programme of government and even less a programme of radical transformation of Syrian society, six months later they had. Upon seizing power, the Ba'th imposed a frantic pace of nationalizations and agrarian reform. It borrowed from Marxist–Leninist ideology the concepts required to justify the new order, such as class struggle, even though it was alien to its own political philosophy. It borrowed the constitutional garb of Soviet bloc regimes to legitimize authoritarian rule in Syria, which had officially become a 'popular democracy'. It restructured its internal organization along the lines of Marxist–Leninist parties and adopted 'democratic centralism' to regulate the party's internal life.

But old demons are not easy to be rid of and the chronic challenges that Syrian political life had experienced before 8 March 1963 soon reappeared, prominent among which was the uneasy cohabitation of the military and civilians, even within one and the same party. Ba'thist officers, grouped as the Ba'th Military Committee, a hermetic and opaque body outside the party body, had no intention of handing power to their civilian comrades. They managed to rally to them the young generation of party members united around the Ba'th Regional Command. The party's founders and the old guard came together within both the party's pan-Arab National Command, and the country's governing body, the National Council of the Revolutionary Command. As Syria remained a trump card for anyone wanting to influence events in the Near East, the traditional rivalry between civilians and the military was compounded by rivalries within the military. These often reflected personal differences and sectarian bonds, but sometimes also political choices and strategic domestic or regional alliances.

One of the particularities of the coup d'état of 8 March 1963 was that, for the first time in the country's history, it established a collegiate governance that lasted seven years. This collegiality was the reflection of existing practice within the Ba'th leadership, namely the National Command – the supreme body capping all the party's structures in the various Arab countries and the party organizations elsewhere in the world – and the Regional Command – the organization tasked with leading the party in Syria. During the first phase of the Revolution from 1963 to 1966, this collegiality was written into the 1964 provisional constitution. The collegiate leadership was to take on a new form during the period of radicalization of the Revolution from 1966 to 1970 but without disappearing. It was finally abandoned after the 'Corrective Movement' that brought Hafez Assad to power in 1970. The collegiate leadership of the state and party soon gave way to the personalization of power.

One of the reasons for the symbiosis of a part of the Syrian population with the Ba'th was that the party made the main features of the Syrian national project its own. The main tenets of the project had initially been developed by the Founding Fathers when the Arab provinces separated from the Ottoman empire in 1918. They had been taken up by the following generations that had fought for the end of the mandate and then led Syria since its independence. Its features formed the cornerstone of any Syrian policy and the Ba'th with its pan-Arab, secular, and socialist ideology comfortably fitted the mould. Ever since it was first formed, the Ba'th had advocated inter-sectarian coexistence and secularism, rejecting the break-up of Arab lands, foreign hegemony, and the Zionist project. These four main characteristics of the Syrian national project had been compounded by a fifth in the early 1960s, the principle of social justice. The Ba'th had largely contributed to propagating this principle and was quick to act on it upon coming to power, even if it imparted to social justice a Marxist orientation that it had not initially had.

The new rulers established an informal social compact with the population: in exchange for handing over political power to the Ba'th, the party ensured the redistribution of wealth through a programme of agrarian reform and nationalizations. In addition, citizens would have free education and medical care; subsidies for basic commodities; various material benefits for the military and government workers; and unemployment would be slashed thanks to an overblown civil service and public sector. The party left domestic trade to the urban bourgeoisie and gradually opened up other sectors to private initiatives. The prime instrument for implementing this social compact was state control of the economy through public-sector hegemony and a very tight rein on civil society.

6.1 The Revolution of 8 March 1963 and the Coming to Power of the Ba'th

Syria had experienced numerous coups since its independence in 1946. They fall into two main categories. The first comprises the coups by which the army meant to divert civilian rule for its own gain and govern the country (March 1949, 1951). The second category includes the coups by which the army meant to hand power back to the civilian authorities (August 1949, 1954, and 1961). The coup d'état of 8 March 1963 definitely belongs to the first category. The army, under the cover of the Ba'th Party, seized power and had no intention of relinquishing it.

The coup of 8 March 1963 was led by officers (Ba'thists, Nasserists, Unionists, and independents) in favour of re-establishing the union with Egypt. There were several reasons for them making their move. First, the majority of the population had remained favourable to the union with Egypt even though many, beginning with the Ba'thists themselves, agreed that the unitary experience of 1958 to 1961 had been marred by errors not to be repeated in the future. But Nasser continued to enthuse crowds and no leader in Syria or elsewhere in the Arab world was nearly so charismatic or popular. Second, the attempt in 1962 by the government of Ma'aruf Dawalibi, supported by a right-wing parliament and president, to backtrack on the social measures (agrarian reform and nationalizations) adopted under the union had deprived the regime that arose from the *infissal* (separation) of the support of large sections of Syrian society (including farmers, workers, and the military from rural areas). Third, the regime had lost its democratic legitimacy since the coup by Colonel Nehlawi in March 1962, which had dissolved the parliament elected four months earlier. The forcible eviction of the assembly from political life plainly reflected the deep crisis besetting a political regime in its final throes. Fourth, independent officers nurtured personal ambitions, feeling that power was within reach of their bayonets, or more accurately their tank tracks.

With less than a thousand men and a few armoured vehicles, General Ziad Hariri, the perpetrator of the coup and commander of the Syrian–Israeli front, marched on Damascus and seized control of the still-sleeping capital on 8 March 1963. No force stood in his way. The insurgents, although few in number, had ensured control of all the garrisons and checkpoints around the capital and secured the support of the key officers on the general staff in Damascus such as the deputy head of the general staff, the head of military intelligence, and the officer in charge of the defence of the headquarters building. The officers who took part in the coup of 8 March 1963 belonged to four, ideologically close, political strands. The Ba'th was represented by Captain Salim Hatum. The army had very few Ba'thist officers at the time. They had been steamrollered by Nasser during the period of the union and by the separatist *infissal* regime that had succeeded him. Upon seizing Damascus, Captain Hatum broadcast a radio appeal for the dismissed Ba'thist officers to re-enlist in accordance with a carefully prepared plan. Ba'thist officers were quickly assigned to sensitive postings. The army also counted very few Nasserist officers. They had been systematically ousted after the break-up of the union in 1961 and the insurrection of the Aleppo units in April 1962. At the time of the 1963 coup, the Nasserists were represented by General Rachid Quaitani, the head of military intelligence, who had been appointed to that sensitive position just a week earlier. Some junior officers belonged to the Socialist Unionist Movement, a spin-off from the Ba'th, and others to the Arab Nationalist Movement.

The largest group of officers involved in the coup of 8 March 1963 was made up of independent, politically neutral officers, although leaning to the left and in favour, in principle, of restoring the union with Egypt. These officers were for the most part driven by personal considerations of furthering their careers. They were grouped around General Ziad Hariri, the highest-ranking among the perpetrators of the coup.

6.1.1 *The Founding of the Regime*

The first period (1963–64) of the Fourth Republic was characterized by the juxtaposition of parallel, often rival, institutions making it impossible to tell at a glance where power really lay and what the decision-making mechanisms were. Having been used to operating clandestinely, at least during the union with Egypt, the Ba'thists took time to reveal and to institutionalize their power.

The National Council of the Revolutionary Command

The supreme ruling body, the National Council of the Revolutionary Command (NCRC),[2] formed on 8 March 1963, initially brought together

---

[2] The name was inspired by the Ba'thists in Baghdad in the Iraqi coup of 8 February 1963.

ten officers representing the various currents that had participated in the coup. The NCRC was chaired by General Lu'ay Atassi, an independent officer won over to the cause of the union with Egypt and appointed by the putschists as president of the NCRC. The composition of this ruling body was not made public. Its members' names transpired only gradually. When tripartite discussions began in Cairo, Nasser insisted on knowing the names of the NCRC members.[3] The Ba'th had two members on the Council, Salah Jadid and Mohammad Umran. The NCRC was extended to new members in the course of March 1963 including the leaders of the Ba'th National and Regional Commands as well as Socialist Unionists. The NCRC gave itself a presidential council and continued to run the country until September 1965, when it was superseded by a National Revolutionary Council also headed by a presidential council.

The NCRC set itself up as a collegiate leadership of Syria. In many respects this was indeed the case although the military in fact held power. The NCRC harboured representatives of all political leanings of the Ba'th and its allies for as long as those alliances lasted. The alliance with the Nasserists was short-lived. Cracks appeared in the NCRC by the end of April when it dismissed forty-seven officers known for their Nasserist sympathies. Two pro-Nasserist members of the NCRC and five Unionist ministers resigned from the government in protest. On 7 and 8 May, pro-Nasserists organized street demonstrations in Damascus and Aleppo. They were violently repressed by the interior minister Amin Hafez.

General Ziad Hariri, the perpetrator of the coup of 8 March, was excluded from the NCRC and discharged as chief of the army general staff in late June 1963 after refusing to join the Ba'th.[4] He was replaced by General Amin Hafez. After the resignations of the pro-Nasserist Unionists in late April and the ousting of General Ziad Hariri in late June, only Ba'thists and the military continued to sit on the NCRC. When the break between Ba'thists and Nasserists occurred, General Lu'ay Atassi resigned as president of the NCRC on 27 July 1963 and retired from politics. He was replaced by General Amin Hafez, the regime's new strongman who had quelled the pro-unionist demonstrations in May 1963 and the attempted coup by Nasserists in July.[5] He remained in the job until the coup of February 1966.

---

[3] Guingamp, *Hafez El Assad et le parti Baath en Syrie*, p. 129.
[4] Al-Jundi, *El Baas* (Arabic), p. 129.
[5] See section 6.1.2.

The Delegitimization of the Old Order

Ba'th historiography does not consider the events of 8 March 1963 as a classical armed coup but as the founding act of a revolution. Taken in this sense, 8 March 1963 was indeed a revolution, but it was only seen as this after the event. Within months, the revolution of which the Ba'th had been joint perpetrators brought about a complete upheaval of the country's political, social, and economic order. To assert their authority, the new leaders in Damascus decided to liquidate the old order and replace it with a new one. This meant liquidating not just the institutions in place but also the political and military personnel.

From the first hours of the coup of 8 March 1963, the officers in the putsch formed the NCRC, which gave itself executive, legislative, and even judicial powers. Purges within the army began immediately. General Lu'ay Atassi proudly informed Nasser in the first tripartite meetings that began days after the coup of 8 March that three hundred officers had already been discharged. The NCRC's hold over the army was total and incontrovertible, to the extent that in June 1963 the NCRC authorized itself by decree to 'discuss and decide on the armament of the active army and the reserve as well as its composition, reduction, and dissolution upon proposal by the Defence Council'.

In addition to purges within the army, the rooting out of the old order affected the whole of the political class who had supported the coup of 28 September 1961 that had led to the break-off of the union with Egypt. All the politicians who had signed the declaration of support for the secessionist officers in 1961 and all the civilians and high-ranking military who had run the separatist (*infissal*) regime were stripped of their civic rights for five to ten years depending on the case.[6] The notorious exception was Salah Bitar, the co-founder of the Ba'th. His ally Akram Hawrani, another Ba'th leader, was among the politicians stripped of their civic rights. Hawrani's supporters had not taken part in the coup of 8 March 1963. The loss of civic rights was a novelty in the arsenal of discretionary and arbitrary decisions by the military who had recently come to power by force of arms. It had never been enforced before and was not to be again. But it was crushingly effective. It eliminated and neutralized the country's traditional political elite at the stroke of a pen.

---

[6] NCRC decrees of 25 March 1963. See Akram Hawrani, *Memoirs* (Arabic), p. 3185.

6.1.2 Legitimization of the New Order by Arab Nationalism and Socialism

A week after the coup of 8 March 1963 discussions began in Cairo for a three-way union of Egypt, Syria, and Iraq. Damascus and Baghdad were recently led by coalitions of mostly Ba'thist officers for whom the quest for union with Nasser was more than a leitmotiv, it would help them to legitimize the new order they were attempting to establish in Syria and Iraq. The officers in power in Syria and Iraq had no intention of legitimizing their regimes through the traditional mechanisms of liberal-style parliamentary democracy. They wished to do so by according their acts with the spirit and principles of the Ba'th, beginning with Arab union. But within the Syrian Ba'th Party, the situation was complicated. The party's leading cadres were ambiguous about union with Egypt because of the strained relations between the Ba'th and Nasser during the union. By contrast, the party's grass roots were all in favour.[7] The tripartite discussions began on 14 March 1963 and ended after three sets of talks on 17 April 1963, the Syrian national day, with the signing of a charter creating the second United Arab Republic of Egypt, Syria, and Iraq.[8]

The Attempted Trilateral Union (Syria–Egypt–Iraq)

The agreement provided not for the merger of the three states into a single republic as had been the case with the union of Syria and Egypt between 1958 and 1961 but for a federation of the three states. Nasser was in favour of an identical arrangement to that of the United Arab Republic of 1958 to 1961. However, both Syria and Iraq insisted on a federation of the three states instead of their merger into a single political entity. The federation was to set up a presidential regime. In each region, 'political fronts' were to federate the various democratic and socialist unionist strands but without dissolving the political parties. The Charter of Union was to be presented for approval by popular referendum in each state within five months of it being signed. It was never submitted to the people further to the abortive putsch by pro-Nasserist Syrian officers on 18 July 1963.

---

[7] Sami Al-Jundi relates in his memoirs that the supporters of the union within the party did not even dare utter the word 'union', whereas the grass roots were deeply unionist. See Al-Jundi, *El Baas* (Arabic), p. 121.

[8] The pan-Arab Charter will be analysed in Chapter 7, 'The Pan-Arab Constitutions'.

The charter of 17 April 1963 provided that Syria and Iraq should be governed by a 'political bureau' during the interim period of five months until the referendum. Divergences soon arose over the bureau's composition. In Syria, the Ba'th demanded half the seats. The Unionists wanted all the factions that had taken part in the coup of 8 March to be represented equally on the political bureau, with one seat each for the Nasserists, Socialist Unionists, Arab Nationalists, and the Ba'th.[9] But the Ba'th had no intention of sharing power. They wished to govern Syria and Iraq within the framework of the charter of 17 April, leaving Nasser to govern Egypt. A Ba'th spokesman put in bluntly, 'In Syria and Iraq, we wish to be the ruling party and not the ruler's party', that is Nasser's party.[10]

The disagreement between Ba'thists and Unionists over the distribution of seats within the Political Bureau forced the Nasserists to resign from their positions in the governing bodies of Syria (NCRC, government). Their supporters attempted to mobilize the masses but were victims of harsh repression by the Ba'th-controlled police and security services. On 18 July, while the NCRC president, General Lu'ay Atassi, was heading for Cairo with a large delegation to try to convince Nasser not to withdraw from the charter of 17 April, Nasserist officers led by Colonel Jasim 'Alwan attempted a coup that was bloodily put down by General Amin Hafez, chief of the general staff, holed up in army headquarters. This failed coup marked the end of Nasserist hopes of controlling Syria and accentuated the distrust and suspicion between Nasser and the Ba'th. Blood had flowed in this attempted coup. Almost 170 were killed, plus some thirty military personnel and civilians shot after summary judgments by a special National Security Court. The Ba'th won the trial of strength. It no longer had any rivals within the army.

The Attempted Bilateral Union (Syria and Iraq)

One month before the coup in Syria, Iraq had experienced a coup d'état that had brought the Ba'th to power there. Being governed by the same party, Syria and Iraq felt closer than ever during this period. Two days after the coup of 8 March 1963, a sizeable Iraqi delegation took the road to Damascus to congratulate their Syrian comrades. As in Damascus, the rulers in Baghdad experienced tension between Ba'thists and Nasserists. In Baghdad, too, Nasser's supporters were ousted from the ruling bodies. On

---

[9] Al-Jundi, *El Baas* (Arabic), p. 123.
[10] Cited in Hawrani, *Memoirs* (Arabic), p. 3197.

the same day as Salah Bitar formed his second government in Damascus in May 1963 dominated by the Ba'th after the resignation of Nasserist and Unionist ministers, Ahmed Baker formed a new cabinet in Iraq also dominated by the Ba'th and from which the Nasserists were also excluded. Damascus and Baghdad joined forces against Cairo. Egypt responded virulently by supporting the attempted coup by the Nasserists in Syria and supporting the Kurd rebellion led by Barzani in northern Iraq. Egypt's support for the Kurdish insurrection was nothing new in itself. In 1959, at the time of the United Arab Republic, when relations between Abdel Karim Qaseem and Nasser had deteriorated, Cairo had already supported the Kurds in northern Iraq via Syria, which was part of the UAR at the time.[11]

The failure of the Nasserist coup d'état in Damascus signalled the end of any possible three-way union. There remained, however, the possibility of a union between Syria and Iraq. The Syrian army entered Iraq to join the Iraqi army in its fight against the Kurdish insurrection in the north. In September 1963, an NCRC delegation went to Baghdad to discuss with the Iraqi NCRC the creation of a single revolutionary command for both countries that would be tasked with taking the necessary measures for the unification of Syria and Iraq. On 8 September 1963, the Syrian and Iraqi armies were proclaimed to have merged.[12] The process of union between Syria and Egypt had begun with a similar merger of the two national armies in 1958.

The union seemed to be making great strides but the Ba'thist position in Iraq was fragile. The Ba'th had terrorized the population via its militia, the National Guard. Moreover, the Iraqi Ba'thists were divided. This split came to a head on 13 November 1963 when the Ba'thists loyal to the National Command and President Abdel Salam Aref turned their weapons on their comrades who supported Ali Saleh Sa'adi. This fratricidal struggle benefited President Aref, who eliminated the two factions of the Ba'th on 18 November 1963.[13] The dramatic developments in Baghdad tolled the bell for any Syrian–Iraqi union. The failed attempt at union under the Ba'th compounded the failed attempts at union between the two countries under the Hashemite banner in the 1950s during the

---

[11] Hawrani, *Memoirs* (Arabic), p. 3199.
[12] See the text of the Charter of Union of the Syrian and Iraqi armies in Tlass, *The Mirror of My Life* (Arabic), vol. II, pp. 492–3.
[13] On the crisis between Abdel-Salam Aref and the Ba'th in November 1963, see *ibid.*, pp. 499–504.

Second Republic, when Syria was led by the People's Party. This caused some to wonder whether fate was not playing a hand.

Legitimization by Socialism

In the space of four months, the Syrian Ba'th had lost all hope of a tripartite and then of a bilateral union. The restoration of the union with Egypt had been presented as the ultimate goal of the coup of 8 March 1963 and had largely legitimized it. The failure of the attempted unions risked stripping the new rulers of any legitimacy internally and costing them valuable alliances regionally. The Syrian Ba'th's only remaining option was to successfully exercise power within Syria – the Ba'th within a single state. To this end it tightened its grip on the country by intensifying its socialist policies. It became more radical so as to put Nasser in difficulty regionally and so as to appear as the champion of socialism, Arab nationalism, and the fight for the liberation of Palestine.

The elimination of political personnel and the re-founding of the army went along with the liquidation of the old economic order and a transformation of the social order. Within months, a cascade of nationalizations transformed the Syrian economy from a liberal to a socialist-style state economy. In May 1963 the new regime nationalized the private banks. The textile sector was nationalized in spring and summer 1964. In October 1964 it was the turn of mining and petroleum resources and heavy industry. Towards the end of 1964, the government nationalized 112 firms, some of which were too small to warrant it.[14] In February 1965 the government nationalized foreign trade. Alongside the sustained pace of nationalization, the Ba'th carried out an agrarian reform from June 1963 that limited ownership of farmland to a maximum of fifty hectares if irrigated and three hundred hectares if not. This measure was supplemented by a decision in December 1964 simplifying expropriation.[15]

The first nationalizations and the redistribution of agricultural land occurred while Syria, Iraq, and Egypt were still negotiating the possibility of creating a tripartite union. They therefore had an immediate use as they were supposed to prove to Nasser the goodwill of the new regime in Damascus with respect to its economic and social policy. They were in a sense 'certificates of socialism' to lay before the Egyptian president, who was very sceptical about the new masters of Syria. In the longer term, the

---

[14] Tlass, *The Mirror of My Life* (Arabic), p. 555.
[15] Sami Al-Jundi argues the logic behind these nationalizations and the land reform was to outdo Nasser in this domain. See Al-Jundi, *El Baas* (Arabic), p. 152.

aim of the nationalizations and the land reform was to transform social relations through a radical change of ownership of the means of production. The rural population was the great beneficiary of these measures that forced the liberal economic elite to leave the country and drove Syrian capital towards more favourable conditions, particularly in neighbouring Lebanon.

The establishment of the Ba'th regime, the break with Egypt, and the authoritarian imposition of socialist measures such as the nationalizations and the land reform all gave rise to resistance movements that were sometimes violent. Between January and April 1964 Syria experienced disorder at Banias and Homs stirred by the Muslim Brotherhood and the Nasserists.[16] In April 1964 disorder was fomented in Hama by a ragbag alliance of Muslim Brothers, Nasserists, and Communists. The troubles resulted in armed confrontation in the city. Once calm had been restored in Hama, the protests shifted to Homs. Muslim Brothers barricaded themselves in the Khaled Ben El-Walid Mosque before being forced out by the army. After Homs, the protests spread to Aleppo and Damascus where strikes hit the markets. It was finally in January 1965 that the army and security forces managed to break this movement that had been largely inspired by the Muslim Brotherhood: 'the backbone of the middle class is broken', wrote Eric Rouleau in *Le Monde* at the time.[17]

6.1.3 *The Ba'thist Governments*

The Syrian governments that arose from the coup d'état of March 1963 at no time truly held power. They acted as the managing body of the country's senior civil service to implement the decisions taken in other spheres such as the NCRC, the Ba'th Military Committee (BMC), the Ba'th National Command (NC), and the Ba'th Regional Command (RC). Governments during this period reflected the balance of power among these four institutions. Salah Bitar, co-founder of the Ba'th, formed the first government after the coup of 8 March at the request of the NCRC. His government was composed of representatives of parties to which the putschist officers belonged, namely Ba'thists, Nasserists, Socialist Unionists, and Arab Unionists. The Ba'th held half the seats with the other three unionist parties sharing the other half. The cabinet was not the prevailing power in terms of decision-making. It was formally subject to the

---

[16] See Tlass, *The Mirror of My Life* (Arabic), pp. 516–18.
[17] Cited in Guingamp, *Hafez El Assad*, p. 150.

NCRC as the supreme body in Syria, while other bodies served in parallel as venues for discussion and decision-making.

After the signing of the charter of 17 April 1963, the Nasserists organized street demonstrations in the country's major cities in support of the union with Egypt. The Ba'thists reacted vigorously through the interior minister, General Amin Hafez, who violently put down the street demonstrations. The seven Nasserist and Arab Unionist ministers left the Bitar government in protest. Bitar resigned but was returned to office by the NCRC after Sami Al-Jundi, who had in the meanwhile left the Socialist Unionists and rejoined the Ba'th, had failed to form a government.

The second Bitar government took office on 14 May 1963. It was composed of four Ba'thist ministers, two Arab Unionists, three military officials, and seven independents.[18] So as not to break all ties with the Nasserists, the Ba'th left seven ministerial portfolios for delegated ministers in the hope that they would shortly be attributed again to Nasserists. But the Nasserists refused and formed a front against the Ba'th. This was the prelude to the Nasserists' loss of influence. The Bitar government became politically radicalized after the Nasserists had been eliminated from the army further to the abortive coup of 18 July 1963, burying the charter of 17 April 1963 for good. These radical political changes on the national stage were accompanied by a radicalization of the regime in Syria and more intensive nationalizations.

The third Bitar government was formed on 29 July 1963. It continued down the road of nationalization and facilitated agricultural expropriation as part of its land reform. Bitar presented his cabinet's resignation after its failure in the elections for the Ba'th First Regional Congress held in Damascus in September 1963. General Mohammad Umran was tasked by the NCRC in November 1963 with forming a new government. He preferred to leave the position to General Amin Hafez, and settled for the position of deputy prime minister.[19] Amin Hafez's government survived until 14 April 1964 after having harshly quelled disorder throughout the country (in Aleppo, Homs, Hama, Banyas, Abu Kamal, and Damascus) in reaction to the enforcement of socialist measures taken at the Sixth National Congress.

The fourth Bitar government formed on 23 May 1964 ushered in a more liberal period. Supporters of the Regional Command gave up some of their seats to the more moderate National Command supporters. The

---

[18] Hawrani, *Memoirs* (Arabic), p. 3196.
[19] See Al-Jundi, *El Baas* (Arabic), p. 141.

new government invited the middle classes to participate in the country's development. This government remained in office until October 1964. The attempt to open up to the private sector proved a failure. On 4 October 1964, Amin Hafez replaced Salah Bitar as head of a more radical government composed solely of regionalists. Nuredin Atassi became deputy prime minister. Amin Hafez's new cabinet implemented markedly left-wing measures such as prohibiting oil concessions to foreign companies.

The Zuayin government was formed after the creation of the National Revolutionary Council (NRC) in September 1965. This government, which was close to the supporters of the Regional Command, remained in office until the end of the year. On 21 December 1965, the National Command dissolved the Regional Command and dismissed the Zuayin cabinet. The National Command then asked Salah Bitar to form a new government. Bitar asked Mohammad Umran to return from Madrid where he had been exiled as ambassador in February 1965 and offered him the defence portfolio. The fifth Bitar government was formed on 1 January 1966 and lasted less than two months. It was dissolved further to the movement of 23 February 1966.

Within the space of three years, Syria had experienced five cabinets headed by Salah Bitar, two headed by Amin Hafez, and one by Yusef Zuayin. This governmental instability was the reflection of dissension and the struggle for power among the comrades controlling the true decision-making bodies that were the NCRC/NRC, the National Command, the Regional Command, and BMC.

6.1.4 Political Life within the Ba'th between 1963 and 1966

After consolidation of the revolution against its domestic enemies (Nasserists, Muslim Brotherhood, and others), political life in Syria between 1963 and 1966 was limited to rivalry among the military within the BMC and the party's Regional and National Commands.

The Ba'th Military Committee

Many commentators viewed the BMC as the true holder of power in Syria.[20] It was a secret organization created by a few Syrian officers when posted to Egypt in the summer of 1959. Unhappy with the turn taken by the union and with their treatment from the Egyptian authorities, and disappointed at the self-dissolution of their party in 1958, these Ba'thist

---

[20] Al-Jundi, *El Baas* (Arabic), p. 133.

officers serving in Egypt decided to set up their own organization in the utmost secrecy.[21] The BMC played no part in the coup of 28 September 1961 that ended the union nor in that which ended the *infissal* regime. After the coup of 8 March 1963, the leading officers of the BMC occupied the strategic posts. Salah Jadid took control of the department of officers' affairs that had the final say on postings and transfers of all the army officer corps. Hafez Assad re-joined after having been discharged by the *infissal* regime. He was entrusted with the Dumeir air base close to the capital before becoming air force commander-in-chief. Mustafa Tlass became the strongman of the Fifth Armoured Division stationed at Homs that controlled the centre of Syria.

The coup of 8 March 1963 seriously shook the army. In a matter of months, nearly seven hundred officers whose loyalty to the new regime was doubtful were dismissed. They were replaced by reservist officers, mostly teachers by profession, who were thought more reliable because they came from the rural classes and sectarian minorities, in particular the Alawis, Druze, and Ismailis.[22] The army and party command were aware the military institution had been substantially weakened by these purges. But it was considered to be a temporary phenomenon (four or five years) until the military colleges had trained up new officer cadets imbued with Ba'th ideology. The immediate advantage of purging the army of its unreliable components was to stabilize the regime.

The dismissal of officers sympathetic to the *infissal* regime, officers whose loyalty was questionable, and Nasserists after the abortive putsch of 18 July 1963 resulted in the army officer corps having more marked sectarian and rural backgrounds. For some, the instigator of this sectarianization seems to have been Salah Jadid. Sami Al-Jundi paints an unforgiving portrait of him and accuses him of having raised sectarianism into a party within the party.[23]

Sectarianization of the key institutions was soon noticed by the party leaders. Before becoming the subject of public debate and being a delight for Western academics in search of orientalism, the sectarianization of the military institution and the regime in general was discussed as from 1965

---

[21] There were supposedly fifteen original members of the BMC. See the list in Guingamp, *Hafez El Assad*, p. 378. The most prominent ones who played leading roles afterwards in Syria were Mohamed Umran, Salah Jadid, Hafez Assad, Salim Hatum, Abdel Karim Al-Jundi, Ahmad Suwaydani, and Mustafa Tlass.

[22] Guingamp, *Hafez El Assad*, p. 127.

[23] Al-Jundi, *El Baas* (Arabic), p. 142.

in a closed session of the Second Regional Congress held in Damascus in February 1964.[24] The former defence minister Mustafa Tlass relates in a critical tone in his memoirs that the head of state, General Amin Hafez, twice expressed his fears about the sectarianization of the regime.[25]

Relations between the founders of the Ba'th and the BMC officers remained strained. They were a throwback to the tension prevailing between politicians and the military at another time and in other circumstances during the Second Republic from the first coup d'état in March 1949 to the fall of the *infissal* regime in March 1963. The head of state and his supporters within the National Command found it increasingly difficult to tolerate the BMC's growing influence. They wanted to regulate relations between the party and army so as to halt interference by officers in the party's internal affairs via the BMC. To clarify relations among the institutions governing Syria, that is the army, the state, the government, and the party, the National Command adopted a set of sixteen decisions in December 1964 including the dissolution of the BMC and its replacement by an elected Bureau of Military Affairs, with limited prerogatives and responsibility for the army's relations with the party. But confronted with the protests of the military, the National Command agreed to postpone enforcement of these decisions until the Eighth National Congress in April 1965.

As planned, that National Congress fixed relations between the party and the army. It decided that the military could represent no more than 20 per cent of the delegates to the National and Regional Congresses and that they would be represented at most by three officers on the National Command and the same for the Regional Command. The BMC was officially dissolved and superseded by an elected Bureau of Military Affairs (BMA) answerable to the Regional Command. The Congress also sought to limit party and government members holding both military and political functions within the ruling bodies. Once these decisions were adopted, the NCRC and the Regional Command called for a congress to be organized in April 1965 for Ba'thist military of at least five years' standing to elect the BMA, which was to have seven members to replace the former BMC.[26] Nearly 200 officers took part in the congress held in the grounds of Qabun college for motorized troops in the Damascus area. So as to

---

[24] See Guingamp, *Hafez El Assad*, p. 152.
[25] See Tlass, *The Mirror of My Life* (Arabic), p. 563.
[26] For details of the military congress and the list of officers elected, see Tlass, *The Mirror of My Life* (Arabic), pp. 560 ff.

separate political and military responsibilities as far as possible, the head of state, General Amin Hafez, abandoned his position as commander-in-chief of the army four months later and the powerful General Salah Jadid resigned as chief of the general staff to hold on to his position as deputy secretary-general of the Ba'th Party.

The Ba'th National and Regional Commands

Political life in this period was limited to struggles of influence within the party between its founders (Aflaq and Bitar) and the new generation, and between civilians and the military. A quick description of the challenges of the various national and regional party congresses provides an understanding of the struggle for power that drove the various clans. The stages in this rivalry reflected the transformation of the Ba'th and its radicalization.[27]

The Ba'th First Regional Congress (11 September 1963)

This congress is numbered as the first party congress or more exactly the first after the seizure of power by the Ba'th in March 1963. This congress brought together, for the first time in the same forum, the party's traditional political organization and the military structure represented by the BMC. The young generation was largely represented by three rising figures – Nuredin Atassi, Yusef Zuayin, and Ibrahim Makhus. The Marxist-leaning Ba'thists were represented by Yasin Hafez.[28] Being used to years in hiding, the main members of the BMC decided to remain in the shadows. The only officer known to the general public was until then Amin Hafez, president of the NCRC and who had never been on the BMC. One of the objectives of this congress was to join the military and political arms of the Ba'th together in a single structure. The task was not an easy one. The officers agreed to join the party's political organization but insisted on keeping an autonomous military structure. The congress was marked by the non-election of Salah Bitar, the party's co-founder. Consequently, he resigned as prime minister. Nuredin Atassi was elected secretary of the Regional Command, which comprised three officers and five civilians. For the first time ever, the military made their appearance

---

[27] For a description of the various Ba'th Congresses, especially between 1963 and 1966, see Sallam, *La Ba'th et la patrie arabe*, 1982.

[28] Yassin Hafez participated actively in the theoretical radicalization of Ba'th ideas and introduced many conceptions from the Marxist–Leninist heritage. He subsequently studied at the Ecole Nationale d'Administration in Paris (1967–68). His writings were published as *The Defeat and the Vanquished Ideology* (Arabic).

within the party's Regional Command and the historical leaders were ousted. The same phenomenon occurred in Iraq, which was also led by the Ba'th at the time.

The Ba'th Sixth National Congress (5–23 October 1963)

This congress was a pivotal date in Ba'th history. It brought together delegates from all Arab countries where the party had any standing and especially Iraq and Syria, which were ruled by the party. The congress-goers adopted the 'Theoretical Bases of the Ba'th', intended to convert the Ba'th into a Marxist party, a far cry from the guiding principles of the Ba'th when it was first formed in 1947.[29] The congress was influenced by the presence of a large number of participants who, as former Communist Party members, had Marxist leanings. Their leader was Yassin Hafez, an intellectual who gave a new Marxist–Leninist impetus to the decisions of the congress.[30] The military members of the Ba'th supported the party's Marxist reorientation not so much out of conviction but more to counter the Ba'th's founders, Michel Aflaq and Salah Bitar, proponents of moderate socialism.[31] The congress invited Iraq and Syria to merge in the two months ahead and recommended appointing General Mohammad Umran, member of the BMC, as prime minister after he had been replaced as chief of the general staff by General Salah Jadid, who was likewise a BMC member.

The hope for a union between Syria and Iraq was short-lived. Just days after the end of the Damascus Congress an Iraqi Regional Congress met on 11 November 1963. Ali Saleh Sa'adi was left with a minority by the Ba'thists allied with certain army officers including President Aref. The congress was followed by armed confrontation between supporters of the two camps, which turned to the advantage of the Ba'th's enemies. Ali Sa'adi had to go into exile, which meant the beginning of the end of the first Ba'th experiment with power in Baghdad.

The Extraordinary Session of the First Ba'th Regional Congress (31 January–5 February 1964)

This session of the party congress was crucial for the future of Syria's institutions. Supporters of two different conceptions of the future constitution were

---

[29] The theoretical changes in the Ba'th doctrine adopted at this congress will be examined in detail in Chapter 8, 'Towards the Fifth Republic'.
[30] See Tlass, *The Mirror of My Life* (Arabic), pp. 496 ff.
[31] Ibid., p. 498.

at loggerheads. General Umran supported an idea whereby an appointed assembly, made up of representatives of the trade unions and the party, would elect a five-member presidential council. Standing against this proposal, Sami Al-Jundi wanted the assembly to be elected and not appointed.[32] After three days of talks, the congress voted for General Umran's proposal. Syria was to head down the road of 'popular democracy' as promised at the Sixth National Congress. A new Regional Command was elected at the end of the meeting. It comprised sixteen members, seven of whom were military personnel. The secretary was Shibli Aysami, who was close to Michel Aflaq, although the regionalists held the majority. The new Regional Command was to prepare Syria's new constitution within two months.

The Seventh National Congress (12–18 February 1964)

The agenda for this national congress, which was held just six months after the previous one, featured the Iraqi crisis and the elimination of the Ba'th in Baghdad. The policy followed by Ali Saleh Sa'adi in Iraq when in power was condemned and he was expelled from the National Command. Three weeks later he was to be expelled from the Ba'th for having tried to mobilize Lebanese militants against the party. The advocates of the Marxist tendency in the party, who had come over to it from the Syrian Communist Party and who had contributed substantially to the drafting of the 'Theoretical Bases' of October 1963, were also expelled from the party. But their expulsion did not benefit the old guard, which was suspected of favouring a moderate, reformist style of socialism. Instead, it benefited the regionalists and the military.

6.1.5 *The 1964 Provisional Constitution and Collegiate Rule*

The provisional constitution was promulgated by a presidential decree dated 25 April 1964. Interestingly, this decree made no reference to the conclusions of the extraordinary session of the First Regional Congress of the Ba'th held in Damascus from 31 January to 5 February 1964, although it was then that the basic principles of the new constitution were adopted. One of the conclusions of the congress provided laconically that the Regional Command should be tasked with finding a suitable formula for governing relations among the various authorities and enable the party to guide and control the ruling powers.[33]

---

[32] Al-Jundi, *El Baas* (Arabic), pp. 141–2.
[33] Arab Socialist Ba'th Party, *The Arab Socialist Ba'th Party Regional Congresses* (Arabic), p. 24.

The 1964 provisional constitution broke with the previous Syrian constitutions in terms of the organization of executive and legislative power. Among the rare points in common with the previous fundamental texts were Islam as the president's religion (art. 3 (1)) and the *fiqh* (Muslim jurisprudence) as the main source of legislation (art. 3 (2)).

The 1964 constitution also kept the title 'Syrian Arab Republic' that had been given to the country by the *infissal* regime and endorsed by the 1962 constitution. Previously, Syria had officially been called the Syrian Republic. From article 1 of chapter I, entitled 'The Syrian Arab Republic', the new constitution defined Syria as a sovereign socialist popular democratic republic that was part of the Arab nation. The pan-Arab and socialist ideological orientation could not be better expressed. The 1964 constitution reflected the conclusions of the Ba'th Sixth National Congress of October 1963, except for the leading role of the party which it was careful not to reveal or codify.

The new direction taken by the country was also to be reflected by the question of the flag. The 1964 constitution altered the Syrian flag, from that of the 1928 constitution, commonly known as the flag of independence, to the flag of the abortive tripartite union of Egypt, Syria, and Iraq.[34] When the provisional Syrian constitution was promulgated in April 1964, the tripartite union was already dead and buried but the Syrian authorities were still eager to adopt its flag. The symbolism was important and a reminder of the meaning of the national project to which the Ba'th aspired.

The 1964 constitution contained in its chapter II entitled 'General Principles' several articles similar to those of a declaration of rights and that took up the constant themes proclaimed in the previous constitutions but also new rights that reflected the ideological orientation of the new regime and the social provisions of the Ba'th party's constitution dated 1947. Equal opportunities were guaranteed by the state (art. 8). This principle was one of the fundamental aspects of the concept of social justice developed by the Ba'th literature since the party's creation. The new constitution guaranteed respect for beliefs, religions, and the exercise of all religious worship (art. 16).

---

[34] Article 6(1) of the 1964 provisional constitution describes the Syrian flag: the flag is twice as long as it is wide. It comprises three colours of equal area from top to bottom red, white, and black. The white part contains three green five-pointed stars. Each star represents a member country of the tripartite union (Egypt, Syria, Iraq). Syria was to keep this flag until the formation of the Federation of United Arab Republics in 1971 (Egypt, Syria, Libya).

The 1964 constitution proclaimed observance of civil liberties (art. 13) without specifying which ones. This was wishful thinking at least for the classical conception of civil liberties. It should be noticed that the constitution did not recognize the right of association other than for trade unions. Thus the right to form political parties did not feature in the constitutional text. Nor did the text recognize the right to freedom of opinion, expression, or the right to freedom of the press. In all these areas, the 1964 constitution appears to be a step backwards compared with the earlier constitutions.

The 1964 constitution innovated in terms of economic and social rights. On education, it recalled the mandatory character of primary schooling and affirmed for the first time the principle of free education at all levels (art. 17(1)). This rule, which was included in the Ba'th party's constitution, was never challenged. Despite the population explosion in Syria over the last five decades, the state has continued to take charge of the education of young Syrians from primary school to university. During his first mandate, Bashar Assad authorized the creation of a private educational sector alongside the state sector. In addition to free education, the 1964 constitution introduced the principle of free health care by affirming in its article 19 that the state insured all citizens and their families, in the event of accidents, illness, incapacity, becoming orphaned, and old age, and that the state protected the health of citizens and provided them with the means of prevention, medication, and treatment. Free medical care was also one of the main provisions of the Ba'th party's constitution.

The 1964 constitution defined work as a right and an obligation. The state was bound to create a socialist national economy enabling citizens to enjoy a decent standard of living (art. 18(1)). The state had to protect workers and guarantee them a fair wage. The state was the guarantor of social security and had to organize workers' rights to rest time and holidays (art. 18(2)). The combined effects of articles 17, 18, and 19 on free education at all levels, state sponsored health care, and social security transformed Syria into a welfare state of a unique kind in the region for the time.

The organization of trade unions was guaranteed provided they were independent and helped to build the national economy on a socialist basis (art. 18(3)). The constitution introduced the principle of a planned economy. To increase the national income, ensure it was fairly shared out, and prevent exploitation, the state was to set out a plan to take account of all of the country's wealth (art. 23).

In its chapter III entitled 'Property, Production, Heritage', the constitution asserted that the collective ownership of the means of production was the basis of socialist society (art. 24(2)). It also defined the different means of production: state ownership, producers' collective ownership, and individual ownership (art. 25(1), (2), (3)) The law was to lay down limits on individual property (art. 27). In fact, when the 1964 constitution was promulgated, the government had already nationalized almost all the means of production. The constitution was therefore describing an existing state of affairs.

Chapter IV of the constitution on 'Powers' defined the relationships among the various forms of power. The National Revolutionary Council (NRC), previously known as the National Council of Revolutionary Command (NCRC), became the state's legislative body (art. 31). The NRC was composed of the members of the NCRC as of the date the provisional constitution was promulgated plus representatives of the popular sectors, whose number and representational standing was to be laid down by law (art. 33).

The NRC was given the power to exercise legislative functions and the power to control the executive (art. 31). It was also to elect the members of the Presidential Council including its president and vice president (art. 32(1)). The NRC was also responsible for revising the provisional constitution and had to prepare the draft for the permanent constitution (art. 32(2)). The NRC could call for a referendum (art. 32(3)), set the number of ministers, and decide on their responsibilities (art. 32(4)). It set the guidelines of state policy and periodic plans (art. 32(5)). It decided on the state budget and taxes (art. 32(6)) and on questions relating to war and peace (art. 32(7)). It could grant confidence to the government and withdraw it either collectively or for an individual minister (art. 32(8)).

The NRC was to elect a president from among its number (art. 34) and had to sit three times a year. The first session had necessarily to be held in early October. The date of the other two sittings could be decided by the NRC's internal rules (art. 35(1)). The NRC could hold extraordinary meetings if convened by its president (art. 35(2)). Members of the NRC enjoyed criminal immunity when council sessions were held (art. 36). The NRC could only sit when an absolute majority of its members was present (art. 42).

Law-making initiative belong to the Presidential Council and to each member of the NRC (art. 43). Any law adopted by the NRC was to be promulgated by the Presidential Council within two weeks (art. 44(1)), except for what were characterized as emergency laws. These had to be published within the time allotted by the NRC (art. 44(2)).

The NRC met for the first time on 1 September 1965. Pursuant to article 33 of the constitution, the ninety-five members had been designated by law. They included the members of the NCRC as of the date the constitution was promulgated in April 1964 and representatives of the various popular categories. At its first session, the NRC members elected Mansur Atrash as their president.

Executive power was exercised jointly by the Presidential Council and the council of ministers (art. 47). The Presidential Council was composed of a president, a vice president, and three members, all of whom were members of the NRC and elected by it (art. 48(1)). The Presidential Council was accountable for all its acts to the NRC (art. 48(1)). It had the authority to appoint ministers and remove them from office (art. 50). The Presidential Council also had the authority to lay down the law and regulations in areas reserved to the NRC when it was not sitting even if it meant submitting all such decisions for the NRC's approval at its next session. Should the NRC rescind the decisions taken by the Presidential Council by a two-thirds majority, they would be abolished and would no longer be effective as from the date they were rescinded by the NRC (art. 51). The requirement of a two-thirds majority to rescind legislative decrees taken by the Presidential Council gave it a certain advantage over the NRC. But this procedure was never applied.

The Presidential Council ratified treaties after the council of ministers had approved them and informed the NRC (art. 52). The Presidential Council set out domestic and foreign policy. It oriented the action of the council of ministers and the ministers and supervised their activities (art. 54(1)). It had the right to cancel or amend decisions made by the council of ministers or by ministers if they were contrary to the constitution or the law, or if they were detrimental to the general interest (art. 54(2)).

The council of ministers was made up of the prime minister, his deputies, the ministers, the ministers of state, and the deputy ministers (art. 59). The prime minister had to be a member of the NRC (art. 60). The cabinet was accountable collectively to the NRC and each minister was individually accountable for the activity of his ministry (art. 61). The cabinet had to manage the affairs of state and coordinate the approaches of the different ministries and public institutions. It had to set out a periodical plan and enforce it once approved. It had to set out the state budget and direct its foreign policy (art. 62).

The council of ministers had to discuss bills (art. 63(1)) although it could not initiate them because this was a matter exclusively for the Presidential Council and each member of the NRC (art. 43). Only the prime minister could bring a motion of confidence in the government before the NRC under article 64(3).

In the final transitional provisions, the 1964 constitution gave notice that the provisional constitution was to remain in place until the people adopted a permanent constitution within less than one year from the date the provisional constitution was promulgated (art. 80). The final transitional provisions also provided for a procedure for modifying the constitution that could be revised upon a proposal by the Presidential Council or a quarter of the NRC members and approval of two-thirds of its members (art. 81).

The 1964 provisional constitution reflected the policies (nationalizations, land reform) already implemented by the leaders in Damascus since March 1963. However, it was innovative in the exercise of executive power by introducing at the top echelon of the state the principle of collegiate power, thus reflecting existing practice within the ruling bodies of the Ba'th. It is worth recalling, though, that the 1964 constitution timorously overlooked the role of the Ba'th Party that already controlled all the seats of power, all the institutions, and openly proclaimed in the conclusions of its congresses that the Ba'th governed the state. Nowhere in the text of the constitution was there any allusion to the Ba'th although it was during a Ba'th Regional Congress that the decision to draw it up was adopted together with its basic principles. But at the time, the Ba'th still preferred not to be in the spotlight constitutionally although politically it already held power. This is why a positivist reading of the 1964 constitution cannot enlighten readers as to where power really lay in Syria at the time. To be understood, the constitution has to be read alongside the political developments in Syria and in particular the Ba'ths takeover of all power. Such a reading readily reveals that the separation of powers provided for by the 1964 constitution was in reality merely a separation of functions.

The 1964 constitution was revised twice. The first revision was on 24 May 1965 and concerned article 80. The new version stated that the 1964 provisional constitution would continue in force until the people approved a permanent constitution before 31 July 1967. Initially article 80 had stipulated that the permanent constitution should be approved by the people within one year after the promulgation of the provisional constitution, that is as from 25 April 1964. This amendment was made upon a proposal from the Presidential Council. The second revision of the 1964 constitution concerned article 33. In its new version, this article stipulated that the NRC would be made up of representatives of the different categories of the people and that their number and representative quality would be laid down by law. Initially this article stated that all members of the NRC at the date the provisional constitution was promulgated would remain ex officio members of the new NRC and representatives of the people, the number and representative capacity of whom would be laid down by law. This revision was made upon a proposal of the Presidential Council dated 14 February 1966, that is nine days before the coup that was to bring the regime down. It allowed the NRC to be expanded from 95 to 135 members.[35] Mansur Atrash, who was already president of the NRC before its enlargement, was returned to office during the few days the regime lasted. It is noteworthy that this second revision also included the possibility of appointing ten non-Syrian members from Arab liberation movements as NRC members. There was no time to enforce this provision because of the coup of 23 February 1966.[36]

The provisional constitution also underwent an attempted revision, the description of which sheds interesting light on the nature of the debates that went on within the NRC and the balance of power within it. Mansur Atrash relates in his memoirs that the BMC wanted to amend the provisional constitution so as to raise the number of members of the Presidential Council from five to seven.[37] This proposed revision had been inspired by General Amin Hafez, the head of state, who complained he was systematically in a minority on the Presidential Council because of a tripartite alliance (Salah Bitar, Mansur Atrash, and Mohammad Umran).[38] The NRC met to discuss it. Mansur Atrash vehemently opposed the constitutional revision in vain. The military members of the NCRC voted en bloc for the change. Mansur Atrash, Mohammad Umran, and Salah Bitar resigned. They were replaced by Yosef Zuayin, Hasan Murayewed, and Shibli Aysami. Having won out, the military decided not to formalize the constitutional revision and modify article 48(1), raising the number of members of the Presidential Council to seven instead of five.

In his memoirs, Mansur Atrash asserts that before the increase to forty-five members there were twenty-two members of the NCRC, including thirteen military officers who, whenever it came to voting, complied with the instructions of the party's military committee. Decisions within the

---

[35] See the lists of the 95 NRC members of 1 September 1965 and the 135 members from 14 February 1966 in Ase'ayed, *Historical Development of the Syrian Parliament* (Arabic), pp. 395 ff.
[36] See Esber, *Political Movements in the Arab Countries* (Arabic), pp. 57–8.
[37] Mansur Atrash does not mention the date of this event, which probably took place in early October 1964 just before the Salah Bitar government resigned.
[38] Atrash, *The Cursed Generation* (Arabic), pp. 356 ff.

BMC were taken by the majority and the minority had to rally to them. This meant in practice that a majority of seven officer members of the BMC could at any time impose their will on the whole of the NCRC. Civilians had no real power.[39] The number of members of the NCRC was raised to forty-five when the 1964 constitution was adopted but its composition was still not made public.[40] According to the provisional constitution, the members of the new NRC elected on 4 May 1964 a Presidential Council of five members: General Amin Hafez as president, General Salah Jadid, General Mohammad Umran, Nuredin Atassi, and Yusef Zuayin. This committee was dissolved the next day so as to include Salah Bitar and was replaced by the following five members: General Amin Hafez as president, Salah Bitar as vice-president, General Umran, Shibli Aysami, and Mansur Atrash.[41] The government tendered its resignation and the Presidential Committee tasked Salah Bitar with forming a new cabinet.

6.1.6 *The End of the Regime of 8 March 1963*

The rivalry among the various ruling bodies intensified in the course of 1965. The struggle for power from the end of 1964 to February 1966 can be summarized as follows: the Presidential Council and National Command on one side versus the BMC and Regional Command on the other. This rivalry showed in the army, the party's governing bodies, and the NCRC, which became the NRC under the 1964 constitution.

The Second Syrian Regional Congress (17 March–5 April 1965)

This congress marked an additional stage in the mobilization of regionalist and military strength against the National Command dominated by the old guard. The congress-goers reportedly discussed in closed session a confidential report on the party organization. This critical report allegedly listed the forms of factionalism within the party (membership of

---

[39] See Atrash, *The Cursed Generation* (Arabic), p. 358.
[40] See Guingamp, *Hafez El Assad*, p. 146. The author asserts that before its enlargement the NCRC comprised just fifteen members.
[41] Sami Al-Jundi claims this 'reshuffle' was designed to appease Michel Aflaq by giving the position of vice president of the NRC to Salah Bitar (see Al-Jundi, *El Baas* (Arabic), p. 146). But according to Mansur Atrash, the Presidential Council was composed of Amin Hafez, Salah Bitar, General Umran, Nuredin Atassi, and Mansur Atrash (see Atrash, *The Cursed Generation* (Arabic), p. 355).

clans, geographical origin, sectarianism, clientelism, etc.).[42] At the end of their work, the participants elected a new regional leadership, the composition of which was kept secret. It comprised seven civilian and four military members. Amin Hafez became secretary of the Regional Command superseding Shibli Aysami who was closer to the old guard of the party's founders.

The Eighth National Congress (April 1965)

This was a congress of reconciliation and compromise between the supporters of the National Command backed by the NRC and the supporters of the Regional Command backed by the army. The national secretary, Michel Aflaq, submitted a document criticizing the regionalists and the military. It stated that within the party there were neither soldiers nor civilians but only members subject to the authority of the National Command. His aim was to try to subject the military to the party's civilian leadership. The congress members followed Aflaq while smoothing the edges so as not to upset the military and the regionalists unduly. The congress reasserted the leading role of the party over all the ruling instances. Among the conclusions was also the revision of the party's internal statute.

The congress adopted two other decisions of capital importance for the future of the party, Syria, and the region. First, the congress decided that the Syrian army was to become an 'ideological army'. This meant the armed forces (army, police, intelligence services) were to have two missions to accomplish: to protect the external borders against Israel and to defend the Ba'th revolution within the borders. To achieve these two objectives, recruitment of army officers was to rely on criteria of ideological loyalty to the regime. The future would show that this was not to be the sole criterion. Other considerations were appended to membership of the Ba'th alone, such as social (working classes and urban lower middle classes), geographic (preferably rural), and sectarian origins. The long-term cumulative effect of the dual functions assigned to the army and the new selective recruitment policy of its officers transformed the Syrian army, for the first time in its history, into a homogenous institution welded together by a strongly partisan *esprit de corps*.

The other important decision adopted by the Eighth National Congress was the support from the party, and therefore from Syria, for the incipient

---

[42] See Guingamp, *Hafez El Assad*, p. 152.

Palestinian resistance, which was considered the embryo of a strategy for the liberation of Palestine. As such, the Eighth Congress marked a turning point in the Arab strategy towards Israel. For the first time, a governing party of an Arab country shifted from a defensive position with regard to Israel and adopted an offensive strategy aimed at freeing Palestine and supporting the effort to create 'a revolutionary Palestinian organization that will lead the Palestinian people'. This unequivocal support for the Palestinian resistance movement symbolized at the time by Yasser Arafat's Fatah, which had launched its first raid against Israel less than four months earlier and whose first *fedayi* to fall as a martyr in occupied Palestine belonged to the Ba'th, forced the other Arab countries and especially Egypt, although bogged down in its war with Yemen, to support the Palestinian armed resistance movement too. Israel was to take the pretext of the growing political and military support from Syria and Egypt for the Palestinian cause and organizations to patiently create two years later in June 1967 the circumstances required for its aggression, presented by Tel Aviv as an action in legitimate self-defence, whereas in fact it was a preemptive and not preventive military action, in complete contravention of international law.

In siding with the Palestinian resistance, the Ba'th was merely espousing certain characteristics inherent in the Syrian national project since 1918, namely the refusal of the Zionist project and the rejection of foreign hegemony. At the end of the congress, Michel Aflaq distanced himself somewhat from the party's political life. He relinquished the position of secretary-general, which was given to the Jordanian, Munif Razzaz. Aflaq left Syria and moved for a time to Brazil.

The First Extraordinary Session of the Ba'th Second Regional Congress (11–13 June 1965)

This session was convened by the party's new secretary-general, Munif Razzaz. The Military Affairs Bureau officially replaced the BMC. Under the rule of non-accumulation of military and political responsibilities adopted at the Eighth National Congress, Salah Jadid stood down as chief of the general staff to remain deputy regional secretary. Amin Hafez gave up his position as commander-in-chief of the army to hold on to his job as president of the NCRC's Presidential Committee. The military and regionalists seemed to be complying with the decisions adopted at the Eighth National Congress.

The Second Extraordinary Session of the Ba'th Second Regional Congress (8–14 August 1965)

This new session was convened once again by the party's secretary-general, Munif Razzaz. The newly elected Regional Command comprised sixteen members including eight military officers. The military and the regionalists failed to abide by the rule that there were to be no more than three military members on the party's National and Regional Commands. No supporter of the National Command was included in the newly elected team. This was a failure for the secretary-general's policy and went back on the decisions adopted by the Eighth National Congress. Two rival personalities emerged as the winners in the new Regional Command: the head of state, General Amin Hafez, who was elected regional secretary, and General Salah Jadid, who was elected deputy regional secretary. But the other Regional Command members quickly rallied around Salah Jadid. As for Amin Hafez, he moved closer to the National Command.

The Crisis between the Ba'th National and Regional Commands

The straw that broke the camel's back of relations between the National and Regional Commands was the incident involving the fifth armoured division in Homs, when Lieutenant-Colonel Mustafa Tlass, acting on the orders of the defence minister, arrested Colonel Salah Nemur, the division's commander and a protégé of the chief of the general staff and the head of state.[43] There followed a crisis meeting of the National Command (8–20 December 1965) with the participation of Michel Aflaq, who was back in Syria. The National Command members considered that the hoped-for limitation of the army's powers further to the replacement of the BMC with the elected Military Affairs Bureau was a failure. The military still eschewed party authority. Most National Command members thought the only solution was to dissolve the Regional Command to regain control of the party and army. On 21 December 1965, the National Command under the authority of Munif Razzaz decided to dissolve the Regional Command, contrary to the party's by-laws, which provided that only the National Congress could do so. The National Command withdrew its confidence from the Zuayin government, which was close to the regionalists, which then resigned, together with three of the five members of the Presidential Committee. Amin Hafez and Mohammad Umran supported the National Command's stance. Mohammad Umran became

---

[43] See Tlass, *The Mirror of My Life* (Arabic), pp. 634 ff.

a member of the Presidential Committee and defence minister. Salah Bitar was appointed prime minister. On the other side, Salah Jadid, Hafez Assad, and their supporters absorbed the blow and prepared their riposte in silence.

On 15 February 1966, the NRC was dissolved and replaced by a new NRC of 135 members after the amendment of the constitution as described earlier. Of the ninety-five members of the previous NRC, sixty-five were returned to office. The thirty who were excluded were all supporters of the dissolved Regional Command. Mansur Atrash was returned to office as president of the NRC. The new NRC was composed of Syrian members of the National Command, members of government, trade union leaders, and representatives of the nationalist and progressive currents. It remained in place eight days until the coup d'état by the regionalists on 23 February 1966.

6.2 The Neo-Ba'th Seizure of Power and the Radicalization of the Revolution (1966–1970)

After two months of assiduous preparation behind the scenes, the members of the Regional Command dissolved by the National Command on 21 December 1965 went into action on 23 February 1966. In the early hours of the morning, their forces took control of strategic locations in Damascus. The president, General Amin Hafez, ensconced in his official residence, fought doggedly. Loyalist forces also resisted in Aleppo. Some estimates put the number of dead in this coup d'état at close to 800. Never before in Syria's history had a coup claimed so many lives.

6.2.1 The Constitutional Arrangement of February 1966

The communiqués announcing the coup did not come from the army, nor a military council, nor revolutionary council as had been the case with earlier coups. They were signed by the Ba'th Provisional Regional Command (PRC).[44] Its first decision, PRC decision number 1 of 23 February 1966, announced the suspension of the 1964 provisional constitution, the dissolution of the NRC and the Presidential Council. On 25 February the radio announced PRC decision 2 appointing Nuredin Atassi head of state. The decision also set out how power would be exercised

---

[44] See excerpts from the first PRC communiqué in Tlass, *The Mirror of My Life* (Arabic), pp. 684 ff.

transitionally until the new regime was institutionalized. It was therefore quasi-constitutional in character.

Legislative power was to be exercised by the council of ministers via legislative decrees that were to be approved by an absolute majority. The head of state could object to a legislative decree adopted by the council of ministers within a period of two weeks. The head of state's objection had to state its reasons. In this event, the council of ministers was to re-examine the legislative decree. If it was confirmed by a two-thirds majority of the council of ministers, the head of state had to promulgate it. The head of state was to appoint the prime minister and ministers by a decision taken within the Ba'th Regional Command. The Regional Command had the power to revoke these appointments and accept resignations. This provisional arrangement for the exercise of power made the Ba'th Regional Command the country's supreme political authority. The council of ministers and the ministers represented administrative and not political authority. As head of state and secretary-general of the Ba'th, a position to which he was elected some weeks later, Nuredin Atassi became the middleman between the collegiate leadership of the Ba'th Regional Command and the council of ministers.[45] He was placed at the apex of the state and the heart of power, a junction between the state institutions and the party, but without being the strongman of the regime, which post was reserved first for Salah Jadid and which Hafez Assad began to challenge from 1968. This constitutional arrangement remained in place until the adoption of a provisional constitution in 1969.

The Ba'th now officially held power and controlled all the institutions in the country. The Ba'th PRC placed all of the executive and legislative power in the hands of the head of state and the council of ministers. But as Mustafa Tlass emphasizes in his memoirs, there was no question of granting absolute power to the government. The powers granted to the cabinet were to be exercised for the implementation of decisions taken within the PRC in the same way as practised in the Communist Party of the Soviet Union.[46] The highest authority in the country was the Ba'th Party or more specifically the PRC, which appointed the head of state, prime minister, and members of the government. On 1 March 1966, the PRC tasked Yusef Zuayin with forming the new government. To confirm its leftist leanings, the cabinet included a Communist minister for the first time under the Ba'th.

---

[45] For Decision number 2, see Al-Ghali, *Principles of Constitutional Law* (Arabic), pp. 553–4.
[46] Tlass, *The Mirror of My Life* (Arabic), p. 688.

Within the Ba'th, the coup of 23 February 1966 was traumatic and spread throughout the party's pan-Arab structures. The Ba'thists in the other Arab countries found it difficult to follow, understand, and approve the action of their Syrian comrades against the National Command that had been legitimately elected at the Eighth National Congress in Damascus in April 1965. Moreover, the National Command included the party's historical leaders, including its co-founders, Michel Aflaq and Salah Bitar, who were highly respected by Arab militants. The armed coup was dismissed by many Arab Ba'thists, beginning with the party's Lebanese branch. The members of the new Syrian PRC in charge of the country had to justify their action. Internally, the explanation was summary and forceful. The new prime minister, Yusef Zuayin, declared at a press conference on 5 March 1966:

> The resort to arms is unusual in the party context. But it was all that was left to us. The Regional Command had been dissolved and that act was illegal, because such a decision belonged to the Regional Congress that elected it ... We were faced with an alternative: give in and we would be playing into the hands of the colonialists; or save the party by putting it back on the revolutionary path.[47]

The historical leaders of the Ba'th and the country's former rulers (Michel Aflaq, Salah Bitar, Munif Razzaz, Amin Hafez, Mohammad Umran, etc.) were either imprisoned or exiled to neighbouring Lebanon. Their supporters in the army were discharged. This new wave of purges again affected mostly civil servants and officers of Sunnite origins who were almost totally rooted out of any important positions in the army and replaced by their Alawi and Druze counterparts.[48] To legitimize their action domestically and elect a new Regional Command, the perpetrators of the coup convened an extraordinary session of the Regional Congress two weeks later in Damascus.

6.2.2 *Political Life under the Neo-Ba'th*

Political life under the neo-Ba'th was confined to confrontations among comrades within the party's Regional Command against a backdrop of transfers, promotions, or discharges of officers supporting one or other camp or clan. The victims were usually supporters of the powerful deputy

---

[47] Guingamp, *Hafez El Assad*, p. 163.
[48] Gunigamp, *Hafez El Assad*, p. 135.

secretary-general of the party, Salah Jadid, who were ousted by his rival Hafez Assad, the defence minister. The only serious attempt to overthrow the regime came in September 1966 from a Druze officer and member of the BMC from the outset, Salim Hatum.[49] It was thwarted by Hafez Assad. The neo-Ba'th regime attempted to institutionalize revolutionary rule by adopting a provisional constitution in 1969 that in many respects can be considered as the 'mother' of the subsequent Ba'th constitutions (of 1971 and 1973). But the political circumstances of the time precluded its implementation.

The Third Extraordinary Session of the Second Regional Congress (10–27 March 1966)

All observers awaited this congress to discover what new direction Syria would take. In addition to legitimizing new leaders, the congress reasserted its attachment to the conclusions of the Sixth National Congress of 1963. The left-wing orientation was not in doubt. It reaffirmed the enforcement of democratic centralism as the mode of regulating relations within the party between the leadership, the militants, and the various sections. It reasserted the principle of 'popular democracy' and recalled the party's role as the revolutionary vanguard. It underscored the importance of trade unions and popular organizations, and the need to intensify the socialist transformation of the economy and society. It evaluated the ongoing experiment with the ideological army adopted at the Eighth National Congress, in other words an army subordinate to the party, although in actual fact, and everyone could still remember the events of February 1966 to prove it, it was the party that was now subordinate to the army, for better or for worse. The Regional Congress legitimized rule in Syria since the coup of 23 February and announced that the arrangement for the rulers and the state institutions to work together, that is decision number 2 of 25 February 1966, would remain in force until such time as the congress should adopt a constitution within a period not to extend beyond 1 July 1967.[50] The congress elected Nuredin Atassi as the

---

[49] Some commentators think that because of Salim Hatum's Druze origins and because the insurrection was triggered in the city of Suweyda, the capital of the Jabal Druze, this uprising was sectarian and reflected rivalry between Alawi and Druze Ba'thist officers. The Druze were supposedly disappointed not to have any leading positions after the coup of 23 February 1966. In April 1966, a Druze officer, Hamad Ubayd, member of the BMC, had attempted an uprising in Aleppo that had also failed. For details, see Guingamp, *Hafez El Assad*, pp. 166–8.

[50] Tlass, *The Mirror of My Life* (Arabic), p. 711.

new secretary-general and Salah Jadid, the country's strongman, as deputy secretary-general.

Once the congress was over, the new leaders set to studying major construction projects that were to be largely financed by eastern bloc countries. The dam on the Euphrates was built thanks to the USSR, for example. Syria moved closer to the USSR, which worried its neighbours in the region, who were all opposed to Moscow. This alignment with the USSR moved the country closer to Egypt too. The country was under a leaden shroud that prevented any political life.

The Third Regional Congress (20–30 September 1966)

This congress was held just days after Salim Hatum's failed putsch. Its primary objective was to prepare the ground for the Ninth National Congress, which was the first of its kind since the coup of 23 February 1966. Among the topics discussed were the reaffirmation of class politics in the recruitment of party members, the evaluation of the ideological army experiment, the purge of hostile elements within the state machinery, cooperation with socialist countries, the call for a people's war of liberation for Palestine, the reassertion of the importance of the Euphrates dam project, and the swiftest possible implementation of land reform. The congress ended with the election of the new Regional Command with Nuredin Atassi as secretary-general and Salah Jadid as deputy secretary-general. Two weeks later, the newly elected Regional Command tasked Yusef Zuayin, the outgoing prime minister, with forming a new government.

The Ninth National Congress (October 1966)

Having legitimized the coup of February 1966 internally through an extraordinary session of the Second Regional Congress, followed six months later by the Third Regional Congress, and having strengthened their rule further to Salim Hatum's failed putsch, and having moved closer to the USSR and Egypt, the Syrian leadership judged the time was right to legitimize their rule with respect to the Arab Ba'th militants. To this end, they convened a National Congress in Damascus to elect a new National Command that would be favourable to them. Organizing this National Congress after the ousting of the National Command and the founders of the Ba'th was no easy matter. The very fact that it was to be held in Damascus confirmed the split in the Ba'th between supporters and opponents of the Syrian Regional Command. Even so, it was indisputably a success for the leaders in Damascus. The congress approved the decisions of the Syrian Regional Command and considered that the coup of 23 February 1966 was the only way to save the party. The congress reaffirmed that the grass roots of the party were to be made up of working people,[51] and decided to convene an extraordinary congress of the party to adopt an ideological report that would develop the party's theoretical foundations and revise its constitution. The congress reiterated its attachment to the Palestinian question, which was considered the main line of the party's strategy in all areas and reaffirmed the need to prepare the war of popular liberation. The congress confirmed the form of power in Syria pending the adoption of a permanent constitution for the country. The congress praised the ideological army experiment, which was the first of its kind in a developing country. At the end of its session, the congress adopted several transitional provisions reaffirming that the National Command was still the party's highest body and the role of the Regional Command with regard to civilian and military matters, and the need for the two instances to hold joint meetings in Syria. The congress elected a new leadership and a new secretary-general, Nuredin Atassi, and a new deputy secretary-general, Salah Jadid.[52]

The strategy adopted by the Syrian Ba'th at its Eighth National Congress in April 1965 of support for Palestinian resistance making the people's war of liberation the spearhead for freeing Palestine, coupled with a virulent pan-Arab and socialist language that was highly critical of what were characterized as reactionary Arab countries, and a spectacular rapprochement with the USSR were aimed at far-reaching changes throughout the Near East. The traditional conservative monarchic regimes in Amman and Riyadh and their western allies were worried about Syrian agitation. Israel denounced Syria's support for the *fedayin* movements and threatened reprisals. Egypt and the USSR feared that Syria might come under Israeli attack. Syria and Egypt signed a common defence agreement in November 1966.[53] But the future was to show that the tension that led

---

[51] Guingamp, *Hafez El Assad*, pp. 169–70 cites among the official documents published for the congress an interpretation of the February 1966 crisis that attributes its origin to 'infiltration in [the party] ranks of offspring of the middle classes that exploited certain theoretical loopholes ... to get into the higher bodies'. These right-wing components 'represented by Michel Aflaq, Salah Bitar, Munif Razzaz ... pushed the party into the ambush of parliamentary interplay, disregarding the people's struggle, and offering alliance with reactionary professional politicians and military adventurers'. It was a bold move indeed to call the founders of the Ba'th representatives of the middle classes who had infiltrated the party!

[52] For more details on this National Congress see Tlass, *The Mirror of My Life* (Arabic), pp. 775 ff.

[53] See the text in Tlass, *The Mirror of My Life* (Arabic), pp. 781 ff.

to the 1967 war had been largely orchestrated by Israel, under the cover of Arab militant talk, in order to justify what was not a preventive but a pre-emptive attack on Syria, Egypt, and Jordan with a view to occupying Jerusalem, the West Bank, Gaza, the Golan Heights, and the Sinai.

The Extraordinary Session of the Third Regional Congress (27–30 August 1967)

Two and a half months after the June 1967 defeat, the Ba'th held an extraordinary session of the Third Regional Congress. The meeting took place in the barracks of the seventieth brigade, the most powerful military unit, according to Mustafa Tlass, to impress the participants and prompt them to support the views of the party leadership, without which the leaders of the Regional Command would probably have failed to gain the confidence of the Congress.[54] The congress concentrated on the need to overcome the consequences of the military defeat and the recognition of armed struggle as the basis of the party strategy supported by political action.

The Extraordinary Session of the Ninth National Congress (September 1967)

This meeting was held the following month, again in the seventieth armoured brigade's barracks. It confirmed the decisions taken at the extraordinary sessions of the Third Regional Congress a few days earlier. Interestingly, this congress formally declared that the joint meeting of the National and Regional Commands was the most appropriate framework for leading the party and the state in all countries governed by the Ba'th.[55] On 28 September 1967, the head of state asked Yusef Zuayin to form a new government.

The period that followed was marked by a disagreement between the defence minister, Hafez Assad, and the chief of staff, Ahmed Suwaydani. All attempts to mediate between the two failed. Suwaydani resigned and was replaced in February 1968 by Mustafa Tlass, a close ally of Hafez Assad. For its part, the orthodox strand that had remained loyal to the Ba'th's traditional leaders organized a Ninth National Congress (bis) in Beirut in March 1968. Most of the congress-goers belonged to the party's Iraqi branch. This congress harshly condemned the Ba'thists in power in Damascus and enshrined the division of the party between supporters

---

[54] Tlass, *The Mirror of My Life* (Arabic), p. 871.
[55] Tlass, *The Mirror of My Life* (Arabic), p. 882.

of the Syrian Ba'th and supporters of the historical National Command. The non-Ba'thist Syrian opposition also created a National Progressive Front in Beirut with the supporters of Akram Hawrani (Arab Socialist Party), the Nasserists (Arab Socialist Union), and Arab nationalists (Arab Nationalist Movement). But neither the Ninth National Congress (bis) nor the creation of the National Progressive Front worried the leadership in Damascus as much as the Ba'th's return to power in Baghdad in July 1968. The party's Iraqi branch had remained loyal to the National Command that had been ousted by the coup of 23 February 1966. The Ba'th's return to power in Iraq in these conditions meant that the supporters of the old guard and the founders were to find a sound base from which to conduct their actions against the Syrian Ba'th and try to destabilize it.

The Fourth Regional Congress (26 September–7 October 1968)

The first clash between Hafez Assad and Salah Jadid's supporters occurred at the Fourth Regional Congress. The defence minister presented a lengthy report in the form of a plea for closer contacts with other Arab countries even if they were 'reactionary' so as to face up to the Israeli challenge and erase the humiliation of the Six Days' War. Assad also recommended reintegrating some of the officers cashiered during the previous period so as to raise army morale and increase its operational capacity. Assad lambasted the Zuayin government's policy. At the end of the Congress, Zuayin was replaced by Nuredin Atassi, who combined the positions of head of state and prime minister.

The Tenth National Congress (October 1968)

This Congress took place three months after the return of the Ba'th in Iraq and just days after the Fourth Regional Congress in Damascus. The congress-goers disregarded the fact that their comrades had come to power in Baghdad. As such, the Congress widened a little further the split in the party since the February 1966 coup. Few decisions were taken at this Congress, which merely reiterated the discussions of the Fourth Regional Congress. Debate centred on the situation in Syria. The Congress reasserted its support for the Palestinian resistance and decided to create an organization of *fedayins* inspired by the Ba'thists, the Saiqa. This politico-military organization was placed under the leadership of the party, in other words of Salah Jadid. This did not go down well with Hafez Assad. For its part, the orthodox Ba'th, now in power in Baghdad, was to hold its own Tenth Congress in March 1970. The great divide in the Ba'th family seemed consummated between the rival branches of the governing party in Syria and Iraq.

The Extraordinary Session of the Fourth Regional Congress (21–31 March 1969)

This extraordinary session was preceded by an open crisis between Hafez Assad and Salah Jadid. Relations between the two had not ceased to deteriorate since the Fourth Regional Congress of 1968. Although in a minority within the party, the defence minister had deployed troops in the capital early in March 1969 to restore an equilibrium with his rival Salah Jadid and bring it home to the Regional Command that, as head of the army, he, and not Salah Jadid, held the country. The troops had then been withdrawn pending the extraordinary session. But a few days before the congress opened, Assad had had the army reoccupy strategic buildings in Damascus. As soon as discussions began, Hafez Assad was in the hot seat and accused by supporters of Salah Jadid of thwarting the party's policy from within the state institutions, namely the army. Assad refuted this accusation. The party's secretary-general, Nuredin Atassi, then asked Hafez Assad if he had a programme for the party to put before the congress. Assad replied not, but that if the congress wished, given time, he could present such a programme. The session was adjourned until the following evening to allow the defence minister to prepare his programme.[56]

The following day, Hafez Assad set out his complaints with the party policy. He fixed as his priority preparing the army to liberate the territories occupied since 1967. This strategy implied modernizing the armed forces, reinstating certain officers, and establishing closer ties with other Arab countries despite their political regimes, and especially with Egypt, Jordan, and Iraq. Assad also advocated closer ties with the Iraqi Ba'th. He called for the establishment of a constitution within one year at most, the creation of a National Revolutionary Council representing the party and the popular sectors in which the Ba'th would have a majority and that would exercise legislative functions, the creation of a Political Bureau the number of members and competences of which would be determined by the future constitution, the creation of a National Progressive Front, and the formation of a coalition government.

The make-up of the new leadership team elected at the end of the congress proved that the strand led by Assad was still in a minority, although

---

[56] See the text of the full memorandum submitted by Hafez Assad to the extraordinary session of the Fourth Regional Congress in Tlass, *The Mirror of My Life* (Arabic), pp. 123–54.

some of his proposals were included in the conclusions of the congress, such as the decision to adopt a constitution within one month, the election of a popular assembly within four months, and the decision to elect a Political Bureau made up of nine members elected by the National Command and Regional Command. The Political Bureau was supposed to be the country's highest authority. The election was held on 27 April 1969. Hafez Assad and Mustafa Tlass became members.

6.2.3 The 1969 Provisional Constitution and the Institutionalization of the Ba'th

The provisional constitution was promulgated on 1 May 1969. It had been prepared and adopted within one month by the Ba'th Regional Command further to the extraordinary sessions of the party's Fourth Regional Congress in March. It was the most socialist and most secular constitution in Syria's history.

The 1969 provisional constitution was preceded by a long preamble describing the constituent assembly's political philosophy. Contrary to the 1964 provisional constitution, which remained silent on the Ba'th affiliation, the 1969 preamble attributed paternity of this constitution to the Ba'th and more specifically to the extraordinary session of the Ba'th Fourth Regional Congress in March 1969. It was decided to elect a People's Assembly to exercise legislative power and draw up a permanent constitution. But according to its preamble, this permanent constitution was to be preceded by a provisional constitution to organize relations among the various branches of government and state institutions temporarily.

The preamble listed the principles underpinning the provisional constitution:

1. The Revolution in Syria is part of the total Arab Revolution, the main aim of which, for the current stage, is the liberation from Zionist occupation.
2. Arab unity is not just a national resurrection of the Arab people, it is the result of an economic and social resurrection and the elimination of underdevelopment;
3. The march towards the establishment of a socialist regime is a necessity arising from the needs of Arab society.
4. Freedom is a sacred objective for society and the individual that cannot be achieved by traditional parliamentary forms that have been experimented by the Syrian people in the past and that have led to the

falsification of the will of the majority to the benefit of restricted categories. The rejection of parliamentarianism does not mean recourse to dictatorial or individual or bureaucratic or military forms of government but rather the transition to a broader, deeper democracy in the form of a popular democracy. This is the exemplary form that guarantees the masses the exercise of their rights and the fulfilment of their obligations.

The constitution began with title I, 'Fundamental Principles of the State and Society' comprising three chapters. Chapter I, 'Political Principles', defined Syria as a sovereign socialist popular democratic state that was part of the Arab nation (art. 1(1)) and a republic (art. 2(1)). Article 2(2) stated that sovereignty belonged to the people, while article 3 added that the Muslim *fiqh* (doctrine and case law) 'is a principal source of legislation'. Unlike any previous constitutions, it did not require Islam to be the religion of the head of state. The 1969 constitution maintained the same flag as in the 1964 constitution, that of the abortive tripartite union among Syria, Egypt, and Iraq (art. 6).

Article 7 formalized Ba'th rule for the first time, stipulating that 'the ruling party of the society and the state is the Arab Socialist Ba'th Party'. In addition to the Ba'th Party, the 1969 provisional constitution enshrined for the first time the existence of 'popular organizations' as subjects of law enjoying constitutional rights. Article 8 defined them: 'Popular organizations, cooperative associations are institutions comprising the forces of the People working to serve its members and participate in social change'. This initial definition is to be read in conjunction with article 42, which asserted: 'Popular sectors have the right to form trade unions, social, and professional organizations and cooperative associations of products or services'.

Article 10 defined the two functions of the armed forces and defence organizations. Like others, the Syrian army was to ensure the security of the national territory against outside attack. In addition, it fell to the armed forces to ensure 'the protection of the objectives of the unitary socialist Revolution', in other words, to protect Ba'th rule from its enemies within its borders. Never before had a Syrian regime set out in the constitutional text an obligation for the army to defend the ruling power, although Syria had in the past experienced many military coups and regimes. The principle of an ideological army adopted by the Eighth National Congress in Damascus in 1965 had prepared the ground for this type of constitutional provision. In this sense, the 1969 constitution merely took up, codified, and formalized the principle of the ideological army devoted to the Ba'th.

Chapter II dealt with 'Economic Principles'. Article 12 recalled that Syria had a socialist planned economy. This principle had already been laid down in the 1964 constitution. Article 13 defined the various types of property: state property (natural resources, state enterprises, nationalized establishments), collective property (common property belonging to popular and professional organizations, production units, cooperative associations), and private ownership, which comprised property belonging to individuals. The law was to determine the maximum limit of private ownership. The article merely restated the various types of ownership listed in the 1964 constitution.

Chapter III was on the 'Principles of Education and Culture'. Article 17 stipulated that the purpose of education and culture was 'to create a socialist, national, Arab generation attached to its history, proud of its heritage, driven by a spirit of combat, to achieve the objectives of the Nation in unity, freedom, and socialism'. The state's educational objective was thus clearly to shape a generation steeped in Ba'th principles that might continue to advance the national project. This purpose of education and culture also featured in the 1964 constitution. Further on, article 34 recalled that primary education was mandatory and that education was free at all levels. Article 40 took up the provisions of the 1964 constitution on free medical care.

Title II was 'On the Rights and Obligations of Citizens, Popular Organizations, and Cooperative Associations'. Chapter I defined the 'Rights and Obligations of Citizens', bringing together individual and collective rights. Like the corresponding chapter of the 1953 constitution, it began with an article on Syrian nationality. Specific articles were given over to the promotion of women's rights (art. 24), the right to work (art. 33), non-paying education (art. 34), health protection and state provision of medical treatment (art. 40). Article 23 was about the equality of citizens in law. Article 25 stipulated that the state ensured citizens' individual freedom and safeguarded their dignity and security. The inviolability of homes was referred to in article 28 and the secrecy of postal and telegraphic correspondence in article 29. Freedom of belief, respect of the state for all religions and the freedom of worship were guaranteed in article 31. Under the provisions of article 32, all citizens were entitled to participate in political, economic, social, and cultural life in accordance with the law. Article 35 of the constitution stated that all citizens were allowed to make their opinions known freely and publicly and participate in control and criticism within the limits of the law. These rights recognized by the 1969 constitution, some of which did not feature in the 1964 constitution, such as freedom of opinion, were wishful thinking. The country had been living under a state of emergency since 1963, which meant that none of the classical individual rights listed above was enforced.

In contrast, the economic and social collective rights were already largely enforced. One of the innovations of the 1969 constitution was article 24 on women's issues. This article stipulated that the state was bound to afford women every opportunity to contribute effectively to public life and allow them to participate in building the Arab socialist society. This article incontrovertibly bears the mark of a progressive, socialist, and secular regime.

The mechanisms regulating relations between the powers and the state institutions were addressed in the final part of the 1969 constitution under title III, 'On the Constitution and Organization of State Administration'. As with the 1964 constitution, the separation of powers gave way to a separation of functions in the style of Communist regimes. Article 45 defined the institutions of state power as being the People's Assembly (parliament), the Head of State, and the Council of Ministers, the local councils, the courts, and the prosecution service.

Chapter I covered 'The People's Assembly', which was presented as the supreme institution of state power (art. 46).[57] The mode of electing the assembly, the number of members, the sessions, and the rights and duties of members were left for the law to specify (art. 47). This provision of the 1969 constitution was specific to it. No previous Syrian constitution had left such prerogatives to the legislature. The constituent assemblies had always decided on these capital points. The political context at the time characterized by the infighting between the two main rival groups led by Salah Jadid and Hafez Assad may explain why these questions were left to the legislative authorities. The 1969 constitution simply laid down the principle of the election of members of parliament instead of their appointment as under the 1964 constitution. The conclusions of the extraordinary session of the Fourth Congress held a month earlier provided that the People's Assembly would be elected within four months, but this provision was not complied with.

Article 48 set out the competences of the assembly. It was to establish a permanent constitution, elect the head of state, pass laws, conduct votes of confidence in the government, adopt the budget and development plans, make treaties, and vote on general amnesties. Although article 47 provided that the rights and duties of assembly members would be laid down

---

[57] Some translations name this institution the 'People's Council'. In Arabic assembly and council are synonymous.

by law, article 49 set out the principle of non-accountability of assembly members for the opinions they expressed, votes they cast, or facts they related. Article 50 defined members' immunity: they were immune from criminal prosecution and no criminal sentence could be enforced against them unless the assembly so authorized.

Chapter II of title III fixed the competences of the 'Head of State and Council of Ministers'. The two institutions together formed the executive branch (art. 52). In addition to his function as commander-in-chief of the armed forces (art. 53), the head of state appointed the prime minister and the ministers upon a proposal from the prime minister, he accepted their resignation, he promulgated laws passed by parliament and legislative decrees adopted by the council of ministers outside sessions of the People's Assembly, he could object to laws by a decree setting out the reasons within two weeks, declare war and order mobilization upon the decision of the council of ministers and approval of the chamber, accredit heads of mission with foreign governments and receive letters of accreditation from heads of foreign missions, and he could proclaim a special amnesty (art. 54).

Under article 55, the head of state was entitled to dissolve the People's Assembly by decree stating the reasons in the council of ministers. In this event, he had to convene the electors to elect a new assembly within three months. The head of state had the right to convene the parliament (art. 56) and the right to convene the council of ministers to meet under his chairmanship (art. 57). In the event the position of head of state should be vacant or if he were prevented from exercising his functions, the speaker was to exercise responsibility as the head of state. In the event of the head of state's resignation or death, the speaker was to convene the assembly within ten days to elect a new head of state. Should the chamber be dissolved or should there remain less than two months to the end of its mandate, the president of the council of ministers would exercise the powers of the head of state until such time as the new assembly met (art. 60). The council of ministers exercised legislative power outside the sessions of parliament and had to submit to parliament at its next meeting the laws and legislative decrees that it had promulgated for approval (art. 61). The council of ministers was accountable jointly before the chamber and each minister was answerable to the president of the council of ministers for his own ministry (art. 65).

Title III included a chapter III on 'Local People's Assemblies' and chapter IV related to 'Courts and the Prosecution Service'. Transitional provisions were collected under title IV. They set out the procedure to be followed for revising the constitution. It could be amended by a decision of the People's Assembly passed by a two-thirds majority (art. 76). Pending the meeting of the parliament, the Ba'th Regional Command could amend the constitution as it saw fit. In addition, it could appoint the head of state or an interim head of state and as necessary accept his resignation or dismiss him, appoint the president and members of the council of ministers, accept their resignation or dismiss them, lay down the general policy of the state, decide to go to war, and order general mobilization (art. 78). Until parliament met, the council of ministers would exercise legislative power except for the responsibilities of the Ba'th Regional Command defined by article 78. The laws it promulgated by this procedure were not to be subject to the provisions of article 61, that is, they need not be submitted to parliament for approval when it next met.

Lastly, in its final article, the 1969 constitution abolished Decision number 2 of 25 February 1966, the de facto constitution that governed relations between the Ba'th party and the state concerning the exercise of executive and legislative functions, just as it abolished the 1964 provisional constitution, which was merely suspended by Decision number 1 of 23 February 1966 further to the coup of that same day (art. 80).

Although in a quite different context, the neo-Ba'th regime, via the policies it pursued and the 1969 provisional constitution, made its own the characteristic features of the Syrian national project as they had been formulated by the Founding Fathers in 1919, namely multi-sectarian coexistence and secularism, refusal of division of the Arabs, refusal of foreign hegemony, and resistance to Israel. The 1969 constitution confirmed the fifth component of the national project that had imposed itself at the end of the Second Republic, namely social justice. It largely codified the informal social compact gradually established between the Ba'th and the population since 1963, that is, an economy largely directed by the public sector, free medical care and education. In addition, it had the merit of seeking to institutionalize power that had become radicalized since the coup of February 1966 after the suspension of the 1964 provisional constitution and dissolution of the National Revolutionary Council. But the circumstances of the time did not allow this constitution to come into force. No law or legislative decree was adopted to define the conditions for electing the People's Assembly. Syrians had to wait until 1973 to elect a legislative assembly in the very closely supervised style dear to popular democracies.

6.2.4 The End of the Neo-Ba'th Regime

The rivalry between Hafez Assad and Salah Jadid became envenomed in the course of 1970. This rivalry was due not just to a struggle for influence to acquire power, but to a genuine choice in Syria's regional and political orientations so as to reinforce the Ba'th revolution.

The Extraordinary Session of the Tenth National Congress in Damascus (November 1970)

The extraordinary session of the Fourth Regional Congress of March 1969 had far-reaching consequences for the party's future. The confrontation between Salah Jadid and Hafez Assad had been postponed but not averted. The two camps stood their ground. Salah Jadid's side argued for a hard line inside and outside Syria. This political stance was characterized by Hafez Assad's supporters as 'childish leftism'. To reinforce their hold over the army, Hafez Assad and Mustafa Tlass decided in the wake of the congress to adopt 'the artichoke strategy' against officers loyal to Salah Jadid.[58] Every week, an officer who supported Salah Jadid was given a different posting. This patient and continual strategy culminated in mid-September 1970, during the tragic Black September events in Jordan and a month and a half before the extraordinary session of the Tenth National Congress, with the transfer of Colonel Izzat Jadid, commander of the powerful seventieth armoured brigade, to a desk job. With this transfer, Salah Jadid had lost his last mainstay within the army.

It was against a backdrop of dramatic events that the extraordinary session of the Tenth National Congress was held in Damascus in November 1970. September had seen the premature death of Nasser and the bloody confrontation between the king of Jordan and the Palestinian organizations. This event, which went down in history as Black September, was traumatic for Arab public opinion, which saw the *fedayin* as contemporary Arab heroes who were to erase the affront of the humiliating defeat of the regular armies in June 1967. Palestinian organizations had developed rapidly in the previous three years and had acquired operational capability that had surprised even the Israelis. In March 1968, the Palestinian resistance had valiantly held off an Israeli army incursion into Jordanian territory for two days in the Al-Karame region and inflicted heavy losses on it. This battle had been applauded throughout Arab countries and

---

[58] On the 'artichoke strategy' and the Izzat Jadid episode, see Tlass, *The Mirror of My Life* (Arabic), vol. III, pp. 345 ff.

reinforced the public's conviction that only popular armed struggle could restore the rights of the Palestinian people and free the occupied Arab territories.

The head-to-head between the Palestinian organizations and the king of Jordan can be attributed to the consequences of the regional realignment further to the Rogers Plan presented by the USA and the United Nations, which provided for the evacuation of the Sinai and the West Bank in exchange for Egypt's and Jordan's recognition of the State of Israel. Whereas those two countries accepted the Rogers Plan and the UN's mediation by Jarring for its implementation, Syria formally rejected the plan at the joint meeting of the National and Regional Commands of the party on 31 July 1970. In August 1970 the Palestinian National Council categorically refused the Rogers Plan, which failed to address the legitimate demands of the Palestinian people. Rightly fearing that it would be the loser in this plan, the Palestinian National Council declared that it wanted to make Jordan the main base for Palestinian resistance for the liberation of Palestine. The trial of strength with the king of Jordan became inevitable.[59]

The Syrian Ba'th could hardly stand idly by as the dramatic events unfolded in Amman. Ever since its Eighth National Congress in April 1965, the Ba'th had been among the first Arab political forces to support the incipient Palestinian resistance. At the Ninth National Congress in October 1966, the Ba'th had advocated a people's war for the liberation of Palestine, even if it meant the war might spread to all Arab territories as required by the necessities of battle. On the basis of this strategy, Syria had allowed Palestinian organizations to develop their activities from its territory including along the front line, even if it meant destabilizing the region. This prompted Itzhak Rabin, chief of staff of the Israeli army, to call Syria the spiritual father of the Fatah in September 1966.[60] From the outbreak of the fratricidal fighting in Amman between Palestinians and Jordanians, the Ba'th National and Regional Commands met in Damascus and decided to support the Palestinian organizations. Concretely, it was decided to send into Jordan the Palestine Liberation Army (PLA), an auxiliary force of the Syrian army stationed in Syria, and the Saiqa, a Palestinian organization obedient to the Ba'th that was created by the party's Tenth National Congress in October 1968, and which therefore

---

[59] On Syria's position on the Rogers plan, see Tlass, *The Mirror of My Life* (Arabic), vol. III, pp. 584 ff.
[60] See Guingamp, *Hafez El Assad*, p. 172.

depended on Salah Jadid. The operation was entrusted to Hafez Assaz, the defence minister, with instructions to support the PLA and Saiqa with Syrian troops, including the air force if necessary.

Assad's opinion of the Arab strategy pursued by Syria and the Ba'th was known to all at least since the extraordinary sessions of the Fourth Regional Congress of March 1969 when he gave the attendees his communication in the form of an indictment of the policy on regional relations. It was likely that he would not be overzealous in enforcing the decisions of the party's National and Regional Commands. Besides, the USSR was advising caution, the USA was threatening, and Israel was massing troops along the border. Direct intervention by Syria might have entangled it in a conflict in which it would have been alone and ill-prepared against the Israeli army, without military support from Egypt and Iraq. Assad decided not to take such a risk with its unfathomable consequences and did not support the PLA and Saiqa units, which, having reached Irbid some 20 km from the border and 80 km from Amman, were forced to turn back by Jordanian air force strikes.

In Damascus, Hafez Assad's opponents wanted to use the opportunity to blame him for the fiasco of the intervention in Jordan and for failing the Palestinian resistance. In the face of the revived rivalry between Salah Jadid and Hafez Assad, Nuredin Atassi resigned as head of state on 18 October. The National Command convened an extraordinary session of the Tenth National Congress for 30 October 1970. The congress met for twelve days. Hafez Assad and his chief of staff, Mustafa Tlass, had to face accusations from the majority of congress-goers who backed Salah Jadid. They were accused of weakening the party, creating power centres within the party, mismanaging the intervention in Jordan, and having forged closer ties with Iraq without a mandate from the party. Hafez Assad recalled the demands he had already presented to the extraordinary session of the Fourth Regional Congress in March 1969 and made a long speech to the Congress.[61] Hafez Assad and Mustafa Tlass were dismissed from office by the National Congress, the party's highest authority, but the army was theirs. The day after the congress, the armed forces occupied the headquarters of the National and Regional Commands on 13 November. Their opponents were placed under house arrest. For three days Assad tried to negotiate. Several approaches were made to Nuredin

---

[61] See the text of Hafez Assad's speech in Tlass, *The Mirror of My Life* (Arabic),vol. III, pp. 357 ff.

Atassi, who held the positions of (resigned) head of state, prime minister, and secretary-general of the party. He refused to condone Assad's coup and preferred to remain within the legal framework of the decision of the extraordinary session of the Tenth National Congress.[62] Finally, on 16 November, Radio Damascus announced the army coup which was referred to simply as a 'Corrective Movement'.

6.3 The 'Corrective Movement' and the Institutionalization of the Revolution (1970–2000)

Salah Jadid pulled no punches in his attempt to be rid of his adversary, Hafez Assad. He had convened a session of the National Congress to dismiss him from office along with the chief of staff, Mustafa Tlass. But the events that followed showed that while Salah Jadid controlled the party, his rival Assad had a firm grip on the army. In February 1966, the army under cover of the dissolved Regional Command, had undertaken a coup and eliminated the National Command. Four years later, the army, this time under no party cover, overthrew the decisions taken by a National Congress and dissolved the party's National and Regional Commands. Unlike the coup of February 1966 which had left almost 800 dead, the army coup of November 1970 went off without bloodshed.

6.3.1 The 1971 Provisional Constitution and the Legitimization of the Regime

It was via a communiqué from the Ba'th PRC broadcast by Radio Damascus in the evening of 16 November 1970 that the population learnt without surprise that the country had changed leadership. To justify the army coup, the PRC communiqué took up the major topics that Hafez Assad had developed since the extraordinary session of the Fourth Regional Congress of 1969, namely, to form a National Progressive Front bringing together political formations with similar objectives to the Ba'th's under Ba'th leadership, to establish a parliament, adopt a permanent constitution, and strengthen the armed forces. The communiqué also took up the traditional issues dear to the Ba'th such as Arab union and socialism. With regard to pan-Arabism, the Ba'th PRC announced from the outset

---

[62] On the details of the contacts with Nuredin Atassi, see Tlass, *The Mirror of My Life* (Arabic), vol. III, p. 441.

that it wished to join the ongoing tripartite negotiations among Egypt, Libya, and Sudan with a view to uniting the three countries. And with regard to socialism, the PRC communiqué simply asserted that the new leaders intended to pursue its socialist orientations and allow popular organizations to play an enhanced role in the social transformation. On foreign policy, the communiqué announced the new leaders' intention to strengthen cooperation with the eastern bloc and especially the Soviet Union. But the promise that many Syrians probably remembered from this communiqué and hoped to see fulfilled was the PRC's undertaking to spare no effort to ensure the freedom and dignity of citizens.[63]

The 1971 Provisional Constitution

As a rare enough feat in Syrian history that merits special mention, the 1970 Corrective Movement was the only coup that kept the existing constitution in place, probably because it had never served to regulate the country's institutions, having no elected People's Assembly, that is a parliament, since the constitution had been promulgated in 1969. A few hours before the communiqué was read out on Radio Damascus, the new Ba'th PRC had appointed Assad secretary-general. The names of the twelve PRC members, including two military members, Hafez Assad and Mustafa Tlass, were not immediately made public.[64] The new PRC hastened to appoint an interim head of state from among its members. Hafez Assad chose age as the selection criterion. The eldest comrade was to be head of state. The honour fell to Ahmad Khatib, former secretary of the teachers union, who became interim head of state on 20 November 1970.[65] On the same day, Hafez Assad formed a cabinet of twenty-five ministers including fourteen Ba'thists and two Communists. Assad held on to his defence portfolio and the position of prime minister.

Institutionalizing the new regime involved amending the 1969 constitution. The PRC adopted an amended version of the 1969 constitution in February 1971. The 1971 provisional constitution took up almost in full the previous constitution save a few exceptions that heralded the presidential style of the new regime. Apart from this, the political philosophy of the two texts remained the same. As promised in the initial communiqué of the PRC broadcast on the evening of 16 November 1970, three

---

[63] For the full Arabic text of the communiqué of 16 November 1970, see Tlass, *The Mirror of My Life* (Arabic), vol. III, pp. 446 ff.
[64] See the list of PRC members in *ibid.*, pp. 455–6.
[65] For details of the circumstances of this appointment, see *ibid.*, p. 457.

months after the introduction of the new regime a People's Assembly was appointed on 16 February 1971. This assembly, which for the first time in five years was to serve as legislative chamber, comprised 173 members, eighty-seven of whom were Ba'th members, with four women representing the different popular and socio-professional sectors. The assembly also included representatives of the Arab Socialist Union (Nasserists), Socialist Unionists (ex-Ba'thists who had become pro-Nasserists), members of the Arab Socialist Party, and the Communist Party.

The next day, the PRC amended the 1969 provisional constitution, in accordance with its article 78, so as to reintroduce the position of president of the republic instead of head of state. The major difference between the 1971 constitution and that of 1969 was that the president was not to be elected by the People's Assembly as provided for in 1969 but by a popular referendum once the candidacy had been proposed by the Regional Command and approved by the assembly. Article 48 of the 1971 constitution described this procedure in detail, which was later taken up by the 1973 permanent constitution. The People's Assembly was to receive from the Ba'th Regional Command the name of its candidate for the position of president. It was to endorse him and then submit the proposal to a popular referendum. In fact, it was a plebiscite to which the electors had to answer yes or no.

Article 9 of both the 1969 and 1971 constitutions provided that the People's Assemblies would be elected. That included both the People's Assembly that served as the parliament and the local assemblies. It is probably for this reason that the 1971 constitution shortened the legislature to two years instead of the four years provided by the 1969 constitution, the 1971 legislature being appointed by the PRC and not elected. The first election of a People's Assembly was to take place two years later under the 1973 permanent constitution and the lifetime of the assembly was then extended to four years. In addition to the shortening of its mandate, the 1971 constitution reduced the powers of parliament. Contrary to what had been provided for by the 1969 constitution, the council of ministers was no longer answerable to the People's Assembly but to the president alone. The 1971 constitution also stripped the chamber of the competence to amend the constitution.

Under the provisions of the 1969 constitution, the council of ministers was jointly accountable to parliament and each minister was accountable to the president of the council of ministers for his own ministry (art. 65). Under the new version of article 65, in the 1971 constitution, the council of ministers was answerable to the president of the republic alone. The president's enhanced role was also manifest in the provisions concerning the competence to legislate between parliamentary sessions. The 1969 constitution provided that the council of ministers could legislate in the intervals between parliamentary sessions. This responsibility was withdrawn from the council of ministers in 1971 and left to the president of the republic alone (art. 54(2)). The 1969 constitution provided that if the position of head of state was vacant or if he was unable to exercise his functions, the speaker of the People's Assembly would act as head of state. In the event of the head of state's resignation or death, the speaker would convene the assembly within ten days to elect a new head of state. Should the assembly be dissolved or if there remained less than two months until its term of office expired, it was the president of the council of ministers (prime minister) who would exercise the powers of head of state until the new assembly met (art. 60). These provisions were cancelled by article 82 of the 1971 constitution, which provided that in the event the supreme office should fall vacant without the president of the republic having named a vice-president, then the prime minister would act as head of state until a presidential referendum could be held.

Article 78 of the 1969 constitution granted extensive powers to the Ba'th. It provided that pending the convening of a People's Assembly, the Ba'th Regional Command could amend the constitution as it wished. In addition, the Regional Command exercised the power to appoint the head of state or interim head of state, accept his resignation or dismiss him, appoint the president and ministers of the council of ministers, accept their resignations or dismiss them, lay down the general policy of the state, decide to go to war, and order general mobilization. Article 78 of the 1971 constitution was radically different and restricted the powers of the party while extending those of the president of the republic. The new version of article 78 stipulated simply that until the adoption of a permanent constitution, the number and appointment of members of the assembly would be decided by the Ba'th Regional Command. Henceforth the Ba'th had simply to present its candidate for the presidency of the republic to the People's Assembly. It no longer had the power to dismiss the president of the republic, to appoint the president of the council of ministers or the ministers, to dismiss them or accept their resignation, to lay down the general policy of the state, or to decide on war or order general mobilization. All of these competences went to the president of the republic alone, except that of amending the provisional constitution, which remained among the Ba'th Party's powers (art. 76).

No Syrian constitution had previously granted so much power to the president of the republic. On this point, the 1971 constitution differed even from the other Ba'thist constitutions of 1964, 1966, and 1969 that were based on collegiate power and granted a greater role to the party. The 1971 provisional constitution gave precedence to the president of the republic to the detriment of the party and the People's Assembly. It contained the seeds of the personalization of power that was to be confirmed subsequently.

The new assembly met on 22 February 1971. Two days later it approved of Hafez Assad's candidacy proposed by the Regional Command for the position of president of the republic. It elected Ahmed Khatib, who had resigned as interim head of state, as speaker of the People's Assembly. On 12 March 1971, Assad was elected president of the republic by universal suffrage for seven years with 99.2 per cent of the votes. The election was held in an ad hoc manner with no regulatory or legislative text to frame it. Assad tasked General Khlefawi with forming a government. The assembly concentrated on its major task of preparing a permanent constitution. On 11 May 1971, it adopted a law on local administration opening the way to local elections, the first elections for ten years, to be held on 3 March 1972. Ahmed Khatib resigned as speaker on 26 December 1971 to become prime minister of the Federation of Arab Republics. He was replaced by Fehmi el-Yusefi, who supervised the preparatory work for the permanent constitution by a special commission directed by Mozhar al-Anbari.

Legitimization of the New Regime by Union (Syria, Egypt, and Libya)

The beginning of the Corrective Movement was reminiscent of the period immediately after the Revolution of 8 March 1963. Both had raised nationalist hopes in terms of regional and especially pan-Arab policy. A few days after the Revolution of 8 March 1963, the new Syrian authorities had made known their intention to begin negotiations to re-establish the union with Egypt but on sounder bases than the 1958 union. The same phenomenon occurred in 1970. On 27 November 1970, eleven days after the Corrective Movement, the new governing authorities announced Syria's intention to join the Cairo agreement between Egypt, Libya, and Sudan with a view to forming a union. But the big difference between 1963 and 1970 was that Nasser, the symbol of Arab unity, was no more. The future was to show the nationalists that his successor had neither his stature, nor his charisma, nor above all the same ambitions. By coincidence, the creation of the Federation of Arab Republics (FAR) was signed by Syria, Egypt, and Libya (without Sudan) on 17 April 1971, that is on the same day that, eight years earlier, the tripartite Charter of Union among Syria, Egypt, and Iraq had been signed on 17 April 1963. It was a ragbag federation among three countries with divergent visions and ambitions. From the time it was created, it was obvious that this experiment at union had very scant chance of success.

As in 1963 when the tripartite Charter of Union had been signed, the FAR served the purposes of the new regime in Damascus by giving it a stamp of approval in terms of Arab nationalism. The same was true for Egypt, where Sadat had just replaced Nasser, who had died in September 1970. The constitution of the Federation of Arab Republics was approved by referendum in the three countries on 1 September 1971. It scored 99.9 per cent of votes in Egypt, 98.0 per cent in Libya, and 96.4 per cent in Syria. In fact, the FAR never saw the light of day because the differences over domestic and foreign policy among its members were too great, but even its virtual existence promoted the process of planning and preparation for the October 1973 war by Syrian and Egyptian armies against Israel. It was under the FAR's flag that the two countries launched their assault on Israeli lines in the Sinai and Golan Heights on 6 October 1973 to liberate their lands occupied by Israel in 1967.

6.3.2 *The Reorganization of Political Life*

Hafez Assad tried to broaden political life in Syria so as to include those parties judged ideologically and sociologically close. This timorous opening favoured historical reconciliation among political movements that were close without, though, calling into question the supreme power of the Ba'th or, of course, the president's authority.

The National Progressive Front

The idea of bringing together within a single political movement those parties, currents, and individuals with similar political sensitivities in order to achieve common objectives was not new in the Syrian context. Such a formation had already proved its worth under the French mandate. The National Bloc had for almost two decades federated all of the lifeblood of Syrian society with a view to achieving two fundamental objectives – total independence and the reunification of the Syrian territories that had been separated by the French authorities.

After the Ba'th came to power, the idea of creating a common front of all the progressive and nationalist parties took seed. Akram Hawrani, the founder of the Arab Socialist Party that merged with the Ba'th in 1952 before hiving off after 8 March 1963, tried unsuccessfully to create such a front in Beirut in 1966 but without the Ba'th. The idea was taken up again some years later, in a very different context, by Hafez Assad at the extraordinary session of the Fourth Congress of the Ba'th in 1969, again unsuccessfully. Assad was in a minority in the party and the mainstream led by Salah Jadid was not favourable to the plan. After the Corrective Movement of November 1970, nothing stood in the way of implementing the scheme for a common front with the nationalist and left-wing parties. The communiqué of the Ba'th Provisional Regional Command of 16 November 1970 took up the idea, which was also adopted some months later by the Ba'th Fifth Regional Congress. Assad wanted to create his own version of the National Bloc.

Talks for the formation of a National Progressive Front (NPF) included parties that were ideologically close to the Ba'th – the Syrian Communist Party, the Union of Arab Socialists, the Socialist Unionist Movement, and the Arab Socialist Union. Negotiations began in May 1971 and were completed on 7 March 1972. The new regime had begun to prepare the ground for such discussions back in February 1971 by appointing among members of the People's Assembly figures who were close or affiliated to the political parties that were to form the future NPF. Although Hafez Assad was a fervent supporter of this arrangement, the idea of creating a front with other political parties was not self-evident for the other party leaders. Mustafa Tlass confessed in his memoirs that the Ba'th leadership, himself included, was at first surprised at the idea of sharing power, as were the leaders of the other political parties.[66]

Experience subsequently proved that the creation of the NPF did not mean sharing power, which remained very much in Ba'th hands. The NPF was rather an opportunity for historical reconciliation with the parties of Nasserist persuasion such as the Arab Socialist Union and the Socialist Union Movement, some of whose members or supporters had opposed the Ba'th, including by arms, during the period 1963 to 1966. The NPF also included a dissident branch of the Arab Socialist Party led by Abdel Ghani Qanut, and the Syrian Communist Party, a traditional ally of the Ba'th since 1966. In 2005, when the Syrian Socialist Nationalist Party was reconciled with the Ba'th, it joined the NPF.

The NPF compact provided that it would be led by the Ba'th and set its priority as the liberation of occupied Arab territories, the development of

---

[66] See Tlass, *The Mirror of My Life* (Arabic), vol. III, p. 468.

five-year plans, discussion of economic policy, the development of plans for civic and socialist education, the development of the popular democratic regime, constitutional institutions, local councils to supplement popular sovereignty, the development of popular organizations, and the strengthening of the armed forces. The compact reserved militant action and the recruitment of new members within the army and the universities to the Ba'th alone. The NPF statutes provided that its president should be the secretary-general of the Ba'th, the president of the republic. They also provided for the creation of a central leadership in Damascus and provincial leaderships. The central leadership had seventeen members, nine of whom were Ba'th members.

The Fifth Regional Congress (8–14 May 1971)

The process of internal legitimization of the new regime required a Regional Congress that was convened after the provisional constitution had been adopted and a council appointed to serve as a constituent and legislative assembly. Although the primary objective of the Fifth Regional Congress was therefore to legitimize the armed coup of 16 November 1970, it was also a chance to make known the new regime's orientations in terms of Syria's domestic and foreign policy. Four main topics dominated this first congress of the Assad era held in Damascus from 8 to 14 May 1971. In terms of the party's domestic policy, the congress marked the end of the collegiate leadership of the Ba'th and therefore of the state – since the party ruled the state – and the beginning of the personalization of power.

One of the most important conclusions adopted by the congress stated that 'The Congress considers that our people, at this stage in their development and in current circumstances, feel the necessity for a leader, a guide around whom to close ranks. It is beginning to see in comrade Hafez Assad this leader that it so badly needs'.[67] The Syrians' leaning towards a guide behind whom they could rally had been demonstrated in the past when the population came together behind the Emir Faysal, who was welcomed as victor by jubilant crowds on his entry into Damascus as liberator after the withdrawal of Ottoman troops in 1918. The Syrians continued to support him after making him king until Damascus was occupied by French troops. The same phenomenon occurred for Nasser, as the herald of Arab nationalism, who was acclaimed as a saviour when

---

[67] Guingamp, *Hafez El Assad*, p. 201.

he visited Damascus in 1958 to sign the Syrian–Egyptian Union. Faysal and Nasser were considered as guides and leaders by Syrians as they each in their own way symbolized the symbiosis between a great cause and a providential man. Given past experience, Hafez Assad's initiative in 1971 to set himself up as the guide and leader of historical dimension was certainly not without its risks. Few commentators would have bet on his rule lasting thirty years.

The second major topic addressed by the congress was the strengthening of what the Ba'thists like to call the 'domestic front' by opening up to other similar political currents, by the joint creation of an NPF under the aegis of the Ba'th and by the invitation to the front's members to become involved with the constitutional institutions. The third important topic was the encouragement of private initiatives to participate in the development of the national economy via a mixed sector that would include both public and private capital. This mixed sector was to play an important role in the Assad era and be a favoured means for injecting private capital into the economy. The fourth topic of significance that was debated at the congress concerned Syria's signing of a compact establishing the Federation of Arab Republics with Egypt and Libya.

The congress ended with Assad predictably being elected secretary-general. This congress marked the end of the transformation of the Ba'th since it first came to power in 1963 and the beginning of a new era in the party's history. From an initially left-wing reformist party that abided by liberal parliamentary democracy, the Ba'th had changed in 1963 and 1966 into a party structured in a similar way to Communist parties and adept in popular democracy, before becoming simply the party of one man, Hafez Assad.

The Eleventh National Congress (August 1971)

Three months later, the Eleventh National Congress was held in Damascus. The holding of a National Congress had been something of a challenge after the movement of 23 February 1966 that saw the Regional Command eliminate the National Command, which was the party's supreme body that had brought together the Ba'th's founders. It was even more of a challenge in light of the movement of 16 November 1970 when the army eliminated both the National and the Regional Commands. The Syrian Ba'thists had at all costs to find Arab Ba'thist militants to endorse the armed coup against the former National Command and legitimize their new power. But in the end this proved to be comparatively easy. The congress was held in a serene atmosphere among comrades of the same stripe. It backed the directions of the new Regional Command expressed at the Fifth Regional Congress in May 1971 such as the creation of the NPF in Syria and the establishment of a Federation of Arab Republics. At the end of proceedings, the congress quite naturally elected Hafez Assad as Ba'th secretary-general.

6.3.3 The 1973 Constitution

The 1973 constitution was drafted by the People's Assembly appointed in February 1971. The initial draft, prepared by a special committee led by Mozhar al-Anbari,[68] was approved by a vote of the People's Assembly on 30 January 1973 and amended on 20 February 1973.[69] The text was adopted by referendum on 12 March 1973 by 97.6 per cent of those voting and promulgated by the president the next day. The 1973 constitution merely developed certain aspects of the 1969 provisional constitution. The 1971 provisional constitution had introduced the office of president of the republic and extended his competences. The 1973 constitution set out in detail the functions of the People's Assembly, which was to be elected, and defined its relations with the president and the government. Like the previous Ba'th constitutions, the 1973 version was built more on a division of functions than on a separation of powers.

The preamble to the 1973 constitution was consistent with those of 1969 and 1971, although more concise. It took up the Ba'th doctrine developed since the Sixth National Congress of 1963 but without referring expressly to that congress. The preamble set out the main themes of the Ba'thist discourse, namely that the party represented the working masses, that it had been the first Arab political party to give its revolutionary meaning to Arab unity and establish a connection between the national struggle and the fight for socialism. Unlike the 1969 and 1971 versions, the 1973 preamble made no allusion to the way power had been organized since the Revolution of 8 March 1963, namely the National Revolutionary Council and the Presidential Council of 1963 and Decisions 1 and 2 of the Ba'th PRC of 23 and 25 February 1966. The period between 8 March 1963 and 16 November 1970 was completely erased. Ba'th official history now included just two dates, the Revolution of 8 March 1963 and the Corrective Movement of 16 November 1970. The preamble described

---

[68] Mozhar al-Anbari was appointed by Bashar Assad in October 2011 to preside over a National Committee to prepare the 2012 constitution.
[69] The circumstances of this amendment are explained below.

the achievements of the new regime since the Corrective Movement. It cited the establishment of the Federation of Arab Republics as a pan-Arab achievement and the creation of the NPF as a national achievement. The remainder of the preamble was identical to the 1969 and 1971 versions.

The structure of the 1973 constitution remained broadly similar to that of the 1969 and 1971 constitutions. It was divided into four main titles on 'Fundamental Principles', 'Powers of the State', 'Amendments of the Constitution', and 'General and Transitional Provisions'.

Title I on 'Fundamental Principles' contained four chapters on 'Political Principles', 'Economic Principles', 'Principles of Education and Culture', and 'Freedoms, Rights and Public Rights'. The political philosophy behind title I remained the same as in the 1969 and 1971 constitutions. However, a few differences should be pointed out. Article 3(1) of the 1973 constitution reintroduces Islam as the president's religion. This provision, which had featured in all previous Syrian constitutions, including the first Ba'thist constitution of 1964, had been deleted from the 1969 and 1971 constitutions. The final text of the constitution proposed in January 1973 by the People's Assembly contained no article on the president's religion. The Islamists and in particular the Muslim Brotherhood took this as a pretext to stir up trouble in Hama, which then spread to Homs and Aleppo. To appease matters, at President Assad's request, the People's Assembly amended the initial draft constitution on 20 February 1973 to reinstate Islam as the president's religion.[70]

The other innovation of the 1973 constitution compared with the 1969 and 1971 ones was a slight reshaping of the article on the leading role of the Ba'th for the state and society. The new article 8, formerly article 7 in the earlier constitutions, added that the Ba'th 'leads a National Progressive Front that seeks to unify the potential of the popular masses and put them in the service of the objectives of the Arab Nation'. Through this article, the NPF achieved a constitutional standing. The function of the armed forces defined in article 10 of the 1969 and 1971 constitutions was extended in the new article 11 to specify that the purpose of the armed forces was to defend 'the security of the homeland and ... safeguard the objectives of the Revolution in union, freedom, and socialism'. In earlier versions of this article, the armed forces had to defend the territory and 'the unitary and socialist objectives of the Revolution'. In the new version, the objectives of the Revolution were replaced by the Ba'th trilogy of union,

---

[70] For details see Jabbour, *The Life of Political Parties* (Arabic), p. 21.

freedom, and socialism. The new regime thus expressed its intention to continue the experiment with the ideological army begun in 1963, that is, an army totally loyal to the Ba'th. With the growing personalization of the regime, loyalty to the party went hand in hand with, or was even subordinate to, loyalty to the person of Hafez Assad.

Chapters I and II of title I contained other new provisions such as the statement that Syria was a member of the Federal State of Arab Republics (art. 1). Article 6 stated that 'the flag of the state, its coat-of-arms, and its anthem are those of the Federal State of Arab Republics'. The People's Assembly revised this article on 16 March 1980 after Egypt signed the Camp David Accords in 1978–79 and opened an embassy in Tel-Aviv. In the new version, it stipulated that 'Syria's flag, coat-of-arms, and national anthem shall be determined by law'. Consequently, Syria took up again the flag and coat-of-arms of the Syrian–Egyptian Union of 1958–61 and kept its own national anthem from the period of the fight for independence during the French mandate.

Chapter I contained a new article 18 stating that saving was a national duty that the state protects, encourages, and regulates. Article 19 provided that 'taxation shall be established on an equitable and progressive basis in application of the principles of equity and social justice'.

Chapter IV of title I served as a Declaration of Rights. It contained new provisions and language that did not feature in the 1969 and 1971 constitutions. Thus article 25 stated that freedom is a sacred right; Article 26 specified that 'all citizens are entitled to participate in political, economic, social, and cultural life'. Article 38 expanded on this, adding that all citizens 'have the right to express their opinions freely and publicly in speech, writing, and by any other means of expression and to contribute through supervision and constructive criticism, to safeguarding the security of the nation and the homeland, and to strengthening the socialist regime. The state guarantees the freedom of the press, printing, and circulation pursuant to the law'; and article 39 asserted that 'citizens are allowed to assemble and protest peacefully in accordance with the principles of the Constitution'. These very liberal provisions unfortunately remained a dead letter. They were neutralized by the emergency law that had been in force since 1963. It was only in 2011, after the beginning of the Syrian crisis, that the authorities finally abolished the emergency law and adopted laws on press freedom and the right to protest under articles 38 and 39 of the constitution. It is noteworthy that the 1973 constitution, like those of 1969 and 1971, did not provide for the possibility of creating political parties. Nor did it recognize the right to strike, which was declared illegal by the 1985 Labour Code.

The greatest innovation of the 1973 constitution compared with the preceding two was in title II, 'On the Powers of the State', chapter I, 'On Legislative Power', which defined the competences of the People's Assembly, the legislative body that was to be elected by the citizens. Syrians had not elected their legislative assembly for twelve years. The last elections of the kind had been in December 1961 after the ending of the union with Egypt. However, those elections had unfolded in a very different political context. In 1961, the voters had been called on to elect a legislative assembly in the context of a western-style liberal democratic regime, whereas in 1973 the electors were invited to elect a legislative assembly under a popular democratic type of regime based on that of Communist bloc countries.

The 1973 constitution set out the details of the People's Assembly: 'It shall exercise legislative power' (art. 50(1)) and 'its members shall be elected by universal suffrage in a secret, direct, egalitarian ballot pursuant to the provisions of the electoral law' (art. 50(2)); 'The legislature shall last for four years' (art. 51); 'The members of the Assembly represent the people in its entirety' (art. 52). The most innovative provision concerned the structure of the parliament: 'The law shall determine the electoral constituencies and the number of Members of the Assembly, half of the seats of which shall be for workers and farmers, and the other half for the remainder of the population' (art. 53). This article took up a similar provision inherited from the tripartite charter of 1963 between Egypt, Iraq, and Syria to be examined in the next chapter. This provision, which was included in the 1973 electoral law, provided that 'the popular and political organizations based on direct free elections shall truly and fairly represent the forces making up the majority. For this workers and farmers shall be guaranteed at least half of the seats on these organizations at all levels, including within the Assembly of the Nation [the parliament].'[71]

By the terms of the constitution, 'the electoral law shall contain provisions ensuring the freedom of electors to choose their representatives, the fair character of elections, the right of candidates to supervise electoral operations, and the penalties for anyone falsifying the outcome' (art. 57). Article 58 stipulated that elections were to be held within ninety days of the Assembly's mandate expiring. If the new Assembly is not elected

---

[71] See the tripartite charter in Khouri, *Plans for Arab Union, 1913–1989* (Arabic), p. 407.

within this time, the former Assembly shall convene as of right upon the ninety days expiring and remain in office until a new Assembly is elected. The provisions of this article were applied in 2011. The mandate of the Assembly in office expired in May 2011, but given the exceptional circumstances since the onset of the crisis in March 2011, elections for a new People's Assembly could not be held. Consequently, the former Assembly met as of right during the first half of August 2011 and remained in office until the election of a new People's Assembly in May 2012 on the basis of the new constitution adopted by referendum in February 2012.[72]

Under article 60(1), The People's Assembly is convened by a decree of the President of the Republic within two weeks of the proclamation of the election results. It shall convene as of right on the following day if the decree convening it is not promulgated. Article 61 added: The Assembly holds three ordinary sessions per year. It may be convened to hold extraordinary sessions if its President so decides, or on written request from the President of the Republic, or further to a request from one-third of its Members. Under article 67, members of the Assembly enjoyed immunity during the life of the Assembly.

Article 70 stated that Assembly members were able to propose laws: They have the right to initiate laws, address questions, and question the Government and Ministers.

Article 71 continued:

> The People's Assembly nominates but in fact endorses the candidate to be submitted by the Ba'th Regional Command for the Presidency of the Republic for the popular referendum; approves the laws, it discusses government policy; it rules on the budget and development plans, on international treaties and agreements concerning state security, rights relating to sovereignty, concessions to foreign companies, treaties and agreements entailing spending for the Treasury that is not planned in the budget or spending that is contrary to the laws in force and whose enforcement requires new legislation; it grants general amnesties; accepts or declines the resignation of any of its Members; votes motions of censure of the Government or Ministers.

The 1971 constitution had stripped the assembly of the power to censure the government by limiting such power to the president of the republic alone. The 1973 constitution restored this competence to the People's Assembly as the 1969 constitution had initially provided. According to article 72, a motion of censure can only be voted after interpellation of the Government or the Minister in question. The censure motion shall be brought by one-fifth of the Assembly Members. The Government or

---

[72] See Chapter 8, 'The Fifth Republic'.

any Minister shall be held liable by the majority of the Members of the Assembly. Article 73 added: The Assembly may form ad hoc commissions of its Members to investigate and collect information on questions pertaining to its responsibilities.

The president's status and powers were addressed in chapter II 'Executive Power' of title II on 'Powers of the State'. The 1971 provisional constitution had already established the preponderance of the president in the workings of the institutions and the 1973 constitution reinforced this pre-eminence. Article 83 stated that 'the candidate for the Presidency must be an Arab Syrian, enjoying his civil and political rights and be aged forty years at least'. The provisions of this article were revised by the People's Assembly on 10 June 2000, the evening of Hafez Assad's death, to allow Bashar Assad to succeed his father as president. The amendment to article 83 was promulgated the next day by the vice president, Abdel Halim Khaddam, and published in the official journal. The provisions of the new article 83 stated that the candidate for the presidency had to be at least thirty-four years old.

The procedure for designating the president was identical to that introduced by the 1971 provisional constitution. Article 84 provided that the name of the candidate for the position of President of the Republic shall emanate from the People's Assembly upon proposal by the Ba'th Regional Command and then be submitted for the people's approval by way of referendum. The election shall take place at least thirty days and at most sixty days before the expiry of the President's term of office. This provision was revised on 1 July 1991 to allow the election of the new president to take place one month at least and six months at most before the term of office of the acting president expired. Article 85 set out that a candidate is elected if he obtains the majority of votes cast. The term of office is for seven years. Article 86 provided that should the President be provisionally unable to carry out his functions, he was to delegate them to the Vice-President. This provision could not be applied in late 1983 and early 1984 when Hafez Assad had heart problems that prevented him from exercising power for a few months because he had not then appointed a vice-president. At the time, he delegated his functions to an ad hoc committee composed of senior officials of the state and the Ba'th Regional Command.

Under article 95, the president was permitted to appoint one or more vice-presidents. Article 88 of the constitution stipulated that 'should the President be unable to fulfil his duties, they shall be performed by the First Vice-President or the designated Vice-President. Should the incapacity be permanent, or in the event of death, a referendum shall be held to elect a new President', while article 89 provided: Should the position be vacant and no Vice-President appointed, the President of the Council of Ministers shall hold the powers and responsibilities of the President of the Republic until a presidential referendum can be held.

The president was the true head of the executive: he decides on the State's general policy after consultation with the Council of Ministers and oversees its implementation (art. 94); the President of the Republic appoints one or more Vice Presidents, the President of the Council of Ministers, the Vice Prime-Ministers, the Ministers, and Vice-Ministers (art. 95); 'The President of the Republic may convene the Council of Ministers to meet under his chairmanship' (art. 97); he may dissolve the People's Assembly by a decision stating the reasons. Dissolution cannot occur twice for the same reason. In the event of dissolution, elections shall be held within ninety days (art. 107); 'The President of the Republic may convene an extraordinary session of the People's Assembly' (art. 108(1)). The President promulgates laws adopted by the People's Assembly. He may object to them within one month by a decision stating its grounds. If the Assembly passes a law again by a two-thirds majority it shall be promulgated by the President of the Republic (art. 98).

Further, 'The President of the Republic has the initiative in law-making. He may present bills to Parliament' (art. 110). Under article 111:

(1) The President exercises legislative power in the interval between sessions of the People's Assembly. He shall submit all legislation that he promulgates in this context to the People's Assembly at its first sitting.
(2) The President of the Republic may legislate during the sessions of the People's Assembly in the event of absolute necessity affecting the nation's interests or the security. Legislation thus promulgated shall be submitted to the People's Assembly at its next sitting.
(3) The Assembly may abolish or amend such legislation by a law voted by a two-thirds majority of the Members present at the session provided that this majority is not less than the absolute majority of Assembly Members. The amendment or abolition cannot be retroactive. If the Assembly does not abolish or amend the legislation in question, it is taken to be approved as of right and need not be passed.
(4) The President may legislate in the gap between legislatures. Legislation thus promulgated is not submitted to the People's Assembly but may be amended or abolished under the terms provided by subsection 3.

Other powers of the president set out in the 1973 constitution were: 'The President of the Republic shall proclaim and abolish the state of emergency pursuant to the law' (art. 101); 'In the event of serious and imminent danger liable to threaten the unity, integrity, and independence of the nation's territory or impede the proper working of its constitutional institutions, the President of the Republic shall take urgent measures required by the circumstances' (art. 113); the President of the Republic exercises all other powers generally attached to his office such as the supreme command of the armed forces (art. 103); the ratification and abrogation of treaties (art. 104), the exercise of the right of pardon (art. 105), the appointment of civil servants and the military (art. 109), submission to referendum of questions concerning the state's higher interests (art. 112).

The responsibilities of the council of ministers were also addressed in title II, chapter II on 'Executive Power'. Compared with the extended role of the president, the powers of the council of ministers appeared modest indeed, although article 115 stipulated that 'the Council of Ministers is the state's highest executive and administrative organ'. Article 117 stated that the president of the Council of Ministers and the ministers were accountable to the President of the Republic and, under article 71, may also be the subject of a censure motion by the People's Assembly. The cabinet had no means of putting pressure on members of the People's Assembly because the right of dissolution was reserved to the head of state alone as per article 107 cited above. When formed, 'the Council of Ministers lays its general policy and its government manifesto before the People's Assembly' (art. 118). No vote of confidence by the members was required. Article 122 provided: 'In the event of expiry of the term of office of the President of the Republic or permanent incapacity to exercise his prerogatives, the Council of Ministers shall take care of current affairs until the appointment of a new Cabinet by the new President of the Republic'. Unlike the 1969 and 1971 constitutions, article 127 of the 1973 constitution listed the responsibilities of the council of ministers carefully. It was to participate with the president in drawing up and performing the state's general policy; it coordinated and performed the activities of the ministers and all the public services and institutions; it established the draft budget, it drew up bills but could not initiate legislation, which fell to the assembly members and the president; it prepared development plans; subscribed and consented to loans, concluded treaties; saw to the enforcement of laws; and set forth administrative decisions.

Title II, chapter III on 'Judicial Power' covered in its section I questions on the judiciary and the prosecution service. It included a High Constitutional Court, which had already existed in various forms in the 1920, 1928, 1950, and 1962 constitutions. The Ba'th constitutions of 1964,

1969, and 1971 had abolished it. It was reintroduced in 1973 as an institution tasked with 'deciding on objections about the election of Members of the People's Assembly' (art. 144); 'the constitutional character of laws' (art. 145); 'the constitutional character of bills and legislative decrees' (art. 147); and 'trying the President of the Republic in the event of high treason after charges proposed by one-third of the members of the People's Assembly followed by a favourable vote of two-thirds of the members' (art. 91). The role of this institution remained largely virtual.

The 1973 constitution could be amended upon a proposal by the president or one-third of the members of the People's Assembly. Wherever it originated, the proposed amendment had first to be examined within a special commission before being submitted to a vote of the Assembly. A two-thirds majority was required for the amendment to be accepted. As stated, this procedure was used in 1980 to change the flag, in 1991 to amend the time for holding a presidential referendum when the president's term of office expired, and in 2000 upon the death of Hafez Assad to amend the minimum age for presidential candidates. It should be noted that for this final amendment, the People's Assembly voted in a plenary session on the amendment without it being discussed in a special commission, probably because of the exceptional circumstances following the president's death.

After the People's Assembly had drafted the text of the permanent constitution, the president promulgated a legislative decree on 14 April 1973 containing a new electoral law, the first under the rule of the Ba'th which had come to power ten years earlier, introducing several innovations into the electoral procedure. The first was to have enlarged the electoral constituencies to coincide with the *mohafazats* or provinces, except for Aleppo which was divided into two covering the city and the rural areas. The change in size of electoral constituencies with the transition from *cazas* to *mohafazats* meant voters were more remote from their elected representatives. This change, introduced under a political regime that presented itself as a 'popular democracy' living in a state of emergency since 1963, favoured candidates of the Ba'th and its allies within the NPF to the detriment of all others. The elections became elections for lists of candidates under the hegemony of the Ba'th and the executive.

The second major innovation of the 1973 electoral law that intensified the influence of the Ba'th and its allies was to introduce, pursuant to the 1973 constitution, the principle of the division of elected representatives in the People's Assembly into workers and farmers (category A) and the remainder of the population (category B). This distinction features in article 53 of the permanent constitution and had first been introduced in the 1963 Tripartite Charter that planned for a federal union between Syria, Egypt, and Iraq, which never came about.[73]

The 1973 law took up a provision introduced by the 1949 electoral law for voting to be extended to a second half-day if turnout was below 60 per cent. The 1973 law lowered the rate to 50 per cent. Opponents criticized this provision, which, they argued, made it possible to manipulate voting slips and facilitated fraud between the two days of voting.

The 1973 electoral law was amended by the legislative decree of 2 November 1980 abolishing electoral lists, the necessary condition for transparent elections, and introduced 'mobile ballot boxes', which, the opposition claimed, made it easier for the executive to manipulate elections. The electoral law was amended a second time by the legislative decree of 12 April 1990 setting the number of deputies in the People's Assembly at 250, cancelling the number of elected officials for each constituency depending on the civil status registry lists, and assigning a set number of elected officials for each *mohafazat*.

Among the other innovations of the 1973 electoral law, mention should be made of the possibility of being both a member of the assembly and holding a ministerial portfolio, despite the principle of the separation of powers. It should also be pointed out that army officers were allowed to stand for parliamentary elections. One of the major shortcomings of the 1973 law was that it contained no provision for judicial control of the electoral procedure.

General elections for the new assembly were held in May 1973. During the campaign, strikes and protests broke out in Hama, Homs, Latakia, and Aleppo. The movement lasted four days and was harshly suppressed by the authorities. The elections gave an unsurprising victory to the NPF candidates, who won 124 out of 186 seats, 104 of which went to the Ba'th. Only a third of the electorate turned out to vote and the elections had to be extended by a day in accordance with the electoral law on low turnout.

Interestingly, although he had the parliament he wanted and that caused him no difficulties, Hafez Assad legislated over the three decades by way of legislative decrees as much as by statutes passed by the People's Assembly. President Assad issued 1134 legislative decrees between 1971 and 1999 while the parliament passed 1158 acts over the same period.[74]

---

[73] See the analysis of the 1963 Tripartite Charter in Chapter 7, 'The Pan-Arab Constitutions'.
[74] Figures obtained from the People's Assembly services in Damascus. These acts and legislative decrees were passed under the provisional constitution of 16 February 1971 and then the constitution of 12 March 1973.

This method of government reflected both the outright presidentialization of the regime with a ubiquitous head of state within all the wheels of power (executive and legislative) and also a crisis of the system, with a parliament that failed to fully assume the primary function attributed to it by the constitution. That the head of state should be bound to submit the legislative decrees he issued between parliamentary sittings to the People's Assembly and that it could abolish or amend them by an act changed nothing fundamentally. In thirty years, the parliament did not reject a single legislative decree.

Syrian governments under Hafez Assad, like their predecessors since the Ba'th had come to power in 1963, remained administrative bodies tasked with implementing decisions taken by the president and the Ba'th Regional Command. At no time did the successive governments become decision centres. They remained organs for performing tasks. This was why, in thirty years, only six prime ministers in addition to Assad himself became heads of government.[75] No specific rule seems to have dictated the appointments and resignations of governments under Hafez Assad. Generally, their timing did not coincide with constitutional events such as the re-election of the president, the election of a new parliament, or the occurrence of a major political event such as a Ba'th Regional or National Congress. The only common point was that the prime minister had to belong to the Ba'th Regional Command.

6.3.4 Political Stability and the Final Challenges to Hafez Assad's Power

Political stability under Hafez Assad was displayed, among other things, by the compliance with all the deadlines laid down by the 1973 constitution, whether the election of the president by referendum (1978, 1985, 1991, 1999) or parliamentary elections (1973, 1977, 1981, 1986, 1990, 1994, 1998). Throughout all of Syria's earlier history only one president had managed to complete his term of office (President Shukri Qwatli, 1943–48) and similarly only one parliament had managed to complete its legislative period (1943–47). After taming the army between 1966 and 1970, Hafez Assad decidedly made the Ba'th Party toe the line after his coup d'état of November 1970.

---

[75] Hafez Assad's prime ministers were Abdel Rahman Khlefawi (1971–72; 1973), Mahmud Ayubi (1972–73; 1973–78), Mohamad Ali Halabi (1978–80), Abdel Rauf Al-Kasm (1980–87), Mahmud Al-Zu'bi (1987–99), and Mustafa Miro (1999–2000).

This political stability was due less to the interplay of constitutional institutions and the electoral law than to the strength of the regime. The two major internal challenges that the Hafez Assad regime had to face during his thirty years in power were the armed opposition of the Muslim Brotherhood (1977–82) and the 1984 crisis with his brother Rifaat Assad. Hafez Assad came out as victor both times: one at the cost of brutal repression and a sizeable military operation to take back control of Hama, which had fallen into the hands of the Muslim Brotherhood in February 1982; the other by exiling Rifaat further to the rallying of army units around their commander in chief. Apart from those two challenges, political life under Assad's rule was limited to the holding of Ba'th National and Regional Congresses with, from 1980 onwards, the formation of a timorous opposition led by Jamal Atassi, who created the Democratic National Rally. The hegemony of the regime led to a freezing of Syria's political life.

The Extraordinary Session of the Fifth Regional Congress (30 May–13 June 1974)

This meeting was the only extraordinary session of a party congress under Hafez Assad. The aim was to discuss with the members of the Regional Congress the consequences of the October 1973 War and of the war of attrition on the Golan Heights and Mount Hermon that ensued for eighty-two days as from 11 March 1974 until a disengagement agreement was concluded through the mediation of US Secretary of State, Henry Kissinger. The disengagement agreement returned to Syria one-third of the Golan including its capital, the martyred city of Kuneitra, which had been entirely razed by the Israeli army before it withdrew. The agreement also provided for peace negotiations in Geneva between Arabs and Israelis at which the thorniest questions of the conflict were to be addressed, including Israeli withdrawal from the remainder of the territories occupied by Israel in June 1967 and the Palestinian question. The congress-goers approved the disengagement accord unanimously. The Geneva talks never came about because Egypt preferred to move unilaterally towards a separate peace that led to the 1978–79 Camp David Accords after Sadat's visit to Jerusalem in 1977.

This extraordinary session of the Fifth Congress recognized for the first time an embarrassing phenomenon for a left-wing party supposed to represent the labouring classes, namely the suspicious enrichment of some of its executives. The opening up of the private sector and financial support from the Gulf States further to the October 1973 War had given rise to what was not always a healthy symbiosis between certain party leaders, state leaders, and a new class of businessmen who supported the regime. The congress did not formally characterize this phenomenon as corruption although that is what it was. It delegated to the secretary-general the creation of a special committee under his authority to investigate comrades whose lifestyle had suddenly changed and ask them to account for it.[76] As an endemic scourge of the regime, corruption was obviously not eradicated by the creation of a special committee of the party. It was not just the expression of the lack of moral compass of certain executives tempted to get rich quick, but more generally the expression of the natural shortcomings of a state-run economy, of civil servants with modest living standards, and the ambition of people from long-marginalized social categories who had finally made it to the top of the state apparatus to rapidly improve their standard of living.

The Sixth Regional Congress (5–14 April 1975)

As something rare enough to be worth pointing out, this congress was held at the date required by the by-laws, that is four years after the previous congress. This compliance with deadlines reflected the stability in the country after the Corrective Movement of 16 November 1970. This stability, though, did not induce the Ba'th to lower its guard. One of the recommendations of the congress was that party members should undergo military training. The congress was preceded by internal elections to choose who would attend. More than five hundred delegates were elected to participate in the biggest congress in the party's history. It convened at the time when Egypt was confirming day after day its great strategic turn towards the United States and its abandoning of armed conflict to settle the dispute with Israel that was to be formally contained in the agreement on disengagement from the Sinai of 1 September 1975. Tension was mounting dangerously in neighbouring Lebanon and was soon to degenerate into a civil war with regional ramifications that would last for nearly fifteen years.

To plainly show that the party led the state in accordance with article 8 of the constitution, the congress adopted recommendations in all areas in which the public authorities acted (foreign policy, Arab policy, domestic policy, agriculture, health, education, taxation, and so on). Among the many recommendations from the congress, one reflects quite well the spirit of the time and the pragmatism of Hafez Assad and his entourage

---

[76] See the Arab Socialist Ba'th Party, *The ASBP Regional Congresses* (Arabic), p. 57.

in terms of regional policy. In reference to the disengagement agreement with Israel secured under the auspices of the USA, the congress made the following recommendation: 'Reminder of the necessity to clearly understand the nature of tactical political action exercised by the authorities to achieve their objectives and the necessity to draw the attention of the party's grass roots to differentiate between positions of principle that remain intangible and methods of political action that require advancement by stages and tactical flexibility'.[77]

The Twelfth National Congress (July 1975)

Egypt's new strategic orientation stoked tension in Lebanon and prompted the Christian militia to launch an assault on Palestinian organizations and their Lebanese allies so as to eliminate them militarily. It also caused a realignment of the position of the main regional actors including Syria, which moved closer to its Jordanian neighbour. This policy of opening up by Syria was encouraged and supported by the members of the Ba'th Twelfth National Congress meeting in Damascus in July 1975. Otherwise, this second national congress to be held since Assad had taken power went off without surprises.

The Seventh Regional Congress (22 December 1979–6 January 1980)

This congress was held at a time when the Syrian authorities felt encircled both internally and externally. Since 1977 the authorities had been confronted with a wave of attacks orchestrated by the Muslim Brotherhood. They concentrated on leading figures, mostly Alawis, whom they took as their targets. Among their victims were dignitaries of the regime, high-ranking army officers, and the dean of Damascus University. Their most notorious feat of arms was the cold-blooded slaughter in the grounds of Aleppo artillery school on 16 June 1979 of thirty-two officer cadets, all of Alawi origin. This attack was the apogee of more than two years of targeted killings by the Muslim Brotherhood. The congress recommended intensifying the security and political campaign until the Muslim Brotherhood was eradicated, reinforcing the propagation of socialist pan-Arab thought, asserting national unity, and widening popular participation in public affairs, re-evaluating religious teaching methods at all levels, and modernizing the ministry of religious affairs (*wakf*).[78] The

---

[77] See Arab Socialist Ba'th Party, *The ASBP Regional Congresses* (Arabic), p. 72.
[78] Carré and Michaud, *Les Frères musulmans*, p. 93.

congress also recommended establishing a central committee of seventy-five members elected by the Regional Congress as an intermediate echelon between the congress and the Regional Command. The confrontation with the Muslim Brothers continued for another two years, climaxing with the tragic events in Hama in 1982.

It is noteworthy that the Congress hardly addressed the Lebanese crisis although the Syrian army had already been deployed there for almost four years. The point of Syrian intervention in Lebanon had been explained by Hafez Assad in a 1976 speech defining his objectives.[79] This intervention, with Washington's tacit agreement, aimed first to restore a balance in the field so as to prevent a military defeat of the Christian camp by Islamic-Progressive forces supported by the PLO and to pre-empt any bid by Israel to intervene in the conflict as protector of the Christians. For Assad it was for the Arabs to ensure the survival and security of Christians of the Orient. After Sadat's visit to Jerusalem in 1977 and the signing of the Camp David Accords in 1978–79, the strategic deal changed in Lebanon. As Israel had set itself the goal of having Lebanon as the second Arab country to sign a peace agreement with the Hebrew State, Damascus became reconciled with the Muslim Lebanese camp and the PLO.[80]

The Thirteenth National Congress (10–25 August 1980)

This was the last National Congress to be organized under Hafez Assad. It was held at a pivotal time of Arab rivalry and regional tension. Sadat had resolutely turned his back on the Arab world and committed himself to a separate peace with Israel by signing the Camp David Accords. Iraq, which had fallen under the control of Saddam Hussein, had moved away from Syria and had buried the National Action Charter signed between the two countries in November 1978 that planned for an eventual union of the two states ruled by the Ba'th.[81] Lebanon continued to plunge deeper into an endless civil war with regional ramifications. This congress proclaimed itself to be 'standing up to the Camp David Accords'. Less than a month after the congress ended, Iraq was to trigger a murderous war of eight years with Iran. Syria found itself alone against Israel, without Egypt or Iraq. To break its isolation, it attempted to create a unitary state

---

[79] See Hafez Assad's speech of 20 July 1976 at the meeting of *mohafazat* councils for local administration, Ba'th National Command, 1976.
[80] For an analysis of Syria's role in Lebanon at this time, see Pakraduni, *La Paix manquée*.
[81] For a Syrian version of the causes of the divorce between Syria and Iraq, see Tlass, *The Mirror of My Life* (Arabic), vol. IV, pp. 53–68.

with Libya in September 1980 based on a merger of the two countries that never came to be.

The Eighth Regional Congress (5–20 January 1985)

The congress-goers reviewed the many developments in Syria and the region since the previous congress in 1980. Domestically, the regime had quelled in bloodshed the armed insurrection of the Muslim Brotherhood in Hama in February 1982. This incident ended the armed opposition of the Muslim Brotherhood whom Damascus claimed were supported by Jordan and Iraq.[82] Following heart problems, Hafez Assad, supported by the vast majority of the Regional Command, the army, and the party, had thwarted the aims of his brother Rifaat, backed by the USA, to claim power.[83] Regionally, Sadat had paid with his life for the separate peace with Israel. His assassination sounded a warning to any Arab leader who might follow in the footsteps of the Egyptian president. Iraq had become bogged down in a far longer war than expected with Iran, to the great satisfaction of Israel, which was for a time rid of two states that were not particularly benevolent towards it. Lebanon had managed to overcome the effects of the Israeli invasion in June 1982. The multinational force had withdrawn from Lebanon in 1984 and Syria's allies had managed to have President Amin Gemayel abolish the 1983 Israeli–Lebanese agreement.

The PLO, defeated by Israel, had had to leave Lebanon and transfer its headquarters to Tunis. The Palestinian forces loyal to Yasser Arafat were transferred to Yemen while the units close to Damascus withdrew to Syria before eventually returning to Lebanon. The 1982 Israeli invasion opened a wound that never really healed between Yasser Arafat and Hafez Assad. The Palestinian leader, concerned for his independence, had always refused to coordinate military actions in Lebanon with Syrian forces, even at the time of the Israeli aggression in June 1982. It followed that Palestinians and Syrians adopted different approaches in response to the Israeli military offensive.[84] Some of Fatah's senior officials found it hard to swallow the order not to fight Israel in southern Lebanon and to fall back on Beirut. One of the main Palestinian military leaders, Colonel Abu Mussa, broke away and with Syria's help created an organization called

---

[82] Arab Socialist Ba'th Party, *Reports of the Eighth Regional Congress* (Arabic), p. 15.
[83] For a version of the crisis with Rifaat by Hafez Assad's supporters, see Tlass, *The Mirror of My Life* (Arabic), pp. 345–407.
[84] For a Syrian version of the war in Lebanon in 1982, see Tlass, *The Israeli Invasion of Lebanon* (Arabic).

'Fatah Intifada' (Fatah Insurrection) that ousted Arafat's Fatah from the Palestinian camps in Lebanon with the support of the Syrian army.[85]

Well before the 1982 invasion, Lebanon had become the leading theatre of confrontation between Syria and Israel, the latter of which was trying to bring the land of the cedar into its fold and to sign a peace accord similar to that signed with Egypt. Syria rose to the challenge and resisted Israeli claims that almost materialized with the eviction of the PLO from Lebanon further to the 1982 Israeli aggression and the agreement between Lebanon and Israel on 17 March 1983, but that was finally abolished further to the resistance of Syria's Lebanese allies. To counterbalance Israeli military superiority and Washington's unflagging politico-military support for Tel-Aviv since the creation of the Hebrew State, in 1980 Syria signed a Treaty of Friendship and Cooperation with Moscow containing a strategic dimension. The immediate effect of this agreement was to sanctuarize Syrian territory. In the medium and longer term, this agreement facilitated Syria's search for a strategic equilibrium with Israel.

The congress reviewed all these developments. Rifaat Assad had been allowed to return from his gilded exile between France and Spain to attend the congress which, it is worth observing, set more store by regional than purely local developments. The political reports published at the end of the congress devoted seventy pages to foreign policy and a mere ten pages to domestic policy.[86]

This was the last Regional Congress of the Hafez Assad era. The party went without a congress for fifteen years. Hafez Assad died weeks before the Ninth Regional Congress that enthroned his son and heir Bashar as the new secretary-general of the party in June 2000.

The Syrian Opposition

Facing the Ba'th and its allies, a timid democratic opposition was to crystallize around Jamal Atassi. A former member of the Ba'th in the 1940s and 1950s,[87] minister after the March 1963 Revolution, a fervent supporter of the union with Egypt, the historical leader of the Arab Socialist Union that brought together Nasser's supporters in Syria, Jamal Atassi backed the Corrective Movement led by Hafez Assad in November 1970 and for a time his party joined the NPF created in 1972 under the aegis of the Ba'th. In January 1980, together with other figures from political parties of

---

[85] Abu Mussa, *Colonel Abu Mussa*.
[86] Arab Socialist Ba'th Party, *Reports of the Eighth Regional Congress* (Arabic).
[87] The Ba'th owes to him its motto, 'A united Arab nation with an eternal message'.

left-wing pan-Arab sensitivity, he created the National Democratic Rally. Initially this movement grouped dissidents from political parties within the NPF criticizing the political line adopted by their leadership in support of the regime. Like Siamese twins opposed to the NPF, the parties within the National Democratic Rally were the Democratic Arab Socialist Union, an offshoot of the Arab Socialist Union; the Syrian Communist Party-Political Bureau, a spin-off from the Syrian Communist Party; the Arab Socialist Movement, a spin-off from the Arab Socialist Party originally formed by Akram Hawrani; the Workers Revolutionary Party, a spin-off of left-wing Ba'th members; and the Democratic Arab Socialist Ba'th Party, a spin-off from the Ba'th led by Ibrahim Makhus, former foreign minister at the time of Salah Jadid. The regime more or less tolerated the members of the National Democratic Rally – although many of them such as the Communist leader Riad Turk spent many years in prison – because their opposition was limited to simple criticism without undertaking any action on the ground. Jamal Atassi led the National Democratic Rally until his death in 2000, a few weeks before that of Hafez Assad. Hassan Abdel Azim was to become head of the party after Jamal Atassi's demise.

6.3.5 *The Assad System*

The longevity of the Assad regime in a country characterized since its independence by chronic political instability and the transformation of Syria under his rule from a pushover for regional and international powers into a major actor on the near-eastern scene capable of projecting its influence beyond its borders led analysts to take an interest in the personality of Hafez Assad and the regime he put in place.[88] The system Assad imposed was a complex regime that cannot readily be grasped by simplistic descriptions and analyses. Several readings are required to grasp the complexity and originality among which feature the economy, society, history, and politics.

The Syrian economy, society, and state were largely conditioned by the overall refoundation programme decided on by the Ba'th since it took power in 1963 and expressed in resolutions adopted by the Sixth National Congress

---

[88] Among the main books on Hafez Assad and his policy are Seale, *Assad. The Struggle for the Middle East*; Bitterlin, *Hafez Assad. Le Parcours d'un combattant*; Maoz and Avner, *Syria under Assad*; and Le Gag, *La Syrie du général Assad*.

in October 1963. The 'Theoretical Foundations' of the Sixth Congress had fixed the structure of ownership of the means of production (public, cooperative, and private) by attributing pride of place to the public sector, which was confirmed and amplified by the massive nationalizations between 1963 and 1965 that mostly affected the industrial sector (70 per cent of industry) and all of the financial sector. Alongside this, the agrarian reform transformed the situation in the countryside. The redistribution of land in rural areas marked the end of the domination of the great landowning families and sapped the foundations of their micro-economic influence. The politicians and military, who were traditionally close to the big landowners and the middle classes who played a leading role in the Second Republic, were stripped of their civil rights and imprisoned or exiled. In this sense, the cumulative effects of the coup d'état of 8 March 1963 in economic, social, and political terms were the equivalent of those of a real revolution.

As the sole master on board, the Ba'th decided to re-shape the economy, society, and state power in its own way. The state played a dominant part in this restructuring work, without claiming to be neutral in any way. Through the public sector, the state was engaged in a deliberate policy to control production flows and the distribution of wealth. As is often the case in such circumstances, the public sector was not always efficient in terms of yields, productivity, and profits. However, it continued to enjoy the virtually unconditional support of the public authorities because, in addition to its primary economic function, the public sector fulfilled a social function that was equally important by offering a chance of employment to people who were often close to the spheres of power, in other words, by camouflaging part of the real unemployment figures. In supporting the public sector, the state promoted the emergence of new economic elites related to its own political elites.

Unlike the large landowners and the industrial and financial middle classes who vanished from the Syrian economic landscape, the commercial middle class prospered under Ba'th rule. Domestic trade was still about 80 per cent controlled by the private sector and Hafez Assad's Corrective Movement in 1970 gave new impetus to foreign trade, which had previously been largely state run.[89] This window of opportunity for private initiative benefited the traditional merchant class of the big cities such as Damascus and Aleppo. The larger-scale profits reaped from domestic and foreign trade by the new dominant economic class related to the political elites in power were primarily invested in property or transferred abroad.

[89] Michel Seurat in Raymond, *La Syrie d'aujourd'hui*, p. 126.

Capital flowed into the property sector because of the absence of other outlets into industry and foreign trade, which were 70 per cent controlled by the public sector, or into agriculture after the agrarian reform, or into a national finance and banking circuit that was completely under state control and unable to attract and absorb the monetary flows and channel them into the economic cycle. The flow of capital into the property sector was to cause price and rent rises incompatible with middle-class purchasing power. The price of the square metre in Damascus reached levels comparable with big European capitals. Hence young Syrians, who made up the majority of the population, found it very difficult to leave their parents' place and start a home of their own. New housing supply failed to keep pace with population growth and demand. The very strict limitation on products that could be legally imported, including for the building industry, favoured smuggling through Lebanon and Jordan. Smuggling was often protected and even organized by officials of the regime or people close to them. But smuggling was not a one-way business. State-subsidized basic necessities such as heating fuel and medicines were smuggled to neighbouring countries by well-organized traffickers with good connections in the bureaucratic apparatus. Ultimately the Syrian state was losing across the board thanks to this two-way smuggling.

The October 1973 War brought a massive inflow of capital from Arab oil states to Syria in support of the war effort against Israel. Syria was the only country remaining from the 'confrontation' at the Arab Summit held in Baghdad in 1978, which saw the exclusion of Egypt from the Arab League further to President Sadat's signing of the Camp David Accords. This financial rent from non-productive origins was used for purchasing weaponry and to strengthen the army, but in doing so it also created a system of rewards for loyalty towards the holders of power and intensified clientelism. Hafez Assad's regime gradually opened up new economic areas to private capital such as the tourism, textile, pharmaceutical, and agri-food industries. After the First Gulf War and Damascus siding with the camp opposed to Iraq, Hafez Assad signed legislative decree no. 10 that was to promote the inflow of foreign, mostly Arab, capital into Syria. These economic opportunities were very carefully studied so as not to challenge the supremacy of the new middle class that had arisen from the Revolution of 8 March 1963 and that was intimately connected with the state bureaucracy and so as not to unduly increase dependence on the outside world. The Syrian economy, which was structured like a war economy with a preponderant share of spending on national defence, had to stand fast against foreign pressure.

Interpretations of the Assad System

The rule instituted by Hafez Assad has been the subject of many analyses. Three types of explanation can be recalled here: the Marxist analysis, the sectarian analysis, and the Ibn Khaldun model.

The Marxist Analysis The traditional Marxist analysis considers that the class struggle of the coup d'état of 8 March 1963 and the Ba'th's control of the country represent the coming to power of the petty bourgeoisie. The Syrian Communists did not back the coup d'état and were even harshly repressed until the neo-Ba'th came to power in February 1966 after the coup d'état of the Jadid faction. With the nationalizations and Ba'thist Syria's rapprochement with the Soviet Union, the Syrian Communists began to change their minds about the Damascus regime. For the Syrian Communist Party, the nationalizations in industry between 1963 and 1965 introduced a form of non-capitalist development in the sector that ought to benefit the working class. However, their secretary-general, Khalid Bakdash, warned in 1965 that, unless safeguards were put in place, the development of the industrial sector might well lead to forms of state capitalism and the formation of a bureaucratic middle class that would exploit the situation and acquire the privileges held by the previous bourgeois without the need to have legally inherited its means of production.[90] It was a prescient vision.

The Syrian Communists were torn between their attachment to the Marxist–Leninist ideology that forced them to a certain disdain for what was considered simplistic Ba'thist doctrine and their loyalty to the Soviet Union, which saw Syria as an important regional ally. Should they support the Syrian regime solely because the Soviet Communist Party asked them to? This question caused an open rift at the Third Congress of the Syrian Communist Party in 1969 between the party's secretary-general, Khalid Bakdash, and Riad Turk, a member of the Political Bureau around whom a majority of the Bureau's members gathered. The crisis was partly resolved in 1971 through joint mediation of the Soviet and Bulgarian Communist Parties. At its Fourth Congress in 1974, the party adopted a compromise on 'non-capitalist development' in Syria. This arrangement did not secure unanimous support and was withdrawn at the party's

---

[90] Khaled Bakdash, 'Syria on a New Path', 1965 reprinted in Nadaf, *The Words of Khaled Bakdash* (Arabic), pp. 188–9.

Sixth Congress.[91] This did not prevent some militants from following Riad Turk and leaving the party in 1976 further to Syrian intervention in Lebanon and Damascus support for the Christian militia against the left-wing Lebanese–Palestinian forces. They founded the Communist Party-Political Bureau. Riad Turk remained an irrepressible opponent of Hafez Assad's policies and spent several years in prison. The Syrian Communist Party was to split again ten years later in 1986 over the policy followed by Mikhail Gorbachev. Khalid Bakdash objected to *perestroika*, which forced some militants to create their own (unified) Syrian Communist Party led by Yusef Faysal. This new formation was admitted to the NPF alongside its elder party.

Despite these two splits, most Syrian Communists remained associated with the Ba'th within the NPF. They officially considered the Syrian regime to be close to 'scientific socialism'.[92] But their position was actually more subtle and more nuanced because, although associated with the ruling party, Khalid Bakdash, the charismatic secretary-general of the Communist Party, did not refrain from stating that in view of Syria's domestic policy alone, his party should have joined the opposition.[93]

The Sectarian Analysis   In basing their analysis on the class struggle alone, but without seeing their rationale through to the end for reasons of international policy, the Syrian Marxists failed to pose the question of the integration of society and assumed consequently that the other divides and in particular religious sects were to be relegated to the level of the superstructure. This was not the case of the 'new Orientalists' who based all of their analysis on the sectarian prism. This interpretation is based on the string of Orientalist works by European travellers to the region between the eighteenth and early twentieth centuries and which served as the intellectual basis for the carve-up of the region in the aftermath of the First World War. The civil war in Lebanon (1975–90) and the invasion of Iraq in 2003 promoted a new literature giving precedence to sectarian divides.

The new Orientalists were not the first to take an interest in the sectarianization of power in Syria. As stated earlier, this line of thinking was first adopted behind closed doors in Damascus at the Ba'th's Second Regional

---

[91] Nadaf, *The Words of Khaled Bakdash* (Arabic), pp. 67–9.
[92] See Majed, 'Le parti communiste syrien', pp. 129–52.
[93] Nadaf, *The Words of Khaled Bakdash* (Arabic), p. 46.

Congress in 1965. As concerns Syria, the adherents of the sectarian prism take as their starting principle that the geographical area of Syria is inhabited by a mosaic of communities on a sectarian or ethnic basis which coexist side by side, unable or unwilling to merge into a modern society with a national character. In this scheme of things, the regime set up by the Ba'th is supposedly just a screen behind which the Alawi community, which is in a minority in the country, can exercise its power and dominance over the other communities and especially the Sunnites, who make up the majority. The most illustrious representative of this school is Nikolaos van Dam, author of the famous *The Struggle for Power in Syria*. The author analyses meticulously the careers of Alawi senior officials in the army and scrutinizes their tribal, clan, and family origins to draw conclusions that are almost explanatory and even causal about their rise and the positions they hold. He argues the army and regime are fully controlled by the Alawi community behind a Ba'thist, socialist, and pan-Arab façade.

This analysis ignores the general will of the Syrians to live together regardless of their community of origin. It may seem enticing superficially, but the circumstances of Syria, including in the army, cannot be reduced to a simple analysis of intercommunity relations. Such an interpretation fails to account for the complexity of the situation and to suitably explain the phenomenon of Alawi intra-community (Jadid–Assad rivalry) or intra-family (Hafez–Rifaat) conflicts. Van Dam suggests in his conclusions that there is a connection between the political stability of Syria and some degree (without specifying what degree) of sectarianism, regionalism, and tribalism.[94] This conclusion does not square with the Syrian crisis in March 2011 that broke out outside the sectarian, regional, or tribal prism and outside the framework of internecine struggles within the army, party, and state.

Although it can be asserted that membership of the Alawi community was instrumentalized by some, it is important to observe that Hafez Assad did not take this as an end in itself but at most as one means among others of consolidating his regime. If he did take advantage of it, it was to strengthen and extend his influence within the army and the state. But this was not an exclusive criterion. Other factors played a paramount part in forming a loyal network around the head of state, such as Arab–Syrian nationalism and personal loyalty. While at the beginning of the Fourth Republic and with the advent of the Ba'th, figures of Alawi origins were

[94] Van Dam, *The Struggle for Power in Syria*, p. 136.

thrust to the fore and, for various reasons, occupied leading positions in the army, party, and state, this trend began slowly to shift after the crisis between Hafez Assad and his brother Rifaat in 1984. The preponderant element became personal loyalty to the head of state. This tendency was intensified after Bashar Assad came to power.

The Ibn Khaldun Model Ibn Khaldun's theory of the state seems to offer a better basic model for understanding the circumstances of the Syrian state and the Assad system. It was the French researcher and sociologist, Michel Seurat – who died prematurely and tragically in Lebanon in 1986 – who took up and adapted this model to the Syrian situation.[95] In his magisterial book *Al-Muqaddima* (*Prolegomena*) written in the fourteenth century, Ibn Khaldun begins with a basic given of physical and human geography in Islamic lands that, as he saw it, produced two separate ways of life, bedouin and settled. For Ibn Khaldun, a settled population is one that produces more than is strictly necessary. Unlike the bedouin population, it accumulates and amasses wealth. In this scheme of things the bedouin are not necessarily nomads. They may also be poor farmers with no stores for the future, reduced to living from hand to mouth. Cities are the brightest aspect of settled life. It is in cities that the most refined trades develop (woodworkers, artists, doctors, jurists, etc.). Science and history, which rely on cumulative memory, also develop in settled and not bedouin societies.

Ibn Khaldun explains the emergence of cities thanks to what he calls *mulk*, that is, the state.

> Ibn Khaldun thus names the coercive force that through taxation concentrates the wealth of the territory it controls in a capital city, for the benefit of elites who redistribute these resources to the craftsmen, merchants, scholars – to all those whose positions and skills are closely dependent on a wealthy clientele, who multiply with them, and who perfect their know-how for them ... The prosperity of the city ..., however, raises demand [for tax], stimulates the subsistence output of peasant taxpayers and enriches them in turn, which enables a rise in taxation, new diversification and new progress in the arts and knowledge, and therefore a new increase in urban demand and prosperity of the countryside, etc. These 'virtuous circles' have but one requisite condition, that subjects be disarmed.[96]

---

[95] Michel Seurat's main contributions to the topic including under the pseudonym of Gérard Michaud are 'La Syrie ou l'Etat de barbarie'; 'Remarques sur l'Etat syrien'; 'Terrorisme d'Etat, terrorisme contre l'Etat: le cas syrien'; Carré and Michaud, *Les Frères musulmans*.
[96] Martinez-Gros, 'Comprendre la marche du monde', p. 25.

The coercive force for levying taxes requires a form of violence that the state cannot find among its own subjects and the populations it controls because it has banned and domesticated it. It is therefore among the bedouin, who live outside the state, that it finds the violence it requires. Bedouin society is characterized by a subsistence economy on the verge of starvation. Violence within it is not centralized. The family, clan, and tribe secure protection for their members in exchange for unfailing solidarity. 'Ibn Kahldun calls 'asabiya (*esprit de corps*) this primitive solidarity that is peculiar to bedouin groups but that the settled state mobilizes and transforms for its own benefit into a force for coercion and for maintaining law and order'.[97] The introduction of bedouin violence into the city and the heart of the state may take two forms: the enrolment of mercenaries (mamluks, janissaries) or the takeover of state control by a single tribe. The natural solidarity of bedouin may sometimes be accompanied by a religious message or *da'wa*.

Once the tribe has integrated the state and the settled way of life, its primitive solidarity, 'asabiya, disintegrates. The head of the tribe, having become king, rushes to disarm his tribe so that it cannot oppose the levying of taxes and so weakens the state.

> Settled society and the sovereign's political will converge therefore to abolish the 'asabiya, the tribe's combined strength. In general, two or three generations, 100 to 120 years, are enough for there to be nothing left of the initial *esprit de corps*. The triumphant monarchy is disarmed and dependent for its defence on expensive ... and ultimately ineffective mercenaries in the face of the assaults of a new 'asabiya from the bedouin world.[98]

In this scheme, settled bedouin violence is the driving force behind a social system with no nuances. One is either dominant or dominated, either ruler or ruled.

This Khaldunian model was taken up, expanded, and adapted to Syrian circumstances by Michel Seurat:

> For this fourteenth-century Maghrebi thinker [Ibn Khaldun], when city-dwelling society is in crisis, all of the clans excluded from the city are stirred up and create a hitherto unknown internal consensus; they form an 'asabiya so as to conquer the seat of power and benefit from the crisis destroying the state. This centripetal movement of taking the city that controls the state leads one of the competitors (the Alawi clan and their allies in Syria, for example) to victory. But straight away, corruption, lust, the

[97] Ibid.
[98] Ibid.

will to rule without sharing destroy the (formerly marginal and now central) group, giving way to another competition, the formation of another *'asabiya*. That is what I have called a *jama't*-state, a concept that is lacking in Ibn Khaldun's theory, because he recognizes that he 'lacks the necessary knowledge of the Orient and its peoples'. The fact is that Ibn Khaldun invariably speaks of marginal tribes and more specifically of bedouins against settled peoples or city dwellers; but this opposition between the minority currently holding power and groups excluded from power, whatever their nature can be generalized: clans or tribes on the one side, with their apparent agnatic line of descent, and religious communities on the other side. ... And it is here that politics arises again, understood not as the formation of a space of citizenship, but as domination, as power without law. To overlook the political dimension of a particular competition that unfolds not in a pluralistic democratic state but in a *jama't*-state is to give in to folkloristic temptation.[99]

This *'asabiya* was grafted onto the pan-Arab and socialist message of the Ba'th, which played a similar role to the *da'wa* in the Khaldunian model. It went along with an informal social compact that widened the base of support for the regime and that may be summarized as: redistribution of land via agrarian reform, free education at all levels, free health care, subsidies for basic necessities, control of industry via a wide public sector while allowing the parallel development of agri-food, textile, pharmaceutical, and tourist industries financed by private capital. Domestic and to some extent foreign trade were left to the city-dwelling, merchant middle class and various advantages were afforded to the military, civil servants, and Ba'th party officials.

Foreign Policy Protection of the Regime

The longevity of the Assad system over the thirty years of his unshared reign over Syria was not due just to this hybrid *'asabiya* which he managed to widen and control. It rested too on his regime's ability to take up for its own benefit, while renewing them, the permanent characteristics of the Syrian national project and transpose them to the regional scale with the tacit agreement of the majority of its citizens. The updated version of the national project under Assad involved the strengthening of multi-sectarian coexistence and the Syrian secular model despite the preponderant influence granted to certain members of the Alawi community within

---

[99] Communication by Michel Seurat to the conference 'Journalistes et chercheurs face au Liban et au Proche-Orient', Lyon, 3–4 January 1985, at the initiative of Lyon II University and the journal *Esprit*, pp. 5–10.

Syria's borders and, beyond its borders, the protection of the Christian minority in Lebanon; the refusal of Israeli or western hegemony while avoiding any direct confrontation with the West except for the brief spell when Andropov ran the Kremlin; the refusal on principle to carve up the Arab nation; the organization of a front to resist Israel, bringing together Lebanese and Palestinian political and military formations; and the quest for greater social justice.

The projection of Syrian ambitions on the regional scale had two objectives. First to propagate certain aspects of the Syrian national project, the fundamental traits of which had barely altered since the separation of the Arab provinces of the Ottoman empire and that still commanded a broad consensus within the Syrian population. Second, to de-territorialize the geographical area of confrontation between the regime and its opponents by taking violence whenever possible outside its national territory that had been sanctuarized against any foreign attack after the signing of a strategic agreement with the Soviet Union in 1980.

Thus Syrian diplomacy, through a skilful balancing act and even brinkmanship at times, based on the astute exploitation of international and regional rivalries, managed to neutralize and counter the designs of the various players on the near-eastern stage. This policy successfully averted dangers that could have turned into a threat to the regime. And yet the period was not short of crises. The architect of this regional policy who was second in command to Hafez Assad in foreign policy was Abdel Halim Khaddam, his foreign affairs minister (1970–84) and then vice-president (1984–2005).

The cornerstone of Syrian regional and international policy during the Hafez Assad period was certainly resistance to Israel and the refusal of any Israeli hegemony over the Near East. To ignore this basic fact would be to fail to recognize the very foundations of Damascus policy over three decades. In order to check the ambitions of Israel backed by its US ally, Syria was constantly forced to seek out regional and international alliances. The regional alliances varied. It was first Egypt with which it waged the October 1973 War. After Sadat's 1977 visit to Jerusalem and the Camp David Accords in 1978–79, Syria's hopes turned briefly towards Iraq. But in 1979 Saddam Hussein aborted the attempt to create a solid Iraqi–Syrian front against Israel and launched a deadly war against Iran (1980–88). Iran, after the fall of the Shah, proved a valuable ally for Damascus. The closer ties between Syria and Iran in the 1980s offset somewhat the loss of the Egyptian ally.

THE 'CORRECTIVE MOVEMENT' 335

Internationally, the ally cut out for Syria was the Soviet Union. The alliance between Moscow and Damascus since the Ba'th came to power in 1963 was cemented by a strategic agreement in 1980 and it reached its zenith under the presidency of Andropov (1983-84) before going into comparative decline under Gorbachev because of a change in Soviet policy together with regime change in Moscow in 1991. It was precisely during this period that Damascus readjusted its regional and foreign policy further to Iraq's invasion of Kuwait. Syria used the opportunity to renew its ties with Egypt and move closer to the Gulf countries; it supported the war launched by the USA to liberate Kuwait by deploying Syrian troops in Saudi Arabia and the United Arab Emirates although they did not take part in the fighting.[100] The Kuwait crisis provided the opportunity for a spectacular rapprochement between Damascus and Washington with substantial regional implications including the entry of Syrian forces into East Beirut in November 1990 and Syria's taking control, with its Lebanese allies, of all of the Land of the Cedar. This privileged position of Syria in Lebanon was formalized by a Treaty of Brotherhood, Cooperation, and Coordination in 1991. After the liberation of Kuwait, Syria took an active part in stabilizing the Gulf and played a leading role in drafting and monitoring the Damascus Declaration signed in 1991 by the Gulf Cooperation Council states, Egypt, and Syria. The good relations between Syria and the USA were strengthened by Syria's participation in the Arab-Israeli peace process initiated in Madrid in 1991 and continued on the Syrians' part with Washington as mediator.[101] The upswing in Syrian-US relations during the final decade of Hafez Assad's reign made up for the waning influence of post-Soviet Russia, which was embroiled in its own domestic affairs.

The last of the Israeli forces occupying southern Lebanon withdrew just days before Hafez Assad died. This defeat of Israel in the face of Lebanese resistance that was largely backed by Syria and Iran illustrated better than anything the deftness of Syrian foreign policy. It was a policy capable of reassuring the Gulf states while allying with Iran, negotiating with Israel while supporting anti-Israeli resistance in Lebanon and Gaza, maintaining good relations with the USA without being herded into its fold and without breaking with Russia. Ultimately, this astute foreign policy of

---

[100] For a Syrian version of the war in Kuwait, see Tlass, *The War of Liberation of Kuwait* (Arabic).

[101] For details of talks between Syria and Israel, see the interview in Arabic by Walid al-Muallem in *Revue d'études palestinnienes*, 29, Winter 1997, 16-28.

reconciling contrary forces bolstered Hafez Assad's regime domestically and protected it from regional and international designs.

By the end of Hafez Assad's reign, the Ba'th had passed its first test, that of holding on to power on a lasting basis. It brought to Syria the stability that its political system had so badly lacked since the country's independence. Syria under Hafez Assad changed its status. Instead of being something of a pushover in the region, it became a major regional player that was both feared and respected. The price the population had to pay domestically was high. Syrians had largely to abdicate their individual and collective political freedoms under the combined effect of the enforcement of the state of emergency since 1963 and the imposition of an authoritarian system under the cover of a popular democracy based on that of former Soviet bloc countries, which was hardly compatible with Syrians' vibrant and instinctive interest in politics. Those who ventured into active opposition to the regime became victims of brutal repression by the security forces. But most of the population managed to live with this because the Ba'th was the first regime since independence that proved capable of taming the army by politicizing it and converting it into an ideological army, although one in which, paradoxically, political activity was banned and restricted to unswerving loyalty to the person of the president, the Ba'th, and the regime.

The Ba'th constitutions (1964, 1966, 1969, 1971, and 1973) setting up the Fourth Republic and the political institutions that derived from them can be characterized at best as a superstructure in the Marxist sense. The stability of power owed more to the strength of the regime than to the formal interplay of the institutions. The absence of any counter-power (political opposition, media, civil society) facilitated excesses (corruption, clientelism, opportunism) of which the regime was aware but could not remedy, despite its efforts.

The stability of the regime was due also to the establishment of an informal social compact that took the form of various mechanisms designed to redistribute national wealth (agrarian reforms, nationalizations, free medical care, and education) for the benefit of the poorest and the least-favoured geographical areas (countryside, coast, mountains) while leaving doors wide open for the traditional city-dwelling merchant class (dealing in domestic and then foreign trade) and private initiatives in domains carefully defined by the state (such as the food industry, pharmaceuticals, textiles, and tourism). This compact largely ensured social peace in Syria, but towards the end of Hafez Assad's reign cracks began to appear because of population growth, the rising cost of social and educational services, and the emergence of a new middle class that was disinclined to share and that was well connected in the spheres of power.

The national project inherited from Syria's Founding Fathers after the separation from the Ottoman empire remained unchanged. It was simply updated to keep abreast of the developments of the day. Syria continued to be a model of multi-sectarian coexistence, in particular among Christians and Muslims, and protected Christians in Lebanon. The Ba'th regime continued as a matter of principle to refuse the division and carve-up of the Arab nation, to reject any foreign hegemony, and to resist Israel directly by force of arms (the October 1973 War), by negotiation (the Madrid process), and indirectly by way of the Lebanese and Palestinian resistance that were largely supported by Damascus. The projection of Syria's influence beyond its borders culminated in the final decade of Hafez Assad's presidency with it laying hands on Lebanon.

Hafez Assad dominated his era like no other politician of his generation. He remained at the forefront of Syrian history for more than three decades and was the origin of three Syrian presidential authoritarian constitutions (1969, 1971, and 1973). After the premature death of his eldest son, Basil, in 1994, Hafez Assad left to his second son and successor, Bashar, a dominant Syria that was stronger than the one he himself had conquered in 1970. In June 2000 Bashar Assad inherited an Imperial Republic.

7

The Pan-Arab Constitutions

The 'Pan-Arab constitutions' is the name given here to the constitutional-type texts Syria signed with a view to forming a union or federation with one or more Arab states. There are three such texts: the 1958 constitution of the United Arab Republic (UAR), the 1963 tripartite charter, and the 1971 constitution of the Federation of Arab Republics (FAR).

In the aftermath of its independence in April 1946, despite the joy at being freed from all foreign military presence and recovering its full sovereignty, independent Syria had a bitter taste left by its still incomplete national construction. The initial ambition of the Founding Fathers was greater than the borders of the Syrian Republic inherited from the mandate. To their mind, the national area was to include Lebanon, Jordan, and Palestine. Syrians concentrated on their own territorial area and continued to implement within their borders the components of the national project inherited from the Founding Fathers and in particular multi-sectarian coexistence within a civilian-governed state, the refusal of any foreign hegemony, and, regionally, resistance to the ambitions of armed Zionist groups towards Palestine, and the stand on principle against the carving up of the country. From the outset, this independent Syria appeared very different to Christian-dominated Lebanon based on a fragile and unstable sectarian system, or conservative and anxious Jordan subjected to British influence and not hesitating to find salvation by dealing if necessary behind the scenes with the new master of Palestine.

With whom should the union be initiated? It was the fate of Palestine that had just fallen into the hands of armed Zionist groups in 1948 that decisively influenced the choice of most Syrians as to national and regional strategy for closer ties with its fellow countries. The 1948 defeat or *nakba* prompted the largest party in the chamber, the People's Party, to explore the possibility of a union or confederation with neighbouring Iraq. Only Iraq seemed capable of joining forces with Syria to stand up to the challenge arising from the creation of the State of Israel. This policy of the People's Party was largely supported by its electorate in the north

(Aleppo), centre (Homs), and east of the country (Jazira). In addition to its strategic aspects, the union of Syria and Iraq also reflected the economic interests of these regions. This plan was opposed by the minority party in parliament, the National Party, the party of the president, Shukri Qwatli, who was from Damascus and historically close to the Saudi royal family, which was very worried about the possible impact of any closer ties between Syria and Iraq, not just for the Near East but for the entire Arabian peninsula. The National Party did everything it could to prevent any rapprochement. Army officers supported by various foreign powers took up the running at different times to prevent the People's Party – in the majority in successive national elections (1947, 1949, and 1954) – from implementing their plan for union with Iraq.

7.1 The 1958 Constitution of the United Arab Republic (Syria and Egypt)

The growing power of a new generation in the 1950s was accompanied by the emergence of an Arab nationalist movement on the Syrian political scene represented by the Ba'th Party first formed in 1947. To general surprise, the Ba'th became the second most powerful party in the 1954 elections, far ahead of the older ideological formations such as the Communist Party, the Syrian nationalists, or the Muslim Brotherhood. The Pan-Arab ideas the Ba'th propagated found the charismatic leader that the Arab nationalists were short of in the person of Nasser. His victory in the 1956 Suez War gave him a dimension as a leader for the entire Arab nation.

From 1956 to 1958, Syria was the stakes in a relentless struggle among local actors supported by regional powers (Iraq, Saudi Arabia, and Egypt), which were themselves supported by foreign powers (Britain, the USA, and the USSR) for control over Syria and its political choices. All were aware that whoever managed to control Syria would have considerable influence over the entire Near East. This fierce fight was reflected in Syria in the way the civilian authorities found it impossible to control the military. Purges among officers and their insubordination convinced Syrians, Arab nationalists, and others that the country could only find salvation in the union with Egypt because only Nasser could make the Syrian army toe the line. Some enlightened minds did point out, however, that the formula proposed by Nasser for a straightforward merger of the democratic and liberal Syrian republic with a military and socialist-tending Egyptian republic would not suit the impassioned temperament and inborn attachment of Syrians to political freedom. Some spoke out to suggest a federation or even a confederation rather than full union. But their recommendations went unheeded because of the principled stance taken by Nasser, who wanted a complete merger, that is, the plain and simple Egyptianization of Syria. The Damascus government and parliament bowed down and amid general euphoria Syria and Egypt formed the United Arab Republic (UAR) from 1958 to 1961.

When in February 1958 Syria was to cast itself within the institutions that arose from the Revolution led by free officers in 1952, it was to become Egyptian for the second time in its history in a little over a century. But the comparison stops there because the circumstances of 1958 had nothing to do with those of 1831. Egypt did not lay hold of Syria through a military campaign like that of Mohamad Ali and Ibrahim Pasha; it was Syria rather that threw itself body and soul into Nasser's arms. Arabism, which had not yet fully emerged in 1831, this time played a fundamental part as a factor of national identity bringing the two countries together. Their shared conception of militant Arabism that was pro-Palestinian and opposed to Israel, of a neutral and progressive third-world stance allied to the Soviet Union, worried the protégés of the western camp in the Near East.

The Syrian–Egyptian union proclaimed in February 1958 sent shock waves through the region. Unrest broke out in Lebanon in March between UAR supporters and opponents. The crisis quickly came to look like a latent civil war. The dividing lines reflected both the sectarian composition and partisan affiliations, Sunni Muslims favourable to the UAR on one side versus violently anti-Nasserist Christians and the Syrian Social Nationalist Party on the other. The crisis ended with the landing in Lebanon of US forces of the sixth fleet stationed in the Mediterranean on 15 July 1958 and the conclusion of a compromise among the main political forces over the election of the head of the army, General Fouad Shebab, as president to replace Camille Shamoun. On the eve of the US intervention on the beaches of Beirut, Iraq experienced a bloody coup d'état on 14 July 1958 that eliminated one of the most powerful and most ancient monarchies of the Arab world in which many Syrians had seen a natural partner for union instead of Nasser's Egypt. The country's new master, General Qassem, advocated a rival Arab nationalism to Nasser's based on an alliance with the local Communist Party. The immediate reason for the coup was the gathering of Iraqi forces to send them to Jordan to defend the Hashemite monarchy that was trapped between the UAR's northern province (Syria) and southern province (Egypt). In reaction to the Syrian–Egyptian union, Hashemite Iraq and Jordan had decided to create on 14 February 1958 the Arab Federal State (AFS) to which they gave a federal constitution on 19 March 1958.[1] This federation was abrogated the day after the Iraqi monarchy fell. Three days after the Baghdad coup and two days after the landing of US troops in Lebanon, British forces were deployed in Jordan to protect the regime of the young King Hussein.

Other regional powers such as Saudi Arabia and Israel were also worried about the possible impact of the Syrian–Egyptian union and developed strategies to deal with it. The Saudi monarchy fought the influence of the Egyptian leader in Yemen, which had signed an association agreement with the UAR on 8 March 1958. The association took the name of the United Arab States. It remained a dead letter but even so did have a constituent charter of a federal character and internal regulations.[2] As for Israel, it bet on the acceleration of its nuclear programme to stand up to the UAR, and it was probably at this time that France transferred to it the technological knowledge required to manufacture the atom bomb.

Syria had abdicated its political system which was a legacy from the time of the mandate in order to merge into the Egyptian political system. The union was approved by a referendum with a majority of 99.98 per cent of votes cast. Nasser promulgated a provisional constitution in Damascus on 5 March 1958. The constitution had just seventy-three articles. Article 1 defined the UAR as an independent democratic republic whose people were part of the Arab nation. Article 58 specified that the UAR was made up of two provinces, Egypt and Syria, each with an executive council appointed by the president and tasked with applying the general policy relating to its province.

According to the provisional constitution, the society of the UAR was based on social solidarity (art. 3). The national economy was organized 'on the basis of predetermined plans taking account of the principles of social justice' (art. 4). Private property was guaranteed (art. 5); taxation based on social justice (art. 6). Under article 7, citizens have equal rights and duties with no discrimination based on sex, origins, language, religion, or belief.

Article 13 provided that the Council of the Nation holds legislative power. The number of members of the Council of the Nation is set by the President of the Republic. He appoints them by a half-and-half distribution between members of the Syrian Assembly of Deputies and members

---

[1] See the texts of the joint Iraqi–Jordanian Declaration on the Federal Arab State and its constitution in Khouri, *Plans for Arab Union* (Arabic), pp. 380–1 and 384–9.
[2] Khouri, *Plans for Arab Union* (Arabic), pp. 367–70.

of the Egyptian Council of the Nation. The Council 'supervises the executive in accordance with the provisions of the Constitution' (art. 14) and 'is convened by the President of the Republic' (art. 17).

As a legislative body, the Council of the Nation proposed the laws. However, the provisional constitution did not describe the procedure for passing ordinary legislation. It simply stated in article 22 that laws shall be passed article by article. Members of the Council may ask questions to the Ministers (art. 24). A debate on a general question could be called by twenty members of the Council. According to article 37, a member having lost trust and consideration could be removed from office by a two-thirds majority vote. In accordance with article 38, 'The President of the Republic has the right to dissolve the Council of the Nation'. Article 39 provided that confidence may be withdrawn from any Minister by a vote of the Council upon a proposal from at least twenty of its members.

The president assumed executive power. Nasser had already been elected president of the UAR by referendum on 21 February 1958 before the provisional constitution was promulgated. Interestingly, because the constitution was provisional it contained no rule for the election of the president or the duration of his term of office. It was agreed that those aspects would be defined in the future permanent constitution, but the union disintegrated before it could be adopted. The president could appoint and dismiss one or more vice-presidents (art. 46) and ministers, ministers of state, and vice-ministers (art. 47). He could refer a Minister to the courts in the event of any crime committed while in office (art. 49) and 'The President of the Republic introduces laws. He promulgates them and may oppose them' (art. 50). According to article 51, the president had a period of thirty days in which to oppose a law and refer it back to the Council of the Nation and article 52 provided that if the Council of the Nation confirms its previous vote by a two-thirds majority the law is definitively adopted. According to article 53, the president had the power to legislate in the domain of the law in the event of necessity or in the absence of the Council of the Nation provided he submits the decisions taken to the approval of the Council when it first convenes. If the Council rejects a decision taken by the Head of State by a two-thirds majority, that decision is then annulled. This provision of the 1958 constitution featured in the 1962 Syrian constitution and was to be taken up by the Ba'thist constitutions to come. It was included in the 1969, 1971, and 1973 constitutions as well as that of 2012. The 1958 constitution contained no mechanism for revising the constitution.

For Syrians, this constitution was reminiscent of Adib Shishakli's presidential constitution between 1953 and 1954, although the latter was far more sophisticated than the 1958 version when it came to constitutional mechanisms.

Syrians were highly enthusiastic about the union with Egypt because of Nasser and their faith in Arab unity. The national project represented by the creation of the UAR galvanized the Syrian population because it took up the main characteristics of the Syrian national project developed by the Founding Fathers from 1919 on: multi-sectarian coexistence strengthened by drastic secularism and the abandoning of any reference to religion in the 1958 constitution; the refusal of the carving up of the nation; the refusal of any foreign hegemony; and resistance with regard to Israel. While the union did reflect Syrian aspirations in terms of their national project, few people realized that in February 1958 at the time the union was proclaimed, the UAR institutions did not correspond to those they had just renounced. Syrians found it difficult to find their place in the institutions of the union. The simplistic character of the presidential-style provisional constitution of 1958 was a striking contrast to the Syrian parliamentary constitution of 1950. Syrians of all stripes, including the declared supporters of the union such as the Ba'thists, found it hard to accept the total absence of political life, the dissolution of parties, the hegemony of Cairo over Damascus, in particular within the army. It was paradoxical that the union with Egypt was imposed on the Syrian political class by the officer corps and that the break-up of the union was also the work of officers who were victims of what they called discrimination by their Egyptian counterparts.

At the moment Syrians and Egyptians decided to join together, Iraq and Jordan also decided to unite as the AFS, which lasted just four months. Interestingly, as a federation, the AFS, unlike the UAR, maintained the existence of its founder members, their constitutions, and all their national institutions. The AFS had its own constitution and federal institution for legislative (federation council), executive (federation president, federation council of ministers), and judicial (supreme court) functions.[3] However, the sophistication of the AFS federal constitution and the mechanisms regulating the relations between the federal institutions and the federated institutions did not mask the lack of appeal of the political project of the Iraqi–Jordanian federation for Arabs and for Syrians in particular. The two Hashemite monarchies' relations with Britain and the presumed complacency of the throne in Amman towards the Israelis

---

[3] See the text of the AFS constitution in Khouri, *Plans for Arab Union* (Arabic), pp. 384–8.

meant the AFS project was hardly attractive, although its authors presented it as a continuation of the 1916 Arab Revolt that had so inspired the Near East.

7.2 The 1963 Charter of the United Arab Republic (Syria, Egypt, and Iraq)

No one should have been more at ease than the Syrians at the time of talks for establishing a tripartite union among Syria, Egypt, and Iraq. During the previous decade, Syrians' hearts had leant towards a union with Baghdad as much as with Cairo. This time Syria was uniting with both. The tripartite union agreement was signed in Cairo on 17 April 1963 by Egypt, Syria, and Iraq at the end of three rounds of talks among the three countries lasting nearly a month.[4] The agreement consisted of a lengthy political text explaining the motives of the contracting parties, the form of the tripartite union, the bases on which it was built, and described the functioning of the federation's main institutions. In the appendix to the agreement was a document describing in detail the institutions of the federal state and the relations governing them. The agreement and its appendix, which are commonly referred to as the 'Tripartite Charter', are virtually a federal constitution, although the charter provides for the formal adoption of a constitution for the federal state after approval of the union by popular referendum in the three countries.

The agreement defines the project of the tripartite union. The spirit of the text reflects the traditional themes dear to Ba'thist literature. In the talks among the delegations of the three countries to adopt the charter, the Founding Fathers of the Ba'th, Michel Aflaq and Salah Bitar, sat among the representatives of the Syrian delegation. The two dominant themes of the charter were nationalism and Arab socialism. The tripartite union was presented as a logical consequence and an end-point of the revolutions of 23 July 1952 in Egypt, 8 February 1963 in Iraq, and 8 March 1963 in Syria. For the contracting parties, the union was a revolution in itself since it was a popular, progressive move linked to the Palestinian question and to the national duty of liberating Palestine. It was the loss of Palestine that revealed the plot by the reactionary classes and lifted the veil on the populist parties that betrayed the aspirations of the people. It was the loss of Palestine that showed up the weakness and underdevelopment of the

---

[4] See the text of the tripartite charter in Khouri, *Plans for Arab Union* (Arabic), pp. 405–17.

economic and social systems in force in Arab countries. It stirred minds and roused the spirit of rebellion against colonialism, oppression, poverty, and underdevelopment. It very clearly pointed the way to go, the way of union, freedom, and socialism. Such was the general framework of the project for tripartite union for implementing policies of social justice, equal opportunities, priority for education, the fight for the liberation of Palestine, against colonialism, against the Arab reaction, and for development.

During the talks in March and April 1963 to set up the tripartite union, the parties took good note of the weaknesses of the defunct bilateral union between Syria and Egypt from 1958 to 1961 and drew their conclusions from it. The first consequence was that the union would take the form of a federation among three federated states termed 'regions' instead of the full merger as had been the case with the Syrian–Egyptian union, when Syria disappeared as an entity and was cast in the mould of the Egyptian institutions. The second consequence was that the three regions maintained a multi-party system limited to the nationalist and socialist formations favourable to the union instead of the dissolution of all political formations, including the fervent supporters of the union such as the Ba'th as had been the case in the earlier union between Syria and Egypt and their replacement by a party at Nasser's orders – the Arab Socialist Union. In practice, that meant Egypt and the federation would be directed by Nasser but Syria and Iraq would continue to be governed by their respective Ba'th parties around which their allies in the union (local Nasserists and others) rallied within a political front.

The tripartite charter stipulated that the federal state would be known as the United Arab Republic and would be formed of Egyptian, Syrian, and Iraqi regions. Its citizens would all have Arab nationality. Islam was the state religion and Arabic the official language. The flag of the union was the UAR flag (red, white, and black with two green stars on the white stripe symbolizing Egypt and Syria) to which a third star was to be added for Iraq. Cairo was to be the state capital. The federal authorities were to handle foreign policy, defence and national security, finance, the treasury, information, culture, justice, coordination of laws, and federal transport.

The legislative power of the federal state was in the hands of the Council of the Nation formed by two separate chambers: the assembly of deputies elected by citizens by direct universal suffrage in proportion to the population of each region and the federal assembly elected by direct suffrage by the citizens and composed of an equal number of members from each of the three regions of the union. Both chambers were elected for four years. The Council of the Nation elected the president and vice-presidents by a two-thirds majority. If such a majority could not be achieved in the first round of voting, a second round would be organized at the end of which the candidate with the absolute majority of votes would be declared the winner. The president could introduce laws as could each member of the two legislative assemblies. The union would be open to other Arab countries. The admission of another member would first require a vote in favour by three-quarters of the members of the Council of the Nation.

The tripartite charter contained a novel provision reflecting the socialist orientation of the signatories and that was to be applied later to Syrian parliaments. It provided that 'the popular and political bodies based on free direct elections shall truly and fairly represent the forces making up the majority. For this workers and peasants must be guaranteed at least half of the seats on these bodies at all levels, including within the Council of the Nation'.[5] This provision was taken up by the Syrian constitutions of 1973 and 2012 and the electoral laws of 1973 and 2011 that divided the elected representatives within parliament into two categories; category A representing workers and farmers and category B representing the remainder of the population.

Executive power within the federal state was in the hands of the president assisted by a council of ministers. The president's term of office was four years. The president had three vice-presidents, one for each region. The council of ministers was answerable to the Council of the Nation, which could dismiss it if an absolute majority of its members so voted. The prime minister and ministers also had to have the confidence of the president to hold office.

Each of the federated regions had its own constitution, president, and parliament. The president of each region was elected by the regional parliament for a four-year term and then approved by the president of the republic. The regional president's competence was to be determined by the federal constitution and the regional constitutions. Each region could adopt its own specific laws. The region's president was assisted in his executive functions by a council of ministers answerable to the local parliament.

The first president of the UAR was not to be elected by the Council of the Nation but by referendum at the same time as the UAR constitution was submitted for approval within no more than five months from the

---

[5] See the text of the tripartite charter in Khouri, *Plans for Arab Union* (Arabic), p. 407. This is the present author's translation.

signing of the Charter on 17 April 1963. The natural candidate was obviously Nasser. But the double referendum was never held, for Nasser, and perhaps other signatories of the tripartite charter, were not entirely happy with the compromise achieved by the agreement. Nasser intended to lead the new union in the way he had led the previous union with Syria between 1958 and 1961. A few days after signing the agreement, Nasserists orchestrated street protests in Syria calling for immediate and unconditional union with Egypt. Nasserists resigned from their positions within the ruling bodies in Syria (the National Council of Revolutionary Command and the government). On 18 July 1963, Nasser's supporters attempted a coup d'état in Damascus that was put down in a bloodbath. This consummated the split between Syria and Egypt, Ba'thists and Nasserists, ending all hope of a tripartite union. Syria and Iraq, both governed by the Ba'th, closed ranks and tried to move towards a bilateral union. The armies of the two countries merged in October 1963. But any hope of a union was short-lived. On 18 November 1963, General Abdel-Salam Aref turned against his former Ba'thist allies and removed them from power.

Despite the appeal of the political project among Arab populations especially in Syria and despite the undeniable advances made in formulating a union by introducing federalism and a limited multi-party system, the tripartite charter remained primarily the work of the military and authoritarian regimes. The internal regime of the future UAR was neither liberal, nor democratic, nor did it purport to be representative of the whole of society. The charter stipulated that sovereignty of the UAR was in the hands of the people, that all freedom belonged to the people with no freedom to the enemies of the people. These were defined as people stripped of their rights by law;[6] anyone tried and convicted as a separatist as well as conspirators and exploiters; anyone having been involved with or being involved in the future with foreign political organizations thereby becoming a foreign agent; or anyone looking to impose the hegemony of the exploitative classes on society. All of these categories were excluded from political life from the outset.

Syrians made only a quick and superficial analysis of the failed tripartite union, ascribing the failure to Nasser, just as they attributed the failure of the bilateral union with Iraq to the coup d'état by General Abdel-Salam

---

[6] Syria's new masters after the coup of 8 March 1963 resorted to this stratagem to exclude all of the political right from public life for supporting the break-up of the union with Egypt in September 1961. See Chapter 6, 'The Fourth Republic'.

Aref. These ready scapegoats saved the Ba'th from thinking about the importance of individual and public freedoms in strengthening the foundations of the regime and from seeking to form a solid union with sister countries. Nearly half a century later such thinking had still not been done, although the concept of freedom remains one of the three pillars of the Ba'th trilogy of union–freedom–socialism.

The national project flowing from the tripartite charter of the new UAR of 1963 took up the themes developed by the Founding Fathers of modern Syria. Once the option of a tripartite federation had been set aside, the Syrian and Iraqi leaders attempted to set up a bilateral union between the two countries governed by the Ba'th. But this attempt was short-lived and when Iraqi Ba'thists were removed from power their Syrian comrades were left alone in a regional environment that was more hostile to them than ever.

7.3 The 1971 Constitution of the Federation of Arab Republics (Syria, Egypt, and Libya)

The Federation of Arab Republics (FAR) came about after two cataclysms that lastingly shook the entire Arab world and especially the Near East: the humiliating defeat of three Arab armies by Israel in June 1967 and President Nasser's sudden death in September 1970.

The negotiating process that lead to the formation of the FAR began in Tripoli, Libya, three months after the coup d'état that brought Colonel Gaddafi to power. The process initially involved Egypt, Sudan, and Libya. The three heads of state, Nasser, Numeiri, and Gaddafi, signed the Tripoli Charter on 27 December 1969 announcing the formation of a common Arab front to face up to 'Zionist challenges and Israeli aggression'. The charter provided for summit meetings every four months and the establishment of joint commissions to lay down the basis for further cooperation among the three countries.[7]

This declaration of intent was followed by a meeting of the three countries' foreign affairs ministers in Cairo from 11–13 January 1970. At the end of this meeting, the participants published a joint communiqué announcing the formation of joint ministerial committees on foreign policy, transport, agriculture, animal resources, education, the economy, and

---

[7] See the text of the Tripoli Charter in Khouri, *Plans for Arab Union* (Arabic), pp. 423–33.

industry.[8] Nasser's death was followed two months later by Hafez Assad easing into the driving seat in Syria after the Corrective Movement of 16 November 1970. Ten days later, he went to Cairo and informed the new Egyptian president, Anwar Sadat, of Syria's intention to join the Cairo tripartite declaration of January 1970.

On 17 April 1971, eight years to the day after the signing of the Cairo Charter of the tripartite union between Syria, Egypt, and Iraq, the FAR was created in Benghazi between Syria, Egypt, and Libya. Sudan, although a participant in talks begun in Tripoli in December 1969, preferred to abstain because of internal problems. The three heads of state jointly adopted the Benghazi Declaration and the Fundamental Principles of the FAR that provided for the drafting of a constitution which, along with the Fundamental Principles, was to be submitted for the approval of the citizens of each of the federation's member republics.[9]

The draft federal constitution was submitted for popular approval in the three countries. Voting took place in September 1971 and it was approved in Syria by a majority of 96.4 per cent without enthusiasm and with no surprises.[10] The proposed text took up in one form or another the permanent themes of the Syrian national project developed by the Founding Fathers at the time of separation from the Ottoman empire such as multi-sectarian coexistence, the refusal of partition, the refusal of foreign hegemony, and above all resistance to Israel. This aspect was fundamental in the formation of the FAR because Egypt and Syria were determined to liberate their territories occupied by Israel in its June 1967 assault.

The constitution stated that 'sovereignty in the Federation is in the hands of the people' (art. 2). According to article 3 the people of the Federation is an integral part of the Arab nation. Unlike the UAR constitution adopted at the time of the Syrian–Egyptian union in 1958 that made no reference to religion, article 6 of the federal constitution asserted that the Federal State is built on the spiritual values of Islam and that *sharia* law was the main source of legislation. In expressly mentioning Islam, the 1971 federal constitution can be likened to the 1963 tripartite union constitution, which also stipulated that Islam was the state religion. Interestingly, the Syrian

---

[8] See the text of the final communiqué of the Cairo meeting in Khouri, *Plans for Arab Union* (Arabic), p. 433.

[9] See the text of the Benghazi Declaration and Fundamental Principles of the FAR in Khouri, *Plans for Arab Union* (Arabic), pp. 434–5.

[10] See the text of the FAR constitution in Khouri, *Plans for Arab Union* (Arabic), pp. 439–44.

constitution in force at the time was the 1969 constitution as amended by the Ba'th Provisional Regional Command (PRC) on 16 February 1971, which did not provide for Islam as the state religion.

The 1971 federal constitution provided for the national constitutions to be maintained. They were not to contain any provisions contrary to the federal constitution (art. 11). Moreover, the 1971 federal constitution contained in its article 12 a list of minimum individual rights that had to feature in the national constitutions of the member states.[11] Unlike the 1963 tripartite charter that planned for a common nationality of the three federated states, the 1971 federal constitution sought to maintain the nationalities of the member states until such time as a common nationality was adopted by a federal law (art. 10). It also granted citizens of the member countries the right to move, live, and work anywhere in the federation's territory. A federal law was to provide for these rights (art. 13).

The federal constitution included a lengthy article 14 setting out the competences of the federal state in terms of unifying foreign policy. Decisions on peace and war were to be taken unanimously with the Council of the Presidency, with coordination over diplomatic and consular representation, the conclusion of treaties with foreign powers and international organizations also being matters of federal competence. In the realm of defence, the federal state's jurisdiction extended also to matters of organization and command, the establishment of a military command responsible for training and operations, the movement of armed forces among the member states' territories, and coordination with respect to the armaments industry. Article 14 defined in detail the federal state's competences for economic questions, education, and the arts.

The federation's institutions were of three kinds; executive, legislative, and judicial. Article 15 provided for the creation of a Council of the Presidency of the Federation made up of the presidents of the member states, which would elect its president for a renewable term of two years (art. 16). Under article 18, decisions of the Council of the Presidency are adopted by a majority except in cases provided for by the Constitution

---

[11] This federal declaration of rights included: equality of citizens in law; absence of discrimination based on sex, origins, or language; inviolability of the home; personal safety within the framework of the law; the right to bring legal actions; the right of defence; freedom of movement and choice of residence; prohibition of exile; freedom of belief and worship; freedom of the press; freedom of assembly; freedom to choose rulers and hold them responsible; inviolability of private property in the framework provided for by the law; the right to work; the right to medical care; protection of children, motherhood, and the family; equal opportunities among citizens.

or in important areas at the express request of one of the parties during the first two years after the Constitution comes into force. According to article 19, the Council of the Presidency had authority to adopt decisions with the character of federal laws as necessary during the periods when the Council of the Nation is not in session.

The Council of the Presidency was to appoint a federal prime minister and federal ministers (art. 23). Federal ministers were to be answerable to the Council of the Presidency (art. 24). Under article 27, the Council of the Presidency puts in place federal councils and institutions in the areas of planning, the economy, social affairs, national security, foreign policy, education, the arts, scientific research, information, and others. These councils and institutions are attached to the Federal Ministries.

According to article 29,

> legislative power within the Federation is in the hands of a Council of the Nation. Each Member Republic of the Federation elects twenty members of its national parliament to the Council of the Nation. Should a Federation Member not have a national parliament, the executive authority of that republic shall lay down rules for selecting members to sit on the Council of the Nation

This provision specifically concerned Libya, which had no parliament at the time. The members of the Council of the Presidency were to elect their president (art. 30) and The Council of the Nation was to hold two sessions per year (art. 31). Under article 34, the decisions of the Council of the Nation 'are adopted by the absolute majority of members except as otherwise provided by the Constitution'. Article 36 provided that the Council of the Nation is competent for adopting federal laws, discussing and adopting the Federation's budget, discussing and adopting treaties signed by the Federation in accordance with the relevant provisions of the Federal Constitution, discussing the Federation's general policy, and questioning Federal Ministers.

The federation provided for a constitutional court whose members were appointed for a four-year term by the Council of the Presidency. Each member state was to have two representatives and the Council of the Presidency was to appoint the President of the Constitutional Court (art. 46). Under article 48,

> The Court has jurisdiction to rule on the constitutional character of federal laws; the conformance of national laws to the Federal Constitution; disputes among federal institutions and Member States' institutions; to give opinions on constitutional or legal questions submitted by the Council of the Presidency, the Federal Ministers, or the Member States.

The federal constitution could be amended by a two-thirds majority vote of members of the Council of the Nation endorsed unanimously by the Council of the Presidency (art. 68). Among the transitional provisions of the federal constitutions, three articles determined the internal dynamics among the three federated states. As was the case with the 1963 tripartite charter, the 1971 federal constitution laid down the nature and form of political life within the member states by providing for the establishment of political fronts within those states. Article 62 provided that 'the Council of the Presidency forms a political front grouping the national political leaders and establishes among them a National Action Charter to further the purposes of the FAR'. The objective was to eventually unify the various political forces within a single Arab national movement. Meanwhile, each member state was to organize political life within its territory.

Article 63 recalled that the armed forces in the member states remained under the authority of the president of each republic. But the most original article of the federal constitution was probably article 64, which stipulated:

> in the event of internal or external disorder threatening any of the Member Republics of the Federation, the Member Republic shall immediately advise the federal authorities so that they can take the necessary measures to restore security and order. Should the authorities of the Republic in question be unable to make such a request for aid, the federal authorities shall nonetheless intervene so as to restore order in the Republic in trouble.

This article went much further than the familiar concept of collective self-defence in international law because it concerned not just external threats but also internal disorder that any of the federated republics might experience. Thus it confirmed the non-liberal and authoritarian character of the FAR just as the regime suggested by the 1963 tripartite charter had been and the one that was put in place at the time of the UAR between Egypt and Syria from 1958 to 1961. The paternity of a mechanism for collective support when confronted with external and internal threats to the left-wing nationalist ideological regimes did not fall to the authors of the FAR constitution, though. It was the Ba'thist Iraq of 1963 that was the first to propose such a project for cooperation among the nationalist and socialist regimes of Syria, Egypt, Algeria, and Yemen.[12] The Iraqi project for cooperation remained dormant but was taken up eight years later by article 64 of the FAR constitution.

---

[12] See the text of the Iraqi project for cooperation among liberated Arab countries in Khouri *Plans for Arab Union* (Arabic), p. 405.

The FAR remained a dead letter although the states parties did take a few symbolic decisions to assert its existence such as the adoption of a common flag, which is still Egypt's flag today. The most important result to attribute to the FAR was to have provided a general framework for the preparation of the October 1973 war when Syrian and Egyptian armies launched simultaneous attacks on Israeli positions in the Golan Heights and Sinai to try to liberate these territories that had been occupied by Israel since June 1967. But the FAR member states did not share the same vision for the region's future. Apart from the October 1973 War, the FAR had no common project. With hindsight, the FAR appears to have been a moment of convergence, an ephemeral coming together of the transient interests of three Arab leaders who had recently come to power, each with a specific conception of his country's role in the region and the choice of its international alliances. The FAR was officially dissolved on October 1984.

After the FAR experiment, Syria sought a rapprochement with Iraq in 1978–79 to make up for Egypt leaving the ranks of the countries confronting Israel. The two nations signed a Charter for Joint National Action in 1978 in anticipation of closer ties between Damascus and Baghdad. But the experiment was curtailed when Saddam Hussein came to power in Baghdad in 1979. The following year Syria and Libya declared their union. But this attempt at unity went no further than statements of intent.

The dramatic thing about all these abortive attempts at Arab union and the Arab nationalist movement in general was the absence of any attachment to the principle of freedom. The Arab nationalists failed to see that individual and collective freedoms give rise to political legitimacy and produce a representativeness of the social body that alone can bring about and protect any union. They failed to see that union is not the business of states alone. It is primarily that of their citizens. This was how the 1958 union between Syria and Egypt was created, by a vote of the democratically elected Syrian parliament followed by a popular referendum. And it was precisely because Nasser had abolished the liberal type of democratic representation that the putschist officers in Damascus were able to break off the union so easily on 28 September 1961.

8

Towards the Fifth Republic

I shall call the political regime established by the constitution adopted by popular referendum in February 2012 'the Fifth Republic'. The march towards the Fifth Republic began with the investiture of Bashar Assad in 2000; it was slow, laborious, and tragic. At its birth this Fifth Republic seemed more fragile than the previous one and there were no grounds for claiming it will endure.

Bashar Assad's investiture as president was more like a dynastic succession than a republican handover of power despite the formal popular referendum which officially opened up the gateway to the presidency for him. The young president was proud of the legacy he held in his hands and conscious of the challenges awaiting him. He officially inherited Syria, but unofficially Lebanon too. He had to prove his worth on both the national and regional scenes. Regionally, he was not to have any period of grace. Just weeks after he took office, the second Palestinian *intifada* broke out as a result of the failure of the Camp David negotiations between Yasser Arafat and Ehud Barak sponsored by President Clinton. One year later, the murderous attacks on New York and Washington prompted the USA to invade Afghanistan before mounting its assault on Iraq.

Such a regional environment was hardly conducive to the young president setting about the substantial reforms the country needed. Reforms need time and stability, but the entire region from Palestine to Iraq was beset by growing instability. And yet upon taking office, President Bashar Assad announced his intention to make changes. This fostered great hope within Syria's political and cultural elite and gave rise to the Damascus Spring, the forerunner of the Arab Springs to come. The mistake the authorities were to make was to come up with only partial (economic, administrative, and judicial) reforms without setting about political reform which alone could give meaning to the partial measures and change the political system as a whole. Without political reform, the partial moves could at best be desperate attempts to modernize an obsolete political system.

The road towards the Fifth Republic began with the president announcing reforms on the very day of his investiture in July 2000. It was taken up by an unprecedented movement of civil society that proposed concrete formulas, first calling for the liberalization of the political system before purely and simply demanding its change. This period, commonly called the Damascus Spring, left as its legacy several political texts that were unfortunately largely overlooked when the crisis broke out in March 2011. For its part, the government set to work on partial reforms but they failed to have the hoped-for impact. In 2005, the Ba'th in turn launched an era of reforms, but finally revised only its economic doctrine integrating into it the market economy with a social purpose called 'the social market economy'. Although it modernized its economic ideology, the Ba'th proved unable to reform its political doctrine and its conception of power. And yet the party's internal constitution adopted in 1947 and the reinterpretation of its trilogy (Union–Freedom–Socialism) in its original meaning could have served as a basis for an overall reform of the Ba'th.

The liberalization of the economy had adverse effects on the regime's social basis. The economic growth that it engendered did not meet expectations. It could not make good the consequences of liberalization, reduce unemployment, or absorb the galloping population growth. It pauperized hundreds of thousands of young Syrians living in mushroom suburbs around the big cities, who threw themselves body and soul into the contestation movement in March 2011. They had little to lose and thought they had everything to win. Almost ten years before the event, Samuel Huntington in his famous book *The Clash of Civilisations* virtually predicted to within a few months the date of a crisis in Syria caused by the population explosion.[1]

The two great dilemmas of the regime will have been how to successfully open up the economy without losing its social basis or the original *'asabiya*, the hybrid *esprit de corps* that brought the Ba'th to power and kept it there for almost half a century, and how to successfully open up and modernize the political system while holding on to that same *'asabiya*. The transition from *'asabiya* to democracy is no easy matter. There is no miracle formula to show the path to follow in terms of economic policy or political reform. The absence of any blueprint for the long term made itself manifest in ideological logjams preventing the development of both the Ba'th and the regime's thinking in terms of individual and public

---

[1] Huntington, *Le choc des civilisations*, p. 128.

freedoms. This was to lead the authorities at the time of the 2011 crisis to count on a security-based solution instead of immediately seeking a national dialogue.

The opposition, although without any common plan, was to prove much more audacious and creative, multiplying its political initiatives, proposals, and texts during the Damascus Spring. The opposition's great weakness since 2011 has remained its division. During the Damascus Spring, the opposition remained loyal to the main themes of the Founding Fathers of the Syrian national project, namely multi-sectarian coexistence and secularism, the refusal of foreign hegemony, the refusal of carve-up, and the rejection of the Zionist project. But after the 2011 crisis, some of these themes seem to have disappeared from the literature of the opposition abroad, probably because of its exaggerated proximity with certain regional actors. However, the opposition within the country and the supporters of the authorities still seem to be standing by the principles of the Founding Fathers. One of the challenges of the crisis will be to see around which national project Syrians finally manage to unite.

8.1 The Settling in of the New President and the Announcement of Reforms

Bashar Assad's succession to his father was programmed in advance. It was orchestrated by Mustafa Tlass, the defence minister and loyal companion of Hafez Assad, who mobilized the military and civil institutions to put Bashar in the saddle.[2] Few Syrians opposed the succession, which was perceived as a sign of stability, admittedly not quite consistent with the republican character of the state but certainly in keeping with the patriarchal not to say monarchic style of Hafez Assad's presidency. The successor had raised great hopes even before his investiture. As *The New York Times* correspondent Judith Miller observed on travelling through Damascus in late 1991, the supporters of a democratic regime in Syria were hoping for a succession like that Franco prepared before his death.[3]

The new president did everything in his power to consolidate the hopes for change. In his inaugural speech, commonly called the 'Oath Speech' in Arabic, made just after swearing the oath before the People's Assembly

---

[2] See the amendment to the 1973 constitution to allow Bashar Assad to take over the presidency in Chapter 6, 'The Fourth Republic'.

[3] See Miller, 'Syria's Game'. At the time, the heir presumptive was Basil, Bashar's elder brother, who met a premature death in a road traffic accident in January 1994.

on 17 July 2000, he found the right words for all categories of society. His speech was welcomed by the population, including the opposition, because it foreshadowed an opening up of the political system and economy, and a reform of the administration. The main themes addressed were:

- The political strategy put in place and enforced by Hafez Assad had proved successful. This was not the case in other domains. There was a need for scientific economic and social strategies to strengthen development and firmness at the same time.
- Citizens should not expect the state to do everything.
- There was a need for economic change through modernization of the law and the removal of bureaucratic obstacles that hampered the flow of domestic and foreign investment and the mobilization of private and public capital.
- Primacy of the sense of the state over that of leadership as it rested on recognition of the way others think. Democracy is a duty towards others before being a right for oneself.
- Democratic thinking is the primary element, democratic practices form the edifice. When the foundations are unsound, the building may collapse under the slightest shock.
- Western democracy is the outcome of a long history that has given rise to customs and traditions that explain western society and culture. To live like them we must live their history with all its setbacks. But that is impossible for us, so we must create our own democratic experience. Our democracy must come from our own history, that derives from our culture, personality, civilization, and which arises from the needs of our society and the givens of our present day.
- The need to reform the administration because it impedes development and construction.
- There is no magic wand to overcome the challenges facing Syria.

The themes raised in this inaugural speech of Bashar Assad's first period of office barely diverged fundamentally from those of his father's time, except for the 'recognition of the way others think'. But the style was different and the allusion to the recognition of the other produced the finest effect. Many intellectuals saw in it the hoped-for beginning of a change in individual and collective political liberties. This hope was reflected by the Damascus Spring. It was only with time that these intellectuals realized that the inaugural speech actually marked the start of a process of modernization that was to be limited to the administration and the economy without claiming to encompass the political arena.

8.2 The Plans for Political Reform during the Damascus Spring

Syrian society reacted positively to the 'oath speech'. The population liked the young president's modern style and his open-minded approach. The intellectual and cultural elite saw in this the signs of a renewal of the political system. The first effects of the inaugural speech began to show a month after its proclamation. On 15 August 2000, the independent member of parliament Riad Seif set up the 'Association of Friends of Civil Society' in Damascus. Intellectuals mobilized and the Damascus Spring began to take shape. On 9 September, the first conference of the National Dialogue Forum was held at Riad Seif's house. In September 2000, the National Democratic Rally, the main opposition grouping, called for the restoration of public and democratic liberties. On 17 September, the government announced the release of 600 prisoners. On 27 September, ninety-nine Syrian intellectuals signed a document that was to become known as the 'Statement of 99'.[4]

The months from October to December 2000 were relatively quiet. In November 2000, Riad Seif called for political reforms in parliament and an end to the Ba'th monopoly on power. On 10 December the creation of a Forum of the Left was announced in Damascus. The Damascus Spring reached its climax early in 2001. On 9 January a new statement was published in the name of the Committees for the Renaissance of Civil Society, signed by 1000 intellectuals and that came to be known as the 'Statement of 1000'.[5] On 12 January came the announcement of the creation of the Jamal Atassi Forum for National Dialogue. On 22 January, fifty-five lawyers wrote to President Assad calling for an end to the courts of special jurisdiction and the restoration of the ordinary courts of law.[6] On 22 January, the minister of information granted the famous cartoonist Ali Ferzat the authorization to publish a satirical weekly *Al-Domari*. On 24 January Riad Seif announced his intention to create a political movement. On 29 January, the information minister declared that emergency law was no longer in force in the country.

From February 2001 onwards, the authorities reacted against the themes raised by the Damascus Spring before turning on their authors. In an interview of 9 February in the Saudi daily *Ash-Sharq Al-Awsat*, the president called the activists of the Damascus Spring witting or unwitting

---

[4] Its contents will be examined later in section 8.2.1.
[5] Its contents will be examined later in section 8.2.2.
[6] See the text in Arabic in the collected texts, documents, and articles presented by Baroud and Keilani, *Syria between Two Reigns* (Arabic), pp. 123 ff.

enemy agents.[7] On 17 February, the Ba'th Regional Command began its counter-offensive against the forums and intellectuals.[8] This counter-offensive was led essentially by the vice-president, Abdel Halim Khaddam, who mobilized the Ba'th sections throughout the country against the supporters of the Damascus Spring. He declared to an audience of students at Damascus University on 18 February that Syria would not become a new Yugoslavia or Algeria. The forums were gradually prohibited. In an interview with the Jordanian newspaper *Al-Majd* on 5 March, President Assad did declare, however, that the Atassi Forum could continue its activities. It was the last political forum to be authorized, finally being closed down in July 2005 on the pretext that a letter from the supreme guide of the Muslim Brotherhood, which was banned in Syria, had been read out.

By the end of 2001, most of the Damascus Spring activists who had wanted to continue to militate publicly for political reforms had been arrested. The political and security offensive launched by the Ba'th and the security services tolled the bell for the Damascus Spring, which was in many respects a forerunner of the Arab Springs to come in 2011, although it was limited to elitist opposition by intellectuals and human rights activists without successfully mobilizing the masses.[9] It left as its legacy four major political writings that reflected the spirit of the time when civil society stepped into the front line brandishing hope and a beacon of change.[10]

8.2.1 The Statement of 99

This text was signed by a group of intellectuals and political activists.[11] It was published on 17 September 2000. The signatories called for:

- an end to the state of emergency in force since 1963;
- a general amnesty for all political prisoners, prisoners of opinion, and those held on political grounds;

---

[7] George, *Syria: Neither Bread nor Freedom*, p. 51.
[8] The Ba'th published Circular 1075 on 17 February 2001 in its internal newspaper *Al-Munadil* (*The Militant*) in which it conceded that the party had made mistakes and recalled that decisions had been taken to allow the opening of private banks, a stock exchange, and private universities. The Circular also accused civil society activists of playing into the hands of Syria's enemies, knowingly or not. See George, *Syria: Neither Bread nor Freedom*, p. 78.
[9] For a description of political life in Syria during the Damascus Spring, see George, *Syria: Neither Bread nor Freedom*.
[10] One might also cite the political programme of the Democratic National Rally grouping the opposition parties and led by Hassan Abdel Azim. See Baroud and Keilani, *Syria between Two Reigns* (Arabic), pp. 154 ff.
[11] See the text of the Statement of 99 and the list of signatories in *ibid.*, pp. 99 ff.

- authorization for exiles and opponents living abroad to return;
- the establishment of the rule of law; the implementation of civil liberties; the recognition of political and ideological pluralism;
- freedom of assembly, freedom of the press, and free speech;
- the release of public life from laws, impediments, and other forms of censorship imposed on it, so that citizens could express their various interests in the context of social concord and peaceful competition; and
- the construction of institutions to allow everyone to participate in the country's development and prosperity.

The statement ended with an assertion that read as a warning. Any economic, administrative, or judicial reform (implying those promised in the inaugural speech) would remain incomplete unless accompanied by political reform. The statement stopped at that and took up no position on the constitution and whether it should be revised or not. Nor did it state any opinion about whether the regime in place since 1963 might undergo political development and peaceful transformation.

8.2.2 The Statement of 1000

This statement of the Committees for the Revival of Civil Society was a continuation of the action of the Association of the Friends of Civil Society created in Damascus by Riad Seif in August 2000. It was signed by a thousand intellectuals, artists, and political activists and published on 9 January 2001. The text developed the themes of the Statement of 99 published four months earlier, emphasizing the need to revive Syrian civil society after it had been put on ice by the advent of the Ba'th in 1963. The main points of the statement were:[12]

- the end of the state of emergency and courts of special jurisdiction;
- the release of all political prisoners and the authorization for those in exile to return;
- the enforcement of civil liberties especially freedom of thought and free speech;
- the adoption of laws on political parties, associations, NGOs, and trade unions;
- the restoration of the law on publications ensuring a free press and publication, which had been interrupted by the state of emergency;

---

[12] See the text of the Statement of 1000 and the list of signatories in Baroud and Keilani, *Syria between Two Reigns* (Arabic), pp. 117 ff.

- the adoption of an electoral law so that elections would come under judicial control and the parliament arising from them should be a true legislative and supervisory institution;
- the independence of the judicial system so as to impose the rule of law on rulers and ruled alike;
- enforcement of economic rights in the constitution and in particular a right of citizens to a fair share of national wealth and national output as well as the right of every citizen to suitable employment and a life of dignity;
- protection of the rights of future generations to national wealth and a clean environment;
- revision of the connections between the parties of the National Progressive Front (NPF) and the authorities;
- revision of the principle of the party (that is, the Ba'th) as a guide for the state and society and of any principle excluding the people from economic life; and
- the abolition of any discrimination against women in laws in force.

On the basis of these principles, the statement called for the creation of committees for the revival of civil society. The Statement of 1000 did not openly take sides on the need to amend the existing constitution nor on the form in which power should be exercised. In appearance, the text therefore came within the framework of constitutional legality. In fact, the statement was more nuanced, since the call for a revision of the ties binding the political parties within the NPF – the leading one of which was the Ba'th – and the authorities, and the call for a revision of the principle of the leading party of society and state were thinly veiled invitations to revise the constitution.

8.2.3 The Social and National Charter

This project was drawn up by the Committees for the Revival of Civil Society and published on 14 April 2001.[13] It was meant as a basis for discussion of a social, political, and moral charter and addressed to all the country's social and political forces.

The charter comprised nine points:

1. A reminder of the declaration of rights in the Syrian constitution and Syria's international commitments on human rights.
2. The Syrian people forms an entity of free citizens and should not be seen as a group bringing together sundry religious, sectarian, or

---

[13] See the text in English in George, *Syria: Neither Bread nor Freedom*, pp. 189–93.

economic components. No effort should be spared in consolidating national identity. National unity should be strengthened by policies and practices based on public interest.
3. The country's independence, freedom, dignity, strength, and unity are common objectives in the fight against the Zionist enemy and hegemonic forces. Democracy is the most powerful arm for winning this battle.
4. The state must be based on the rule of law, a state that belongs to all of its citizens without ethnic, political, or religious discrimination.
5. The need for economic reforms.
6. The occupied Arab territories cannot be liberated without a democratic Arab system. Patriotism must be connected with pan-Arabism and both connected with democracy. This is the only method for establishing true nationalism which alone is able to defeat Zionism, imperialism, and recover the nation's rights.
7. The reconstruction of Arab solidarity and the creation of a common Arab market.
8. The political emancipation of the Syrian people and their right to choose their political, economic, and social system.
9. The resort to dialogue and consensus as the means to settle disputes and the rejection of violence in all forms.

The Social and National Charter was one of the most important texts drawn up by the Syrian opposition during the Damascus Spring. The intellectual Michel Kilo played a leading role in drafting it among the Committees for the Revival of Civil Society.

8.2.4 *The Damascus Declaration*

The text that most faithfully reflects the political demands of the Damascus Spring in the most complete form is certainly the Damascus Declaration. The declaration was drafted at a crucial time for Syria in October 2005, four months after the Ba'th had missed the opportunity to reform its political ideology at its Tenth Regional Congress, settling for simply modernizing its economic thinking, and three months after the shutdown of the Atassi Forum, the last space for the opposition to come together to discuss the country's affairs, and a time when Syria, having withdrawn from Lebanon six months earlier, was isolated on the regional and international stages. Contrary to the Statement of 99 and the Statement of 1000, the Damascus Declaration proposed radical change by the peaceful means of the Syrian political system. This transformation was to involve the supporters of the regime who wished to join it. Their involvement was welcome. The Damascus Declaration was also the first major political text of the opposition to set out the method for regime change, namely a national dialogue, the convening of a National Congress, the election of a constituent assembly to prepare a new constitution and then free and transparent elections for a lawful government.[14]

The Damascus Declaration was signed by many political groups and by mostly left-wing opponents but also by some close to the Muslim Brotherhood. The Declaration created a movement that continued to keep the flame of the Damascus Spring burning. Repression by the forces of law and order split the movement into two, the internal members living in Syria and the external members living abroad, who enjoyed greater freedom to act.

8.2.5 *The National Salvation Front Project*

The National Salvation Front (NSF) was created in March 2006 by the former vice-president Abdel Halim Khaddam and several leading opposition political formations and personalities including the Muslim Brotherhood and a number of Kurdish political movements. It may seem paradoxical that the NSF should stand by the Damascus Declaration since it was Abdel Halim Khaddam, while still in the high office of the state and Ba'th party, who directed the Ba'th counter-offensive in February 2001 against the Damascus Spring. But in the meantime Khaddam had joined the opposition and the virulent provisions of the NSF political project fitted in with the themes featured in the Social and National Charter proposed by the Committees for the Revival of Civil Society and the Damascus Declaration.

The NSF project is more radical than all the other political projects proposed during the Damascus Spring. From the outset it called for regime change in Syria. The main points of the project include an inquiry into abuses of power by the regime; cooperating with international human rights organizations to expose mass graves, massacres, and have access to 'vanished' persons held by the government; encouraging the people to

---

[14] For the English text of the Damascus Declaration, see faculty-staff.ou.edu/L/Joshua.M.Landis-1/syriablog/2005/11/damascus-declaration-in-english.htm.

civil disobedience by emphasizing that regime change must be brought about by peaceful, democratic means from within the country; mutual aid for all opponents inside and outside the country to overcome the regime followed by free elections the results of which will be accepted by all; rejection of all forms of totalitarianism and the use of violence; introduction of a modern regime, a civil government based on a social contract that will emerge from a new constitution respecting religious, ethnic, political, and ideological differences and will ensure peaceful handovers of power by democratic means and consider citizenship as the basis for rights and duties; preparation of a national alternative conceptually and structurally to ensure stability and security and remove the threat of civil war and disorder that the regime proffers in the event of its destitution; eliminating the causes of the profound injustice against the Kurdish population because of political exclusion by the regime, the Kurdish people having the right to enjoy their political and cultural rights like the remainder of the population; meeting the needs of the economy, encouraging the private sector, and accepting the market economy while ensuring citizens' basic needs.

The NSF project also calls for the return of the Golan Heights occupied by Israel in 1967 and supports the Palestinian people in their fight to recover their national rights, including their right to return, self-determination, and the establishment of an independent state with Jerusalem as its capital.

After setting out the guidelines in terms of domestic, regional, and international policy, the NSF project proposed a mechanism for political handover of power in Syria. The mechanism provided for the formation of a transitional government with executive and legislative powers and as guarantor of judicial power. The transitional government was to abolish the 1973 constitution and restore the 1950 constitution as a benchmark for all its political actions. Furthermore, the transitional government was to abolish the state of emergency in force since 1963; dissolve the special courts and courts of special jurisdiction; abolish law 49 of 1980 that made the Muslim Brotherhood liable to capital punishment; release all political prisoners and investigate the fate of missing persons; remove all statutory provisions preventing Syrians from returning to their country; grant citizenship to all those who had been excluded from it or stripped of it; adopt a law on political parties, a law guaranteeing the freedom of the press, and a new electoral law based on proportional representation.

After which the transitional government was to call for elections to elect members of a constituent assembly to adopt a new constitution, choose a new government from among its members that would take on executive authority and be accountable to the constituent assembly and would also have legislative authority.

The main characteristic of the NSF project was that it was a shared platform of the Muslim Brotherhood and a former senior official of the state and the Ba'th, which had been joined by Kurdish groups. It was therefore both a synthesis between political Islam and secular Arab nationalism and a synthesis in the form of recognition of Kurdish diversity in Syria in all its dimensions by the two major political movements on the national stage, namely Islam and pan-Arabism. No political project from the opposition had gone so far into the details of political changes to be introduced in Syria. The Statement of 99 and the Statement of 1000, and even the Damascus Declaration, paled in comparison to the radical political discourse and the demands of the opposition. The NSF was to experience internal dissension as from 2007 that eventually led to it imploding when the Muslim Brotherhood suspended their participation before breaking away following the Israeli offensive against Gaza in late 2008 and early 2009.

8.3 From Partial Reforms to Revision of Ba'th Economic Doctrine

Upon taking office, Bashar Assad realized the country urgently needed reforms in various domains (such as administration, justice, and the economy). But such reforms first required an overall political vision of a future Syria. Reform of the administration, the judicial system, or the public sector is impossible without an overall theoretical framework for change. How could the judicial system become effective unless it first secured the status and guarantees of a truly independent branch of power? There was little chance of reforming the judicial system while it was considered a function with a special status as provided for by the 1973 constitution that was still in force when Bashar Assad came to power, a constitution that, it should be recalled, was largely inspired by the constitutions of former eastern bloc countries. And how could the judicial system be converted into an independent branch of power without altering the very spirit of the constitution and the essence of the other branches of power, namely a virtually unbridled executive and an impotent legislative branch?

The same was true of the administration. How could it be modernized and reformed while the Ba'th, under article 8 of the constitution, headed the state and so held de facto all the higher and intermediate positions in the civil service? No serious reform of the administration could bear fruit in such an environment. There was also the matter of the low pay of government workers, who often had to hold down two or even three jobs to survive or had to depart from the moral code and accept bribes in kind or in cash for services rendered, at least in the case of those who thought they could ward off any risk of investigation for corruption or unjust enrichment. Such protection, like everything else in Syria, came at a price.

It was in the economic domain that the will to modernize outside any pre-established conceptual framework compatible with Ba'th political and economic framework very quickly came to a dead-end and met resistance from the defenders of the system who failed to understand the need for urgent reform if the regime were to endure and remain in place. The resistance of the old guard was made manifest by its scepticism over the reforms in the banking and public sectors. Reform of the banking sector, which had been entirely in the hands of the state since the March 1963 coup d'état and the rise to power of the Ba'th, was essential to attract domestic and foreign investments that had to replace the direct aid that Hafez Assad's Syria was used to receiving from generous donors, especially from the Gulf. The lack of any banking sector capable of channelling financial flows and injecting them into the economic cycle was the main cause of the absence of growth according to the International Monetary Fund. Ghassan Rifai, an expatriate working at the World Bank in Washington, was recalled as minister of the economy in 2001 as part of the economic reforms promised by the new president.[15] Although the decision to authorize private banks was taken rapidly by late 2000, the minister of the economy still encountered fierce opposition from the Ba'thists within the government and the party who failed to see the necessity to open up banking to the private sector. The unfortunate experience of Ghassan Rifai, who did not remain long in the job, showed it was difficult to reform any particular sector without a comprehensive theoretical framework.

As the same causes produce the same effects, another experiment with partial reform met with an identical fate. The attempted reform of the public sector (2001–03) was entrusted to Issam Al-Za'im, an expatriate economist working for the United Nations Development programme, whose Marxist leaning meant he opposed any privatization on principle. Issam Al-Za'im recommended separating the running of public

---

[15] Cited in Donati, *L'Exception syrienne*, p. 219.

undertakings from their supervision.[16] The economic bureau of the Ba'th Regional Command opposed this categorically. The attempt to reform the public sector was a failure. Once again, the absence of any pre-established conceptual framework for change that was accepted by the Ba'thists was to blame.

A third attempt at partial reform, the reform of the administration, was undertaken in close consultation with France during the honeymoon period between the two countries that followed Bashar Assad's coming to office. Syria asked France to audit its administration in 2000. The conclusions of the first mission despatched by Paris reflected the disastrous state of the Syrian administration: vast numbers of employees, low pay, insufficient recognition of merit, lack of clarity in the demarcation of responsibilities, lack of team work, functional deterioration, corruption at all levels, and arbitrary controls.[17] To complete the lamentable review, the report denounced the controlling role of the party and the various intelligence services. The French experts recommended revising all of the Syrian administration's control mechanisms. Nibras Fadel, an expatriate graduate of France's Ecole Nationale d'Administration and Ecole polytechnique, was assigned to reform the administration.[18] But the French recommendations had little chance of being understood and followed in a context in which the Ba'th was still officially, under the constitution, the guide of state and society. Again, this reform of the administration lacked a comprehensive political framework for it to fit into the Ba'th's vision of its own future and that of Syria.

8.4 Interpretations of the Ba'th Trilogy

The attempts to reform the economy, public sector, and administration without a coherent political framework and without a Ba'thist vision of the future had proved impossible. Finally, only the banking reform was brought about out of concern not just to modernize the economy, but also to bring Syria out of its regional and international isolation after its withdrawal from Lebanon

---

[16] Donati, *L'Exception syrienne*, p. 221.
[17] *Ibid.*, p. 222.
[18] *Ibid.*, p. 223. Nibras Fadel's responsibilities seem to have changed during his stay in Damascus. First he was attached to the president's office as economic affairs adviser, and then to the prime minister's office. See the interview he gave to the Saudi newspaper *Ash Sharq Al-Awsat* on 26 February 2005.

in 2005. Resistance primarily from the Ba'thists themselves had scuppered the initial attempts at reform just as it had done during the Damascus Spring (2000–01). Before heading down the path of reform, the Ba'th had first to set about its own modernization. This was the ambition of the Ba'th's Tenth Regional Congress in June 2005 held in difficult regional circumstances after the withdrawal of Syrian forces from Lebanon a few weeks earlier.

The trouble with the Ba'th Tenth Regional Congress was that the party leaders wanted to make it a modernizing rather than a reforming congress. Modernization and reform are processes that often flow together but they are not identical. Modernizing the Ba'th did not necessarily mean reforming it. The great principle around which the modernization of Ba'th economic thinking was organized at this congress was the adoption of the concept of the 'social market economy' borrowed from the Chinese model of development, that could not succeed in Syria without very strong annual economic growth. Thus the stated intention of the Syrian leaders was clearly to modernize the economy while keeping intact, as far as possible, the political power structure and its social base. And yet, the approach adopted to legitimize this change of economic heading had suggested a genuine determination to overhaul Ba'th political thinking.

It was not until nearly four years after the Ba'th Tenth Regional Congress that a senior party official described the approach that led to the conclusions of the congress being adopted. In an interview with the Lebanese newspaper *Assafir*, Hatham Sattahyi, a member of the Ba'th Regional Command explained that the renewal of the party's theoretical bases had been raised even before the Tenth Regional Congress in 2005, but that the party Command decided to put on hold the studies and proposals made. According to Haytham Sattayhi, the debate about the renewal of the party's theoretical bases continued later, looking into the development of the concepts of 'union', 'freedom', and 'socialism' so as to take account of internal developments and economic and social changes under way as well as international changes and the experience of other political parties.[19] The economic opening-up and the adoption of the 'social market economy' by the Tenth Congress therefore marked the beginning of a new interpretation of the Ba'th trilogy, Union–Freedom–Socialism. The renewed interpretation was only partial in 2005 because the Tenth Congress only revised the concept of 'socialism' in its economic dimension, leaving till later the job of reforming the concept of 'freedom' which

---

[19] Haytham Sattayhi's interview with the newspaper *Assafir*, 'Ba'th cadre announces party redefining its relations with power', Beirut, 28 May 2009.

was much more substantial and consequential, and to a lesser extent that of 'union'. To understand the intellectual development that enabled the Ba'th to modernize its economic doctrine by adopting the principle of the 'social market economy' at its 2005 Congress and how this was in fact a return to the Ba'th's original thinking, we must briefly describe the Ba'th trilogy and the various changes in its interpretation.

8.4.1 The First Interpretation (1947–1963)

The Ba'th's fundamental political ideas were expressed in a number of texts by the party's co-founder, Michel Aflaq, with which must be associated the writings of Zaki Arzuzi, Elias Farah, and later former Marxists such as Antoine Makdessi, Elias Murkoss, Yassine Hafez, and yet others. The Ba'th trilogy (Union–Freedom–Socialism) features in the two most important documents in the party's history, its 1947 constitution and the Theoretical Foundations adopted by the Sixth National Congress in 1963. Unfortunately they give opposing interpretations of it.

The Ba'th Party considers itself to be the foremost pan-Arab political party. It stands apart in that it was historically the first to raise the Arab national question in its totality. Thus the Ba'th does not consider that the Arab question is limited to the union of the nation, but rather to the resurrection[20] of Arab civilization that had fallen into decline after a long period characterized by decadence, carve-up, occupation, and colonialism. In this sense, the Ba'th is a direct heir to the various strands of thought that impelled the Arab *nahda* in the nineteenth and the first half of the twentieth centuries.[21]

The two founders of the Ba'th, Michel Aflaq and Salah Bitar, were influenced by several European movements while they were students in France in the 1930s and in particular by personalism and socialism. With this dual Arab and European inheritance of the Founding Fathers, the Ba'th set itself as its ultimate objective the resurrection of the Arab nation. For the Ba'th, the Arab renaissance can only come about by a purposeful individual and collective approach encompassing the moral, intellectual, social, economic, and political aspects of the nation. From this perspective, political power is not an end in itself but an instrument to promote and create the objective circumstances that should lead to the rebirth of the Arab nation and its political unity.

---

[20] The word Ba'th means resurrection or renaissance in Arabic.
[21] See Chapter 1, 'The Syrian Question'.

Such is the ambitious mission for which the Ba'th was created on 7 April 1947 in Damascus, a year after Syria had become independent. No sooner was it done than it began to take an impassioned part in politics. From the outset, the party gave itself a trilogy designed to enable it to achieve its ultimate objective.

The Concept of Union

The founding texts of the Ba'th addressed the problem of union[22] from two different angles. First, the national union among the various Arab countries (pan-Arabism) and second, the national union within the Arab state. The Ba'th constitution states that the Arab nation is made up of all Arabs without exception. Article 10 of the constitution defines the Arab. Unlike other nationalist movements, Ba'th Arab nationalism is not based on race or religion (like Zionism), or the ties of blood or land. The definition of who is an Arab has two components: an objective one, 'Arabs are those whose language is Arabic and who live in an Arab country' and a subjective or intentional component 'and who consider they belong to the Arab nation'. It is a form of nationalism that sees itself as humanist, cultural, and far removed from any racist, religious, or xenophobic considerations.

The Ba'th constitution has defined the specificities of the Arab nation. The Arab nation forms a single cultural unit characterized by its vitality, its creative spirit, and its aptitude for renewal. The Arab nation holds an eternal message that can be renewed according to the times. This message aims to renew humanist values, the progress of humanity, and harmonious developments among nations.

The Ba'th party constitution has delimited the Arab homeland as the territory inhabited by the Arab nation and extending from the Taurus mountains to the Gulf of Basra, to the Arabian Sea, to the mountains of Abyssinia, to the Great Desert, as far as the Atlantic Ocean and the Mediterranean (art. 7).

The ambition of the Ba'th did not stop at calling for the creation of a unitary Arab state. The founding texts also addressed the question of the national union within this unitary Arab state. Article 15 of the constitution states that the national bond is the only bond in the Arab state; it ensures harmony among citizens and their merger in the melting pot of a single nation; and it allows the fight against all forms of *'asabiya*, whether

---

[22] Union is sometimes translated as unity.

religious, sectarian, tribal, racial, or regional. Article 16 stipulates that the Arab State is based on decentralization. There is no national unity without a solution to the question of minorities. Michel Aflaq addressed the question of national minorities and saw the solution in the advent of socialism.

The Concept of Freedom

The Ba'th constitution has addressed the question of freedom from several angles. Freedom means first the liberation of Arabs from colonialism (art. 6). The character of the political regime of the Arab state is defined quite unambiguously. It is a constitutional parliamentary state and the executive is accountable to the legislature, which is directly elected by the people (art. 14). The Ba'th party strives to establish a constitution guaranteeing Arab citizens absolute equality before the law, the free expression of their will, and the sincere choice of their representatives (art. 17).

The Concept of Socialism

Michel Aflaq began to outline Ba'th socialism in the 1930s. This stood apart from other conceptions of socialism in two ways. First, was its connection with its political and cultural environment. It was Arab socialism, contrary to Marxist-type socialism that proclaimed itself overtly internationalist. Second, it was socialism derived from the principle of Arab national union and not from the country's socio-economic situation as were reformist types of socialism generally (socialist, labour, or social democratic parties).

Several articles of the Ba'th constitution give a fairly precise idea of the party's initial conception of socialism. Article 13 states that it is first a question of ensuring for citizens the principle of 'equal opportunities in the areas of education and economics'. Further on in the text, article 42 defines the social dimension of Ba'th socialism resting on the notion of a 'fair social regime'. The Ba'th is therefore far closer to reformist socialist parties because it does not fundamentally challenge the principle of private property or the market economy Article 29 provides for partial nationalizations only: major natural resources, major means of production, means of transport, monopolies, and foreign companies. Similarly, article 30 maintains private agricultural ownership although regulating it, and article 33 does the same for real estate. The Marxist terminology, however, created ambiguity in the party doctrine.

The Ba'th also had the ambition of transforming the future unified Arab state into a welfare state. The party's constitution defined free medical care in article 39, free state education in article 45, social security for workers in article 40, and the redistribution of national wealth among citizens in article 27, without specifying how this would be done (nationalization, or redistribution through taxation or other means). This type of socialism presupposes a state that is very active in economic and social life, but it remains a reformist type of socialism rather than a revolutionary one.

8.4.2 The Second Interpretation (1963–1970)

Six months after the movement of 8 March 1963 was triggered the Ba'th held its Sixth National Congress. It was an opportunity for the party to review its ideology to make it square with the seizure of power by the Ba'th military.

The Concept of Freedom

The greatest turnaround in the Theoretical Foundations adopted by the National Congress in 1963 concerned the principles of freedom. The seizure of power by the Ba'th in March 1963 further to a coup d'état organized by the party's military branch was in flagrant contradiction with the party's belief in parliamentary democracy. In order to legitimize this seizure of power ideologically without touching the constitution of the party adopted when it was formed in 1947, the party decided to amend its conception of freedom. With the new ideology adopted in 1963, freedom came to mean Marxist liberties of the type in popular democracies. Here are a few excerpts from the 1963 Theoretical Foundations to illustrate this change:

> Despite the party's theoretical foundations containing a revolutionary concept of social change, even so in the states with political life allowing (at irregular intervals) the development of a political façade, the party engaged in the parliamentary game in a way that might suggest it accepted the parliamentary system in its liberal bourgeois conception as a permanent and adequate framework for the struggle and political action. Because of its revolutionary character, the party did not doubt the utility of bourgeois parliaments as a path towards socialist transformation. Thus, it [the party] became bogged down – at times – in parliamentary action, forgetting that the fundamental question was that of the organization of the masses and ignoring the fact that the objective circumstances in the Arab homeland indicated that parliamentary government in its liberal

bourgeois form could in no way be a means of radical social transformation and was merely a formal façade hiding the influence of feudalism and the upper middle classes.[23]

After justifying the Ba'th's participation in the liberal democratic process (elections, parliaments) since its creation in 1947 as purely tactical, the Sixth National Congress tolled the bell for parliamentary democracy:

> Under present circumstances, at a time when several Arab states are seeing the transition from a near-feudal and capitalist society, power must be passed from the feudal and bourgeois classes to the working classes. This is why we must go beyond parliamentary government because it is one of the forms of [feudal and bourgeois] class domination over the mass of the people.[24]

Once buried, liberal democracy was immediately replaced by 'popular democracy':

> Going beyond parliamentary government does not mean a transition to a dictatorial, individual bureaucratic or military form of power. It means the abolition of the bourgeois and near-feudal framework of democracy and the transition to a wider, deeper, solid and sound democracy; it is popular democracy that can both quell the reaction and mobilize the energy of the masses and their abilities in the socialist and revolutionary construction of Arab society ...[25]

Alongside the adoption of popular democracy, the Ba'th was to proclaim itself the ruling party of the state, promote mass organizations of the people, and adopt democratic centralism borrowed from the communist parties as its internal mode of operation.

The Concept of Union

The concept of union was also greatly changed in 1963 in its two dimensions of pan-Arab union and national union. The concept of Arab union that features first in the Ba'th trilogy lost its pride of place. Officially it continued to feature in first position, but the spirit of the time was first to promote the revolution within Syria, rivalry with the Arab regimes that were characterized as reactionary, and rapprochement with the eastern bloc. This is why another element of the trilogy, socialism, gained the

---

[23] Arab Socialist Ba'th Party, *Some Theoretical Foundations Adopted by the Sixth National Congress*, (Arabic), p. 44 (our translation).
[24] Ibid., p. 50.
[25] Ibid.

upper hand over the other two and imbued them with its new Marxist-leaning tenets.

Likewise socialism permeated the concept of union in terms of national unity. A popular democracy style of socialism stole a march on national unity and called for discrimination against the bourgeoisie:

> The conception of popular democracy includes [both] a broad democracy for the mass of the people and the need to isolate the forces of [the bourgeoisie] class and the political forces hostile to the socialist revolution. This isolation must take a legal form and a popular form. The remains of 'class collaboration' that [still] persist among the backward categories of the masses must fall and be liquidated ... the masses must commit themselves to the class struggle against the reactionary classes in a clear and determined way; either we shall survive or the reaction will survive.[26]

The adoption of popular democracy as the foundation of Ba'thist Syria's regime shows how far the party had moved from its 1947 constitution. The stated principles of equal opportunities for citizens and social justice were superseded by the refusal of class collaboration, discrimination against a part of the population – the bourgeoisie – by law and outright class struggle. Such discrimination did not claim to attain the level of Marxist dictatorship of the proletariat but theoretically it did not fall short of it.

The Concept of Socialism

The Theoretical Foundations of 1963 recommended a programme of action to put the party on the road to revolutionary socialism. This programme took up the socialist provisions of the party's 1947 constitution but emphasizing them in three areas: the intention to strictly regulate private property (agricultural and industrial); nationalization (of the banking sector and the great estates), and the adoption of the principle of collective farms as the socialist solution to the agricultural question.

> Recognition of private property, in absolute terms, despite the fact that it has been limited, nevertheless remains the expression of a petty bourgeois conception because scientific socialism considers human labour as the sole source of value. So, should private property exceed the limit of individual needs it can only be a source of exploitation.[27]
>
> The problem of land, to be solved by the principles of socialism, must be based on the principle of 'the land to those who work it', thus avoiding any tendency to individual and private appropriation. The important thing, the essential thing is to create new socialist relations and to ensure

---

[26] Ibid., p. 56.
[27] Ibid., p. 67.

that collective farms provide the definitive framework for socialization in the countryside.[28]

In these three areas, the Theoretical Foundations bring an innovation to the socialist construction imagined by the party's constitution. When it was adopted in 1947, the constitution was less severe with respect to private property, it did not provide for nationalization of the banking sector, and it envisaged limiting private agricultural property as a response to the land question. Economically, the 1963 Theoretical Foundations were a turning point in the party's history as they moved Ba'th socialism closer to that of Marxist popular democracies.

8.4.3 The Third Interpretation (1970–2005)

The Corrective Movement led by Hafez Assad in November 1970 led to the components of the Ba'th trilogy being balanced anew.

The Concept of Union

The concept of socialism that, during the radical period of the neo-Ba'th between 1966 and 1970, had prevailed over the other components of the trilogy leading Syria towards a regional policy that entailed Damascus being isolated from other Arab countries that were judged reactionary, was put on stand-by in favour of the concept of union. This variation in the order of priorities of the components of the trilogy and their interpretation meant Syria could renew ties with its Arab environment by adopting a regional policy characterized by realism. Hafez Assad expressed this new approach in his address to the final session of the Ba'th Twelfth National Congress in Damascus in 1975:

> We have confirmed in the writings of the party and at our regional and national Congresses the bond between the fight for union and the fight for socialism. This bond between the fight for union and the fight for socialism does not mean that achieving union rests on achieving socialism.

The Concept of Socialism

The changes to the concept of socialism and the loss of its primacy led to the recognition of a role for the private and the mixed (public and private collaboration) sectors in the economy. Hafez Assad's policy in this area was prudent and pragmatic. On several occasions, when Syria was

---

[28] *Ibid.*, p. 84.

isolated on the regional and international stage (1985–86) or short of capital (1990), Hafez Assad opened the floodgates to the private sector so that it could inject capital into the economic cycle.

The Concept of Freedom

This concept was revived a little in Hafez Assad's time without returning to the initial conception of the Ba'th's Founding Fathers. Hafez Assad stood by a Marxist-type conception of freedom as accepted in the context of a 'popular democracy' modelled on those in eastern European countries. Even so, he allowed certain left-wing Arab nationalist political parties to operate and included them in the NPF. He also tolerated a sheepish opposition in the National Democratic Rally led by Jamal Atassi and including mostly dissident formations from parties in the NPF.

8.4.4 The Fourth Interpretation (2005)

It has been stated that the Ba'th Tenth Regional Congress was one of modernization and not of reform. And yet, as recalled earlier, a well-informed member of the Regional Command later acknowledged that the theoretical framework of a global reform of Ba'th doctrine had been thought out by this date. Proposals for simultaneous reinterpretation of the three components of the Ba'th trilogy had been shared with members of the Regional Command. However, they decided to revise the concept of socialism alone during the Tenth Congress, leaving freedom and union for later. The congress thus adopted the principle of 'social market economy' and considered that such an organization of the economy was not in contradiction with the principle of socialism advocated by the Ba'th. This spelt the end of the 'scientific socialism' proposed by the party's Theoretical Foundations in 1963. The Ba'th was turning the page on a Marxist-style conception of the economy and returning to its origins as a reformist and not revolutionary socialist party.

The Ba'th's error was that it failed to see that such a conception of the economy and consequently society would be incompatible with a 'popular democracy' type of political system. By postponing the revision of the concept of freedom, the Ba'th sought to maintain a type of political regime that did not correspond to a market economy, albeit a social market economy, and a society that was inevitably to suffer from economic liberalization. The Ba'th in 2005 failed to see that a society based on a market economy could not be governed top-down as in a state-run economy. A market economy has too many actors for this and their decisions are based on individual interests. The various social and economic partners defend contradictory sectorial and regional interests. In such an environment, it is in the state's interest to appear neutral while laying down the safeguarding rules that apply to all. The categories that suffer most, workers in the sectors hit hardest by liberalization, must be able to express their frustration without it being perceived as a threat to the regime's survival. To operate smoothly, a market economy must provide safety valves for social and political protest. Such an economy must have a political system based on multiparty government with free periodic elections and the possibility of changing government and majority precisely so the political system can be maintained and can endure. Political openness is a safety net for market economy regimes. The other equally crucial safety net for the regime's survival is the introduction of a social security system for the worst off. In refusing to reform the concept of freedom, the Ba'th backed itself into an ideological dead-end, forcing it, when the crisis broke in 2011, to opt for a security clamp-down rather than dialogue and the search for a compromise.

To seek solely to reform the content of one of the components of the trilogy, namely socialism, was attempting the impossible, because the three terms are interconnected. What the Ba'th needed was a fresh interpretation of the three terms of the trilogy and a new balance among them. The new conception of socialism based on social justice while adopting the principle of a market economy with social security safety nets required a new conception of freedom based on the recognition and guarantee of individual and collective liberties including multiparty government and free elections. Such a reformulation of the principle of freedom would have opened the path to historical reconciliation between not just the Ba'th and democracy, but the Arab nationalist movement, which was all too often authoritarian about the exercise of power, and democracy. As for the principle of union, it too needed to be revised and based on the principles of solidarity and shared interests of the various Arab states.

The final declaration of the Tenth Regional Congress indicated that the party was to propose a revision of certain articles of the constitution, a law on political parties, a law on the press, and the revision of the electoral law.[29] This might have suggested the party was also going to modernize the concept of freedom. But those promises were never fulfilled. The unfinished reform of Ba'th ideology in 2005 was a missed opportunity to reform the

---

[29] The final declaration did not specify which articles of the 1973 constitution were to be amended. It seems that various viewpoints were later expressed about the necessity to alter the constitution to make it compatible with the principle of a social market economy. Finally, the opinion that prevailed was that no revision was necessary because there was no contradiction in principle between socialism and the social market economy.

party, to change it gradually into a modern social-democratic-type party. The Ba'th should have been clear-sighted enough to modernize the concept of freedom along liberal lines. Such a step would have prepared the militants for the concessions later made urgently after the outbreak of the crisis in 2011, such as the abandoning of article 8 of the constitution making the Ba'th the ruling party of the state and society, the adoption of a law on political parties, a law on the press, and a new electoral law. All were adopted under the pressure of events but without any change to the party dogma on the concept of freedom. By the end of the Tenth Congress, the Ba'th, which officially still had a socialist ideology, found itself with a lopsided trilogy whose economic dimension of liberal inspiration was soon to be at loggerheads with an authoritarian political system modelled on former communist regimes. These contradictions led to an identity crisis for the party.

The Theoretical Foundations adopted at the Sixth National Congress in 1963 that gave a Marxian aspect to the Ba'th trilogy were implicitly abandoned at the Fourteenth National Congress held in Damascus in May 2017. The meeting was held thirty-two years behind time, the preceding national congress having been in 1980. The congress decided to dissolve the National Command as the party's highest body and replace it by a consultative 'National Council' representing the various political organizations of the Ba'th in Arab countries. The Theoretical Foundations were abandoned tacitly and without fuss, without referring to them by name, and without any critical review. The final communiqué of the congress merely made a laconic reference to the party's historical constitution of 1947 and its experience and the contributions amassed over the last seventy years forming the common intellectual basis of all the Ba'th's political organizations. The communiqué added that at its first meeting the National Council should adopt a National Charter to modernize the party's thinking. While the National Congress was thirty-two years late, the praiseworthy determination to reform the party and rehabilitate its 1947 constitution came sixteen to seventeen years too late. It would probably have been in everyone's best interests for the reform to have been introduced during the Damascus Spring in 2000–01 or the Ba'th Tenth Regional Congress in 2005.

8.5 The Missed Opportunity to Reform the Political System in 2006–2007

Since its refusal to endorse or at least not to counter the US occupation of Iraq, Syria became an embarrassing regional actor. The six

Gulf countries began to distance themselves from Syria after the honeymoon period that had joined them with Damascus and Cairo for almost a decade as part of the 1991 Damascus Declaration after the liberation of Kuwait. The separation intensified in 2004 with the UN Security Council's adoption of resolution 1559 and the withdrawal of Syrian forces from Lebanon in 2005 after the assassination of former prime minister Rafic Hariri. Assad was to have his revenge in 2006 with the victory of the Hizbullah in Lebanon and the Hamas in Gaza at the time of the failed Israeli offensive in 2008–09 to eliminate Palestinian resistance in the territory. The victories of the Lebanese and Palestinian resistance movement supported by Damascus, the development of Iraqi resistance in Iraq also supported by Damascus, the coming to power in Iran of Ahmadinajad, a supporter of a tough foreign policy line, and the historic reconciliation with Turkey all put Syria back in the saddle as a regional power. In 2008–10 Bashar Assad had managed to make new ties with the Gulf states, with Sarkozy's France, and even with the USA, which after a five-year gap sent a new ambassador to Damascus in 2010 further to mediation by John Kerry, then chair of the senate's foreign affairs committee.

These regional developments directly impacted the domestic situation in Syria. To escape its isolation, Damascus had to liberalize and open up its economy at the Ba'th Tenth Regional Congress in 2005. This policy was personified by Abdallah Dardari who was appointed vice-prime minister in charge of economic affairs in June 2005. The defection of the former vice-president, Abdel Halim Khaddam, in late 2005 was not just the expression of disagreement at the highest level in the state over Syrian policy in Lebanon or the choice of domestic policy, it was also a harbinger of the crisis of confidence between Damascus and the Gulf states on Syria's regional policy. To face the growing threats, President Assad thought at one point in 2006 of liberalizing the Syrian political system somewhat in anticipation of increased foreign pressure and with an eye to the 2007 elections.

The beginning of 2006 was rather feverish, suggesting for a moment a possible development in the Syrian political system. In his opening address to the 22nd Congress of the Union of Arab Lawyers in Damascus on 21 January 2006, President Assad indicated that Syria was preparing to adopt laws on political parties, elections, and local administration. The bill on political parties was indeed discussed within the Ba'th, its parliamentary bloc, and by the parties in the NPF. The Ba'th asked its partners in the NPF for their views on the future law, complying with two principles: the prohibition of any political party based on religion, race, and ethnic origin; and compliance with the separation of religion and the state.

Various proposals were discussed such as authorizing only pan-Arab political parties, reminiscent of a similar provision in the 1953 law on political parties. In March 2006, the chair of the parliamentary committee in charge of drafting the law on political parties declared the committee had studied the laws on political parties in Egypt and Jordan but that the Syrian law would reflect its own needs. He added that the law on political parties would probably be submitted for popular approval by referendum. He also specified that the law on political parties would include 'red lines' such as the prohibition of parties with sectarian, racial, or ethnic connotations. By adopting the law by referendum the voters would thus have approved those red lines.

Around mid-May 2006 the NPF adopted the bill. In its final version, it authorized the formation of political parties, but without accepting the principle of political changeover, which was deemed contrary to article 8 of the constitution stipulating that the Ba'th ruled the state and society. According to the reports of the press close to government sources, two questions were debated. The first concerned the possibility of political changeover defended by the Syrian Communist Party (the Yussef Faysal branch) and the second the possibility of membership for non-Syrian Arabs. The NPF dismissed both with an exception for Palestinians who were authorized to be affiliated to Syrian political parties. This was perceived as a concession by the Ba'th, which had a pan-Arab structure formed of non-Syrian militants. The concession was made in a context in which the Ba'th seriously thought of ridding itself of its pan-Arab structure and maintaining just the Syrian branch.

Alongside the preparation of the new law on political parties, the People's Assembly set up a special committee on 11 May 2006 to draw up a new law for legislative and municipal elections. The committee had until the end of May to complete its work. The parliamentary blocs and independent members presented proposals for a proportional system in the *mohafazats* (administrative divisions) or for the entire country considered as a single electoral constituency. Hunein Nemer, member of parliament and general secretary of the Communist Party, claimed the new electoral law was one component of the political reform of the country alongside the law on political parties and the revision to come of the law on the state of emergency.

Had these bills been enacted, they would have been a timid but not insignificant advance on the road to democratic reforms. They would have opened up a breach in the monolithic thinking of the Ba'thist old guard. This political and legislative agitation during the first half of 2006 perhaps suggested that Syria was preparing to develop its political system for the following year's elections, the legislative elections in April 2007, followed by the presidential referendum in May. Such modernization of the political system, even if partial, would have consolidated the economic opening-up by the Ba'th Tenth Regional Congress the previous year. The reform of the concept of freedom of the Ba'th trilogy would have reflected the reform of the concept of socialism. Unfortunately this will to reform came to a sudden stop after the war in Lebanon in July–August 2006. Israel's defeat and the Hizbullah's victory had led to a new deal in the Near East. Israel, the USA, and their allies had suffered a stinging defeat. The USA was bogged down in Iraq. As for the Israelis, before their defeat in Lebanon, they had had to withdraw their forces from Gaza in 2005 under the impact of the resistance of Hamas, whose political leadership was based in Damascus. Syria, through its allies in Lebanon and Gaza, was in the victors' camp. President Assad had nothing more to fear regionally, which probably prompted him to put on hold his plans for domestic political reform … until things exploded in 2011.

8.6 The Crisis of March 2011

Several factors can explain the explosion of March 2011 and its amplitude, beginning with a mistaken appreciation of the country's economic and social situation and an underestimation of the rancour of some regional actors with regard to the policy followed by Damascus. Some commentators seem convinced it was the economic policy that was the immediate cause of the March 2011 explosion. This may be so, but it was certainly not the only cause because it was grafted on to a sclerotic political system and amplified by the intervention of regional and international actors in the crisis. Bashar Assad's time in power was marked by liberalization of the economy that accelerated from 2005 onwards after the disengagement of Syrian troops from Lebanon and the adoption of the social market economy principle some weeks later. The immediate aim of opening up the market economy was to bring Syria out of its isolation and attract Arab investment instead of the direct aid Syria had customarily received from Gulf countries over the last four decades. It was also meant to instil trust so that Syrian capital that had been expatriated would flow back home. Syrian assets abroad were estimated at about US $50 billion.

The leaders in Damascus were aware that opening the economy in this way would have adverse social consequences on a population in which the least-favoured sectors were already suffering from poverty.[30] What they may not have realized was that it would hit the regime's grass roots full on, that it would partly dismantle the *'asabiya* that the Ba'th and Hafez Assad in particular had put in place and that had propped up the authorities during the most difficult times (the uprising of the Muslim Brotherhood in 1965, armed opposition of the Muslim Brotherhood in the period 1977–82, and during the serious economic crisis of 1986–88).

To appraise the damage economic liberalization did to the regime's power base means returning to the Khaldunian model and recalling how the *'asabiya* was formed.[31] The various divides in Syrian society and in particular the urban/rural opposition had given rise to an *esprit de corps*, an *'asabiya* that developed mainly among the young generation of the period after independence in 1946 in rural areas and the hinterland. This *'asabiya* was grafted onto the message of the Ba'th (Arab nationalism and socialism) that played the role of religious belief or *da'wa* in the Khaldunian model. The Founding Fathers of the Ba'th who spread their message primarily among high school and university students and intellectuals failed to realize at the time that some of their supporters were recruiting party sympathizers and members by a dynamic of *'asabiya*, concentrating their efforts on their rural or sectarian community of origin. The modern and progressive Ba'thist ideology meant that the initial support systems (sectarian, clannish, geographical, etc.) could be extended and strengthened by associating them with the ambitions of young people from other horizons (Sunni urbanites, or other sectarian minorities). The Ba'th's implantation among the urban population of the major cities was more laborious.[32]

---

[30] See UNDP report, 'Poverty in Syria': 1996–2004. Diagnosis and Pro-poor Policy Considerations', June 2005.

[31] See Chapter 6, 'The Fourth Republic'.

[32] The country's third largest city, Homs, unlike Damascus and Aleppo, was one of the few big cities where the Ba'th managed to implant itself firmly in the late 1940s and early 1950s. Many young members of the Atassi family joined the party ranks including Nurredin Atassi, the future head of state and general secretary of the Ba'th (1966–70); Jamal Atassi, future minister (1963) and head of the left-wing democratic opposition to Hafez Assad from 1973 until his death in 2000, a few days before Assad's death; Khulusi Atassi, a militant of the first hour, at whose home the works of the 1962 Ba'th National Congress were held; Abdul Wadoud Atassi, who published under his name the local newspaper *Al-'Orouba* (*Arabism*) from 1954 to 1958 that propagated Ba'th ideas in Homs, before having a diplomatic career, becoming the *chef de cabinet* to four ministers of foreign affairs and then Syria's ambassador to Japan (1978–86).

The army was the favoured domain of this rising *'asabiya*. Once they came to power further to the coup d'état of 8 March 1963, the Ba'thists and military of rural origins who were mostly from sectarian minorities eliminated the right-wing and/or Sunni officers. Then, they gathered in circles or groups (*jama't*) around a higher-ranking officer and eliminated each other.[33] Hafez Assad's *jama't*, supported by his loyal associate Mustafa Tlass, emerged as victorious from all these internecine struggles. In this scheme of things, the main role of the big cities and in particular the capital, Damascus, was to legitimize the power of the new rulers by accepting the pan-Arab, socialist ideology of the Ba'th and the popular democratic regime that it introduced in exchange for the protection of the interests of the city-dwelling merchant class.

According to this schema, the *'asabiya* that brought Hafez Assad to power in 1970 and kept him in the upper spheres of the state until his death in 2000 cannot be reduced to a simple *esprit de corps* of the Alawi. His base was far broader. It included people of various origins (Alawi, Sunni, Druze, Christian, manual workers, peasants, shopkeepers, industrialists, city dwellers, rural folk, civilians, the military, etc.) all driven by the same spirit and who played a fundamental role under Hafez Assad's rule. This geographically, sectarian, and socially hybrid *'asabiya* took up the national project of the Founding Fathers and supplemented it with an unwritten, informal, social convention between the Ba'th and large sectors of the population. This social compact can be summarized as follows: distribution of national wealth via the redistribution of land to farmers through the agrarian reform; control over the economy by the intermediary of a broad public sector allowing the marginal development of agrifood, textile, and pharmaceutical industries in the hands of the private sector with ties to the authorities; abandoning domestic trade and to a lesser extent foreign trade and tourism to the urban commercial middle class; free education at all levels and free health care; subsidies for basic necessities; various privileges and benefits in kind for the military, government workers, and Ba'th party members.

The system was topped by modern political institutions including the NPF that brought together a spectrum of national and progressive political parties and by a popular democratic type of constitution that was ideally suited to the regime's outer construction but without reflecting the

---

[33] The principal *jama't* were those of Mohammad Umran in 1965–66, Salim Hatum in 1966–68, Salah Jadid in 1966–70, and Rifaat Assad in 1984.

system's intrinsic nature. This made it extremely difficult for observers unaccustomed to Syrian life to understand the nature of the regime (military or civilian, left- or right-wing, minority or secular, progressive or traditional), its strengths and weaknesses, and the reasons underpinning its decisions.

The changes introduced since 2005 to modernize the economy, prepare for the post-oil period, preserve macro-economic equilibria, and integrate the Syrian economy into its regional environment have ignored the fact that it is in many respects a war economy. The authorities therefore faced a double challenge. They had not just to successfully liberalize a state-run socialist economy but also a war economy characterized by massive military spending that could not readily be cut back. Only double-figure annual growth could have met the challenge.

The changes introduced since 2005 also challenged certain fundamental components of the informal social compact established by the Ba'th since 1963 without offering alternatives. By seeking to institutionalize authoritarian practices that by nature were not amenable to the dogma of rational economics and the idea of a neutral state; by seeking to submit acquired benefits to the laws of the market; by liberalizing the imports of foreign products some of which competed with domestic production, this opening-up benefited a well-connected minority.[34] It partly broke the *esprit de corps*, the umbilical cord joining Ba'thist rule to its traditional social base. The living conditions of the former beneficiaries of the regime's largesse deteriorated rapidly, weakening sectorial and geographical pillars of the regime. The situation was exacerbated by the deterioration of social services (education and health) that had to cope with a population boom and the inflow of more than a million Iraqi refugees from 2005, equivalent to almost a 5 per cent rise in the country's population,[35] and a drought in eastern Syria that pushed some 800,000 impoverished people towards the west of the country.

The spark that ignited the powder was the arrest in the city of Dara'a in the south of the country near the Jordanian border of a group of high-school children who had written slogans on walls calling for the fall of the regime, imitating the slogans of the revolts in Tunisia and Egypt. The intelligence services arrested the teenagers on 6 March 2011 and subjected

---

[34] On the regime's new clientele, see 'La république des copains' in Donati, *L'Exception syrienne*, p. 233.
[35] On the population increase in Syria see Courbage, 'Des réticences à la transition (démographique)' in Dupret et al., *La Syrie au présent*, pp. 177–213.

them to degrading and inhumane corporal punishment. The population of Dara'a took to the streets calling for their release. The students were freed on 19 March 2011 and returned to their families. Other demonstrations broke out in various parts of the country calling for political liberties. In the face of repression by the authorities, the moderate watchwords were soon abandoned for a simpler but more radical demand that had serious consequences for the country, namely the fall of the regime and the departure of the president.

The authorities urgently passed a series of measures to meet the protesters' demands. On 24 March 2011, presidential adviser Buthaina Sha'aban announced the possibility of lifting the state of emergency and authorizing political parties. On 19 April 2011, a little over a month after the first protests, the president enjoined the government to adopt three draft legislative decrees for the head of state's approval. The procedure was rare enough to be worth pointing out because legislative decrees were usually drawn up directly by the president without prior consultation with the government. On that day, the entire cabinet put to the head of state a draft legislative decree to abolish the state of emergency that had been in force in the country since 1963. The government also proposed a bill to abolish the Supreme Court of State Security, a court with special jurisdiction that was decried by the regime's opponents and human rights activists. The cabinet also proposed a third draft legislative decree on the right to demonstrate. In addition, the cabinet asked the relevant ministers to quickly draw up a bill on political parties, another on the press, and a third on local administration.

The three legislative decrees were signed by the president two days later. On 10 May 2011, the prime minister created a committee to prepare a new electoral law. Special committees were set up to prepare laws on political parties, press freedom, and local administration. The committee tasked with drafting the bill on political parties presented its work on 21 June 2011. The one preparing the law on the press completed its work in July 2011. The two texts were signed by the president and then the legislative decrees were submitted to parliament, whose term had been extended under article 58(2) of the constitution since it had been impossible to hold legislative elections in May 2011 because of the situation within the country. This People's Assembly was to remain in place until the election of a new assembly in May 2012. In October 2011, President Assad tasked a special committee composed of members appointed by him to propose a new constitution for Syria. The committee submitted its work early in February 2012. The draft constitution was submitted for approval by referendum on 26 February and obtained 89.4 per cent of the votes cast, in a 57.4 per cent turnout.

This raft of political reforms, which had been unthinkable a few months earlier, and that would have been highly beneficial if it had been adopted in peaceful circumstances, for example further to the recommendations of the Ba'th's Tenth Congress in 2005, or in 2006 when the authorities looked as though they wanted to reform the political system, had no effect on the crisis in 2011-12. It rang hollow. The responses proposed were not just too little too late compared with the demands of the street protesters, but they were not taken in consultation with the opposition or accompanied by any dialogue with it. One of the dramatic features of the crisis is that the protagonists refused to talk to each other. The opposition openly refused to talk with the president and his representatives while the repression continued. As for the regime, from the outset of the crisis it gave the use of force precedence over dialogue.[36]

On 6 April 2011, President Assad signed a decree that was to grant Syrian nationality to nearly 300,000 Kurds who had been deprived of it because of a controversial census of inhabitants in the province of Hassake in 1962. This decision probably appeased the Kurdish population some of whom had rebelled in 2004 and prompted them not to join in with the 2011 uprising.

8.7 The 2012 Constitution or Continuity in the Midst of Change

In October 2011 the president set up a national committee to draft a new constitution composed exclusively of figures appointed by him.[37] The committee's chair handed the results of its work to President Assad on 14 February 2012.

---

[36] On repression, see the damning reports of the UN Independent International Commission of Inquiry on Syria on the website of the Office of the High Commissioner for Human Rights: www.ohchr.org/en/countries/menaregion/pages/syindex.aspx. From 2013 onwards, the commission of inquiry also criticized armed opposition groups for violations of humanitarian law.

[37] The committee was headed by Mazhar al-Anbari and included Abdel-Karim Adi, Kamal Charaf, Moharam Tayara, Mohamed Adel Jamouss, Moumtaz Fouakhri, Aziz Choukri, Aboud Al-Sarraj, Fouad Dib, Sam Delah, Saiid Nahili, Mikhael Nekoul, Nizar Skeif, Ahmad Eido, Abdel-Rahman Eskahi, Jassem Zakariya, Mohamed Kheir Al-Akam, Kinda Al-Chamat, Jamila Al-Shourbaji, Amal Jazji, Qadri Jamil, Ahmad Saleh Ibrahim, Omran Al-Zobi, Nabih Jalah, Osmat Ghebari, Mahmoud Younés.

This new constitution was approved by referendum on 26 February 2012. It contains 165 articles. It is more a logical continuation and modernization of the 1973 constitution than a radical departure from it. This general assertion as to the spirit of the 2012 constitution must be relativized because certain new provisions reflect real democratic advances and a substantial change, at least in theoretical terms, although they are yet to be confirmed in practice. It is possible therefore to follow a thread linking the constitutions of 1969, 1971, 1973, and 2012. Each has modernized and moved forward the initial parent constitution of 1969.

The 2012 constitution contains a preamble and six titles. Its overall structure does not depart unduly from that of the previous constitution that includes a preamble and just four titles. The new constitution contains additionally a title II on 'Rights, Freedoms and the Rule of Law' and a title IV on 'The Supreme Constitutional Court'.

The preamble is an integral part of the constitution (art. 151). It has been shortened somewhat compared to the 1973 constitution. In fact, since the 1969 parent constitution both those 1971 and 1973 saw their preamble reduced in size and in ideological intensity. As such, the preamble to the 2012 constitution is probably the most neutral politically because it is stripped of all reference to socialism, it only included a reference to social justice. The 2012 preamble recalls nonetheless that Syria belongs to the Arab nation and takes up Nasser's famous expression calling Syria the 'beating heart of Arabism'. The preamble also emphasizes Syria's role in the confrontation with the Zionist enemy and its role as defender of the resistance to colonial hegemony.

8.7.1 Title I: 'Basic Principles'

As in the 1973 constitution, the new title I is on 'Basic Principles'. It contains four separate chapters. Three keep the same names in both constitutions (Political Principles, Economic Principles, Educational and Cultural Principles), although their contents sometimes diverge radically. In the 1973 constitution 'Freedoms, Rights and the Rule of Law' were contained in a chapter IV that has become title II in the 2012 constitution. Instead, the new title I contains a chapter III on 'Social Principles' that were not to be found in the earlier constitution.

The Basic Principles in title I and its four chapters that run from articles 1 to 32 of the constitution reflect the spirit of the regime, its vision of national identity, Syrian society, the place of the individual, the purpose of laws, and long-term objectives that every Syrian government should set itself.

Chapter I is the hard core of the constitution. Its twelve articles describe Syria's identity. Article 1 is similar to that of the previous constitution except that it no longer says that Syria is a 'popular socialist' democracy. The mention of the Federation of Arab Republics has also been removed. Article 2 recalls the republican form of the regime of government and states that sovereignty lies with the people. It is virtually the same as in the 1973 constitution. The new article 3 takes up the first two paragraphs of its predecessor in the earlier constitution about Islam being the religion of the president of the republic (art. 3(1)) and Islamic jurisprudence as the main source of legislation (art. 3(2)), to which it adds two new paragraphs. Article 3(3) states that the state shall respect all religions, ensure freedom of practice of all forms of worship, provided they do not infringe public policy. These provisions featured in article 35 of the 1973 constitution. In its new version, article 3 also has a paragraph 4 guaranteeing the personal status of the different religious communities. This last provision confirms 'Syrian-style secularism' developed by all successive regimes since the separation from the Ottoman empire in 1918, namely the secular character of the state and its institutions, but not the personal status of individuals who continue to be governed by rules specific each to their own sectarian origin (such as those concerning marriage, divorce, and inheritance).[38] This notorious exception to secularism will continue to prevent all Syrians from being integrated as citizens in the national melting pot and preclude the absence of any differentiation among citizens on the basis of religion.

Article 4 of the new constitution stating that Arabic is the official language is similar to that of the 1973 constitution except that it adds that Arabic is the official language of the state.[39] This clarification will open the path to the 2012 constitution recognizing other languages used within Syrian society. Indeed, the new article 9 should be read together with article 4. Article 9 supplements article 4 and stipulates that the constitution protects cultural diversity within Syrian society with all its components and considers diversity to be a national heritage that promotes national

---

[38] The new version of article 3 with its four paragraphs featured is almost as it stands in the 1953 constitution that ushered in the Third Republic.

[39] Here again, interestingly, the new version of article 4 is the same as article 4(1) of the 1953 constitution.

unity within the framework of the territorial integrity of the Syrian Arab Republic. This article is certainly one of the major advances of the 2012 constitution. From now on, all of the languages spoken in Syrian society such as Kurdish, Assyrian, Aramaic, Syriac and others will be able to flourish. Nothing should now prevent the opening of private schools in these various languages, provided of course that they comply with the official curriculum in Arabic. This cultural openness principally towards the Kurdish component within the Syrian population comes in addition to the rapprochement between the Damascus authorities and the main Kurdish politico-military movement the Democratic Union Party (PYD) since the onset of the 2011 crisis. This rapprochement was facilitated by the legislative decree of April 2011 granting Syrian citizenship to stateless Kurds and was to be confirmed subsequently on the ground. Some Kurdish activists evoked the possible creation of an autonomous Kurdish region or more within the Syrian Republic.

Another major and probably the greatest innovation of the 2012 constitution is the amendment of article 8 of the previous constitution on the leading role of the Ba'th party in the state and society. Article 8 of the 1973 constitution had merely reiterated article 7 of the 1969 provisional constitution and article 7 of the 1971 provisional constitution.[40] The removal of this clause of article 8 was the leading demand of all of the opposition factions. The new version of article 8 states:

(1) The political system of the state shall be based on the principle of political pluralism, and exercising power democratically through the ballot box.
(2) Licensed political parties and constituencies shall contribute to the national political life, and shall respect the principles of national sovereignty and democracy.
(3) The law shall regulate the provisions and procedures related to the formation of political parties.
(4) Carrying out any political activity or forming any political parties or groupings on the basis of religious, sectarian, tribal, regional, class-based, professional, or on discrimination based on gender, origin, race or color may not be undertaken.
(5) Public office or public money may not be exploited for a political, electoral or party interest.[41]

---

[40] See Chapter 6, 'The Fourth Republic'. Article 8 of the 1973 constitution further provided that the Ba'th should lead a National Progressive Front.
[41] See constituteproject.org.

The hopes for a multiparty system and growing participation of Syrians in the country's political life rest mostly on this article. Through this article, the legitimacy of rule through the ballot box, in the liberal sense, is now a matter of national consensus among Syrians. It remains to be seen how it will be applied. It can now be said that the concept of liberty is henceforth a new consensus-based component of the Syrian national project alongside multi-sectarian coexistence, the refusal of foreign hegemony, the refusal of division, the refusal of Zionist ambitions in Palestine, and the principle of social justice.

Article 10 of the constitution supplements the provisions on political pluralism in article 8 with specific provisions on public organizations and trade unions. The 1973 constitution had done much the same in its article 9, except that it made no reference to trade unions. It simply stated that popular organizations and cooperative associations brought together the active forces of the people so as to ensure the gradual change of society and achieve the interests of their members. As a sign of the times and the abandoning of any reference to socialism, article 10 of the 2012 constitution makes no mention of cooperative associations. Article 10 states that 'Public organizations, professional unions and associations shall be bodies that group citizens in order to develop society and attain [that is, defend] the interests of its members. The State shall guarantee the independence of these bodies and the right to exercise public control and participation in the various sectors and councils defined in laws.'

It should also be pointed out that the new article 11 of the 2012 constitution is a re-write. In its earlier version, article 11 set out two main missions for the armed forces: to secure the territory and safeguard the objectives of the Revolution, namely (Arab) union, freedom, and socialism – the objectives of the Ba'th. In the new version, article 11 of the 2012 constitution still assigns two missions to the armed forces: defending territorial integrity and sovereignty for one; for the other, the armed forces 'shall be in the service of the people's interests and the protection of its objectives and national security'. This second objective of the Syrian armed forces is somewhat hazy. The former version of article 11 had laid down the constitutional basis justifying the Ba'th's hold over the officer class. Loyalty first to the party and subsequently to the president, after the personalization of the regime under Hafez Assad, had been the basis on which the policy of recruitment, training, promotion, postings, and allocation of privileges in favour of Ba'thist officers had been built. What will the new version of article 11 mean for the Syrian army? Will the military academies be more open to applications from young Syrians not affiliated to the Ba'th? Time will tell.

The final article of chapter I, article 12, merely takes up the provisions of the former article 10 on the role of elected councils. So chapter I, while retaining the overall structure of chapter I of the 1973 constitution, is radically different from it. But the spirit of the article tends to show that the change introduced is in reality just a form of continuity.

Like the previous constitution, chapter II of title I of the 2012 constitution relates to 'Economic Principles'. Article 13 states:

(1) The national economy shall be based on the principle of developing public and private economic activity through economic and social plans aiming at increasing the national income, developing production, raising the individual's living standards and creating jobs.
(2) Economic policy of the state shall aim at meeting the basic needs of individuals and society through the achievement of economic growth and social justice in order to reach comprehensive, balanced and sustainable development.
(3) The state shall guarantee the protection of producers and consumers, foster trade and investment, prevent monopoly in various economic fields and work on developing human resources and protecting the labour force in a way that serves the national economy.

The difference between this new article 13 and the previous one in the 1973 constitution is striking. The earlier version stipulated that the state economy was a socialist planned economy designed to abolish all forms of exploitation (art. 13(1)). The country's economic planning was to bring about economic complementarity in the Arab homeland (art. 13(2)). References to socialism and Arabism have completely vanished from the new version of article 13. Syria is now a state seeking its economic salvation on its own, through a liberal type of national development policy for social purposes. The reference to 'social justice' in article 13(2) refers implicitly to 'Arab socialism' based on social justice and equal opportunity. This conception of socialism was that of the Ba'th since its creation in 1947 and until the great ideological turning point that occurred with the Sixth National Congress in October 1963 after the Ba'th had taken power in Syria in March that same year.

Article 15(1) states that 'Collective and individual private ownership shall be protected in accordance with the following basis: 1. General confiscation of funds shall be prohibited; a. Private ownership shall not be removed except in the public interest by a decree and against fair compensation according to the law; b. Confiscation of private property shall not be imposed without a final court ruling'. These three provisions already featured in the former version of article 15. The new version of article 15 introduces two important new provisions that were not in the previous one: 'c. Private property may be confiscated for necessities of war and disasters by a law and against fair compensation'. In the previous version such compensation was of a general character and was not limited to the two exceptions mentioned. But above all, the new article 15(2) states that 'Compensation shall be equivalent to the real value of the property'. This provision, if construed retroactively, will give rise to numerous actions for the re-evaluation of property and land confiscated by the Ba'th since 1963. This could satisfy the middle classes who felt they had been stripped of their property against derisory compensation at the time of the nationalizations.

The maximum area of agricultural holdings shall be determined by law 'to ensure the protection of the farmer and the agricultural laborer from exploitation and to ensure increased production'. This article 16 is much the same in the 1973 and 2012 constitutions.

Chapter III of title I of the 2012 constitution relates to 'Social Principles'. It did not feature in the previous constitution. It comprises eight articles, five of which are new. The other three were in chapter IV on 'Freedoms, Rights, and Public Duties' of the previous constitution. The most important article in this chapter is probably the new article 19 which states that 'Society in the Syrian Arab Republic shall be based on [the basis of] solidarity, symbiosis and respect for the principles of social justice, freedom, equality and maintenance of human dignity of every individual'. Then article 20 on the family merely reiterates the provisions of the former article 44. Article 22 restates the provisions of the former article 46 on state guarantees for citizens in terms of prevention, medication, and treatment in the event of accident, illness, disability, orphanhood, old age, and health protection. Article 23 takes up the provisions of the former article 45 on women and their involvement in building society, except that the former version of the article referred to 'building Arab socialist society'. Article 25 reiterates the former article 47 on education, health, and social services provided by the state, adding that they are designed for 'achieving balanced development among all regions of the Syrian Arab Republic'.

As for the other articles newly added by the 2012 constitution, article 24 introduces the principle of mutual aid and solidarity between the state and society in dealing with natural disasters. This new article was probably inspired by the devastating drought the country experienced for the three years before the adoption of the constitution forcing nearly 800,000 people to flee the affected areas and crowd into the suburbs of the main cities. Mention should also be made of article 27, which for the first time introduces protection of the environment into a Syrian constitution and makes it the shared responsibility of the state, society, and every citizen.

Article 26 of the constitution contains a new provision on citizens being equal in assuming positions in public service. Only time will tell how this provision is applied under the 2012 constitution. Practice since the advent of the Ba'th has been to favour party members in joining public service and to reserve the main positions for Ba'thists. Lastly, new article 21 holds laying down one's life for the homeland as a supreme value and guarantees martyrs' families state aid in accordance with the law.

Chapter IV of title I of the 2012 constitution is about 'Educational and Cultural Principles'. In its earlier version, this chapter ran to five articles. They have been cut to four in the 2012 constitution. The most important change is the absence of any reference to socialism and Arabism in education and culture. The provisions of former article 21 stating that 'the system of education and culture shall aim to create a national, Arab generation with scientific training, attached to its history and its land proud of its heritage, driven by a spirit of struggle to achieve the objectives of the nation in unity, freedom, and socialism' have completely vanished from the new version of chapter IV, just as the provisions of the former article 23(1) have disappeared that stated that socialist national culture was the basis for building the unified socialist Arab society.

From now on, education and culture have a purely Syrian aspect. Article 28 of the new constitution states that 'The educational system shall be based on creating a generation committed to its identity, heritage, belonging and national unity'. The constitution stops short of specifying what this identity and heritage are and what future generations belong to. To answer this question, one must probably read article 28 in conjunction with article 1(2), which states that the Syrian people are part of the Arab nation. The combined reading of the two articles suggests the constitution intended to confine the state to a position of relative neutrality with respect to education. It is because Syrians are part of the Arab nation that education seeks to produce a generation attached to its identity, its heritage, to its sense of belonging. Arab-ness, the Arab identity, which is a hard fact, as the vast majority of Syrians are Arabs, has discreetly replaced Arabism as the dominant ideology.

Article 29 recalls a fundamental social *acquis*, namely that education is free at all levels. But article 29(1) adds that the law determines in what cases education shall be fee-paying in universities and government institutions, thus opening up the way for future fee-paying state higher education establishments. Article 29(2) recalls that primary education is compulsory, but adds that the state works to extend compulsory education to subsequent stages. So the constitution sets out the objectives for future governments to achieve. Article 29(3) recalls that the state oversees education and adds that it is for the state to relate education to the needs of society and requirements of development. Article 29(4) states that 'The law shall regulate the state's supervision of private educational institutions'. The final article of chapter IV, article 32, introduces a new topic into the constitution by stating that 'The state shall protect antiquities, archaeological and heritage sites and objects of artistic, historical and cultural value'.

As with the other three chapters of title I, chapter IV dusts down and modernizes certain provisions that had become obsolete and outdated in the earlier constitution. Title I introduces fundamental changes that might make a big impact on Syrian society, but in a spirit of continuity and not of a break with the past.

8.7.2   Title II: 'Rights, Freedoms, and the Rule of Law'

Title II of the 2012 constitution bears on 'Rights, Freedoms and the Rule of Law'. It is the equivalent of a declaration of rights and continues the dusting down of the articles of the earlier constitution that have outlived their usefulness. The new title II is divided into two chapters. It takes up the themes from the former chapter IV 'Freedoms, Rights and Public Duties' of title I of the 1973 constitution. Chapter I of title II covers 'Rights and Freedoms'. Its articles concern both individual and collective freedoms. Article 33(1) states that 'Freedom shall be a sacred right'. This provision already featured in article 25(1) of the earlier constitution. However, article 33(2) is an innovation. It introduces the concept of citizenship and states that 'Citizenship shall be a fundamental principle which involves rights and duties enjoyed by every citizen and exercised according to law'. This is supplemented by article 33(3) proclaiming that citizens shall have equal rights and duties. This provision existed already in article 25(3) of the previous constitution, but the 2012 version further states there shall be no discrimination among citizens 'on grounds of sex, origin, language, religion or creed'.

For some commentators, this provision goes against several other articles of the constitution including article 3(1) stating that Islam is the religion of the president, and other provisions to be mentioned later. In addition to the principle of non-discrimination, the state shall guarantee the principle of equal opportunities among citizens. This principle already featured in article 25(4) of the 1973 constitution. As noted earlier, the principle of equal opportunity forms the second pillar of Arab socialism of the Ba'th in addition to the principle of social justice already mentioned several times in the 2012 constitution (arts 13(2) and 19).

Article 34 confirms 'Every citizen shall have the right to participate in the political, economic, social and cultural life' of the country. Article 42(1) guarantees freedom of belief. 'Every citizen shall have the right to freely and openly express his views whether in writing or orally or by all other means of expression' (art. 42(2)). This provision was already in the 1973 constitution as article 38 that gave as the purpose of citizens' freedom of expression 'to contribute through control and constructive criticism to ensuring the security of the nation and homeland and strengthening the socialist system'. Article 43 says that 'The state shall guarantee freedom of the press, printing and publishing, the media and its independence in accordance with the law'. This provision was in article 38 of the 1973 constitution except for the media and its independence. However, no law governed this right until the 2011 crisis and the adoption of the press law during the second half of 2011.

On collective rights, article 44 of the 2012 constitution grants citizens the right of assembly, peaceful demonstration, and the right to strike in compliance with the principles of the constitution. The exercise of these rights is to be regulated by law. Apart from the right to strike, these rights were in the previous constitution (art. 39). But as with the provisions on press freedom, no law was enacted to regulate and guarantee these rights until the 2011 crisis and the adoption in April of that year of a law on the right to demonstrate that has proved a dead letter.

Recognition of the right to strike is one of the major advances of the new constitution. It remains for it to be put into practice within a statutory framework. Article 45 of the new constitution supplements the previous article by guaranteeing the right to form associations and unions on a national basis to achieve lawful objectives by peaceful means on terms to be determined by law. This article is an innovation on the earlier constitution that restricted the possibilities of forming associations and unions. The 1973 constitution referred to 'popular organizations and cooperative associations' (art. 9), but only the popular sectors were allowed to form unions, social or professional associations, or cooperative associations for production or services (art. 48). The law was to define the framework of operation, mutual relations, and the sphere of activities for these organizations. This provision was never implemented.

Another progressive innovation of the 2012 constitution is article 47 stipulating that 'The state shall guarantee the protection of national unity, and the citizens' duty is to maintain it'. However, article 48 on Syrian nationality is a step backward compared with article 43 of the previous constitution. In its 1973 version, the article on Syrian nationality stated that it was governed by law that had to include special facilities for Syrian Arab expatriates, their descendants, and citizens from countries of the Arab homeland. This favoured treatment for Syrian expatriates and other Arab citizens that was one of the constants of all Syrian constitutions since that of 1950 has completely vanished from article 48 of the 2012 constitution. This is probably because of the active part played by certain Syrian expatriates or their descendants in the 2011 crisis and their open support for the opposition and the attitude of most Arab countries toward the Damascus government. This removal of the favoured treatment for the descendants of Syrian expatriates in acquiring citizenship is supplemented by other articles that discriminate against Syrian expatriates, which will be addressed later. It remains to be seen what effect this article will have on the law regulating Syrian nationality. This article runs so obviously against the stream of earlier constitutional provisions on the subject that it seems to be dictated by circumstances and motivated by the events besetting the country at the time it was adopted. Some future amendment should by no means be ruled out.

Article 36(1) lays down the principle that private life shall be inviolable and protected by the law. This is a new provision that did not appear in any previous constitution. It remains for the legislature to enact a law to this effect. Article 36(2) confirms that people's homes shall be inviolable. This provision was in the 1973 constitution (art. 31), but was not implemented because of the state of emergency that gave the security forces special power of search. Article 37 specifies that postal correspondence, wire-operated and wireless telecommunications, and other means of communication shall be confidential in accordance with the law. This article picks up on and extends to all means of communication the principle of freedom of correspondence that was in the earlier constitutions (art. 32). That article stipulated that the law was to ensure that correspondence remained confidential, but no such statute was ever enacted.

Article 38 of the constitution covers the provisions of the former article 33 of the 1973 constitution about not deporting citizens and the right to return, and the freedom of movement within the national territory.

The new article of 2012 adds a provision that was not in the earlier constitution, namely that Syrian citizens may not be extradited (art. 38(2)). During the years before the 2012 constitution, the Syrian authorities had consistently adopted this position for any Syrian citizens found guilty by the Special Tribunal for Lebanon set up by the United Nations further to the assassination of former Lebanese prime minister Rafic Hariri.

Article 39 of the new constitution takes up the provisions of the former article 34 on the non-refoulement of political refugees because of their political ideals. This provision has featured in all the constitutions since 1950. It is clumsily drafted. It does not correspond to the definition of a refugee as per the 1951 UN convention relating to the status of refugees. Syria is not a signatory of this international instrument probably because of the presence of a large number of Palestinian refugees in its territory and because the 1951 convention contains no provision on the right of refugees to return to the country of origin as one of the lasting solutions to the refugee problem. Even so the definition in this convention is now the cornerstone for the protection of refugees worldwide. By this definition, a refugee is any person who is outside his country of origin because of a well-founded fear of being persecuted for reasons of race, religion, nationality, membership of a particular social group, or political opinion. The political factor is just one among others giving entitlement to refugee status.

Article 40 of the new constitution on work takes up the main provisions of the former article 36, introducing the idea of a 'minimum wage' to cover everyday necessities. Article 40(3) says that the state shall guarantee social security and health care for workers. In the Syrian context, 'workers' has a very broad meaning including all government employees and public sector workers.

Article 41 of the new constitution on taxation is similar to article 41 of the 1973 constitution. It states that 'Payment of taxes, fees and public costs shall be a duty in accordance with the law'. This provision should be read together with article 18 (2) which stated that the tax system shall be based on a fair basis and taxes shall be progressive in a way that achieves the principles of equality and social justice.

Chapter II of title II deals with 'The Rule of Law'. There was no such chapter in the 1973 constitution. It comprises five articles, two of which are new. The other three featured in title I, chapter IV of the 1973 constitution. The two new articles are article 50, which states that 'The rule of law shall be the basis of governance in the state' and article 54, which states that 'Any assault on individual freedom, on the inviolability of private life or any other rights and public freedoms guaranteed by the Constitution shall be considered a punishable crime by the law'. These two articles are incontrovertibly a step forward in the protection of individual rights. It remains to be seen when and by what mechanisms they will be implemented. The three articles that already featured in the previous constitution cover personal safety, the legislative character of punishments, and the non-retroactive effect of criminal law, although for non-criminal matters the law may decide otherwise. Articles 51, 52, and 53 of the new constitution take up the main provisions of articles 28, 29, and 30 of the 1973 constitution and introduce a few new features. Article 51(3) states that any accused who are unable to retain the services of a lawyer in their defence will be provided with legal aid by the state in accordance with the law. But the most important innovation is probably that made by article 53(3) stating that the administrative authority cannot continue to hold any person without an order of the competent judicial authority. However, the constitutional text does not set out the duration of such detention nor refer to the law to determine this.

8.7.3   Title III: 'State Authorities'

Title III on the 'State Authorities' contains fewer new elements than title I 'Basic Principles' and title II 'Rights, Freedoms and the Rule of Law'. The only major innovation compared with the previous system is that the president is elected in open competition with other candidates instead of by presidential referendum as under the 1973 constitution.

Chapter I of title III concerns the 'Legislative Authority'. This chapter takes up almost all of the provisions of the corresponding chapter in the earlier constitution. The legislative authority set up by the 2012 constitution consists of a single chamber, although further to the Ba'th Tenth Regional Congress in June 2005 some party leaders had announced the reform of the Syrian political system would include the introduction of a second chamber (senate or consultative council, *majles shura*).[42] The People's Assembly under the 2012 constitution (art. 75) has the same attributes as that of 1973 (art. 71) except that it no longer proposes the candidate for the office of president of the republic suggested by the Ba'th for popular referendum because the method for electing candidates to supreme office has changed. It is disappointing that the 2012 constitution maintained in its article 60 the means of election of members as provided

---

[42] Interview with President Assad by the Italian daily newspaper *La Repubblica*, 19 March 2009.

for by the previous constitution (art. 53) and the division of the members of the People's Assembly into two separate groups: workers/farmers and other citizens. Maintaining this anachronistic division inherited from the 1963 Tripartite Charter can only make the People's Assembly less representative. The previous political system already suffered from a crisis of representativeness and maintaining this provision can only reflect negatively on the representative character of the new legislative assembly elected in May 2012. Besides, this provision clearly contradicts the principle of non-discrimination among citizens in article 33 of the constitution, cited earlier. Logically such a provision should be considered contrary to the very spirit of the constitution.

Among the minor changes in this chapter made by the 2012 constitution, it is worth mentioning the last two paragraphs of article 61 on the electoral law. This article takes up the same provisions on the electoral law as article 57 of the previous constitution but adds as article 61(4) that it must include provisions on the financing of election campaigns and in article 61(5) the need to regulate electoral advertising and the use of the media. It should be noted that the electoral law provided for by the 1973 constitution was finally adopted in 2011 after the beginning of the Syrian crisis. It contains provisions on the points stipulated in article 61(4) and (5).[43]

Title III, chapter II of the 2012 constitution covers the 'Executive Authority', that is both the president of the republic and the government. This chapter takes up the main provisions of chapter II of title II of the 1973 constitution. The big difference is the way the president is elected directly by the voters plus the restriction of the number of terms of office to two consecutive seven-year terms and the conditions for being eligible to stand for the office of president.

The new conditions for standing as a candidate for the office of president are set out in article 84 of the 2012 constitution. Article 84(1) restores the minimum of forty years of age for any candidate for the highest office. This rule had been in force in the 1950, 1953, 1962, and 1973 constitutions but was amended by the People's Assembly on the day President Hafez Assad died, 10 June 2000, to enable his son to succeed him. Article 84(2) adds that the candidate must be Syrian by birth, as must his parents. This rule did not figure in the previous constitution. Article 83 of the 1973 constitution stated that the candidate for the office of president had to

---

[43] The 2011 electoral law will be examined in section 8.8.

be a Syrian Arab. That article could be construed as excluding non-Arab Syrian candidates. The 2012 constitution has corrected the drafting of that provision by stating that the candidate has to be Arab Syrian by nationality, excluding any discrimination based on origin.

Article 84(3) states that the candidate must 'Enjoy civil and political rights and not [have been] convicted of a dishonorable felony, even if he was reinstated'. Article 83 of the 1973 constitution confined itself to saying that the candidate had not to have been stripped of his civil and political rights. Article 84(4) stipulates that the candidate must not be married to a non-Syrian wife. This rule did not feature in the previous constitution either. Lastly article 84(5) stipulates that any candidate must have resided in Syria for an uninterrupted period of ten years at the time of standing for presidential office. All these conditions of eligibility for the position of president of the republic are new to Syrian constitutional history, except for the rule on being aged forty years and in possession of one's civic and political rights.

The new rules on eligibility to the highest office are particularly discriminatory towards Syrians living abroad. Article 152 adds that any Syrian with dual nationality is ineligible for office as president. This extends the non-eligibility of Syrians with dual nationality to the positions of vice-president, prime minister, deputy prime minister, ministers, members of the People's Assembly or members of the Supreme Constitutional Court. All of these discriminatory measures against Syrian citizens living abroad or with dual nationality go against article 33 of the constitution, which states that Syrian citizens have equal rights and duties. The explanation for the adoption of such discriminatory measures is probably the intense mobilization of Syrians abroad and their active support for the opposition since the beginning of the 2011 crisis. It is to be hoped that these articles will be revised at the first opportunity so as to ensure a return to former practice rather than create second-class citizens.

In addition to the conditions of eligibility, the great innovation of the 2012 constitution with respect to the office of president of the republic is that the candidacy for the highest office no longer comes from parliament on the proposal of the Ba'th Regional Command to be submitted to referendum for popular approval, as was the case with the provisions of article 84 of the 1973 constitution. The new mode of electing the president is defined in article 85 of the 2012 constitution. The speaker of the People's Assembly calls for the election of the president at least sixty and at most ninety days before the end of the term of office of the outgoing president (art. 85(1)). Candidacies must be filed with the Supreme Constitutional

Court within ten days of the announcement of the election of a new president (art. 85(2)). Article 85 continues:

(3) The candidacy application shall not be accepted unless the applicant has acquired the support of at least thirty-five members of the People's Assembly; and no member of the assembly might support more than one candidate.
(4) Applications shall be examined by the Supreme Constitutional Court; and should be ruled on within five days of the deadline for application.
(5) If the conditions required for candidacy were met by only one candidate during the period set for applying, the Speaker of the People's Assembly should call for fresh nominations according to the same conditions.

The president of the republic is to be elected by direct universal suffrage (art. 86(1)). The winner is the candidate who secures an absolute majority of votes cast. Should no candidate win an absolute majority, a second round is organized within two weeks between the two candidates with the most votes in the first round (art. 86(2)). The president of the republic is elected for a seven-year term and can be re-elected for one successive term (art. 88). However, the terms of this article do not apply to the president of the republic in office at the time the constitution comes into force, who may stand for a further two terms of office under article 155.

This new procedure for electing the president is certainly a step in the right direction. However, it is still hard on minor candidates who will find it difficult to obtain the thirty-five signatures required among a legislative assembly of 250 members. By setting the number of sponsors required at thirty-five to stand for election, that is almost 28 per cent of the legislative body, the constitution penalizes candidates from small parties and sets the maximum number of candidates to seven, as each member can only support one candidate. Moreover, because the eligibility of candidates for the presidential election depends on sponsors from among the members of the People's Assembly, the constitution has tied the legitimacy of the future president to that of the members of the assembly. Anyone doubting the legitimacy of the assembly members, whose representative character is subject to caution as stated earlier because of the division of the legislative assembly into workers/farmers on one side and other categories on the other, not to mention the accusation of interference by the authorities in the election of assembly members, will ipso facto cast doubt on the legitimacy of the representative character of a president sponsored by members of a doubtfully representative assembly. It would probably have been preferable for the 2012 constitution to completely separate the legislative assembly, however formed, from the presidential election. The country would then have had two major elections that were unrelated.

The golden rule of any democratic system, namely that the legislative and executive powers be separated, has unfortunately not been strictly observed by the 2012 constitution. The earlier Ba'thist constitutions (1964, 1969, 1971, and 1973) disregarded it for ideological reasons. They were all part of a 'popular democracy' political philosophy borrowed from communist regimes in which the separation of powers was merely a separation of functions. This should not have been the case for the 2012 constitution, which eliminated all ideological mention of socialism. It is difficult, then, to follow the 2012 constitution in some of its provisions, which do not comply with the precious rule of separation of powers. Article 113 takes up and widens the provisions of article 111 of the 1973 constitution and grants the president the power to legislate when parliament is not in session and under certain circumstances even when it is. Article 113(1) states that 'The President of the Republic assumes the authority of legislation when the People's Assembly is not in session, or during sessions if absolute necessity requires this, or in the period during which the Assembly is dissolved'. In its earlier version, article 111(2) limited the instances when the president could exercise legislative power when parliament was in session to cases of absolute necessity affecting the national interests or security only.

Article 113(2) of the 2012 constitution specifies that legislation enacted by the president shall be submitted to the People's Assembly within fifteen days of its first session. Article 113(3) goes on to state that the Assembly may revoke or amend such legislation by a law passed by a two-thirds majority of members attending the session provided the majority is not less than the absolute majority of the members of the People's Assembly. Such amendment or revocation cannot have a retroactive effect. Should the People's Assembly fail to make such an amendment or revocation, the legislation in question is considered to be approved as of right and does not need to be passed.

The practice of legislative decrees is an old-established one in the history of Syria. All systems have resorted to it since the First Republic set up under the French mandate, but differently. The 1928 constitution that introduced the First Republic was inspired in part by the practices of the French Third Republic. It entitled the executive to legislate via an 'authorizing statute'. The 1950 constitution that brought in the Second Republic banished this practice (art. 59), although at the beginning of the Second Republic when the new regime was being established, the constituent assembly adopted a provisional constitution authorizing the head of state to exercise legislative powers with the council of ministers, except for international treaties, until the adoption of a new constitution and its coming into force within three months.

The practice of legislative decrees reappeared during the third phase of the Second Republic (1961–63), although for different reasons. During this very tense phase in Syrian history and especially after the dissolution of parliament further to the second coup d'état by colonel Nehlawi, the executive had no choice but to govern the country by legislative decrees. The 1962 constitution adopted in very difficult circumstances by a parliament that had been officially dissolved, but that was nonetheless authorized by the army to meet one last time outside the parliament building, at the home of the prime minister, Kahled Al-Azzem, gave the government free rein to run the country by legislative decrees (art. 59). The Ba'th regimes inherited this practice and what was initially an exceptional rule for the circumstances. They reinforced it so that after thirty-nine years of power under the 1973 constitution, the executive under Presidents Hafez and then Bashar Assad shared nearly 50 per cent of legislative activity by means of legislative decrees with the legislature. The only periods in the history of Syria when the executive did not resort to legislative decrees and parliament fully assumed its legislative function were during the second period of the Second Republic (1954–58) and the short-lived Third Republic (June 1953–February 1954).

The constitutional provision of legislative decrees and the intensive practice that followed led after more than forty years of practice to a 'downgrading' of the hierarchy of norms. Under Hafez Assad almost 50 per cent of legislation was adopted by presidential legislative decrees and almost 50 per cent by acts passed by parliament. The percentage increased in favour of legislative decrees under Bashar Assad.[44] The 2012 constitution would have done well to end this practice by abolishing legislative decrees.

---

[44] According to figures obtained from the People's Assembly services in Damascus, from 2001 until 2010 the parliament adopted 542 statutes and the President issued 699 legislative decrees. These figures exclude the exceptional years of 2000 and 2011, the former marking the transition between Hafez Assad and Bashar Assad and the latter the crisis that broke out in March of that year.

Any serious political development or reform of the Syrian political system must necessarily involve a rebalancing of power between the executive and legislative arms and therefore include the abolition of legislative decrees. Given the hierarchy of norms, allowing a decree to modify an act is a 'legal monstrosity' to take up the expression of Professor Philippe Ardant.[45] So what if the decree should replace the act of parliament? While it is conceivable that such a practice might exist in exceptional moments in the life of the nation, it is to say the least odd that a constitution should grant one person in ordinary circumstances the right to legislate directly without any control, without even having to consult the council of ministers or parliament.

The only article in which the president consented to relinquish a little power in the new constitution compared with the previous one is in article 103 on proclaiming a state of emergency. New article 101 stipulated that the president could proclaim and abolish a state of emergency by decree in the council of ministers gathered under his presidency with a two-thirds majority. The decree then had to be presented to the People's Assembly when it first met.

The executive under the 2012 constitution is two-headed and includes the council of ministers alongside the president of the republic. Article 83 states that the president of the republic and the council of ministers exercise executive power. The government's place and role are the same as under the previous regime. The articles are much the same in both constitutions. The council of ministers is the highest executive and administrative authority of the state (art. 118(1)). The president of the republic appoints the president of the council of ministers (prime minister), his deputies, the ministers and vice ministers. He accepts their resignation and can dismiss them (art. 97). There is no constitutional rule limiting the president's choice of prime minister, by restricting the appointment to a member of the majority party in the assembly, for example, or insisting on consultation of parliamentary political groups. Nor does the prime minister need to win an investiture vote from the People's Assembly. He must simply present his programme to it within thirty days (art. 76). The parliament may withdraw its confidence in the government or a minister by a vote (art. 75(3)). 'The Prime Minister, his deputies and the ministers shall be responsible before the President of the Republic and the People's Assembly' (art. 121). The only new article

---

[45] Ardant, *Institutions politiques et droit constitutionnel*, p. 395 where the author develops his theory of 'downgrading'.

concerning the government is article 125, which provides for the cases in which the government shall be considered to have resigned: in the event of election of a new head of state, the election of a new parliament or the resignation of the majority of its members. Otherwise the provisions of the 2012 constitution concerning the cabinet are the same as in the previous constitution.

The political system the 2012 constitution seeks to set up is very similar to that of the 1973 constitution with two notable exceptions: political pluralism (art. 8) and the election of the president from among several candidates (art. 85). For the rest, the constitutional mechanisms governing the relations between the executive and the legislature and between the institutions (office of president of the republic and council of ministers) within the executive remain the same. It is therefore a presidential regime with a touch of parliamentary government. Time will tell whether the law on political parties, the law on freedom of the press, the abolition of the state of emergency, and other liberal laws will free up the Syrian political system and increase popular participation in public life so that it is no longer an authoritarian regime.

Title III of the new constitution deals also with 'The Judicial Authority'. It takes up the provisions of chapter III of title II of the previous constitution. The president of the republic assisted by the Supreme Judicial Council guarantees the independence of the judicial authority (art. 132). The head of state chairs the Supreme Judicial Council (art. 133). These provisions have raised certain criticisms about the actual independence of the judicial authority with respect to the president's prerogatives.

8.7.4 Title IV: 'The Supreme Constitutional Court'

It is fortunate that the 2012 constitution has not included the Supreme Constitutional Court among the articles on the judicial authority. It now comes under its own title, title IV. Article 140 states that it is an independent judicial body. It is made up of at least seven members, including a president, all appointed by the president of the republic (art. 141). These two articles are contradictory. The very fact that all the members of the court are appointed by the head of state leaves doubt as to the institution's independence and impartiality. There is little risk that such a body should ever censure an instrument enacted by the head of state. The members of the court are appointed for a renewable four-year period (art. 143). They must not hold dual nationality (art. 152). They may only be removed under the conditions laid down by law (art. 144). The Supreme Constitutional Court controls the constitutionality of laws and legislative decrees (art. 146(1)). It states an opinion at the request of the president of the republic on the constitutionality of bills, draft legislative decrees, and on the legality of draft decrees (art. 146(2)). It oversees the election of the president of the republic and organizes the procedures relating to it (art. 146(3)). It investigates challenges to the validity of the election of the head of state and assembly members (art. 146(4)). It tries the president of the republic in the case of high treason (art. 146(5)). It has no right to check the constitutionality of laws submitted by the head of state to a referendum and approved by the people (art. 148).

Article 147 sets out the procedures for bringing cases before the Supreme Constitutional Court for examination of the constitutionality of legal texts and introduces for the first time in the Syrian legal system the possibility for individuals to challenge the constitutionality of a law before an ordinary court. The system set up by article 147 is therefore mixed. It includes an a priori control of constitutionality via a right of action and an a posteriori control via a right of defence.

The procedures for bringing matters before the court are as follows: the president of the republic or a fifth of the members of the People's Assembly may challenge the constitutional character of a law before it is enacted. In this event, the enactment is suspended until the Supreme Constitutional Court rules on it within fifteen days for an ordinary law or seven days for an urgent law (art. 147(1a). A fifth of the members of the People's Assembly may object to the constitutionality of a legislative decree within fifteen days of it being brought before the assembly. In this event, the Supreme Constitutional Court must rule within fifteen days (art. 147(1b)). If the court is to rule on the unconstitutionality of a law or legislative decree, the non-constitutional provisions are repealed retroactively and have no effect (art. 147(1c)). This provision may well create problems for some legislative decrees. For contrary to laws, the control by the Supreme Constitutional Court is not necessarily exercised a priori, and may in some cases be a posteriori control once the legislative decree in dispute has come into force and produced legal effects that may not always be easy to cancel. This provision was to be found in the previous constitution (art. 145) but was never implemented because of the specific conditions the article laid down for bringing cases before the Supreme Constitutional Court. The minimum number of members required to bring a bill or draft legislative decree before the Supreme Court was set at one quarter of the members, that is, sixty-three members of the People's

Assembly. It was impossible to achieve this figure in the political context of the time. The new constitution has reduced the limit on the number of members required to bring cases before the Supreme Constitutional Court to one fifth.

As mentioned, the 2012 constitution has introduced a procedure for control of the constitutionality of laws by individuals in the ordinary courts. The procedure rests upon the preliminary question. A plaintiff may raise at appeal the non-constitutional character of a law enforced by the court. Should the court accept the application is well founded, it must stay its ruling and refer the question to the Supreme Constitutional Court (art. 147(2a)). The Supreme Constitutional Court must make a ruling within thirty days (art. 147 (2b)). Should the Constitutional Court accept the plaintiff's argument, its decision will not have effect *erga omnes* as with the control by way of action. The judgment handed down will be confined to the case at hand and the provisions of the law simply set aside from the dispute. One hypothesis that might engender many preliminary questions would be if the law were not harmonized with the new constitution. The constitution maintained in force all the laws already in existence and granted a maximum of three years from its adoption for such harmonization (art. 154). Beyond this time limit, individuals may raise preliminary question before the courts. This provision of article 154 together with those of article 147(2) are a clear step forward compared with the previous constitution in which the legislator often failed in its duty to adopt the laws stipulated by the constitution.[46]

The credibility of the mechanism for controlling constitutionality rests in the final analysis in the hands of the Supreme Constitutional Court. It is a body whose neutrality, impartiality, and objectiveness are subject to caution because of the way its members are appointed. However, it should not be ruled out that the joint effects of widening the control of constitutionality by right of action and the introduction of control by right of defence introduce the beginnings of constitutionalism in Syria.

8.7.5 Title V: 'Amending the Constitution'

Title V of the 2012 constitution relates to 'Amending the Constitution'. The procedure is the same as in the 1973 constitution. It enshrines in this area the ubiquity of the head of state, who is a true republican monarch.

---

[46] The People's Assembly was unable to harmonize the pre-existing laws with the 2012 constitution within the three-year period.

The president of the republic and a third of the members of the assembly may propose to amend the constitution (art. 150(1)). Upon receiving the proposed revision, the parliament sets up a special commission to examine it (art. 150(3)). The People's Assembly discusses the proposed amendment and if a three-quarters majority of its members approve it, it is considered final provided the president of the republic approves it (art. 150(4)). 'The Constitution shall not be amended within eighteen months of its coming into force' (art. 153), that is, until 28 August 2013.

Notwithstanding this last provision, the Syrian government accepted in principle the recommendations of the Action Group for Syria made on 30 June 2012 in Geneva and more commonly referred to as 'Geneva 1', which included among other provisions for the settlement of the political crisis the recommendation that 'there can be a review of the constitutional order and the legal system. The result of constitutional drafting would be subject to popular approval'.[47]

8.8 The 2011 Laws on Elections, Political Parties, and the 2012 Legislative Elections

The parliamentary elections of May 2012 needed to be different after a year of crisis that had turned into civil war. They were held under the aegis of the new constitution adopted three months earlier and in accordance with a new electoral law enacted by legislative decree in July 2011. They also took place after the introduction by legislative decree of legislation on political parties in July 2011, a law on the press also adopted by legislative decree in August 2011, the suspension in April of the state of emergency in force since 1963, the abolition of the Supreme State Security Court, and the adoption of legislation by legislative decree on the right to demonstrate.[48]

The 2011 electoral law was passed urgently by legislative decree in a context of incipient civil war and hasty political reforms that were little more than cosmetic. These reforms came late in the day and were unconvincing. The authorities were probably not convinced themselves by the

---

[47] See www.un.org/News/dh/infocus/Syria/FinalCommuniqueActionGroupforSyria.pdf.
[48] See for political parties legislative decree no. 100 of July 2011, for the electoral law legislative decree 101 of July 2011, for the law on the press legislative decree 108 of August 2011, for the suspension of the state of emergency decree no 161 of April 2011, for the abolition of the State Security Courts legislative decree 53 of April 2011, and for the right to demonstrate legislative decree no 54 of April 2011.

contents of the reforms although they realized they could be useful for the time being. To be convinced of the need for far-reaching political reforms, the regime should have begun with a reform of Ba'thist political thinking before claiming to reform the country's entire political system. The Ba'th Tenth Regional Congress in 2005 will remain in this respect the great lost opportunity for the ruling party to overhaul its political thinking and reinterpret its trilogy in a moderate, liberal, and pluralistic way.

The 2011 electoral law sets out the procedure for the legislative and local elections but omits the presidential election. It is supposed to reflect a political system in which the Ba'th is no longer the ruling party of the state and society. It places the whole electoral procedure under the supervision of the judicial authorities in the shape of a Supreme Judicial Commission for Elections, contrary to the previous electoral law that placed proceedings under the authority of the interior ministry. The electoral constituency remains at the level of the *mohafazats* or provinces except for Aleppo which is still divided in two between the city and the neighbouring areas. The new electoral law maintains one-round majority voting (first past the post) and the division of elected representatives into category A, representing workers and farmers, and category B, representing the remainder of the population. It limits the elections to a single day, unlike the previous law that allowed for a second half-day should the turnout not exceed 50 per cent. Pursuant to the law on political parties adopted in 2011 prohibiting the creation of any political parties on a sectarian, religious, ethnic, or tribal basis, the new law specifies that candidates' election campaigns must not contain any sectarian, religious, ethnic, or tribal reference. The 2011 law, though, maintains the compatibility between a ministerial portfolio and a seat in the assembly and for the first time prohibits candidates from using public property during their election campaign.

The opposition criticized the electoral law. Anwar Buni, in foreign exile, expressed his misgivings about the role of the judicial authorities, which were tasked with overseeing the elections, and were not truly independent of the executive and especially the head of state, who presides over the Supreme Judicial Council and appoints five of its seven members.

Anwar Buni also criticized the little importance attributed by the new election procedure to electoral rolls, although they are a fundamental element for any transparent election and pointed out how easy it would be for an elector to vote several times in different places. He also criticized the size of the electoral constituencies, which correspond to provinces or *mohafazats* and are too large for independent candidates to cover. Anwar Buni also criticized elections being held on weekdays and not on a public holiday, thereby favouring near-mandatory voting for government workers at the workplace under pressure from their supervisors.

In addition to these remarks, the fundamental criticism agreed by both opposition abroad and at home, including the fringe of the opposition reputed to be close to the authorities, is the need to abandon the majority voting based geographically on *mohafazats* for proportional representation. All agree that such a system could promote debates and competition among national policy manifestos in today's Syria. The current 'first past the post' system based on provinces favours the candidates from the big parties and especially the Ba'th and its allies within the NPF. The candidates of the small parties cannot campaign over such wide areas, nor can they have their supporters ensure the elections go off smoothly and are fairly counted. One of the perverse effects of this system has been the arrival in parliament of a large number of officially independent candidates who are in fact very close to the authorities and in particular a number of businessmen tied to ruling spheres and with no interest in politics and no manifesto.

Among the other criticisms of the new electoral law is the fact that it maintains, in keeping with the constitution, the division between the elected representatives into two separate categories, with one side for workers and farmers and the other for other categories of the population. Syria would certainly have everything to gain by abolishing this anachronistic and discriminatory provision that dates from the time of the Tripartite Charter with Egypt and Iraq in 1963. Legitimate interests of workers and farmers ought to be represented in the programmes of the competing political parties rather than in the division of the electorate.

The 2011 electoral procedure was applied for the local elections in December 2011 and the legislative elections in May 2012. Its impact remains very mixed. In terms of the results, voters will probably not have felt much difference between the period before and after the 2011 electoral law. The makeover of the constitutional architecture and the reform of the political system changed nothing in the way of results. The Ba'th and its allies won almost all the seats in the local and legislative elections, confirming that the changes did not prevent the continuation of business as usual. Some responsibility certainly lies with the opposition, which, by boycotting the elections, refused to give a chance to the very principle of gradual development of the political system and knowingly or not promoted the militarization of the crisis and the civil war. But the main responsibility lies with the manner in which the spirit and the letter of the main texts were drafted and adopted unilaterally, with little if any consultation with the opposition and civil society, although they were meant to reflect the change from a system based on the constitutional pre-eminence of the Ba'th to a pluralistic, multiparty regime. The results of the 2012 legislative elections saw the NPF win 168 of the 250 seats in the assembly, 134 of which went to the Ba'th, 5 to the opposition supported by the Ba'th, and 77 to independents.

The 2012 elections were disappointing. This can be gleaned from the scathing declarations on the electoral law made by the opposition, including some members of the home-based opposition although reputed close to the authorities such as Qadri Jamil, a communist, who later became deputy prime minister.[49] In the wake of the legislative elections, he wrote in an opinion column that the judicial supervision of the elections – the great innovation of the 2011 electoral law – was in practice merely a formal control because the entire election procedure remained within the state's hands.

The law on political parties adopted by legislative decree in July 2011 was also drafted in the spirit of change as part of continuity. This legislation on political parties is the second in the history of Syria after that of 1953 adopted under the Third Republic and that remained in force for just a few months. The new legislation recognizes first off all of the political formations within the NPF. It provides for a regulatory mechanism, the Committee for Party Matters, headed by the interior minister and composed of a judge appointed by the president of the Supreme Court and three figures appointed by the president of the republic. The call for creation of a political party must be accompanied by the signature of fifty founder members, the party's by-laws, its objectives, the principles underpinning it, and the rules on which its organization, its finances, and its management are based. The application must also contain the party's name, its head office, its branches, its principles, its manifesto, the terms of membership, the organization of its structures, the election of its leaders, and its finances.

Political parties must abide by the constitution, democratic principles, the rule of law, collective freedoms, the Universal Declaration of Human Rights, and the treaties and conventions ratified by Syria. Parties must look to maintain the unity of the homeland and national unity. No party can be formed on a religious, sectarian, tribal, or geographical basis nor discriminate in terms of race, gender, or colour. Parties cannot create military or paramilitary structures or resort to, incite, or threaten to use violence in any form whatsoever. No Syrian political party can be affiliated to or dependent on any non-Syrian political party.

---

[49] See kassioun.org/index.php?mode=article&id=19968.

Contrary to the law of 1953, the new legislation contains detailed provisions on financing political parties. Party finances are provided by their members. Parties cannot receive donations from foreigners but they may receive donations from Syrian donors. All donations must be made by a transaction through a Syrian bank. An annual ceiling is set for donations. Political parties receive public funding from the state. Forty per cent of such funding is attributed to parties depending on the number of parliamentary seats they hold and the remaining 60 per cent depending on the number of votes cast for them in the legislative elections, provided they exceed 3 per cent of the votes. Each political party has the right to publish a newspaper and to have its own website.

The new legislation on political parties was criticized by the opposition in terms of its form and content. Formally, the opposition criticized the unilateral way the law was adopted. Substantially, it criticized the hold exerted by the executive via the interior ministry and the persons appointed by the head of state to sit on the committee for political parties.

8.9   The New Electoral Law and the 2014 Presidential Election

For the fourth time in its history, Syria held presidential elections with multiple candidates in 2014. But unlike earlier elections, these were by single-round direct universal suffrage. The three earlier elections with several candidates had all taken place within parliament because it was for the members to elect the president of the republic under the First and Second Republics.[50]

The 2014 presidential election, the first of its kind under the Fifth Republic, was, like the 2012 legislative election, part of this movement of change within continuity. The opposition as a whole both at home and abroad criticized the holding of the election. The foreign powers opposed to the Damascus regime and supporting the opposition abroad and the armed groups within Syria did the same. The most moderate fringe of the opposition, represented by the strand of Qadri Jamal who had joined the government after the 2012 legislative elections, also kept their distance and did not approve the presidential election being held at that particular

---

[50] The first presidential election with more than one candidate was in 1932 when Mohamed Ali Abed came ahead of Hashim Atassi. The second was in 1955 when Shukri Qwatli beat Khaled Al-Azzem. The third saw Nazem Kudsi beat Khaled Al-Azzem in 1961.

time.[51] The main reason for this near-general refusal by the opposition was that the presidential election could not be held against the backdrop of civil war with almost six million people displaced within the country, nearly three million refugees in neighbouring countries, and large parts of the country outside the control of central government. Besides, the opposition abroad and the majority of the opposition at home had rejected the constitutional framework, that of the 2012 constitution, and the legislative framework, that of the 2014 electoral law, in which the election was to be held. In short, for the opposition, the political circumstances in the country and the military situation on the ground were not amenable to a free and transparent presidential election.

The authorities in Damascus had a very different reading of the political times in which the election was to be held. Since the second half of 2013, the Syrian army was in the ascendant, winning crucial battles against armed groups in strategic locations such as Al-Qusair in June 2013, Yabrud and the Qalamon region in Anti-Lebanon in March 2014, Homs in May 2014 and most of the Ghouta region around the capital. These advances by the army were accompanied by 'local reconciliations' in the context of which local fighters who had risen against the central authorities were allowed to keep their light weapons and would be tasked with keeping law and order in their area in conjunction with the army and the paramilitary forces close to it.[52] These victories by the army, supported by the Lebanese Hizbullah, had managed to create a fairly uniform space stretching south to the Jordanian border, to the Lebanese border and the Mediterranean coast in the west, and to part of the north and east of the country. The area under government control included Suyeda, Damascus, Homs, Hama, Tartous, Latakia, Idlib, most of Aleppo, and a part of Deir Ezzor in the east of the country. The cities of Hassake and Qameshli were dominated by the Kurdish militia of the PYD, which although it defined itself as affiliated to the domestic opposition, did not question the symbols of the Syrian state in the regions it controlled. The areas around Dera'a and

---

[51] See the communiqué of 24 April 2014 published by the Front for Change and Liberation led by Qadri Jamil and the communiqué of 6 May 2014 published by Ali Heidar, minister for national reconciliation and secretary general of the Syrian National Social Party, who, although a member of the government, described himself as a member of the opposition. In the communiqué, he decided to withdraw from the Front for Change and Liberation and announced his support for Bashar Assad's candidacy.

[52] In the old city of Homs, the agreement between the authorities and fighters was that the latter could leave the city with their light arms and go to places further north held by armed groups.

the neighbouring regions close to the Jordanian border, certain localities near the occupied Golan Heights, the region of Rastan in the centre of the country, part of the city of Aleppo, almost all of the rural areas in the north on the border with Turkey, and the province of Raqqa continued to escape from the control of the central authorities. All the major urban centres except for Raqqa, part of Aleppo, and part of Deir Ezzor were therefore still under the control of the army or of forces not opposed to it. This area concentrated the vast majority of the population including persons displaced within the country because of the fighting, who for the most part had fallen back on zones held by the army. Given these geographical and demographic facts, the Syrian authorities concluded that circumstances on the ground were suitable for the presidential election to be held within the time laid down by the constitution.

Seen from Damascus, the regional and international circumstances were also right for the election. Since the USA and UK had abandoned the idea of air strikes against Syria in September 2013, the Damascus authorities had nothing more to fear from a western military intervention. The coalition of states styling themselves 'The Friends of Syria', which included more than 120 countries at the start of the crisis, had dwindled to eleven members. The failure of the Geneva 2 talks in January and February 2014 had ruled out any way out of the political crisis between the authorities and the opposition abroad. This weakening of the front opposed to the regime both inside and outside the country and the Syrian army's advances on the ground prompted the Damascus authorities to go ahead with the presidential election within the constitutional time frame.

Towards the end of 2013, some commentators began to call for the presidential election planned for 2014 to be delayed and President Assad's mandate extended for two years. According to some media reports a proposal to this effect had been made by the UN mediator, Lahkdar Brahimi to the Syrian delegation involved in the Geneva talks in February 2014. According to the press reports, Brahimi told Syrian delegates that the USA and its western allies would be favourable to an extension of President Assad's term of office for a further two years if it went along with the establishment of a transitional government with full powers including in defence and security and whose primary function would be to fight terrorism. There would follow a national congress tasked with adopting a new constitution that would define the country's future political system. It was reported that Damascus refused this proposal.

Some members of the moderate opposition expressed their agreement with the extension of the presidential term of office and the postponement of the election for two years.[53] But Damascus was resolved to capitalize on its army's advances on the ground in terms of political gains and create an irreversible situation with the re-election of Bashar Assad for a new seven-year term. Had the Syrian authorities wanted to extended the president's term of office for two more years, they could have invoked article 87(2) of the constitution, which stipulates that if the president's term of office expires without a new president being elected, the incumbent continues in office until a new president is elected. The provisions of that paragraph together with a declaration of principle, or better still a constitutional revision under article 150, could have created a suitable framework for justifying delaying the presidential election given the exceptional circumstances in the country. Three years earlier, the onset of the Syrian crisis and the instability in the country had justified delaying the parliamentary elections at the time for one year under article 58(2) of the 1973 constitution that was then in force.

The 2014 presidential election was preceded by the adoption of a new electoral law three months before. It was passed by parliament and promulgated by the president on 24 March 2014. The new legislation took up the provisions of the former electoral law of 2011 described earlier for local and parliamentary elections. It supplemented them with provisions laying down the procedure for the election of the president of the republic and referendums. This electoral law was intended to govern all forms of political voting in Syria. This is a novelty worth pointing out. In the past, only the Third Republic under Shishakli had adopted similar legislation but it concerned only the parliamentary and presidential elections.

The overall architecture of the new law is similar to the previous one. The entire electoral procedure is placed under the judicial authority, whose independence from the executive has been called into question by the opposition as described earlier. As the new law made no changes to the provisions for local and parliamentary elections, all the criticisms made before for the 2011 law remain valid for that of 2014. During the parliamentary debate that preceded the adoption of this law, some members called into question the one-round majority voting for the legislative elections and proposed replacing it by a proportional system. It is also worth observing that an official of the Communist Party suggested abolishing the division of the electorate into two sections, workers and farmers on one side and the other sectors of the population on the other. The assembly dismissed these proposals.

---

[53] Interview with Syrian intellectual Samir Aita by the Lebanese satellite channel Al-Mayadeen on 30 April 2014.

The new electoral law took up the constitutional provisions about the conditions of eligibility for the office of president, the procedure for filing candidacies with the Supreme Constitutional Court, and the required backing of at least thirty-five members of the assembly to validate a candidacy, with each member being able to back a single candidate only. The electoral law supplemented these provisions by specifying that the national territory formed a single constituency for the presidential election and for referendums. The Supreme Judicial Commission in charge of elections acts under the supervision of the Supreme Constitutional Court when organizing the presidential election. All elections must be held on a single day. The commission may extend voting by five hours in certain locations.

One of the great innovations of the 2014 electoral law concerns the conditions in which Syrians abroad could vote in the presidential election. In the early nineteenth century many Syrians emigrated to the Americas. That migratory flow has never ceased. In the last fifty years, a large number of Syrians has continued to emigrate to the Americas and also to Europe, the Gulf countries, and Africa. Some have become integrated in their host countries and have become naturalized, especially in Europe and the New World. In some regions, such as the Gulf, naturalization is not an option. The exodus of Syrian refugees fleeing the conflict to seek international protection in neighbouring countries has been adding to this continuous migratory flow. At the time of the 2014 presidential election, close to three million Syrians had taken refuge in neighbouring countries and probably nearly one million were living in the Gulf, mostly in Saudi Arabia.

The vote of these expatriate Syrian communities was one of the challenges of the presidential election. Not because the vote could have influenced the outcome of an election the result of which was a foregone conclusion but rather because of the behaviour of Syrians abroad. Would they take part in the election and so approve the principle of it or just ignore it? The 2014 electoral law set out the framework for Syrians abroad to take part in the process of electing the president of the republic in its chapter 13 (arts 99–107). The foreign vote had to be held ten days before the national vote within the country. Expatriates were able to vote in the presidential election in Syrian embassies abroad. This means that Syrians living in countries with no embassy could not participate. Each elector needed to have a current Syrian passport with a border exit stamp. This excluded refugees who had fled the country without passports and without going through border posts. Relations between the Damascus authorities and several governments actively supporting the opposition deteriorated in March 2014, which led to the closure of Syrian embassies in North America (USA and Canada) and the Gulf (Saudi Arabia and Kuwait), thus denying many Syrians the right to vote, or at least those who planned to do so. France, Germany, and the United Arab Emirates asked the Syrian embassies in their capitals not to organize votes for the presidential election.

On 21 April 2014, the speaker of the People's Assembly announced in line with the relevant provisions of the constitution (arts 84 and 85) and the electoral law (arts 30–37) that candidacy applications for the election of the president of the republic could be filed. Between 22 April and 1 May 2014, twenty-four applications were filed with the Supreme Constitutional Court. Only three met all the conditions for eligibility, in particular the support of at least thirty-five members of the assembly. The three candidates selected were Bashar Assad, Hassan Nouri, and Maher Hajjar. President Assad's two competitors presented themselves more as reformers than adversaries from the opposition. Hassan Nouri, from Damascus and a former minister, positioned himself as a liberal economist concerned for the interests of the merchant class and business. Maher Hajjar, from Aleppo, a member of the assembly, formerly affiliated with the political group of Qadri Jamil in parliament, stood as a candidate of the left and concerned for the interests of the working class. The election campaign on the ground was short and sober. It was limited to a few demonstrations of support, public meetings, and TV appearances by President Assad's adversaries, while he himself chose not to appear. However, and this was one of the new features of this election, the candidates were very active on social media. It was on his personal page on one of the social media that President Assad invited Syrians to cut back on advertising spending during the campaign, to help those in need, and not forget those who had lost family and friends in the war. President Assad's campaign slogan was a single word that sought to rally support, 'Together'. Hassan Nouri used several slogans such as 'A free and intelligent economy', 'The return of the middle class'. Maher Hajjar used slogans illustrating his political commitment such as 'Secular Syria' and 'Syria for Palestine'.

Voting took place on 28 May 2014 for Syrians living abroad and on 3 June for those in the country. The particularly high turnout attracted the attention of observers. Officially it exceeded 73 per cent. In Beirut, the surge of Syrians heading to the embassy to vote created huge traffic congestion. The embassy had to extend voting by a day. In Syria itself, Syrians turned out in large numbers despite the risks, as several armed groups had said they would target polling stations. On that day more than a hundred mortar shells fell on Damascus. The result was unsurprising. President Assad was re-elected with 88.7 per cent of the votes. His two opponents scored 4.3 per cent for Hassan Nouri and 3.8 per cent for Maher Hajjar.

What does the election mean? For opponents of the Damascus authorities, it is meaningless because President Assad had no legitimacy before the election and still none after. For the supporters of the authorities, the holding of elections at this particular time in the crisis and the high turn-out are clear and unequivocal messages about the population's support for the regime and the state of mind of most Syrians exhausted by three years of civil war and aspiring to stability and security. Supporters and opponents of the regime will continue to debate how to interpret the election and President Assad's political legitimacy. It might be useful to attempt a re-reading of Max Weber on the various ideal types or categories of political legitimacy, if possible, to reconcile the opposing views. To those who argue against Bashar Assad's domination saying that he has no electoral legitimacy – or what Max Weber calls legal–rational legitimacy – others might reply that in any event and notwithstanding the controversy over President Assad's representative legitimacy – again according to Max Weber's ideal types – he can claim traditional and/or charismatic legitimacy.[54] If no political compromise comes about to get out of the crisis, the debate may last a long time and prove costly for Syrians. For ordinary Syrians, this election will have opened the door, even if in a small way, to a new political culture, a culture in which the president of the republic might face candidates who are not just competitors as in 2014 but perhaps one day actual opponents.

8.10 The 2016 Legislative Elections

The second legislature under the 2012 constitution was elected by direct universal suffrage on 13 April 2016. These elections could have been dispensed with, not just because of the war still raging in the country and that alone could have justified postponing voting, but they could also have been postponed had the Geneva talks advanced towards the formation of

---

[54] Max Weber argues that none of these three ideal types of political legitimacy (legal–rational, traditional, and charismatic) occur in a historically 'pure' state. For example, it is possible to consider a 'hereditary charismatic' domination. Moreover, Max Weber does not exclude the possibility of 'charismatic authority becom[ing] routine' and transforming in the long term into a legal–rational or a traditional type of authority. See Weber, *Economie et société 1*.

a transitional government, widened to include the opposition and independents, and tasked with preparing for elections under international supervision and a new constitution. Unfortunately this was not to be. The Geneva meeting was very disappointing and fell short of the hopes raised by UN resolution 2254. Accordingly, President Assad decided to comply with the deadline for the elections so as to avoid a legislative void.

These elections were held in a more difficult context than those of four years earlier. This time Raqqa and Idlib provinces lay outside the control of the central authorities in Damascus. The cities of Aleppo, Deir Ezzor, and Dara'a were divided into pro- and anti-government areas. Some 6.5 million people had been displaced within the country, many to zones that were surrounded or difficult to reach, and the number of refugees approached 5 million.

The elections were boycotted by the main opposition movements within the country, primarily by the National Coordination Committee of the Forces for Democratic Change in Syria, commonly called the National Coordination or more simply the Coordination. The procedure was the same as in 2012. The elections were organized under the control of the judicial authorities and protests examined by the Supreme Constitutional Court. The turnout rate stood at 56.57 per cent, which was 5 per cent up on the previous elections. The results were unsurprising. The lists of the Ba'th and its traditional allies won an absolute majority. The new chamber counted 180 new members out of 250, making a 72 per cent renewal rate. That was probably the only novelty compared with the previous assembly. Otherwise the elections were consistent with those organized ever since 1973.

8.11 The Draft Constitutions Proposed by the Opposition

Three draft constitutions have been proposed by Syrian opposition members since Bashar Assad has been in power and prior to the adoption of the 2012 constitution. One was proposed by a political party based in the USA in 2006 and supported by the neo-conservative Bush administration. The other two were proposed by Syrian activists in their own name. More draft constitutions were put forward after 2012, which will be analysed in Chapter 9.

8.11.1 The Syrian Reform Party's 2006 Draft Constitution

Although this draft constitution was prepared by an opposition party formed in 2001 at the time when Syrian intellectuals were hoping to change the political system, it would be unfair to relate it to the Damascus Spring. This draft constitution is more the mixed offspring of the September 2001 terrorist attacks and the US invasion of Iraq in 2003, which some in Washington considered as a first step towards an attack on Syria after occupying Iraq.

The Reform Party that published this draft constitution in English[55] on its website in 2006 was created in the United States in 2001 by a Syrian businessman, Farid Ghadry, a naturalized American known to be close to the neo-conservatives then in power in Washington. He was born in Aleppo in 1954 and grew up and studied in Lebanon between 1964 and 1975 before his family settled in the USA. Farid Ghadry is a member of the pro-Israeli lobby, the American Israel Public Affairs Committee.[56] His ambition was to be the Syrian Ahmed Shalabi.[57] He joined the Committee on the Present Danger, a group of mostly right-wing politicians including leading neo-conservatives such as Newt Gingrich, Jeane Kirkpatrick, and James Woolsey II, was close to Elizabeth Cheney, the daughter of the US vice-president of the time, who became deputy secretary of state for the Near East and headed a special working group in the State Department, the Iran–Syria Operations Group, working on strategies to 'democratize' the two countries. Elizabeth Cheney saw that the political party created by Ghadry was among the lucky beneficiaries of the funds generously distributed by the State Department under the Middle East Partnership Initiative to opposition groups in the Middle East and North Africa. In September 2007, Farid Ghadry was stripped of his Syrian citizenship by President Bashar Assad after he appeared before the Foreign Affairs and Defence Committee of Israel's Knesset.[58]

The Syrian Reform Party's draft constitution comprises 253 articles, called sections, and is entirely at odds with all earlier Syrian constitutions. Its objective is to create a federal state with a presidential-type regime subordinated to the assembly. This constitution makes no allusion to the Arab identity of Syria or to its cultural and spiritual heritage. It makes no reference to Islam, which has always been presented as the religion of the

---

[55] To the best of my knowledge, there is no Arabic version.
[56] 'As a Syrian and a Muslim, I have always had this affinity for the State of Israel. As a businessman and an advocate of the free economic system of governance, Israel to me represents an astounding economic success in the midst of so many Arab failures ... While many Arabs view Israel as a sore implant, I view it as a blessing.' *Vanity Fair*, March 2007.
[57] Farid Ghadri declared 'Ahmed paved the way in Iraq for what we want to do in Syria'.
[58] See www.haaretz.com/news/assad-revokes-citizenship-of-politician-who-visited-knesset-1.229382.

head of state, except in the 1969 and 1971 constitutions. It makes no reference to the Arab character of Syria, nor to Arabism, nor to Syria's people belonging to a broader whole, the Arab nation or natural Syria as all previous constitutions had. This draft constitution does not even mention Damascus as the capital of the republic. Section 42(6) states timidly that the seat of parliament is in Damascus.

But it is in section 6 on language that the determination to weaken the national fabric comes out most clearly. Whereas almost 90 per cent of the Syrian population is Arabic speaking, this article states that the official languages of the republic shall be Arabic and Kurdish (s. 6.1) and adds that the state recognizes all other languages spoken in Syria and takes all necessary measures to promote their use (s. 6.2). Moreover, the national government and governments of the provinces may choose any language to perform their duties depending on circumstances and the preference of the population, but in any event, they shall use at least two official languages (s. 6.3.a). Cities must take into account the usual language and the preference of residents (s. 6.3.b). All official languages are to be treated identically and fairly (s. 6.4). A Syrian language council is to be created by law to promote and favour the development and use of all official languages and all minority languages used among the population (s. 6.5.a); the council will also promote and ensure respect for all languages in use in Syrian communities such as Assyrian, English, French (s. 6.5.b.i), Hebrew, Hindu, Urdu, and all other languages used in Syria for religious reasons (s. 6.5.b.ii).

This section summarizes better than all others the sprit of the constitution proposed by the Syrian Reform Party. The draft constitution was probably drawn up by Americans affiliated to neo-conservative think tanks with the minimal participation of a few expatriate Syrians in the USA who have long been out of touch with the real situation in their country of origin. Wanting to promote Kurdish or Assyrian (why not also Syriac?) or even Hebrew, assuming that some members of this community are still in the country, at a push may pass muster, but Hindu and Urdu have never been practised by any religious or ethnic community in Syria.

The 2006 draft constitution organizes Syria as a federal state. Its section 40 provides for three levels of administration: national government, provincial (*mohafazat*) government, and local administration. Alongside this, the draft constitution defines three levels of competence for exercising legislative authority: a national parliament, provincial assemblies, and municipal or local councils (s. 43.a., b., c.)

The planned parliament would have two chambers that participate in developing legislation: the national assembly and the national council of the provinces (s. 42.1). The national assembly represents the people. It chooses the president of the republic, participates in drawing up the law, controls the executive, and provides a forum for discussion of national affairs (s. 42.3). The national council of the provinces represents the provinces. It ensures that their interests are taken into account by the national government. It participates in developing laws and provides a forum for discussion with respect to the provinces (s. 42.3).

Distrust of all authority, including that of the legislative authorities, extends to the speaker of the national assembly. He is always elected by his peers but they may revoke his position at any time by a majority vote of the assembly members (s. 52.4). The same goes for the deputy speaker. The national council of the provinces is the second chamber of the legislature. It comprises a delegation for each province of ten members each. The provincial delegation comprises four special delegates including the prime minister of the province, or if unavailable any other member of the provincial parliament designated by him, and six permanent delegates. The provincial delegation sitting in the national council of the provinces is led by the prime minister and if he is unavailable by a member of his choosing (s. 60). There are to be fourteen provinces corresponding to the existing Syrian *mohafazats* (s. 103).

The president of the republic is the head of state and the executive at the national level. The national assembly elects the president from among its members (s. 86). The draft constitution does not explicitly set out the presidential term of office. However, it can be inferred from reading sections 86 and 88 that it is normally for five years and coincides with the length of the legislature. Under the provisions of section 86, each national assembly must, when it first meets or when exceptional circumstances so require, elect a president of the republic from among its number. The holder of the office remains in office until a new president is elected. The president cannot serve for more than two terms. Should a president be elected to complete the term of office of his predecessor, this period shall not be considered as a term of office and the holder may subsequently run for two terms (s. 88).

The president of the republic may be revoked by the national assembly on the basis of serious violation of the constitution, serious misconduct, or if he is unable to carry out his duties (s. 89). No Syrian constitution had ever made the president so vulnerable with respect to parliament.

The national assembly can pass a no confidence vote in two ways. It may vote a motion of censure by the majority of its members that does not extend to the president of the republic. In this case, the president must form a new government. It may also vote a censure motion by the majority of members against the president of the republic. In this case, the head of state and all of the ministers and deputy ministers must resign. The revocation of the president and all of the government by an absolute majority vote by the lower chamber puts the entire executive in a position of weakness and vulnerability, and it enshrines the power of the national assembly in an assembly-led regime. No other Syrian constitution or political regime had established such a system in the past. In this, the 2006 draft constitution truly proposes a complete break with the country's political, institutional, and constitutional history.

The intention of the authors of the draft constitution to dismantle any strong state in Syria continues with the role and duties of the provinces. Having considerably weakened the executive for the benefit of the legislature, the draft constitution grants powers to what it terms 'provinces' that no other territorial division has ever experienced in the history of Syria. As indicated earlier, the draft constitution maintains the territorial division existing in Syria of fourteen *mohafazats* but grants them a different status. Whereas they were initially simple administrative constituencies, by the wave of a magic wand they become political entities with the status of near-federated states within a federation. Each has its own constitution, prime minister, government, and parliament.

Each province has an elected parliament, which adopts the province's constitution (s. 142). The provincial constitution must be consistent with the constitution of the republic (s. 143.1). It can make provisions concerning the laws of the province and the structure of the province's executive (s. 143.1.a). It can also make provisions for the institution, role, authority, and status of a traditional monarch (*sic*) where required (s. 143.1.b). There is no such category of 'traditional monarch' in Syria. This last clause is a further indication that the authors of this draft constitution know nothing of the history and sociology of Syria.

This draft constitution is plainly totally at odds with Syria's political and constitutional history. Never had a Syrian constitution sought to create a federal regime, except perhaps for the abortive 1920 monarchic constitution, but in the minds of its drafters it was to include present-day Syria, Lebanon, Jordan, and Palestine/Israel. No Syrian constitution had to this extent weakened the executive for the benefit of the legislature, which itself is divided between two chambers and much reduced by the existence of fourteen provincial legislative assemblies. Never had a Syrian constitution so promoted separation among communities to the detriment of integration of those communities within the national melting pot that respected their differences. The 2006 draft constitution is a draft for planned disintegration of a country left to its own devices with no executive authority capable of governing and guiding it. It fits in with the analyses that consider Syria to be a mosaic of communities that are not conducive to any form of national integration.

Section 235 is probably the best reflection of this view. It states that the Syrian people's right to self-determination as expressed in the draft constitution does not exclude recognition within a legal framework of the notion of the right to self-determination for any community sharing a common culture and linguistic heritage, in the form of a territorial entity within the republic or otherwise, to be determined by national legislation. Finally, it is certainly no chance matter that the Syrian Reform Party, created in the USA and financed and supported by the most hard-line American neo-conservatives of the Bush administration, should make a gift of a project for disintegration – all done up in constitutional wrapping paper – to a proud unitary Arab country.

8.11.2 Anwar Buni's 2011 Draft Constitution

Anwar Buni is the director of the Centre for Legal Research and Studies. He is an activist who participated in the Damascus Spring. He spent several years in prison. Once released, he published this draft constitution online first in 2008 and again in 2011. For a while he joined the Istanbul Syrian National Council before leaving it in 2012. It is the 2011 version of the draft constitution that is examined here.[59] His draft is characterized by its great suspicion of the executive and in particular the president of the republic although it provides for his election by direct universal suffrage.

The preamble to the draft constitution begins by regretting the disappearance of democracy and what he calls the 'assassination' of political life by the declaration of union with Egypt in 1958 and the onset of the collapse of the social compact that ensued. The preamble asserts the need for a new social compact to rebuild civil society on a new basis and goes on to say that the constitution is the best social compact for rebuilding Syria.

Syria is a democratic parliamentary republic (art. 1). It is multi-national, multi-religious, and multi-sectarian (art. 2). It is part of a regional and

---

[59] See the text in Arabic at www.ahewar.org/debat.show.art.asp.aid=46673.

international Arab grouping (art. 4). Sovereignty lies with the people who exercise it through democratic elections based on a fair and transparent electoral law that rests on the principle of proportional representation and considers all of Syria as a single electoral constituency (art. 5). The principle language of the state is Arabic. Kurdish is the second language. Other minorities have the right to teach their language and national culture (art. 6).

Work is a right and a duty for all. The state must implement a fair system of social protection (art. 26). Education is a right for all citizens. The state guarantees free education until the end of secondary education (art. 27). This provision is a step backward compared with the Ba'th constitutions of 1964, 1969, 1971, 1973, and even 2012, which all guaranteed free education at all levels including higher education. It is to be observed that the draft constitution makes no reference to Islam as the religion of the president of the republic nor to Muslim jurisprudence (*fiqh*) as the main source of legislation, as all Syrian constitutions have done except those of 1920, 1928, and 1969.

Legislative authority lies with a single chamber and in the hands of the assembly of deputies. Article 33 defines the assembly's powers. It adopts laws, ratifies international treaties, votes confidence in the government, adopts the state budget, controls the court of auditors, controls the activities of the government, and chooses the members of the Supreme Constitutional Court.

The assembly is elected by direct universal suffrage (art. 35). Each legislature lasts four years (art. 38). The president of the republic and each member of the assembly may table bills (art. 61). The assembly cannot relinquish its legislative responsibility or delegate it to any other authority (art. 62). This fundamental provision tends to show that the legislative authority cannot grant the executive the right to legislate by means of legislative decrees and that this endemic practice since the 1962 constitution is not taken up by this draft. Unfortunately, bad habits die hard because further on in the text, article 102(9) states that the president submits legislative decrees to the assembly for approval. The draft takes up a provision of the 1953 constitution by attaching the court of auditors to parliament.

The president of the republic has executive power (art. 81). The president is elected by the people by direct universal suffrage in a secret ballot (art. 82). The term of office is for five years and the president may be reelected for one more term (art. 86). The president may appoint a vice president with the agreement of the assembly (art. 90). The president appoints the prime minister and ministers (art. 94). The government must present its programme to the parliament within one month and secure a vote of confidence by an absolute majority (art. 96). The cabinet is collectively accountable to the assembly for the application of the general policy on which it has won a vote of confidence (art. 97). The council of ministers meets under the leadership of the prime minister or the head of state (art. 98). The president of the republic is answerable in the event of violation of the constitution on charges of high treason (art. 89(1)) and in the event of any crime under ordinary law (art. 89(2)). He can only be tried by the constitutional court (art. 89(3)) upon a proposal from the assembly passed by an absolute majority of its members and presented by at least a quarter of the members and previously debated by the members of the constitutional commission and the judicial commission convened for the occasion (art. 89(4)).

This project reflects distrust of the executive, although it does provide for the president to be elected by universal suffrage. His political legitimacy is therefore equal to that of the assembly. But there is no real counterweight between executive and legislature. Parliament can withdraw its confidence in the government. It cannot dismiss the head of state from office, but it can refer him for trial by the supreme constitutional court by what is a fairly elementary procedure on so simple a charge as 'violation of the constitution'. The executive has no countermove vis-à-vis the legislature. It has no possibility of dissolving the assembly. Moreover, the constitution is confusing on the issue of legislative decrees. Are there any or not? One article states the parliament cannot delegate its legislative prerogatives, but another states the president must submit legislative decrees for the assembly's approval. The draft constitution provides for a greater role for the court of auditors and the Supreme Constitutional Court, but the appointment and revocation of their members make them handmaidens to parliament rather than instruments for the control and impartial regulation of the institutions.

8.11.3 *The Labwani–Muqdad Draft Constitution of 2011*

This draft constitution was published in September 2011, six months after the outbreak of the Syrian crisis. One of its authors, Luay Muqdad, was then in prison. The other, Kamal Labwani, had just been released after serving five years after his visit to Washington at the end of 2005 and his meeting with President Bush at the White House, which Damascus saw as conniving with a foreign power and inciting US military action against Syria. When released in May 2011, Kamal Labwani joined the Syrian

National Council (Istanbul Council) for a few months before defecting with other liberal-minded intellectuals.

The Labwani–Muqdad draft constitution purports to be democratic and liberal.[60] Like the other draft constitutions presented by the Syrian opposition, that suggested by Labwani and Muqdad is highly suspicious of the executive and especially the president of the republic. The legislature dominates and in the Labwani–Muqdad draft, an institution that is barely known in Syrian political history, the senate, plays a dominant role.[61]

The Labwani–Muqdad draft has no preamble but many of its articles, to be mentioned later, have no operative character and could have been placed in a preamble. Article 1 defines Syria as a civil, democratic, and parliamentary state. The term 'civil', which is synonymous in Arabic with 'secular' but with no pejorative connation that for many relates secular to atheist, was not previously used except in the 1920 monarchic constitution. The official language is Arabic (art. 4).

Articles 6–11 are examples of non-operative clauses that could have featured in a preamble to the constitution. Article 6 goes over the main lines of the history and geography of Syria, as a crossroads of three continents, the cradle of monotheist religions and ancient civilizations. The Arab identity and Muslim culture prevail there. Article 7 recalls that Syria was created by an international decision and that previously it did not exist as an independent political entity. Article 7 also recalls that the current borders of Syria are not natural barriers separating national, cultural, religious, economic, and geographical influences from its neighbours. Its borders rest on negotiation and mutual recognition. Any change would require approval of the majority of the population by referendum.

Article 9 asserts the multi-ethnic, multi-religious, and multi-sectarian character of the Syrian population and dismisses any discrimination based on race, religion, or gender. The unity of the Syrian people is based on the recognition of its diversity and not negation of it. The prevailing character is the Arab identity and Islam alongside other ethnic and religious characters, the most important of which are the Kurds and Christianity.

Sovereignty belongs to the people (art. 12). Article 13 states that the Syrian people are represented differently by the two assemblies. The

---

[60] See all4syria.info/Archive/27540.

[61] Only the monarchic constitution adopted in its first reading by the Syrian congress in July 1920 but never enforced because of the French mandate in Syria provided for a senate. See Chapter 2, 'The Syrian Monarchy'.

senate represents the *mujtam'a ahli* that might be translated as 'civil categories' and the assembly represents 'civil society' or *mujtam'a madani*. In Arabic *ahli* and *madani* are often synonymous. The senate is composed of one hundred members divided by 'civil category'. Each individual declares which category he plans to belong to and for which he intends to vote depending on his religion, sectarian origin, ethnic group, or statelessness (bedouin), or a civil or secular category. In this novel scheme, the senate does not represent regions (provinces or other forms of local authorities) but pre-established categories. The draft constitution, however, does not specify how to establish these 'civil categories'.

Article 16 states that the election of the assembly is based on proportional representation with a list for the entire country. Syria forms a single electoral constituency. This draft constitution contains provisions that are to say the least original. Article 24 states that political parties replace those parliamentarians who die in office or resign. They may also revoke their representatives within the assembly and replace them with others. Moreover, an absolute majority of the senate, in agreement with the head of state, may revoke any member of the assembly or senate.

Again among the novel provisions of the draft constitution it is worth mentioning article 25, which stipulates that the senate controls the duties of the head of state in the areas of internal and external security, protection of fundamental rights, establishment of justice, protection of civil peace, common (sectarian) coexistence, ratification of international treaties, and foreign coalitions. Article 26 states that the senate supervises the supreme judicial council, constitutional court, national security council, and supreme defence council. The senate also oversees the activities of three ministers: defence, justice, and foreign affairs. Readers remain doubtful about so broad a mandate being granted to the senate and wonder what remains of the separation of executive and legislative powers.

The head of state may be elected in several ways: either by the absolute majority of the members of the senate, or failing that by the relative majority of the two chambers, or failing that by national referendum (art. 27). Similarly a government may be appointed in several ways under article 28. The head of state appoints the prime minister after parliamentary consultations. Should the cabinet secure the confidence of the assembly, the head of state approves the government by decree. Should the assembly not give a vote of confidence in the cabinet, the formation of the new government would then be transferred to the senate. Should it fail to form a government within three months, early by-elections would be held. The head of state, who is not a president of the republic, can appoint vice heads of state from among members of the senate (art. 41). The head of state may preside over the works of the council of ministers with no right to vote. He may propose to remove the government or a minister, or to dissolve the assembly. His proposals require the agreement of both chambers, one by an absolute majority, or the decision can be taken by popular referendum (art. 30).

In the event of conflict between the head of state and the chambers, a referendum is to be held to settle matters. The referendum may be called for by the head of state or by the majority of either of the chambers. A referendum may also be organized at the instigation of ten members of parliament in each chamber supported by 10,000 signatures from at least ten *mohafazats* with at least 500 signatures from each *mohafazat*. For the referendum result to be taken into account, more than half of the electorate must turn out to vote (art. 34). The ease with which a referendum can be organized suggests the country will be voting non-stop.

This draft constitution also contains original provisions on the enforcement and amendment of constitutional articles. The chambers may suspend application of some articles for a set period by an absolute majority vote of both chambers. They may also add articles to the constitution temporarily in the same way. Any permanent change to the constitution has to be approved by a referendum approved by the majority of voters (art. 46).

8.12 What National Compact for Syria?

These three draft constitutions hardly convinced the remainder of the opposition, many of whom seem to lean towards restoring the 1950 constitution if only provisionally until the election of a constituent assembly to draft a new constitution. But even on this point the opposition has failed to reach a consensus.

The opposition was unable to adopt a common strategy to bring about regime change. Schematically, the Syrian opposition during the first years of the crisis can be divided into two main strands. The domestic opposition, although it has structures outside the country, and the opposition abroad, although it has its relay points inside the country. It should not be imagined that the division between the two major strands is geographical. It is first and foremost political. The main internal opposition was grouped within the Coordination. The leader of this organization is Hassan Abdel Azim, a historical opponent and successor to Jamal Atassi at the head of the Democratic Arab Socialist Union Party and the National

Democratic Rally. This movement brings together left-wing intellectuals, nationalists, Kurdish movements including the PYD, the Syrian branch of the Turkish PKK according to Ankara, and dissident branches of political parties that have split from their original parties because of their participation in the NPF. The supporters of the Damascus Declaration within Syria also joined the Coordination, which advocates peaceful change and rejects both violence wherever it comes from and the calls for foreign armed intervention. The Coordination was represented in Europe until 2015 by a long-standing opponent of the Ba'th regime, Haytham Manaa, a man of strong convictions, who has been living in France for more than thirty years.

After several meetings in the first months of the uprising in 2011 (including in Antalya, Istanbul, Paris, and Brussels), the opposition abroad managed in August 2011 to gather some of its components around Islamists and especially the Muslim Brotherhood within the Syrian National Council, which is sometimes called the Istanbul Council or more simply the Council. There were to be several defections from it, including those of Basma Kudmani, Haytham Maleh, Anwar Buni, and Kamal Labwani. The Council was criticized for being dominated by Sunni Islamist political outlooks, for over-representing the Muslim Brotherhood with respect to their actual presence within the country, for not being representative enough of the other schools of thought on the Syrian stage, and in particular the left-wing and the nationalists, for not fairly representing minorities and having only a limited influence within Syria. The major division precluding any agreement between the Council and the Coordination has been over their positions on possible foreign intervention in Syria. The Council was in favour and the Coordination against. This fundamental divergence prevented the two from reaching a political agreement at Cairo in January 2012.[62] In addition, the Council supports the armed rebellion within Syria whereas the Coordination rejects violence from any quarter, whether the regime or the opposition.

The representative character of the Council and its actual influence within Syria were soon treated with caution. The USA insisted on creating a new, more representative opposition body that would amalgamate the Council with political figures and other political movements. This new arrangement gave rise in Doha in November 2012 to the National Coalition for Syrian Opposition and Revolution Forces, more commonly

---

[62] The negotiators in Cairo signed an agreement rejecting any foreign intervention but the Council quickly withdrew the agreement signed by its representatives.

called the Doha Coalition or simply the Coalition. This body shares the same objective as the Council, namely the fall of the regime, militarization of the crisis, the refusal of any compromise with the regime, and calls for foreign military intervention.

The most important text the opposition managed to come up with jointly at the onset of the crisis was the National Compact, sometimes called National Commitment, adopted in 2012 in Cairo at the invitation of the Arab League.[63] This document contains the fundamental principles that should figure in the next constitution. The Compact recognizes that the Syrian people are part of the Arab nation just as it recognizes Kurdish nationalism and the national identity and rights of Assyrians (Syriacs) and Turkmens. No part of the territory can be ceded, including the Golan Heights. The Syrian people reserve the right to fight by all means to recover their occupied territory and support the Palestinian people in their right to found a state with Jerusalem as its capital. The future constitution shall lay the foundations for a civilian, multi-party, democratic system and a modern and fair means of voting. The institutions shall be renewed on the basis of regular elections and respect a strict separation of power. The state is to guarantee public freedoms, including the right to information, the right to form civilian associations, unions, and parties. The state guarantees freedom of conscience and the right to protest and to strike. The state undertakes to eliminate all forms of poverty and discrimination and ensure basic services for all citizens. The Compact was supplemented by another document that was adopted in Cairo and contains the characteristics of the transitional period.

This consensus-based approach masked deep divergences within the opposition with some vague provisions. Some days after the National Compact was signed, opposition members close to the Coordination published the Rome Appeal inviting Syrians to engage in dialogue for a political rather than military solution to the crisis.[64] The most important part of this declaration is that it did not set any conditions on engaging in dialogue such as the fall of the regime or the departure of the president. It was therefore consistent with the Geneva 1 declaration adopted a month earlier. This position was taken up by the Coordination and confirmed in the final communiqué of its meeting in Geneva on 29 January 2013.

---

[63] On the Cairo meeting and the text of the National Compact, see the Arab Orient Center; The Congress of the Syrian Opposition in Cairo, 4.7.2012 (Arabic) at www.asharqalarabi.org.uk/barq/b-qiraat-296.htm.

[64] See the text in English at carnegie-mec.org/diwan/49832?lang=en.

The absence of any pre-condition for a national dialogue in the form of a Geneva 2 meeting proposed in 2013 by the Russians and Americans and the refusal of any foreign intervention are the two main dividing lines between the Coordination and the Coalition.

To offset the absence of any common strategy, some opposition members set about making draft studies for the transitional period after the fall of the regime. These studies were financed by foreign governments and drafted with the support of US, German, and Canadian research institutes. The first study 'Syria the Day After' was published by the US Institute for Peace in July 2012. The second study worth citing is the 'Syria Transition Roadmap' published by the Syrian Centre for Political and Strategic Studies and Syria Expert House in 2013. These are interesting but cannot fill the void created by the lack of any common vision for the end of the crisis, because they are built on the hypothesis of a total victory of the opposition.

The civil war has shattered Syrian society. For the first time in a century certain initial components of the national project defined by the Founding Fathers in 1919 seem to have been called into question by part of the population. This questioning was not reflected so much in the political programmes of the moderate opposition, although it was perceptible, but rather in the stances taken, the foreign alliances, the absence of perception of Israel as a common enemy, and the support of some of the opposition for the most extreme armed groups that do not frighten minorities alone.[65] The militarization of the crisis has led to the moderate opposition, including the Free Syrian Army, being outflanked on the ground by various Islamist groups and jihadists such as the Islamic Front actively supported by certain regional powers, and the emergence of extremist groups affiliated or close to Al-Qaida, including many foreign combatants such as Islamic State of Iraq and Sham and the Al-Nusra Front. The precedence taken by these various Islamist armed groups, often in opposition with each other, is reflected on the ground by practices and values that are marked by extreme violence and are very different from those

---

[65] See for example the text in Arabic of the Coalition's political programme (www.etilaf.org/2013-08-12-15-50-47.html), the Council's political programme (www.syriancouncil.org), the interview of Burhan Ghalioun, then president of the Council, with the *Wall Street Journal* of 2 December 2011. These texts do not reflect, among other things, the content of the Syrian national project on the Palestinian question and Israel. In March 2014, the opposition figure Kamal Labwani went further still in proposing that Israel keep the Golan in exchange for helping overturn the regime in Damascus.

advocated by the moderate opposition when the crisis began. The same goes for the political programmes of Islamist armed groups that openly advocate the Islamization of the state and society, and even the establishment of a caliphate for ISIS, in place of a secular civilian state as in the national project of the Founding Fathers.

In a speech at the Damascus Opera House on 6 January 2013, President Bashar Assad suggested that the opposition should engage in a political process for the settlement of the crisis that would begin with a national dialogue for the adoption of a national compact that would then be submitted for the approval of the people. President Assad said the compact should reassert Syrian sovereignty, national unity, territorial integrity, the refusal of any foreign intervention in its internal affairs, the rejection of terrorism and of any form of violence. For President Assad, the compact should also map out Syria's political future, its constitutional regime, legal system, political and economic matters, electoral law, law on political parties, and law on local elections.

Were such a compact to see the light of day, it is likely to reflect, in one way or another, the main characteristics of the Founding Fathers' national project. The opposition supporters in the Coordination seem to want to maintain the features of the Syrian national project while developing them in a pluralist and democratic direction that is dear to them. The supporters of the Coalition, on the contrary, seem to want to change them substantially. Is this just tactical positioning to please some of their sponsors and generous foreign donors? Are Syrians in the process of changing their national project? Or are they extending it, rather, to include and confirm a new component, which it is to be hoped after so much suffering should never more be called into question, namely individual and collective freedom? Time will tell.

What will become of the Founding Fathers' national project is certainly one of the major issues of the war in Syria. On the fate of that project hangs the nature of the post-war Syrian political system and its constitutional architecture.

9

Towards the Sixth Republic

The Sixth Republic is the term I use for the political regime that will have to be established after the adoption of a new constitution at the end of the war in Syria. As the English-language manuscript of this book nears completion towards the end of 2017 it seems that the new constitution will be adopted pursuant to Security Council Resolution 2254 of December 2015. The march towards the Sixth Republic can be dated from the beginning of 2015 with the rallying of much of the opposition around a common project and more realistic positions, with points of agreement between the government and the moderate opposition being identified, but without denying the many points of disagreement between the two sides, and with the repositioning of the leading regional and international players after the onset of the Russian intervention and the refugee crisis in Europe in the autumn of that same year which consisted mainly of Syrians fleeing war and sanctions.

It is a Syria that is exhausted, battered, and bled dry that seems to be moving towards the Sixth Republic. This was no foregone conclusion. Few experts would have wagered in 2011–12 at the outbreak of the war that the country would remain united in the aftermath of this horrendous ordeal. How many doomsayers have predicted and even seemed to want Syria to be divided up along sectarian or geographical lines? The march towards the Sixth Republic seems to crown the victory of the nation state and the defeat of the schemes for sectarian partition. It is a victory for inclusion over exclusion. It is a victory for a continued desire to live together as a community inherited from the century-old national project of the Founding Fathers. But to be complete and lasting, this victory must be collective and ought necessarily to include the latest component of the national project called for by the current generation in blood – democracy.

Unlike the previous constitutions devised within a national framework without foreign influence, the origins of the Sixth Republic are to be sought jointly in military developments on the ground and in the political and diplomatic initiatives that have accompanied them. In this respect, 2013 will remain the year in which US military intervention to bring down President Assad's regime was abandoned despite the petitions of Washington's closest allies such as Turkey, Saudi Arabia, Qatar, and France, but, importantly, not Britain, which was the first to distance itself from any action supposedly in response to the Syrian army's alleged use of chemical weapons.[1]

That same year saw the battle of Al-Qusair and the engagement of Hezbollah forces that halted the ambitions of armed rebel groups to extend their zone of influence towards the centre of Syria from the Lebanese border in the west. The armed groups then had three options left for reaching Damascus: to launch an attack from the north, that is, from positions close to the Turkish border, or from the south close to the Jordanian border, or alternatively from the east across the Syrian–Iraqi desert. The most dramatic development came in the east in the next year with the taking of the city of Raqqa in January 2014 and then Mosul in June 2014 by ISIS or Daesh after a lightning attack allegedly launched in part from Turkish territory. This feat of arms was followed up by Daesh's proclamation of the Caliphate of the Islamic State. On the ground, this new entity astride the border between Syria and Iraq was an immediate threat for the region of Kurdistan, the Iraqi capital Baghdad, the remainder of Iraq, and in the longer term for inland Syria and even for Jordan. Faced with the risk of losing Irbil and Baghdad, the Americans and Iranians mobilized, separately, to oppose Daesh. Washington put in place an international coalition for air attacks on the terrorist group in Iraq and also in Syria without the agreement of the Damascus government.

The following year, the Al-Nusra Front and its allies launched a massive attack in Spring 2015 against the province of Idlib in north-western Syria. The taking of Idlib was a threat to the province of Latakia in the west, the Ghab plain, and the province of Hama to the south. Damascus claimed the attack was supported and remote-controlled by the Turkish-based military operations centre, known as the MOM from its initials in Turkish, which brought together military advisers from the regional and international powers hostile to President Assad. A few weeks later, Al-Nusra and other armed groups dug in close to the Jordanian border

---

[1] In an article on the Obama doctrine, journalist Jeffrey Goldberg says of this incident, 'Obama was also unsettled by a surprise visit early in the week from James Clapper, his director of national intelligence, who interrupted the President's Daily Brief, the threat report Obama receives each morning from Clapper's analysts, to make clear that the intelligence on Syria's use of sarin gas, while robust, was not a "slam dunk". See 'The Obama Doctrine' by Jeffrey Goldberg, *The Atlantic*, April 2016.

launched five successive waves of attack in an attempt to seize control of the south of the country, in particular the city of Dara'a, with the intention of then marching towards Damascus and joining up the enclaves in rebel hands in rural areas around the capital. All failed. Again according to Damascus, the attacks were allegedly supported and planned by a military operations centre in Jordan known as Military Operation Command (MOC), the twin of the operating centre in Turkey. On the eastern front, Daesh managed to take control of the symbolic city of Palmyra. Plainly the Islamic State group had not been seriously weakened by the US-led air strikes.

The Syrian army and its allies were fighting on all fronts, nearly five hundred of them. True, the army was on the back foot in the north-west and the east, but it was falling back in good order, without collapsing.[2] Nor was the Syrian state machinery collapsing. Its central administration and public services were still operating, albeit at a slower pace. The Syrian model established on the basis of the Founding Fathers' national project close to a century earlier remained the basis for national coexistence to which most of the population were still attached and who chose to remain under the protection of the central government rather than place themselves under the protection of rebel groups in the areas under their control or to seek refuge abroad. Initially the Syrian project included four components, namely secularism in the form of egalitarian and harmonious coexistence of all components of society in their religious and sectarian diversity; the refusal of foreign hegemony; the refusal of partition; and the attachment to Palestine. Two other components had subsequently grafted themselves on to this Syrian model, namely social justice and democracy.

The solidity and endurance of the Syrian nation-state model in the face of adversity surprised the opponents of Damascus. The attachment of most Syrians to the values of a modern, tolerant way of life derived from their national project and their perseverance in defending them probably encouraged Russia to continue to invest in this country with which Moscow had maintained privileged relations since the 1950s. It is for these two reasons that Russia decided to intervene massively at the end of September 2015, not just to support the Syrian army, or the Damascus regime, or President Assad, as Moscow's adversaries claimed, but rather

---

[2] In January 2017 the Russian foreign minister, Sergey Lavrov, declared that Damascus was two to three weeks away from falling into rebel hands at the time of the Russian army's intervention in September 2015. This was also the opinion of the Israelis whose defence minister, Moshe Ya'alon, declared in June 2015 that the Damascus government might collapse very shortly.

to prevent the establishment of a centre for jihadists, to save the Syrian nation-state model, one of the few in the region, and to protect long-term Russian interests in the Near East and the eastern Mediterranean.[3]

9.1 The Search for a Unifying Political Project

The independent moderate opposition held two meetings in Cairo in January and June 2015, in parallel with the Moscow discussions, to try to agree on a political project. It was a praiseworthy initiative and had been too long in coming. In nearly four years of crisis, the only political text adopted by joint agreement by the opposition inside and outside Syria was the National Compact, ratified in Cairo in July 2012.[4] But as Haytham Manaa points out, that text contains many confused passages.[5]

9.1.1 *The Cairo 1 and 2 Opposition Meetings*

The Cairo meetings were held under the aegis of what was officially a non-governmental organization, the Foreign Relations Council, but in reality it was quite close to the authorities. The first gathering lasted three days from 22 to 25 January 2015. It brought together almost fifty participants representing various political formations and independent opponents living in the country or abroad, including certain personalities affiliated to the National Coalition. Some participants proposed setting up a transitional council with executive and legislative competences, others called for a presidential council reflecting collegially held power, and others wanted the formation of a government of national union including those in power, the opposition, and independents.

This first gathering ended with the adoption of a ten-point Cairo Declaration. The declaration planned the transition towards a democratic regime and sovereign civil state, the adoption of confidence-building measures in humanitarian terms (such as the release of detained or abducted persons, cessation of bombardments, and allowing emergency aid to get through), an agreement among all Syrian parties to end the presence of non-Syrian military forces, restriction to the state of the possession of

---

[3] The basis of Damascus' request for Russia's intervention is the Treaty of Friendship and Cooperation signed by the USSR and Syria in Moscow in 1980. The initial duration of the treaty was twenty years and it has been automatically extended every five years.
[4] The text is sometimes referred to as the National Commitment.
[5] See http://haythammanna.net/bilan-du-congres-de-lopposition-democratique-et-patriotique-du-caire-8-9-juin-20015/.

weapons in any negotiated solution, restructuring of military and security institutions, the incorporation of the military opposition having participated in the political solution, the criminalization of violence and sectarianism, and the preparation of a Syrian national congress.

The Cairo Declaration also planned for the adoption of a founding national charter and a social compact. Readers of this book will remember from the previous chapters that it can be inferred from the history of Syria ever since its separation from the Ottoman empire in 1918 that the country's Founding Fathers had set out the basis for a national project containing four main principles[6] that were taken up by successive generations and to which two new principles were added later.[7] Readers will also recall the existence of what is called here an informal social compact between the Ba'th and certain categories of society since the party came to power in 1963.[8] So the initiative of the authors of the Cairo Declaration about adopting a national declaration and social compact can only be applauded, particularly since none of the provisions of the Cairo Declaration contradict the themes of the Syrian national project developed by the Founding Fathers and supplemented by the following generations. On the contrary, they consolidate them.

The moderate opposition met as a congress in Cairo on 8 and 9 June 2015. This gathering brought together more than a hundred participants including some twenty members of the Coalition who had come in their own names. The congress adopted the national declaration but instead of the social compact, it adopted a roadmap for a negotiated political solution.

The National Charter can legitimately be considered the most important political text developed by the opposition since the outbreak of the crisis, or even since the 2005 Damascus Declaration. It contains principles on which the immense majority of Syrians should agree. The Charter asserts:

> the Syrian people is one. Citizenship is underpinned by equal rights and duties without distinction as to colour, sex, language, or sectarian denomination. This citizenship shall be based on a comprehensive national compact in which religion belongs to God and the homeland to all citizens. The Charter provides that Women enjoy equality with men. No going back on this law shall be tolerated. Likewise, any citizen, man or woman, may seek to hold any public position, including the office of President of the

---

[6] See Chapters 2 and 3.
[7] See Chapters 4 and 6.
[8] See Chapters 6 and 8.

Republic ... The Syrian people is free and sovereign within its territory; these are two inseparable components (people and territory), of which it is prohibited to give up the least part, in particular the occupied Golan Heights. The Syrian people claims the right to fight to recover its occupied lands by all means decided on pursuant to international legitimacy concerning resistance to occupation.

On minorities, the Charter announces that 'The Syrian state guarantees observance of social diversity, the diversity of beliefs and the specific characteristics of all components of the Syrian people. It recognizes the cultural and political rights of all those components and shall see that they are advanced.' The Charter confirms the criminalization of communitarism and political sectarianism and rejects terrorism and violence. The Charter recognizes the diversity of Syrian society by asserting that the Syrian people is one, composed of Arabs, Kurds, Syriacs, Assyrians, Turkmens, and others. Its component parts have the same internationally recognized legitimate rights. The Charter recognizes Arab identity and signals its solidarity with the Palestinians:

> Syria is an integral part of the Arab nation, tied with the Arab peoples by cultural bonds, history, shared interests and objectives, and a common destiny. Syria, as a founding member of the Arab League, shall make sure to strengthen various forms of cooperation and ties among Arab countries. The Syrian people undertakes to provide its support to the Palestinian people and its right to build a free, sovereign, independent state with Jerusalem as its capital.

The Charter contains provisions on the military institution: the Syrian army is the national institution tasked with protecting the country, preserving its independence, its sovereignty over its territory, and watching over national security. It does not intervene in political activities. The Charter provides for a system of administrative decentralization: the state abides by the principle of democratic decentralization. Local administration is performed by representative executive bodies in charge of administering the population and developing areas and regions in such a way as to achieve sustainable and egalitarian development under the sovereignty of the state and the territorial unity of the country. The Charter sets out social provisions:

> the Syrian state undertakes to eradicate all forms of poverty and discrimination, to combat unemployment by seeking to achieve full employment with a decent wage, to achieve justice through the redistribution of wealth, to secure balanced development and protection of the environment, to provide basic services for all citizens: housing, town planning, drinking

water, sewage systems, electricity, telephone service, the Internet, transport routes, education, socio-professional rehabilitation, medical care, retirement pensions, and unemployment benefits consistent with the standard of living.[9]

The Charter provisions reflect in modern terms the four main principles developed by the Founding Fathers since the 1919 Damascus Programme and taken up by the following generations, namely: Syrian secularism in the form of equality and peaceful coexistence among all beliefs, the refusal of foreign hegemony, the refusal to divide up Syria, and the attachment to Palestine. It also contains the two main principles added subsequently, namely social justice and democracy. When the time for national reconciliation comes, it is likely that many themes in this Charter will be taken up by the supporters of the ruling authorities.

It is regrettable that the social clause of the Charter gives only an expeditious and vague list of certain welfare provisions. Syrians in general and in particular those on the lowest incomes have benefited for more than half a century under the Ba'th from state generosity in terms of free education, medical care for all, various welfare provisions, and benefits in kind for cadres of the state, party, and army. The state under the Ba'th has also delimited an economic space for the middle and upper merchant class. This space has expanded continually from self-employed craftsmen and domestic commerce to banks, insurance, and the stock exchange by way of the agro-food, pharmaceutical, textile, and tourism industries, and so on, so much so that I spoke earlier of an informal social compact between the Ba'th and broad sectors of society including both the working, middle and upper classes.[10] This social compact acted not just as an umbilical cord between the Ba'th and its social base. It has also benefited the entire population and has contributed to legitimizing the rule of the Ba'th at times when there were no elections or when elections had little meaning. Since the Ba'th came to power in 1963, the redistribution of the national wealth through welfare has been inseparable from the regime in place in Damascus. This is why the vague social provisions of the Charter cannot make up for the failure to set out a social compact as initially planned by the organizers of the Cairo meeting.

---

[9] For the full version in Arabic see http://m-syria-d.com/.
[10] See Chapter 6.

9.1.2 *The Moscow 1 and 2 Consultative Meetings*

With the failure of the Geneva 2 meetings in 2014, the political process for ending the crisis was stalled. Credit goes to the Russian authorities for having successfully restarted the process by organizing two meetings in Moscow in preparation for a subsequent round of talks in Geneva. The importance of those two consecutive meetings organized under the auspices of the Institute of Oriental Studies in January and April 2015 lies not just in the conclusion adopted under the 'Ten Moscow Principles' but in the fact that, for the first time since the outbreak of the political crisis and its transformation into a civil war with regional ramifications, representatives of the Damascus government talked openly with certain representatives of the opposition inside and outside Syria and with representatives of civil society. Those absent outnumbered those attending, but the important thing was to make a start with Syro-Syrian talks rather than to reach any particular conclusion or secure comprehensive participation. The National Coalition supported by Qatar, Saudi Arabia, and Turkey was among the most notable absentees, as was the moderate and independent opposition, which during this period was beginning to organize itself in Cairo. The National Coordination Committee for Democratic Change left those of its members who were invited the free choice of whether or not to participate in this first meeting in Moscow.

The priority for the government delegation led by its United Nations representative in New York, ambassador Bashar Jaafari, was the fight against terrorism, whereas, for the opposition, the priority was the political transition under the Geneva 1 provisions. The opposition delegation also wished to discuss the humanitarian question and the implementation by the government of confidence-building measures to facilitate talks. These divergences meant no joint declaration could be signed by the participants after two days of talks. But they should not hide from view the ten points of agreement that were presented by Professor Vitaly Naumkin, the Institute's president, in a personal statement and that may be summarized as follows: to protect Syria's sovereignty and to safeguard the unity of its territory and its security; to combat international terrorism and its manifestations in whatever form; to solve the crisis in Syria by peaceful political means pursuant to the principles of the 2012 Geneva Communiqué; to ensure Syria's future was to be decided by the Syrian people freely and democratically; to refuse any foreign intervention in Syrian affairs; to ensure the continued action of the state institutions and the participation of all components of the Syrian people in the country's political and economic life; to observe the rule of law and equal rights for citizens; to refuse any foreign military presence in Syria without the agreement of its government; to end the occupation of the Golan; and to lift the sanctions imposed on the Syrian people.

Critics were not slow to emphasize the difficulty in implementing this declaration, particularly as it did not call for the departure of President Assad.[11] The opposition delegation asked for the mediation of the Russian authorities to pursue discussions with Damascus on humanitarian issues and announced it was to provide Moscow with all the documents in its possession concerning prisoners and detainees. Despite all the criticism they came in for, the Ten Moscow Principles are nonetheless far from negligible and are in keeping with the national project developed by the Founding Fathers of Syria almost a century ago.

The participants in the talks accepted to meet for a second time. This meeting took place from 6 to 9 April 2015. The participants' priorities had not changed; the fight against terrorism for the government delegation and confidence-building measures and the humanitarian aspect for the opposition. Although the participants separated without reaching agreement on all the points dividing them, Professor Vitaly Naumkin, who hosted the talks, was glad that the meeting threw down the basis for a peaceful resolution of the crisis through the adoption, for the first time, of a political document he termed 'The Moscow Platform', which was acceptable to both the opposition and the government.

The Platform set out the points of agreement among the participants. It consolidated and developed the Ten Principles from the previous talks. It supplemented them by introducing two important aspects: (1) the refusal of any political solution based on ethnic, sectarian, or religious considerations, thus confirming the Syrian model of coexistence and secularism developed over almost a century; (2) the solemn assertion of the monopoly over possession of weapons and therefore of the use of armed force by the state. The Platform also recalled the refusal of any outside interference in Syrian affairs and the need to liberate the occupied territories. In this it was also fully consistent with the national project of the Founding Fathers.

Because the second Moscow meeting was unable to limit the divergences among the participants or to advance the humanitarian dossiers such as that on prisoners, some commentators claimed it was a failure. That verdict is probably overstating things. It was impossible to reach a

---

[11] For criticism of the Moscow meeting see: http://syrie.blog.lemonde.fr/2015/02/01/rencontre-consultative-de-moscou-petits-et-bas-cotes-dun-non-evenement/.

comprehensive agreement in three days. But with hindsight, it can be asserted, by listing the points of agreement among the participants and leaving aside the points of disagreement to be negotiated later, that the Moscow 2 meeting favourably paved the way for the international conferences to come.[12]

9.1.3 The Vienna 1 and 2 Conferences

The two Cairo meetings gathered the independent opposition around a common political programme. The two Moscow meetings identified the points of convergence between the regime and the moderate opposition, leaving aside the points of divergence. Thus these four meetings in two different capital cities indirectly laid the groundwork for two important diplomatic conferences that were held in Vienna in October and November 2015, a few weeks after the beginning of the Russian army's intervention in Syria and at a time when the refugee crisis from Turkey towards Europe was seeing record arrivals in Greece, including a large majority of Syrians fleeing the war, and the degradation of their living conditions since 2011 that had been made worse by sanctions against the country.

The first Vienna conference on 30 October 2015 was the result of an agreement between the Russians and Americans. The primary objective of the conference was to convince their respective regional allies, the Damascus government and the rebels, of the necessity to implement a ceasefire. All the regional and international powers involved in the Syrian crisis, including Iran – which a year earlier had reached an agreement on nuclear issues with the Five Plus One Group – were invited to this meeting at the outcome of which the participants adopted a Final Declaration taking up some of the provisions developed in Cairo and Moscow. The declaration set out the general framework for a political solution that was to be completed by the adoption of a new constitution and by elections under UN supervision as well as the implementation of a ceasefire.

---

[12] In addition to the Cairo and Moscow meetings, it is worth mentioning two less ambitious meetings organized in Astana in May and October 2015 between representatives of Syrian civil society, the domestic opposition, and some opponents living abroad. The discussions focused on the unity of the Syrian state, the humanitarian question, the withdrawal of foreign fighters, the need for a common front against terrorism, and a political solution to the crisis. It is also to be mentioned that the Norwegian Peacebuilding Resource Center has facilitated the adoption in 2015 of the 'Oslo Principles' by a group of Syrian religious and academics individuals who have developed the concept of citizenship in post-conflict Syria.

The main points of the declaration can be summarized as follows. The declaration stated that Syria's unity, independence, territorial integrity, and secular character are fundamental. State institutions are to remain intact. The rights of all Syrians, regardless of ethnicity or religious denomination, must be protected. Humanitarian access will be ensured throughout the territory of Syria, and the participants will increase support for internally displaced persons, refugees, and their host countries. Daesh, and other terrorist groups, as designated by the UN Security Council, and others, as agreed by the participants, must be defeated. Pursuant to the 2012 Geneva Communiqué and UN Security Council resolution 2118, the participants invited the UN to convene representatives of the Government of Syria and the Syrian opposition for a political process leading to credible, inclusive, non-sectarian governance, followed by a new constitution and elections. These elections must be administered under UN supervision to the satisfaction of the governance and to the highest international standards of transparency and accountability, free and fair, with all Syrians, including the diaspora, eligible to participate. This political process will be Syrian led and Syrian owned, and the Syrian people will decide the future of Syria. The participants together with the United Nations will explore modalities for, and implementation of, a nationwide ceasefire to be initiated on a given date and in parallel with this renewed political process.

This declaration worried the opposition as it remained unclear about President Assad's future and the mechanisms of the transitional period. The second conference was held on 14 November within the framework of what was to become the International Syria Support Group. It adopted a declaration inviting participants to support efforts to stop the fighting except against Daesh, the Al-Nusra Front, and the armed groups affiliated to them. The declaration provided for the application of humanitarian confidence-building measures, the adoption of a Security Council resolution, and the resumption of peace talks among the protagonists. The declaration provided for a transitional period in keeping with the Geneva 1 provisions that would include establishing within six months a credible political process with a non-sectarian government, the preparation of a new constitution, and the holding of elections under UN supervision within eighteen months on the basis of that constitution.[13]

---

[13] See https://eeas.europa.eu/headquarters/headquarters-homepage/3088/node/3088_en.

9.1.4 *The UNSCR 2254*

All of these initiatives (in Cairo, Moscow, and Vienna) might appear disordered at first sight, and they undoubtedly were, but in the end they reflected an unchanging joint Russo-American determination to reach a political solution to the crisis that would conserve the Syrian state and sideline the most radical groups linked to the Al-Qaida terrorist network. The undertaking was a bold one because, before getting to that stage, the USA had to convince its closest regional allies that in the Syrian crisis the ends could not justify the means and that supporting – even if secretly and tactically – groups affiliated to Al-Qaida to bring down the Assad regime was unacceptable.[14]

The two Vienna declarations that accompanied the turnaround in the situation on the ground in favour of the Syrian army and its allies further to Russian intervention paved the way for the Security Council to adopt, in December 2015, resolution 2254, which contained a political roadmap for the settlement of the Syria crisis and opened up the way to a third round of talks in Geneva in 2016. The resolution expressed 'its support for a Syrian-led political process that is facilitated by the United Nations and, within a target of six months, establishes credible, inclusive and non-sectarian governance and sets a schedule and process for drafting a new

---

[14] US Vice-president Joe Biden had to apologize for having made the following comments on 2 October 2014 at Harvard University's Kennedy School of Government: 'Our allies in the region were our largest problem in Syria. The Turks were great friends, and I have a great relationship with Erdogan, [who] I just spent a lot of time with, [and] the Saudis, the Emirates, etcetera. What were they doing? They were so determined to take down Assad, and essentially have a proxy Sunni-Shia war, what did they do? They poured hundreds of millions of dollars and tens of tons of weapons into anyone who would fight against Assad – except that the people who were being supplied, were al-Nusra, and al-Qaeda, and the extremist elements of jihadis who were coming from other parts of the world. Now, you think I'm exaggerating? Take a look. Where did all of this go? So now that's happening, all of a sudden, everybody is awakened because this outfit called ISIS, which was al-Qaeda in Iraq, when they were essentially thrown out of Iraq, found open space and territory in [eastern] Syria, [and they] work with al-Nusra, who we declared a terrorist group early on. And we could not convince our colleagues to stop supplying them. So what happened? Now, all of a sudden – I don't want to be too facetious – but they have seen the lord. Now we have ... been able to put together a coalition of our Sunni neighbors, because America can't once again go into a Muslim nation and be the aggressor. It has to be led by Sunnis. To go and attack a Sunni organization. And so what do we have for the first time? [Audio cuts out]' at www.washingtonpost.com/news/worldviews/wp/2014/10/06/behind-bidens-gaffe-some-legitimate-concerns-about-americas-middle-east-allies/?utm_term=.9f7f0f284ff5.

constitution, and further expresse[d] its support for free and fair elections, pursuant to the new constitution, to be held within 18 months and administered under supervision of the United Nations'.[15]

The contents of the resolution were confirmed a year later in the provisions of resolution 2336 after the fall of Aleppo that called for a ceasefire, negotiations in Astana between the government and opposition, and the resumption of the Geneva peace talk. A new round of negotiations was held in early 2017. Geneva 4 ended with United Nations special envoy Staffan de Mistura announcing a promising agenda for future talks with 'four baskets', namely, political transition, constitution, elections, and combatting terrorism.

9.2 The Search for a Constitutional Formula

The points of agreement expressed by the participants at the various meetings on the Syrian crisis in 2015 and resolution 2254 created an environment conducive to the development of proposed constitutions to reflect them. Three such projects were put forward in 2016; two by the Carter Center and a third by Russia. Some of the media spoke also of an Iranian initiative. For the first time in their modern political history, the initiative behind the constitutional proposals did not come from Syrians themselves, although some were consulted and contributed to the wording of the documents.

The three constitutional texts of 2016 were all written from a different perspective to the draft constitutions presented by the opposition since the Damascus Spring, all of which adopted a scenario of regime change. The Carter Center proposals involved a substantial revision to the 2012 constitution or the adoption of a provisional constitution. The Russian project proposed a new constitution. These documents were presented before Syrians had agreed on a political project. This is palpable in the texts. The intrinsic failing of all three texts is precisely the absence of any national dimension reflecting Syrian identity or taking up in some form or other the major themes of the national project that have been adopted down the generations. These themes were developed in 2015 in various texts such as the Cairo Declaration, Moscow Declaration, Moscow Platform, and National Charter, but not in either the Russian proposal or in those of the Carter Center. This is why, without wishing to offend their authors, those constitutional projects must be considered to be

---

[15] See www.un.org/press/en/2015/sc12171.doc.htm.

mere working documents, technical, apolitical projects designed to begin rather than end the constitutional debate.

9.2.1 The Carter Center's Proposed Revision of the 2012 Constitution

In July 2013, the Carter Center started to discreetly organize meetings among Syrians from all sides and international experts to discuss constitutional and legislative options for a political transition within the framework of the Geneva 1 communiqué dated 2012. After the Security Council adopted resolution 2254 in December 2015 providing for the establishment of a transitional governmental authority, the adoption of a new constitution within eighteen months followed by elections under international supervision, the Center organized six new workshops bringing together Syrian jurists to examine what was presented as shortcomings in the UN resolution, namely what constitutional arrangements should be put in place during the eighteen-month period in which the transitional governing authority was to assume power. Materially, the work of the Center looked into what an inclusive transitional governing body endowed with executive competences should be and what constitutional and legislative amendments would be necessary during the transitional period for resolution 2254 to be applied. That work was published in June 2016.[16] Three options were explored: the revision of the 2012 constitution to include the provisions of resolution 2254; the adoption of a provisional constitution for the transitional period in the form of a constitutional declaration; and a return to the 1950 constitution. This last option was ruled out as unrealistic. Only the first two were expanded upon.

The preferred approach was to revise the 2012 constitution so as to overhaul the composition of the council of ministers in order to include representatives of the opposition and independents and transform it into a transitional governing body. Executive power would be exercised jointly by the president of the republic and the president of the council of ministers. The revision also suggested changing the make-up of the People's Assembly and the Supreme Constitutional Court so as to include opposition and independent representatives. Revision of the constitution would also entail the amending of twenty-one articles of the 2012 constitution granting unchecked power to the president, cancellation of twenty

---

[16] See 'Syria's Transition, Governance and Constitutional Options under U.N. Security Council Resolution 2254', June 2016 on the Carter Center website: www.cartercenter.org/.

decrees, the elimination of extra-judicial tribunals, and the adoption of a supra-constitutional declaration.

This declaration states that during the transition foreseen in United Nations Security Council Resolution (UNSCR) 2254, the principles adopted in the revised constitution would supersede any contradictory constitutional provisions, legislation, and decrees. All obligations undertaken by Syria in respect of international humanitarian laws and human rights instruments would be proclaimed as the law of the country, would prevail in cases where there is a contradiction with Syrian law, and would be enforceable by the judicial authorities of the country. This provision is innovative because it introduces monism for the first time in the country's constitutional history by according international law primacy over municipal law in place of the previously existing dualism. There would be separation of powers between the executive, legislature, and judiciary. The independence of the judiciary would be ensured.

One of the main features of the model is that it leaves the institution of the presidency intact during the transitional period. In other words, President Assad would remain in office during the eighteen months of the transition but with restricted powers.

The Carter Center suggested two options for the Transitional Governing Body and the exercise of executive powers:

(a) For the 18-month transitional period foreseen in UNSCR 2254, the Council of Ministers assumes the functions of the Transitional Governing Body with full executive powers. [Option 1a]
(b) For the 18-month transitional period foreseen in UNSCR 2254, an ad hoc Transitional Governing Body is constituted by combining the institutions of the President of the Republic and the Council of Ministers under the current Constitution as amended. [Option 1b]

> [if Option 1a] All executive powers exercised by the President of the Republic are transferred to the President of the Council of Ministers under the following articles of the Constitution: 96, 98, 100, 101, 102, 103, 105, 106, 107, 108, 111, 112, 113, 114, 115, 116, 124(2), 132, 141.
> [if Option 1b] The President of the Republic exercises powers granted to him under articles 96, 98, 100, 101, 102, 103, 105, 106, 107, 108, 111, 112, 113, 114, 115, 116, 124(2), 132, 141 of the Constitution with the consent of the President of the Council of Ministers.

The Carter Center made specific suggestions regarding the Transitional Legislative Authority:

> For the 18-months transition period foreseen in UNSCR 2254, the People's Assembly is reconstituted as follows – the current People's Assembly shall elect a caucus of [50] from its members to constitute one-third of the membership of a Transitional People's Assembly, the opposition High Negotiation Committee shall select the second caucus of one-third, and a [neutral third party, i.e. an international institution] shall select the remaining caucus of one-third. Such a reconstitution of the People's Assembly shall be agreed at the Geneva negotiations as an extraordinary measure. The term of office of the reconstituted Transitional People's Assembly shall expire with the election of a new legislature under the new constitution to be adopted at the conclusion of the 18-month transition period. For the 18-month transition period foreseen in UNSCR 2254, the following articles of the current Constitution shall be suspended: 56, 57, 59, 60, 61, 62, 63, 75.3 and 77.
>
> The president of the Council of Minister and members of the cabinet, shall be initially appointed for the transition period mandated by UNSCR 2254 by the peace conference convened in Geneva. Deputy ministers are appointed by the president of the Council of Ministers. The president of the Council of Ministers [with the consent of the President of the Republic] accepts the resignation of the deputies of the president of the Council of Ministers, ministers and their deputies, and appoints their replacement. The Transitional People's Assembly accepts with a [qualified][simple] majority vote their resignation of the president of the Council of Ministers and the Council of Ministers in its entirety. Following the Transitional People's Assembly's acceptance of the resignation of the president of the Council of Ministers and the Council of Ministers in its entirety, the speaker of the Transitional People's Assembly with the consent of the President of the Republic appoints the new president of the Council of Ministers and new Council of Ministers, and submits the new appointments for the approval of the Transitional People's Assembly with a qualified majority vote.[17]

According to the Carter Center, such a model based on a revision of the 2012 constitution would allow for an inclusive transitional governing body with full executive power formed on the basis of mutual consent while ensuring continuity of government institutions as per UNSCR 2254.

---

[17] See www.cartercenter.org/.

9.2.2 The Carter Center's Suggested Provisional Constitution

The Carter Center came up with another option in the form of a provisional constitution for the transitional period that would consist of a constitutional declaration and would replace the current Syrian constitution. Under this model, the president and the transitional governing authority would jointly govern the country.

Just as in the previous option that planned for maintaining the 2012 constitution while revising it, the provisional constitution option did not call into question President Assad's remaining in power during the eighteen months of the transition but gave him restricted powers.

Under the constitutional declaration, the president of the republic and the transitional governing body would jointly exercise executive authority. The president would have three vice presidents, one selected from the independents, the second from the loyalists, and the third from the opposition. The president would delegate some of his authority to them.

> The President will lead the Transitional Governing Body, he is the commander in chief of the army and armed forces. The President may veto any decree by the Transitional Governing Body within 10 days of its issue by letter to the body explaining the reasons for his veto. If the body reconsiders the matter and approves it by a simple majority, the decree will come into effect.
>
> The Transitional Governing Body is the supreme authority in the nation during the transitional phase, and all security, military, and civil state institutions are directly subject to it. It is composed of 30 members; 10 appointed by the government, 10 appointed by the opposition, and 10 others appointed from independent individuals selected by a representative of the secretary general of the U.N. from a list containing 20 names approved by the opposition and the loyalists. The chairman will be elected from among its independent members by simple majority.
>
> The Transitional Governing Body will exercise both legislative and executive authority. It will set general policies for the nation during the transitional phase, which will cease when the authoritative agency begins operations after the results of elections conducted under the framework of the new constitution.
>
> The Transitional Governing Body will form a military council containing representatives of the military authorities from the regime and the opposition having a considerable presence on the ground. The council will be headed by a high-level military person acceptable to both parties to be selected with the assistance of a representative of the secretary general of the U.N. This council will be entrusted with undertaking measures to stop the fighting among these authorities and coordinate their efforts in fighting terrorist organizations, regaining the unity and integrity of

Syrian territory, and securing the exit of foreign forces from it. It will also be entrusted with proposing the restructuring of the police, security, and military agencies.

The judiciary is independent. The President and the Transitional Governing Body will guarantee this independence, with assistance from the Supreme Judicial Council. The Supreme Judicial Council is headed by the president of the Supreme Constitutional Court. The Supreme Constitutional Court is an independent judicial organization with sole jurisdiction for oversight of the constitutionality of laws and regulations.[18]

9.2.3 *Russia's Constitutional Proposal*

In May 2016, some of the media reported on a proposed constitution for Syria prepared by Russia. This news was denied in Damascus by the president, who asserted that only Syrians were entitled to discuss and prepare their constitution and that any constitutional project would be submitted for popular approval by referendum. The matter rested at that until the first round of Astana talks in January of the following year when the Russian delegate handed the representatives of the armed groups a draft constitution for Syria prepared by Moscow and invited them to comment on it. The draft was quickly leaked and the press made it big news. It was rejected by almost all of the Syrian political class across the board. Moscow presented it as a 'guide'.[19]

The Russian proposal contains innovative provisions that are worth some thought, but it strips Syria of its Arab character and its regional attachment. Article 1 states that 'The Syrian Republic is an independent and sovereign democratic state'. Syria's name would therefore no longer be the 'Syrian Arab Republic' but simply the 'Syrian Republic' as before the 1958 union with Egypt. Even the *infissal* regime that ended the union in 1961 did not dare restore the country's earlier name but preferred the 'Syrian Arab Republic'. The great majority of Syrians remain very much attached to their Arab identity. To remove it would be to leave the country without its soul.

Article 2.2 defines the Syrian people as being of several ethnic and sectarian backgrounds. Article 4 continues:

(2) The institutions of the Kurdish cultural autonomous authorities and its organizations shall equally use Arabic and Kurdish languages.

---

[18] See www.cartercenter.org/.
[19] See the Arabic version of the Russian-sponsored draft constitution at https://arabic.rt.com/news/860757.

(3) Syrian citizens have the right to have their children educated in their mother tongue in public and private educational institutions.
(4) Each region has the right to decide by referendum on the use of the language of the majority of its population in addition to the official language.

According to article 7.3, 'The recognized general principles of international law and the international conventions binding Syria are an integral part of the legal order. In the event of conflict between a law and an international convention, the latter shall prevail.' Article 8.2 stipulates that Syria rejects war as a means of settling international disputes. Under article 9.2, Syria's borders may be modified by referendum. Article 10.4 adds: 'The army and armed forces are under the control of society, they protect the unity of its territory ... and do not intervene in political matters.'

Syria is made up of decentralized administrative units (art. 15). The constitutional oath that a citizen must take before entering office begins 'I swear...' (art. 17.4) and no longer contains the expression 'I swear by Almighty God ...'. Article 19.2 provided that all citizens, men or women, 'are equally entitled to participate in state affairs and enjoy the same political rights including the right to vote and the right to stand for election'.

The legislative authority was to be composed of the People's Assembly and the Assembly of Regions (art. 34). The members of the People's Assembly are elected by secret universal ballot (art. 35.1). 'The Assembly of Regions is established to ensure the participation of representatives of the administrative units in preparing legislation and ruling the country' (art. 40.1). 'The Assembly of Regions is composed of representatives of the administrative units' (art. 40.2). Article 44.4 stated that the People's Assembly had the power to remove the President of the Republic.

The executive authority was to be formed by the President of the Republic and the Council of Ministers (art. 48), with the president elected by a secret universal ballot for a term of office of seven years (art. 49.1) who 'may be re-elected once only' (art. 49.2). The President of the Republic was to command the armed forces (art. 60). The President of the Republic may be removed in a complex procedure by a two-thirds majority vote of the members of the two legislative assemblies (art. 61.2) in the event that he has been accused of high treason or serious crime by the People's Assembly based on a decision taken by the Supreme Constitutional Court.

The President of the Republic was to appoint the President of the Council and the ministers and remove them from office and accept their resignation (art. 64.1). The appointments of vice prime ministers and ministers 'must take account of the proportional representation of all ethnic and religious components of the Syrian population. Positions shall be reserved for national and ethnic minorities' (art. 64.3).

Under article 72.1, the two legislative assemblies could withdraw their confidence in the government at a joint meeting by an absolute majority vote of their respective members. The Supreme Constitutional Court was to be based in Damascus and composed of seven members at least appointed by the Council of the Regions for a term of four years (art. 77). A revision of the Constitution may be instigated by one-third of the members of each of the two assemblies as well as by the President of the Republic. The revision is passed by a majority vote of three-quarters of the two assemblies (art. 80).

The Russian proposal certainly contains some innovative aspects for the Syrian constitutional order. It introduces, or more accurately it reintroduces, the bicameral arrangement planned for by the 1920 monarchical constitution that was never applied. The supporters of human rights will applaud the introduction of monism into the Syrian constitutional order, in other words the primacy of international law over municipal law. The supporters of Kurdish autonomy will be happy about the marked decentralization and the scope given to the Kurdish language and the Assembly of the Regions. The supporters of increased secularism will have appreciated the absence of any reference to the president's religion and to Islamic law as the main source of legislation. Feminists will have welcomed the greater emphasis on equal rights of men and women. President Assad's supporters will certainly have been happy that he would be entitled to stand for a second term of office in 2021 and continue to head the army and the executive. Reformists will have been glad to see the shift in the balance of executive authority to the president of the Council of Ministers and the end of the legislative decrees that allowed the President of the Republic to legislate, just as they will be glad to see the independence of the judiciary and the Supreme Constitutional Court.

That said, this proposed constitution leads to Syria becoming detached from its environment. In addition, the proposal weakens secularism despite the absence of reference to the president's religion and to Muslim law because it introduces a system of sectarian and ethnic quotas in government. Besides, the rejection on principle of any resort to armed force, when part of the national territory is still occupied and can, according to international law, be liberated by the legitimate use of armed force amounts to separating the fate of the Golan Heights from that of Syria. It is also tantamount to leaving the Palestinians and the Occupied Palestinian Territories at the mercy of Israel's intransigence. The article stating that the borders could be altered by referendum has been construed as abandoning the part of the Golan Heights occupied by Israel. That is unacceptable for almost all Syrians. The weakening of secularism, the absence of any reference to Arab identity, and the negation of Syria's regional dimension are all contrary to the Founding Fathers' national project that has been taken up by each generation for close on a century. For all these reasons, the Russian proposal can only be considered to be a working document.

9.2.4 The 2015 Iranian Initiative

There is no need to discuss at length the privileged relations between Damascus and Tehran ever since the 1979 Iranian Revolution. This strategic relation between the two countries has become even stronger during the Syrian crisis. In this context, any criticism of Iran in the Syrian press close to the government is rare enough to be noteworthy. And this is what happened in August 2015 when some of the media reported on a four-point Iranian initiative for Syria: (1) an immediate ceasefire; (2) the formation of a government of national union; (3) revision of the constitution so as to reassure the ethnic and sectarian components in Syria; (4) early elections under international supervision.

Reaction from Damascus was not slow in coming. It was voiced via a major national daily newspaper close to the government that called the third point of the Iranian initiative 'unacceptable'.[20] The author of the article asserted that such a revision of the constitution to reassure the various ethnic and sectarian groups in Syria would not contribute in any way to ending the current conflict but on the contrary would engender a religious and ethnic war for centuries to come. The article recalled that Syria continued to proclaim its Arab character precisely so as to dilute under its banner the various sectarian, ethnic, and racial groups. It affirmed that to make such a revision would be to recognize that each sectarian group would have political and religious features justifying ties outside Syria. It concluded by asserting that this would lead to the break-up of the country.

The criticisms levelled at the Iranian initiative reflect the political and constitutional development Syria has undergone in almost a century. The same kind of remarks were made about the Russian proposed constitution presented in January 2017 that provided for the introduction of religious, sectarian, and ethnic quotas within government. It is interesting that even

---

[20] *Al-Watan*, 5 August 2015.

the closest allies of Damascus have not always understood the essence of Syrian identity and personality based on a national project established by the Founding Fathers in 1919 and then developed by the next generations, which has been discussed at length here. That Syria's allies have not fully understood it to some extent excuses its opponents for not having understood it at all.

9.3 The Search for Post-war Partners

The magnitude of human distress and the extent of physical destruction means that regardless of whoever ultimately wins the war in Syria, everyone will have lost. While it has been commonly accepted since resolution 2254 that the war will have to end by the defeat of the most fanatical of those involved such as Daesh, Al-Nusra, and the armed groups affiliated to them, it is also understood that a purely military solution is unattainable. This does not preclude one camp from gaining an advantage over the other in the field as has been the case since the Russian intervention in 2015. But ultimately the solution has to be a political one. It will have to include new protagonists such as the armed groups that have marked themselves apart from Daesh and Al-Nusra, the Kurdish component, and for the opposition it will have to include specific provisions on the military establishment.

9.3.1 The Joint Military Council

During the crisis, the military institution proved to be the true backbone of the state, the regime, and the country. Several ideas have been proposed about the form the military might take in the aftermath of the war. The Geneva 1 communiqué of June 2012 mentioned the need to maintain the army and security forces and place them under the authority of the Transitional Governing Body. The National Charter (or National Commitment) of Cairo in July 2012 provided for the establishment of a National Security Council made up of officers of the regular army, the Free Syrian Army, armed groups, and civilians. The participants in the opposition meeting in Cairo in January 2015 laid down the principle of the state monopoly on possession of weapons and called for the military and security institutions to be restructured and merged with the armed opposition that had participated in the peaceful solution. The participants at the Moscow 1 meeting agreed on the necessity to ensure the state institutions, including the army, continued to function. The Vienna Declaration of October 2015 adopted a similar terminology by calling for the state institutions to remain intact. The idea of creating a body to bring together the officers of the regime and commanders of the armed opposition groups was again evoked in the roadmap adopted by the opposition in Cairo in June 2015. It was also taken up by UN special envoy Staffan de Mistura in his draft framework for settlement of the crisis announced in September 2015 suggesting the creation of a Joint Military Council. The High Negotiations Committee formed in December 2015 called for the army and intelligence services to be restructured. It too proposed that the Transitional Governing Authority should create a Joint Military Council as one of the institutions for the transitional period on which loyalist and opposition officers would sit in equal numbers.

The idea of a Joint Military Council seems then to be widely shared by the various factions of the opposition and by the UN emissary. It remains to be seen what the position of the Damascus government will be. The concept of the ideological army adopted by the Ba'th in 1965 has placed the military institution at the heart of the hybrid '*asabiya* characteristic of the political system since the beginning of the Fourth Republic. The change of the constitution in 2012 and of the previous political system where the state was ruled by the Ba'th do not seem to have entailed changes as to the nature of the army, its functions, its mode of recruitment, and its military doctrine. The Ba'th may no longer officially be the ruling party but it remains nevertheless the party of the ruler. It is a safe enough bet that the central authorities and the general staff will be cautious about any possibility of amalgamating armed opposition groups within the military institution as that would call into question its homogeneity.

9.3.2 *The Moderate Armed Groups*

The Russian intervention turned around the dynamics of the conflict and from December 2015 onwards gave rise to a general framework for the post-war period reflected by the terms of resolution 2254 adopted unanimously by the members of the UN Security Council. The two groups historically derived from Al-Qaida in Syria, that is, Daesh and the Al-Nusra Front, as well as the fanatical armed groups affiliated to them were automatically excluded. Unfortunately what seemed to be obvious was not self-evident for all the opponents of the Damascus regime. While abandoning Daesh to its fate did not raise too many questions,[21] at least on the

---

[21] In September 2017, the Syrian army lifted a three years siege of Deir Ezzor and the following month the Kurdish lead militia, Syrian Democratic Forces (SDF), liberated Raqqa from Daesh.

surface of things, giving up on the Al-Nusra Front was a dilemma not to say a torment for its regional and international sponsors and even among certain Syrian opponents who purported to be moderates, to the extent that, at times, some members of the opposition attending the Geneva talks gave the impression they were nothing other than Al-Nusra's political wing. In fact, many of the Damascus government's opponents did not want to abandon the Al-Nusra Front because they considered it to be the most effective armed group in the fight against the Syrian army; but they could not say so openly nor support them publicly because of Al-Nusra's terrorist affiliation.

Most of 2016 was spent by Russian diplomacy looking for a practical way to remove Al-Nusra from the military and political equation. Jordan had been tasked by the International Syria Support Group at the second Vienna conference in November 2015 with identifying the terrorist groups so as to separate them from the other armed groups. It failed in this. At the same time, Saudi Arabia saw to the establishment of a common opposition delegation to negotiate with the Syrian government in Geneva. This led to the creation of the High Negotiations Committee that included the Coalition, the Coordination, the main components of the domestic opposition, and other entities based abroad, including certain armed groups that could have been included on the list of terrorist groups had it been drawn up. But the High Negotiations Committee left out some major components of the opposition such as those gathered around the Cairo Platform, the Moscow Platform, and the Kurds affiliated to the PYD. That is why the representative character and the credibility of the High Negotiations Committee were contested from the outset. The attitude of its members during the 2016 Geneva negotiations, who were more eager to grant interviews to the big international media than to negotiate even indirectly with the government delegation, was also criticized. The composition and sponsorship of this institution made it heavily dependent on Saudi Arabia.

The powers hostile to Damascus who knew full well that the Al-Nusra Front was the mainstay of the rebel armed groups, except for Daesh, mobilized so that a list of terrorist groups could not be established. They did all they could to save the groups affiliated to Al-Nusra, not to say Al-Nusra itself. Some even suggested it change its name and officially cut all ties with Al-Qaida. It did so in July 2016 becoming 'The Front for the Conquest of the Levant'. But this subterfuge made no difference to the group's ideology and practices. In supporting Al-Nusra, its sponsors aborted the application of the Vienna Declaration, the Geneva 3 talks, the ending of hostilities called for by the Munich Declaration of February 2016, and the Russo-American agreement of September 2016. It was only with the partial turnaround of Turkey, Aleppo being taken by the Syrian army and its allies in December 2016, the tripartite Moscow declaration by Russia, Iran, and Turkey, the UN Security Council resolution 2236, and the Astana talks in January 2017 in which several armed groups participated that such a list began to see the light of day.

Potential partners for peace talks among the armed opposition groups were identified during the Astana process. In 2017, several rounds of indirect talks between the Syrian government and representatives from the armed groups took place in Astana. Having Russia, Turkey, and Iran as guarantors made the Astana process an efficient forum to reduce tension. Several important decisions were taken during the different rounds of the talks, such as the establishment and consolidation of a ceasefire, and the establishment and implementation of several de-escalation zones. However, progress could not be achieved on all humanitarian issues and in particular the adoption of confidence-building measures on the release of detainees, abductees, the handover of bodies, and identification of missing persons. At the end of the seventh round of the Astana talks in October 2017, Russia announced its intention to host in Sotchi a Syrian congress for national dialogue. The Astana process has therefore contributed to identifying a political solution to the crisis in parallel to the Geneva process that had limited success during Geneva 4 in March 2017. The Geneva talks focused afterwards on organizing expert meetings that were by nature exploratory and non-binding in preparation for the next round of intra-Syria talks in Geneva.

9.3.3 *The Kurdish Component*

Bolstered by the progression of Kurdish forces and their allies on the ground against Daesh in 2015 with the retaking of the cities of Ain Al-Arab (Kobane) in January followed by Tel Al-Abyad in June, and then their advance towards the Euphrates, and disappointed at the PYD being kept out of the Geneva talks, the three cantons of Rajova (Jezira, Kobane, and Afrin) with large Kurdish populations that proclaimed themselves autonomous announced unilaterally in March 2016 their intention to create a Kurdish federation in northern Syria. This announcement was rejected out of hand by all the components of the opposition, across the board, including those closest to the Kurdish movements such as Haytham Manna as well as by the central authority in Damascus. The announcement caused great concern in Turkey, which feared seeing a Kurdish belt developing on its southern border running from Afrin as far as the border with Iraq and that would adjoin the Turkish provinces with high concentrations of Kurds. Towards the end of 2017 the Kurdish-led militias controlled 20 to 25 per cent of Syria's territory.

The areas predominantly populated by Syrian Kurds have experienced the civil war in a specific way. After the withdrawal of most of the Syrian armed forces from the extreme north of the country in 2012, except for the cities of Qamishli and Hassake, the PYD close to the Turkish PKK according to Ankara and the Kurd National Council, which was a new body created in 2012 and close to the authorities of Iraqi Kurdistan, grouped within the Kurd Supreme Council to set up an autonomous administration to fill the void created by the paralysis and even the disappearance of certain basic services provided by the Syrian state and its territorial administration. The PYD, through its armed branch (YPG), became the main force in the three self-proclaimed autonomous cantons. In January 2014, elected assemblies in the three cantons brought together under the Movement for a Democratic Society adopted a constitution for the autonomous region of Rajova entitled the Social Contract Charter. Although tailor-made for a population that in principle was mainly Kurd, the constitution was multi-ethnic and multicultural in character and set itself within the framework of the Syrian state. Article 12 stated that 'the autonomous regions are an integral part of Syria and form a model for a future decentralized system of governance of Syria'. In October 2015, the PYD and local militias close to it (Syriac-Assyrians, Arabs, etc.) formed a military coalition named the Syrian Democratic Forces. Two months later, a Federal Assembly grouping representatives of the assemblies of the three cantons elected a political body, the Democratic Syrian Council. This Council was to be the political branch of the Syrian Democratic Forces. In March 2016, after the PYD members had been kept out of the Geneva 3 negotiations by a Turkish veto, the autonomous assemblies grouped under the Movement for a Democratic Society met in congress in the city of Roumeilane in Hassake province and unilaterally proclaimed the Federation of Northern Syria-Rajova. A draft constitution was presented in July 2016. It was revised and then adopted in December 2016. The word 'Rajova' was dropped from the federation's name in the end. The constitution took up the multicultural and multi-ethnic aspects of the 2014 constitution.[22]

Damascus gave tacit support to the administration of the three self-proclaimed autonomous cantons. This experiment fitted into the framework of a local administration adapted to the exceptional circumstances the country was going through. This position also reflected a de facto alliance on the ground between the PYD and the Syrian army both of which were fighting Daesh. However, Damascus openly criticized the PYD's stated intention of moving from autonomy to federation.

Is Syria called upon to become a federal or bi-national state because of the presence of a Kurd community among its population? The question is worth asking. Before answering, it is worth recalling a few facts and figures. Syria reportedly had 17 million inhabitants in 2016 after the departure of some 5 million refugees for neighbouring countries and 1 million to Europe. Arabs make up 90 per cent of the population. The remaining 10 per cent, nearly 1.7 million, are mostly Kurds but also Turkmens, Armenians, Assyrians, Syriac, Circassians, and others. By way of comparison it can be recalled that Turkey reportedly has nearly 19 per cent of Kurds in a population of 80 million, which corresponds to almost 15.2 million. Iraq supposedly has 15–20 per cent of Kurds in a population of 38 million, so between 5.7 and 7.6 million.[23] In Iran, the number of Kurds is put at between 4 and 5 million out of a total population of 82 million.

The number of Kurds in Syria is far lower than in other countries because the historic sites of the Kurdish people are mainly in Turkey and Iraq. In Syria, neither history, nor geography, nor numbers can serve as a basis for calling for a federal or bi-national state between a population that is made up of 90 per cent Arabs and just 10 per cent Kurds. Separation is impossible too, because northern Syria is a region where the population is tangled, multi-ethnic, and multicultural. The Kurds are certainly in the majority in some areas but not necessarily so over the entire space that is supposed to be part of the future federation. Nor is it certain that most Syrian Kurds are in favour of a federal project. What is certain, though, is that the legitimate rights of Kurds and other components of Syria must be fully recognized, guaranteed by the future constitution, and implemented

---

[22] For an English version of the constitution of the Federation of Northern Syria, see https://en.wikisource.org/wiki/Constitution_of_Rojava.

[23] The figures for Syria, Turkey, and Iraq come from the Central Intelligence Agency's 'The World Factbook' at www.cia.gov/library/publications/the-world-factbook/. Those for Iran are an estimation from the Wikipedia page on 'Iranian Kurdistan'.

through ingenious and generous democratic administrative decentralization. The institutions, structures, and mechanisms for doing this will have to be negotiated and approved in the framework of the future constitution.

The circumstances for drawing up the constitution that will bring about the Sixth Republic are very different from those that engendered the previous ones. Syrians would like the process to unfold without foreign intervention. But is this realistic, given the multiple foreign interventions and interferences, both military and political, with and without the central government's authorization, not forgetting the Security Council resolutions? And yet, regardless of circumstances, this constitution will ultimately have to be discussed and drafted by Syrians and then approved by popular vote. If it is to be Syrian, it will have to reflect the values of its society and the historical personality of the national community. Will it once again take up the national project of the Founding Fathers? This will only be known once the war is over. What is for sure is that the war has traumatized society and individuals. Some questioning of identities or cultures cannot be excluded, such as the accentuation of the Syrian identity and the propagation of secular and liberal values. But it is unlikely such questioning will affect the major principles of the Syrian national project established by the Founding Fathers and developed by subsequent generations.

Conclusion

Return to the Syrian Question

Over close on two centuries, various schemes have been proposed and trialled for Syria. Some, such as Mohamad Ali and Ibrahim Pasha between 1831 and 1841, Napoleon III, the Victorian British government in 1860, King Faysal under the Syrian monarchy 1918–20, and the US King–Crane commission despatched by President Woodrow Wilson in 1919, saw Syria as stretching over all of the Near East, encompassing the territories that now form Syria, Lebanon, Jordan, Palestine/Israel, and a part of Turkey. In contrast to this expansive Syria embracing and including all sectarian and ethnic diversity, others saw a retiring Syria, carved up into local political and religious entities. In the forefront of these were the colonial party in France under the Third Republic, Robert de Caix and the supporters of a return of the Jews to Palestine such as Lloyd George and Lord Balfour in 1917–19. These two antithetical conceptions of Syria survive today in one form or another. The idea of an integrated Syria as it exists today, or even an integral Syria if it were to extend to the whole of the Near East, continues to stand against the idea of a disintegrated or even non-existent Syria.

With independence, Syrians managed to partially piece back together some of the territories hived off by France (the States of Damascus and Aleppo, the Alawi and Druze territories). But that was not enough and Syrians attempted to forge unions with variable geometries. Syria agreed to merge with others into states that did not always come about, but whose territory was in principle to extend, depending on the case, from the Iranian border to the Libyan desert by way of Egypt, or from the Tigris and Euphrates to the Algerian border, again by way of Egypt.

While Syria agreed to commit its body to pan-Arab states, it never gave up its soul. Whatever its actual or supposed borders, whatever the extent of its national territory, ranging from near-disappearance to resurrection, from the infinitely small to the infinitely large, Syria has continued for a century to pursue the main objectives of a national project set out by its Founding Fathers in 1919, even through its merger with other Arab states. Syria's grandeur has never been tied to the extent of its territorial space, but rather to the character of its national project. In this sense, Syria remains first and foremost an idea and an ideal to be achieved.

When the French version of this book came out in 2014 Syria was mired in a bloodbath with no one able to predict whether what it was facing were growing pains or an existential crisis. The very foundations of its national project and of the nation state seemed threatened. In some respects, the crisis resembled that of 1860 in terms of local and regional dynamics and the stands taken by the major powers, one of the major challenges being the creation of a new regional order. As the English version of the book comes out in 2018, Syria seems, to the surprise of many, to have overcome the risk of disintegration and to have preserved its national project and survived as a nation state. But no one can yet predict what form the end of the conflict will take or what the new regional order, in which Syria will have to find its place, will be like.

What is certain, though, is that with or without a Syrian crisis, the absence of a peaceful solution to the Palestinian question may well eventually entail the disintegration of the Near East into small sectarian or ethnic entities, much like Israel itself.[1] Israel's leaders have taken out of mothballs the plans concocted in 1982 at the height of the confrontation between the authorities in Damascus and the Muslim Brotherhood on the eve of the invasion of Lebanon and are beginning again to envision the possibility of Syria breaking up into a State of Aleppo that would be opposed to another state based in Damascus and other micro-entities on the Alawite coast and in the Druze mountains. In short, a return to General Gouraud's Syria of 1920.[2] Any dismembering of Syria along sectarian and ethnic lines would have dramatic repercussions and could spread throughout the region. The cohesion of the Syrian army, despite

---

[1] See Labévière and El-Atrache, *Quand la Syrie s'éveillera ...*, pp. 62–92.
[2] 'The break down of Lebanon into five provinces foreshadows the fate awaiting the entire Arab world, including Egypt, Syria, Iraq, and the whole of the Arabian peninsula. In Lebanon it is a *fait accompli*. The break-up of Syria and Iraq into ethnically and religiously homogeneous provinces as in Lebanon is Israel's long-term priority on its eastern front; in the short term, the aim is the military dissolution of these states. Syria is going to divide up into several states, by ethnic communities, in such a way that the coast will become a Shi'ite Alawi state; the Aleppo region a Sunnite state; Damascus another Sunnite state hostile to its northern neighbour; the Druze will form their own state, which will stretch to our (*sic*) Golan Heights and in any event to the Hawran and northern Jordan. This state will guarantee long-term peace and security in the region: it is an objective that is now within our reach.' Oded Yinon, senior official at the Israeli ministry of foreign affairs, in the journal of the World Zionist Organization, *Kivunim* (*Orientations*), 14 February 1982, quoted in Labévière and El-Atrache, *Quand la Syrie s'éveillera...*, pp. 62 and 85 (our translation).

some painful defections, and the support of broad sectors of public opinion for the military and the regime have so far prevented such a scenario.[3]

The instinctive and immediate satisfaction of Israel and its allies with the possible dismemberment of Syria was to be short-lived. For no state in the region, even the most powerful – namely, Israel – has yet successfully formed a modern nation-state based on the concept of citizenship. Since 1967 the whole of the former British mandate territory of Palestine has been under the control of Israel and the population living there today is ethnically practically half Jewish, citizens of the State of Israel, and half Palestinian, some of whom are second-class Israeli citizens while the others live under occupation and in conditions of apartheid.[4]

The Jewish State has worked itself into an ideological and strategic blind alley from which it is finding it hard to escape. Israel is unable to accept the possibility of a long-term presence of Arab Israelis whose numbers are growing incessantly. Similarly Israel is unable to find a solution to the Palestinian question, refusing the only two possible options; an independent Palestinian state on the West Bank and in Gaza with East Jerusalem as its capital, or that of a bi-national Israeli–Palestinian state. These two options would be contrary to the national project of the Founding Fathers of Israel to create a Jewish State in Palestine. The only way for Israel to be able to continue its occupation for some time to come is through the disintegration of the Near East until a Palestinian state can be created there, in Jordan or the Sinai, and most of the Palestinians transferred there including perhaps those who currently have Israeli nationality.

Failing this scenario, Israelis will have to face the consequences and acknowledge what today is a hard political fact and an inescapable demographic reality, namely, that it is impossible to create a Jewish state covering the whole of mandate Palestine and that their national project in its

---

[3] The most significant defection was by General Manaf Tlass, commander of the 105th regiment of the presidential guard, a personal friend of President Bashar Assad, son of the former defence minister, General Mustafa Tlass, a staunch ally of President Hafez Assad. Having taken a firm position against the use of violence against civilians and having supported a policy of reconciliation, General Manaf Tlass found his initiatives overruled by hardliners. Refusing to be implicated in acts and decisions against his military principles, he thus decided to retreat, attempting from France to gather moderates from both sides to work towards an exit plan solution.

[4] On the apartheid of the Israeli occupation policy, see the book by former US President and Nobel prize winner, Jimmy Carter, *Palestine: Peace Not Apartheid*. See also former Israeli prime minister Ehud Barak's June 2016 speech at the conference on Israel's security at Herzliya at: www.herzliyaconference.org/eng/?CategoryID=555&ArticleID=2760.

initial form has failed. Unfortunately, such a realization does not seem to be on the agenda. Since the October 1973 War, Israeli society has grown more radical and has shifted to the right mainly because of an electoral law based on full proportional representation. This electoral system has favoured small religious and nationalist parties that are little inclined to compromise and that for four decades have imposed values on the entire electorate and the major political formations that they did not necessarily share initially. And yet, this society is changing despite its radicalization. It is paradoxical to see that some of the courageous stances taken by senior military personnel exhibit a lucidity and critical faculties that the great majority of the political class has long since lost.[5] It is equally paradoxical and heartening to see on the bestsellers lists a book that goes against the tide in praising a passionate relationship between an Israeli woman and Palestinian man.[6]

The failure to settle the Palestinian question because of the intransigent policies pursued by successive Israeli governments has characterized the Near East since Bashar Assad came to power in July 2000. It has also exacerbated the Syrian and Israeli national projects, that were already antithetical, by opposing them one against the other more than ever. For as long as these two national projects continue to be mutually exclusive, it will probably be difficult to reach a peace agreement between Syrians and Israelis and more broadly between Arabs and Israelis. All the formulas that have been tried so far have proved to be limited.[7] Talks held

---

[5] In a speech in honour of Holocaust Remembrance Day in May 2016, Israel's deputy chief of staff, General Yair Golan, likened developments in Israeli society to processes that unfolded in Europe before the Holocaust. 'If there's something that frightens me about Holocaust remembrance it's the recognition of the revolting processes that occurred in Europe in general, and particularly in Germany, back then – 70, 80 and 90 years ago – and finding signs of them here among us today in 2016.' Two weeks later, Israeli minister of defence General Moshe Ya'alon, who backed his deputy chief of staff, resigned saying, 'But to my great sorrow, extremist and dangerous elements have taken over Israel and the Likud Party and are shaking the foundations and threatening to hurt its residents.'

[6] Dorit Rabinyan, *Geder Haya* (Am Oved, 2014); published in English as *All The Rivers* (Random House, 2017).

[7] The peace agreements between Egypt and Israel (1978–79), Jordan and Israel (1994), the Oslo Accords between Palestinians and Israelis (1993), and the various bilateral relations woven between the Jewish State and certain countries of the Gulf and North Africa have not extended to all Arab countries. Only a negotiated agreement with Syria could have such a geopolitical impact because, historically, when the Arab provinces of the Ottoman empire separated a century ago, of all the Arab states that emerged only Syria developed a national project with a regional dimension including Palestine.

in the Madrid process between Damascus and Tel Aviv failed in 2000 after nine years of negotiations with the active support of the USA, probably because they mainly focused on the territorial aspect of the conflict between the two countries, namely the extent of the Golan Heights to be returned to Syria, instead of concentrating on conciliation between two antagonistic national projects. Territorial negotiation is a sterile attempt to clear up a past in which Syrians and Israelis were always in disagreement whereas an attempted conciliation between two opposing national projects would be about exploring a common future.

One month after Bashar Assad became president, the failure of the Israeli–Palestinian peace process begun in Madrid in 1991 was consecrated at Camp David because of Ehud Barak's inflexibility, while President Clinton looked on powerless despite the painful concessions made by Arafat since the signing of the Oslo Accords in September 1993. The failure at Camp David heralded a second *intifada* that effectively began in September 2000.

Despite their dramatic character, developments on the Palestinian stage did not directly affect Syria. It was Al-Qaeda's terrorist attacks on the USA in September 2001 that were to have the greatest impact on the Near East and on Syria. The USA used them as a pretext, after having unsurprisingly attacked Afghanistan and driven out Al-Qaeda, to launch an assault on Iraq, which had strictly nothing to do with those attacks. This detail did not weigh heavily in the Bush administration's decision to attack Iraq at any cost, without any mandate from the United Nations Security Council, to destroy supposed weapons of mass destruction and establish democracy there. Having occupied Iraq and dismantled its national institutions, the Americans realized that the country had no weapons of mass destruction. Undaunted, the neoconservatives in Washington decided to pursue their ideological intent and by way of democracy endowed Iraq with a constitution and electoral law that promoted sectarian and ethnic identities. The invasion of Iraq and its reshaping at the cost of millions of victims, refugees, and displaced persons was just the first step in the creation of a new 'Greater Middle East' dear to the Bush administration and that was bound at one point or other to include Syria unless it changed its policy primarily with respect to the USA and Israel.[8]

---

[8] See the list of US complaints against Syria in Frum and Perle, *An End to Evil*, pp. 97–8.

CONCLUSION

While the USA was bogged down in Iraq, Iran emerged as the main beneficiary of the fall of Saddam Hussein's regime. The two wars of the Bush administration (Afghanistan and Iraq) had eliminated the two neighbours most hostile to the Tehran regime. The Americans had pulled down the barriers that had contained Iran within its borders. From then on, nothing could stop Iran from projecting its influence towards the Eastern Mediterranean and Central Asia. The adoption of resolution 1559 in September 2004 and the campaign by the western nations and Gulf states against Syria after the assassination of former Lebanese prime minister Rafic Hariri for which political responsibility was immediately ascribed to Damascus, isolated Syria within its Arab environment, led to the withdrawal of Syrian forces from Lebanon, and pushed Damascus even closer to Iran. This phenomenon was accentuated when Ahmadinajad came to power in Tehran in 2005. When Israel launched its attack against Hizbullah in Lebanon in July 2006, Damascus and Tehran lent their unflagging support to the Lebanese resistance.

The 2006 war confirmed the deep divisions running through the Arab world. For the first time in the history of the Arab–Israeli conflict, some Arab leaders lent towards Israel without daring to admit as much in public. The victory of the Lebanese resistance was felt to be a weakening of the 'moderate' Arab camp. In Damascus, the victory was considered a victory for Syria and its regional political choices. This defeat of Israel was repeated two years later when the Israeli army, despite its crushing superiority, was unable to penetrate more than a few hundred metres into the Gaza Strip. Two humiliating defeats for Israel in the space of two years. It was something to worry the supporters of the Greater Middle East and reassure their opponents, in the vanguard of which was Syria, which set greater store than ever on support for resistance movements, as attested by Bashar Assad's speech at Deir Ezzor, on 30 April 2007 during the campaign for his re-election for a second term of office:

> Syria as well as the Arab region and the Near East are now at the turning point of a new stage that is just as dangerous as the previous stages they have been through. They have to face up to colonialist schemes to occupy, destroy, or carve up the region to create a new Sykes–Picot agreement. What we observe in our region generally is a fight between the possible success or failure of these schemes. To be more specific, we are witnessing the likely failure of the plan for a new Near East. Results so far do not seem to be favourable for this project. Iraq is resisting to the east, Lebanon is resisting to the west, and the Palestinians are resisting to the south. We in Syria are not in the centre but at the heart of these resistances. There

> is a big difference between being in the centre and being at the heart of these events. However, we must not underestimate our enemies and our rivals despite their failures. They still have cards up their sleeves which they pull out from time to time to revive their dead plans. And today they have pulled out their last card, that of discord and break up. The card that prompts one resistance force to fight another! The card that impels the resistance force to defend the occupier ... that is their plan.[9]

This speech clearly reflects the Syrian president's state of mind and sounds like a warning of the dangers to come. The victories of his Lebanese and Palestinian allies gave President Assad an opportunity to concentrate on the country's internal affairs. His popularity would probably have enabled him to amend a political system that had become obsolete and was barely representative of Syrian society. The Syrian president was unable to take the opportunity to look to the country's internal affairs. In supporting the resistance movements against Israel, in fighting foreign hegemony over the Near East in the form of the Greater Middle East, in refusing sectarian division and the break-up of the region, Bashar Assad was following the line of the national project of Syria's Founding Fathers. But in the regional context of 2011, this position was perceived as a radicalization not so much because of the Syrian national project, which was almost a century old, but more because of the strategic relations tied with Iran, a country rightly or wrongly considered a threat by the Gulf leaders, the West, and Israel. The hardening of Iran's regional policy between 2005 and 2015 under the Ahmadinajad presidency had dramatic repercussions on Syria's position within its regional setting. So did Syria's refusal to allow its territory to be crossed by a gas pipeline from Qatar to Turkey that would have competed with Russia's gas supply to Europe and a similar Iranian plan.

Syria's future and more broadly the future of the region is in danger of wavering further between integration and disintegration until a solution is found to the Palestinian problem. The concept of Syria is an antidote to the region's disintegration. This concept has proved to be a generous framework that brings people together and protects minorities; it is a formula that makes it easier to live together as a multi-religious, multi-sectarian, and multicultural community. If, at the end of this crisis, Syria manages to hold together and to bestow on itself an authentically

---

[9] See www.youtube.com/watch?v=6I8D9BsI_IQ.

pluralistic, liberal, and democratic political regime, then the concept of Syria will enjoy a new lease of life. Syria will once again be seen as an idea that holds promise for the future; as an inclusive setting open to all and excluding none; as a setting that integrates without assimilating; a setting that is respectful of everyone's personality and the historical road they have travelled.

Annex

Summary Table of Constitutional Architectures

Political regime	Constitution	Constituent assembly	Legislative assembly	President	Electoral law	Law on political parties
Monarchy 1918–20	1920	1919 [1]	1919 [1]	King [20]	1876 [14]	No
First Republic 1928–49	1928	1928 [2]	1931/1932, 1936, 1943, 1947 [3]	(1932, 1936, 1943, 1948) [9]	1928 [21], 1947 [15]	No
Second Republic						
1949–51	1949 [4]	1949 [1]	1949 [1]	(1949, 1950, 1955, 1961) [9]	1949 [15]	No
1954–58	1950	1961 [1]	1954 [3]		1954 [15]	
1961–63	1961 [4] [5]		1961 [1]		1957 [16]	
	1962				1961 [16]	
Third Republic 1951–54	1953 [5]	No	1953 [3]	1953 [10]	1953 [16]	1953 [17]
Fourth Republic 1963–2012	1964 [4]	1971 [7]	(1964, 1965, 1966, 1971) [8] (1973, 1977, 1981, 1986, 1990, 1994, 1998, 2003, 2007) [3]	(1964, 1965, 1966) [11] 1966 [12] (1971, 1978, 1985, 1991, 1999, 2000, 2007) [13]	1973 [16] 2011 [16]	2011 [17]
	1966 [6]					
	1969 [4]					
	1971 [4]					
	1973 [5]					
Fifth Republic 2012–present	2012 [5]	No	(2012, 2016) [3]	2014 [18]	2014 [19]	

The table omits:

- The 1923 electoral procedure and elections organized by France for representative councils in the States of Damascus and Aleppo and in the Alawite State during the period of the Syrian Federation (1922–25).
- The partial elections organized by France in 1926 during the State of Syria period (1926–28/30).
- The constitutional referendum organized by Husni Al-Zaim in June 1949 to legitimize his regime.
- The United Arab Republic regime and constitution (1958–61), the Federation of Arab Republics constitution (1970), and the United Arab Republic Tripartite Charter (1963).

[1] Election of a constituent and legislative assembly. Members of the 1919 assembly, the Syrian Congress, were elected in the east zone and co-opted in the west and south zones.
[2] Partial elections organized by France in 1926 during the State of Syria period (1926–28/30).
[3] Election of legislative assembly.
[4] Provisional constitution.
[5] Constitution approved by popular referendum.
[6] Constitutional arrangement implemented by Ba'th.
[7] Constituent and legislative assembly appointed by Ba'th.
[8] Councils with legislative functions appointed by Ba'th.
[9] Election of president by assembly members.
[10] Election of president by direct universal suffrage with single candidate.
[11] Collegiate power exercised by presidential council that elects a president from among its members.
[12] Head of state appointed by Ba'th.
[13] Election of president of the republic by popular referendum.
[14] 1876 Ottoman law (two-tier ballot).
[15] Electoral law or legislative decree (two-round majority ballot).
[16] Electoral law or legislative decree (single-round majority ballot).
[17] Legislative decree on political parties.
[18] Presidential election by single-round direct universal ballot with multiple candidates.
[19] Law on local, legislative, presidential elections, and referendums.
[20] Faysal I proclaimed King of Syria by Syrian Congress on 8 March 1920.
[21] 1928 order of high commissioner on electoral procedure (two-tier ballot).

ARABIC BIBLIOGRAPHY

Books

Abou Saleh Abdel Qadous and Al-Hachemi Mohamad Ali, *Mouzakarat Al-Doctor Ma'arouf Al-Dawalibi (The Memoirs of Doctor Ma'arouf Dawalibi)* (Al-'Obeikat, Riyadh, 2005).

Abu Mussa, *Al-'Aquid Abou Moussa Yatakalam 'An Al-Harb Al-Khamissa Wa Soumoud Beirut (Colonel Abu Mussa Speaks of the Fifth War and Resistance of Beirut)* (Dar Al-Jalil, Damascus, 1984).

Aflaq Michel, *Fi Sabil Al-Baath, Al-Kitabat Al-Siyasiya Al-Kamila, (For the Ba'th, Complete Works)*, vols I, II, III, IV, V (Arab Socialist Ba'th Party, Baghdad, 1986).

Nouqtat Al Bidayya (The Starting Point) (Al Mou'assa Al-Arabia Lilnacher, Beirut, 1975).

Al-Amin Hassan, *Sarab Al-Istiqlal Fi Bilad Al-Cham 1918–1920 (The Mirage of Independence in the Land of Sham 1918–1920)* (Riad El-Rayyes Books, Beirut 1998).

Al-Armanazi Najib, *Souriya Min Al-Ihtilal Hata Al-Jala'a (Syria from Occupation to Independence)* (Dar Al-Kitab Al-Jadid, Beirut, 2nd edition, 1973).

Al-'Ayssami Chibli, *Rissalat Al-Ouma Al-Arabia (The Message of the Arab Nation)* (Al-Moassassa Al-Arabia lil-Dirassat Wa Al-Nacher, Beirut, 1980).

Al-Ba'ini Hassan Amin, *Drouz souriya wa lubnan fi 'ahd al-intidab al-faransi 1920–1934 (The Druze in Syria and Lebanon during the Period of the French Mandate 1920–1934)* (Al-Markaz Al-Arabi Li-Al-Abhath Wa Al-Taouthiq, Beirut, 1993).

Alaywi Hadi Hassan, *Faysal Bin Al-Hussein, Mou'assess Al-Hikm Al-Arabi Fi Souriya Wa Al-Irak, 1883–1933 (Faysal Bin Al-Hussein, Founder of the Arab Government in Syria and in Iraq, 1883–1933)* (Riad El-Rayyes, Beirut, 2003).

Al-Ghali Kamal, *Mabade' Al-Qanoun Al-Doustouri Wa Al-Nozom Al-Siyassiya (The Principles of Constitutional Law and Political Regimes)* (Damascus University, 2000–2001).

Al-Hakim Hassan, *Al-Watha'ek Al-Tarikhia Al-Muta'alika Bi-Al-Quadiya Al-Souriya Fi Al-'Ahdienne Al-Arabi Al-Faysali Wa Al-Intidab Al-Faransi 1915–1946*

(Historical Records on the Syrian Question during the Arab Period of Faysal and the French Mandate 1915–1946) (Dar Sader, Beirut, 1974).

Al-Hakim Youssef, *Beyrout Wa Loubnan Fi Al-'Ahd Al-Osmani (Beirut and Lebanon during the Ottoman Period)*, vol. II (Dar Al-Nahar, Beirut, 1991).

Souriya Wa Al-'Ahd Al-Osmani (Syria during the Ottoman Period), vol. I (Dar Al-Nahar, Beirut, 1991).

Souriya Wa Al-Ahd Al-Faysali (Syria under Faysal's Reign), vol. III (Dar Al-Nahar, Beirut, 1986).

Souriya Wa Al-Intitab Al-Faransi (Syria and the French Mandate), vol. IV (Dar Al-Nahar, Beirut, 1983).

Al-Husri Sati, *Yaoum Mayssaloun, Safaha Min Tarikh Al-Arab Al-Hadith (The Day of Maysalun, A Page of the Arabs' Contemporary History)* (Ministry of Culture Publications, Damascus, 2004).

Al-Jundi Sami, *El-Baas (The Ba'th)* (Dar Al-Nahar, Beirut 1969).

Al-Kayali Nizar, *Dirassa Fi Tarikh Souriya Al-Siyassi Al-Mou'aser 1920–1950 (Study of Syrian Contemporary Political History 1920–1950)* (Tlass, Damascus, 1997).

Al-Khani Abdallah Fakri, *Jihad Choukri Qouwatli Fi Sabil Al-Istiklal Wa Al-Wahda (Shukri Qwatli's Fight for Independence and Union)* (Al-Nafaeiss, Beirut, 2003).

Souriya Bayn Al-Dimoucratiya Wa Al-Hokm Al-Fardi, 'Achr Sanaouat Fi Al-Amana Al-'Ayma Li-Riassat Al-Joumhouriya, 1948–1958 (Syria between Democracy and Personal Power, Ten Years in the General Secretariat of the Office of President of the Republic, 1948–1958) (Dar Al-Nafaess, Damascus, 2004).

Al-Mouallem Walid, *Souriya 1918–1958 Al-Tahadi Wa Al-Mouwajaha (Syria 1918–1958, Challenge and Confrontation)* (Babel, Nicosia, 1985).

Al-Omari Soubhi, *Al-Ma'arek Al-Oula, Al-Tarik Ila Dimashq (The First Combats, The Road to Damascus)*, (Riad El-Rayyes, Cyprus, 1991).

Lorens, Al-Haquiqua Wa Al-Oukzouba (Lawrence, Truth and Lies) (Riad El-Rayyes, Cyprus, 1991).

Mayssaloun, Nihayet 'Ahd (Maysalun, The End of A Regime) (Riad El-Rayyes, Cyprus, 1991).

Al-Sayyed Jalal, *Hizb Al-Ba'th Al-Arabi (The Ba'th Arab Party)* (Dar Al-Nahar, Beirut, 1973).

Al-Sharaa Farouk, *Al-Riwaya Al-Mafkouda (The Missing Account)* (Arab Center for Research & Policy Studies, Doha, 2015).

Arab Socialist Ba'th Party, *Al-Mou'tamarat Al-Qotriya Lihizb Al-Baas Al-Arabi Al-Ichtiraki Fi Al-Qotr Al-Arabi Al-Souri (The Arab Socialist Ba'th Party Regional Congresses in the Syrian Arab Region)* (National Command, Office for Culture and Executive Training, Dar Al-Baas Printers).

Taquarir Al Mou'tamar Al Qotri Al-Khames (Reports of the Eighth Regional Congress) (Publications of the Regional Command of the Ba'th Party, Damascus, 1986).

Some Theoretical Foundations Adopted by the Sixth National Congress (Damascus, 6th edition, 1976).

Ase'ayed Mohamed Shaker, *Al Barlaman Al Sury Fi Tatawurihi Al Tarikhi (Historical Development of the Syrian Parliament)* (Dar Al Mada Lil Thakafeh Wa Al Nachr, Damascus, 2002).

Atassi Mohammed Radwan, *Hachem Atassi, Hayatahou – 'Asrahou (Hashim Atassi, His Life – His Times)* (Damascus 2005).

Atrash Mansour, *Al-Jil Al-Moudan (The Cursed Generation)* (Riyyad El-Rayyes Books, Beirut, 2008).

Al-Azzem Khaled, *Mouzakarat Khaled Al-Azzem (Memoirs of Khaled Al-Azzem)*, vols I, II, III (Dar Al-Moutahida Lil-Nacher, Beirut, 2003).

Al-Azzme Béchir, *Jil Al Hazima Min Al-Zakira (The Generation of the Defeat of Memory)*, (Al-Mo'assassa Al-Arabiya Lil-'Ilam Wa Al-Nachr, Beirut, 2nd edition, 1998).

Babeel Nassouh, *Sahafeh Wa Siyasset Souria Fi Al-Quarn Al-Echrin (Twentieth-Century Syrian Journalism and Politics)* (Riad El-Rayyes Books, Great Britain, 2nd edition, 2001).

Balqziz Abdel-Ilah, *Riyah Al-Takhyir Fi Al-Watan Al-Arabi (Winds of Change in the Arab World)*, Discussion Workshops on Egypt, Morocco, and Syria (Markaz Dirassat Al-Wahde Al-Arabiya, Beirut, 2011).

Baroud Jamal Mohamed and Keilani Chams Al-Din, *Souria Bayn Ahdayin Qadaya Al-Marhala Al-Intiqalia (Syria Between Two Reigns: The Questions of the Transitional Period)* (Dar Sindibad, Amman, 2003).

Darwaza Mohamed Ezzat, *Hawl Al-Harake Al-Arabiya Al-Haditha (On the Modern Arab Movement)* Part One (Al-Matba'a Al-Assriye, Saïda, 1950).

Esber Amin, *Tataour Al-Nozom Al-Siyassiya Wa Al-Dastouiya FI Souriya, 1946–1973 (The Development of Political and Constitutional Regimes in Syria, 1946–1973)* (Dar Al-Nahar, Beirut, 1979).

Fansa Nazir, *Ayam Hosni al-Za'im, 137 Yaouman Hazat Souriya, (The Days of Husni Al-Zaim, 137 Days that Shook Syria)* (Dar al-afaq al-jadida, Beirut, 1983).

Farah Elias, *Qiraa Manhajiya Fi Kitab Fi Sabil Al-Baath Al-Jize Al-Awal (A Methodological Reading of 'For the Ba'th' Volume I)* (Al-Mouassa Al-Arabiya Lil-Dirassat Wa Al-Nacher, Beirut, 1981).

Hafez Yassin, *Al-Hazima Wa Al-Ideologia Al-Mahsouma (The Defeat and the Vanquished Ideology)* (Dar Al-Tali'a, Beirut, 1979).

Haidar Rustom, *Muzakarat Rustom Haidar (The Memoirs of Rustom Haidar)*, presented by Najdat Fathi (Al Dar Al-Arabia Lil-Maoussou'at, Beirut, 1988).

Hallak Abdallah Yorki, *Al-Thaourat Al-Souriya Al-Kubra Fi Rub' Quarn 1918–1945 (The Great Syrian Revolts in the Quarter Century 1918–1945)* (Tlass, Damascus, 1990).

Hamdan Hamdan, *Akram Haurani, Rajol Lil-Tarikh (Akram Hawrani, A Man for History)* (Bisan, Beirut, 1996).

Hawrani Akram, *Mouzakarat (Memoirs)*, vols I, II, III, IV (Madbouli, Cairo, 2000).
Hussein Lu'ay, Al-Azzem Sadek Jalal, Ghalioun Burhan, Tarabishi George, Ezzedin Fayez, Tezini Tayeb, Sa'id Jawdat, Neirabiye Mowafak, and Barut Jamal, *Hiwarat Fi Al-Wataniya Al-Souriya (Dialogues on Syrian Patriotism)* (Dar Petra, Damascus, 2005).
Ismaël Hikmat Ali, *Nizam Al-Intitab Al-Faransi Ala Souriya, 1920–1928 (The Regime of the French Mandate in Syria 1920–1928)* (Tlass, Damascus, 1998).
Issa Ghassan, *Al-'Alakat Al-Loubnania Al-Souriya (Lebanese–Syrian Relations)* (Charikat Al-Matbou'at Lil-Di'ayya Wa Al-Nachr, Beirut, 2007).
Jabbour Georges, *Al-Hayat Al-Hizbiya Fi Souriya Wa Mustaqbalaha (The Life of Political Parties in Syria and its Future)* (Damascus, 2004).
Joum'aa Souad and Zaza Hassan, *Al-Hokoumat Al-Souriya Fi Al-Qarn Al-'Ichrin (Twentieth-Century Syrian Governments)* (Dar Al-Raou'ya, Damascus, 2001).
Kalthoum Faysal, *Dirassat Fi Al-Qanoun Al-Doustouri Was Al-Nozom Al-Siyassiyah, (Studies of Constitutional Law and Political Regimes)* (Damascus University, 2005–2006).
Kasmiyé Khayriyé, *Al-Hokouma Al-Arabiya Fi Dimashq 1918–1920 (The Arab Government in Damascus 1918–1920)* (Al-Mou'assa Al-Arabia, Beirut, 1982).
Al Ra'il Al-Arabi Al-Awal, Hayat Wa Aouraq Nabih Wa Adel Al-Azzmé (The Arab Vanguard. Life and Records of Nabih and Adel Azzmé) (Riad El-Rayyes Books Ltd, London, 1991).
Mouzakarat Fawzi Al-Qaouqji (The Memoirs of Fawzi Al-Qaouqji) (Al-Rouwad, Beirut, 1995).
Mouzakarat d'Aouni Abdel-Hadi (Memoirs of Aouni Abdel-Hadi) (Centre d'Etudes de l'Union Arabe, Beirut, 2002).
Khaddam Abdel Halim, *Al-Nizam Al-Arabi Al-Mou'asser, Quira'at Al-Waque' Wa Istichfaf Al-Mustaqubal (The Contemporary Arab Regime, Reading of Reality and Predictions for the Future)* (Arab Cultural Centre, Casablanca, 2003).
Khadoury Majid, *Quadiyet Al-Iskandarona (The Question of Alexandretta)* (Dar Al-Salam, Damascus, 1992).
Khouri Youssef, *Al-Macharie Al-Wahdaouiya Al-Arabiya, 1913–1989 (Plans for Arab Union, 1913–1989)* (Arab Union Research Centre, Beirut, 1989).
Khoury Farés, *Aouraq Fares Khoury (Farés Khoury's Documents)*, vols I and II (Tlass, Damascus, 2001).
Kourani Asaad, *Zikrayat Wa Khawater Mima Ra'ayt Wa Sama't Wa Fa'alt (Recollections and Impressions of What I Have Seen, Heard, and Done)* (Riad El-Rayyes, Beyrouth, 2000).
Ma'arouf Mohammad, *Ayam 'Ichtaha 1949–1969, Al-Inkalabat Al-Askariya Wa Assrarouha Fi Sourya (Days I Lived, 1949–1969, The Secret of Military Coups in Syria)* (Riad El-Rayyes Books, Beirut, 2003).
Mardam Beik Salma, *Awrak Jamil Mardam Beik, Istiqlal Souriya 1939–1945 (Jamil Mardam Beik's Notes, The Independence of Syria 1939–1945)* (Charikat Al-Matbou'at Lil-Di'ayya Wa Al-Nachr, Beirut, 1994).

Moussa Sulaiman, *Al-Harakka Al Arabia, Al-Marhala Al-Oula Lilnahda Al-Arabia Al-Haditha 1908–1924 (The Arab Movement, The First Period of Arab Renaissance, 1908–1924)* (Dar An-Nahar, Beirut, 1986).

Nadaf Imad, *Khaled Bagdache Yatahadath (The Words of Khaled Bakdash)* (Dar Al-Tali'a, Damascus, 1993).

Qarqout Thouquan, *Michel Aflaq, Al-Kitabat Al-Oula Ma'a Dirassa Jadida 'An Sirat Hayatihi (The First Works of Michel Aflaq with a New Study of his Journey)* (Al-Mouassa Al-Arabiya Lil-Dirassat Wa Al-Nacher, Beirut, 1993).

Tatawor Al-Harake Al-Watania Fi Souriya 1920–1939 (The Development of the National Movement in Syria 1920–1939) (Tlass, Damascus, 1989).

Qassab Hassan Najat, *Sani'ou Al-Jalaa Fi Sourya (The Makers of Syrian Independence)* (Chariket Al-Matbou'at Lil-Taouzi'e Wa Al-Nacher, Damascus, 1999).

Rabbath Edmond, *Al-Takouin Al-Tarikhi Lilubnan Al-Siyassi Wa Al-Doustouri, (The Historical Formation of Political and Constitutional Lebanon)*, vols I and II (Lebanese University Publications, Beirut, 2002).

Razzaz Mounif, *Tataour Ma'ana Al-Quaoumiya (The Development of the National Idea)* (Dar Al-'Elm Lil-Malayin, Beirut, 1960).

Shahbandar Abdel-Rahman, *Al-Makalat (The articles)* (Ministry of Culture Publications, Damascus, 1993).

Al-Qadaya Al-Ijtima'ya Al-Koubra Fi Al-Watan Al-Arabi 1936 (The Great Social Questions in the Arab World 1936) (Ministry of Culture Publications, Damascus, 1993).

Al-Thaoura Al-Souriya Al-Watania (The Syrian National Revolt) (Ministry of Culture Publications, Damascus, 1993).

Mouzakarat Wa Khotob (Memoirs and Speeches) (Ministry of Culture Publications, Damascus, 1993).

Sheherstan Mari Almaz, *Al-Mou'tamar Al-Souri Al-'Am 1919–1920 (The Syrian General Congress 1919–1920)* (Amouage, Beirut, 2000).

Soulaiman Abou Izz Al-Din, *Ibrahim Pacha Fi Sourya (Ibrahim Pasha in Syria)* (Dar Al-Chorouk, Cairo, 2009).

Sultan Ali, *Tarikh Souriya 1908–1918, Nihayat Al Hokm Al-Turki (The History of Syria 1908–1918. The End of Turkish Reign)* (Tlass, Damascus, 1996).

Tarikh Souriya, 1918–1920. Hokm Faysal Bin Al-Hussein (The History of Syria 1918–1920. The Reign of Faysal Bin Hussein) (Tlass, Damascus, 1996).

Tlass Moustapha, *Al-Khazou Al-Isra'ili Liloubnan (The Israeli Invasion of Lebanon)* (Techrine, Damascus, 1983).

Harb Tahrir Al-Koweït (The War of Liberation of Kuwait) (Tlass, Damascus, 1994).

Mour'at Hayati, Al-Nidal (The Mirror of My Life, The Struggle), vol. I, 1948–1958 (Tlass, Damascus, 1990).

Mour'at Hayati, Al-Thaoura (The Mirror of My Life, The Revolution), vol. II, 1958–1968 (Tlass, Damascus, 1995).

Mour'at Hayati, Al-Zolzal (The Mirror of My Life, The Earthquake), vol. III, 1968–1978 (Tlass, Damascus, 2003).

Mour'at Hayati, Al-Somoud (The Mirror of My Life, The Firm Hold), vol. IV, 1978–1988 (Tlass, Damascus, 2004).

Souriya Al-Tabi'ya (Natural Syria), vols I and II (Tlass, Damascus, 2001).

Wadi' Bachour, *Sourya Son' Dawla Wa Wiladat Ouma (Syria, Creation of a State and Birth of a Nation)* (Al-Yazji Printers, Damascus, 1996).

Zahr El-Din Abdel-Karim, *Mouzakarati 'An Al-Infissal Fi Souriya Ma Bayn 28 Eylul 1961 Wa 8 Azar 1963 (My Memoirs on the Era of the Infissal in Syria from 28 September 1961 to 8 March 1963)* (Beirut, 1968).

Zakaria Ghassan, *Al-Sultan al-Ahmar (The Red Sultan)* (Arados Publishing Ltd, London, 1991).

Articles

Al-Mouallem Walid, 'The reality of Syrian-Israeli negotations', *Journal of Palestinian Studies* 29 (1997) 16–28.

Arab Orient Center for Strategic and Civilization Studies, London, The, File of the Arab Orient Center, The Congress of the Syrian Opposition in Cairo, 04.07.2012. Available at: www.asharqalarabi.org.uk/barq/b-qiraat-296.htm.

Atassi Mohamad Ali, 'The story of Nourredine Atassi told by his son', *Al-Hayat* 18 December 1993, number 11266.

Haurani Fida'a 'Election is our right however …' www.maaber.org/independance/independance_7.htm.

Sattayhi Haytham, 'Ba'th cadre announces party redefining its relations with power', interview with the Lebanese daily, *Assafir*, Beirut, 28 May 2009.

FRENCH AND ENGLISH BIBLIOGRAPHY

Books

Ajlani Munir, *La Constitution de la Syrie*, PhD thesis (Les presses modernes, Paris, 1932).

Anonymous, *La Syrie et le Liban sous l'occupation et le mandat français 1919-1927* (Librairie et éditions Babylon, Lebanon, 2008).

Ardant Philippe, *Institutions politiques et droit constitutionnel* (17th edition, LGDJ, Paris, 2005).

Atassi Karim, *Syrie, la force d'une idée. Architectures constitutionnelles des régimes politiques* (L'Harmattan, Paris, 2014).

Balanche Fabrice, *La région alaouite et le pouvoir syrien* (Karthala, Paris, 2006).

Barr James, *A Line in the Sand. Britain, France and the Struggle that Shaped the Middle East* (Simon and Schuster, London, 2011).

Setting the Desert on Fire (Bloomsbury, London, 2007).

Bitterlin Lucien, *Alexandrette, le Munich de l'Orient* (J. Picollec, Paris, 2000).

Hafez Assad, le parcours d'un combattant (Jaguar, Paris, 1986).

Bokova Lenka, *La confrontation franco-syrienne à l'époque du mandat 1925-1927* (L'Harmattan, Paris, 1990).

Brown Nathan J., *Constitutions in a Nonconstitutional World* (State University of New York Press, Albany, NY, 2002).

Carré Olivier, *L'Islam laïque ou le retour à la grande tradition* (Armand Colin, Paris, 1993).

Le nationalisme arabe (Fayard, Paris, 1993).

Carré Olivier and Michaud Gérard (alias Michel Seurat), *Les Frères Musulmans en Égypte et en Syrie 1928-1982*, Collections Archives (Gallimard Julliard, Paris, 1983).

Carter Jimmy, *Palestine: Peace not Apartheid* (Simon and Schuster, New York, 2006).

Chagnollaud Jean-Paul and Souiah Sid-Ahmed, *Les frontières au Moyen-Orient* (L'Harmattan, Paris, 2004).

Cloarec Vincent, *La France et la question de Syrie 1914-1918* (CNRS, Paris, 2002).

Corm Georges, *Conflits et identités au Moyen-Orient (1919-1991)* (Arcantere, Paris, 1992).

L'Europe et l'Orient, de la balkanisation à la libanisation, histoire d'une modernité inaccomplie (La Découverte, Paris, 1989).

Orient–Occident, la fracture imaginaire (La Découverte, Paris, 2002).

Davet Michel-Christian, *La double affaire de Syrie* (Fayard, Paris, 1967).

David Philippe, *Un gouvernement arabe à Damas, le Congrès syrien* (Thesis, Paris, 1923).

De Gontaut-Biron Comte R., *Comment la France s'est installée en Syrie* (Plon, Paris, 1922).

De Wailly Henri, *Syrie 1941, la guerre occultée, vichystes contre gaullistes* (Perrin, Paris, 2006).

Delpal Bernard, Hours Bernard, and Prudhomme Claude (eds), *France-Levant, de la fin du XVIIe siècle à la Première Guerre Mondiale* (Geuthner, Paris, 2005).

Donati Caroline, *L'exception syrienne entre modernisation et résistance* (La Découverte, Paris, 2009).

Droz-Vincent Philippe, *Moyen-Orient: pouvoirs autoritaires, sociétés bloquées* (PUF, Paris, 2004).

Dupret Baudouin, Ghazzal Zouhair, Courbage Youssef, and Al-Dbiyat Mohammed (eds), *La Syrie au présent, reflet d'une société* (Sindbad Actes Sud, Paris, 2007).

Foucher Michel, *Fronts et frontières, un tour du monde géopolitique* (Fayard, Paris, 1991).

Fournier Pierre and Riccoli Jean-Louis, *La France et le Proche-Orient 1916–1946* (Casterman, Paris, 1996).

Fromkin David, *A Peace to End All Peace, The Fall of the Ottoman Empire and the Creation of the Modern Middle East* (Henry Holt and Company, New York, 2001).

Frum David and Perle Richard, *An End to Evil: How to Win the War on Terror* (Ballantine Books, New York, 2004).

Garnier Jean-Paul, *La fin de l'Empire Ottoman, du Sultan rouge à Mustafa Kemal* (Plon, Paris, 1973).

Gelvin James L., *Divided Loyalties. Nationalism and Mass Politics in Syria at the Close of Empire* (University of California Press, Berkeley and Los Angeles, CA, 1998).

George Alan, *Syria: Neither Bread Nor Freedom* (Zed Books, London and New York, 2003).

Guingamp Pierre, *Hafez El Assad et le parti Baath en Syrie* (L'Harmattan, Paris, 1996).

Hajjar Joseph, *La Syrie (bilâd al-Schâm). Démembrement d'un pays* (Tlass, Damascus, 1999).

Homet Marcel, *L'histoire secrète du traité franco-syrien, où va le Proche-Orient?* (J. Peyronnet & Cie, Paris, 1938).

Hourani Albert, *A History of the Arab People* (Faber and Faber, London, 2002).

Huntington Samuel, *Le choc des civilisations* (Edile Jacob, Paris, 2000).

Kaminsky Catherine and Kruk Simon, *La Syrie: politiques et stratégies de 1961 à nos jours* (Presses Universitaires de France, Paris, 1987).

Kauffer Rémi, *La saga des Hachémites* (Stock, Paris, 2009).
Kayali Hasan, *Arabs and Young Turks* (University of California Press, London, 1997).
Kessel Joseph, *En Syrie* (KRA, Paris, 1927).
Khoury Gérard D, *La France et l'Orient arabe, Naissance du Liban moderne 1914–1920* (Albin Michel, Paris, 2009).
  Une tutelle coloniale, le mandat français en Syrie et au Liban, Écrits politiques de Robert de Caix (Belin, France, 2006).
Khoury Gérard D and Méouchy Nadine (eds), *États et Sociétés de l'Orient Arabe en Quête d'Avenir 1945–2005, Fondement et Sources*, vol. I (Geuthner, Paris, 2006).
  (eds), *États et Sociétés de l'Orient Arabe en Quête d'Avenir 1945–2005, Dynamiques et Enjeux*, vol. II (Geuthner, Paris, 2007).
Labévière Richard, *Le grand retournement Bagdad–Beyrouth* (Seuil, Paris, 2006).
Labévière Richard and El-Atrache Talal, *Quand la Syrie s'éveillera ...* (Perrin, Paris 2011).
Lacouture Jean, Tuéni Ghassan, and Khoury Gérard D, *Un siècle pour rien, Le Moyen-Orient arabe de l'Empire ottoman a l'Empire américain* (Albin Michel & Éditions Dar An-Nahar, Beirut, 2004).
Landis Joshua, 'Early U.S. policy toward Palestinian refugees: The Syria option' in Joseph Ginat and Edward J. Perkins (eds), *The Palestinian Refugees: Old Problems – New Solutions* (University of Oklahoma Press, Norman, OK, 2001).
Laurens Henry, *Le grand jeu, Orient arabe et rivalités internationales* (Armand Colin, Paris, 1991).
  L'Orient Arabe. Arabisme et islamisme de 1789 à 1945 (Armand Colin, Paris, 2008).
  Le royaume impossible, la France et la genèse du monde arabe (Armand Colin, Paris, 1990).
Lawrence T. E., *Seven Pillars of Wisdom* (Penguin Classics, London, 2000 (first published 1926)).
Le Gag Daniel, *La Syrie du général Assad* (Editions complexes, Paris, 1991).
Leverett Flynt, *Inheriting Syria. Bashar's Trial by Fire* (Brookings Institution Press, Washington, DC, 2005).
Mansfield Peter, *A History of the Middle East* (Penguin Books, London, 2003).
Mantoux Paul, *Les délibérations du Conseil des Quatre*, vols I and II (CNRS, Paris, 1955).
Maoz Moshe, *Asad, The Sphinx of Damascus. A Political Biography* (Weidenfeld & Nicolson, New York, 1988).
Maoz Moshe and Yaniv Avner, *Syria under Assad* (Croom Helm Ltd, Australia, 1987).
Mardam-Bey Farouk and Sanbar Elias, *Être arabe* (Actes Sud/Sindbad, Paris, 2005).
Martinez-Gros Gabriel, *Brèves histoires des empires* (Seuil, Paris, 2014).
Méouchy Nadine, *France, Syrie et Liban 1918–1946, les ambigüités et les dynamiques de la relation mandataire* (Institut Français d'Études Arabes de Damas, Damascus, 2002).

Moubayed Sami, *Steel and Silk, Men and Women who Shaped Syria 1900–2000* (Cune Press, Seattle, WA, 2006).

Moubayed Sami M., *The Politics of Damascus, 1920–1946. Urban Notables and the French Mandate* (Tlass, Damascus, 1999).

Olivier-Saidi Marie-Thérèse, *Le Liban et la Syrie au miroir français (1946–1991)* (L'Harmattan, Paris, 2010).

Pakradouni Karim. *La paix manquée* (FMA, Beirut, 1984).

Palazzoli Claude, *La Syrie, le rêve et la rupture* (Le Sycomore, Paris, 1977).

Picaudoux Nadine, *La décennie qui ébranla le Moyen-Orient 1914–1923* (Editions complexes, Paris, 1922).

Pierret Thomas, *Baas et islam en Syrie* (Presses Universitaires de France, Paris, 2011).

Pipes Daniel, *Greater Syria. The History of an Ambition* (Oxford University Press, New York, 1990).

Prévost Philippe, *La France et la tragédie palestinienne, retour sur les accords de Sykes-Picot* (Erick Bonnier, Paris, 2012).

Puaux Gabriel, *Deux années au Levant. Souvenirs de Syrie et du Liban 1939–1940* (Hachette, Paris, 1952).

Rabbath Edmond, *Unité syrienne et devenir arabe* (Marcel Rivière et Compagnie, Paris, 1937).

Raymond André (ed.), *La Syrie d'aujourd'hui* (CNRS, Aix-en-Provence, 1980).

Roberts David, *The Ba'th and the Creation of Modern Syria* (Croom Helm, Kent, 1987).

Russell Malcom B., *The First Modern Arab State, Syria under Faysal 1918–1920* (Bibliotheca Islamica, Minneapolis, MN, 1985).

Saab Edouard, *La Syrie ou la révolution dans la rancœur* (Julliard, Paris, 1968).

Sallam Kassim, *La Ba'th et la patrie arabe* (Editions du Monde Arabe, Paris, 1982).

Savir Uri, *The Process, 1100 days that Changed the Middle East* (Vintage Books, New York, 1998).

Sartre Maurice, *D'Alexandre à Zénobie: Histoire du Levant antique (IVe siècle av. J.-C. – IIIe siècle ap. J.-C.)* (Fayard, Paris, 2001).

Seale Patrick, *Assad. The Struggle for the Middle East* (I.B.Tauris & Co Ltd, London, 1988).

The Struggle for Syria A Study of Post-War Arab Politics 1945–1958, Arabic translation (Tlass, Damascus, 1983).

Seurat Michel, *L'État de barbarie* (Esprit Seuil, Paris, 2012).

Shaaban Bouthaina, *Damascus Diary: An Inside Account of Hafez Assad's Peace Diplomacy 1990–2000* (Lynne Rienner Publishers, Inc, Boulder, CO, 2013).

Sinoué Gilbert, *Le dernier pharaon* (J'ai Lu, Paris, 2000).

Sorman Guy, *Les enfants de Rifaa, musulmans et modernes* (Fayard, Paris, 2003).

Tharaud Jean and Tharaud Jérôme, *Le chemin de Damas* (Plon, Paris, 1923).

Torrey Gordon H., *Syrian Politics and the Military 1945–1958* (Ohio State University Press, 1964).

Valter Stéphane, *La construction nationale syrienne. Légitimation de la nature communautaire du pouvoir par le discours historique* (CNRS, Paris, 2002).
Van Dam Nikolaos, *The Struggle for Power in Syria* (I.B.Tauris, London, 4th edition, 2011).
Weber Max, *Economie et société 1, les catégories de la sociologie* (Editions Pocket, Paris, 1995).

Articles

Barak Ehud, Speech to the annual conference on Israel's security at Herzliya, 2016. Available at: www.herzliyaconference.org/eng/?CategoryID=555&ArticleID=2760.
Eberhard Kienle, 'Entre jama'a et classe', *Revue des mondes musulmans et de la Méditerranée* 59(1) (1991) 211–39.
Égypte/Monde Arabe, 'Les architectures constitutionnelles des régimes politiques arabes. De l'autoritarisme à la démocratisation', edited by Nathalie Bernard-Maugiron and Jean Noël Ferrié, CEDEJ, number 2, 2005.
Grey Mary, 'Preparing the Ground for Balfour – the Contribution of Shaftesbury', in balfourproject.org.
Majed Nehmé, 'Le parti communiste syrien de la stratégie "internationaliste" à la contestation "nationaliste"', *Communisme* 6 (1984) 129–52.
Martinez-Gros Gabriel, 'Comprendre la marche du monde', *Qantara* 60(2) (July 2006) 25 ff.
Miller Judith, 'Syria's Game', *The New York Times*, 26 January 1992.
Picaudou Nadine, 'La tradition constitutionnelle arabe', *Égypte/Monde arabe* 2 (2005) 24 ff.
Seurat Michel, 'Journalistes et chercheurs face au Liban et au Proche-Orient'. Text reconstructed from notes taken by Jean-François Clément, as 'Ce que le Liban m'a appris'. *Esprit* 1667 (June 1986).
'Remarques sur l'État syrien', reconstructed from notes taken by Jean-François Clément in a presentation to the 'Développement' group of the journal Esprit in 1984 and published in *Esprit* 115 (June 1986) 11–13.
'La Syrie ou l'État de barbarie' written under the pseudonym Gérard Michaud, *Esprit*, 83 (November 1983) 16–30.
'Terrorisme d'État, terrorisme contre l'État: le cas syrien' written under the pseudonym Gérard Michaud, *Esprit* 94–95 (October–November 1984) 188–201.

INDEX

1920 constitution
  adoption of 80
  Declaration of Rights 73–74
  drafting of 69–70
  executive powers of the General Government 75–76
  executive powers of the King 74–75
  legislative powers 76–78
  the national question in 184
  parliamentary monarchy 71–72, 75
  the provinces under 72–73, 79–80
  separation of religion and politics 71
  and Syrian independence 4
1928 constitution
  1948 revision of 148–50, 156
  Article 116 109, 139
  Assembly of Deputies 104–5
  the Executive 105–7
  first reading of 101
  French objections to 108–9
  government's ten points 98–99
  high commission's revisions to 108–9, 139
  legislative powers 104
  the national question in 102–4, 180, 184
  overview of 4–5, 101–2
  as pan-Syrian 162, 184
  restoration of 136–37
1949 constitutional referendum 159–60
1949 draft constitution
  draft constitution 160–63, 207
  executive powers 162–63
  legislative powers 162
1949 draft provisional constitution 170–71, 208–9

1950 constitution
  adoption of 176, 179
  agrarian question 6, 181
  Assembly of Deputies 186–88
  constitutional revision 191–92
  executive power constraints 5–6, 180
  executive powers 188–90
  government 190–91
  interruptions to 5
  legislative powers 186
  military influence and 173–74
  the national question 184–85
  overview of 5–6, 153
  restoration of 193
  social issues 6, 179–83, 207–8
  sovereignty 185–86
1953 constitution
  abolition of 193
  democratic guarantees 233–35
  duration of 225
  government 244
  legislative powers 237
  national wealth organization 236–37
  the president 241–44
  for a presidential regime 225, 231–33
  the assembly 237–41
1961 provisional constitution 208–10
1962 constitution
  adoption of 217–20
  as emergency constitution 215–17
  overview of 6
1964 provisional constitution
  Arab socialism 273
  citizens' rights 271–72
  collegiate governance 7, 275
  council of ministers 274–75

484 INDEX

executive and legislative powers 271, 273–75
and the First Regional Congress 270
National Revolutionary Council (NRC) 265, 273–74, 275–76
Presidential Council 273–74, 276
revisions to 275–76
Syrian Arab Republic 271
the Syrian flag 271
1966 constitutional arrangement 7, 281–82
1969 provisional constitution
and the 1971 provisional constitution 300–3
citizens' rights 292–93
economic principles 292
education and culture 292
fundamental principles 291
head of state and council of ministers 294
institutions of state power 293–95
local people's assemblies 294–95
people's assemblies 293–94
preamble 290–91
role of the army 291
role of the Ba'th party 290, 291, 292, 295
1971 provisional constitution
as amended version of 1969 constitution 300
council of ministers 301–2
People's Assembly 300–1
and personalization of the regime 7
President of the Republic 301, 302–3
role of the Ba'th party 301, 302–3
role of the Regional Command 302
1973 constitution
council of ministers 315
Declaration of Rights 310–11
drafting of 308
electoral law 316–17
Fundamental Principles 309–11
future amendments to 316
judicial powers 315–16
legislative powers 311
People's Assembly 311–13
and personalization of the regime 7
preamble 308–9

President of the Republic 313–15
role of the army 309–10
role of the Ba'th 7–8, 309
2012 constitution
Arabic language 388–89
control of the constitutionality of laws 406–7
economic principles 391–92
educational and cultural principles 393–94
electoral law 399
executive powers 404–5
future amendments to 407–8
judicial powers 405–7
legislative powers 398
legislative powers of the president 402–4
overview of 8, 386–87
People's Assembly 398
political pluralism 389–90, 405
political principles 388
popular democracy 402
preamble 387
president of the republic 399–402
public organizations 390
rights and freedoms 394–97
role of the army 390–91
rule of law 398
social principles 392–93
Syrian nationality 396
2014 presidential elections
2014 electoral law 415–17
candidates and campaigns 417
domestic situation 413–14
expatriate Syrian votes 416–17
extension of Bashar Assad's term 414–15
the opposition and 412–13
regional and international situation 414
result 417–18
significance of 418
2015 Iranian initiative 454–55
2016 constitutional texts
absence of dimension reflecting Syrian identity 447
Carter Center revision of the 2012 constitution 447–49

INDEX

provisional constitution for the
transitional period 450–51
the Russian constitutional
proposal 451–54

Abed, Ali 112, 113–15, 122
Al-Afghani, Jamal Din 24
Aflaq, Michel
  Ba'th ideology 253, 369
  Ba'th socialism 269, 371
  cabinet of national unity 166
  exile in Lebanon 245, 248, 283
  as founder of the Ba'th 158, 369
  as national secretary 278, 279
  tripartite discussions 344
Agrarian reforms
  Assad regime 326
  under the 1950 constitutions 6, 181, 207–8
  under the Fourth Republic 262–63
  under the military republic 230
  and reformist socialism 208
Alaa' el-Din Droubi 69
Al-'Ahd (The Covenant) 26, 30, 39–40, 72–73
Al-Arabia Al-Fatat (Arab Youth) 26, 29, 30, 39–40, 58
Alassar, Colonel Badr 214, 215
Alawi territory
  reattachment, Franco-Syrian treaty 119, 121, 122–23, 131, 136
  separation of under the French mandate 4, 85, 88, 95, 101, 102, 113–14, 115–16
  within the Syrian Federation grouping 90
Aleppo
  under Ibrahim Pasha 15
  pashalik, Ottoman Empire 13
  reattachment, Franco-Syrian treaty 119, 121, 122–23, 131, 136
  and reintegration under French mandate 90–92
  separation of under the French mandate 4, 85, 88, 95, 101, 102, 113–14, 115–16
  territory of 145–46

Ali, Mohamad
  and the Arab renaissance 23–24
  and Ibrahim Pasha 12
  invasion of Syria (1831) 11, 13–14
  military involvement in the Greek crisis 12–13
  and the Sharif of Mecca 32
  as threat to British commercial interests 19–20
  withdrawal from Syria 16–17
Al-Kahtania 25–26
Allenby, Edmund, 1st Viscount Allenby 41, 42, 54
Amer, General Abdel-Hakim 203–4
Arab Congress (1913) 26–28
Arab Federal State (AFS) 340–41, 343–44
Arab Liberation Movement (ALM) 230–31, 248
Arab renaissance (*nahda*) 23–24
Arab socialism
  in the Ba'th trilogy 371–72, 374–77
  and the 2012 constitution 391
  and social issues 206–8, 262–63
  United Arab Republic of Egypt, Syria, and Iraq 344–45
Arab Socialist Party
  initial support for 1949 coup d'état 157, 164–65
  merger with the Arab Ba'th Party 245
Arab Spring 8
Arab state
  under the revised Sykes-Picot agreement 53–55
  territorial division of 32–33, 41, 42, 47–48
Arabism
  Faysal's nation state 44
  transition from Arab-ness 34
  and the union with Egypt 340
Arafat, Yasser 279, 323–24, 354, 466
Army *see also* coup d'états
  1969 provisional constitution and 291
  1973 constitution and 309–10
  2012 constitution and 390–91
  Ba'th civilian/military relations 253
  checks on, 1950 constitution 180

Army (*cont.*)
  and the civil war 436
  collapse of the United Arab Republic 204–6
  form of, post-civil war 455–56
  function of during Husni Al-Zaim's regime 158
  as an ideological army 278, 284, 285, 286, 291, 310, 336, 456
  military ties with Egypt 202, 203–4
  National Security Council (NSC) 211–12
  officers in the 1963 coup 256
  opposition to General Shishakli 249
  and the Palestinian war 150
  political involvement of, 1949-51 174–79
  post-1963 coup 266
  proscription of SSNP 197–98, 201
  protection of the government, 1948/9 150–51
  reinforcement of 228
  relations with the People's Party 178–79, 226–27
  role in the Second Republic 153–54, 158
  role in the Third Republic 228, 245–46, 251
  stance on federation with Iraq 171–73
  union with Iraq 261, 347
'Asabiya 332–33, 355, 370, 382–83, 456
Assad regime *see also* 1973 constitution; Assad, Hafez
  agrarian reforms 326
  corruption 319–20
  the economy 326–27
  Eighth Regional Congress 323–24
  extraordinary session of the Fifth Regional Congress 319–20
  foreign policy 334–36
  Ibn Khaldun model 331–33
  Israel's invasion of Lebanon (1982) 323–24
  Marxist analysis of 328–29
  Muslim Brotherhood's armed opposition to 319, 321–22, 323
  National Democratic Rally 324–25
  national project in the regional arena 333–34, 337
  opposition to 324–25
  overview of 336–37
  political stability under 318–19
  sectarian analysis of (New Orientalists) 329–31
  Seventh Regional Congress 321–22
  Sixth National Congress 325–26
  Sixth Regional Congress 320–21
  Syrian–US relations 335
  Thirteenth National Congress 322–23
  Twelfth National Congress 321
Assad, Bashar *see also* 2014 presidential elections; Fifth Republic
  call for national compact 433
  inaugural speech 356–58
  investiture 354
  partial reforms under 7
  role during proposed transition period 448
  succession of 356
  support for resistance movements, wider Middle East 467–68
Assad, Hafez
  air force commander-in-chief 266
  alliance with USSR 335
  clash with Ahmed Suwaydani 287
  common front of progressive and nationalist parties 305
  governments under 318
  as guide for the Syrian people 306–7
  legislative decrees 317–18
  personalization of the regime 7, 307, 310
  political stability under 318–19
  as President of the Republic 303
  rivalry with Salah Jadid 288, 289–90, 293, 296, 298, 299
  as secretary-general 300
  support base for 382–83
Assad, Rifaat 319, 323, 324
Al-Assali, Sabri 193, 200, 201, 250
Association for Arab–Ottoman Brotherhood 24–25

Astana Conference 446, 451, 458
Atassi, Adnan 201
Atassi, Faydi 91, 178
Atassi, Colonel Faysal 249
Atassi, General Lu'ay 214–15, 257, 258, 260
Atassi, Hashim
  1931–32 elections 109, 112
  as caretaker president, 1949 166, 171, 173, 175, 177
  constituent assembly, 1928 101, 108
  constitutional commission 69
  first session of the Syrian congress 61–62
  and the Franco-Syrian treaty 113–14, 118, 120, 131
  the General Strike, 1936 117–18
  negotiations with the French, 1943 135, 136–37
  neutrality of 145
  opposition to General Shishakli 245–46, 248
  political career 250–51
  presidency, 1936 122
  presidency, 1954 192, 193, 196, 250
  president of the congress, 1920 68–69
  proposed federation with Iraq 167
  resignation of 227
Atassi, Jamal 324–25
Atassi, Nuredin 281–82, 286, 289, 298–99
Atrash, Mansur 274, 276, 277
Al-Azzem, Haqqi
  1931-32 elections 109, 112
  as Prime Minister 113
Al-Azzem, Khaled
  1955 presidential elections 198–99
  assembly elections, 1961 210
  assembly meeting outside the chamber, 1962 218–19, 220
  government of, 1950 175–76
  government of, 1951 177
  opposition to Azzme government 216–17
  the Progressive Front 200
Al-Azzme, Beshir 216–17

Balfour Declaration 20, 52, 56, 63, 65, 116–17
Balfour, Lord 52–53, 54
Barazi, Mohsen 157, 159, 160, 164–65
Ba'th Military Committee (BMC) 265–68, 276–77
Ba'th Party *see also* Fourth Republic; neo-Ba'th regime; Union-Freedom-Socialism trilogy
  1954 elections 339
  alliance with the People's Party 147
  civilian/military relations 253
  coming to power of 6
  formation of 158
  ideology of 6–7, 252–53
  initial support for 1949 coup d'état 157
  Marxist reorientation 269
  merger with the Arab Socialist Party 245
  modernization of 368, 376, 377–78
  national identity and 254
  and the 1964 provisional constitution 275
  under the 1973 constitution 309
  policy towards Israel 278–79
  social issues 254–55
  support base for 383, 384
Ba'th Provisional Regional Council (PRC) 299–300
battle of Maysalun 81–82, 84
Bitar, Salah
  exile in Lebanon 245, 248, 283
  as foreign minister 202
  formation of governments 260–61, 263–65
  as founder of the Ba'th 158, 369
  governments of 277
  maintenance of civic rights 258
  moderate socialism of 269
  on the Presidential Council 277
  resignation of 268
  tripartite discussions 344
Buni, Anwar 409–10, 424
Bureau of Military Affairs (BMA) 267

Camp David Accords 310, 319, 322, 327, 334
Carter Center 447–49
Catroux, General Georges 135–36, 138, 139
Cheney, Elizabeth 420
Christians
　1860 religious crisis 11, 21
　Christians of the Orient 25
　equal rights with Muslims 34, 42–43, 44
　interests of, Arab Congress 28
　minority rights of 60
　oath of allegiance to King Faysal 45–46
　reservations of Christians from Mt Lebanon on the Damascus Programme 65
Churchill, Winston 138, 141
Clemenceau, Georges 52–53, 57–59, 65–66, 80, 82
Committee of Union and Progress (CUP) 11
constitutional texts, overview of 2–3
Corrective Movement *see also* 1971 provisional constitution
　communiqué, November 1970 299–300
　coup November 1970 298–99
　Eleventh National Congress 307–8
　Federation of Arab Republics (FAR) 303–4, 307
　Fifth Regional Congress 306–7
　first actions of the assembly 303
　mixed-sector economics 307
　National Progressive Front (NPF) 304–6, 307
　PRC during 300
Coup d'états
　attempted coup, 1963 221
　August 1949 165–67, 226
　categories of 255
　December 1949 5, 6, 171–72, 226
　February 1966 281
　March 1949 5, 6, 151, 156–58
　March 1962 212–15
　March 1963 252, 254, 255–56, 258, 347
　November 1951 178–79, 192, 225–26
　November 1970 (Corrective Movement) 298–99
　and restoration of civilian authorities 165–66
　September 1961 203–4
Covenant of the League of Nations 86–87, 99, 124

Daesh (ISIS) 435, 456
Damascus
　bombing of, 1945 141
　bombing of, Great Revolt 93
　post-Ottoman 44
　riots against the French 140–41
Damascus Programme
　Christians of Mt Lebanon's criticism of 65
　enduring values of 3
　geographical boundaries of Syria 63–64
　King–Crane commission's response to 64–65
　main points of 62–63, 64
　overview of 4
　preparation of 61–62
　strengths of 63
Damascus Protocol
　calls for national independence 28
　within the context of WWI alliances 29–30
　future relations with the Turks 31
　geographical borders of an Arab state 31
　relations with Sharif Hussein of Mecca 31–32, 40
　withdrawal of foreigners' privileges 31
Damascus Spring
　Ba'th counter-offensive 358–59
　Damascus Declaration 362–63
　legacy of 359
　National Salvation Front (NSF) 363–65
　opposition movement and 356
　plans for political reforms 354–55, 358
　Social and National Charter 361–62
　Statement of 1000 358, 360–61
　Statement of 99 358, 359–60

Damascus, State of
  partial elections, 1926 97
  and reintegration under French mandate 90–92
Dawalibi, Ma'aruf 178, 227, 250
Declaration of Independence 65–68
democracy
  democratic guarantees, 1953 constitution 233–35
  Fifth Republic 357
  popular democracy, Ba'th ideology 374, 402
Dentz, Henri 132–33
Druze territories
  lack of support for Husni Al-Zaim 165
  opposition to General Shishakli 248–49
  reattachment, Franco-Syrian treaty 119, 121, 122–23, 131, 136
  under the French mandate 88

Eastern Question *10–11*
economy
  1969 constitutions 292
  under the Assad regime 326–27
  liberalization of 355
  mixed-sector economics 307
  modernization of 368, 381–82
  social market economy 208, 355, 368, 376–77, 379
education
  1964 constitution 272
  1969 constitution 292
  2012 constitution 393–94
Egypt *see also* Ali, Mohamad; United Arab Republic (Egypt and Syria); United Arab Republic of Egypt, Syria, and Iraq
  administration of province of Syria 15–16
  disengagement from Sinai 320
  exiled Syrian nationals in 25
  military ties with Syria 202, 203–4
  support for Kurd rebellion 261
  Syria–Egypt–Iraq federation 259–60
  Syrian campaign 11
  Syria's political move towards 196–98
  union with Syria 5, 200–3

electoral law
  1947 electoral law reforms 146–47
  1953 constitution 246–47
  1954 constitution (amended 1957) 194
  1973 constitution 316–17
  2011 electoral law 409–11
  2012 constitution 399
  2014 presidential elections 415–17
Emir Abdel Kader
  during the 1860 crisis 21
  refusal to take the Syrian throne 22
Europe *see also* France; Great Britain
  impact of increased tensions, pre-WWII 128
  involvement in Syrian campaigns 14–15, 16
  support for Ottoman Empire 19

Faysal I bin Hussein bin Ali al-Hashemi
  Christian and Jewish oaths of allegiance to 45–46
  downside to his reign 142–43
  early life 39
  executive powers of 74–75
  Faysal–Clemenceau agreement 57–59, 65–66, 80, 82
  Faysal–Weizmann agreement 55–57
  formation of an Arab government 41–44
  formation of the constitutional state 4, 41–44
  the Great Arab Revolt 33, 40–41
  as guide for the Syrian people 306–7
  meetings with Syrian nationalists 29–30, 39–40
  the nation state under 44–45
  objectives for the Syrian Congress 59–60
  possible restoration of 110–11
  promotion of equal rights for Christians and Muslims 34

490   INDEX

Faysal I bin Hussein bin Ali al-Hashemi (*cont.*)
  revisions to the Sykes-Picot agreement 52–54, 55
  Syrian Congress's proclamation as King of Syria 66, 67
  territorial division of Syria 41
Federation of Arab Republics (FAR)
  debates, Fifth Regional Congress 307
  executive powers 350–51
  federal constitution 349–50, 352
  formation of 348–49
  internal and external security provisions 352
  judicial powers 351
  legislative powers 351
  overview of 303–4, 353
Fertile Crescent 167, 185, 229
Fifth Republic *see also* 2012 constitution; 2014 presidential elections; Assad Bashar
  2011 electoral law 409–11
  2012 elections 410–11
  2016 legislative elections 418–19
  administration reforms 367
  crisis of March 2011 384–85
  economic reforms 355, 366, 376–77, 381–82
  Fourteenth National Congress 378
  law on political parties 411–12
  missed opportunities for reform 378
  opposition movement and 356
  political reforms 354–56, 379–81, 385–86, 408–9
  proposed reforms 356–57, 365–66
  public sector reforms 366–67
  social impact of economic reforms 383–84
  Tenth Regional Congress 367–69, 376–78, 379
  wider regional situation 354, 378–79, 381
First Republic *see also* 1928 constitution; Franco-Syrian treaty; French mandates
  1928 elections 99–101
  1931–32 elections 109–11
  1936 elections 122

1943 elections 136–37
1947 elections 147–48
1947 electoral law reforms 146–47
challenges to authority of political classes 143–44, 152
under de Gaulle's Free French 134–37
division of French territories 88–89
election of the President, 1932 111–12
the General Strike, 1936 116–18
the Great Revolt (1925-26) 92–94
independent Syria's challenges 143–44
insurgents' demands, post-Great Revolt 94–96
last government of 151
overview of 84–85
partial elections, 1926 96–97
political crisis, 1939 131–33
revision of 1928 constitution 148–50, 156
sanjak of Alexandretta crisis 124–28
State of Syria 91–92
Syrian Federation 90–91
Syrian–Lebanese relations 138–39
flags
  1928 constitution (flag of independence) 102, 271
  1964 provisional constitution 271
  under the 1973 constitution 310
  UAR flag (1958) 310
  UAR flag (1963) 345
Fourth Republic *see also* 1964 provisional constitution; 1969 provisional constitution; Ba'th Party
  agrarian reforms 262–63
  Ba'th governments 263–65
  Ba'th Military Committee (BMC) 265–68, 276–77
  Bureau of Military Affairs (BMA) 267
  collegiate governance 254
  Eighth National Congress 278–79
  Extraordinary Session of the First Ba'th Regional Congress 269–70

extraordinary sessions, Ba'th Second Regional Congress 279–80
First Regional Congress 268–70
National Command/Regional Command power struggles 280–81
National Council of the Revolutionary Command (NCRC) 256–57, 258, 273, 277
nationalizations 262–63
1963 coup d'état 252, 254, 255–56, 258, 347
Presidential Council 273–74
resistance movements to 263
Second Syrian Regional Congress 277–78
sectarianism of 266–67
Seventh National Congress 270
Sixth National Congress 269
Syria–Egypt–Iraq federation 259–60
union with Iraq 260–62, 269, 347, 348
France
backing of Abdel Kader for the throne 11, 21, 22
battle of Maysalun 81–82
and the Declaration of Independence 66
fall of the Syrian monarchy 81–82
Faysal–Clemenceau agreement 57–59, 65–66, 82
fears of Turko-Syrian alliance 80–81
Franco-Turkish talks over the sanjak of Alexandretta 125–26
misunderstanding of the Arabo-Syrian national phenomenon 33, 82
Ottoman policy 22–23
petite politique 58, 88–89
position on the Ottoman Empire during WWI 46–47
reaction to monarchical constitution 4
revisions to the Sykes–Picot agreement 52–55
territorial aims of the Sykes–Picot agreement 49

Vichy government's collaboration with Germany 133–34
Vichy/Gaullist battle over Syria 134–35
Franco-Syrian treaty
1933 version 114–16
1936 version 118–21
delayed ratification of 128, 129–30, 131
the General Strike, 1936 116–18
impact of the sanjak of Alexandretta crisis 125
Lebanon and 119–20
localized opposition to 123–24
negotiations 112–14
reintegration of Alawi and Druze territories 121, 122–23, 131, 136
right-wing opposition to 121
French mandates
bombing of Damascus 141
Covenant of the League of Nations 87, 99
division of the French territories 88–89
end of in Lebanon 142
end of in Syria 139–42
end of, British stance on 140, 141
French political stance towards 81, 87, 96, 99
independent Lebanon 137–38
military resistance to 89–90
nationalist movement under 84, 85
reintegration of French territories 90–92
removal of French troops 139–40, 141–42
republican government 142–43
restoration of a monarchy 110
riots against the French 140–41
Syrian political classes under 151–52
transfer of common interests 139

Gaulle, Charles de 134–35, 136, 138, 141
General Syrian Congress *see also* 1920 Constitution
Damascus Programme 61–62
declaration of independence 65–68

General Syrian Congress (*cont.*)
  election of members of 60–61
  Faysal's objectives for 59–60
  as a legislative assembly 68–69
  proclamation of Faysal as King of Syria 66, 67
Geneva 1 408, 431, 441, 455
Geneva 2 414, 418–19, 431–32, 441, 444
Geneva 3 445, 458, 459
Geneva 4 446, 457
Geneva Communiqué (2012) 441–42, 444, 447
Germany
  increased threat of, pre-WWII 128
  Iraqi support for 133
  Vichy government's collaboration with 133–34
Ghadry, Farid 420
Ghazi, Said 194, 199
Golan Heights and Mount Hermon war of attrition 319
Gouraud, Henri 81, 90, 91, 138
Great Arab Revolt 29, 31–34, 40–41
Great Britain
  Arab support for the allies, WWI 29, 30–31
  the Declaration of Independence 66
  end of the French Mandate 140, 141
  imperialist doctrine 19–20
  interests in the Syrian question 19–20
  middle eastern policy under Lloyd George 51–52
  misunderstanding of the Arabo-Syrian national phenomenon 33
  personal religious views and British policies 20
  position on the Ottoman Empire during WWI 47
  proposed Greater Syria 22
  reaction to Franco-German collaboration, WWII 134–35
  relations with the First Republic 85
  relations with France over Lebanon 138
  revisions to the Sykes–Picot agreement 52–55
  role in the Great Arab Revolt 33, 40
  territorial aims of the Sykes–Picot agreement 50
Great Revolt (1925–26) 91, 92–96
Greek crisis 10–11, 12–13

Hafez, General Amin
  fears of sectarianism 267
  governments 264–65
  Presidential Council 277, 279, 281
  public knowledge of 268
  as regime's strongman 257, 264
  secretary of the Regional Command 278
Al-Hakim, Hassan 177
Al-Hasni, Sheikh Tajeddine 98–99, 109, 116, 135
Hawrani, Akram
  Arab Socialist Party merger with the Ba'th 231, 245
  early political career 157–58
  loss of civic rights 258
  opposition to Al-Zaim's regime 164–65
  as speaker 202
  third coup, 1949 173
Hinnawi, General Sami 165, 172
Hizb Al-Ahrar (Liberal Party) 147

Ibn Khaldun 331–33
Ibrahim Pasha
  administration of province of Syria 15–16, 17–18
  awareness of Arab identity 18–19, 23–24
  invasion of Syria (1831) 13–14
Iran 454–55, 467
Iraq
  1958 coup d'état 340–41
  Arab Federal State (AFS) 340–41, 343–44
  Ba'th Party 260, 261, 269, 270, 288
  Egyptian support for Kurd rebellion 261
  financing of 1956 plot 200–1

INDEX

proposed federation with Syria 146, 167–68, 169–70, 171–73, 196–98, 229, 338–39
under Saddam Hussein 322
support for Germany, WWII 133
Syria–Egypt–Iraq federation 259–60
union with Syria 260–62, 269, 347, 348
US invasion of 466
ISIS (Daesh) 435, 456
Israel
  Assad regime's policy towards 334
  Ba'th strategy towards 278–79
  Egypt's disengagement from Sinai 320
  Fertile Crescent as Arab challenge to 167
  Gaza war, 2008 467
  Golan heights 319
  invasion of Lebanon (1982) 323–24
  the Palestinian question 464–66
  potential break-up of Syria 463–64
  response to UAR 341
  Rogers Plan 297
  Syria's support for resistance against 467–68
  war with Lebanon, 2006 381, 467
Italy 51

Jabri, Saadallah 111, 137, 140, 145, 146
Jadid, Salah
  chief of the general staff 269, 279
  department of officers' affairs 266
  as deputy secretary-general 285, 286
  on NCRC 257
  rivalry with Hafez Assad 288, 289, 293, 296, 298, 299
  and sectarianism 266
Jamal Pasha 11, 32
Jews *see also* Israel
  Faysal–Weizmann agreement 55–57
  oath of allegiance to King Faysal 45–46
  Palestine as homeland for 51–52, 65
Jordan
  Arab Federal State (AFS) 340–41, 343–44
  confrontation with Palestine resistance 296–97
Jouvenel, Henri de 94, 95–96, 97, 98

Khaddam, Abdel-Halim 313, 334, 359, 363, 379
King–Crane commission 4, 53–54, 59, 61–62, 64–65
Kudsi, Nazem 175, 176–77, 195, 212–13, 215–16
Kurds, Syrian
  1962 census 221–22
  Kurdish forces, post-war 458–59
  and the National Salvation Front 364, 365
  population 460–61
  restoration of Syrian nationality 386, 389
  Social Contract Charter 459–60
Kuzbari, Ma'amun 205, 210, 218, 220, 248, 249

Labwani, Kamal 426–27
Lawrence, T. E. 40, 56–57
League of Nations *see also* Covenant of the League of Nations
  France's withdrawal from 133
  and the sanjak of Alexandretta 126–27
  Syria's membership of 113–14
Lebanon
  1943 elections 137
  in 1985 323
  civil war 320, 322
  end of the French mandate 137–38, 142
  execution of Antun Sa'ada 164, 165
  Franco-Syrian treaty and 119–20
  Israeli invasion of (1982) 323–24
  Syrian intervention in 322
  unrest over United Arab Republic 340
  war, 2006 381, 467
Lloyd George, David
  Christian Zionism of 51–52
  revisions to the Sykes-Picot agreement 52, 54
  stance on the Middle East 51, 65

Al-Malki, Adnan 197, 201
Mardam, Jamil 122, 129, 130, 131, 146, 151

Martel, Count Damien de 114, 115, 116, 117, 120, 130–31
McMahon, Henry 32, 40, 47–49
monarchy, Syrian *see also* 1920 constitution; Faysal I bin Hussein bin Ali al Hashemi; General Syrian Congress
    fall of 81–82
    formation of an Arab government 41–44
    formation of the constitutional state 4, 41–44
    French mandate over Syria, 1920 81
    French support for 143
    legacy of 82–83
    nation state under 44–45
    overview of 37–38
    pan-Syrianism of 184–85
    possible restoration of, 1931-2 elections 110–11
Muqdad, Luay 426
Muslim Brotherhood
    and the National Salvation Front 365
    opposition to Assad regime 319, 321–22, 323
    prohibition of 228
    resistance to Ba'th 263
Muslims
    1860 religious crisis 11, 21
    equal rights with Christians 34, 42–43, 44
    interests of, Arab Congress 28
    Islamic renewal (Arab renaissance) 24
    support of during WWI 29

Nahda (Arab renaissance) 23–24
Nami, Damad Ahmad 97–98
Nasser, Gamal Abdel
    charisma of 255
    collapse of Egypt-Syria union 203, 204, 206
    as guide for the Arab people 306–7
    pro-Russian stance 196
    on Syria 1
    Syria-Egypt-Iraq federation 259, 347
    tripartite discussions 257
    union with Syria 339–40

National Bloc
    1931–32 elections 109, 111, 112–13
    1936 election victory 122
    1939 government 131–32
    1943 elections 137
    challenges to authority of 122–24
    formation of 100
    Franco-Syrian treaty 112–14, 115–16
    the General Strike, 1936 117–18
    impact of sanjak of Alexandretta crisis 129
    the National Covenant 116–17
    political crisis, 1944 140
    split of, 1947 144–45
National Council of the Revolutionary Command (NCRC) 256–57, 258, 273, 277
National Democratic Rally 324–25
national identity
    Arab Congress (1913) 26–28
    Arab nationalism 369, 370
    Arabism 340
    Association for Arab–Ottoman Brotherhood 24–25
    equal Christian and Muslim rights and 34
    exiled emancipation associations 25–26
    Great Arab Revolt 29, 31–34, 40–41
    Ibrahim Pasha's Arab identity 18–19
    nahda (Arab renaissance) 23–24
    in the 1949 draft constitution 161–62
    pan-Arabism 185
    pan-Syrianism 162, 184–85
    and the Syrian campaign 18
National Party
    1947 elections 147
    opposition to union with Iraq 339
    overview of 145
National Progressive Front (NPF) 304–6, 307
national project
    1920 constitution 184
    1928 constitution 102–4, 180, 184
    1950 constitution 184–85
    and the 2016 constitutional texts 446–47
    Ba'th ideology and 254

and the Cairo Declaration 438
future relevance of 468–69
impact of the civil war 432–33, 436–37, 463
independent Syria 338
under the military republic 229
and the National Charter 440
under the neo-Ba'th 295
and the Palestinian question 464–66
and SSNP ideology 164
and the United Arab Republic 343
nationalist movement *see also* National Bloc
and the 1928 elections 100
Arab support for the allies, WWI 29–31
boycott of the 1926 elections 97
British and French understandings of 33
communiqués, Great Revolt 92–93
demands, post-Great Revolt 94–96
under the French mandate 84, 85
geographical boundaries of future Arab state 32–33, 139
Great Revolt (1925–26) 92–94
military resistance to the French mandate 89–90
opposition to Faysal–Clemenceau agreement 65–66, 80
potential for revolt against the Turks 32, 33
support from Emir Faysal 30, 39–40
and union with Egypt 197
Nehlawi, Lieutenant-Colonel Abdel-Karim 203, 205, 214
Neo-Ba'th regime *see also* 1969 provisional constitution
1966 coup 281
Arab responses to 1966 coup 283
constitutional arrangement, 1966 7, 281–82
extraordinary session of the Fourth Regional Congress 289–90, 296
extraordinary session of the Ninth Regional Congress 287–88
extraordinary session of the Second Regional Congress 284–85
extraordinary session of the Tenth National Congress 296, 298
extraordinary session of the Third Regional Congress 287
Fourth Regional Congress 288
institutional control 282
national identity under 295
Ninth National Congress 285–87
political life under 283–84
Tenth National Congress 288–89
Third Regional Congress 285

October 1973 War 319
Opposition draft constitutions
Anwar Buni's 2011 draft constitution 424–26
Labwani–Muqdad 2011 draft constitution 426–29
Reform Party of Syria 2006 420–24
Opposition movements
Al-Nusra Front 435–36, 456–57
battle of Al-Qusair 435
Cairo Declaration 437–38
Cairo meetings 437, 438, 455
Doha Coalition 430–31
Istanbul Council 430
National Charter 438–40, 455
National Compact (National Commitment) 431–32
national compact and the national project 433
National Coordination Committee of the Forces for Democratic Change in Syria 429–30
transitional period studies 432
Ottoman Administrative Decentralization Party 25, 26–27
Ottoman Empire *see also* Syrian campaign
aims for, Arab Congress 27–28
alliances during WWI 28
British position on during WWI 47
and the Eastern Question 10–11
European support for 19
French policy towards 22–23
French position on during WWI 46–47
the Greek crisis 10–11, 12–13

Ottoman Empire (*cont.*)
  implementation of recommendations of Arab Congress 28
  Ottoman Syria 13
  re-established control of Syrian provinces (1860) 21, 22
  separation of Arab provinces 11–12

Palestine
  during the Second Republic 154–55
  effects of the Palestine war 150–51, 156
  Faysal–Weizmann agreement 55–57
  impacts on Israeli and Syrian national projects 464–66
  Jewish homeland 65
  personal religious views and British policies 20, 51–52
  resistance confrontation with Jordan 296–97
  Rogers Plan 297
  strategic importance to the British 51
  support from Ba'th for resistance movement 278–79, 286–87, 288, 297–98
  and the tripartite union 344–45
  Zionism and 338
Palestine Liberation Organization (PLO) 323–24
Palestine war 150–51, 156
Palmerston, Henry John Temple, 3rd Viscount Lord 19, 20, 22, 51–52
Pan-Arabism 185
Pan-Syrianism 162, 184–85
Paris Peace Conference 4, 46, 59
People's Party
  alliance with Ba'th Party 147
  draft provisional constitution, 1949 170
  initial support for 1949 coup d'état 157
  pro-Iraqi overthrow plot 200–1
  proposed federation with Iraq 146, 167–68, 169–70, 338–39
  relations with the Al-Hakim government 177–78
  relations with the military 178–79, 226–27

political solutions to the civil war
  Moscow 1 and 2 consultative meetings 441–43, 455
  UNSCR 2254 445–46, 447
  Vienna 1 and 2 conferences 443–44, 455–56
Ponsot, Henri 98–99, 100, 108–9, 110, 112, 113–14, 143
President of the Republic (office of)
  1928 constitution 105–7
  1932 elections 111–12
  1950 constitutions 188–90
  1953 constitution 241–44
  1962 constitution 215–16, 219
  1971 provisional constitution 301, 302–3
  1973 constitution 313–15
  2012 constitution 399–402, 404
  Carter Center revision of the 2012 constitution 448
  election for a second term 148–50
  legislative decrees 317–18, 402–4
  provisional constitution for the transitional period 450
  religion of 163, 179, 232, 271, 291, 309, 388, 394–95
  Russian constitutional proposal 452–53
press 310
Puaux, Gabriel 130–31, 143

Qwatli, Shukri
  1943 presidential elections 137, 145
  1948 re-election for a second term 105, 148–49
  1955 presidential elections 198–99
  end of the French mandate 140
  pro-Egyptian union 202
  proposed restoration as President 166
  second term of office 105, 148, 149–50, 156

Reform Committee 26, 27
religion
  1860 religious crisis 11, 21
  changes of religion 130–31
  minority Christian rights 60

mixed marriages 130–31
multi-religious coexistence, unitary
  Syria 18, 34, 42–43, 44
and the *nahda* 24
of the President 163, 179, 232, 271,
  291, 309, 388, 394–95
separation of from politics, 1920
  Constitution 71
Rikabi, General Rida
  1931–32 elections 110, 111
  as head of government 41, 42,
    43, 60
  as head of monarchic government
    68, 109
  and independence negotiations 65
Russia
  2016 constitutional texts 446
  constitutional proposal 451–54
  European suspicion of 19
  intervention in Syria 436–37, 456
  Moscow 1 and 2 consultative
    meetings 441–43, 455
  political solution for the civil
    war 445
  Soviet alliance with Syria 335
  Soviet relations with the
    neo-Ba'th 285
  Sykes–Picot–Sazanov
    agreement 51, 52
  the Syrian campaign (1831) 14
  and the Syrian–Egyptian
    union 201–2

Sa'ada, Antun 164, 165
Sadat, Anwar 304, 319, 322,
  323, 327
San Remo Conference 46, 59, 81,
  88, 124
Sanjak of Alexandretta
  constitutional status of 127
  Franco-Turkish talks over 125–26
  impact on the Franco-Syrian
    treaty 125
  impact on the National Bloc
    government 129
  League of Nations status of 126–27
  overview of 124–25
  transference to Turkey 127–29

Saudi Arabia
  High Negotiations Committee 457
  response to UAR 341
Second Republic *see also* 1949
    constitution; 1950 constitution;
    United Arab Republic
  1954 electoral law (amended 1957) 194
  1954 legislative elections 193–95
  1961 elections 210
  1961 provisional constitution 208–10
  army's function 153–54, 158
  constituent assembly elections,
    1949 168–69
  fall of 220–21
  government/military tensions,
    1949 172–79
  Husni Al-Zaim's regime 158, 164–65
  international and regional
    policies 163–64
  National Security Council
    (NSC) 211–12
  overview of 153–55, 222
  plot to overthrow the government,
    1956 200–1
  political classes, post-1954 199–200
  proposed federation with Iraq
    146, 167–68, 169–70, 171–73,
    196–98, 229
  provisional government, August
    1949 165–67, 168
  second legislature 195–98
  second presidency, 1955 198–200
  social issues 155
  strength of independent
    candidates 194–95
  union with Egypt 196–98, 200–3
Seif, Riad 358
Selo, General Fawzi 163, 176, 225, 228
Seurat, Michel 331, 332–33
Shahbandar, Abdel-Rahman
  assassination of 132
  Declaration to the Seven 49
  exile in Cairo 100, 111, 129
  formation of the People's Party 144
  letter to the French foreign
    ministry 93–94
  political head of the Great Revolt
    92, 100

Sharif Hussein of Mecca
  alliance with the nationalists 31–32
  appointment of 39
  correspondence with McMahon 32,
    40, 47–49
  relations with the Ottoman
    Empire/Allies, WWI 29, 31
  as trigger for Great Arab Revolt
    32, 33, 40
Shishakli, Colonel Adib *see also* Third
    Republic
  1949 coup d'états 172, 226
  1951 coup d'état 178–79
  alliance negotiations 174
  fall of the Shishakli regime 192
  head of first armoured division 165
  military republic of 5, 6, 225–26
  opposition to 245–46, 248, 249
  political activities, pre-1951 226–27
  SSNP armed resistance movement 158
Sixth Republic *see also* 2016
    constitutional texts; opposition
    movements; political solutions to
    the civil war
  conflict during 434–36
  move towards 434
  the nation-state model under 436–37
social issues
  1950 constitution 6, 179–83, 207–8
  Arab socialism 206–8, 262–63
  under the Ba'th 254–55
  during the *infissal* regime
    206–8, 212–13
  modernization, 1949 158
Supreme Arab Revolutionary
    Command of the Armed Forces
    (SARCAF) 203, 205, 214
Sykes–Picot agreements
  British aims 50
  final form of 50–51
  French aims 49
  and international law 86
  revisions to 46, 52–55, 88
  and the three occupied zones 41, 43
Syria
  geographical significance of 1–2, 12, 13
  history overview 1

Syrian Arab Republic 271
Syrian campaign
  European understanding of 13
  as fight for national
    independence 18
  invasion of Syria (1831) 13–14
  Mohamad Ali's withdrawal 16–17
  overview of 11
  Russian involvement 14
  second war (1839-40) 16
  Treaty of London 16–17, 18
Syrian Federation 90–91
Syrian Question *see also* Syrian campaign
  British interests in 19–20
  early twentieth century 11–12
  nineteenth century 11
Syrian Social Nationalist Party (SSNP)
  Akram Hawrani's ties with 157–58
  assassination of Adnan Al-Malki
    197, 201
  deportation of Antun Sa'ada 164
  ideology of 164

Territories, Syrian *see also* Alawi
    territory; Aleppo, State of; Druze
    territories
  Arab homeland 370
  of the Arab state, post-Ottoman
    empire 32–33, 41, 42, 47–48
  and the break-up of Syria 463–64
  conceptions of 462–63
  and the Damascus Protocol 31
  division of the French
    territories 50–51
  division of under the French
    mandate 88–89
  France's legacy of 142
  of the newly independent Syria 338
  and the Palestinian question 464–66
  pan-Syrianism 162, 184–85
  proposed federation with Iraq 146,
    167–68, 169–70, 171–73, 196–98
  regional policy and military
    influence 174
  reintegration of French
    territories 90–92
  SSNP ideology and 164

and the Sykes–Picot agreement 49
union with Egypt 5, 196–98,
  200–3
Third Republic *see also* 1953
  constitution
Arab Liberation Movement (ALM)
  230–31, 248
characteristics of 227–29
constitutional and presidential
  referenda 246
electoral law 246–47
establishment of 226–27
fall of 248–50
ideology of 229–31
legislative elections 247–48
as military republic 225–26
political opposition to 245–46,
  248
relations with the army 228,
  245–46, 251
Tlass, General Manaf 482
Tlass, General Mustafa
as minister of defence 356
as chief of staff 287, 296, 298
common front of progressive and
  nationalist parties 305
fifth armoured division 266, 280
memoirs of 267, 282, 287
on the Political Bureau 290
succession planning 356
Turkey *see also* Ottoman Empire
aid to Syrian resistance
  fighters 89–90
and the First Republic 85
Franco-Turkish talks over the sanjak
  of Alexandretta 125–26
French fears of Turko-Syrian
  alliance 80–81
transference of the sanjak of
  Alexandretta to 124–29

Union–Freedom–Socialism trilogy
1947–63 interpretation 369–72
1963–70 interpretation 372–75
1970–2005 interpretation 375–76
2005 interpretation 368–69,
  376–78, 381

and Arab nationalism 369, 370
concepts of freedom 371, 372–73,
  376, 377, 378, 381
concepts of socialism 371–72,
  374–77
concepts of union in 370–71,
  373–74, 375, 377
as enshrined in the 1973
  constitution 7–8
United Arab Republic (Egypt and
  Syria) (UAR)
and the 1950 constitution 5
Constitution of the United Arab
  Republic 341–43
formation of 339–40
the national project 343
regional impact of 340–41
separation of (*infissal*) 204–6
and the September 1961 coup
  d'état 203–4
United Arab Republic (Egypt, Syria,
  and Iraq) (UAR)
Arab socialism 344–45
civil liberties under 347
collapse of 347
executive powers 346–47
legislative powers 345–46
and the liberation of
  Palestine 344–45
overview of 259–60
regional structure of 345
Tripartite Charter 344–45, 346
United Nations Security Council
  (UNSC) 445–46, 447
United States of America (USA)
coalition against ISIS 435
invasion of Iraq 466
military intervention in
  Syria 434–35
opposition movements
  and 430–31
political solution for the civil
  war 445
Syrian–US relations 335

Weber, Max 418
Weizmann, Chaim 55–57

Women
  rights under the 1969 constitution 293
  suffrage, 1920 constitution 77–78
  suffrage, 1949 158, 168–69
Woodrow Wilson, US President
  Fourteen Points 86
  and the King–Crane commission 3, 4, 46, 54, 59
World War I
  Muslim support during 29
  operations in the East 28–29
  Ottoman Empire's alliances 28

World War II
  British reaction to Franco-German collaboration 134–35
  increased tensions, pre-WWII 128
  Iraqi support for Germany 133

Zahr El-Din, General Abdel-Karim 204, 205, 214
Al-Zaim, General Husni 6, 151, 156, 157, 159, 163, 225
Zionism
  David Lloyd George 51–52
  Palestine and 338
Zuayin, Yusef 265, 280, 282, 283, 285, 287